D1610636

KING ALFRED'S COLLEGE
WINCHESTER

To be returned on or before the day marked
below :—

20. JUL 1986

— 5 APR 2012

PLEASE ENTER ON ISSUE SLIP:

AUTHOR WELLINGTON

TITLE Political correspondence. Vol. 1

ACCESSION No. 66584

THE DUKE OF WELLINGTON as Chancellor of Oxford University.
From a mezzotint by Samuel Cousins after the painting (c. 1839) by John Lucas

Reproduced by courtesy of the Trustees of the British Museum

ROYAL COMMISSION ON
HISTORICAL MANUSCRIPTS

The Prime Ministers' Papers:

WELLINGTON

POLITICAL CORRESPONDENCE
1: 1833–November 1834

EDITED BY JOHN BROOKE
AND JULIA GANDY

LONDON
HER MAJESTY'S STATIONERY OFFICE

© *Crown copyright* 1975
First published 1975

ISBN 0 11 440051 2*

CONTENTS

ACKNOWLEDGEMENTS

The Commissioners wish to express their thanks to the Duke of Wellington for permission to publish these papers of his ancestor. The work was begun during the lifetime of the late Duke, who kindly allowed the manuscripts to be deposited at the Commission's offices for listing and transcribing.

Their dutiful thanks are due to Her Majesty The Queen for her gracious permission to quote from the papers of King William IV and Lord Melbourne in the Royal Archives.

The late Marquess of Salisbury kindly gave permission to consult and quote from the diary of Lady Salisbury, first wife of the 2nd Marquess, and to publish Wellington's letters to Lord and Lady Salisbury.

For permission to publish other letters, the Commissioners are indebted to Major-General E. H. Goulburn, the Marquess of Lothian, Mr. Oliver Williams, and the National Trust.

The Editors wish to thank the staffs of the following repositories for help in consulting the collections of manuscripts in their charge: the Department of Manuscripts of the British Library (the papers of the 4th Earl of Aberdeen, John Wilson Croker, John Charles Herries, Sir Robert Peel, Sir Robert Wilson); Kent Archives Office (the papers of the 5th Earl Stanhope); McGill University, Montreal (the papers of Sir Henry Hardinge); the National Library of Scotland (the papers of Edward Ellice senior and Sir George Murray); the Scottish Record Office (the papers of the 7th Marquess of Lothian); and Surrey County Record Office (the papers of Henry Goulburn); also to Mr. R. H. Harcourt Williams, Librarian and Archivist at Hatfield House.

All documents printed are taken from the Wellington Papers unless otherwise stated. For other collections the following abbreviations are used:

ADD MS: British Library Additional Manuscript
NLS: National Library of Scotland
RA: Royal Archives
SRO: Scottish Record Office

INTRODUCTION

(i)

The papers of Arthur Wellesley, 1st Duke of Wellington, have remained at Apsley House in the possession of his family. They comprise many thousands of documents, both military and political, and cover most of the Duke's adult life.

About 1832 Lieutenant-Colonel John Gurwood began under the Duke's supervision to prepare for publication the military correspondence and papers. Gurwood's edition, *The Dispatches of Field-Marshal the Duke of Wellington*, was published in thirteen volumes between 1834 and 1839. It was a great success, and by 1847 two revised and enlarged editions had appeared. After Wellington's death the 2nd Duke continued the task of editing his father's papers, and between 1858 and 1880 published a further twenty volumes. As well as military papers omitted from Gurwood's edition these contain an extensive selection of political correspondence to the end of the year 1832. The papers from 1833 to 1852 remained unpublished, and these form the basis of the present edition.

Even this vast collection of papers, partially published in twenty-eight large volumes, is but a proportion of the total number of letters the Duke wrote or received. He habitually destroyed his personal correspondence, and few letters of this nature have survived among his papers. Nor did he always preserve his public correspondence, as is evident by gaps in this volume. But he tried to keep his papers in an orderly manner, and he had the assistance of a private secretary. For the period covered by this volume Algernon Greville, brother of Charles Greville, the diarist, was the Duke's secretary.

During the last twenty years of his life Wellington held a unique position in public esteem, such as no other Englishman has held. As the great military hero, the victor of Waterloo, he was revered by all. Even those who disliked his politics respected his sense of duty and his devotion to what he regarded as the true interests of the nation, irrespective of considerations of party advantage. His honesty, straightforwardness, and total lack of vanity disarmed his critics. But this unique position brought with it certain disadvantages. He became the target for every crank with a scheme to propound or a grievance to be redressed, and to secure the approbation of the Duke of Wellington seemed a universal desire. Thus General Sir Charles Colville was hurt when the Duke failed to acknowledge his 'respectful bow' in the House of Lords—'thus shewing that I must have either fallen out of your Grace's recollection or into your displeasure'—and wrote to entreat an explanation. Wellington wrote to one of these correspondents on 23 March 1833:

> The fact is that my whole time is taken up from morning till night in receiving written suggestions for the public benefit from gentlemen with whom I have no connection or even acquaintance. Nobody is satisfied unless I write an answer. It is not surprising if these answers are at times not given at great length, and are not satisfactory to those to whom they are addressed.

And to another correspondent on 8 April 1834: 'The Duke certainly receives more letters and applications than any man that now exists.'

Yet almost all who wrote to the Duke received some sort of a reply. To correspondents whom he knew he wrote in his own hand, often keeping a draft of the letter. To the majority, whom he did not know, he would sometimes turn the paper round and write his reply across the letter which would be afterwards copied fair by his secretary. This was how he answered the young Disraeli's request to be allowed to dedicate to the Duke his poem *The Revolutionary Epick*. These replies usually begin: 'F.M. the Duke of Wellington presents his compliments to . . .' On many letters Wellington simply noted as an instruction to his secretary: 'Compliments. Received.' He wrote standing at a desk which is still preserved at Apsley House.

Wellington's surviving correspondence during the last twenty years of his life falls into four classes:

1. Letters on political affairs. His correspondents include the Sovereign and other members of the Royal Family (the Duke of Cumberland was a regular and not altogether welcome correspondent); close colleagues such as Peel or Aberdeen; Conservative peers who regarded Wellington as their leader; and a variety of miscellaneous people.

2. Letters on business connected with Wellington's appointments as Chancellor of Oxford University, Lord Warden of the Cinque Ports, Constable of the Tower of London, Master of the Trinity House, etc. This business frequently involved political action, e.g. Oxford University's attempt to prevent the admission of Dissenters; but in general this correspondence is not political.

3. Letters on military affairs. Until Wellington resumed the command of the army in 1842, these usually concern the regiments of which he was colonel-in-chief (the Grenadier Guards and the Rifle Brigade), or else are applications for commissions.

4. Begging letters; letters appealing for the Duke's aid in righting some real or imagined wrong; letters advocating some new invention or some political scheme—what, in short, may be called the 'crank' correspondence. Some of these letters are funny, others pathetic, but few are important.

When the late Duke of Wellington allowed the Historical Manuscripts Commission to inspect his family papers, it was decided to give priority to those from 1833 onwards. Much of the earlier correspondence had been published, though with suitable omissions to avoid offending living people, and it seemed best to begin with the unpublished correspondence. It was decided to deal with this in two ways:

1. To prepare a list of the papers, giving certain essential information about each document: name of writer, date, address, and a brief summary of its contents.

2. To prepare and publish an edition of Wellington's political correspondence, 1833–1846, of which this volume is the first.

The word 'political' has been given a wide interpretation. Thus correspondence dealing with military affairs has been included (e.g. a proposal to abolish flogging in the army) if these were likely to have political repercussions. Letters dealing with strictly military business (e.g. the design of uniforms or the type of weapons) have been omitted. Correspondence dealing with Oxford University, the Cinque Ports, etc. has been included or omitted on the same principles. Also included are a number of letters from people whose names are unknown to history favouring the Duke with advice on political affairs, but letters from people who were clearly mentally unbalanced have been omitted. Letters from Wellington found in other collections have also been included.

(ii)

The political interest of these papers is the contribution they make to the history of the Conservative party from its revival after the Reform Act of 1832 to its split over the repeal of the Corn Laws in 1846. Peel was the dominant figure in the party and Wellington no more than his first lieutenant, yet it is doubtful if Peel could have led the party effectively without the Duke's prestige and influence. Even so, it was difficult. The Conservatives were not a united body, nor was party allegiance so strong a factor in politics as it became later in the century.

The word Conservative was first used as a party designation in British politics to distinguish those who opposed the Reform Act of 1832. On Wellington's resignation as Prime Minister in 1830 the Whigs had returned to office pledged to a measure of parliamentary reform. Wellington by his public pronouncements was equally pledged against reform. When the bill was defeated in the House of Lords in May 1832 and the King refused to create sufficient peers to give the Whigs a majority, the ministers resigned. William IV sent for Wellington, who attempted to form a ministry which would be responsible for the bill. He found little enthusiasm for the project; Peel refused to take office; and Wellington gave up the attempt. The Whigs returned to office, and Wellington advised the Conservative peers not to vote against the bill.

Some account of these events is necessary to explain the state of relations which existed between Wellington and Peel when this volume opens. Wellington had not yet forgiven Peel for refusing to stand by him in May 1832. He hardly appreciated what he was asking or the difficulties of Peel's position. Peel felt unable to propose to the House of Commons to enact the very bill which for the last eighteen months he had been advising the House to reject. He had already made one such political volte-face over Catholic Emancipation, and he would not make another. Wellington could only see that the King's government must be carried on, and that the Reform Bill, bad as he believed it to be, was preferable to continued disturbances in the country and to a lavish creation of peerages. Political consistency meant little to him. 'I felt that my duty to the King', he wrote subsequently, 'required that I should make a great sacrifice to serve him, and to save His Majesty and the country from what I considered a great evil.'

There are few letters between Wellington and Peel in this volume, and there seems to have been little communication between them even on day-to-day business in Parliament. In February 1833 Wellington wrote to Aberdeen:

My opinion has long been that Sir Robert Peel and I would never again serve the publick in the same council. I entertained this opinion previously to the occurrences of May 1832.

But it is possible for two men to serve the publick out of office. But there must exist candour, truth and fairness in the views of both; and the line of proceeding of each should be taken without the desire of contradicting and opposing himself to the views of the other.

'It is evident the Duke feels he cannot do without him', Lady Salisbury wrote about Peel on 22 December 1833, 'though he never can entirely depend upon him.' Their relations had improved little by the time Peel left for the Continent in October 1834.

Wellington took a gloomy view of the country's prospects under the reformed Parliament. 'It is my opinion', he wrote on 2 February 1833, 'that the Reform Bill has effected a compleat revolution in this country, as it has taken the political power of the House of Commons out of the hands of those who possess property in order to place it in the hands of those who keep shops and exercise trades.' The political influence of the Crown and the House of Lords had diminished, and further revolutionary changes must be expected. 'We have a House of Commons all powerful', he wrote on 15 May 1833, 'which has no community of interest or feeling with the property, the establishment, the institutions, the commerce, or the policy of the country.' And on 9 July 1833: 'I would do anything to quit this unfortunate and unhappy country.'

When reading such declarations two facts about Wellington have to be borne in mind. He was a man of the eighteenth century who had completed his education by the time the French Revolution broke out; and he had sat only three years in the House of Commons. Peel on the other hand was born only the year before the French Revolution and had entered the House of Commons as soon as he came of age. Wellington was ill equipped by his age and experience of politics to understand the problems of Great Britain in the post-Reform Act era. During the years covered by this volume he is found opposing almost every change put forward by the Whig Government and prophesying disaster if they were adopted. Nor was he more willing to adapt himself to new techniques in politics. He never hesitated to show his contempt for the press or public opinion. 'The Duke has nothing to say to the newspapers', he wrote in February 1833 to a journalist who had offered his services to the Conservatives, 'and he is desirous of avoiding to have any communication of any description with any of them.'

Another fact to be borne in mind is that Wellington came from the Anglo-Irish gentry and was concerned to maintain the political supremacy of Great Britain over Ireland. Perhaps he cared more for this than for any other object in politics. He had advocated Catholic Emancipation as a final concession to Irish demands. There was no going beyond this. On 10 February 1833 he wrote to Henry Phillpotts, Bishop of Exeter: 'I have no notion of the Union lasting if the Government give a blow to the Protestant religion in Ireland. The Protestants of the Church of England or in other words the proprietors of the soil are its only friends.' And on 29 August 1834: 'We support the Church of England in Ireland not only as a system of religion, but as one of property and imperial policy.' The Irish Protestants looked to the Duke as their leader, though he had little sympathy with the Orange movement.

Wellington also believed that a successful attack on the privileged position of the Church of Ireland would be followed by an attempt to disestablish the Church of England. This would be a triumph for the Dissenters and Radicals. The maintenance of the Church of England as an establishment was dear to the heart of every Conservative. 'I look upon you as the head of the Church', wrote Lord Francis Egerton on 13 June 1834. Wellington undertook to defend the position of the two universities as exclusively Anglican seminaries. In an age of violent political changes he thought of the Conservative party as the defender of property and the established order. Even a proposal to abolish the monopoly rights of the patent London theatres seemed to him 'highly revolutionary'. Yet he did not sympathise with the Ultra wing of the Conservatives who had opposed him over Catholic Emancipation and had brought about his downfall in November 1830, and he tried to avoid meeting the Duke of Cumberland in society.

Perhaps the key to Wellington's character was his sense of public duty. 'I am always ready to come forward when it is thought that I can be useful to any class of His Majesty's subjects', he wrote on 13 February 1833. This can best be seen in the documents relating to his acceptance of the chancellorship of Oxford University. Because of his never having had a university education he regarded himself as 'incapable and unfit' for the office, and pressed the Oxford Conservatives to take Peel. He was told that they wished for a Chancellor who sat in the House of Lords and that he alone could unite the Conservatives in the university. 'I then said that in all cases of this kind I considered myself as an instrument to be used by the publick when it was deemed necessary.'

CORRESPONDENCE

CORRESPONDENCE

The Marquess of Londonderry to Wellington, 1 January 1833

Mount Stewart. The fates are against us in all quarters. And what will become of us as a party? Or how we are to act appears to me an enigma no human wisdom can solve.

Providence can alone save us from revolution.

I send poor McDonnell's letter *where* they were *quite* sure of bringing in two Conservatives for Antrim.

In short we were all *quite sure.* But alas! nothing can stand the war cry of reform, that will not cease until State, Church and King are pulled down.

I sail for England tomorrow. Pray direct [to] Wynyards.

Dated (incorrectly) January 1st 1832. *Docketed* 1833.

Wellington to the Earl of Elgin, 1 January 1833

Apethorpe. I have received and am much obliged to you for your letter of the 28th and its inclosure.

This last, of which I can vouch for the truth of some of the facts stated, shews clearly that we have proceeded upon false principles in respect to the slave trade. I have always been of that opinion.

God knows how the mischief of those proceedings or others more nearly affecting us are now to be remedied. I believe that there is not a man in the country who does not see the evil. Where is the one who can avert it?

Viscount Beresford to Wellington, 2 January 1833

Deepdene. You will recollect about two years since, you were so good to say you could put on your list for the Rifle Brigade Lady Anna Beresford's son, William, and I have just received a letter from her, on the subject, asking me what are the prospects for him, and I hope you may be able to give me a favourable answer for her.

Our expectations in the elections we were concerned in have sadly failed, as I am sorry to see, those of our friends have so generally done. Leitrim was lost by the same method as most others in Ireland, violence and the indefatigable workings and influence of the priests. Armagh the same with the personal active exertions of Lord Charlemont, and the Lord Lieutenant of the county, two of the least scrupulous and out and outs of the Whigs at least. Berwick was also a curious and unexpected loss, but on this there is some idea of a petition, though with such a House of Commons, little can be expected by those on our side, and it would probably be but adding to the great expense I have already incurred. I suppose we shall all meet on the 29th inst.

Viscount Melbourne to Wellington, 2 January 1833

Whitehall. I have had the honour to lay before the King, the address of the owners and occupiers of land, tradesmen and other inhabitants of the county of Somerset, against the measures adopted towards the King of the Netherlands, which accompanied your Grace's letter of the 27th ultimo.

Signature only in Melbourne's hand.

Charles Manners Sutton to Wellington, 2 January 1833

Palace Yard. From sincere respect, and also flattering myself that what may happen to me in public station will not be without interest to your Grace, I venture to enclose copies of a letter I have received from Lord Althorp and of my answer. I hope your Grace will think I have done right.

Of general news your Grace knows much more than I can send; but from all I hear from various quarters I fully expect a grand crash when we first meet.

Docketed The offer to him by Government of their support for the Chair of the House of Commons.

The Earl of Carnarvon to Wellington, 2 January 1833

Highclere. I received your letter this morning at Pusey just as they were preparing to lift me into my carriage, to end a tedious fit of gout at home. This is the very day for which you were good enough to invite me, but I am quite unable to move without assistance, and I cannot hope for much more than to be with you before the opening of Parliament, which is at present either on the fourth or fifth of February. If possible I will endeavour to be in town on the Saturday preceding. I should be glad to hear what you think of the measures we ought to follow, and whether our game may not at first rather be the backward game, at all events our position is an awkward and difficult one. I regret much having been unable [to] meet their Royal Highnesses at Stratfield Saye, and nothing would have given me greater pleasure than to have passed two days with you there, especially at this time.

Dated Wednesday. *Docketed (incorrectly)* 1833. January 1.

The Earl of Bandon to Wellington, 4 January 1833

Castle Bernard. Lord Aberdeen's absence in Scotland will I trust plead my apology, for the liberty I take in being myself the person to presume to bring to your Grace's recollection a conversation which his Lordship had the honor of having with your Grace on the subject of the anxiety I felt to obtain your Grace's sanction and influence whenever a vacancy might enable me to become a candidate for the Irish representative peerage. I was then gratified by hearing, that your Grace was pleased to express yourself favourably to my pretensions, which has emboldened me, on the occasion of the present vacancy caused by the death of Lord Conyngham, to enquire whether I might hope for the honor of your Grace's influence. My political opinions have ever been in conformity with those of His Majesty's late Government and my son during a short time he was in Parliament firmly opposed the Reform Bill. My exertions have not been wanting during the late elections, and although my son was ultimately defeated by a combination of Popish priests and agitators we maintained a hard struggle in the county of Cork and were nobly supported by the property of the county. I have the satisfaction however of stating that my brother has been returned for Bandon and in him the good cause will find a steady supporter.

The Earl of Roden to Wellington, 4 January 1833

Dundalk. I have to acknowledge *half* of your kind communication in answer to my letter on the important concerns of the situation of this country. In your envelope was contained two sheets of the correspondence I enclosed you and *half* a sheet of your own letter to me evidently the end of a much longer communication. This I received on Monday last and have not since heard any thing of the former part of your letter. I think you may have mislaid it perhaps but I cannot help feeling uneasy lest it may have fallen into improper hands. Should I receive it before I get your answer to this I will apprize you of it. I am sorry to say the state of this country is getting more awful every day. The poor Protestant inhabitants are alarmed night and day with threats of the Romish mob, who are really marching about the country enforcing club law and keeping the poor Protestant families in such a state of terror that I can conceive nothing to be compared to it since the days of 1641. The Government have appointed men magistrates who no gentleman will associate with, and who being Roman Catholics refuse to go out with the Protestant magistrates to enforce the payment of the tithe for the reimbursement of the Government. I could have no idea of such a change having taken place in the country in so short a period as I witness about me in the neighbourhood of this town. While the Popish mob is denouncing the Protestants with threats within our hearing, they are pairing up the King and the Ministers who they say are on their side and such is the peril in which the poor Protestants here consider themselves that they are uniting into bands for each other's protection and none of them dare venture out after dark. Even the little Popish children are taught to bully the children of the Protestants and their parents are obliged to go to the schools to bring them home with them for protection. I have had several deputations from the Protestants with me and have given them the best advice I can. They are all united here which is one advantage arising from the temper and violence of the opposite party. What is quite impossible without witnessing it [is] to describe the conduct of the priests and the manner in which they goad on the poor misguided peasantry to every species of violence. You are aware I am here in the midst of a very Popish town and population. Nothing can reach this state of things but some strong measures to establish and maintain the law. Things have been permitted to go to such a length, that no common proceedings can give confidence or restore peace. All trade and improvement in this flourishing town has ceased and every one is barricading his house for the preservation of himself and family. Further to the north all is right and the Protestants are united and determined to follow the advice of their leaders.

I trust we shall have Lord Downes in for a representative peerage. I wrote to you upon the subject and since to him as I was aware no time was to be lost. I am sure you will do what you can on your side of the water to serve him. I shall remain here for a fortnight or three weeks. I find the poor Protestants are so much encouraged by my being among them, and their devotion to our interests at the time of the election one and all is not soon to be forgotten.

Robert Henry Jenkinson to Wellington, 4 January 1833

Norbiton. I have the honor to return herewith Mr. Courtenay's letter to your Grace, and at the same time to acknowledge the receipt, by this morning's post, of the copy of your answer to Mr. Courtenay; I should doubt his succeeding, should he ultimately decide upon coming forward, at least from what I hear of the disposition of some of Sir John Reid's committee. In the meantime I learn that upon the intelligence being received of Mr. Grant's success at Inverness, Mr. Rice, who had previously obtained the promise of the support of the Treasury, provided Mr. Grant did not stand, had commenced his canvass, and that Captain Stanhope, with Halcomb, was also in the field and at Dover, but that Stanhope was not himself sanguine, and I should think would not persevere.

I have taken care not to commit your Grace with reference to the proposal contained in your letter of the 29th. I fear there is little chance of such an union of parties, and upon such principles, as to make it likely that your Grace will be called upon. Many of Sir John Reid's friends have declared themselves for Halcomb, while others of them are averse to another Conservative being brought forward, for reasons which your Grace is already apprized of.

Enclosure: Thomas Peregrine Courtenay to Wellington, 28 December 1832.

30 Upper Harley Street. I take the earliest opportunity, after receiving permission to do so, of acquainting your Grace with the probability of my standing for Dover.

The party which supported Sir John Reid has made an overture to Sir Charles Wetherell; but what has passed hitherto makes it probable in the opinion of the gentleman who has communicated with him (Mr. Manning) that he will ultimately decline it.

I am assured that in this event, the same party will support me.

Although this interest, at the last election, only brought in their candidate second, there are great hopes that no Whig will at a single election unite as many votes as Mr. Thomson had.

Your Grace's countenance would be equally gratifying and valuable to me.

I cannot spend money, but I will use every other sort of exertion towards replacing myself in the rank in which I lately served in the House of Commons.

It has been reported that Mr. Fector means to offer himself, but he will not be of age at the time of election.

Should there be any alteration in to [*sic*] Sir Charles Wetherell, from whom a letter has been expected for several days, I will take the liberty of writing to your Grace again.

John Parkinson to Wellington, 5 January 1833

66 Lincoln's Inn Fields. I had a consultation with Sir James Scarlett and Mr. Follett yesterday and they have written an opinion of which I enclose a copy.

My own strong impression is, that, in your Grace's elevated station, you ought not to prosecute, except there was in the opinion of the most eminent common lawyers, something like a certainty of conviction.

I shall see your Grace at the time you appoint—viz. on the 9th instant.

Enclosure: Copy [of] opinion

We have read both the newspapers and it does not appear to us that any paragraph in the second throws any light upon the intention of the writer in the first to designate the Duke of Wellington. We have no doubt however that the Duke of Wellington is the individual designated in the leading article of the first newspaper, although not in terms so entirely free from ambiguity as to preclude the possibility of the editor or printer swearing that his Grace was not the person to whom he meant to allude. If such an affidavit should be made the court would probably consider it proper to make the rule for the information absolute in order to submit the question to a jury, but it is of course impossible to pronounce with certainty or even any great degree of confidence what might be the result of a question that would depend entirely on the discretion of the court and not upon any known rule or practice of law.

If the object of the Duke of Wellington is to acquit himself of the imputations, this might be attained by the application to the court upon an affidavit denying the charges contained in the article whatever might be the issue of the application.

J. Scarlett   W. W. Follett
Temple   4 January 1833

Wellington to John Charles Herries, 5 January 1833

Belvoir Castle. Arbuthnot has shewn me a letter from you on the subject of the paragraph in the *Morning Post, Standard* etc. respecting my intention of going abroad. It is difficult to judge what was the *intention* of these gentry in publishing such an article; which till I saw your letter I considered a matter of indifference. It is still more difficult to contradict the existence of an *intention* excepting from authority; but as I never have had so I never will have any thing to say to any of the newspapers.

But the *intention* is supposed to exist because there has been a reduction of establishments, servants etc. This fact may be contradicted if it is judged necessary. In fact I have as many servants as I have ever had; and more horses because I am in the habit of going out hunting more frequently than heretofore.

No establishment has been diminished, not even that for preserving game; notwithstanding that since the enactment of the Game Bill to put down poaching, there has been such an increase of that since [*sic*], as that there is no game to preserve.

This is all that can be said upon the subject. But I would prefer to say nothing; and to leave this lie to take the usual course; that is to be the wonder of nine days; and to be the subject of various anonymous and abusive letters to myself; and then be forgotten, unless others should wish it to be contradicted by a contradiction of the facts.

ADD MS 57368

Robert Henry Jenkinson to Wellington, 6 January 1833

Norbiton. The enclosed is in reply to a letter which I wrote to Mr. Pain upon the receipt of your Grace's letter of the 29th. It is not an encouraging picture of the state of publick feeling or of parties at Dover, but it does not surprise me after the knowledge and experience I have had of the place and persons we have to deal with.

It should appear from Mr. Pain's postscript that Rice retires, which I shall regret, if no Conservative comes forward. He was respectable and disposed to be moderate, and indeed in his heart may be said to be Conservative from what I have heard of his sentiments. I cannot suppose that such a place as Dover will be left to two such men as Halcomb and Stanhope to contest, without some person of more consideration and character, of one side or the other, coming forward.

John Charles Herries to Wellington, 7 January 1833

Albemarle Street. I see in the *Post* of this day a contradiction of the foolish paragraph about your going abroad. It is I believe, copied from some other paper in which a similar contradiction appeared. I think the best way will be to take no farther notice of the matter.

How such a falsehood could originate I cannot well understand, but I think it more likely to have been a contrivance than a mistake on the part of the person who supplied the paragraph.

It made some sensation at first among the few persons who now frequent the Carlton Club, but it was soon generally disbelieved.

Goulburn has received and communicated to me a long letter from Sir Robert Peel containing some of his views upon the present position of the Conservative party in Parliament and of the conduct which it will be right and expedient for them to pursue. He says—'I presume the chief object of the party which is called Conservative—whatever its number may be—will be to resist Radicalism and to prevent those farther encroachments of democratic influence which will be attempted (probably successfully attempted) as the natural consequence of the triumph already achieved. I certainly think that as that party will be comparatively weak in numbers, all victories gained by mere union with the Radicals will promote mainly the view of the Radicals. As there is no use in defeating—no use in excluding—a Government, unless you can replace it by one formed on principles more consonant to your own, that our policy ought to be rather to conciliate the good wishes of the sober minded and well disposed portion of the community, and thus lay the foundation of future strength, than to urge an opposition on mere party grounds and for any purposes of mere temporary triumph.'

'I think it very difficult to lay down any course of action in detail. Circumstances which we cannot foresee or controul will determine that. I should recommend a system of caution and observation at the first commencement of the session rather than that we should be the first to take the field, or instantly begin hostilities. *We* act on the defensive. The Radicals must move—they must attack—we can, in my opinion, act with more effect after that attack shall have commenced than before.'

'Take the first day of the session for instance. Surely it is much better that Cobbett and O'Connell should move an amendment to the Address than that *we* should. The party that interposes between the two others will have the greatest advantage—relatively I mean to its own intrinsic strength. The best position the Government could assume would be that of moderation between opposite extremes of ultra-Toryism and Radicalism. We should appear to the greatest advantage in defending the Government whenever they espoused our principles —as I apprehend they must do if they mean to maintain the cause of authority and order.'

'Possibly we shall find them indifferent to this and afraid of an open rupture with the Radicals. In that case we must oppose their united forces with all the energy we can. But even in that case our power will be greater should the union which we resist appear the voluntary deliberate act of the Government rather than an act forced upon them by our precipitate or unreasonable opposition.'

He then goes on to observe that these principles apply only to domestic politics, and that on the subject of foreign policy we could not with advantage or even propriety *lie by* while measures were in progress which we can not sanction.

He also expresses himself totally disinclined to make any *concessions of opinion* in order to gain support or increase our strength in the House. He mentions the *currency* as one of the topics to which this observation applies.

I have thought that as you will possibly not have learnt his opinions from himself or from other quarters on these points it might be worth while to send you this sketch and extract of his letter.

For my own part, I confess that I concur very much in opinion with Sir R. Peel as to the course which we ought to pursue as members of the Conservative party in Parliament. And I sincerely wish that in pursuing it, he may keep together, better than he has hitherto done, all those who are ready with proper encouragement to act cordially with him.

The Earl Bathurst to Wellington, 7 January 1833

Arlington Street. I received your letter just as I was setting off from Cirencester to Lord Abingdon's on Thursday, and I shewed it to Apsley, who was much pleased with your invitation.

I will certainly meet the Duke of Cumberland on the 18th inst. Lady Bathurst will tell you her doubts of being able to do so. My daughter will come with me, if you think she will be acceptable to the Duchess of Cumberland.

If the Dutch answer is come, it is at least not announced, but by the funds having fallen one per cent. the beginning of the day it is suspected that they who are in the secret, have reason to suspect it will not be favourable. There seems however to be such an indifference to foreign concerns at present in this country, that I do not expect that the three Continental powers will be willing to make any head against France, and that the Dutch King must submit in the end.

You will see Lord Sandon's speech at Liverpool, exhorting all men to support the Ministers. He, being a Whig, always supported them. But with the knowledge of what is the foreign policy of the Ministers, and the ignorance of what is to be their domestic policy, it seems at least premature to promise support. Great credit is however given them for having declared (two of them only by the bye) that their Reform Bill is a final measure—so is a man being shot by a highwayman, a final measure; and afterwards the highwayman proceeds to plunder the man he has shot, an act as liberal as what Lord Sandon seems to recommend—provided it be done with caution.

Lord Downes to Wellington, 7 January 1833

Merrion Square, Dublin. Understanding from Lord Roden that he has written to your Grace on the subject of the vacancy in the representative peerage, for which the Conservative Society have decided on putting me forward, I hasten to assure your Grace that if there is any other person whom you would prefer supporting, or any one who you think would be more likely to succeed against a Government candidate I shall be happy to withdraw and to place my vote and all the influence I can command at your Grace's disposal.

In the meantime I am sure that you will approve of my carrying on my canvass with activity—for this purpose I am come to Dublin where I shall be more in the way of hearing what is going forward. Lords Howth, Lismore, and Garvagh are spoken of as candidates, but they have no chance of success except by a concentration of their force.

I enclose a list of peers to whom I believe your Grace applied on the occasion of Lord Rathdown's contest, in case you should feel inclined to write to them, and I also enclose a letter from Lord Hertford as I conceive that it has direct reference to your Grace and if you decide in my favor you will probably have the goodness to write to Lord Hertford on the subject.

Enclosure: List of peers to be applied to

7 January 1833

Lord Jersey ⎫
Lord Dungannon ⎬
Lord Mexborough ⎭

Lord Lucan   by Mr. Arbuthnot
Lord Carbery   do.

Lord Chetwynd ⎫
Lord Rokeby   ⎬ by Mr. Goulburn
Lord Gort   ⎭

Query   Duke of Cumberland ⎫ to be applied to
         Duke of Gloucester ⎭

The Earl of Roden to Wellington, 7 January 1833

Dundalk. I have just got your letter respecting the representative peerage and I am delighted to think I have anticipated your wish in the choice of Burgh.[1] I have had a communication with him and he is at work and I trust will succeed—but I hope you will make our friends on the other side *active also*. I have never received the first part of the letter you wrote me in answer to my communication. I received but *one* cover enclosing the two sheets of the letter I had sent you and a half sheet, the end of your reply to me. But the first part has never appeared. It seems very odd that it has not arrived, but I hope you will be able to account for it.

Wellington to the Earl of Bandon, 8 January 1833

London. Private and confidential. I have had the honor of receiving your Lordship's letter and I perfectly recollect the conversation which I had with Lord Aberdeen upon the subject of your Lordship's wish to become one of the representative peers of Ireland.

I have but little powers to promote the views of any noble Lord to obtain this honor, and that little depends upon my recommending the claims which the peers of Ireland in general are disposed to favour. The letters which I have received upon this subject since the death of the Marquis Conyngham afford ground for the belief that many peers favour the pretensions of Lord Downes, and I had therefore considered it proper to support his pretensions as far as I could promote them.

I am very sorry therefore that it is not in my power upon this occasion to promote the views of your Lordship.

Lieutenant-Colonel Sir John Woodford to Wellington, 8 January 1833

Orderly Room. I have the honor of reporting to your Grace that a communication has been received at the Commander-in-Chief's office from the Secretary of State for the Home Department respecting the attendance of a soldier of the regiment at a political union meeting.

There seems every reason to believe that it is a man of the name of Simmons (of the 3rd Battalion) already known and noted as having been in the habit of attending Reform meetings, for which he was

---

[1] Lord Downes, whose family name was Burgh.

bantered and ridiculed by his comrades and they reported him for something which he said. He also attends, or pretends to attend, a temperance society, but as he says that his father and grandfather attended it before him, it is probably some other kind of meeting which has adopted that modern denomination. He is a weaver from Lancashire—a sullen discontented soldier, having no associates among his comrades, but is rather shunned by them.

He has books and reads a good deal.

I beg to submit to your Grace whether it would not be best to discharge this man at once, without assigning any reason. Some objection to this course is made at the Horse Guards, and I am well aware that to discharge men for misconduct as a general plan would be very objectionable; but this is a particular case. The man is recruiting for a political union. He may entrap one or two other soldiers by exciting their curiosity or cupidity to accompany him occasionally, and then it will appear that a committee of the Grenadier Guards are members of a revolutionary club.

The regiment from its strength, station, and name is the most important in the service. Its good spirit is unquestionable, and it seems hardly dealing justly with it to allow this contamination to exist.

We enlist no men now in manufacturing towns. The account given as the soldier's statement by the informant is very true in that respect.

I should think the man is unlikely to wish to enlist in a marching regiment, but at all events the seeds of revolutionary doctrine may be more prejudicial in the Guards than any where else.

That other men should seek their discharge by similar means is not probable. No publicity will attend the discharge of this man. Under the present system of discharges that great anxiety to be released from the service which formerly existed is no longer apparent. I entreat your Grace to let the regiment get rid of this politician.

I have procured a copy of the informant's statement which your Grace will find enclosed herewith.

Enclosure: Copy of a report made to the Home Office. December 24th 1832.

I should have stated before, that about a month since I saw a young man in the undress regimentals of the Foot Guards at the meeting of the union, who seemed to take much pleasure in the speeches and proceedings, but I have several times since then tried to know more of him and could not do so. On Monday evening last he was there again (Theobald's Road) and mixed with the groups standing about waiting for the speakers. I met them and him and found him though a young man, about 22, of some political knowledge and ability, and a decided republican. We were talking of the riot at Sheffield, and other election riots, and he was asked by Davies, 'If a row was to take place in London would the Guards fire on the people?' He said, 'He was afraid they would unless the people were once to make a stand and not run, which if they did, he did not know how it would be then.' He added, 'I have not been long a soldier, nor should I be if I could have lived by my work. I know there are many good men and good politicians in our regiment and some bad men. I often talk to them and as I take in the *Guardian* regularly I often shew it and read it to those I know and who think as I do, but there is one, a raw country lad, who I often try to reason with, and who I asked a few days ago, "If he was called out would he fire on his own countrymen?", and his answer was, "Yes, on my own father if my commanding officer ordered me." Thus you see ignorance and military discipline makes man his fellow man's enemy. Our regiment used to be much recruiting in the north and manu-facturing towns, but the wiseacre Government have found out that there is too much knowledge in these towns, and our commanding officer has issued orders that, in future, no recruiting parties, or men on furlough, are to enlist any more from these districts—but to go into Kent, Hampshire, Sussex, Somerset, where the more recruits they get with a straw hat and smock frock the better, as their plan was the more ignorant, the better soldiers.' I had found that he belonged to the 1st Regiment of Foot Guards and that he is stationed in the King's Mews, and that he is a weaver from Manchester where he has long followed the political meetings, and is particularly attached to Hunt and his principles.

On Friday evening I met him in Holborn and found that he had been to Theobald's Road to see Russell, the secretary to the union, but was too late (Russell's hour is from 10 to 3) and finding from him that he belongs to the 35th class of the union, of which Oliver, one of the shopmen of the Exchange Bazaar, is leader, I went with him to see Oliver, but he was out. His motive for going was, that as that class meets on Sundays he cannot attend, and he wishes to be moved into some other class who meet on a week evening. This can be done and he asked me to select the nearest class leader to his barracks. In our conversation he stated that their time was so taken up by their duty, and the humbug of going to church on a Sunday, that they were a great deal worse than slaves, for in the morning they had a knapsack drill to shew their necessaries, and just as that was over their commanding officer walks in with his Prayer Book in his hand and marches them off to a damned hole where they are stuck for an hour or two to hear a lot of humbug and nonsense, and he added, 'I am sure the commanding officer has got about as much religion in him as I have.' I have seen Russell since to know his name but he does not know it and as the Bazaar is in a falling state as to means Oliver is seldom there, but I will soon know his name, and will state it.

Wellington to Lieutenant-Colonel Sir John Woodford, 8 January 1833

London. I am very averse to give a soldier his discharge because he has been guilty of a crime, unless the crime should render him infamous in which case it is my opinion that he ought invariably to be discharged with infamy. I don't think that attendance upon a political union however improper in a soldier and inconvenient as an example can be deemed infamous. It would not be so considered by the class of persons from whom soldiers are enlisted, nor possibly would the legislature or others so consider it.

There is no doubt that the attendance of a soldier upon these political unions is a great inconvenience. These societies if not illegal, and liable to be punished in a summary way by a magistrate, are very nearly so, and I believe that their members avoid punishment only because the proof of their real conduct is very difficult.

The paper which you have inclosed giving the report of a conversation between this soldier and another member of the society is of itself a proof of the objects of the society, of the illegal nature of them and the danger that will result from allowing soldiers to associate with such bodies.

I don't like giving opinions upon abstract points of discipline and conduct without discussion and communication with the General commanding the army in chief. I will delay therefore for a day or two to give you my opinion respecting the mode of dealing with this soldier.

That which I earnestly recommend to you is the strictest attention to the interior discipline of the regiment and to the conduct of the non-commissioned officers and soldiers from hour to hour. They should never be exempt from observation and free from controul. You see from this report the benefit resulting from both and I earnestly recommend to you to attend most particularly to the subject.

PS. Since writing the above I have conversed with Lord Fitzroy Somerset on the subject to which it relates.

I don't think it quite certain that you have discovered the man complained of, and at all events the discharge of him from the regiment appears to me to be a measure of extremity which ought not to be adopted without first trying every thing else. I would recommend to you to have the man supposed by you to be the soldier indicated by the Secretary of State, watched by the police. You will then know exactly what he does, where he goes etc. and you can judge whether you ought to punish him in a military manner or to discharge him from the service. He should be kept in observation besides by the non-commissioned officers and steady men of the regiment.

The Earl of Roden to Wellington, 9 January 1833

Dundalk. I have just received your letter of the 3rd. I have promised my vote to Lord Downes and I am doing all I can in his favour, believing that he was the individual most agreable to you. I could not put him for a moment in competition with Lord FitzGerald who I don't think would ever have any chance of succeeding to the representative peerage. The Government have sent to Lord Dunsany who is a candidate and of our principles to say they will not oppose *him*. This I conceive is just out of spite to you knowing that Downes would naturally be your friend but I trust we shall be able to meet them and bring him in though every exertion should be made. I have never received the first part of your letter which you were so kind as to write to me, it was not in the envelope with the end of it or the letters returned. I came back from the north last night where I had had much intercourse with the Protestant strength of the country and I believe as yet they are firm with Repeal. I will send you their address to me and their answer, both of which I hope you will approve of.

The Earl Belmore to Wellington, 9 January 1833

Dublin. I was on the point of writing to your Grace today when Lord Downes called on me soliciting my vote on the vacancy in the representative peerage. I felt anxious to communicate with your Grace, because I am certain the present Ministers can have no chance of influencing the return on the ensuing election, unless the Conservative party weaken their power, by division on personal considerations.

I have received applications from three candidates—Lord Garvagh, Lord Downes, and Lord Bandon, but Lord Downes informs me Lord Dunsany is a candidate, and that Government feel disposed to favour his election.

I think it probable your Grace may feel disposed to support Lord Downes but in accordance with the intention I had previously formed, I shall abstain from declaring my vote until I may hear from your Grace, for I should greatly regret that a Ministerial candidate should succeed for want of concert among the Conservative party.

PS. I forgot to say that I purpose sailing for Holyhead tomorrow morning on my way to St. Giles's where I shall probably remain with Lord Shaftesbury until towards the period when Parliament will assemble.

Wellington to Viscount Mahon, 9 January 1833

Stratfield Saye. I return your account. I have seen something of the same sort in the *Morning Post*.

I do not derive much consolation from this view of our prospects. It is taken of counties only in England alone. It is here that we are strongest. But even here the property is beat by the democratic interest. The towns in England are not; and no part of Ireland or Scotland are taken with the account.

It is a miracle if we should escape another revolution.

I expect the Duke of Cumberland to come here on the 18th of this month. If you would come at the same time I should be delighted to receive you.

CHEVENING PAPERS 685.

The Earl of Wicklow to Wellington, 11 January 1833

Shelton, Arklow. I take the liberty of addressing you on the subject of the Irish representative peerage now vacant. There are several candidates in the field, and it is quite clear that if all stand the peer supported by the Government will succeed. It becomes therefore absolutely necessary for the sake of the Conservative cause more than for the interest of any individual, that some authority or influence should be exerted amongst us to prevent the evil result of division, to procure for one candidate the united support of our party and to induce the others to retire from the contest.

I need not say that it is to your Grace we all look up as the head of our party, or that the great body of the Irish peerage professing Conservative principles would with alacrity attend to your Grace's suggestions. I would therefore take the liberty of requesting of your Grace to consider the comparative merits of the several candidates and to say to whom our support should be given.

I have already been canvassed by the Earl of Bandon, Lord Downes, Lord Dunsany and Lord Garvagh; the latter probably has the Government support, but I have also heard that they intend to set up Lord De Vesci.

I confess that amongst those candidates Lord Bandon appears to me to be the best qualified. He is the first in rank and possesses probably the largest fortune of any peer in this kingdom. He has lately undertaken two severe contests for the Conservative cause, one in the county of Cork in which his son Lord Bernard was defeated, the other in the town of Bandon where his brother was successful.

He also ventures to hope that your Grace's influence will be exerted in his favour in consequence of an application made to you last spring in London by Lord Aberdeen to which he conceives he received a favourable reply. However, upon that point there may be some mistake, and I can undertake to assure your Grace on the part of Lord Bandon that he is quite ready upon this occasion to take whatever part you may consider to be most conducive to the interest of the Conservative party.

The Earl of Aberdeen to Wellington, 11 January 1833

Haddo. We are this day about to begin our journey; but as we have several visits to make in our way, it will be towards the end of the month before we can arrive in London.

The ensuing session will commence under auspices more unfavorable to the monarchy, and to the general interests of the country, than any which has existed since the meeting of the Long Parliament; and I have little doubt that the Long Parliament, when first it assembled, contained as large a proportion of moderate men, and as few decided republicans as the present House of Commons. Whether the same change will take place in the conduct and character of the House, time, and perhaps a very short time, will shew.

I shall be glad, when we meet, to hear what you think, and to learn what you propose to do; if indeed, it should be possible to attempt to do anything which can afford the slightest prospect of good.

After the events of the last six months, and from the necessary topicks of the King's Speech, I imagine it would be difficult for us consistently to avoid bringing forward an amendment; not for the purpose of pressing the matter to a division; but in order to assert and record our own opinions on questions of such importance. Unless you feel inclined to take the business in hand yourself, I should be much disposed to do so. There might be various subjects perhaps deserving of notice in such an amendment; but I think we could scarcely abstain from giving some opinion on the Dutch war, and from expressing a desire to renew our friendly relations with Portugal.

We shall have time however, to discuss these matters when we meet. If you have anything to communicate to me before my arrival in London, the porter at Argyll House will always know my address.

The Earl of Rosslyn to Wellington, 13 January 1833

St. James's Square. I fear some difficulty may arise in the Irish peerage from Lord Bandon having also started, but I hope as Lord Downes has a much greater number of votes, I hope some means will be found to unite their forces against the common enemy.

I am told that Zea Bermudez thinks the Queen of Spain coming round from her liberalism, and it is true that he has obtained an order to remove the vessels belonging to Dom Pedro from Vigo and the Spanish harbours.

It is reported that our Cabinet has sent a more violent and more threatening message to The Hague; but that was before the receipt of the last communication.

I send your Grace a note from Pearse stating the funds for the Duke of York's monument and the disposition of them so far as it has gone.

Wyatt has sent his certificate and applied for payment; but I will not encourage Maitland to give an order till I receive your Grace's commands. I think it may wait for a week when Pearse will be in town, and we may know what arrangements are to be made for raising the statue which Westmacott says he cannot finish before March 1834, a year longer than his contract, which delay he justifies upon the ground of the increase of size from 12 to 14 feet.

I send a sketch of a report which if you approve I will sign and send to Maitland.

I hope to see you on your way to or from Hatfield.

Undated. Docketed 1833, January 13.

Enclosure: John Pearse to Lord Rosslyn, Chilton Lodge, 12 *January* 1833, *and a statement of payments made for the Duke of York's monument.*

The Duke of Cumberland to Wellington, 13 January 1833

Hastings. Many thanks for your kind letter and explanation of the roads. I propose leaving this on Thursday next, sleeping in town that night, and being with you the Friday to dinner, which I take is at 7 o'clock. And hope that the weather will favour our hunting and shooting projects. My horses will leave this that day to be fresh for the sport. I perceive by the papers you also passed through London and arrived there the very day I left it. Had I had the least idea of your coming to town, I would have postponed my departure for a day to have seen you.

I am told Ministers do *not* mean *this session* to bring in their *Church Reform Bill* but merely a *commutation of tythes. This* however strikes me as requiring very *serious* and deep attention and reflection, as this very step may bring us dreadful changes. We shall be able when we meet to talk upon this as many other very weighty points.

Wellington to Sir Henry Hardinge, 14 January 1833

Stratfield Saye. I return Booth's paper, which I consider excellent. I believe that the King has determined that he will not allow of the proposed alteration. I don't know how they can get rid of the Treasurer's office. They may make the board draw upon the Bank. But there must be an accountant for payments. They cannot have a general accountant for army, navy and ordnance. This will be serving God and mammon with a vengeance. I believe that the object was to make the master-general of the ordnance a civil officer at the head of a board of which the Secretary at War and the Paymaster General were to be members; to have had a military officer at the board to do the military ordnance business; and by the moral and political influence of this board to have extinguished the office of the Commander-in-Chief. I cannot understand what other object can be in view.

I could understand loading the ordnance with more business by putting the commissariat under that board. But I cannot see the object of the other scheme, excepting it be determined hostility against every body who wears an uniform.

VISCOUNT HARDINGE PAPERS.

The Earl Howe to Wellington, 14 January 1833

Gopsall. I remember once asking you to have the goodness to put down the name of my eldest boy as an *aspirant* for the honour of having a commission in your regiment of Grenadier Guards. Will you be so good as to enter him now? He is 12 years old and by the time he is 18 will have a chance.

We reached home on Saturday from Brighton, and as I had reason to think the poor King wished to appoint some one in my place at the head of Her Majesty's establishment, I thought it my duty to *force* him to state whether such really was his desire and induce the Queen to consent to make another appointment. He said that such certainly was his wish, but begged me not to *hurry matters*. Still as my situation was anomolous I at last prevailed on Her Majesty to name my friend Lord Denbigh, not a violent politician and most honourable man. This I effected before quitting Brighton and enabled the King to provide for a second son by giving him Lord Denbigh's Bedchamber office. The long negotiation respecting my humble self is thus set at rest and I hope I have done right in settling a question which may have effected [*sic*] in some measure our good Queen's popularity. I shall be in town for the meeting of Parliament. There is a doubt whether the King will be able to come up owing to the allocation of the rooms at St. James's but I *think* it will end in his coming.

Dated Saturday (*i.e. 12 January 1833*). *Docketed* 1833, January 14.
It would seem from the second paragraph that the docketed date is the correct one.

Sir Robert Wilson to Wellington, 14 January 1833

Chapel Street. I shall have very great pleasure in accepting your Grace's flattering and agreable permission to pay my respects at Stratfieldsay on Friday.

I find the French Government throws upon Marshal Gérard the imprisonment of the Dutch garrison and that France and England are seeking pretext to direct its release and return to Holland. The request of the King accompanied with any conciliating expressions could I am assured be even sufficient.

Some verbal communications accompanied the last propositions, and it was hoped they might produce a reply which would permit the renewal of negotiations.

Some letters from Belgium which I have seen describe the distress and discontent there to be heavily on the increase and to menace a crisis in the country.

Wellington to the Earl Belmore, 15 January 1833

London. I am much flattered by your Lordship's letter about the representative peer in Ireland, and the deference which your Lordship is disposed to pay to my opinion.

I have thought it best to support the pretensions of Lord Downes, as this course appears to me to afford upon the whole the best chance of keeping united the whole party.

I judge from your letter that you do not disapprove of this course.

Wellington to the Earl of Wicklow, 15 January 1833

London. I am very much obliged to you for your letter of the 11th and flattered by your deference to my opinion upon the election of a representative peer for Ireland.

I quite concur in your view of the necessity for unanimity. It is for this reason that I have consented to support Lord Downes, and I shall be obliged to you if you will give him your vote.

Viscount Melville to Wellington, 15 January 1833

Melville Castle. In case you should not have heard from any person at Edinburgh by last night's post the details of the peers' election yesterday, I sent you by this post an Edinburgh newspaper containing them. You will perceive that we have carried the election of all our 15 candidates, and if we could have produced a good sixteenth we should [have] brought him in also. Lord Elphinstone is the sixteenth. Lords Queensberry and Napier are excluded, and Lords Airlie, Orkney, and Sinclair are new on our side. We have been put in jeopardy this time, and damaged on former occasions, by a little piece of vanity on the part of some of our friends from whom we should least expect it (Lords Saltoun and Gray for instance) in striving, though perfectly secure, to have more numbers than some of the other candidates, and for that purpose exchanging votes with some of the enemy, who in return take especial care not to vote for any of our friends whom they suspect to be weak. I never will meddle with it again unless every one of the 16 candidates on our side pledges himself to vote for our list exclusively, including himself. By doing so, we can in the present state of the Scotch peerage secure the return of the whole 16. Lord Balcarres's vote on our side this time is bad, and if challenged will be set aside by the House of Lords. Per contra, our opponents have brought forth as one of their voters a soi-disant Earl of Crauford, who, I understand, has lately returned from New South Wales, having been invited to travel in that region for 7 or 14 years, in consequence of his having forged an instrument to establish his right to succeed to the title and estate.

Lord Aberdeen called here today apparently in rustic health. He came to Edinburgh yesterday and proceeds tomorrow to Lord Haddington's in East Lothian, and from thence I believe to Harewood and to London. I expect to see Sir George Murray in a day or two, also on his way to London.

The Bishop of London (Charles James Blomfield) to Wellington, 16 January 1833

London House. I take the liberty of submitting the enclosed statement to your Grace's consideration, in the hopes that if your Grace should be disposed to promote our object, we may have the advantage of your name before we *publish* any advertisement.

Wellington to the Earl of Aberdeen, 18 January 1833

Stratfield Saye. I have received your letter; and I confess that I find great difficulty in answering it. I have never relished as you know the seeking opportunities to carp at and oppose the measures of the Government. The whole course of my life has been different. I dislike such conduct at present even more than I did heretofore. In truth we do not know what sort of constitution we have got; whether a monarchy or a republick under the government of the people; or that best of republick, La Démocratie Royale!

I have seen a letter from Peel upon the subject of our course in Parliament, which in my opinion does not touch the point. We ought to consider what they will do; and what we ought to do on the first day. The rest may be matter for consideration and more general consultation. The proceedings of the first day in the House of Lords depend a good deal upon me and a few others to whom I might write and with whom I might consult.

Will they make the King applaud the Reform Act and its working? If they do we must talk a great deal and shew what its working has been. We might possibly propose an amendment; at all events we ought to enter a protest with our reasons for not joining in the applause, which will contain all our complaints against the working of the bill.

If they should say nothing about the Reform Bill in the Speech we ought to say nothing in the way of amendment to the Address or of course of protest.

They will not say anything about foreign affairs excepting [to] promise information. Of course we cannot move an amendment. But we may say what we think.

The principal field of battle of the campaign will be Ireland; and if they are at all fair upon that subject we must support them.

I think that our friends are much less eager for opposition to the

Government than they were. I have received from many recommendations of moderation.

If we look at our position in the House of Lords we shall be found with a very large majority against or rather not connected with Lord Grey's Government. We cannot avoid however to consider Lord Grey's Government as the last prop of the monarchy, however bad it is and however unworthy of confidence. After him comes Lord Radnor probably and chaos! It will not be wise for us to endeavour to break down Lord Grey without knowing what is to follow him. I happen to know likewise that the King did lately consent to create 25 peers! It is not desirable therefore to engage the House of Lords in an opposition to the Government which will tend to the annihilation of its power to do any good if a great occasion should offer.

The course then which I would recommend on the whole is one of attentive observation rather than of action. That we should observe the measures of the Government whether of foreign or home policy when necessary; but that we should not oppose and bring an opposition to the test of a division excepting in a case of paramount importance essential to the best interests of the country.

ADD MS 43060, ff. 74–75. *Draft in Wellington Papers.*

Wellington to the Bishop of London, 18 January 1833

Stratfield Saye. I have had the honor of receiving your Lordship's letter and I return the inclosure with the addition of my name and subscription for the momentary[1] relief of the unfortunate sufferers.

Knowing Ireland as I do (from having been employed in it) and considering that the disasters which we have witnessed there for the last two years are a disgrace to our times, I cannot avoid to avail myself of this opportunity of writing to your Lordship earnestly to recommend to you to exert the influence which your character and station and the respect which the King's Ministers must feel for your person, must give you over their councils to induce them to adopt some decided steps in respect not only to the Church of England established in Ireland and the property in tithes, and the property of the

---

[1] The word seems to be 'momentary' but perhaps Wellington intended to write 'monetary'.

King's subjects in Ireland, but in relation to the government of Ireland and the protection of the Protestant clergy, gentry, and inhabitants of that country.

Draft.

Lord Downes to Wellington, 18 January 1833

Bert House, Athy. I had a few days ago the pleasure of receiving your Grace's letter of the 11th for which I feel more thankful than I can express. I deferred answering it in the hope of being able to reply to your Grace's question respecting the time of the election. I find that the writ has not yet been received at the Hanaper office, although I know that the certificate of Lord Conyngham's death was signed some days ago by Lord Beresford and Lord Strangford, and forwarded to the Lord Chancellor, according to the form prescribed[1] by the Act of Union. There are 52 days allowed for voting after the writ is issued, so that I shall have sufficient time to send an Irish magistrate round the country parts of England with the writs for the signature of the peers who support me.

To obviate all difficulties in getting the writs out of the Hanaper office, your Grace would oblige me by getting from the several peers who promise you to vote for me, an authority to take out their writs. The enclosed form will I think answer the purpose.

Lord Hertford is qualified to vote now, as it is not necessary for a peer ever to qualify a second time for *this* object. His writ can be sent to him to Naples, where he can sign it in presence of an Irish magistrate if there happens to be one there, but I do not think that I shall be so hard pressed as to require his vote, as your Grace will perceive by the enclosed list that I have already got a majority over any Government candidate that can be set up.

I have marked those of whom I am certain with a D and those who I understand have promised Lord Bandon and Lord Garvagh with their initials B and G. Those with an X after their name I consider the probable supporters of any Government candidate, and I have left without any mark those who I am still uncertain of, of this last number I may reasonably expect one half to vote for me.

---

[1] MS: proscribed.

Lord Fife promised me two years ago, but as he is in the Household I shall probably lose him, if the Government set up a candidate, as I should be unwilling to press him on the subject.

I hear that Lord Anglesey leaves Dublin on Wednesday next for England and that he is not to return. All parties seem to agree that he is the worst Lord Lieutenant that ever came to this country and he leaves it in a state of the greatest anarchy and confusion. Nothing can now save us, but martial law, or the Insurrection Act, with the addition of military tribunals permanently established in the disturbed districts for the trial of prisoners, as neither witness nor juries can be found to do their duty under the present system of intimidation.

First enclosure: Be pleased to deliver to Lord Downes my writ for the election of a representative peer of Ireland in the room of the late Marquis Conyngham.

signature

To
The Clerk of the Crown and Hanaper,
Dublin.

Second enclosure: List of qualified peers—January 1833

Cumberland	D	Meath	x	Howth	Italy
Gloucester		Fingall	x	Kingston1	
Leinster	x	Cavan	D	Sefton	x
Waterford	D	Shrewsbury	x	Roden	D
Downshire		Granard	D	Lisburn	D
Donegall	x	Fitzwilliam	x	Buckingham	D
Wellesley	x	Lansdowne	x	Aldborough	D
Thomond	D	Bessborough	x	Mountcashell	
Headford	x	Carrick		Longford	D
Sligo		Shannon	B	Portarlington	
Ely	B	Fife	D	Mayo	D
Londonderry	G	Tyrconnell		Enniskillen	D
Westmeath		Arran		Mountnorris	D
Ormond	x	Courtown	D	Wicklow	B
Clanricarde	x	Milltown	x	Lucan	D
Cork		Charlemont	x	Belmore	D
Roscommon		Mexborough	D	Kilkenny1	insane

1Deleted in MS.

Clare[1] India		Dungannon	D	Cloncurry	
Landaff		Southwell	x	Clonbrock	
O'Neill		De Vesci	D	Bridport	
Bandon	B	Lifford	D	Rancliffe	D
Castle Stewart	D	Bangor	x	Carrington	D
Caledon	D	Clifden	x	Rossmore	x
Kenmare	x	Doneraile	B	Teignmouth	D
Limerick		Hawarden		Crofton	D
Clancarty	B	Ferrard	D	Langford	D
Gosford	x	Templetown	x	Dufferin	D
Rosse	D	Lismore	x	Henniker	
Normanton		Lorton		Mount Sandford	D
Charleville	D	Frankfort	D	Dunally	
Bantry		Gort	D	Hartland	
Glengall	D	Castlemaine	B	Radstock[1]	
Sheffield	G	Trimleston	x	Ashtown	
Rathdown	D	Dunsany	D	Clarina	D
Dunraven	x	Blayney	D	Rendlesham	
Listowell	D	Hertford	D	Decies	D
Norbury	D	Carbery		Garvagh	
Ranfurley	x	Aylmer		Howden	D
Gormanston	x	Farnham	D	Downes	D
Jersey	D	Mulgrave		Bloomfield[1] 138	
Strangford	D	Arden	B		
Kingsland		Macdonald	D	Downes	53
Molesworth		Kensington	x	Bandon	9
Chetwynd	D	Massy		Garvagh	4
Middleton		Rokeby	D	Government	31
Boyne		Riversdale	B	Uncertain	34
Barrington	D	Muncaster		Abroad etc.	7
Galway	D	Auckland	x		138
Ashbrook	x	Kilmaine			

Sir Robert Wilson to Wellington, 22 January 1833

27 Chapel Street. In a letter which I have received from Sir Robert

[1]Deleted in MS.

Adair in answer to a communication I made him of my inability to pay him a visit at Brussels, he states: 'The whole Belgian affair is a strange one but I hope by a straightforward course to get out of my difficulties before long.' But he told my son that King Leopold was very unhappy and sorry he had gone to Belgium instead of Greece for which he had still a hankering. That he had not a single general in whom he could repose any confidence. That France had offered him 500 officers of all ranks, but he could not accept their services. That he should wish to have some British generals but thought he would not be allowed. That more than half his subjects were Orangists. That the state of the Ministry and temper of the Chamber were further evils. That the French had been induced to go out of Belgium the first time with much difficulty, that the second time they went out without any difficulty, but he was satisfied when they were in a third time they *would never* withdraw *again*.

This last opinion quite coincides with a remark of Count Montrond to myself when he was dining at Prince Talleyrand's. He said: 'The French would withdraw the instant the citadel of Antwerp was taken because it was well known things in Belgium could not remain as they were. That another state of things must occur, the initiative and *dénouement* of which no one could foresee, but it was certain that it would afford France an opportunity to get rid of present complicated engagements and restraints and pursue a free unshackled course there in union with her interests.'

Begging your Grace to accept my sincere acknowledgements for all your hospitable kindness and the very pleasant time I passed at Strathfieldsay.

The Earl of Lauderdale to Wellington, 22 January 1833

Dunbar House. I am a little annoyed at those paragraphs in *The Times* and other newspapers attributing to my management the return made at the Scotch peers election.

If it were true I should have been proud of it, but of all things I hate assuming merit that does not belong to me.

The general state of the peerage of Scotland was that we had about 37. They about 26 peers who were ready to support any body the Minister chose to name, to which five may be added more inclined to us than to them but no way decided. In this state of things there was nothing that could prevent our success but some of our friends giving way to the calls of private friendship or relationship rather than adhering to the political principles which guided them. All we had to do therefore was as much as possible to check this propensity, and in doing so I only took my part with the Duke of Buccleuch and Lord Melville both of whom as well as myself did our utmost and I can assure you I am no ways conscious of any peculiarity of management in which they did not fairly cooperate with me.

I believe I owe this extreme praise to the spleen of my old friends which is evaporating through the medium of their newspapers. All I can say is this that if any person will examine the characters of the only eight candidates they could get they will find ample reason for their want of success, without resorting to the belief of any extraordinary degree of dexterity of management which I am sure neither I nor the two friends I have mentioned are foolish enough to boast of.

There is a young gentleman a Mr. Spottiswood whose name has been down for a commission for some time. He is now nearly 20 which is a little late in life but if you could give Lord Fitzroy Somerset a hint to expedite it he would purchase either in dragoons or infantry which ever he could get soonest. Nobody knows that I have written to you on the subject and I do not intend they should be informed but it will be a great obligation to me if it can be managed.

I have been very unwell since this election.

PS. The name of my friend is Andrew Spottiswoode.

Signature only in Lauderdale's hand.

Lord Downes to Wellington, 22 January 1833

Merrion Square, Dublin. I have received your Grace's note with the enclosure from Mr. Follett respecting the mode of voting, for which I am much obliged to you. I have heard of one or two Irish magistrates who are at Naples—Lord Ossory and Charles Butler Clarke. The oath could be administered by either of these to Lord Hertford. For this purpose the writ can be sent to him by post or by a messenger. Lord Mountcashell is also in Italy, but as he is one of the 28 representative peers he need not take any oath. I understand from his friends that he will vote for me. He would have preferred Lord Bandon but as he (Lord Bandon) either has withdrawn or intends to withdraw immediately, I may count upon himself and all his friends (except probably Lords Shannon and Riversdale) voting for me.

I came to town yesterday on hearing that Lord Lismore had commenced a canvass. He is connected with Lord Grey through the Ponsonbys and I hear that every exertion is to be made in his favor. I have however got so much the start of him that I am under no apprehension. I will not cease however to exert myself and we may not only secure this, but the two or three next vacancies by shewing a strong force now.

Lord *Normanton* has not answered my application. I am told that the Duke of Northumberland, Sir Robert Peel or Goulburn would be the most likely people to influence him. I think that Dowager Lady Salisbury could get *Lord Arran* for me. I wrote to him to remind him of Lady Salisbury's having applied to him two years ago in my favor but I have got no answer yet. May I beg your Grace to see whether these two votes Lord Normanton and Arran can be got for me.

I will send your Grace a list tomorrow of the peers who have promised me and those who are likely to vote for Lord Lismore, and the undeclared. The writ for the election has not yet been received at the Hanaper office here.

Lord Downes to Wellington, 23 January 1833

Merrion Square. I received this morning a letter from Lord Arran promising me his support, and I regret that I gave your Grace so much trouble about him in my letter of yesterday.

I saw a letter today from Lord Roden in which he says that Lord Bandon has withdrawn, and that he had had a letter from Lord Wicklow (Lord Bandon's great friend) saying that he would support me. I think that all Lord Bandon's friends will support me and Lord Garvagh's also as I think that Garvagh may be persuaded to release them, having so small a number.

I send a list made out in a clearer form than the last in which your Grace will see how the numbers stand, as well as we can ascertain them here. Lord Lismore is not canvassing very actively. He is now in Tipperary.

Although Lord Carrick, Limerick, Bantry, Molesworth, Massey, Boyne and Muncaster are in the undeclared list, yet I feel very certain of getting their votes.

Enclosure

For Lord Downes	De Vesci	Castlemaine	x	
Cumberland	Lifford	Arden	x	
Waterford	Ferrard	Riversdale		
Thomond	Frankfort	Lorton	x	
Cavan	Gort	Carbery	x	12
Fife	Dunsany			
Arran	Blayney	*For Lord Garvagh*		
Courtown	Hertford[1] abroad	Londonderry		
Mexborough	Farnham	Mountnorris		
Roden	Macdonald	Sheffield		
Lisburn	Rokeby	Clonbrock		
Buckingham	Rancliffe	Garvagh 5		
Aldborough	Carrington			
Longford	Teignmouth	*Government*		
Mayo	Crofton	Leinster		
Enniskillen	Langford	Donegal		
Lucan	Dufferin	Wellesley		
Belmore	Mount Sandford	Headfort		
Castle Stewart	Hartland	Ormonde		
Caledon	Clarina	Clanricarde		
Rosse	Decies	Meath		
Charleville	Howden	Fingall		
Glengall	Downes 54	Shrewsbury		
Rathdown		Fitzwilliam		
Listowel	*For Lord Bandon*	Lansdowne		
Norbury	Ely x	Bessborough		
Jersey	Shannon	Tyrconnell		
Strangford	Wicklow x	Milltown		
Chetwynd	Bandon x	Charlemont		
Barrington	Clancarty x	Sefton		
Galway	Middleton x	Kenmare		
Dungannon	Doneraile	Gosford		

[1]Deleted in MS.

Dunraven doubtful	Downshire		Hawarden
Ranfurley	Sligo		Kilmaine
Ashbrook	Westmeath		Massy
Southwell	Cork		Muncaster 22
Bangor	Roscommon		
Clifden	Carrick	x	*Abroad, ill etc*
Templetown	Bridport		Howth Italy
Lismore	Dunally		Kingston ill
Trimlestown	Portarlington		Kilkenny ill
Kingston	Landaff		Clare India
Auckland	O'Neill		Aylmer Canada
Cloncurry	Limerick	x	Mulgrave Jamaica
Rossmore doubtful	Normanton		Radstock never voted
Ashtown 32	Bantry	x	Bloomfield Stockholm
	Kingsland		Mountcashel Italy
Not declared	Molesworth	x	Granard Paris
Gloucester	Boyne	x	Hertford Naples

The Earl Bathurst to Wellington, 24 January 1833

Arlington Street. Three months ago the Colonial Office referred to Sir Howard Douglas the American propositions with respect to the boundary question in New Brunswick, having refused to accede to the decision of the King of the Netherlands, to whom that question had been referred. Those propositions contained among other matters the demand of the free navigation of St. John's river.

Sir Howard Douglas transmitted his paper in the beginning of the month of November, and it almost exclusively applied to the river question. He represents at great length that the admission of this right would be ruinous to the province, and by leading to the same claim with regard to the river St. Lawrence, it would be equally ruinous to the whole of our North American possessions. He then contends that the right claimed by them of a free navigation through countries belonging to foreign states, is in itself untenable, and proceeds to quote Mr. Canning's dispatch in 1824 on a similar claim made by the Americans. This paper of Mr. Canning not being in the dispatches published and the quotations being curious with reference to the Dutch question, induce me to send some of them. Mr. Canning says that 'the usages of Europe discountenance the principle of the American claim. That in the case of the Scheldt the treaty of Westphalia confirmed to the Dutch the right to close the mouths of that river and that after the lapse of more than an hundred years, during which the exercise of that right was disputed by the Emperor of Germany the Dutch were left in possession of it in 1785. That the right contended for must be left to the sole discretion of the territorial sovereign, with whom it must exclusively remain to decide in what cases the exercise by foreigners of any of the above mentioned privileges would be attended with prejudice to the national interests. And that the engagements entered into at Vienna shew a disposition to *facilitate* commercial intercourse without however losing sight of the sovereign rights of each particular state.'

In another part of this paper Sir Howard Douglas says that the American Minister at The Hague avowed at an early stage in the Belgian business his delight in the separation of Belgium from Holland, as it would unite France with Belgium in demanding the free navigation of the Dutch waters as a natural and independent right, and that they (the Americans) would find their advantage in it as well in Europe as in America; and Sir Howard in shewing how the Belgium question affects the American question, makes that as his apology for entering so much in the Belgian question.

I understand that Bülow had a conference with Lord Grey last Saturday to explain the principle on which French and British ships are excluded from the Scheldt. He says that it is only in strict conformity with the Dutch declaration of the 16th of November. In that declaration the King says that he will not seize the British and French ships which are in his ports, although they have done so by his ships; that he will only order them to quit his ports within a given time, and will forbid French and British ships from entering his ports, as long as his ships are detained by the two nations. This was at the time considered as a very mild act of retaliation, and must still continue to be so considered. Bülow flatters himself that Lord Grey thought there was a good deal in this explanation, as he said 'Well, but why shut out the Belgian ships; they were not excluded in the November declaration.' The answer was, the Dutch have now acknowledged the Belgian flag, and therefore did not name it in the declaration; they allowed at first Belgian ships to go down, but under foreign flags, but now as the Belgians have seized their boats at Antwerp and have raised their own flags in them, the least which the Dutch could do in return is to withdraw that practical indulgence which has hitherto been shewn them and now inforce the restriction.

You may probably have heard this by another channel, and I therefore doubted whether I should write it.

Talleyrand called upon *my ladies* the day before yesterday. Of course dealt in great encomiums upon you, and his own intention of retiring into the south of France as soon as the interminable Belgian question (as he called it) was concluded. I do not know for what reason, but he chose to tell them, in talking of our revolutionary propensities, that the truth was that they in France were internally in a much more uncertain position.

I hear that Lord Grey has written a strong letter to Lord Hill for the vacant regiment to be given to Ponsonby.

PS. Sir Howard Douglas saw Lord Goderich a week or ten days after he had delivered his paper, and he saw that Lord Goderich had not been aware of Canning's argument about the Scheldt.

Wellington to Viscount Arbuthnott, 24 January 1833

Stratfield Saye. I should think that you and Lord Airlie will be anxious to take your seats, and I should say that the sooner you do so the better.

I cannot foresee however that there will be any occasion for a collection of Conservative forces for some time.

I should say that we ought not to *seek* occasions to oppose the Government, and much time must elapse before any measure can be brought to such a state of maturity as to be in a state to be opposed in the House of Lords, whether brought forward by the Government or by their Radical friends.

The Duke of Northumberland to Wellington, 25 January 1833

Alnwick Castle. Confidential. As I hear that the business of Parliament is likely to commence the first week in February, and I shall have business in the north at the latter end of that month, I am anxious to consult your Grace's opinion as to the necessity of my vote. If it will be required I must go to town at the beginning of February and leave my proxy—if it will not be wanted I should remain here till the end of the month.

We have a report here that your Grace and Sir Robert Peel have been consulted by Ministers on the present state of Ireland, with a view of ascertaining whether the Opposition would support them in an endeavour to re-establish tranquillity and the supremacy of the law in that unfortunate country. I fear that the report is much too good to be true, for I have not yet observed any symptoms of a lucid interval.

I conclude that the same scandalous trick will again be resorted to as before and that the reform of the Church like the reform of Parliament will be introduced into the King's Speech, unless His Majesty has gained by experience.

In this part of the country a general discontent seems to prevail, arising out of disappointed expectations on our side, and disgust on the other side at the breaking up of every thing established and of all social and friendly feeling.

The Marquess Camden to Wellington, 25 January 1833

Hastings. Private. The illness of my sister Lady Londonderry, brought me to this place and the event which occurred, even before I could arrive, has kept me here till the present time.

I did not write to you, after I left Brighton some weeks ago, and after I received your letter, although I had some conversation with the King of rather an interesting nature, but as I did not think the communication of it could be serviceable I did not trouble you with any report of it.

I had some hope I made an impression upon one of the subjects, now impending and a most important one and I still trust it is not effaced— I mean, *Church reform*, but when I left Brighton I was assured no Chamberlain would be appointed and no peer made, and saw soon after Lord Denbigh's appointment and the promotions and Mr. Western's creation. It appeared to me quite clear that although they are acknowledged to be offensive the commands of the Minister can not be withstood. Upon Church reform I strongly advised His Majesty to insist upon the whole plan being laid before *him* before he gave even an implied consent and not to give any answer till he had seen the Archbishop. He admitted that my advice was sound. Not satisfied with my personal appeal, I wrote a letter to which I have not received and I particularly expressed the wish *not* to receive an answer and I have some hope it had some effect, at the same time it is quite as likely he communicated it to Lord Grey, and thinking it not impossible it might have that destiny I so worded it as to make me very indifferent whether he did so or not. When I come to London I will mention other circumstances rather for your amusement than for other reasons.

I propose to be in London on Thursday and will take an early opportunity of calling upon you. There never existed any period of so much danger and which required prudent conduct on the part of the Conservative party, at the same time the country must feel it exists and their conduct alone can save it.

PS. I have twice seen the Archbishop of Canterbury on the subject of the Church reform. He anxiously wishes its postponement. I fear he is too much inclined to give way.

The Earl of Rosslyn to Wellington, 27 January 1833

St. James's Square. I do not know how far your other correspondents keep you *au courant* of the events and reports of the day, and I may therefore trouble you with much that you have from better authority— but very little will serve to restrain me if I do.

1.   Lord Morpeth is to propose, and Sir Francis Burdett to second Manners Sutton as Speaker.

2.   It appears from all accounts to be settled beyond all doubt that the Ministers are to concede the slave question and to propose a measure of emancipation. They stopped the meeting the other day by an assurance that they would take it up themselves. I have not been able in the course of the morning to learn the extent or modifications of the measure, but Holmes seems to believe that it is to be coupled with some assurance of indemnification for the owners of property. It would be foolish to hazard any conjecture in the present state of the business; but it is obvious that the indemnification held out must be illusory or very inadequate to the loss to be sustained, considering the immense British capital imbarked in mortgages on West India property independent of the interests of the proprietors themselves.

It seems probable that the public disclosure of this scheme will produce the greatest alarm in the City and the commercial towns connected with the West Indies. I heard from Chin Grant who had it from Lord Goderich himself that the delegates from Jamaica had proposed to his Lordship to release them (i.e. the colonies) from their allegiance to the Crown; and there is some reason to suspect that they may take upon themselves to relieve them from that burthen, if the course proposed be persevered in.

Lord Chandos, as I hear, must either resign or be turned out of the chair of the West Indian committee tomorrow. They resent his vote with Buxton against them last year, and still more his speech at the Buckingham election; and I don't think his excuse likely to conciliate, viz. that if he had voted according to his opinion, or neglected to flatter the violent feelings of his constituents, he would have lost his election.

This is the less satisfactory that I was assured today that on the previous dissolution of 1831 the West Indian body subscribed and paid in 2000 guineas in aid of the expense of the Marquess's election!

I have seen but few people, but the impression I have received from the general conversation is that the Government has resolved to follow the '*Movement*'; or to speak more correctly that they are incapable of stopping in their downward career, or at least are afraid to incur the hazard. Holmes said, that they have a bill prepared for the reform of the Irish Church in which twelve bishops are ultimately to be reduced, but I have no other authority or rumor to support the credit of the supposition.

It is very currently believed that Lord Melbourne is to go to Ireland, and Stanley to take his seals.

Hobhouse is expected to be the new Secretary; and it is a speculation that before these and other changes, they are to propose a bill to repeal so much of the Place Act as vacates seats upon acceptance of offices.

Two regiments are ordered to Jamaica and the West Indies one from Gibraltar and one from Halifax, from neither of which they can be spared without inconvenience.

I have heard that the Government wishes to augment the army but that as yet they are afraid of losing the support of their friends who will not go with them.

With 15,000 men wanted for the West Indies and 20,000 for Ireland the position is very embarrassing; but if every thing is to be sacrificed to the populor clamour, the Administration may go on for a time whatever may be the ultimate fate of the country.

If I learn anything tomorrow to add to, or correct these reports I will write by the post.

I am persuaded that your Grace ought not to delay your arrival in town beyond the day for it is *now* fixed. Every hour teems with important events, upon which it is desirable that you should have the earliest information, more perhaps to guide the conduct of others than to form your own judgment.

Dated Sunday 27. 1833. *Docketed* 1833, January 27.

Lord Forbes to Wellington, 29 January 1833

Castle Forbes, Aberdeen. Lord Forbes presents his respectful compliments to the Duke of Wellington, and being uncertain whether the proxy which his Grace did him the honor to accept from him last year may not have been vacated by his (Lord Forbes's) presence in the House of Lords since the date of it, and wishing to avoid the chance of any mistake, he requests his Grace, in the above event, to desire a fresh form to be sent to him, which he will immediately sign and seal, and return to his Grace, to be used as he may deem proper.

Draft reply 3 February 1834. Compliments to Lord Forbes. The Duke incloses him two blank proxies; and is much flattered by this mark of his confidence.

Octavius Temple to Wellington, 29 January 1833

Culmstock, near Cullompton, Devon. Confidential. From the station your Grace holds in the country in regard to politicks, and from my great respect for your character as a statesman, I think it a duty to explain to you the objects of an association, recently established in this county, and which if extended may have a most powerful influence in publick affairs.

In ordinary times and under ordinary circumstances it would have been idle and perhaps ridiculous for an individual like myself to have attempted an undertaking of this nature, but in the present '*inverted*' position of society purposes are accomplished by means so totally inadequate, that no one ought to be deterred by such considerations from doing the best for the publick good.

The enclosed proceedings and resolutions of publick meetings held in the parishes of Culmstock and Hemyock and now extending in other parishes will explain the general bearing and object of the measure. Independent however of this declared object the collateral consequences are of the most importance. It is evident by the result of the elections that the Conservative interest has failed altogether as a party. It is also clear that the associations on the same principle, intended as a counterpoise to the political unions and Radicals have likewise failed. This failure is to be attributed in a great degree to the want of a just view of the present state of the kingdom in regard to the two great internal interests, agriculture (the grower of corn) and manufactures (the consumer). Hitherto these two great interests have been united in politicks. The great desideratum then is to create a question which shall cause a schism in these two interests, and thus ultimately raise a strong Conservative party in the state. This question is the repeal or alteration of the Corn Laws. The farmers are fully sensible of the views of the manufacturers in this respect, and know full well success in such views would be followed by their ruin. There will therefore be no difficulty in the plan, *provided every thing like party be avoided,* and that the formation and progress of the society be left *entirely in the hands of the yeomanry themselves.* It may be said by the timid and shortsighted another union will be thus formed, and the present evils increased. This is a vain fear. It is true another union will be formed—but it will be the union of good principles against bad—a union of the property, respectability and orderly habits of the country against the profligate, penniless and vicious population of towns. It will be a union also, not subject as other large bodies to sudden impulses, or to be acted on by designing men for party purposes, since all their proceedings must of necessity require time and will have the advantage of consideration, both from the character of the members and their local separation from each other. It will moreover be a union which from self interest, the great spring of human action, will finally fall under the controul of their landlords—the gentry—and thus restore to that body that influence so essential to the well being of society. Lastly and above all things, as the great majority of the farmers belong to the establishment, it will be a union, once settled the tithe question, that will form a sure bulwark to the Church, and save us from the horrors and misery of fanaticism and infidelity.

The plan has hitherto worked well and all parties have joined, Radicals or Tories, but it is still to be feared, that the Tories from dread of associations in general, and the Radicals, who are too sharp sighted, from seeing the true Conservative tendency of the measure, will both oppose it.

I have taken the liberty of marking my letter confidential because it is evident were the ulterior object known, the measure would fail altogether and should your Grace consider this communication worth notice, I would be thankful that your answer were not addressed to me in your Grace's frank.

Signed: Octavius Temple, late a major in the army and now residing on and cultivating a small farm.

The Duke of Buckingham and Chandos to Wellington, 29 January 1833

Avington. As I shall not be in London on the 4th of February I regret that I cannot dine with you on that day.

I should have been happy to have had some conversation with you on the present state of things. As it is I suppose that the less one thinks of politicks the better. Nothing *can* be done without a strong blow in our House, and we must bide our time and see whether any opportunity for striking it with effect presents itself. Nothing *ought* to be done without the fullest communication between those who are likely to act together, as I am convinced that loose and desultory attacks, without any preconcerted arrangement, will only dissolve the Conservative party like a rope of sand.

Lord Downes to Wellington, 29 January 1833

Bert House, Athy. The writ for the election has not yet been received at the Hanaper office, and I fear that it is intentionally delayed with a view of giving time to some of the friends of Government to qualify on the meeting of Parliament, although by the Act of Union the writ ought to have been sent by the Lord Chancellor of England to the Lord Chancellor of Ireland as soon as the former received the certificate of Lord Conyngham's death. There is no time mentioned in the Act of Union to which the Lord Chancellor is limited, but precedents would go hard with him. In the House of Commons there is no delay allowed. I have written on this subject to Lord Beresford and Lord Strangford, the two peers who signed the certificate of Lord Conyngham's death.

I enclose a list of the peers who are not qualified to vote. There are some of our friends in the list who may qualify in time for the *next* election after this. The operation of qualifying is troublesome and expensive to many peers. The first thing to be done is for the peer to present a petition to the House of Lords praying that his claim to vote may be allowed. The petition is referred to a committee of privileges, who require to see a certificate of the marriage of his parents, and of his own birth and also some proof that he is the eldest son. There were no registers kept in this country in former times, and consequently the difficulty is greater here. Lord Allen would be glad to qualify and vote for me, but as he twice petitioned the House of Lords and was refused as he could not prove his father's marriage, he does not like to try it again. Lord FitzGerald told me a few days ago that he would find it very difficult to qualify for the same reason, but he had put the business into his solicitor's hands, and as his father is alive he hoped to be able to manage it by affidavits etc.

I enclose a list of peers, of whose intentions I am still very doubtful. Probably your Grace could assist me with some of them.

Lord Bandon was withdrawn and I shall have all those who had promised him excepting Lord Shannon, Riversdale, and Doneraile, who I fear will be against me.

Enclosure:

List of peers whose intentions are not known—29 January 1833

Duke of Gloucester	Glengall	Doneraile
Sligo	Normanton	Hawarden
Roscommon	Dunraven	Riversdale
Shannon	Molesworth	Kilmaine
Landaff	Clifden	Muncaster
Kenmare	Boyne	Bridport

List of Irish peers who have not qualified

Drogheda[1] confined	Lanesborough[1]	Carysfort
Hastings	confined	Desart[1] a minor
Conyngham	Ludlow	Clonmel
Denbigh	Winterton	Leitrim
Athlone	Clanwilliam	Kilmorey
Egmont	Annesley	Donoughmore
Darnley	Erne[1] ill	Dillon

[1]Deleted in MS.

Guillamore
Scarborough
Ranelagh
Massereene[1]
  a minor
Cholmondeley
Downe—
  of Yorkshire
Abercorn
Allen
Verulam
Gage
Palmerston[1] House
  of Commons
Powerscourt[1]
  a minor
Mountmorres
Melbourne
Harberton

Avonmore
Dunboyne
Louth
Digby
Harborough
Lisle
Powis
Newborough
Kingsale
Lyttelton
Ongley
Muskerry
Hood
Eardley
St. Helens
Waterpark[1] House
  of Commons
Graves
Huntingfield

Hotham[1] House
  of Commons
Cremorne[1] a minor
Headley
Ffrench
Henley
De Blaquiere
Henniker[1] House
  of Commons
Ventry
Wallscourt
Clanmorris
Gardner
Nugent
Rendlesham
FitzGerald 67

The Earl of Falmouth to Wellington, 30 January 1833

Tregothnan, Truro. Private. I have to regret that my absence at this distance from London must prevent the pleasure I should otherwise have in waiting upon your Grace next Monday according to the card I have today received. Allow me also to say that I shall look with the greatest anxiety to the aspect which public affairs may assume upon the opening of the Reform Parliament.

The Bill has worked precisely in the way I never had a particle of doubt it must and would work, only worse than any one could expect but the framers of it, and I have no hope whatever but that a revolution must rapidly take place if the King should still continue to countenance the measures of his wholly unprincipled and reckless Government.

I have therefore considered it quite useless for me as an individual to leave my business here for the present, but if your Grace should be able to take a less unpromising view of our case after observing the course

---

[1]Deleted in MS.

Lord Grey means to pursue and the chances which may still exist of the Lords being able to stay the revolutionary torrent, I beg to assure you that any intimation of your opinions and intentions with which I may be favoured will receive the earliest attention I can give it, as well as my best thanks for your remembrance of my unaltered principles, and desire to maintain them.

The Earl Bathurst to Wellington, 30 January 1833

Arlington Street. The argument of Mr. Canning with respect to the Scheldt was brought forward in Sir Howard's memorandum for the same purpose that Mr. Canning used it, viz. to contend with the arguments of the United States with respect to the navigation of their rivers: but he undoubtedly thought it was more applicable to the Belgic question than your reference to the Vienna Treaty makes it to be. It is however still a good answer to any claim of Belgium on the general principle of the natural freedom of rivers.

I understand that the language of the Dutch Minister is now that the state of parties in this country since the general election is such, as will not make it advisable for them to look for much support from hence: that they will shape their course accordingly requiring a very moderate, almost a nominal tariff on the navigation of the Scheldt, but standing stout, first in not agreeing to postpone the commencement of the Belgic share of the debt later than the 1st of this month, as that would be indirectly paying the French claim upon Belgium for the use of the French army in their two expeditions, and secondly in refusing to settle the question with respect to internal navigation except by treaty between themselves and Belgium after the treaty with the conference shall have been signed. If they keep to these two points and persist over the exclusion of British and French ships until the embargo on their vessels shall be taken off, I do not think that a conclusion of the business is very near. Whether it be the prospect of this question continuing longer than was expected, or the Turkish question having arisen to make matters more complicated than Talleyrand expected, I do not know, but he announced to us yesterday that he should not go before *October*.

Have you seen the swaggering speeches of Lord Palmerston in Hampshire last week?

I am sorry that I cannot meet you at the Duke of Cumberland's on Friday.

PS. Apsley was much gratified by your keeping him on so long at Stratfield Saye.

The Rev. George Robert Gleig to Wellington, 1 February 1833

Ash, near Wingham. This is not a mere Bible Society. It is one intimately connected with the Established Church, and strictly under the management of the bishops and clergy. I am myself a member of the district committee of which your Grace is requested to become president. I was not present when the resolution passed, but I trust you will accede to it.

I have just sent to the press a letter to the Bishop of London on Church reform; not suggesting any new plans, of which by far too many have been proposed, but pointing out some of the consequences which will inevitably follow the abandonment of any principle, and the rash interference with established rights and property. I am told that the Bishop means to betray us. It is by no means impossible—but of course I assume the reverse—and treat him as if he were the most staunch and faithful of our defenders.

I am going to London on Monday, and will leave a copy at Apsley House.

Docketed Mr. Gleig. Hopes the Duke will accept the office of president of the Dover and Sandwich Society for Promoting Christian Knowledge.

William Murray to Wellington, 1 February 1833

60 St. James's Street. By direction of the standing committee of West India planters and merchants, I beg leave to enclose to your Grace a copy of a memorial agreed to by that body, in consequence of what took place at a conference had with Earl Grey and Viscount Goderich on the 28th ultimo and which has been addressed and sent to each individual of his Majesty's Ministers.

The body trust that the same will receive your Grace's attention.

Signed: William Murray. Chairman pro. tem.

Enclosure: To the Right Honourable the Earl Grey, K.G., First Lord of His Majesty's Treasury, etc. etc. etc. and the other Ministers of the Crown.

The memorial of the standing committee of the West India planters and merchants

Respectfully sheweth

That we, your memorialists, have heard, with feelings of the greatest dismay, the report made to us of the conference held between your Lordship and a deputation of our body, on the 28th instant.

We respectfully recall to your Lordship's recollection, that in the year 1831, your memorialists, as well as the agents of the several legislative colonies, renewed their application to His Majesty's Government that an enquiry upon oath into the condition of our slave population, should be instituted in order to remove erroneous impressions from the public mind.

In the justice and necessity of such an enquiry a numerous meeting of all classes of the commercial and manufacturing interests of the City of London concurred; and by a resolution adopted at that meeting, on the 5th of April 1832, declared that

'As an act of justice to the colonists, and with a view of preventing the fatal effects of that continual excitement, which has already brought them to the brink of destruction, and of removing from the public mind erroneous impressions in regard to the state of slavery in the British colonies, this meeting is of opinion that a full and impartial parliamentary enquiry on oath should be immediately instituted for the purpose of ascertaining the laws and usages of the colonies, the actual condition and treatment of the slaves, their habits and dispositions, and the degree of their progressive improvement and civilization. The information obtained from such authority would not only remove erroneous impressions, but lead to the consideration of such further constitutional measures of amelioration as in the words of the parliamentary resolution of 1823 "shall be compatible with the well being of the slaves themselves, with the safety of the colonies and with a fair and equitable consideration of the interests of private property".'

A petition founded on that resolution was presented to the House of Lords; and their Lordships, on the 17th of April last, appointed a select committee

'To enquire into the laws and usages of the several West India colonies in relation to the slave population, the actual condition and treatment of the slaves, their habits and dispositions; the means which are adopted in the several colonies for their progressive improvement and civilization, and the degree of improvement and civilization which they have at present attained, and also to enquire into the distressed condition of those colonies.'

This committee proceeded in its enquiries until they were terminated by the prorogation of Parliament, and then reported to the House, that, 'considering that there was no prospect of their being able to examine into the state of all the West India colonies during the continuance of the then present session, they had come to an early determination to confine their enquiry in the first instance to the island of Jamaica, and though they had collected much evidence upon the condition of the slaves in that island, some of which is of the most contradictory description, yet they had not found it possible to enter into a detailed examination of many of the other points referred to them, and upon none had their enquiry been so complete as to enable them to submit to the House any definitive opinion'. Their Lordships further state that 'adverting to the advanced period of the session, and to the probable arrival of persons of authority from Jamaica, whose evidence would be most desirable, they have determined to postpone the consideration of any detailed report'.

Since their Lordships have thus reported, persons of authority have arrived in England from different colonies, amongst others the late Governors of Jamaica and of Barbados, of whom the former personally investigated the causes of the insurrection in Jamaica and the state and condition of the slaves taking a part in it. Several eminent persons have, also, been specially appointed and sent to this country by the colonies, at considerable expense, for the express purpose of giving evidence before their Lordships' committee.

A committee of the House of Commons was afterwards appointed (not however at the instance of your memorialists) 'to consider and report upon the measures which it may be expedient to adopt for the purpose of effecting the extinction of slavery throughout the British dominions, at the earliest period compatible with the safety of all classes in the colonies, and in conformity with the resolutions of the Commons' House on the 15th day of May 1823'.

That the committee have made only a partial report. They report, that, 'with some few exceptions the enquiry has been confined to the island of Jamaica and the important question of what is due "to the fair and equitable consideration of the interests of private property" as connected with emancipation has not been investigated by your committee'. 'Some opinions (also) have been pronounced' says the report 'and some expressions used, by witnesses, which may seem to be injurious to the character of persons in high stations in the colonies. Unwilling to present the evidence in a garbled state, your committee have resolved not to exclude from their minutes, testimony thus implicating the conduct of public functionaries; but they are bound to impress on the House the consideration, which it is just constantly to remember, that no opportunity of contradicting or of explaining these statements has been offered to the parties accused; and evidence of this description must be received with peculiar caution.' The committee further declare that 'even the limited examination to which they have been confined' had not been fully accomplished, 'and that they had been compelled to close their labours in an abrupt and unfinished state'.

In a despatch to the Governor of Dominica, dated 5th June, 1832, Viscount Goderich says—'In the present posture of. this controversy, the only course which remains open to His Majesty, with regard to the colonies possessing legislative assemblies, is, to abstain from any measure whatever, until the labors of the two parliamentary committees have been brought to a close.'

The Governor of Jamaica, who had been recently in personal communication with his Majesty's Ministers, in his speech to the legislature of that island on the 30th October last, said—

'Since you last met, both branches of the imperial legislature have been engaged in an enquiry as to the actual relations of society in the slave colonies.' 'The proceedings of these committees have been interrupted by the close of the session, but will be resumed at the next meeting; and their final report, when prepared will be the dispassionate and impartial result of ample and patient examination.'

Your memorialists respectfully submit, that the want of that information which called for the appointment of these committees has not yet been supplied; and that the Government and the nation are now as little qualified to deal with these difficult and momentous subjects as they were when those committees were appointed. Your memorialists therefore respectfully urge on the consideration of His Majesty's Government, the great injustice of taking any substantive measures in relation to the institutions or properties of the colonists, without the completion of these inquiries to which the Government itself may be considered as pledged, no less by the appointment and reports of the committees than by the despatch and the speech above quoted.

Your memorialists are convinced that from the magnitude of the property invested in the West India colonies, and the numerous and extensive commercial relations in this country involved in their fate, any substantive proceeding or declaration affecting their rights and interests rashly adopted or given must be followed by a commercial crisis unparalleled in the history of the Empire.

The recent insurrection in Jamaica, which is proved to have been mainly excited by the mischievous representations impressed on the Negro mind, that 'the King had wished them to be free but that their masters withheld their freedom' cannot fail to establish to your Lordship's conviction the extreme danger to which the lives and properties of the free population resident in the colonies will be exposed by any such proceedings or declaration.

In the view which your memorialists take they beg to be understood as not admitting that any distinction can be made between the legislative and the Crown colonies.

Under these circumstances and considerations your memorialists claim that 'ample and patient examination' of their case which the renewal of, and a report from, the committees of the two Houses of Parliament can alone afford—and they more especially protest against any substantive measures being taken, or declaration made, affecting their rights or properties in the colonies, without previous communication with themselves.

60 St. James's Street.   William Murray
31st January 1833.   Chairman (pro tem.)

Wellington to Octavius Temple, 2 February 1833

London. I have received your letter of the 29 last marked *confidential.* It is my opinion that the Reform Bill has effected a compleat revolution in this country, as it has taken the political power of the House of Commons out of the hands of those who possess property in order to place it in the hands of those who keep shops and exercise trades who are doubtless very respectable, but who are not connected with some of our establishments, and many of them are inimical and opposed to them. I do not know that what is proposed in your letter would be any remedy for this state of things. The political power in the House of Commons cannot be altered by such means.

I confess likewise that I feel a great disinclination to any class of the

King's subjects to associate or combine for any purpose that is not manifest and avowed, and that is not recognized by the laws and by the Government of the country.

Wellington to the Earl of Falmouth, 2 February 1833

London. I have received your letter and I am very sorry that I shall not have the pleasure of seeing you.

It is my opinion that *the revolution* is effected, that is to say that the power in the House of Commons is transferred from the property of the country to those who keep shops and carry on trades.

The first and immediate effect is to annihilate the influence and power of the House of Lords. Indeed the democratick power in the last House of Commons constituted as heretofore, and the conduct of the King had already attained these objects. That which is to follow depends upon circumstances. No man can venture to predict what will happen.

It is obvious that the revolution is compleat. Some may think that the democratick influence ought to be still farther strengthened, and this feeling may lead to farther discussions upon the form. My own opinion is that the work of plunder will begin and that the Church of England in Ireland will be the first victim.

Baron Hugo van Zuylen van Nyevelt to Wellington, 4 February 1833

Londres. On était très pressé aujourd'hui à Stanhope Street, et après un court entretien, dans le quel on traita ma proposition de *curiosité diplomatique*, on m'a proposé une entrevue demain à deux heures. Il me semble qu'on veut gagner du temps et dire peutêtre que des négociations sont en train. La virulence du Vicomte ne me fait rien augurer de bon. Il m'a fait une violente sortie par rapport à mes entretiens avec Lord Grey le 9 novembre. Il prétend que j'ai *parlé* au Premier autrement que je lui ai écrit. Je lui ai demandé pourquoi, dans ce cas, Lord Grey dans ses deux lettres n'a pas relevé cette prétendue inconséquence? Et comme Lord Grey ne l'a pas fait, j'ai trouvé extraordinaire qu'au bout de trois mois on vienne opposer de prétendues paroles à une correspondance écrite. Lord Palmerston m'a prévenu qu'il me poursuivrait dans les discussions du Parlement. Je lui ai répondu, 'Milord, ma correspondance est là.'

PS. Veuiller communiquer cette lettre à Lord Aberdeen.

Dated Lundi, 4 février. *Docketed* 1833, February 4.

Memorandum. Communicated by Viscount Goderich to the West India body. February 4th 1833.

1st His Majesty's Government will be ready to communicate confidentially with the West India body before they submit to Parliament any propositions upon the subject of West India affairs.

2nd The Government retain their original opinion upon the subject of a committee of the House of Lords, of which the West India body now seek the renewal. They felt at the time confident that it would necessarily be followed by the appointment of a committee of the House of Commons, which in all probability would aim at different objects, and be conducted upon different principles; and they apprehended, that the result of the enquiries would be to increase the vehemence of the controversy upon the subject of slavery, to irritate rather than moderate the excited feelings of the public, and aggravate the acknowledged difficulties of the whole question.

What has occurred since the close of the last session has not altered, but has on the contrary confirmed these views; and they would earnestly press upon the West India body the expediency of not calling, upon the present occasion, for a renewal of the committee of the House of Lords.

They admit at the same time that there prevailed, when the committees closed their labours, an impression that their enquiries would be resumed in the present session, and that that impression was countenanced by the language of the respective reports. Nor are they disposed to deny that they themselves looked forward to that course. Considering however every thing which has subsequently passed, and the actual state of the question, they feel that they would best consult the interest of the West Indies, by not inviting the House of Lords to reappoint the committee. If nevertheless the West India body should continue to think its revival essential to their interests, His Majesty's Government will not oppose such a proposition if brought forward from any other quarter.

Feeling it, however, to be their duty in the present crisis of West India affairs, to act upon their own responsibility, they deem it incumbent upon them to state, that the appointment of such a committee would not cause them to abstain from maturing and proposing such measures as they may upon full consideration, and after communication with the West India body, deem to be best calculated to bring this important subject to a safe and satisfactory termination.

Memorial of the standing committee of West India planters and merchants consequent upon the foregoing communication.

To the Right Honorable The Earl Grey, K.G., First Lord of His Majesty's Treasury, etc. etc. etc. and to the other Ministers of the Crown.

Your memorialists beg respectfully to acknowledge the receipt of a communication in the form of a minute bearing date the 4th instant, having reference to the conference of the 28th ultimo; and beg to express their satisfaction at the King's Government having assured them that they will 'communicate confidentially with the West India body before they submit to Parliament any propositions upon the subject of West India affairs'.

Your memorialists submit that if the appointment of the committee of the House of Commons, consequent upon the granting that in the House of Lords, has by the result of its enquiries 'increased the vehemence of the controversy and irritated rather than moderated the excited feelings of the public', that effect is attributable to the publication of the evidence in an incomplete and inconclusive state; and although your memorialists have no desire to aggravate the difficulties of the question, yet they deem it essential to the just and safe settlement of it, that the real extent of those difficulties should be made apparent.

The committee reported that 'the important question, of what is due to the fair and equitable consideration of private property as connected with the extinction of slavery had not been investigated by them'.

Until however, that part of the question shall have been investigated, the further one of the extinction of slavery itself cannot be dealt with. And as the slaves are by the laws of England the property, and necessary to the value of the estates of their masters, in which 'by no fault of their own, and through the encouragement of various acts of the legislature' (as allowed by Mr. Canning) they or their predecessors have invested their fortunes, 'the fair and equitable consideration due to the rights of private property' must in this case involve previous provision of funds to an amount which will be of an appalling magnitude.

Your memorialists submit, that as the committee in the House of Commons was conceded to their opponents, and the evidence for the case of those opponents made public, its labors should not stop at the precise point most prejudicial to the colonists. And they further submit, that the committee is also bound, if it shall report in favor of the extinction of slavery at any definite period, to found that report upon an investigation of the details of a plan upon which it shall be practicable, consistently with the safety of the colonies, and the well being of the slaves themselves, as well as the rights of property.

For these reasons your memorialists do not see that evil in the renewal of the committee of the House of Commons (trusting if such renewal shall be inevitable, to the justice of the King's Government for its impartial constitution) which should deter them from their demand for the renewal of that in the Lords in which House they consider it indispensable to their interests, not only that enquiries should be extended to the other colonies as well as Jamaica, but that the evidence upon oath of Lord Belmore, of Sir James Lyon, and of the deputies especially sent from the different colonies for the express purpose of giving evidence upon their case, should be taken.

With regard to the announcement of His Majesty's Ministers, that the Government means to act upon its own responsibility, and to mature and propose such measures as may seem to them best calculated to bring the important subject to a safe and satisfactory termination, notwithstanding the renewal of the committee, and consequently pending its enquiries, your memorialists must protest against the inconsistency of a course nullifying the only purposes for which the committee shall be granted, and therefore destroying the value of the concession itself. They continue to maintain, that until that committee shall have reported the 'dispassionate and impartial result of an ample and patient examination' of the whole case, in reference to the rights of the colonists themselves, the rights of their creditors in this country, the well-being of the slaves, the safety of the colonies, and their incalculable importance as a constituent part of this empire, the Government are as little qualified to deal with these difficult and momentous subjects as they were previously to granting the committee in the last Parliament.

60 St. James's Street.   W. H. Cooper Bart.
7th February 1833   Chairman pro. tem.

The Earl Belmore to Wellington, 6 February 1833

Grafton Street. I have no desire to precipitate any measure in regard of the papers relating to my recall which I had the honor to submit for your inspection, or to call your Grace's attention further unto them, until the time may arrive when it may appear convenient that they should be noticed, but with your Grace's permission I am desirous of being guided by your advice on the course I should pursue, and I shall be happy to wait on your Grace whenever you may please to see me.

Dated February 6th. *Docketed* 1833, February 6.

Wellington to the Earl Belmore, 7 February 1833

Stratfield Saye. I left town yesterday and have received here your letter.

I should think it desireable on publick grounds to avoid any discussion in the House of Lords for the present, till it will be seen what is likely to be the course followed by the House of Commons.

I should think this the case particularly with respect to the West Indies, but if you should think otherwise and will be so kind as to state what is the course that you would propose to follow I am ready to go to town at any time to attend you, or in my place in the House of Lords.

I am persuaded however that it is not desireable to bring in an early discussion upon any subject connected with the West Indies, and it appears to me that as you was not in the House on the day of the meeting of Parliament you might omit to take your seat for some time longer till you could move for the papers which you require without publick inconvenience.

Lord Downes to Wellington, 7 February 1833

Merrion Square, Dublin. The writ has been at last issued, and I now send to your Grace the papers for Lord Hertford's signature. I am not certain that there is at present any Irish magistrate at Naples—the two who were lately there, Lord Ossory and Butler Clarke, have left it. The election will not close until the 28th of March. So that there may be time for sending the enclosed packet upon the chance of there being an Irish magistrate at Naples. Considering however that I have got 74 promises without counting Lord Hertford's and that Lord Lismore cannot get more than 40—it is scarce worth while giving your Grace or Lord Hertford any trouble about his vote. There are nine peers whose intentions are still unknown to me. I have annexed their names on the other side. Holmes has I believe written to Lord Powis and Clive about Lord Boyne and to Lord Lonsdale about Lord Muncaster.

PS. I have got several votes lately that I had little expectation of. Lord Ormond, O'Neill, Roscommon, Downshire have all promised to vote for me.

[*On the other side*].

Duke of Gloucester	
Marquess of Donegall	
Earl of Normanton	
Earl of Glengall[1]	
Viscount Boyne	
Viscount Hawarden	
Viscount Molesworth	
Lord Kilmaine	
Lord Muncaster	
Lord Bridport	10

The Earl of Aberdeen to Wellington, 8 February 1833

Argyll House. The absence of your name from the protest relating to the capture of Antwerp may possibly produce a bad effect in Holland, as giving rise to the notion that you entertained a different opinion of that transaction.

I suppose you were too late on Wednesday as the House adjourned at two o'clock. If I find from Lord Shaftesbury, that it is usual, and that permission will be granted, have you any objection to my moving on Monday that you have leave to sign the protest on your return to town, in consideration of the early rising of the House before you left London?

I am promised some important information relative to the state of affairs, as regards Portugal, which I will communicate to you, in case you should not be returned to town. The three powers are now beginning to take up this question seriously.

---

[1] Added later.

The Bishop of Exeter (Henry Phillpotts) to Wellington, 8 February 1833

34 St. James's Place. The Archbishop of Canterbury has communicated to us yesterday a letter from Lord Grey, dated some days before the meeting of Parliament, stating that he was not prepared to lay before the bishops any plan of Church reform, though he felt the consideration of that subject to be *necessary and pressing.*

This fully justifies your Grace's suspicion, that Church reform was not to have been mentioned in the King's Speech, had not the mention been rendered necessary by the failure of other matters.

The Archbishop will communicate with Lord Grey on particulars, offering his communication privately on *separate* particulars.

The Irish Church reform is to be announced on Thursday next. I find, that it is intended to pay the Roman Catholic priests, but *not out of the Church property.* On this property—rather on the tythes—is to be saddled (besides 15 per cent to the landlords) the same sum for Church 'sesse [*sic*] making together 30 per cent!

There is to be considerable reduction of the number of bishops, and also, I believe, of their revenues, in Ireland—all the lands of the bishops being to be taken into the hands of commissioners.

All this is very bad in itself, and as a precedent for further measures. Unhappily, the particular circumstances of the Church in Ireland create difficulties in resisting the proposed change, or rather impair the hope of resisting with success. Yet, as at present advised, I think it ought to be resisted, whether there be any hope of success, or not.

It seems certain, that no plan of English Church reform is yet matured. It may therefore be not necessary to bring your Grace to town, before your meditated time of return. When you are here, you will, I am confident, be of inestimable service by speaking on such occasions as shall arise, and as petitions, or attacks of Lord King, may create.

Lord Grey appears to be desirous of sparing the Church. But I have no confidence in these appearances; and, even if he is sincere, I have little doubt, that he would still be ready to abandon us on the first call of party, or ministerial, expediency.

I have ventured to obtrude these particulars on your Grace.

The Duke of Cumberland to Wellington, 8 February 1833

St. James's Palace. I have just heard from Lord Wynford from something that Lord Grey said to him, he rather suspects that the proposition for Ireland will be made on Thursday next in our House; the *bill* is I distinctly understood from *W* to begin in our House though Lord Grey said he objected giving notice this day as he said 'Not to prolong the present debate in the House four days longer'. I give it you as I have heard. We had as you will see a pretty smart brush in the Lords last night. The circumstance I forgot to mention which makes me believe that the notice will be given on Monday night is that Brougham gives as an excuse for *his* not acceding to the postponement of the second reading of his Lunatic Bill was that there could be on Monday night business which could probably lead to *some debate*.

The Earl Belmore to Wellington, 9 February 1833

Grafton Street. I was not aware when I forwarded my letter to Apsley House that your Grace had left London or I should have delayed making any communication until I had heard of your return. I certainly concur in opinion with your Grace that it is advisable to defer any discussion in the House of Lords until it may be seen what is likely to be the course followed by the House of Commons, and further that it may be inexpedient at the present time to allude to West India affairs, especially as Lord Althorp has declared his intention to bring forward a measure on negro slavery in the course of the session. My only object in referring thus early to your Grace is to convey my desire of being guided entirely by your opinion both as to time, and the manner your Grace would recommend me to proceed.

It may be right however for me to observe, that in any step I may take for the purpose of having Lord Goderich's despatch with my reply laid before Parliament, it has been always my intention to avoid expressing any opinion whatever on the contents of his Lordship's despatch, or in any way to question the propriety of His Majesty's Ministers' decision in advising my recall—in fact carefully abstaining from raising any question personally relating to myself, or in any way reflecting on their colonial policy—leaving it to the House and the publick to form their opinion on these points by an examination of the charge and the defence; but that as His Majesty's Ministers have

65

thought fit not only to advise my recall, but to detail the reasons for this proceeding in separate charges made against my Administration—some of which proceed from public bodies in this country; the explanation I offer may be suffered to obtain equal publicity with the charges which have been preferred, which only can be attained by making both public documents.

In furtherance of this, it was my intention had your Grace been in town to have submitted to you the propriety of my waiting on Lord Goderich, to express my hope that on further consideration he would not object to lay his despatch of the 18th February, together with my reply, before Parliament. If he still continued unwilling, to inform him I should feel it necessary to apply to this effect from my place in the House; and then if the papers were refused to give notice of a motion on a convenient day for their production—when if all other efforts failed I should read both despatches as part of my speech. I perceive that your Grace is not aware that I had taken my seat, and was in the House during the whole of the debate on Tuesday evening.

Dated February 9th. *Docketed* 1833, February 9th.

The Earl of Hopetoun to Wellington, 9 February 1833

Stevens Hotel, Clifford Street. Lord Hopetoun has taken the liberty of sending the accompanying form of proxy to the Duke of Wellington which he trusts his Grace will allow to remain with him as on several former occasions.

Draft reply 11 *February* 1833. Compliments to Lord Hopetoun. The Duke will take charge of his proxy with great satisfaction. He is much flattered by this proof of his Lordship's confidence.

Wellington to Lord Downes, 10 February 1833

Stratfield Saye. I have not written to you lately about election writ. But I have not been unmindful of it.

Lord Chetwynd, Lord Hawarden, Lord Lifford, and Lord Charleville will vote for you. Lord Clonmell and Lord Rokeby will if they can qualify; which I think they cannot after the issue of the writ. You will see that you have Lord Hawarden out of your list of doubtful inclosed in your letter of the 7th which I have received this morning. I think that I may be able to get you the Duke of Gloucester, the Earl of Normanton, the Earl of Glengall. I will send the papers to Lord Hertford however; informing him of what you say in case he should find that he cannot qualify without great inconvenience.

Wellington to the Bishop of Exeter, 10 February 1833

Stratfield Saye. You may rely upon it that I was right. The first attack upon the Church was to be made upon that part of it in Ireland. They are not prepared with any plan in relation to the Church of England; nor had they considered the language in which they should mention the subject in the King's Speech.

There is much to be said about the Church of Ireland. I will consider what is best to be done between this and my return to London. But I am very much afraid that between Liberals and Saints and opposers of the Roman Catholic Relief Bill I shall stand nearly alone in my opposition to these measures founded as it will be upon the principles of the Reformation in England as well as in Ireland.

I have no notion of the union lasting if the Government give a blow to the Protestant religion in Ireland. The Protestants of the Church of England or in other words the proprietors of the soil are its only friends. They will quit the country if they should think that Government abandon them.

The King's oath militates with the idea of depriving the Church of England of its sees that is 'its churches' and with the measure of taking the property of the Church into the hands of commissioners. This last measure as well as that respecting the cess are thought to be inconsistent with the Act of Union.

The payment of the priests is in my opinion inconsistent with the principles on which the Reformation was established and now stands in England. We have gone very far in educating priests. We shall go further if we pay them, particularly if the King does not appoint them. But whether he does or not if the appointment should be made by the consent of the Pope the payment of them becomes a very important State question; and as well worthy of the consideration of the R[ight] R[everend] bench and of this Protestant country.

Draft, greatly over written.

Wellington to the Earl Belmore, 10 February 1833

Stratfield Saye. I have received this morning your letter of the 9th. It is impossible to suggest any course to be adopted in Parliament on a question connected with the West Indies which if not attended by inconveniences is not liable to the imputation of being attended by inconveniences by which many may suffer.

It appears true however that the course suggested by your Lordship is as little likely to be liable to such imputations as any that could be pointed out. It leaves the case very much in the hands of the Government. They can avoid discussion altogether if they wish it; and there is this further advantage attending it that if forced to discuss the subject you can with perfect propriety delay to make your motion till the subject will have been forced into discussion by others. I think therefore that the sooner you commence this kind of proceeding by your communication with Lord Goderich the better. I quite agree with you in thinking that it is important for you that the public should hear the truth upon your recall.

Captain W. White to Wellington, 10 February 1833

65 Quadrant, Regent Street. Permit me to offer my humble acknowledgments for the honor you have conferred by condescending to acknowledge the acceptance of my little pamphlet.

Knowing the great interest your Grace takes in every thing connected with your country, least you might not have seen the *British Traveller* of last night, I have taken the liberty to transmit it, as there is a very important article, taken from the *Guardian*, relative to the imputations cast by *The Times* upon the Dutch Minister, your Grace will be pleased to see. There are also two leading articles upon Portugal written by myself and X. I beg also to forward the *Alfred* of today in which there are four of the leaders by me. They were written for the *Naval and Military Gazette*, but for want of space transferred to the *Alfred*.

In making this communication to your Grace, the object I have in view is to explain the nature of my connexion with the press. I am intimately acquainted with the editors of four out of six of the morning papers, and contribute leading articles to them all notwithstanding we differ upon some points. This affords me a facility of communication which probably no other individual in London possesses. My services are greatly at your Grace's command or that of your friends, and you may be assured that the most implicit confidence may be placed in my honor and inviolate secrecy where required. It is in consequence of this, I possess the influence I do with so many papers professing different views. *The Times* alone, and which was also in the habit of receiving constant communications, has quarrelled, or even evinced displeasure, with me upon the Portuguese question, although they were the last that ought to have done it, as the cause of my turning upon and abandoning the Pedroit cause was the liberty which had been taken by the Pedroit Ministers here to make me the channel of propagating falsehoods; which upon the faith of their honor I had received implicitly as truth, and circulated in *The Times* as well as *Chronicle*. Notice at page 93 of my pamphlet: 'When the poor deluded wretches' etc. The editors of all the other journals were satisfied with my explanation, and they one and all, the *Chronicle*, the *Herald*, the *Advertiser*, have ever since been silent; although they have declined noticing the truths set forth in the pamphlet. *The Times* to prevent its being read condescended to abuse the author, that too strange to say, after having three years ago praised him and his truths up to the skies.

I would take the liberty to draw your Grace's attention to page 52 and 80 in answer to Lord Grey's denunciations of '*Perjury and usurpation*'.

Humbly begging of your Grace's pardon for this intrusion I beg to conclude with stating, I shall be proud to attend to any call, or to any command you may condescend to honor me with.

The Earl of Rosslyn to Wellington, 10 February 1833

St. James's Square. I know from Holmes that he gave your Grace some intimation of the purpose of Ministers with respect to Ireland; but having had it confirmed from indisputable authority, I thought it better to repeat the information that tomorrow notice will be given in the House of Lords of the intention to propose the coercive measure for Ireland, and to present a Bill for that purpose upon Tuesday, of which the second reading will be fixed for Thursday.

There will probably be little conversation on Tuesday; but considering the immense importance of the question, and the very high station your Grace occupies in the public estimation, I cannot help feeling very anxious that you should be present on Tuesday.

The measure as I understand is to enable the Crown to change the venue in all criminal cases at its own discretion from any county in Ireland to any other county in that kingdom or to the English counties of Cheshire and Lancashire, or any in the principality of Wales. This extends to all capital cases.

In cases not capital the ordinary course of the law including trial by jury is to be suspended; and power will be given to the Lord Lieutenant to declare any county or district subject to the provisions of this Act to be passed; and then criminals are to be tried by courts martial to be appointed for that purpose, and those courts are to have power to inflict all punishment short of death including even transportation for life.

I have heard this account from two or three quarters, and in substance I believe it to be true; I know not what power of appeal is to be given in any case, or what limitations may be introduced and Holmes who saw the rough outline of the Bill seems to have thought it then in a very crude state.

I presume but do not actually know that this must also be accompanied by the suspension of the *habeas corpus* either by a Bill, or by authority under the old Irish law.

I hear that when Stanley heard of Lord Anglesey's return he broke out, and said in private if that man goes back any measure is useless.

Dated Sunday evening 10 February 1833.

Wellington to the Earl of Aberdeen, 10 February 1833

Stratfield Saye. The omission to sign the protest occurred exactly as you state. I went to the House of Lords, and was informed that the House had adjourned; and I concluded that I was too late to sign the protest; and wishing to arrive here by dinner time I did not dismount from my horse. If I had gone into the House I should have found that provision had been made to enable those to sign who had not counted upon the early adjournment of the House. I am therefore alone to blame. I must ask a favour in order to be permitted to sign; and that I will not do from those who now guide the decisions of the House. The boon would be refused; or some impertinence said which may as well be avoided.

If we and our friends in the House of Commons could understand each other better, we should under existing circumstances possibly be able to do some good in the Lords. But what can be expected when we see Sir Robert Peel in contradiction to our assertions and proofs, and to the known facts of the case, assert that he does not believe that the Government had violated its neutrality in the case of Portugal.

Holmes writes me that Lord Melbourne makes his motion about Ireland on Tuesday. I have not seen any notice of this intention. But if he should give his notice tomorrow and I should hear of it by Tuesday morning's post, I will go to town on Tuesday.

ADD MS 43060, ff. 74–75. *Copy of the first two paragraphs in Wellington Papers.*

The Earl of Aberdeen to Wellington, 11 February 1833

House of Lords. The protest is of no consequence, especially if you should take some opportunity, when the affair of Antwerp may be under discussion, to express your assent to the sentiments contained in it. I find that a good many peers abstained from signing it, in consequence of imagining that some difference of opinion existed between us on the subject.

I am quite certain that you have been greatly misinformed respecting Peel's language, whether you received the impression from a newspaper, or from any other source. I know that he not only agrees entirely with us about the scandalous violation of neutrality in Portugal, but carries his indignation still further, and expresses himself still more strongly. Towards the close of the last session, his principal attack on the Government was in consequence of their manifest breach of neutrality. He was in the House while you were speaking the other night; I saw him the day after, and in mentioning your compendious method of putting an end to what is called the civil war in Portugal, by a proclamation recalling the King's subjects; he not only agreed, but added, that the honest execution of the existing law of the country would be amply sufficient. I have never known him vary an instant in his manner of treating this subject, and therefore it is quite impossible that he should have expressed himself as you imagine. I have not seen him today, but I feel quite certain that he will himself confirm what I state.

I take this opportunity of letting you know that there will be no business, at least relating to Ireland, in the House tomorrow. The Address is not finally carried in the House of Commons, and if the nature of the coercive measures were explained before this is the case, they fear it would give rise to a debate of another week. On Friday therefore, it is at present intended to give notice; and on that day Lord Grey will also explain the whole measure which it is intended to introduce. But on this matter, you will of course hear more correctly from Rosslyn.

The Earl of Rosslyn to Wellington, 12 February 1833

St. James's Square. Grey, as you will have seen, has given notice for Friday, and I have no doubt that it will come on as fixed. If there be any change tomorrow I will write by the post; but if things remain as they now stand I need not trouble your Grace farther.

You see that contrary to the supposition of Ellice, the Church plan has been received with open arms by O'Connell and hailed by all his followers except Ruthven.

Lord King is dissatisfied with it as being much too little a reform.

The question in all its bearings, is one to require the utmost consideration and caution; and even if the outlines of the principle were acceded to require a great deal of examination in the details.

It seems rather preposterous to begin with a heavy tax upon the incomes of the clergy exclusively; while they are the only persons in the country who have no income at all; and for all that I can see not much hope of getting one.

Sir Alexander Grant to Wellington, 12 February 1833

Carlton Gardens. Your return to Strathfieldsay deprived me of all opportunity of thanking your Grace for your kindness in taking the trouble of telling me that the West India memorial of the 31st ultimo had at length reached you.

From the copy of a Cabinet minute, communicated immediately after its receipt by Lord Goderich, which has since been sent to your Grace you will have seen that we produced considerable effect upon the Government—and from that of the second memorial (that of the 7th instant) which we presented in rejoinder, you will perceive that we accept the offer of permitting us to renew the committee in the Lords.

Lord Harewood upon whose motion it was granted last year is not in town—and, as your Grace was upon the committee, I am deputed by the West India body to express their anxious hope that you will not refuse to give that weight and consideration to their cause which your moving for its reappointment would confer. If your Grace will kindly consent to this, perhaps it will be best to enter the notice of the motion for some day next week—which, should you not intend coming to town for some days, Lord Ellenborough would do in your name.

I apprehend that this would be the ordinary course but should your Grace be of opinion that it would be better that the West India body should petition for the reappointment of the committee, that step will be adopted without hesitation.

The Bishop of Exeter to Wellington, 12 February 1833

House of Lords. Lord Althorp has announced his plan.

Ten bishoprics are to be extinguished, after the life of present holders. There is to be a tax of 5% on all livings of £500 per annum—of 7% above £800—of 10% above £1000—of 15% above £1200.

On all bishoprics of 5% above £4000—7% above £6000—10% above £8000—15% above £10,000 per annum. This is to operate on all present incumbents.

The reduction of bishoprics not to take place till after death of present incumbents.

Armagh is to be £10,000 per annum (with the tax of 10%) making it £9000.

Derry is to be reduced to £8000 with the tax.

The most objectionable part is this. The tenant of bishop's lands, by offering to pay six years purchase, is to be enabled to make his interest perpetual—and the amount so obtained is to be at the disposal of Parliament for any purposes not Church purposes—in other words, I fear, though this is not stated, for paying Popish priests.

Lord Althorp is so very obscure, that it is not easy to catch his plan. This and the hurry in which I write will render my statement scarce intelligible.

Dated 6 p.m. *Docketed* 1833, February 12.

William Holmes to Wellington, 12 February 1833

I am still confined to my bed, and I therefore wrote to Wood to send me some news. I inclose you his note just received. The first part refers to the Irish Church reform which Althorp brings in this evening. The latter to the coercive measure which Lord Grey will state on Friday.

Dated Tuesday evening. *Docketed* 1833, February 12.

Enclosure: Charles Wood to William Holmes, 12 February 1833.
Private. I suppose we shall have the devil to pay and no pitch put: but as you know I am all for being abused by the Tories: though I am anxious for, and most ready to acknowledge their gallant support.

Inglis will of course quarrel with the principle; but your people can hardly do so, after agreeing to the tythe report—they must quarrel a good deal or *degree.*

I suppose you say if our people are satisfied, your's won't; and though I think our's except some 100 or so will hear reason we shall have grumbling enough at first. We give you a *sweeping* measure.

Lord Grey *states* his measure on bringing it in on Friday.

PS. I got your message by Scanlan but could not come up.

Wellington to the Earl of Aberdeen, 12 February 1833

Stratfield Saye. In consequence of the receipt of a note from Lord Rosslyn I have postponed my departure from hence for two or three days.

I did not hear Sir Robert Peel speak. But I have read his speech in four newspapers. In all he is represented as having acquitted the Government of any breach of their neutrality in Portugal! My opinion has long been that Sir Robert Peel and I would never again serve the publick in the same council. I entertained this opinion previously to the occurrences of May 1832.

But it is possible for two men to serve the publick out of office. But there must exist candour, truth and fairness in the views of both; and the line of proceeding of each should be taken without the desire of contradicting and opposing himself to the views of the other.

ADD MS 43060, ff. 76–77. *Copy of the last two paragraphs in Wellington Papers.*

Wellington to Captain W. White, 13 February 1833

The Duke of Wellington presents his compliments to Captain White. The Duke has returned the newspapers which Captain White inclosed to him.

The Duke has nothing to say to the newspapers; and he is desirous of avoiding to have any communication of any description with any of them.

Wellington to Sir Alexander Grant, 13 February 1833

Stratfield Saye. I have just now received your letter of the 12th.

I am always ready to come forward when it is thought that I can be useful to any class of His Majesty's subjects. I think it very desirable that the committee in the House of Lords should be reappointed and should continue its labours. But I doubt my being the individual to move for its reappointment with most advantage.

In the first place I did not attend the committee for the same reason that has prevented [me] from attending other committees. I don't hear much that passes; and I find my time thrown away in giving such attendances.

Secondly my interference will be concluded one of party which in the existing state of West Indian affairs had better be avoided. This will be the case particularly if the motion for the renewal of the committee in the House of Lords should be the first mention of the subject during the session.

I recommend you to get Lord St. Vincent or any Lord interested in the West Indian committee to make the motion. I will attend and support it. If however you and your friends think it best that it should be made by me I shall be in the House of Lords on Friday and you can let me know by a line to my house in London what you determine upon.

I think that the committee ought to be appointed in consequence of a motion made in the House.

The Bishop of Exeter to Wellington, 13 February 1833

34 St. James's Place. In the very hurried scrawl which I sent to your Grace from the House of Lords last night, I fear I made but a most imperfect sketch of Lord Althorp's, or rather of Lord Grey's, plan of Church reform in Ireland. I will not now attempt to supply the defects of that sketch, because you will see the plan more accurately reported in the newspapers. But I am desirous of troubling your Grace with my view of the result of this scheme, and I will take the liberty of stating my own impressions, before I read what was said by any of the speakers who followed Lord Althorp, and before I see any one who can give me his views. In the course of the day I hope to see more than one of our staunchest bishops.

The effect produced on my mind is that of deep, unmitigated, unmixed, dismay. To me, after the reflection of sixteen hours, it appears on the coolest consideration, that no better course is left, than to save the only thing, which an unprincipled Government cannot take away, the integrity of our own character, and the consciousness of an unflinching adherence to honest principles, by seizing, or making, an early opportunity of avowing those principles, and putting on record our unaltered and unalterable spirit of resistance to the wicked views of His Majesty's Ministers.

Your Grace will believe that in saying this, I am far from excluding— on the contrary, I feel the duty, as well as the expediency, of including —a wish for cool, sober, unimpassioned proceedings. Your Grace's absence I deeply lament. I dare not take the liberty of urging your return. Yet I should certainly think we had one chance the more, under Providence, of doing wisely, if not effectually, if you were here.

I have been interrupted by Mr. Shaw (Member for University of Dublin). His report of what passed after Lord Althorp's speech—of the tone of the House—the base truckling of Ministers—the flirting between O'Connell and Mr. Stanley, with Sir F. Burdett as the go-between—has only embittered and deepened my former feeling. But I will not say more, till I have seen the Bishop of Durham, on whom I am about to call. One thing, I conceive, must be quite clear—that they who before thought that the Church in Ireland might be treated very differently from the *same* Church (for such it is, and by every honest Churchman must be avouched to be) in England, must now see their error. The principle of despoiling the Church by taking to the disposal of Parliament the price to be paid by the tenants of bishops' lands for extinguishing the right of ownership in the bishops, and transferring it to the tenants, is put forward so unnecessarily, and for so trumpery a pecuniary gain, that it can only be put forward at all, as the small end of the wedge. Had this price been to be employed in advancing the cause of true religion, the measure, however dangerous, would not have been, what it is, absolutely and simply wicked. To be sure, the principle is equally formidable to all other property—and as such ought to excite alarm in all who possess property of any kind; but it will not. For men are determined to blind themselves.

Mr. Shaw told me, that an Irish Member, Mr. O'Connor, son of a personage of that name, who was tried many years ago for stopping and robbing a mail coach, said to him in the simplicity of his heart, 'I wonder that O'Connell, and our people, are so much pleased with this plan. I am sure I am not, nor will the country be, while there is to be a *sixpence* paid in any way for tythe.'

Dr. Elrington has just been here. He is at the head of a deputation from the Irish clergy, soliciting the protection and aid of Government. He is just come from Mr. Stanley, and has given me an account of what little passed on the subject of last night's business. Mr. Stanley declared that 'the measure had the assent of the *Primate*—that although they differed as to details, he (the Primate) assented to the principle'. Dr. Elrington doubts this, and is astonished to hear it—he writes by this post to the Primate, asking him, whether this be so.

Mr. Stanley said that he had great hopes, from what O'Connell said last night, that the tythes would now be paid without resistance. Dr. Elrington expressed himself as of a different opinion. 'Oh!', replied Mr. Stanley, 'he is committed'—seeming, or pretending to believe, that such a man cared whether he was committed, or not.

The commissioners are to be the Primate, the Lord Chancellor, some other official person (I forget who), three bishops to be named by the Crown, and three paid functionaries.

In conclusion, Dr. Elrington taking his leave said, 'Sir, you last night stated, that you had been in communication with some of the leading clergy of Ireland, who had assented to the plan. I had no right to expect to be consulted, but as it is known, that I am here on a mission from the Irish clergy, it may probably be supposed, that I and my brethren here are those persons who have given their assent. I feel it necessary therefore now to state that it has not mine.' 'Oh!', said Mr. Stanley, 'we can hardly expect to agree in all details.' 'No, Sir—my dissent is to *principles*.' This was received with a scowl, and a bow.

I hope your Grace will think this was no more than a prudent declaration on the part of Dr. Elrington.

I have seen the Bishop of Durham—but he had only just arrived in town, and had not seen his newspaper. He was, besides, obliged to attend a commission. I had, therefore, no opportunity of much conversation. He is as much alarmed, as other honest men.

I am ashamed of trespassing on your Grace's patience with so long a detail. But the occasion will excuse, if not justify it.

The Earl of Aberdeen to Wellington, 14 February 1833

Argyll House. I took an opportunity last night of mentioning to Peel that a notion had prevailed, supported by the reports of his speech in the newspapers, that he had taken a different view of the conduct of Government with respect to their neutrality in Portugal, from that which had been expressed by us in the House of Lords. He confirmed my belief of this being entirely a misconception; and this day, I have received a letter from him, which I inclose, in order to put you in possession of his real sentiments, and in the hope of removing an impression which appears to be erroneous. He was certainly surprised that I should have entertained any doubt on the subject.

Enclosure: Sir Robert Peel to the Earl of Aberdeen, 14 February 1833.

Whitehall Gardens. I shall be very glad to see you tomorrow morning at eleven. Pray look in the interval at the debate on the 11th February 1805 on the war with Spain and particularly at Sir John Nicholl's speech (then Advocate-General). I have no doubt that speech contains what will be urged in defence of the present embargo—and fully accounts for Sir John's hesitation to pronounce it illegal.

I had not a conception until you mentioned it to me, that I had in the opinion of any one taken a different line from that taken in the Lords respecting our conduct to Portugal. I have not referred to any newspapers and know not what I may be reported to have said, and in truth on any matter of foreign policy or any matter not perfectly familiar to the reporters I should be not much surprized at mistakes which slight as to words, give a totally different character to the tenor of expressions.

In substance I said that our fleet off Portugal might have abstained from direct interference, and so far have avoided a breach of neutrality —but that the neutrality had been nominal and not real; that the Government that now pretended to lament it were themselves the cause of the civil war in Portugal, were direct parties to it by allowing the use of our ports and military means to Don Pedro, and that their duty was to enforce the Foreign Enlistment Act, and to recall the British officers serving either with Miguel or Pedro. I added that every event that had taken place confirmed the view I had taken last session.

I recollect also that I said that if Donna Maria had attempted to recover Portugal by an expedition fitted out with her own means and sailing from any port of Brazil—or any place not under our jurisdiction —I should not have advised forcible intervention to prevent her. All this is in exact conformity with what I said last year, and moreover is my exact opinion on the matter.

I heard your speech in the House of Lords, and never till you spoke to me last night, had for an instant an impression that there was any difference in substance between your language and mine. I insisted on the necessity of the recognition of Don Miguel, and recollect praising him, saying that he had been exposed to a severer trial than any Prince in modern times.

Robert Henry Jenkinson to Wellington, 14 February 1833

Norbiton. I have the honor to submit to your Grace's consideration the enclosed letter which I have received from Mr. Pain, and I beg leave to suggest that your Grace should authorize some member of the House of Commons to endeavour to ascertain from Sir Thomas Troubridge the occasion and object of his proposed motion, and whether any communication upon the subject has been with the Trinity House. I do not know Sir Thomas Troubridge's politics, but I am disposed to think the matter does not originate with him, but that he has been put forward by others who are anxious to do away with this particular patronage of the Lord Warden, without any real regard for the interests of the public, or just ground of complaint against the present system; I cannot however speak positively upon this point, and infer it only from circumstances that have come to my knowledge. In the mean time I would not have your Grace move in the matter beyond what I have ventured to suggest until we have *quietly* obtained, if possible, some further and more precise information of Sir Thomas Troubridge's intentions. It is to be presumed that he is aware that the subject underwent a full and thorough investigation before the committee under Lord Wallace some twelve or fourteen years ago.

Enclosure: Thomas Pain to Robert Henry Jenkinson, 11 February 1833.

Dover. I beg to call your attention to a notice given on Friday in the House of Commons by Sir Thomas Troubridge, of his intention to move on the 19th of March for a select committee to take into consideration the laws of pilotage with a view to amend them.

Sir Alexander Grant to Wellington, 15 February 1833

Carlton Gardens. Permit me to return my grateful thanks for your kind reply to my application on behalf of the West Indians.

Your Grace's suggestions will be implicitly followed. We shall endeavor in the course of this morning to find a peer, connected with the body, to give notice of a motion (for any future day that will suit your convenience) for the renewal of the committee: when your support upon a subject of this magnitude may surely be attributed with more fairness to the views of a statesman than to those of party.

Mr. Burge and myself will be at the House of Lords this evening in hopes of seeing your Grace.

PS. Mr. Fowell Buxton assured Lord Chandos in the House last night that 'the Government had all but completed their Bill for the extinction of slavery and that it would be *quite ready* by tomorrow (Saturday) evening'.

Dr. Lushington appears to have made assertions to a similar effect two nights since at a meeting in the Tower Hamlets.

Dated February 15. *Docketed* 1833, February 15.

George Loggan to Wellington, 15 February 1833

London. As an officer who served with some credit in the Royal Fusiliers during the Peninsular War—and having in the cause of that service been severely wounded—and never having been brought before your Grace's notice otherwise than favorably, I most respectfully presume to intrude in the full assurance of at least obtaining that ready attention which those officers always experience who had the honor and happiness of serving under your Grace.

It will be readily perceived that this communication is confidential, and that, with the single exception of F. T. de Sampayo Esq. (Portuguese Consul-General) no other individual in this country is aware of the circumstances. To your Grace I most unhesitatingly and unreservedly state the facts.

From having been much in Portugal, and speaking the language, my inclinations entered deeply into the present contest in that country. No man can well account for his political bias. Your Grace need not, therefore be detained by any such explanation of mine—suffice it that *Dom Miguel's cause* has long interested all my wishes—and so far back as last September I applied to several officers, under whom I had served, for testimonials.

Their replies (copies of some of which are transmitted herewith) I had forwarded to Lisbon by Mr. Sampayo, the Consul-General, together with an offer of my services to H.M. Dom Miguel. In the interim I have contributed to the support of the cause by writing and publishing paragraphs, letters, etc.

It is now intended that I shall proceed forthwith to Oporto there to ascertain, by personal observation, the following points (viz.) The number of batteries by which the place is defended, their nature and construction, the quality etc. of the ground round these batteries, the number and nature of the guns etc. the ammunition and shot, the strength of the detachments stationed in or near them, of what nation etc. Also the real strength of the whole garrison, their state of armament, discipline, etc., whether content or otherwise and if vigilant, likely to remain faithful. The weakest points of the defences etc. together with the true state of their stores, ammunition, provisions, military chest— state of politicks etc. with such other remarks as may occur to me. I am then to proceed, by the best method I may, to Lisbon to the Marquis Santarem, to give such a picture as my knowledge of gunnery, fortification, etc. may enable me.

I am fully aware of all the danger and difficulty of this undertaking, and of the careful and guarded manner in which it must be conducted, nor must this explanation to your Grace be taken as any breach as I distinctly stipulated for permission to do so if I wished. Of course to carry such an undertaking through with success sufficient pecuniary means ought to be in my power, for to break down in the midst, would be worse than not make the attempt at all. And the Consul-General finding himself not in a condition to advance *sufficient funds* equal to the casualties to be expected, I am therefore thrown upon my own resources for the deficiency at present, and am under the necessity of borrowing, on my own responsibility, £50 more.

It is also more than probable I may be obliged to return from Oporto to Falmouth in order to proceed by the packet to Lisbon.

Under these circumstances I most humbly presume to solicit of your Grace the loan of £50 for three months, and which loan I solemnly pledge my word and honor to replace within that period, to enable me to carry through an undertaking on which my whole soul is bent. I also most humbly beg that any favor your Grace may please to confer may be addressed to me under cover to F. T. de Sampayo Esq., Portuguese Consul-General, No. 2, Albemarle Street, Piccadilly.

Signed: George Loggan, Captain late Royal Fusiliers.

Enclosed: Copies of testimonials from Major-General Sir Edward Blakeney; Lieutenant-Colonel John Thomas Leahy; Lieutenant-Colonel John Freemantle; Major Digby Mackworth.

Wellington to George Loggan, 16 February 1833

London. I have received your letter. You are perhaps not aware that you are about to undertake a service the performance of which without the King's permission is contrary to the laws of this country.

It is impossible for me so far to encourage you to undertake this service, as to lend you money to enable you to set out upon this service.

Isaac L. Goldsmid to Wellington, 16 February 1833

Bryanston Square. I am desired to request that a deputation from a committee of the Jews may be permitted to have the honor of waiting upon your Grace in order to solicit your support of a bill about to be submitted to Parliament for the removal of the disabilities affecting His Majesty's Jewish subjects in this kingdom. The committee believe that they can offer for your Grace's consideration some circumstances which have occurred since they last applied to Parliament which strengthen their claims for relief.

Draft reply 21 February 1833. Compliments. The Duke is going out of town. But he will be happy to receive the deputation which Mr. Goldsmid announces to the Duke as feeling a wish to see the Duke whenever they will think proper to call upon him after his return.

The Earl of Glengall to Wellington, 18 February 1833

Being unable to go to the House, I beg to remark to you an oversight in the Irish Bill.

No provision is made for coroners' juries. Now if the magistrates, military, or police fire in their own defence and a homicide ensues the juries are so intimidated or *affect* to be so, that they bring in wilful murder against them, and send them to jail for months.

At Tipperary three of one jury were notoriously concerned in the fray!

Coroners' juries should most certainly be placed in some different situation, or no magistrate, officer, or policeman is safe.

I moved last session for documents to be printed, of 'outrages committed in three months in six counties'. I never could succeed in getting them printed, nor have they been, up to this moment.

If I was not ill I would not thus trouble your Grace.

Dated Monday. *Docketed* 1833, February 17th (*a Sunday*).

Wellington to Robert Henry Jenkinson, 18 February 1833

London. I have spoken to Mr. Herries respecting the motion intended to be made by Captain Troubridge on the subject of the Cinque Port pilots.

Of course our officers at Dover must give the gentlemen of the Trinity House as the officers of Government every information they can require.

Sir Hudson Lowe to Wellington, 20 February 1833

10 Hertford Street. I should ill satisfy my own sense of the strong obligation I feel for your Grace's prompt and generous support of my character against the aspersions sought to be cast upon it, by Lord Teynham in the debate of last night, if I delayed any time in waiting upon your Grace to convey the assurance of my most sincere and grateful thanks for the distinguished honor conferred upon me by it. Praying your Grace to believe that this feeling will be indelibly impressed on my mind, I have the honor to remain *etc.*

Viscount Beresford to Wellington, 22 February 1833

London. You asked me the other night in the House, if the Primate had given his sanction to the Bill now in the Commons, respecting the Church of Ireland. I was then unaware of what part he had in that measure, or rather I thought he could not have had any. I regret to say that I have to some extent been mistaken, and by the enclosed, which I received from him yesterday, you will see the extent to which he has gone, and I lament that he has in any manner given his sanction to any part of it. I went yesterday to Apsley House with it, but you were gone out of town, and as you may wish to know this circumstance I send you the letter.

Enclosure: The Archbishop of Armagh (Lord John George Beresford) to Viscount Beresford, 18 February 1833.

Armagh. I have been so hurried in writing letters for some days past, that I have not been able to state to you my opinion upon the measures for the reform of the Church which have been brought forward by Government. It appears that Lord Althorp and Mr. Stanley have declared that in its general features, it had met with the concurrence of some of the highest dignitaries of the Church, and I have been asked to what extent my alleged concurrence has been given, and what are my views upon the subject. To this I have replied that I acquiesced in some parts of the Government plan, namely in abolishing the parochial assessments, for Church purposes; in the suppression of a certain number of the smaller bishopricks, as a means of supplying a fund to meet the charges which would be thus imposed on the Church. The Ministers have suppressed more bishopricks than I contemplated. I have dissented from other parts of the plan which I thought and still think objectionable, namely the conversion of the bishops' leases into perpetuities, and the alienation of the surplus value. I cannot but hope that Government will see the equity of not alienating from the Church a property which is on every fair principle her own; especially as the laity would be relieved by the removal of the parochial assessment. I have also objected to the non-appointment of clergymen to parishes in Popish districts as the most dangerous part of the measure, and calculated to produce the greatest evils to our establishment.

PS. I have been in correspondence with Mr. Stanley, and I would send you my letters to him, if I did not feel a reluctance in communicating even to you letters which might be considered confidential. The suggestions came from Government and I have no fears in regard to the part which I have taken. I am confident that my own conduct will be approved of by all the friends of the Church.

Copy

John Irving to Wellington, 23 February 1833

Richmond Terrace. Your Grace expressed a desire to have the case of the Mauritius. The accompanying documents will furnish it. The inhabitants have sent home volumes, but it is needless to trouble your Grace with them. I may just mention that the strongest remonstrances were made against Jeremie's original appointment, anticipating, with the truth of prophesy, what took place upon his arrival, and a petition signed by the chief merchants connected with the colony against his return. Not the least attention was paid to either at the Colonial Office. Sending Mr. Jeremie back, after the outrage committed by him, of firing a pistol at the people, upon very slight provocation, is certainly a strong measure.

I have no doubt of the consequence of these violent measures—it will throw the colony into rebellion, and be the loss of upwards of a million of British property. I left, a long while ago, the printed papers, upon slavery, in which there is a letter of mine to Lord Goderich, printed without my authority, which will let your Grace into my views on that subject, especially upon the Order of Council.

First enclosure: Case of the Isle of France. Short statement of the grievances complained of by the inhabitants of that colony.

To go into the history and detail of these grievances would occupy too much space for the object of this statement. Their causes have been of long growth, suffice it to say that they have been daily encreasing in strength and if these grievances shall be found on due enquiry to exist to anything like the degree herein alleged it must give rise to the serious question whether the colonial policy of this empire does not require immediate and extensive revision.

It should be observed that several of the grievances complained of in the printed memorial that accompanies this statement prevail in most of the other colonies both chartered as well as ceded in a greater or less degree and in precise proportion to the power that exists there to check them in loco and *mutatis mutandis* much would apply in common to them all, but it is solely and exclusively in what are termed the Crown colonies that the application of new and untried principles of legislation by the Government at home in the shape of Orders in Council from time to time can be said to take the widest range and to reign uncontrolled by local experience or authority and thus the present condition of these colonies affords the best means of judging whether this is a safe, just, or wise way of governing them. This question might perhaps be more satisfactorily answered by a review of the present and actual state of each of them and the loudness of the expressions of their discontent when comparing their present condition with that of the foreign colonies still retained by the Dutch, Spanish, and French* from whom they say they have had the misfortune to be separated by conquest or cession; but it would occupy too much space at this moment. We shall proceed therefore with a very brief summary of these heads of complaint without further comment or more than reference to the memorial annexed for the authority when necessary to establish any particular fact, already not notorious *per se*.

Heads of complaint

1. The people of the Isle of France complain that the articles of capitulation have not been observed and that their laws, usages, and customs, solemnly guaranteed to them have been violated.
2. That under the British Government they have been oppressed with an overpaid colonial administration.
3. That they have been excluded from office in their own colony on the ground of their being colonists in opposition to the practice of their ancient French Government to give a preference to the colonists duly qualified and that raw uneducated English boys are sent from home to supplant them.
4. That clergymen foreign to the colony and in a great part incapable of preaching in the language have been appointed to the best livings and that great scandal has thereby arisen.
5. That judges have been appointed from England ignorant of French law and in some cases of the language.
6. That a most extensive system of monopolies and licences to the prejudice of all trades and handicrafts has been created under the English colonial government and sold at an enormous rate.
7. That the schools of the colony have been neglected and the funds appropriated for the poor dilapidated.
8. That Orders in Council have been framed without due knowledge and with haste and precipitation and without their being consulted;

---

* See report of the Governor of Martinique to the Secretary of Marine and Colonies marked A and which appeared in the *Chronicle* of the 12th January last.

some of them of an impracticable, others of an humiliating, nature, others again of a nature to place in jeopardy their property and their lives.

9.   That these ordinances are marked with distrust of the colonists and seem dictated by the spirit of party and their execution confided to persons strangers to the colony and who are unqualified for their respective offices.

10.   That a summary of these their grievances with others was laid before the Secretary for the Colonies in the year 1831 by the agent of the colony, who listened to him with apparent conviction and made certain concessions which had the prospect of restoring peace to the colony, when it was again disturbed to the utmost and all its prospects blighted by the sudden and unexpected announcement of the ruinous and impracticable Order in Council of the 2nd November of the same year.

11.   That the most alarming changes have been made in their judicial system without any regard to their ancient laws, usages, and customs or even consulting those who were versed in them, by the appointment from England of persons to hold high legal offices in the colony, wholly incompatible with each other by its laws and institutions and wholly impossible in practice and displacing for this purpose functionaries against whom no complaint had ever been heard.

12.   That the alarm and discontent occasioned by such measures have been rendered still greater by the choice of the persons selected to fill these important offices and in particular by the recent appointment of a gentleman to hold two incompatible offices of Procureur Général and Avocat Général, who had already it is conceived rendered himself unfit to unite in his person two high judicial offices or to act in any judicial capacity in any colony by having previously to his appointment distinguished himself as a partizan in print, influenced by the most violent prejudices against the colonists whose lives and properties it would have been his office and his duty to watch over and protect.

13.   That the pertinacity of the Government in persisting to force upon the colony such a judicial functionary and under such circumstances, notwithstanding previous knowledge on their part of this fact, and remonstrances and even entreaty on the part of the best informed to pause before it adopted so dangerous a measure, can only it is feared lead to the most disastrous results.

Second enclosure: French West India colonies (Extract from the *Gazette of Martinique*). Report made to the Minister of Marine and Colonies by Admiral Dupotet, Governor of Martinique (inserted in the *Morning Chronicle* of 12th January 1833).

My Lord—I have the honor to inform you, that in a progress that I have just made from north to south of Martinique, remaining some time in each parish, and quartering myself on a large portion of its inhabitants, after announcing that I would receive all complaints and petitions, I had the high satisfaction of completing my tour without the slightest complaint having been brought to me by the different classes of the population. Everywhere I found perfect tranquillity, docile and tractable slaves treated with kindness and publicly displaying their joy during my progress by their dances, as in a time of feasting or public cessation from labour. Misery is not experienced by this class; they cultivate ground, provisions and vegetables, they rear cattle, and profit by the dearness of provisions to sell their produce at a very high price; privations are now only felt by the master, who, in whatever circumstances he may be placed or whatever may be his means, is obliged to keep up and maintain his establishment, and to furnish the labourers on the estate with the quantity of food, nourishment and clothing required by law, and the regulations of the colonial legislators.

How much Europeans, who do not know the colonies, would be astonished at the comfort which this class enjoys, that is considered to be very unhappy; but which, possessing little properties or portions of land, which they cultivate for their own profits, although slaves, apply the produce of this occupation (for which they have time given them) to their own interests and to the purchase of objects of luxury, which our peasants in France are far from ever dreaming of possessing.

In my visit to the different plantations in my progress through the island, I was not called upon to remit any punishment in my character as Governor, to any convict slave; and the strongest proof of this state of the colony is, that I found the greatest part of the prisons or places of confinement on the several estates either demolished or inclosed.

The position of the colonists is certainly yet very painful but on the other hand, Government and discipline required privations that we could wished to have been spared; however, it will serve as a lesson for the future, and enormous colonial expenditure will no longer be favoured or protected.

I am satisfied with the good sense and discretion of the population of the chief towns of this colony, although this population has sometimes been excited by pamphlets disseminated, it is true, having for their object to disturb the tranquillity of the colony. I continue to proceed in the way that your excellency has recommended for the improvement of the condition of the freed people.

Finally, my Lord, in referring to the epochs since I have been acquainted with the French and foreign colonies, I can assure your excellency, that for several years, a sensible amelioration has taken place in the condition of the slave population; in fact to such a degree, that several would refuse their liberty in order to preserve the advantages which they enjoy in their present state.

I take the liberty of giving your excellency an instance. In my progress through the colony I stopped at the plantation Peter Maillet, at St. Esprit. I entered one of the negro houses, where they did not expect to see me, for my departure was fixed for the hour when I made this visit. I found two rooms one of which served for the kitchen, and the other was a sleeping room. This room had a good bed; a wardrobe of mahogany, a looking glass, and a gold watch suspended from it. I begged Mr. Peter Maillet, the proprietor, who had not followed me on my visit on the estate to come to me; and I asked him whom this cottage belonged to? He answered that it belonged to his head carpenter. The carpenter came to me with his wife. I questioned them upon the manner in which they lived. After having exchanged looks with each other, the wife answered, that at that moment they had not above five doubloons or ten pounds sterling in their possession; but that they had several oxen to sell, pigs, rabbits, and fowls, with a pretty good quantity of Indian corn, not yet cut; and some articles of furniture, which he had not yet finished. I visited also the house of the black overseer, which was as well furnished as the other. He had horses to sell, and provisions from his garden. The cottages of the other negroes that I visited were convenient; and were more or less so, according to their own industry or habits; for I satisfied myself that, after their daily task labour, they have quite sufficient time to attend to their own domestic comforts. A good negro cooper can furnish his master with one sugar barrel a day, but he can easily make two. In this case, if he chooses to work, he may receive from his master for the second barrel or hogshead, three francs, or $3\frac{1}{2}$ francs, that is nearly three shillings sterling.

In general almost the whole of the ground provisions, fruit, fish, cattle, pigs, and poultry, eggs and butter, are sold by the slaves (who have the monopoly of the market and supply) at a high price, to their masters.

Your excellency will, perhaps, be able to conceive an idea, even without visiting these countries, of the pernicious change that would be effected in the condition of the negro slaves if their position with respect to the whites under their present circumstances, were to be suddenly altered.

Deprived of the protection of their masters, they would, in becoming free, have to provide for their wives and children; they would lose the life interest they now have in their cottages on the estates, and the grounds they have a free controul and use of to rear cattle and grow provisions—and finally, the confidence of having the best medical attendance gratis when they are ill. It has been said, my Lord, 'usque ad nauseam' that the slaves who are no longer able to work are abandoned by their master to the most frightful misery; I have my Lord, seen the contrary in visiting the infirmaries of the different plantations; old, infirm, or enfeebled negroes, are treated with all the care that is bestowed in hospitals in Europe. This is a picture which speaks to the eyes of the slaves at Martinique, and which relieves them from all care for the future.

My Lord, I have furnished you with details perhaps very minute respecting this colony, but which I humbly thought ought to be submitted to you.

A great amelioration has taken place in this colony. There will always be bad subjects in every colony, but the general opinion of the inhabitants is right.

I have the honor *etc.*

Dupotet, Contre-Amiral Martinique

Note by the translator. The position of our Crown colonies ceded by France, Spain, and Holland, is any thing but flattering, as compared with the report of the French Admiral; like Hamlet's pair of portraits, it is as 'Hyperion to a satyr'. To what can this be owing?

In Trinidad, St. Lucia, the Mauritius, Demerara and Berbice, the colonists complain that their ancient laws, and usages have been subverted—that they have been inundated by English employés—that their property has been depreciated 60 per cent—and that they are no longer able to raise the taxes or imposts.

On the contrary, in Cuba and the Havana, Martinique and Guadeloupe, in Surinam and Curacoa, the colonists are flourishing and the slaves happy and contented.

There is something in this which deserves serious inquiry. While the ceded colonies remained under their paternal governments they were flourishing; they say they are now the reverse, and that their negroes are as badly off as themselves. English negro philanthropy seems to have made almost as great a mistake in this instance as in the beautiful axiom that England is essentially a commercial country, and that therefore all the young white children of poor parents must be worked to death from the age of seven to seventeen in our cotton manufactories.

But the whole of this question, not only the colonial but the manufacturing system, must undergo a deep and searching inquiry under the new Parliament; we shall then be enabled to see what the former governments of this country have done for the happiness of the people or rather not done.

Lord Downes to Wellington, 23 February 1833

Merrion Square. I have to return your Grace many thanks for the kind communications which you have lately made to me respecting the Duke of Gloucester, Lord Hawarden, and Lord Mountcashell. I have written to them all and I have sent to Lord Mountcashell the papers for his signature in the hope that some Irish magistrate may pass through or near Schaffhausen within the prescribed time, viz. the 29th of March, and as the post takes 12 or 13 days from hence to Schaffhausen, the documents should be signed and dispatched on or before the 16th of March.

I will make enquiry at the bankers and other places and endeavour to find out a magistrate in that neighbourhood, and I will acquaint Lord Mountcashell, if I can find one.

Lord Normanton and Lord Molesworth, who were in the list of doubtfuls which I sent to your Grace on the 7th instant have promised to support me.

Lords Donegall, Fife, Kilmaine and Bridport will either not vote at all or be against me.

Lords Glengall, Boyne and Muncaster are the only doubtful ones at present.

I have got 78 promises—of these 50 have already signed the returns
Lord Lismore 43   and 28 are in progress to be signed
Doubtful 3
Abroad etc. 10
_____
134
With a thousand thanks for your Grace's kind exertions in my favor.

The Rev. George Robert Gleig to Wellington, 25 February 1833

Ash, near Wingham. Private. I am going to trouble your Grace with one
or two questions, which I hope you will be so good as [to] answer truly,
and in full reliance on the discretion and honor of one whom you have
now known some years.

I find among many of the gentlemen and yeomanry of this country
a considerable disposition to form a constitutional society, somewhat of
the model of the constitutional society of Ireland. In ordinary times
and under common circumstances no man dislikes these things more
than I; and the only doubt in my mind is whether we have as yet come
to such a pass, as that ordinary rules may be violated. You can solve
that doubt at once. If you say that the step would be a judicious one,
I think it may be taken; if otherwise, the question will not be mooted. I
write for my own satisfaction; because I have been requested to draw
out a plan for the consideration of others; and I am not willing to do
any thing, which may embarrass, even slightly, those to whom we must
look as our leaders.

I have not forgotten that two years ago your Grace disapproved of
such societies. But we are not now in the position which we occupied
then. Possibly your views may be changed.

My next question is with reference to the Irish Church Bill. What is
to be done? Is it to be fought? for if it be, every man, whatever his
means may be, is bound to aid in the struggle. My own opinion is
decided; that the measure is fraught with ruin. But there may be causes,
which I cannot discern, which would render a marked or violent
opposition unwise. There would be no difficulty in writing another
pamphlet on that subject; or in making out as strong a case for the
Church in Ireland as for the Church in England.

I hope you got my letter to the Bishop of London, and that the
opinions taught there accord with yours.

Wellington to the Rev. George Robert Gleig, 26 February 1833

London. I have received your letter of yesterday. I do not recommend the formation of a constitutional society, as such are called. It is very easy to turn the society with the best name and rules and regulations to the worst purposes; and I know that it is impossible for Government to propose such a measure as has lately passed the House of Lords without including in its provisions, and rendering the best, such as the Irish constitutional society, equally with the worst, liable to be put down.

It is impossible for me now to say what is to be done with the Irish Church Bill. The Irish Primate has conceded the principle. He has departed from the ground on which he could have maintained a battle; that of the Act of Union. How the battle is to be fought in Parliament I do not know.

Lord Downes to Lord Fitzroy Somerset, 27 February 1833

Merrion Square. I received this morning your letter of the 25th inclosing Lady Kenmare's note. Lord Kenmare votes against me which is quite natural.

I have been afraid of boring you with my concerns, if I wrote too often, but since you desire it, I will give you some detail of the progress that I am making.

The election commenced on the 5th of February and it closes on the 29th of March, when I expect to be declared in the *Gazette* 'duly elected'—'having the majority of votes'.

I have every reason to expect 78 votes and I do not think that Lord Lismore will have more than 45. 59 votes for me have already been given in, so that in point of fact the election is decided, but it is quite necessary that I should take steps to get the remaining 19 writs signed. You will much oblige me by giving the enclosed packet for Lord Jersey to the Duke of Wellington. Lord Jersey has not answered my letter, but I understood from the Duke that he will certainly vote for me. There are several Irish magistrates now in London who have taken an active part in my election. Lord Roden, Lord Wicklow, Lord Gort, and Mr. H. Maxwell M.P. have all administered the oaths to different peers for me, and before any one of these Lord Jersey can subscribe the oaths, and sign the documents. He is aware that he must sign his Irish title, Grandison.

I have not heard from Lord Fife, but I find that Lord Anglesey has sent to the Hanaper office for his writ, so I suppose that they intend to make Fife vote against me. Lord Glengall cannot vote against his Tipperary friend, but I think it likely he will not vote at all.

There are 14 peers who live in country quarters to whom it will be necessary for me to depute an Irish magistrate before whom they can subscribe the oaths. I enclose a map of the route that the gentleman will take and he proposes to set off in a week or 10 days. In the mean-time I am endeavouring to ascertain whether the 14 peers whose names are inserted on the enclosed map are likely to be at home during the period between the 10th and 25th of March. It is very possible that some of them may be in London during that period, and if so it would save my friend a good deal of travelling if I could now find that out. You may possibly know something of Lord Rancliffe's movements.

I received Lord Edward's letter respecting Lord Lisburne's letter for which I feel much obliged to him. You will see Lord Lisburne's name in rather an out of the way place, but I must send to him, as I conclude that he will not leave home soon.

I do not like troubling the Duke of Wellington too often but probably you will have the goodness on the first favourable opportunity to shew him this letter and the enclosed map in order that he may see the progress that I am making.

PS. O'Connell appears to be playing off some of his Irish tricks in London. I hope soon to hear that you have sent him to the Tower— or to the treadmill—a fitter place for him.

Enclosure: A sketch map showing the route to be followed by Lord Downes's messenger. The peers to be visited are: Lord Dungannon at Chirk; Lord Lisburne at Aberystwyth; Lord Ashtown at Bath; Lord Mount Sandford at Down; Lord Normanton; Lord Cavan; Duke of Buckingham at Winchester; Lord Chetwynd at Bicester; Lord Lifford at Coventry; Lord Rancliffe at Nottingham; Lord Galway at Bawtry; Lord Mexborough at Leeds; Lord Macdonald at Bridlington; Lord Londonderry at Stockton.

Viscount Melbourne to Wellington, 28 February 1833

Whitehall. Viscount Melbourne presents his compliments to the Duke of Wellington, and, in compliance with his Grace's request, begs to return the two original papers which accompanied his Grace's letter to Lord Melbourne on the 26th instant.

Alfred Mallalieu to Wellington, 3 March 1833

13 Brownlow Street, Holborn. I have been emboldened to address myself to your Grace respecting the affairs of *The Guardian and Public Ledger* morning paper in consequence of the favourable manner in which my original suggestions with regard to that paper and the press generally were formerly received by your Grace.

It may perchance be known to your Grace that I had last year the honour to be entrusted by several distinguished friends of the cause with the sum of £2,000 for the purpose of purchasing an interest in the lease of the *Public Ledger*, respecting which I had about the same time the honour of submitting various calculations to your Grace. Notwithstanding the inadequacy of the sum as contrasted with my calculations, I considered myself bound to answer to the confidence thus reposed in me, by embarking at some risk to myself in a perilous undertaking with inadequate means.

My own opinions as developed in a memoir I had the honour of submitting to your Grace at the time, pointed out the almost certainty with the expenditure of £10,000 diffused over a period of *three* years, of making the *Public Ledger* in every respect equal to *The Times*, whether for ability, circulation, or profit; my conviction being that at the close of the third year it would have so gained, and taken such a position, as must have ensured its gradual and safe advance afterwards.

My second proposition was that for a sum of £5,000 it might be made equal to *The Times* in every respect, save some *portion* of the foreign intelligence which would become too heavy a charge upon that capital.

Circumstances were not favourable to the carrying of these plans into effect. I resolved therefore to do what was possible with the £2,000. The results are as follows.

The Guardian has had the Paris expresses regularly until Christmas—which no other papers but *The Times* and the *Herald* have had, and I cannot help thinking that the abundance and variety of our matter by those expresses has been much superior to those papers. The circulation of *The Guardian* has been increased *two-thirds*; its advertisements, always slow to come in, have increased about *one-fourth*. Its moral influence is acknowledged on all hands to be very much greater than its circulation would seem to warrant—it is the only paper in the City that counter-acts and can enter into competition with *The Times*; and one of its feats—that of the general meeting on the Dutch question—is sufficient to attest it, were there nothing else. It circulates very well in the City; among the coffee houses and club houses; and in all the news rooms and exchange rooms of the larger towns throughout the empire. It is fair to say that it has not a great circulation among families; one great reason being that we are not able to go to the expence of giving the miscellaneous department as it ought to be given; this being for families the great desideratum.

The following is the rate of loss at which these objects have been effected up to Christmas last—a period of *six months*. The account will include also the *British Traveller*, a daily evening paper also printed at the same office, and for our account.

> Loss by *Guardian*—six months— £1300
> *British Traveller*—do.   800
> ———
> £2100

There has been I trust little extravagance or jobs in the management. The following is a statement of the heaviest amounts paid for salary or profit of any kind.

> To myself as chief editor and manager   £7.7.0 per week
> To Mr. Alexander   £7.0.0
> To Mr. Harwood (partner and acting sub-editor) £7.7.0
> To Mr. Richards (partner and book-keeping)   £7.7.0
> City reporter (partner also)   £4.4.0
> French correspondent (partner also)   £5.5.0

Other contributors, when any there have been, have been paid in pro-portion. In the month of November last, finding that we were losing money too fast, three of the partners—myself, Mr. Harwood, and Richards—lowered our own salaries one-third. At the full rate I myself was not paid more than one-half of what persons similarly placed consider regular. I may add that since the end of December not one partner has drawn a shilling from the concern either as salary or in any other way. This resolution we have come to that we might in the event of giving up the concern, at least be able to fulfill our engagements.

Such my Lord Duke is a statement of the affairs of *The Guardian* up to Christmas. Ours has been an uphill battle; we have daily broken ground though slowly, and maintained it. Our prospects have daily become more cheering, in despite of difficulties; yet at the moment when more than ever our position is improved and improveable, we are placed in the mortifying necessity of abandoning our enterprise—on which success seems just dawning. Our loss upon the last month is not more than £80; our paper the last week (for *the first time*) paid its own expences. This however is not a calculation to be depended upon—for we happened to have an influx of more advertisements than even with our manifest and gradual improvement in that respect, can be calculated upon for lasting—although a few months more would enable us probably to realise such a state of things.

In the meantime our progress is suspended, as well as our existence threatened. The very circumstance of the obligation to pay to the Stamp Office our advertisement duty once a month is a serious inconvenience to us with a small capital; and it is the more so as our advertisements increase; so that the very source of our prosperity threatens or will be one cause of our ruin. Our advertisements are chiefly on credit—and are paid on the average not so soon as in four months, so that we have to pay the Stamp Office nearly four times before we can receive from our customers. Thus, suppose our duty amounts monthly to £280, we have to pay four times that, say £1120, before we receive. Besides covering our weekly loss and expenditure (so long as the loss exists) we have need therefore of an intangible floating capital to at least that amount—besides some means of meeting our loss for a time.

It will therefore be seen that my calculations originally submitted to your Grace with respect to the necessity of £5000 have so far been borne out fully and satisfactorily. That sum would have been more than sufficient, but £2000 was too little.

I have endeavoured to find persons of property to join us but the circumstances of the *paper being held under a lease* (although for 21 years) and therefore not considered a property, has and does prove an obstacle. But for that I could find plenty of persons with money to any amount to join a concern with such prospects.

I have taken the liberty to open these circumstances to your Grace thus minutely, in order to show that we have made some return for the money bestowed upon us; and that we have the fair prospect of making that return still more striking and effective in another six months. But without assistance we must sink, and that immediately. We are now narrowing our expences instead of enlarging them to improve the advantages already gained. The property we hold on lease, is let to us in our personal character, *without security*; the former lessee, Mr. Alderman Crowder, a man of great property, having given security for £4000 towards managing the paper. We pay a heavy rental for the paper—representing the interest of capital sunk. But notwithstanding all, I feel assured that it may be made of infinite use to the good cause, and that very soon it would be able to walk alone. And your Grace will remember that I expressed the same sentiments before I had the experience I now have. Our economy I hope will bear comparison with any paper. Our industry I can speak to—without reference to myself. And whereas all other papers have great disadvantages (especially *The Times* and *Herald*) of *heavy and expensive* establishments which they cannot reform, we are few—young in business—and under the necessity of doing double duty in order to succeed and become efficient. I know that *The Times*, through their great—often useless expenditure, is far from being so lucrative as usually considered.

I should be greatly concerned to see *The Guardian* fall; not so much on account of interested motives I hope, as others more suitable to a man of principle. It is useful—it is becoming more so—it may be made greatly so. I consider myself only as a trustee for the friends who have supported me and the party which I believe the only one calculated to serve my country. The shares I hold are therefore one and all at their service—or yours my Lord Duke—to dispose of as best may seem. I hold *five* shares; my Paris friend *three*—out of fifteen; those I can answer for. I believe also I can answer for three more. I am content to serve anyhow—or not at all when more efficient servants offer. For I never coveted to be chief—that was forced upon me by circumstances; and I am conscious of my own deficiencies.

But I do entreat of your Grace not to let *The Guardian* fall. I repeat my conviction that it may and would succeed with some help, and that it has more than realized all that I predicted of it. It will be almost a discredit as well as loss that it should fall.

I fear that I have so ill expressed what I would say that I shall make little impression upon your Grace. I should be very proud to offer any further explanations should your Grace do me the honour to command me.

Signed: Alfred Mallalieu, editor *Guardian*.

The Marquess of Londonderry to Wellington, 4 March 1833

Wynyard Park. I have followed with great anxiety the course of the public discussions.

Did ever men cut so ridiculous a figure as the present Ministers, depending alternately upon one party or the other of their opponents for their ability to carry any measures. I should not be at all surprised at the secession of some of the Cabinet with a view to the formation of a government on principles that would allow the moderate Conservatives to take office. This is a wretched alternative to be reduced to, and nothing but the impossibility of preserving any thing like the constitution as at present established could justify such a coalition.

Has any one the political courage for such an attempt?

In such a case we should not be long without a dissolution, for between such an arrangement and a Radical Administration we shall shortly have no option. I hope to God the Conservatives will feel the impolicy of the smallest semblance of divergence. The King will soon be thrown upon their conduct and their efforts, and although I don't despair, I consider nothing but their union can rally the voice of the loyal in the nation.

I shall come up whenever there is any want of attendance. At present, our coal trade in the north is in a state of ruin and requires my constant and unremitting attendance.

I hope your health is good and equal to the perilous trials before us.

Baron von Wessenberg to Wellington, 4 March 1833

J'ai passé hier matin à votre porte pour vous communiquer les dernières nouvelles de la Turquie. Les nouvelles portent: que le Général Muravieff et le Consul Général d'Autriche, M. Acerbi, ayant fait connaître à Mahomed Ali que leurs cours respectives ne sauraient rester indifférentes si la lutte d'insurrection continuait, celui-ci leur déclara formellement qu'il se considérait déjà en paix avec son souverain, qu'il allait envoyer des ordres positifs à son fils Ibrahim de l'arrêter et de suspendre les hostilités—qu'il attendait avec impatience l'arrivée de Halil Pasha, que sa hautesse avait daigné déléguer pour lui faire connaître son intention, et qu'il recevrait avec les plus grandes distinctions—enfin qu'il donnait l'assurance qu'il s'arrangerait avec l'envoyé de la Porte.

Ces déclarations ont été faites le 17 au Général Muravieff et le 19 au Consul Général d'Autriche. Halil Pasha n'était pas encore arrivé ce dernier jour, mais on savait à Constantinople le 8 février qu'Ibrahim Pasha avait effectivement reçu les ordres de cesser s'avancer et qu'il s'était arrêté à Kutakia à peu près moitié chemin entre Koniah et Broussa.

Voilà la véritable teneur des nouvelles qui nous sont parvenues hier. J'ai pensé qu'il vous serait agréable de les connaître quoique les journeaux en donnent déjà aujourd'hui la substance. Enfin la chute de l'Empire Ottoman est encore ajournée. On se flatte que tout s'arrangera moyennant le Pashalik d'Acre dont Mahomed Ali serait investi en qualité de vassal ou feudataire. La Porte tient avec raison de réserver sous sa domination immédiate les Pashaliks d'Alepp et de Bagdad, le premier couvrant les avenues du Taurus et l'autre comprenant le bassin de l'Euphrate et séparant la Syrie de la Perse avec lequel la Porte ne voudra pas mettre Mahomed Ali en contact.

John Wilson Croker to Wellington, 4 March 1833

West Molesey. I want very much to obtain some information relative to the new Parliament—some of which I think you are likely to have, and the rest of which I know no one but *Holmes* who can give—but I think he is more likely to do it *readily* and *accurately* at *your Grace's* request than at *mine*. If you have no objection, I should, therefore, solicit your Grace to write to him (not mentioning me) for as much of the following information as you may not already have had.

The next sheet of the letter is missing.

. . . O'Connell's recommendations.

I want this information for an essay on the prospects of the country under the working of the Reform Bill; and though I know that even Holmes may not be able to make it accurate in all its details, yet I have no doubt he will be able to approximate to the truth.

I know not how the Ministers may feel but I know that some of their principal supporters are as Conservative as I am. Burdett for instance, whom I met at dinner, by his own desire, on Sunday last, and whose sentiments appeared to concur with—even if they did not exceed mine in Toryism.

I ought to apologise for venturing to give your Grace this kind of trouble, but I know you think nothing of any trouble that may tend to help the good cause.

I have not been in town, except once for one hour to see a doctor, since I saw your Grace. I mention this only to excuse myself for not having been to pay my duty to your Grace.

Wellington to Alfred Mallalieu, 5 March 1833

Stratfield Saye. I have received your letter of the 3rd instant. I assure you that you are quite mistaken in thinking that I had anything [to say] to the establishment of *The Guardian* newspaper, or had any knowledge of the facts to which you refer. Your letter ought to be addressed to some other person. I have no knowledge whatever of the transaction.

I knew so little of the establishment of *The Guardian* that I did not take in that newspaper till the 1st of January last.

The Duke of Cumberland to Wellington, 5 March 1833

St. James's. I called this morning at Apsley House to put a copy of my correspondence with the Primate into your hands, which I trust may meet with your approbation, and if you fully agree with me, I think it would not be unadvisable to let *Peel* see it, in order that we may *all* know fully the line we mean to take upon this momentous question, which it will be necessary should be known in order to prepare every one for the consideration of points so important, on which in my humble opinion the existence or non existence of the Protestants must depend. I wish to know your opinion respecting Peel.

First enclosure: The Duke of Cumberland to the Archbishop of Armagh (Lord John George Beresford), 18 February 1833.

St. James's. I trust you will excuse me writing you these few lines, but I really am so much astonished, and I may add appalled, at what has taken place within the last week with respect to the proposed reform in the Church of Ireland, that I feel called upon to ask your Grace's opinion, having constantly and invariably agreed with your Grace on all subjects respecting the Church there. Is it possible that the hierarchy there can have acquiesced in such a plan? Either they have or have not been consulted; in the former case I should wish to know what can be the grounds for their acquiescence? if the latter, would it not be absolutely necessary, if they disapprove of the measure, boldly and manfully to express the same either by coming over in a body and laying at the feet of His Majesty their protest or presenting a petition to Parliament expressing their sentiments? My Lord, depend upon it, from what transpired the night Lord Althorp opened the business, there can be little or no doubt in any thinking mind that *this* is only the beginning and that ere long the whole Protestant Church will be annihilated; it is evident to me that the surplus of the resources arising from the suppression of bishoprics will sooner or later be devoted to the Catholics. I may be wrong in this conclusion, but I do not deny that this is the conviction of my mind and that if the hierarchy of Ireland remain passive they will be then guilty of suicide, for how can we be called upon to stand up and shield that Church which the natural guardians abandon to its fate? Knowing your Grace's determination, courage and prudence, so often proved, I think I need not impress more upon your attention this subject, but hope that you will pardon my calling on you in order that I may know what line is best to be taken. I fear your not being one of the representatives on the bishops' bench this session will be a vital loss to the cause. One of my chief reasons for believing that the surplus will be handed over to the Catholics was the manner in which the Catholic Members in the Commons hailed the proposal.

Copy.

Second enclosure: The Archbishop of Armagh to the Duke of Cumberland, 21 February 1833.

Armagh. I have been honoured with your Royal Highness's letter of the 18th instant and I am happy to have an opportunity thus afforded me of explaining to your Royal Highness how far and on what principles my qualified assent has been given to the measure of Government affecting the Irish branch of the united Church; begging it to be understood that in any communications with Mr. Stanley upon the subject I neither meant nor could I be thought to convey any other than my own sentiments. It had been urged upon me by many of the clergy collectively and individually and it was my own persuasion that the power of assessing Roman Catholics for Church purposes in a vestry exclusively Protestant was of all others the most invidious in its exercise, and that which brought the incumbent into the most frequent collision with his Roman Catholic and dissenting parishioners. When therefore the abolition of such assessments was proposed to me as a preparatory and necessary step to the intended alterations, I gave to it an unhesitating assent, declaring however at the same time that I felt the concession to be a departure from the just pretensions of a national church and a sacrifice to the prejudices rather than to the real advantage of the people, who were but little affected by an imposition so trifling in amount. In order to provide for the charge of Church assessments it became necessary to draw upon the Church's own resources. To have attempted to lay upon the Protestant landlords any part of the burthen taken from Roman Catholics would have been as fruitless as impolitic, since by such a proceeding the Church would have converted into new enemies those whom she calculated upon as friends. Supposing then that sacrifices were unavoidable, and that the abolition of Church assessments was among the first looked to by all parties, I expressed my opinion on the proposal being made to me for the consolidation of certain of the smaller sees (although I object to the extent to which it has been carried) that such a measure was as little objectionable as any other, if the revenues of these sees were to be strictly applied to the exigencies of the Church in aid of a moderate and graduated tax upon parochial incomes to be taken in lieu of the litigated claims of first fruits. The suppression of any of the sees I distinctly stated was even in a secular point of view in itself an evil instead of a good in a country which laboured under the want of a resident gentry.

The imposition of first fruits was a remnant of Papal usurpations, but as far as my own voice went I was willing and I am still so to concede these points under the persuasion, that circumstanced as the Church is in Ireland, it is wiser to recede from than strenuously to insist upon rights which render the Church unpopular with a large proportion both of the Protestant and Roman Catholic population.

If I have erred in consenting to these concessions, I am willing to bear the blame. My view is that pecuniary sacrifices were to be chosen in preference to others and my declared principle was that what was taken from one part of the Church endowments should be religiously appropriated to her other uses. Mr. Stanley will do me the justice to admit that I never for a moment sanctioned the alienation of the Church revenue to foreign purposes; on the contrary, I protested against the proposed application to objects of the State of the surplus funds to be raised by the sale of see lands as most unfair, and the sale itself as a measure neither desirable for the bishop nor desired by the tenant. I urged as strongly as I could do that if this alteration in the see property should be persisted in, that the funds thence to be raised ought to be applied in diminution of the onerous tax which it was proposed to lay upon parochial incomes. On the remaining points alluded to in your Royal Highness's letter, namely the non-appointment to benefices in which the church service may not have been performed during the last three years, I have endeavoured to convince His Majesty's Ministers of the dangers with which such a measure was fraught to the establishment. In fact, so far from approving of it I consider it one of the objectionable parts of the scheme. I have now laid before your Royal Highness as briefly as I could and with an explicitness in which I shall be borne out by my letters to Mr. Stanley should they ever be produced, in what sense and to what extent I have acquiesced in the measure lately brought forward and on what points I have totally differed from the view taken by His Majesty's Ministers. I would beg to add that throughout my communications with Mr. Stanley he has evinced the greatest openness and candour and in adhering to his own views on the points on which we differed he will I am confident give me full credit for the fairness of this representation.

Copy.

Third enclosure: The Duke of Cumberland to the Archbishop of Armagh, 27 February 1833.

St. James's Palace. I received your Grace's letter of the 21st in reply to mine of the 18th the day before yesterday, and cannot conceal from you the deep grief it has caused me. When I say this, I trust you will not misunderstand me or believe that I for a moment suppose your Grace to have acted but for the most upright and conscientious motives; still, differing on this occasion so widely from your Grace, I think it but fair towards you, who have so candidly and kindly explained to me your altered views on this momentous subject of the Church, to state to you equally distinctly my opinion, especially as till now our views upon Church questions (English or Irish) have never differed. Both Churches must in my humble opinion be considered as one and the same, for if the principle of separation be once recognised, both must inevitably fall, the ruin of the Irish Church preceding the ruin of the English Church by a few short years. Your Grace says that in your communications with Mr. Stanley you only conveyed your own sentiments. Alas! what hope can there be of preserving the integrity of the Church of Ireland when the Primate has found it advisable to declare his assent to a concession which he 'felt to be a departure from the just pretensions of a national church, and a sacrifice to its prejudices rather than to the real advantage of the people who were but little affected by an imposition so trifling in amount'. Your Grace's words apply to the Irish Church assessments. Surely, if this position be admitted as a ground for extinguishing the Irish Church rates, it applies equally to English ones; and if the argument be a good one as to Catholics in Ireland, it must equally be good for all Dissenters in England; and depend upon it, the precedent which your Grace will sanction in Ireland will tell with tremendous force in England in a few months, especially when it is known that you have given your consent however reluctantly, acknowledging at the same time as you do that this is a sacrifice to the prejudices of the people at the expense of the Church for no one tangible benefit to them. With respect to your Grace's assent, given as it appears to me from your letter, against your better judgment, to the proposed extinction or consolidation of the Irish sees, I have but one short remark to offer to your Grace's conscience: viz., the last oath taken by the Sovereign at the altar at Westminster on the day of his Coronation and the last sentence of that oath, which is as follows, and as you know put to him by your brother Primate in England, 'And will you preserve unto the bishops and clergy of England and Ireland and to the Churches committed to their charge all such rights and privileges as by law do and shall appertain to them or any of them?' Now, my Lord, the King having sworn to the archbishops and bishops to defend their rights and privileges, can the archbishops and bishops consent or volunteer to sacrifice themselves and their rights when their Sovereign has so solemnly pledged himself by a solemn oath taken at the altar to maintain them? I put this to you in a religious point of view. No man can justly pretend that such an alteration as now proposed is not *essential and fundamental*; the very words used in the fifth article of the Union, with which the King's oath is in accordance. I am truly glad that we so fully concur in our opinions as to the other two leading features of the bill, namely the conversion of the present leasehold interests in see lands into perpetuities and the non-appointment to benefices where divine service has not been performed for three years. This first measure I consider the most flagrant and I may add useless violation of every principle discernible in the whole plan. The defence of it is founded on sophistry, the calculation as to its pecuniary results I believe to be incorrect, and that the measure will consequently be inoperative; but whether it be so or not, the principle of appropriating Church property to secular purposes is established by it and will therefore form a precedent for future Church spoliation, the extent of which no man can foresee. With respect to the last named part of the scheme, the non-appointments to benefices, it appears to me a most artful one, for in times like these when residence almost ensures destruction to clergymen, and when they are in a state of absolute starvation, even when in the normal possession of their benefices, there could not be a more summary mode of cashiering Protestant clergymen and robbing them of a vested claim to the compassion of the public than this proposal. The more I consider this, the more convinced I am that by conceding principles you lose your strong and best ground, and only increase the appetite and the means of demanding more.

Excuse, my dear Lord, the length of this letter, which nothing but the paramount importance of these awful changes could have induced me to have written; but I thought I owed it in candour to your Grace to do so, in order that I might record to you my unchanged opinions.

Copy.

Wellington to John Wilson Croker, 6 March 1833

Stratfield Saye. I will endeavour to obtain for you the details which you require regarding the state of the representation in the House of Commons. I know none excepting regarding this county. I have compared notes with others; and I think that all agree in the same story. The revolution is made: that is to say that power is transferred from one class of society, the gentlemen of England, professing the faith of the Church of England, to another class of society, the shopkeepers being dissenters from the Church, many of them Socinians, others Atheists.

I don't think that the influence of property in this country is in the abstract diminished. That is to say that the gentry have as many followers and influence as many voters at elections, as ever they did.

But a new democratick influence has been introduced into elections, the copy holders and freeholders and leaseholders residing in towns which do not themselves return Members to Parliament. These are all dissenters from the Church; and are every where a formidably active party against the aristocratical influence of the landed gentry. But this is not all. There are Dissenters in every village in the country; they are the blacksmith, the carpenter, the mason, etc., etc. The new influence established in the towns has drawn these to their party; and it is curious to see to what a degree it is a dissenting interest. I have known instances of a dissenting clerk in the office of the agent in a county of an aristocratical candidate making himself active in the canvass of these Dissenters to support the party in the town at the election.

Then add intimidation and audacity which always accompany revolutionary proceedings; occasioning breach of promise to vote for the aristocratical candidate and forcing some to stay away to guard their property and you have the history of many unsuccessful contests in counties.

That which passed here, passed in Northamptonshire, Gloucestershire, but most particularly in the Scotch and Irish counties. The mischief of the reform is that whereas democracy prevailed heretofore only in some places, it now prevails every where. There is no place exempt from it. In the great majority it is preponderant.

To this add the practice of requiring candidates to pledge themselves to certain measures, which is too common even among the best class of electors; and readiness of candidates to give these pledges; and you will see reason to be astonished that we should even now exist as a nation.

What do you think of Lord Douro pledging himself to revive the currency!!!

I was aware of Sir Francis Burdett's opinions and fears. The truth is that he is one of the largest and most prosperous land proprietors in England. He receives above forty thousand a year from his land. He does not owe a shilling; and has money in the funds. He has discovered that they have gone too far; and thinks it not unlikely that the destruction of one description of property will draw after it the destruction of all.

I happen to know that his opinion upon the state of affairs does not much differ from my own.

ADD MS 38078, ff. 16–20.

The Earl of Aberdeen to Wellington, 6 March 1833

Argyll House. You had left London before I called at Apsley House on Sunday. I was desirous of submitting to you the propriety of our coming forward in the present state of the Belgian question, by a motion in the House of Lords. I admit that the mere question of the embargo has been so well treated in the House of Commons that it need not be revived; but I think that we might unite the questions of law and policy with very good effect. Indeed, it is not easy to separate them; for even if the embargo were perfectly legal, it would still be equally unjustifiable. This view of the subject would naturally open as much of the whole question for discussion as might be thought expedient.

It should be recollected that our present situation is not that of interfering during a pending negociation, for we have the facts compleated. We have the commerce of the country actually prohibited with Holland for the last four months. We have a convention laid upon the table of the House which stipulates the performance of the very act of which we complain. It seems to me that if ever anything required parliamentary notice, it is the present state of this affair. Silence here, is virtual approbation.

I am aware of the propriety of keeping our proceedings comparatively quiet in the House of Lords, at this time. But this system may perhaps be carried too far. We have already inflicted upon ourselves a sentence of humiliation, from which under any circumstances, it will be difficult to recover. To abandon the parliamentary notice of the facts which I have mentioned, I cannot but fear will hasten the time when we may find ourselves without the power of acting at all.

If it should still be thought right to originate no discussion upon any subject, I acquiesce, and will remain quiet; but if we could with propriety bring any before the House, the existing facts connected with the Belgian question offer the best opportunity. With this view, I inclose a series of resolutions which I have drawn up, and which if you approved of, I should like very well to move, or something like them. The subject is not one which could bring us into collision with the House of Commons. Our friends, who are listless and disheartened, would be glad to be brought together. We should have a good cause, and at all events succeed in exposing the misconduct of the Government. And we might possibly be of some use to Holland in resisting the tyranny and oppression of the allied Governments. The last note from The Hague, which you will have seen yesterday in all the newspapers, is firm, and even assumes a higher tone than usual.

I submit all this however entirely to your better judgment, whatever it may be.

PS. I have spoken to Scarlett on the subject, and believe that the assertions of law, contained in the resolutions, may be considered as safe and correct.

Enclosure:

Resolved:

1st   That by the common law, the seas are open to the commerce of all His Majesty's subjects, without any force or restraint being put upon their persons or goods; and that in conformity with the principles of the law of nations, and by the special provisions of divers statutes, the resort of merchant strangers is encouraged, and their persons and property are protected while carrying on their peaceable and lawful traffick within this realm.

2nd   That it is the acknowledged prerogative of the King to declare war against any state or sovereign; and in contemplation of war, His Majesty, by the advice of his Privy Council, may order a general embargo or stop to be made of all ships and vessels within the ports of his dominions; and may order the commanders of His Majesty's ships of war to detain and bring into port all merchant ships and vessels bearing the flag of any foreign state; and may further order that no ships or vessels belonging to any of His Majesty's subjects, be permitted to enter and clear out for any of the ports within the dominions of any such state.

3rd   That these restraints laid upon the commerce of friendly nations, and upon the enjoyment of the undoubted rights and liberties of His Majesty's subjects, can only be justified by the apprehension of war, or by some unforeseen and urgent necessity; and in such cases, may be the result of a due regard for the safety and welfare of His Majesty's subjects. But that it is highly unconstitutional and illegal, except under such pressing and temporary emergencies, to advise His Majesty to suspend or dispense with any of the statutes of the realm, or with the permanent obligations of public law.

4th   That by His Majesty's Order in Council of the 6th of November last, a general embargo was laid upon all Netherland vessels, and the commerce of His Majesty's subjects was prohibited with all such ports as are situated within the dominions of His Majesty the King of the Netherlands. But that it has not been shown by any communications which have been made to this House, that this exercise of the war prerogative of the Crown, was influenced by any reasonable expectation of hostilities; or that this violation of the principles of the constitution was justified by any sudden emergency, and by a necessary attention to the public welfare.

5th   That by the articles of a convention between His Majesty and the King of the French, signed on the 22nd of October last, it is stipulated, together with other measures of force and violence, that the above mentioned embargo shall be laid upon all Netherland vessels, in the event of the King of the Netherlands refusing to enter into an engagement to evacuate the citadel of Antwerp, and the forts and places dependent thereupon, and to withdraw all his troops from the Belgian territory on or before the 12th day of November last. By this convention, a mediation, entered into for the purpose of deliberating, in concert with the King of the Netherlands, upon the best means of putting an end to the disturbances which had broken out in his states, has been converted into an arbitrary and forcible interference; but that this House is unable to discover any interests peculiarly British, which could authorize an act highly injurious to the commerce of His Majesty's subjects, or any emergency which could justify the violation of the law of nations. Believing, on the contrary, that the universal prevalence of this law offers the best security for the peace and happiness of mankind; and being of opinion that its obligations should ever be most scrupulously observed in the relations of powerful states with such as are comparatively weak, this House has seen with deep regret that measures have been adopted which are alike impolitic and unjust, which violate the principles of all publick law, and which are pregnant with danger to the freedom and independence of all states.

In Aberdeen's hand.

Wellington to the Earl of Aberdeen, 7 March 1833

Stratfield Saye. I am very sorry that I did not see you before I left town.

I went to town on Saturday sennight intending on Tuesday to support Lord Colville's motion for the reappointment of the committee on West Indian affairs, when I should have discussed the conduct of the Government in respect to the West Indians. The gentlemen interested in the West Indies suggested that this motion should be postponed. Consequently I came out of town again.

The House of Lords is precisely in the position in which it must be under the reform system. Property has lost its political influence, and a division of the House of Lords upon any question can have no political consequence whatever. A discussion by any men with the habits, education and information of the members of the House of Lords might have some moral influence. But it must be well timed. A fair opportunity for it must be offered. In this case I don't think that there is such an opportunity.

You and I and the King's servants know the history of the removal of Zuylen and the appointment of Dedel. But the publick do not. All that the publick know is that the King says that Zuylen has resigned, and that he has appointed 'a minister charged with the necessary powers to negociate a preliminary convention with the plenipotentiaries of France and Great Britain, and to reestablish the relations with those powers on their former footing', etc., etc. I should say that this is not only not the opportunity for a discussion in the House of Lords upon this subject, but that those who should be instrumental in bringing it under discussion would expose themselves to the imputation of bringing forward the subject purposely to prevent the work of peace.

The tranquillity of the House of Lords does not suit noble lords. They would have a Whig Government; they would have reform; they would have abolition of slavery, they would have other notions and they must make up their minds to the loss of political influence by property and by themselves to the absence of all political influence in their own body, and to the other consequences of the revolution which is in progress.

It appears to me that your resolutions turn entirely upon the embargo. I am convinced that we shall do more harm than good to that question by discussing it in the House of Lords.

ADD MS 43060, ff. 80–82. *Draft in Wellington Papers.*

Wellington to the Marquess of Londonderry, 7 March 1833

Stratfield Saye. I have received your note. I do not see any prospect of the necessity for an attendance in the House of Lords. In truth the revolution is effected. The question is what will it do. In the meantime property and the House of Lords in particular have lost their political influence.

Any deliberative body composed of men of education, of habits of business, and of talent may by their discussions have a moral effect in society and over the legislature and the mob. But their discussions must be opportune, and those of the House of Lords in particular, which still possesses a legislative power but no political influence, ought to be very cautiously managed.

I have been here generally amusing myself with the fox hounds. When I was in London last week there was a report that the King had said to somebody that all the Ministers had resigned excepting Lord Brougham and Mr. Stanley. However they are still in office. I understand that it is now reported that Lord Grey wishes to abdicate into the hands of the Duke of Portland.

I think that Lord Grey's resignation will be just the most blackguard act that any statesman was ever guilty of. He first destroys the constitution of his country. He is repeatedly warned that neither he nor anybody else would be able to carry on a government under the new system which his Act of Parliament would establish. He perseveres, carries his measure, and as soon as he experiences the difficulties into which he has brought the country, he says that he is grown old, is tired, and must retire.

I am sorry to learn that the coal trade is not thriving.

Addressed: My dear Charles. *Londonderry's letter of 4 March 1833, to which this is a reply, was addressed 'My dear Duke'.*

Wellington to the Duke of Cumberland, 7 March 1833

I have had the honor of receiving your Royal Highness's letter of the 5th instant and its enclosures, and I am very grateful to your Royal Highness for this communication. I don't know what course Sir Robert Peel and his friends propose to take in the House of Commons upon this question. It is very probable that his judgement in deciding upon the course which he should follow would be assisted by the circulation by your Royal Highness of a copy of the letter from the Lord Primate to your Royal Highness.

Lord Downes to Wellington, 8 March 1833

Merrion Square. I have received your Grace's note of the 5th and I am much obliged to your Grace for having got Lord Jersey to execute his writ. My friend and relative Mr. Henry Maxwell has administered the oaths to 15 or 16 peers in London, and he has now got nine or ten writs ready signed in his possession; if your Grace will have the goodness to send to him, at no. 15 Abingdon Street, Westminster, Lord Jersey's writ he will forward it to me with the others.

On Wednesday next Captain Cottingham will take from hence, writs for the following peers and wait upon them at their residences for the purpose of administering the oaths, viz.

Lord Dungannon near Chirk
      Mexborough near Leeds
      Londonderry—Stockton-on-Tees
      Rancliffe—Nottingham
      Chetwynd—Bicester
Duke of Buckingham—Avington, near Winchester
Lord Normanton—Ringwood

He will from Ringwood go to Bristol and thence to Dublin.

Lords Rokeby and Macdonald whom I had counted upon cannot vote, as it was by mistake that their names were inserted in the Gazette. They have since qualified, but no peer can vote who had not qualified before the issue of the King's writ. If that privilege was admitted, the Government candidate would be the gainer by it, as they have got Lords Melbourne, Hood, Leitrim, and Dillon to qualify. I hope that before the session is over we may be able to get Lords Abercorn, Clanwilliam, Cholmondeley, Clonmell, Digby, Powis, Verulam, to qualify, in order to be ready for future elections.

I wrote to Lord Muncaster some time ago; and Lord Lonsdale and Lady Anne Becket were requested to apply to him in my favour, but I have not yet heard anything of, or from him.

Wellington to John Bruce Bruce of Duffryn, Glamorgan, 8 March 1833

London. I have had the honor of receiving your letter of the 6th instant.

The libel which you have inclosed is about similar to others which I have endeavoured to prosecute. But the gentlemen of the learned profession, whether from a want of confidence in the law or in the disposition of juries to convict those who take upon themselves to misrepresent and libel the conduct of others, are very unwilling to recommend that they should be prosecuted.

However I will make another attempt in relation to the paper which you have sent me. If I should not be discouraged from prosecuting, I will certainly prosecute those who have published this libel.

I beg leave to return you my thanks for having drawn my attention to it.

Viscount Mahon to Wellington, 11 March 1833

Hertford Committee. The kind interest which your Grace has several times been pleased to take about me makes me consider it quite incumbent upon me to give you a short account of this committee and will I hope prevent your Grace from considering that communication as an importunity.

Your Grace is no doubt already aware by the public prints of the composition of this committee; it consists of eleven most decided political enemies; and Harrison, the counsel, assured me that during his twenty-eight years of parliamentary practice, he had never known any drawn with such complete ill-luck. Nor have I in any degree to complain of any of my friends as having been absent during the ballot and thereby led to its unfortunate result; on the contrary there was a fuller attendance than on any former occasion this session and a great many persons have been named to me (and with whom my degree of acquaintance is much too slight to have given me any expectation of such conduct) who, when solicited to go down to other election ballots earlier in the session, refused, and declared that they would reserve themselves for mine.

It is gratifying in any position of life to have to complain of one's fortune, rather than of one's friends. The committee, thus unfavourably selected, has now sat for three days. In these it has become very evident to me that the case stands thus on my part—a very good case and a very bad committee—and that the question is whether the case or the committee will finally prevail.

The committee decided this afternoon a very important point against me—a point on which the decision of every one committee had been the other way since 1820; namely whether proof of the agency of any individual ought to be adduced before proof of the wrong acts of that individual. Proof of the acts have now been allowed to be given first. Several other minor points have been ruled against us. On the other hand the hostile evidence hitherto has either completely failed or been demolished in cross-examination. The case too on their part was so completely over-stated and over-argued that there appears already and must appear still more hereafter a most monstrous *hiatus* between the allegation and the testimony. These two last considerations have in the opinion of Mr. Follett already produced a visible effect on the minds of the committee and begun to make them relax from their unfavourable bias. On the whole therefore I still see great reason to hope for a triumphant issue to this very harassing and vexatious opposition.

We are I understand to divide tonight—but not on Mr. Hume's amendment. It is to be withdrawn and another differently worded is to be moved either by Mr. Hawkins or by Mr. Buller—that is the one is to move and the other to second. Mr. Hawkins is known by two Reform speeches—the first remarkably good and the latter remarkably bad, and Mr. Buller is a Radical who defeated Lord Eliot at Liskeard.

I have heard that the Ministers are to have a Cabinet council today in order to consider the currency question.

Lord Carrington and my mother are at Deal Castle which they describe as dreadfully cold at this season.

The Earl of Rosslyn to Wellington, 12 March 1833

St. James's Square. I will write again after I shall have seen the Chancellor.

I now write in consequence of the proceedings yesterday in the Commons on the Irish Church Reform Bill.

I saw Sir Robert Peel this morning, who desired me to communicate to you that the Duke of Cumberland had sent him his correspondence with the Primate respecting the Irish Church; and had asked for his (Peel's) opinion upon it; which he had determined not to give to his Royal Highness. The leaning of Sir Robert's opinion at present is *not* to enter into any debate at all on Thursday, declaring that the extreme importance and excessive length of the Bill made it impossible for him to make himself sufficiently master of it to enter into such a discussion upon it as its nature required, and that after protesting against the indecent haste with which it had been pressed on to refuse to submit to the farce of a discussion before he could deliberately examine it. This view however he wished to keep secret to the last. There is to be a small meeting on Thursday when the course to be pursued will be finally settled and declared.

Sir Robert sees great inconvenience in letting the Ministers have any previous knowledge of his purpose. I understand some of the Irish Lords and Commons propose to meet tomorrow to consider the line to be taken; and a few of them had intended to go to Sir Robert to put themselves under his command, and to try to learn his opinions, which as well as I could collect he will not state in any way till Thursday.

In the little conversation I had with him, I understood that he was quite ready to give up the Church cess upon whatever fund the charge may be imposed. I think his objections to the tax upon the present incomes of the clergy and especially upon the scale of graduation proposed, whereby the proportion is to be increased upon the higher incomes is very decided.

He evidently has not made up his mind with respect to the reduction of the bishops.

He seems not disposed to oppose the principle, but to require information, and opportunity for deliberation with respect to the extent of the reduction.

I think he looks to a consultation with your Grace and some few confidential friends before he determines upon any course with respect to the leading provisions of the Bill; and I expect that he will write to you or authorize me to communicate to you on Thursday what passes at his house.

Lord Plunket has given notice of opening his Jury Bill on Friday. I don't at present see any urgent necessity for your coming up for that and in the present aspect of things I can hardly see that your presence will be immediately required upon the Church Bill. This however may take a new face from day to day, and it is impossible to feel secure that the Duke of Cumberland, Lord Kenyon, or Lord Chandos may not do something that will leave no other hope of keeping off some decided split; and regulating and modifying the ultra opinions of our friends but the influence of your Grace's authority. I will keep my eyes and ears open and make known to you whatever I hear that can inform you, and keep you *au courant* of what is passing.

It is a singular fact that I am afraid the Church of Ireland have had no communication upon this very important question with the Church of England, which I suppose means none between the bishops as a body.

The Bishop of Rochester mentioned this to Ellenborough at dinner on Saturday last.

With respect to the provision for the Irish Church cess Sir R. Peel seemed to think it might be made the first charge upon the produce of any saving to accrue from the projected reduction, but this was evidently a very loose and undigested suggestion, and I should not have thought it necessary to mention it, but that even the lightest hints may be of use in considering the various complicated bearings of this great reform.

The Earl of Rosslyn to Wellington, 12 March 1833

House of Lords. I have seen the Chancellor who wishes to consult the Solicitor General before he decides but his present opinion goes along with you, and I think he will adopt your clause. He has had it copied, and means to keep your manuscript himself. I have sent your copy of the Irish Church Reform Bill, of which but a smaller number than are called for, have yet come from the press. I mention this as an aggravation of the violence of pressing it on to a second reading on Thursday; for the man of the Vote Office, when he gave it me, begged me not to let it be seen, and not to mention it.

I think from all accounts Don Pedro is either off or has capitulated. I rather suspect the former. The paragraph in *The Times* leaves no doubt of his ruin.

PS. I sent the copy of the clause and a long letter on the Irish Church under Lord Fitzroy's frank.

The Earl of Roden to Wellington, 12 March 1833

1 Devonshire Place. You will see by the papers that Lord Plunket has given notice for his Jury Bill for Friday and my subject respecting education will come on on Tuesday week (this day week). They are pressing the Irish Church Bill through the House of Commons in order to have it in our House before Easter. Under these circumstances I think it most important that some effort should be made by the House of Lords to save some of the wreck. If we are to stand at all there is no question in my mind so suitable as the Church. My letters from the sober thinking people throughout the country shew that they expect us to do something—we have no proxies and many of our people have not taken their seats. I should like much to know whether you are likely to be in town, that I might wait upon you on this subject. Things seem drawing to a close as respects Ireland, but surely we should shew some sign of life and anxiety to preserve what these Ministers are taking from us, and which are so important to the poor Protestants of that part of the Empire.

Dated Tuesday, 12 March. *Docketed* 1833.

The Earl of Aberdeen to Wellington, 12 March 1833

Argyll House. There seems good reason to believe that Don Pedro has proposed to capitulate; or, if the weather should have enabled him to do so, that he has already left Oporto. It is certain that the Government have received intelligence much more disastrous than anything which has appeared in the newspapers, and that we may expect to hear of the termination of the affair at any moment. It is to be presumed that our Government will at last avail themselves of this new opportunity of getting out of their difficulty. At all events, the other powers profess a determination to delay their recognition no longer.

We hear nothing yet of the arrival of M. Dedel; but I fear we cannot expect any very good ending of the Dutch affair. In the resolutions which I sent you the other day, the two or three first resolutions respecting the embargo, were only intended as introductory of that which stigmatized the treaty of the 22nd of October. This treaty is the real outrage against the law of nations, and against the law of this country too. I have not seen the remark made, but I doubt if the treaty is not one which absolutely requires the sanction of Parliament, like all those which are in opposition to existing law. I still fear that we may have, some day, to repent letting an act like this pass without notice.

There is another point, which perhaps may require some passing notice from us. You may have seen that the Duc de Broglie and Marshal Soult have both declared that France is perfectly free to do as she likes with Algiers, and that they have never come under any engagement, and may turn it into a colony whenever they please. This is a direct contradiction to our assertions made in publick.

Wellington to Viscount Mahon, 13 March 1833

Stratfield Saye. I have received and am much obliged to you for your account of your prospects. A prejudiced and corrupt court is a very bad thing. But I still hope that your cause is so good that you will get the better even of that difficulty.

CHEVENING PAPERS 685.

Wellington to the Earl of Aberdeen, 13 March 1833

Stratfield Saye. I am quite certain that the best course for us at present is to be quiet excepting upon measures brought forward by the Government which we may think proper to oppose.

I shall be in town on Saturday and will judge of the course which I will take about the Jury Bill.

ADD MS 43060, f. 83.

Wellington to the Earl of Rosslyn, 13 March 1833

Stratfield Saye. I am very much obliged to you for the trouble that you have taken about my memorandum, the Church Bill, etc. I desired Lord Fitzroy to shew you the memorandum upon the military governments.

It appears to me that the Duke of Cumberland has made a little mistake. I did not desire him or suggest to him to ask Sir R. Peel's opinion upon the Primate's letter. I knew that Sir Robert would not give him an opinion upon it. The Duke sent me the correspondence and suggested to me to obtain Sir R. Peel's opinion upon it; and upon the course to be pursued. I have, but not by me, a copy of my answer. I recollect it perfectly, as I was most guarded in writing it. I recommended to his Royal Highness himself to communicate to Sir R. Peel the letter from the Lord Primate, as it might be of use in enabling Sir R. Peel to decide upon the course which he should take upon the Irish Church Bill in the House of Commons.

I think that Sir R. Peel is quite right in declining to give his opinion to his Royal Highness. To tell you the truth one of my reasons for keeping out of town is not only to avoid the appearance of seeking for opportunities to oppose a government which I wish to keep in power although I detest their principles and policy and object to their course of action, but likewise because I wish to avoid the perpetual bavardage about public affairs which does no good and can throw no fresh light upon any subject whatever.

119

I don't know when I felt more pain than upon reading the proceedings of Monday. They manifest on the part of the Government an eagerness to seek to please the Radicals by their measures of English and Irish Church reform and Irish jury, all brought forward at the same time. On the other hand there is no pack of fox hounds in this county half so eager for its game as their followers and supporters shewed themselves to be on Monday evening to run down the Church of England.

I shall be in town on Saturday; and will then decide upon the course which I will take next week.

Wellington to the Earl of Mansfield, 13 March 1833

London. I have received your letter. The lady whose letter you sent me is like many others at large in this country—stark staring mad! When I was in office she wrote to tell me that she had by accident obtained some important intelligence that she could not communicate to anybody but myself personally and by word of mouth. I went to her at Hampstead; and then after locking the door and urging me to secrecy and searching all the cupboards and hiding places in the room, she disclosed that Bonaparte was alive and in England, that she had seen him, etc.

After some time I got out of the house. She has written to me several times since; but I have always destroyed her letters after an acknowledgment of the receipt of the two or three first.

The cover which you sent me contained two letters which I send you. I don't recollect the receipt of the pacquet mentioned in that of the 22nd February. I dare say that I received the pacquet and burnt it.

Wellington to the Earl of Roden, 13 March 1833

Stratfield Saye. I have received your letter of the 12th. I shall be in town on Saturday, and I shall then hear what course the Government have determined upon as well regarding the Jury Bill as the Church Reform Bills, and I will determine upon the course which I will follow in respect to these measures.

There is no man who dislikes more than I do the principles and the policy of the existing Administration; or is more opposed to their course of action. But I cannot shut my eyes to the state in which Parliament and the country are. That there is no power in it excepting to do mischief; and I cannot wish to remove from office men who profess at least to have good intentions in order to place the power in the hands of those who have not the grace even to make such professions. I besides feel that I am a member of the House of Lords, an assembly still powerful in legislation; but without political influence and whose character it is the object of the malevolent press of the day and of those who wish to destroy our institutions to pull down, because they feel that the destruction of the character of the House of Lords will lead to the destruction of their power as a legislative body and remove the only barrier to the attainment of their objects.

I wish therefore as far at least as I am personally concerned to afford no ground for the charge of 'faction'. Other noble Lords may entertain a different opinion. But I confess that it appears to me that it behoves those who possess large properties and who must feel that the political influence over the councils of the country is in the hands of those who possess nothing, to consider well the course which they ought to follow particularly in the House of Lords.

I do not intend to avoid to deliver my opinions upon any question that may be brought forward by the Government. But I cannot think it desirable to bring questions forward in the House of Lords solely to annoy the Ministers.

I think that if any individual can entertain a doubt of our position he ought to peruse with attention the proceedings of last Monday. He will there see the Government *coquetting* with the Radicals; and giving them in one day's sitting three important measures. Church reform in the two countries, and the Irish Jury Bill.

Then let him contemplate the eagerness with which the friends of the Government rush to the destruction of the Church of England; and will not allow the Ministers to allow even a decent time for consideration to the opponents of the measure; and he will have I think sufficient food for a day's reflection which will open his eyes to the real views of the Government and to the future proceedings of Parliament.

Wellington to John Charles Herries, 13 March 1833

Stratfield Saye. I inclose you two letters from Mr. Jenkinson on the subject of the Cinque Port pilots.

Let me know if you would wish that Mr. Payne or Mr. Iron or any of the pilots should be brought up to London.

ADD MS 57368.

The Earl of Rosslyn to Wellington, 14 March 1833

St. James's Square. I took an opportunity of explaining to Sir Robert Peel shortly the substance of your letter and particularly that you had not given the least encouragement to the Duke of Cumberland to ask his opinion, but simply had suggested that he ought to be put in possession of the Primate's letter for his information.

He appeared to be pleased and satisfied with what I said on the subject, but I must at the same time add that it did not appear to me when I saw him on Tuesday to consider you as having encouraged the Duke of Cumberland to make the application he did.

He told me for your information that they proposed to try to put off the second reading of the Irish Church till Monday; and if they failed in that to protest against the precipitancy and leave the House, announcing their intention of debating it on the Speaker's leaving the Chair.

There is besides an idea of stopping it today upon a point of form.

It appears to be a tax bill, and as such it ought to have proceeded upon resolutions voted in a committee of the whole House.

In all events the discussion will not be before Monday.

The alterations in the courts martial, particularly the unanimity in courts of five only and the concurrence of four in seven and seven in nine, appear to be very ill advised both from the real difficulties they will throw in the way of forming the courts and the risk of paralysing their proceedings; but I still more lament the symptoms it shews of weakness and irresolution.

I hear good accounts of Hope's canvass; but I tremble for Hertford from the scandalous conduct of the committee.

The Liverpool committee is a most dangerous precedent and they seem to intend to extend it to Stafford and other places. This mode of proceeding will entail a great expence upon Government, and lead to great injustice and oppression, as indeed will be the case with the corporation, where from its constitution and numbers there will be abundant scope for the display of all the bad passions of resentment and revenge from Members to whom the corporations may have been opposed at their late elections.

There have been great crowds seeking admission to our column, and the Woods and Forests are afraid of the complaints of their lessees. I think the curiosity will soon pass away, and I should be sorry to be obliged to charge any money for the entrance to it.

A week or ten days will enable you to judge better.

I will write from the House of Lords if there is anything worth while before the post.

The Earl of Lauderdale to Wellington, 14 March 1833

Dunbar. Young Coventry, in whom I feel so much interest, and who you was so good as to place in the Rifle Brigade, is ordered out next month.

I have advised him to go straight there by the steam packet instead of applying for leave to go overland; I am very anxious however that he should get into the Guards, as soon as it can be managed, and you would oblige me much if you would let me know if there is any chance of his success for a year or two.

I suppose you have heard of Praed's petition accusing me of a breach of privilege by my interference in the election of the borough of St. Ives. It is really the most unjustifiable attack that ever was made on man. I have had for some years some property in the mines there, three general elections have taken place since I possessed it. I never interfered or was asked to interfere till this general election; nor did I dream or do I now believe that I had any influence whatever.

At this general election however Mr. Praed applied to me and my sons urging interference in his favor; applications were made by Harris, Arbuthnot, Holmes, Hardinge, John Hope, Ross, and I believe others. I declined all interference, and I can only conceive that he has done this out of revenge; but I am firmly of opinion that I have no influence whatever, and that my power is a creature of his own imagination.

Signature only in Lauderdale's hand.

Viscount Mahon to Wellington, 15 March 1833

Hertford Committee. I gratefully acknowledge your Grace's kind expressions as to my present election annoyances, and am happy to say that the proceedings up to this time (Friday afternoon) continue to confirm my former opinion as to the utter weakness of Duncombe's case and the undoubted vindication of our's. At the same time with such a committee, as we have got, it is impossible to feel very confident of justice.

I will take the liberty of submitting to your Grace a short narrative of some transactions relative to the currency, which have occurred within the last week or ten days, and in which I have borne a part, since the accounts which have been given of them by some of the newspapers were both imperfect and incorrect, and since they appear to me to be of considerable political importance.

I was informed ten or twelve days ago that a considerable number of Members of Parliament attributed the present depression of business and restlessness of the people in a great measure to the state of our monetary system, and were desirous of obtaining a parliamentary committee of inquiry into that subject. I was informed also that though comprising some Conservatives, such as Duncombe of Yorkshire and Stanley of Cumberland, and some moderate Whigs such as Lord George Bentinck and Mr. Nicholson Calvert, they would nevertheless in all probability consent to be guided on this question by that most outrageous Radical Mr. Thomas Attwood, who has conferred upon this country the blessing of political unions and whose plans of 'equitable adjustment' and 'inconvertible paper money' are in fact nothing but schemes for public bankruptcy and personal enrichment. Under these circumstances two things appeared to me very desirable. First that there should be a committee of inquiry into the most critical state of our currency. I am persuaded that this question is pressing upon us with rapid strides—that it will not admit of being staved off very much longer—that it is now causing in all our manufacturing towns those constant and fierce demands for reduction of taxation to a vast extent, demands which cannot safely either be granted or refused and which would die away if a greater supply of money afforded the people ease and facility in paying the taxes which now exist. And as to us land-owners I believe that it will daily become more evident that there is now only one plain alternative before us—immense reductions in our rents—or moderate enlargement in our currency. On these grounds I think that without the slightest pledge as to ulterior measures, it is desirable to see appointed a committee of investigation. But, secondly it appeared to me not less important and desireable to draw the question from the hands of such a person as Mr. Thomas Attwood. I knew indeed that Sir Robert Peel unfortunately considers himself too much pledged by the Act which bears his name, to originate any such inquiry, and I found that Mr. Baring on many points reserved himself for the parliamentary discussion, though on one point (the adoption of silver as a legal tender) he was, like myself, very decided.

With these views I went to a meeting of Members of Parliament held at the house of Sir Charles Burrell on Friday last. There were about sixty present, and several of them very absurd, and all very divided in their views of this question. I made them a speech declaring that I for one would pledge myself to nothing beyond voting for a committee of inquiry if brought forward by a person of whom I approved and I advised the meeting not to go any further in their resolution. They did adhere to this suggestion and passed a resolution stating in substance that a committee was desireable to ascertain whether any connection existed between the public distresses and our monetary system and if so to consider whether it might admit of any safe and prudent amelioration. The first point after this, was to ascertain how far the Government would allow of such a committee in the House of Commons and a deputation of eight—I was named one but did not go with it—was appointed to go to Lord Althorp and submit that inquiry to him. The deputation saw his Lordship on Saturday and he promised to summon a Cabinet Council on Monday with that view. He did so; and on Tuesday we had his answer which was addressed to one of the deputation (Mr. Cayley, M.P. for North Yorkshire) but not marked 'Private'. In this, he in the name of his colleagues most positively refused their assent to any such committee, and declared that they would oppose its appointment to the utmost of their power.

On the ensuing day (last Monday) [*sic*] another meeting of Members of Parliament was held at Sir Charles Burrell's to receive this answer. They expressed great regret at its purport and though mostly consisting of friends of the Government determined nevertheless to persevere in supporting the motion for a committee. The greater number apparently wished to see it in the hands of Mr. Thomas Attwood and had I not been present I believe it would have been decided in that manner. But I stated explicitly to that gentleman himself, and still more explicitly to the other leading characters present, that neither I nor any of those who concurred with me in political opinions could, consistently with our sense of duty, vote for that motion if brought forward by the parent of the Birmingham Political Union. The point is still I believe un-decided. I have however since, been empowered by several of our friends such as Lord Chandos, Lord Lincoln and Sir Richard Vyvyan to state to Sir Charles Burrell that they entirely concur in my course on this occasion, that they are most willing to vote for such a committee of inquiry but that like myself they make it a *sine qua non* that it be not moved for by Mr. Thomas Attwood.

I apologize to your Grace for the length of these details. But you will perceive by them how strong and growing an impression in favour of some change in the currency is pervading a large portion both of our enemies and friends. For my own part I should be satisfied with the adoption of silver as a legal tender and the repeal of the Small Note Act of 1826. I take up the question only from a deep and thorough convic-tion that it is not a party question but one of immense national impor-tance—that nearly all parties equally concurred in the Acts of 1819 and 1826, and that the advantage of our subsequent experience may therefore with equal justice and consistency modify the views of all. And I cannot but respectfully entreat your Grace—on whom all good men in the country now fix their anxious eyes, as the only standard round which to rally, as the chief head to direct, or hand to execute, in these evil and ominous days—I entreat your Grace I say, not positively to pledge yourself against any future reconsideration of this momentous question, and to remember that the force of circumstances—a force to which all other forces in politics must sometimes yield—may, and I am persuaded will, irresistibly press the question forward against any Government, combine men of all parties for its promotion, and loudly call upon your Grace's wisdom and public spirit to effect some safe and satisfactory settlement.

Again apologizing for this long and tedious letter I have the honour to remain *etc.*

Wellington to Viscount Mahon, 16 March 1833

London. I am rejoiced to learn that you keep up your hopes of the result of your committee.

I am much obliged to you for your note upon the currency.

I can give no opinion upon the subject. I wish that you had coad-jutors with whom you would yourself be better satisfied.

CHEVENING PAPERS 685.

Baron Zuylen van Nyevelt to Wellington, 16 March 1833

Londres. Je n'ai pas la présomption de croire que l'annonce de mon départ de Londres puisse avoir un intérêt spécial à vos yeux, mais je croirais manquer à la franchise que commande l'amitié, dont Votre Grâce m'honore, si je lui cachais que parmi les principaux griefs énoncés contre moi afin d'amener ce résultat, d'ailleurs conformé à mes désirs, on a articulé les rapports, que j'avais l'honneur d'entretenir avec votre Grâce et avec Lord Aberdeen: j'allais à Apsley et à Argyll House pour y chercher mes instructions, et (chose assez contradictoire) pour y dicter les discours de l'Opposition.

Quoique l'approbation que mon souverain a daigné faire exprîmer sur ma conduite ne me fasse attacher qu'un intérêt très secondaire à l'opinion d'autrui, je vous avoue my Lord que devant ces inculpations je n'ai pu m'empêcher de me demander, si j'étais à Venise, à l'époque la plus ombrageuse de son aristocratie, ou bien si je me trouvais sur le sol, réputé le plus libre de l'Europe? C'était bien la peine de faire suivre mes pas dans Piccadilly et Argyll Street! Que ne m'a t'on demandé franchement ce que j'y allais faire? Ma réponse eut été prompte: j'y cherchais en plein midi, la tête haute, et par les propos à deux battans, un grand homme et un noble caractère; j'y entretenais par un sentiment bien juste de reconnaissance, des relations cimentées par la confiance, dont le Cabinet Britannique, sous l'administration de votre Grâce, rehaussa pendant dix-huit mois l'importance de mon Ambassade à Constantinople, en me chargeant avec les intérêts de la Grèce, de ceux de l'Angleterre, privées de leur protection naturelle par le départ de mon très honorable ami, Sir Stratford Canning: j'y acquittais ma dette de gratitude pour les preuves flatteuses et éclatantes de haute approbation, que Lord Aberdeen m'avait fait parvenir, d'après les ordres du feu Roi Georges IV; je cédais en un mot à ces émotions qu'éprouve l'âme en se rapprochant de ceux qu'on respecte, et avec lesquels on sympathise d'affections et de sentimens.

Dans l'histoire moderne de ma patrie, votre illustre nom est associé à tout ce qu'elle renferme d'important et de glorieux; il est surtout inséparable de la fondation du royaume des Pays Bas, vous l'avez défendu par votre épée, et lorsqu'il fallut céder au torrent insurrectionnel de 1830, vous employâtes, d'accord avec votre noble ami, dans le conseil et hors du conseil, votre autorité et votre influence, pour mettre des bornes aux innovations, en aidant à établir entre la Hollande et la Belgique un régime administratif séparé, puisque tel était le vœu général. Plus tard lorsque, conjointement avec l'Ambassadeur Falck, j'eus signé le protocole du 18 février 1831, qui aurait dû être le dernier de cette déplorable série, vous fûtes d'opinion que les bases de séparation contractées avec un souverain, dépouillé de deux tiers de ses états, devraient être franchement et loyalement exécutées, comme gage de paix et comme dette d'honneur.

Si depuis lors un traité fut conclu, sans le consentement de mon souverain, et avec des réserves de la part des trois monarques du nord, vos vœux se sont bornés, vu que les négotiations avaient été de nouveau ouvertes, à désirer qu'elles fussent terminées le plus conformément que possible aux bases de séparation, acceptées par le roi. Si ce vœu est répréhensible, si parler, penser, et agir dans ce sens est digne de blâme, je crains que votre Grâce, son noble ami et moi, ne soyons de grands coupables.

My Lord, j'ai défendu les droits de mon souverain et les intérêts de ma patrie, qui en sont inséparables avec zèle, quelquefois avec chaleur; ma ligne de conduite était simple, je n'étais pas arrêté par aucune complication, car je n'avais engagé mon gouvernement que par *un seul protocole;* et cependant je me suis constamment prêté à modifier, dans l'intérêt de la paix, ce qu'en vertu de cet acte solennel j'avais droit de regarder comme irrévocablement résolu.

Mais au milieu de ces débats vous n'avez pas my Lord, ainsi que le noble comte, entretenu ce qu'on appelle communément nos illusions: supérieur en tout, vous vous êtes montré sans cesse, l'ami éclairé de mon roi et de mon pays; veuillez en agréer le tribut de ma reconnaissance, et nous permettre de compter sur une amitié, qui nous est chère, puisqu'elle tend vers la consolidation de ces anciens et utiles rapports entre la Hollande et la Grande Bretagne, dont les Princes de la maison d'Orange, toutes les fois que leurs vues ne furent point contrariées en Hollande par des divisions, qui heureusement n'y existent plus, ont été de tous tems les plus sûrs garants.

Dieu veuille que les nouveaux efforts de mon Cabinet amènent bientôt le rétablissement de nos relations commerciales, si brusquement interrompus au grand détriment des intérêts des deux pays, et soyent couronnés sans délai par un arrangement final, sur la stabilité duquel l'Europe puisse d'autant plus compter, que pour l'obtenir elle y aura sacrifié jusqu'à ses convictions.

Adieu, Monsieur le Duc, j'espère que nous nous reverrons un jour sous de meilleurs auspices.

The Earl of Aberdeen to Wellington, 18 March 1833

House of Lords. I have not seen the evening papers, and therefore I do not know if they contain the intelligence received yesterday from the Levant. It appears that Roussin on his arrival at Constantinople, undertook to settle the whole affair on behalf of the Pacha. The terms sent to Alexandria by the Sultan, of which Halil Pacha was the bearer, were I believe accepted by Roussin on his behalf, and the acceptance of the Pacha guaranteed by the French Admiral. The affair was settled, and the treaty made, without the knowledge of the Russian or the Austrian Ministers. I cannot quite ascertain whether the English chargé was consulted, and what part he took in the transaction; but he had no instructions, and I presume therefore, that he could not venture to join in the guarantee. Lord Ponsonby, who had not left Naples before the end of February, was on his passage to Constantinople. The whole business proves pretty clearly the nature of the connection between the French Government and the Pacha. I do not find that our Government think they have been treated with any want of respect.

Wessenberg gave me this information last night, having received it himself from Talleyrand.

Wellington to the Earl of Aberdeen, 19 March 1833

Stratfield Saye. I have not seen in the evening papers any reference to Admiral Roussin's negociations. In truth our Government are so much occupied by internal affairs and by their revolutionary negociations in the Peninsula and in Holland that they have not leisure to attend to nor means to interfere effectually in affairs at a greater distance and of minor importance. Then they now prefer the establishment of French influence to that of the Russians in the Levant; and I dare say that there is no man in the Cabinet who has taken the trouble of ascertaining facts and of considering how the interests of this nation might be affected by this arrangement.

I send you my answer to Nyevelt's letter in order that you may write for yourself anything that you may think proper. Send it to Monsieur Dedel, the plenipotentiary of Holland to His Majesty, to be forwarded to Nyevelt.

ADD MS 43060, ff. 84–85. *Draft in Wellington Papers.*

Wellington to Baron Zuylen van Nyevelt, 19 March 1833

Stratfield Saye. I have had the honor of receiving your letter of the 16th and at the same time that I return you my thanks for its flattering expressions towards myself I cannot avoid to express my concern that the noblemen and gentlemen who enjoy the confidence of the King my master should have considered it their duty to require from His Majesty the King of the Netherlands that His Majesty should deprive himself of your valuable services on account of the communications between yourself and Lord Aberdeen and me.

It is true as is well observed by your Excellency that there is an evident and ridiculous inconsistency in the terms of the charge itself. But I have been too often the object of the calumnies of the same parties in the course of my long life of public service not to be aware that there is no inconsistency of which they will not be guilty to attain the purpose of the moment. The ability and firmness with which you maintained the interests of your sovereign in negociation was inconvenient to them; and they found themselves pressed in Parliament by the facts recalled to the recollection of the public by Lord Aberdeen and myself; for they were well known, having been published and discussed in every gazette of Europe.

The calumny therefore is invented of an improper communication between you and Lord Aberdeen and me. One equally injurious to the honor and to the loyalty of all the parties between whom the communication is supposed to have taken place; and by means of it your sovereign is deprived of your services.

As long as it remains concealed in the secrecy of the boxes and confidential despatches I shall treat it with the contempt which it deserves and with which I have treated other misinformations as far as it related to myself.

If it should be made public I shall know how to defend myself.

In the course of my service to my own sovereign I had the good fortune of being the instrument of rendering an important service to His Majesty the King of the Netherlands. I had other occasions [of] rendering to His Majesty many services all of which he received most [*sic*] and I am indebted to him for many marks of his most gracious favour and kindness.

I am one of those who consider the intimate union and alliance between this kingdom and Holland to be essential to the best interests of both; and that the best times for both countries those in which men of the highest reputation for talents, integrity and honor conducted the affairs of each were those in which the two countries were most firmly united in alliance and councils to the exclusion from the councils of each whether

The above two paragraphs were deleted and the following substituted:

The nature of my service to my sovereign in foreign countries and the relations which I have formed in most of them have naturally placed me in intimate acquaintance with most of the foreign ministers in London; and with none more than with the Ambassadors from the King of the Netherlands.

The following draft of the second half of the letter is on a separate sheet:

. . . such relations is criminal; and it will rest with those who found upon their existence such calumnious charges to prove the truth of their assertions.

I never said one word in private whether to your Excellency or your colleague that I did not state in public; and that I do not believe nay that I cannot prove to be true from the documents which are before the public and ought to be before Parliament. I have not concealed my opinion upon any part of these transactions; and if you or your colleague ever entertained any illusions you could not have imbibed them from me, if you was so kind as to attend to and reflect upon what I said.

In the course of my services to my sovereign I have upon more than one occasion been the instrument of rendering services to His Majesty the King of the Netherlands; which services His Majesty received most graciously; and I am indebted to him for many marks of his most gracious favor and kindness.

But my offence towards the party which has invented this calumny is that I am one of those who consider the intimate union and alliance between this kingdom and Holland to be essential to the best interests of both; and that the best times for both countries those in which men of the highest reputation for talents, integrity and honor conducted the affairs of each, were those in which the two countries were most firmly united in alliance and in councils, to the exclusion from the councils of each whether in peace or in war of all Gallick influence.

This opinion frequently expressed in public, has exposed me to the calumny from which I trust that the well known ability and wisdom of the councils of the King of the Netherlands will exempt him from suffering inconvenience.

Draft in Wellington's hand.

Signed: Wellington, Prince de Waterloo.

Wellington to the Earl of Lauderdale, 19 March 1833

Stratfield Saye. I omitted to write you an answer to your former letter respecting a protégé of yours, in favour of whom I applied to Lord Hill for the purchase of a commission. I think he told me that he had recommended him.

It related likewise to some accusations made against you for influencing the elections of the peers to represent the peers of Scotland in the House of Lords. I spoke to the gentlemen who interest themselves about the press upon this last mentioned subject. The Government and the Radicals will not understand that the peers of Scotland as well as the peers of Ireland and the peers of England do not consider the system which has been successfully adopted of depriving property of all political influence as advantageous to the existence of property itself. It is not surprising therefore that the largest properties in the three kingdoms should combine against those who are the patrons of this system. It does not require the exercise of your influence or mine to induce them to do so.

I recommend that young Coventry should apprize the proper department of the Horse Guards of his intention to proceed to his destination by sea. I mean supposing that he has the option. I shall remove him to the Grenadier Guards as soon as it will be in my power. But I have still a very long list.

It is very difficult to understand the proceedings of many of our gentlemen. They never fail to require all the support that can be afforded to them which is fair enough that they should require. But there is a sort of reciprocity in matters of this description. If a man situated as you are cannot or does not think proper to interfere in such a case as that which you describe; or I will go farther and suppose the case to be true which is charged against him, or that he had supported by his influence another party, there can be no reason for attacking that man.

When men are acting together for a common purpose they ought to look steadily to their object, and not deviate from it for any little dirty advantage to be obtained against an adversary.

Would you wish me to say any thing to Mr. Praed or his friends? If I was in your situation I would not notice their conduct.

The Earl of Rosslyn to Wellington, 21 March 1833

House of Lords. I mentioned to you a letter I received from the Comissioners of Woods and Forests respecting the crowds that assemble for admission to the interior of the monumental column. I answered by saying that I would lay their letter before the committee at its next meeting and I submitted to them whether it would not be expedient that the Commissioners should suggest for the consideration of the committee such regulations as they would wish to recommend. I did this that the responsibility of those regulations may in a great degree rest upon them.

I have a note from Maitland stating that there was considerable disturbance yesterday; and upon enquiry late today I found that the disorder had been very great, but that the serjeant with the assistance of the police had succeeded in preventing the people from forcing their way.

I saw great violence myself today and I propose to repeat the direction I gave upon reading Maitland's note, viz. that in consequence of these irregularities the serjeant should keep the door shut tomorrow and until the orders of the committee.

If your Grace stays in town I could assemble a committee for Tuesday.

I have heard but a part of Lord Plunket who was very short, but all our friends agree that his bill is a very great improvement upon that of last year. The second reading is fixed for Thursday sevennight.

Enclosure: General Frederick Maitland to the Earl of Rosslyn, 21 March 1833.

Wellington to Viscount Melbourne, 21 March 1833

Stratfield Saye. I send herewith a petition to the King under the common seal of the corporation of Hull in which that body beseeches His Majesty to appoint me High Steward of Hull *vice* the late Earl of Fitzwilliam.

Upon being apprised of the intention of the corporation to submit this petition to His Majesty I requested that its members would consider of the expediency of recommending to His Majesty a person connected with the corporation or with the county of York; and who might be enabled to promote their views for the interests of the town of Hull by his knowledge of them and by his connection with the town. The corporation has however thought proper to persevere in expressing their wish that I should be appointed to the office, and I beg your Lordship to submit their petition to His Majesty's most gracious pleasure.

Viscount Melbourne to Wellington, 22 March 1833

Home Office. I have the honour to acknowledge the receipt of your Grace's letter of the 20th instant [*sic*], and also of the petition of the corporation of Hull, and I beg leave to acquaint your Grace, that I shall lose no time in submitting to His Majesty, for his royal signature, the warrant appointing your Grace High Steward of Hull; in the room of the late Earl Fitzwilliam.

Signature only in Melbourne's hand.

The Earl of Aberdeen to Wellington, 22 March 1833

Argyll House. I have forwarded your letter to Zuylen, and have added a short one from myself, pretty much in the same strain. The first attempt of M. Dedel has been unsuccessful. They have refused to agree to his proposal of an armistice with any limitation, and insist that it shall be indefinite. They have also brought forward the proposal of a definitive treaty with the two powers; but this M. Dedel has peremptorily rejected, and they do not appear to have persevered in the suggestion.

The Constantinople affair does not become more agreable to the Russians on reflection. Pozzo has remonstrated very warmly at Paris, and I have never heard Lieven express himself with so much bitterness of the French Government, and so much contempt of our own, as he did last night. I understand our Ministers profess to be satisfied. While the French newspapers boast of the exclusive influence and power of France in the Levant, ours are instructed to say that every thing is done in concert.

I have procured the French note respecting Algiers, which I will bring you on Sunday morning, as I understand you are to be in town tomorrow.

By all accounts, the Irish Jury Bill is no longer liable to the former objection; and so far as could be gathered from Lord Plunket's explanation yesterday, does not appear to call for opposition. How O'Connell and his friends may like it is another affair; and possibly in the House of Commons, after the example of the Coercion Bill, it may be so altered as to come back to us in a very different shape.

Wellington to the Rev. L. Sullivan, 23 March 1833

London. I have received your letter of the 20th and I assure you that I am not aware what the contents of mine were which have occasioned any uneasiness to you.

The fact is that my whole time is taken up from morning till night in receiving written suggestions for the public benefit from gentlemen with whom I have no connection or even acquaintance. Nobody is satisfied unless I write an answer. It is not surprising if these answers are at times not given at great length, and are not satisfactory to those to whom they are addressed.

It cannot be supposed to be intended by me to write anything offensive or calculated to hurt the feelings of any gentleman.

Sir Henry Frederick Cooke to Wellington, 23 March 1833

I herewith forward a letter from Naples, which may be worth your Grace's perusal.

Strange and important events have occurred, *even* since I had the honor of walking with your Grace. The machine called monarchy seems within the attractive influence of a destructive comet, and we hasten with the rapidity, which as in matter, augments by approaching.

I perceive but one *certainty* in all this danger—the inevitability of an awful event of *some sort*. You may be ruined legislatively—if the people are patient, it will be so—if not, by a short cut.

If a battalion of Guards marched to the parade tomorrow morning and threw their caps into the air, the present Government could not extricate us. I am not deceived when I say, that the spirit of the army *here* requires only the *abolition* of corporal punishment, to render them ungovernable.

The late election speaks volumes, and Government have made *theirs;* preferring the danger of alliance with the Radicals, to the loss of place. Aware of the danger themselves, they think to controul it by cajolerie, and tricks, and money.

They have bought Colonel Jones! It is through him they think to know the feeling of the people.

He told me yesterday, that my fears were exaggerated. The danger he said 'does not consist in the want of power; but the abuse of it'.

Reform (he added) has been conceded upon an honest avowal of a principle. 'Great concessions must be made to satisfy their real wants— if you fail to do this, the consequences may be fatal.' It were waste of time to listen to more from a rogue or an idiot.

When Hope's committee canvassed an apothecary in Marylebone the man said, 'Sir, I admit the eligibility and propriety of Mr. Hope's pretensions—but he is no longer of *any party*. I will not give him my vote. I prefer him to a Whig, for that party add *crime* with deceit to ignorance—my conscience forbids my voting for Whalley. When King William dissolved his last Parliament he said he would take the voice of his people. They demand positive and immediate *good*. I well know, no Government can obtain it. But the people will have it, thinking they see the sure road. It is really not their fault to entertain an error that has blinded wiser heads. But, Sir, the King appealed to them. Those who advised it will now count their cost—and if the legislature do not produce a crisis, the people will. You may save yourself the trouble of canvassing, for you cannot remove these impressions. I have property, and I desire quiet. I was a Tory, and if you ask me my party now I could not define it unless I was fool enough to imagine I saw safety (*now*) in any—but I am one of two-thirds of England.'

I am convinced this is plain and concise *truth*, and that it *is* the true feeling now alive. All men's minds are upon the stretch looking for something.

Dated 10 p.m. 23 March. *Docketed* 1833. From Sir Henry Cooke. March 23. Sends a letter from Lord Hertford. State of publick mind in London.

The Marquess Camden to Wellington, 23 March 1833

Arlington Street. I send to you under another cover, my proxy (as I am going out of town, on Monday, for the next fortnight) although I do not imagine, there will be a necessity for its being available upon any probable occasion. The Irish Disturbance Bill will be returned to the House of Lords before Easter, but so altered, that I think it cannot be supported but it would not be politic to oppose it, though it is not rendered less constitutional whilst it has become so much less efficient. The conduct of Government on the Marylebone election demonstrates that they have decided upon a connexion with the Radicals. Whalley abused the Government and its candidate Murray grossly and yet when its candidate was beat—Lord Duncannon, Sir J. Byng and Murray's committee openly supported Whalley and there appears to be a very different tone on O'Connell's part and on the part of Government towards each other. On the Church Bill I trust our friends in the House of Lords will attend regularly and act in earnest.

John Wilson Croker to Wellington, 24 March 1833

West Molesey, Surrey. Lord Hertford has executed the papers before the Consul and has returned them to Lord Downes. He says that the Act 6 George IV, c. 87, s. 20 has, unintentionally perhaps but certainly, repealed the instruction as to the Irish magistrate and made valid the act done before the Consul. I have written to this effect to Lord Downes.

I was in town on Friday and found the *knowing ones* in great wonder at the strength of the minority on the currency question the night before. No one had any idea of the strength of that party. Attwood was very doubtful about venturing to divide. I myself think it was not so much the strength of the currency question as the *ad captandum* of a committee on enquiring into the distresses of the poor which made so formidable a division, but the wise ones think otherwise and say that it was a wound of which the Ministry will linger till Easter and then die. Heaven forbid—for I, like your Grace, think that if these men were now to go out, chaos would come again.

Lord Hertford took a world of pains to find an Irish magistrate; he even advertised for one as you will see by the inclosed—which I send to show how anxious he was to fulfill your Grace's wishes.

Enclosure: cutting from an Italian newspaper, headed Avviso particolare: Any gentleman at Naples in the commission of the peace for an

Irish county will confer a favour upon an Irish peer by sending word where and when he may be waited upon to administer some oaths to Valles Inn n. 226 Chiaja.

Wellington to the King, 25 March 1833

Stratfield Saye. The Duke of Wellington presents his humble duty to Your Majesty.

When he was in London in the end of last week he heard a report that it was intended by Your Majesty's servants to propose to Parliament an alteration of the Mutiny Act, by which corporal punishment should be restricted if not entirely abolished in Your Majesty's army; and as the Duke has from the nature and length of his services with the army acquired more experience upon that subject than most officers now alive, and adverting to his position in Your Majesty's military service he considers it his duty to submit to Your Majesty some observations which may deserve Your Majesty's attention and the enquiry of your servants.

The Duke is the more inclined to adopt this mode of drawing Your Majesty's attention to the subject because it is probable that it may be brought under the consideration of Parliament in the discussions on the Mutiny Bill in this week; and considering that the Mutiny Bill must pass by the 1st of May and that Easter holydays intervene, it appears to the Duke that there is not time and opportunity for the enquiries which it is obvious ought to be made before a measure of such importance is adopted, unless Your Majesty should desire that a different course should be taken.

A year has elapsed since the general commanding Your Majesty's forces desired Field Marshal the Duke of Wellington to give him his opinion upon this subject. The Duke then wrote a memorandum upon it, of which he unfortunately has not by him a copy. But he entreats Your Majesty to call for this paper. The perusal of it will shew your Majesty the difference between the constitution of Your Majesty's army, and that of others; upon whose example is founded the reasoning of those who urge the proposed alteration. He will likewise point out the importance of maintaining in full force the power of inflicting this description of punishment not only for the purpose of maintaining discipline and good order in the army, but likewise for the purpose of insuring the unresisting submission of the soldiers of the army to regulations for their conduct, and to minor punishments for breaches of discipline and good order, which would have the effect of rendering it practically unnecessary to inflict corporal punishment in any but very flagrant cases if at all. In that paper the Field Marshal has shewn that no punishment can be substituted for corporal punishment in the British service. If the Field Marshal is not misinformed all the attempts which have been lately made to discover such a punishment have failed. He will not fatigue the attention of Your Majesty by entering into details although fully prepared to do so. He cannot but observe however that it must be mortifying to those who feel a respect for the army, and who are aware of the nature of the duties which even a private soldier has to perform, to see dozens of the soldiers of Your Majesty's Guards confined in British prisons for breaches of military discipline with the pickpockets and thieves of the suburbs of the City of London; and I know moreover that the same confinement has been the occasion of acts of mutiny and outrage.

If the circumstances of the times were such as to give reason to hope that Your Majesty's civil government could be carried on, or that Your Majesty's authority or the law of the country could be put in execution without requiring the aid of Your Majesty's army the Duke would lament the state of indiscipline and disorder into which the army would fall, but he would not consider it incumbent upon him to trouble Your Majesty upon this subject. The Duke however begs leave to recall to Your Majesty's recollection the occurrences in Great Britain of the years 1831 and 1832. He puts out of the question those of the year 1830; and likewise those in Ireland.

He ventures to assert that in these two years 1831 and 1832 there was more outrage upon person and more loss of property by popular violence, and there was more loss of lives in conflicts with Your Majesty's troops within Great Britain, than had occurred in fifty years from the year 1781 to the year 1830 inclusive. There is no reason to believe that even in Great Britain the services of the troops will be less frequently called for to protect the lives and properties of Your Majesty's subjects, and the authority of the law and of Your Majesty.

Yet Field Marshal the Duke of Wellington ventures to tell Your Majesty that an army undisciplined and disorderly is unequal and unfit to perform[1] such services. He adds that it would be better for Your Majesty and the State to have no army than such a one.

---

[1] The word 'even' has been added in pencil, possibly later.

The army now in Your Majesty's service is avowedly unrivalled for its conduct in peace as well as in war, at home as well as abroad. Surely if there be any doubt respecting the discipline and efficiency of the army after this important change in the means of maintaining both will have been effected[1] it would be reasonable and right to take time and to make enquiry before such alteration should be made.

Before he concludes this address[2] the Field Marshal would submit one farther observation to Your Majesty. In the course of his experience as well in command of a regiment as of the King's armies abroad, and of His Majesty's forces, he has frequently had complaints from soldiers of the conduct of officers who endeavoured to maintain discipline and order by regulations enforcing minute restraints and minor punishments, in order to avoid the necessity of inflicting corporal punishment. The Field Marshal recollects one instance upon record at the Horse Guards of a mutiny caused in a corps by such attempts. But he never yet heard any where of any complaint on the part of any military men whatever of corporal punishment.

All of which is humbly submitted to Your Majesty by Your Majesty's most dutiful subject.

Postscript (separate)

Although Field Marshal the Duke of Wellington has omitted to advert to the service in Ireland in the accompanying address to Your Majesty there is a most important consideration involved in this question as relating to Ireland.

A large proportion of Your Majesty's army in Ireland are Irishmen, and Roman Catholicks. Your Majesty can know at any time how many in each regiment.

The Field Marshal entertains no doubt that the discipline of the army is now too strong for the agitator and the priest, certainly when acting upon the mass of the men; but probably upon each individual.

The agitator and the priest would find discipline, and the influence of the officer and non-commissioned officer to be powerless if corporal punishment was discontinued. In truth if the efficiency of His Majesty's service in Ireland should not be destroyed equally with that in England by the natural operation of this measure upon all soldiers it would be dependent upon the goodwill of the agitator and the priest.

---

[1] 'Made' substituted in pencil.
[2] 'Paper' substituted in pencil.

Which is likewise humbly submitted to Your Majesty by Your Majesty's most dutiful subject.

There is also a draft of this paper, docketed 'not sent'.

Viscount Melbourne to Wellington, 25 March 1833

Home Office. Since I had the honour of receiving your Grace's communication upon the subject of the High Stewardship of Hull, I have received an intimation that proceedings are likely to be adopted in that city, calling in question the validity of the petition transmitted to me by your Grace. In these circumstances I am confident your Grace will feel that I cannot do otherwise than advise His Majesty to delay the completion of the warrant, until the import of the elections shall have been enquired into and ascertained.

Wellington to the Marquess Camden, 26 March 1833

London. I have received and will take care of your proxy. It is very difficult to satisfy noble Lords. I have done exactly what I said I would on the day before the session commenced, which course I thought was highly approved of by all present. They now require a more active and harassing Opposition; and when they should discover as they infallibly would that such Opposition would answer no purpose excepting to disgust the publick, and to prepare the publick mind for putting down entirely the institution of the House of Lords or for depriving it of independent functions; they would complain of the course of Opposition, which we should have adopted.

However I will see what ought to be done when the Coercion Bill returns to the House of Lords, which will be next Monday.

Wellington to Viscount Melbourne, 26 March 1833

Stratfield Saye. I am very much obliged to your Lordship for having advised His Majesty to delay the completion of the warrant appointing me to be High Steward of Hull.

I request your Lordship not to advise the King to compleat it until I shall have consented to accept the office after having enquired respecting the opposition of my appointment.

I was not aware that such opposition existed excepting on my own part. To accept an office of honour proffered by a whole community is a very different thing from the acceptance of the same office conferred by a party after a contested election, the result of which is disputed. I think it very possible that my original objections to the acceptance of the office at all will be confirmed by the result of the enquiry which I propose to make into the nature and circumstances of the contest and of the election; and I am desirous of avoiding to decline to accept the office after the King will have signed the warrant to appoint me to fill it.

RA MELBOURNE PAPERS. *Copy in Wellington Papers.*

Lord Downes to Wellington, 26 March 1833

Dublin. I have the pleasure to acquaint your Grace that I have received Lord Hertford's writs from Naples. The documents were duly executed in the presence of the British Consul, who it appears is authorised by an Act of Parliament, 6 George IV, chapter 87, section 20, to administer abroad all oaths etc. in like manner as English or *Irish* magistrates are empowered to administer them at home.

I have now got 76 writs perfected and I may still hope to get Lord Mountcashell's and Lord Bloomfield's in time. Lord Kingsland has expressed a wish not to vote unless his vote is *absolutely* necessary. I shall not therefore press him, as my majority will be very large. There have been only 28 writs sent in for Lord Lismore but there may be some more for him before Friday. There was a paragraph in the papers about ten days ago, stating that Lord Lismore had withdrawn from the contest, but several writs have been sent in for him since that paragraph appeared. He has not however taken out his own writ, and in that respect I had better follow his example, although it has been the custom for the candidates to vote for themselves in all former contests.

On Friday night the election will close, and I will then send your Grace a list of the peers, shewing how they have all voted.

PS. As the Easter recess takes place so soon, I should scarcely have time to take my seat before the House adjourned, but I shall be in London so as to take my place the first day that the House meets after the holydays.

The Earl of Lauderdale to Wellington, 26 March 1833

Dunbar. Many thanks to you for your kind letter on the subject of Coventry's getting into the Guards.

I would not wish you to do any thing about Praed; I meant to have raised an action against him, but I hear he has been so generally condemned even by his friends, that it is not consistent with the feelings of common charity to persevere in exposing him.

People won't let me alone. The Duke of Bedford has thought proper to turn my bust out of what he calls the Temple of Liberty, erected to the memory of Mr. Fox. To that I should have had nothing to say, the bust was his, and the temple was his, and he was of course free to do with either as he chose.

But he took it into his head to write me a letter arraigning my political conduct, and accusing me of having joined a faction for the purpose of overturning an Administration in which Lord Grey and Lord Holland took prominent parts. Now whatever he might do with the bust, I am sure you will agree with me, that he had no right to arraign my political conduct in a private letter, and that at least he laid himself open to receive a reply which I certainly seized the opportunity of sending him, and of therein treating him as he deserved.

I received another letter from him which in some degree excited my pity, at the same time as he explains that you and Sir Robert Peel and the late Government are what he chooses to denominate a faction, and to rest his accusation of me as having joined the faction on my conduct at the last election of peers, I found it necessary to make a few further comments.

It is altogether a most foolish business on his part. I don't know whether he will write any more, I should fancy he must think he has enough of it; but whenever I know that the correspondence is concluded I will send you a copy of the whole for your *private* information.

PS. Coventry sails in the packet on the 5th April.

Signature only in Lauderdale's hand.

Wellington to John Wilson Croker, 26 March 1833

Stratfield Saye. I write to Lord Downes and suggest to him to have that question respecting the legal effect of the oaths taken before a Consul well considered before he tenders Lord Hertford's and other votes depending upon the decision, and in the mean time to keep the secret. This is very important, as I believe that the Government have now withdrawn their candidate. They would set him up again if it should be found that many of Lord Downes's voters had qualified themselves in this manner.

I have a very peculiar way of viewing what is called the currency question. I mean that part of it which relates to the circulation of one pound bank notes which is in fact the whole question. I consider it neither more nor less than a system to force men of property to give their property in their goods as the security for the capital in which men of no property may trade. It is not wonderful therefore that men like Attwood should press for the adoption of such a system, nor that my tenants should wish for it, as they are aware that if they mortgaged their stock for a hundred pounds to a banker in Reading or in Basingstoke and the said banker should become bankrupt, the loss will be mine and not theirs, but it would be extraordinary that I should wish for such a system and it is another instance of the folly of this besotted nation that it is in general wished for.

It is in fact neither more nor less than a system to enable every body, not to coin money, for that would be comparatively innocuous, as in a coined piece there would at least be some value, but to create a fictitious credit, and to force those who possess property in goods either to keep them till they will rot, or the owner can consume them, or else to give them for paper in reality not worth one farthing; of which the issuer has not one shilling of capital, nothing more than a decent[1] coat on his back and as much education as will enable him to sign his name in a running hand. That is the currency question.

Sir William Gordon Gordon-Cumming to Wellington, 27 March 1833

Altyre, Forres, North Britain. I had the honor of addressing your Grace some months ago requesting you would do me the favour of placing my son's name on your list for purchase in the Guards; not having received an answer I fear my letter did not reach your Grace.

I might have applied to you through Lord Burghersh who did me

---

[1] Paper torn.

the honor of introducing me to your Grace some years ago; but I felt I had some personal claim though one I could not urge, in having been the means of sending my brother Major Cumming Bruce into the last Parliament and having gone in myself with the view of doing every thing in my power to support your Grace's Administration.

My son is well known to Lord Charles Wellesley who will I am sure inform your Grace that he will be no discredit to your nomination if you will honor him by placing him on your list.

Alexander Finlay to Wellington, 27 March 1833

6 Dean Terrace, Edinburgh. The meetings between the colonial interest and Lord Goderich with a view of some amicable arrangement, seem to have hitherto proved abortive—and I perceive that Lord Althorp, to prevent Mr. Buxton's motion from coming on, has pledged himself to bring forward a plan on the 23rd of next month. As therefore there is too much reason to fear that the *immediate* abolition of slavery (from the numerous pledges given for election purposes) may be carried, from the great preponderance of Members thus situated, over those who think it ought to be gradual and progressive, there appears little hope of averting the effects of this fatal piece of legislation, but from what may be accomplished by the timely exertions of the peers.

It would be well therefore, I humbly submit, that such noblemen as have not hitherto directed their attention to this important question, should lose no time in doing so, as I cannot help thinking it scarcely less vital to the interests of the whole country than the measure of *Reform* itself. Under the latter, it is barely possible that the returning good sense of the people may yet abate the evil and prevent utter destruction —but should the colonies be lost, the consequent defalcation of *six millions* in the revenue must of itself produce immediate and universal ruin.

The advocates of this measure being almost all mere *theorists* their opinion as to its practical operation is not entitled to much weight. Where the results of such rash and headlong legislation are at all events hazardous in the extreme, to the slaves, the colonists and the country, surely where no necessity exists for this reckless haste, a little caution would be adviseable upon the part of prudent senators, but wisdom seems now to yield to *clamour* in our reformed Parliament.

I do not deny that I am personally concerned in the matter, being interested to the extent of about 500 slaves in Jamaica, but though I may thence have given somewhat more consideration to the question than others not possessed of colonial property, I am fully persuaded that every one of the King's subjects, from the rank of your Grace downwards, is deeply, nay *vitally*, interested in its results.

It is scarcely denied, being proved by a host of evidence, that the West India slaves are a very indolent race, and that the planters by no means attempt to make them perform *all* the work of which they are capable. Were they to be made free labourers therefore, they would be so merely in name, for they would at once become idle and fly to the woods, where they would form hordes of banditti. The value of colonial property, already so much depressed, would be totally annihilated, and the British merchants, who are under such enormous advances, trusting to the good faith of Government, would be swept away in the common ruin. Besides, from the intricate ramification of our trading concerns, this ruin would spread itself to an extent which at first sight could hardly be imagined, and thousands of families not only connected with the West Indies, but with the commercial and manufacturing interests of the Empire, would be at once reduced to absolute beggary.

Your Grace is, I doubt not well aware of this—but having already experienced your kind indulgence I venture to send these my views by way of *memorandum*, should you feel inclined to use your powerful influence with such of your brethren in the House of Lords as have not hitherto given due consideration to this momentous question.

PS. I trouble your Grace with an extract of a letter from a friend of mine in Jamaica. His plan seems at least more prudent than any proposal for *immediate* emancipation.

Enclosure: Extract [from a] letter to Mr. Finlay, dated Trelawny, Jamaica, 3rd August 1833 [*sic*].

So much has been declaimed, said and written on the *slavery question*, that perhaps I can add little that is new, but as I have thought long and anxiously upon it, and as I have now upwards of ten years experience of the negro character and capabilities, I have thought it might not be unamusing to you to state a plan which I have not seen started by any writer *pro* or *con*, on 'the consummation so devoutly to be wished', *negro freedom*.

As history gives us the unquestionable fact that England furnished the colonies with slaves, it follows that they are both guilty, the one as thief, the other as receiver of stolen men. Therefore, let the value of one day's labour of the whole slave population be ascertained, which could be easily done by the registry returns; let the colonies lose *one half* of this sum as their share of the guilt, and let the mother country take off taxes to amount of the *other half* from colonial produce as her share. A day thus purchased might be given to the negroes, who would by this means have 80 days, exclusive of Sundays. The domestic legislatures could then pass a law for enabling the masters to hire them on those days, at the usual rate of 2/6 per day, or some such sum. This would create habits of industry, and accustom the negro to earn the fruits of his labour, and at the same time the planter would get his produce to market under better circumstances, the reduction of the taxes making up for the loss of the labour, and the increased consumption cause but little decrease in the revenue. When this shall be found to answer, another day might be bought up in the same manner, and they would then have (including Sundays) 182 days, or one half of the year to themselves, and doubtless the remaining three days in the week might be granted not only with safety but with absolute benefit to all parties, from the improvement which must necessarily take place by that time in the habits of the negroes. Thus would a virtuous, industrious class of free labourers be formed, without asking the inhabitants of Britain to *compensate* the slave owners, and at the same time without violating the rights of the latter; the dominion of these beautiful countries would be secured to Great Britain, and continued one of its brightest ornaments instead of a howling wilderness, and a national stain would be wiped away, without 'doing evil that good may come', by making education, religion and time the agents of freedom, instead of oppression, robbery and bloodshed.

The Duke of Buckingham and Chandos to Wellington, 27 March 1833

Buckingham House. Private. Having so often during the last autumn and winter failed in seeing you, or opening any communication with you, I am at last obliged to beg that you will be so good as to tell me what your intentions are. My wish is to regulate my movements by yours in the House of Lords, as nearly as I can consistently with my own political feelings and opinions.

I have a strong opinion against what is called the Irish Coercion Bill as returned to us by the Commons. Do these alterations induce you to alter your sentiments respecting that measure?

Do you mean to oppose by a division including proxies the bill for the dismemberment of the Protestant Church of Ireland, if it is brought into our House in the shape in which it stood in the House of Commons previous to its being withdrawn by Ministers?

I should have preferred discussing these matters with you personally. But as my stay in town depends upon the line which I shall take when I know what yours is to be, and as I am desirous of getting into the country as soon as I can, perhaps you will pardon my requesting a communication of your intentions, as soon as you can make it convenient to tell me.

The Marquess Camden to Wellington, 28 March 1833

Hastings. I would not have troubled you with any remarks upon the note I received from you in answer to my communication enclosing the proxy, unless I had been desirous to separate myself from the Ultra Opposition, with whom I was fearful you might rank me, from the expression 'that I thought we ought to oppose the Church Bill in earnest'. I can assure you I did and have approved of your non-attendance, and I think the same line should be pursued except on some *very* important questions. When I return to London, I shall hope to see you when I can explain in a few words my sentiments.

PS. The Duke of Cumberland and some others have been very desirous to enlist me in a constant attendance and in encouraging active opposition.

Wellington to the Marchioness of Salisbury, 28 March 1833

Stratfield Saye. I have received your note about dining with the Lord Mayor; which is a ceremony which I confess that I am anxious to avoid unless you wish it very much. I wish to avoid for three reasons. First I think that all in the City, Conservatives as well as the others, behaved most shamefully to me in the year 1830 on the occasion of the King's intended visit to the City. I then determined that I would not go again either to the Mansion House or to dine at Guildhall.

Secondly I am very anxious to avoid to meet the Ministers any where; but particularly in the City at the Lord Mayor's where they must be toasted, applauded etc. etc.

Thirdly it is not quite clear to me that if the Ministers know as they must that I intended to be present they would not favour me by having a mob ready to receive me on arriving at or going away from the Mansion House, as Mr. Canning's Government had on an occasion that I attended a dinner given by the East India Company when he was present.

My own inclination therefore would induce me not to go.

I shall be in town on Saturday.

SALISBURY MSS.

Wellington to the Duke of Buckingham and Chandos, 29 March 1833

Stratfield Saye. I have received only this morning your note of the 27th instant. I have not seen either of the bills to which you refer; and I could not decide positively upon the course which I should recommend to be taken in regard to either till I should see them and converse with others.

I propose to return to London tomorrow and to stay there as short a time as possible. But I conclude that I must wait for the discussion on the amendments of the Irish Coercion Bill.

Lord Downes to Wellington, 30 March 1833

Dublin. I enclose a list of the Irish peers shewing how they voted at the election which terminated last night. Although I have put down 31 in Lord Lismore's favor, yet there were only 27 of them admitted by the Clerk of the Hanaper in consequence of informalities which he had not time to get corrected, as they were only sent in a few days ago. I have marked the informal votes thus 'x'. *I did not* object to these votes, as I thought it better that the election should have the appearance, as well as the reality, of being contested, but the Clerk of the Hanaper considers it his duty to object to them.

Lord Hertford's vote was admitted. 76 is the largest number of votes ever given in favor of a candidate at a representative peerage election.

Lord Westmeath had	55
Lord Rathdowne	49
And on two former occasions:	
Lord Farnham	49
Lord Mountcashell	43
Lord Dunally	50
Lord Castlemaine	30

I need not say how grateful I shall ever feel for the assistance which your Grace has so very kindly rendered me on this occasion.

PS. Lord Downes	76
Lord Lismore	31

Enclosure:

List of the majority who voted for Lord Downes on the 29th March 1833

Duke of Cumberland	Earl Listowel
Gloucester	Norbury
Marquess of Waterford	Jersey
Downshire	Viscount Strangford
Thomond	Molesworth
Ely	Chetwynd
Londonderry	Middleton
Ormonde	Galway
Earl of Roscommon	Dungannon
Cavan	De Vesci
Arran	Lifford
Courtown	Doneraile
Mexborough	Hawarden
Roden	Ferrard
Lisburne	Lorton
Duke of Buckingham	Frankfort
Earl of Aldborough	Gort
Longford	Castlemaine
Mayo	Lord Dunsany
Enniskillen	Blayney

Earl of Mount Norris
    Wicklow
    Lucan
    Belmore
    O'Neill
    Bandon
    Castle Stewart
    Caledon
    Clancarty
    Carrick
    Limerick
    Rosse
    Normanton
    Charleville
    Bantry
    Sheffield
    Rathdown

Lord Hertford
    Carbery
    Farnham
    Arden
    Muncaster
    Massey
    Clonbrock
    Rancliffe
    Carrington
    Teignmouth
    Crofton
    Langford
    Dufferin
    Mount Sandford
    Hartland
    Ashtown
    Clarina
    Decies
    Howden

List of peers who voted for Lord Lismore

Duke of Leinster
Marquess of Donegall
    Wellesley
    Sligo
    Westmeath
    Clanricarde
Earl of Cork
    Meath
    Fingal
    Shrewsbury   x
    Granard
Marquess of Lansdowne
Earl of Bessborough
    Shannon
    Tyrconnell
    Charlemont
    Portarlington
    Gosford
    Dunraven

Earl of Ranfurley
Viscount Ashbrook   x
    Southwell
    Bangor
    Clifden   x
    Templetown
Lord Riversdale
    Auckland
    Kilmaine
    Cloncurry
    Dunally
    Garvagh

List of peers who did not vote

Marquess of Headfort	Lord Kensington
Earl of Fife	Bridport
Milltown	Rossmore
Howth	Radstock
Kingston	Downes
Sefton	Bloomfield
Mountcashell	Trimlestown
Kilkenny	Aylmer
Clare	Mulgrave
Kenmare	
Glengall	
Viscount Gormanston	
Kingsland	
Boyne	
Barrington	
Lismore	

For Lord Downes	76
Lord Lismore	31
Did not vote	25
	132

Viscount Sidmouth to Wellington, 30 March 1833

Richmond Park. Private. Be so good as to enable me to return an answer to the inclosed letter from the Rev. John Keble, one of the most distinguished members of the University of Oxford. If you should wish for any further information on the subject of it, I shall have great pleasure in procuring it.

Enclosure: The Rev. John Keble to Viscount Sidmouth, 21 March 1833

Oriel College, Oxford. I am directed by the committee of the subscribers to the Wellington testimonial, most respectfully to request that your Lordship, having favoured the subscription with your countenance, would do us the further honour of communicating with his Grace the Duke of Wellington on the subject.

We are desirous of submitting to his Grace, that a few persons connected with this university, anxious to express, however inadequately, their deep sense of the noble example of loyalty, set by him in the month of May last, have contributed for the purpose of obtaining a memorial of his Grace, to be presented by them to the university: and with this view they intreat him to do them the honour of sitting for his bust to Mr. Chantrey, or to any other artist whom his Grace may be pleased to nominate.

If your Lordship can without inconvenience make our request known to his Grace, you will confer a real obligation on all the subscribers, and more especially on the members of the committee.

Should further particulars be judged desirable, I shall be most happy to communicate them to your Lordship, either directly, or through the Dean of Norwich, who has kindly interested himself in our project from the beginning.

Vere Fane to Wellington, 30 March 1833

Fleet Street. Mr. Vere Fane presents his most respectful compliments to the Duke of Wellington and takes the liberty to send his Grace this year (as last) a statement of the working of an estate in Jamaica, under his care as a trustee.

Mr. Fane's principal object is to furnish authentic data to shew that the question of emancipation, if it produce as he thinks it will the non-cultivation of the estates, is a question much more between the abolitionists and the public than between the former and the planter, for the inclosed account will shew that when about one fourth of the value of negro labour is enjoyed by the owner, the other three fourths are distributed to the public in various channels.

Enclosures: details of profits and payments on two estates in Jamaica; 'Detail of the Island expenditure in 1830'; 'List of supplies required for West Prospect estate, 1832'.

The Duke of Buckingham and Chandos to Wellington, 31 March 1833

Buckingham House. I think it right to communicate to you my intention, on the debate upon the Commons' amendments in the Irish Coercion Bill tomorrow in the House of Lords, to move to strike out the words introduced by the House of Commons in the third page of the enclosed printed copy of that bill, enacting that the provisions of the law shall not extend to counties or districts, merely because tythes shall not have been paid in such county or district, and to take the sense of the House of Lords upon that motion.

Wellington to the Duke of Buckingham and Chandos, 31 March 1833

London. I am very much obliged to you for your note in which you inform me that you think it right to communicate to me your intention in relation to the proceedings of the House of Lords on the Coercion Bill tomorrow.

Wellington to the Earl of Lauderdale, 2 April 1833

London. I write one line to thank you for your letter of the 26th.

The Duke has a talent for letter writing; the exercise of which is very dangerous and always requires a great deal of judgement and foresight.

Wellington to Sir William Gordon Gordon-Cumming, 2 April 1833

London. I have had the honor of receiving your letter of the 27th March. You have not stated the name of your son nor his age.

As soon as I receive both I will insert his name on the list of candidates for the purchase of a commission in the Grenadier Guards, but I beg you to bear in mind that the list is a very numerous one and that much time must elapse before I shall have it in my power to recommend your son for a commission.

Wellington to Alexander Finlay, 2 April 1833

The Duke of Wellington presents his compliments to Mr. Finlay. There is no man more sensible than the Duke is of the injury that would result to the public from any imprudent or premature step in relation to the colonies. The Duke has stated in Parliament his conviction that much of the distress complained of at the present moment is occasioned by the sense of insecurity which exists in respect to the tenure of all property; and most particularly in the colonies and in Ireland.

The Duke has given and will continue to give his attention to this subject.

Wellington to Viscount Sidmouth, 2 April 1833

London. Till I received your note of the 30th March I had not an idea that any body of His Majesty's subjects thought proper to approve of the course which I followed upon the occasion referred to. I felt that my duty to the King required that I should make a great sacrifice of opinion to serve him, and to save His Majesty and the country from what I considered a great evil. Others were not of the same opinion. I failed in performing the service which I intended to perform, and I imagined that I had satisfied nobody but myself and those of my friends who were aware of my motives, and who knew what I was doing and the course which I intended to follow. It is very gratifying to me to learn that Mr. Keble and the other gentlemen of the University of Oxford observed and approved of my conduct upon the occasion referred to and that they are desirous of testifying their sense of it in the manner stated in the letter addressed to your Lordship. They may rely upon it that I will attend Mr. Chantrey or any body they please with the greatest satisfaction. I will do so not only because I am personally gratified by their approbation but I am grateful to them as a public man, and a faithful subject of the King, for the encouragement which they give to others to devote themselves to the King's service by their applause of the course which I followed on the occasion referred to.

Wellington to Lady Cowley, 2 April 1833

London. I enclose you a note which I have received from Lady Salisbury.

Mr. Stevenson mentioned therein is the gentleman who under Providence deprived me of the use of my left ear. God knows that I have no feeling towards Mr. Stevenson excepting one of good will. I have never endeavoured to do him an injury. He has frequently endeavoured to prevail upon me to put myself forward as the ostensible protector of schemes of his, and for his benefit. To do him an injury is one thing, that I never will do. But I think that I ought not, and I certainly do not feel any disposition to put myself forward to promote schemes of his which might put it in his power to do to others the injury that he certainly did to me. I think that my compliance with

Lady Salisbury's desire would tend to convince many that I at least was satisfied that I had no reason to complain of Mr. Stevenson. I entreat you to explain to Lady Salisbury my wish to decline complying with her desire without annoying her with any explanation, or exposing me to the necessity of having one with Mr. Stevenson.

Wellington to Sir Herbert Taylor, 3 April 1833

London. You will see with what a narrow majority the Mutiny Bill escaped last night from being castrated.

I know the army well; its virtues and its faults; the services which it renders to the State in the existing state of its discipline; and the mischief and ruin which must follow the deterioration of that quality. I have no interest in the question which is not that of every good subject in the kingdom. I don't suppose it will ever happen to me again to exercise personally any command over troops. But I cannot in tranquillity see such ruin in prospect as must be the consequence of the proposed alteration of the Mutiny Bill without intreating you who have knowledge and who possess power and influence to make an effort in the proper quarter to prevent this mischief.

This subject has long been under discussion. Lord Hill last year called upon me to give him my opinion upon it which I did in a memorandum which I sent him in March 1832 from Stratfield Saye. He laid a copy of this paper before Sir John Hobhouse, who I understand was quite satisfied with it.

I intreat you to read that paper. It shews first the difference between the original constitution of the British army and that of those armies in which corporal punishment has been discontinued, whose example is the principal argument of those who urge this alteration.

It shews secondly what the description of the man is of whom the army is formed; the necessity which exists on account of the nature and the severity of the duty on which he must be employed to render him the best soldier that can be found to exist; and above all to prevent those irregularities and excesses but too common in all armies but to which the British army would be peculiarly disposed on account of the description of man enlisted to serve; and that in most instances he will be found to have enlisted purposely for the gratification of those very vices and propensities from which he must by discipline be weaned.

Thirdly this paper shews that there is no other punishment by which such men can be kept in order excepting corporal punishment. It shews the effect of the power of inflicting corporal punishment, in enabling commanding officers to maintain discipline by the use of regulation and minor punishments. In fact if this power is taken away no other punishment can be inflicted, no regulation enforced. Soldiers, particularly those in the British army, always desire to be discharged from the service. This desire proceeds not from their being insensible to the benefits of the situation in which they are placed. But they do not like the severity of their duty; the restraints, the regularity and order in which it is necessary to keep them, in order that they may be capable of performing the duty required from them, and may not be a nuisance instead of a benefit to the publick.

Let any man consider for a moment what would be the case in his own family if he could not dismiss his servants. He has no other power over them to keep them in order.

This is the state in which every commanding officer of a battalion will be placed after he will be deprived of the power of inflicting corporal punishment. He cannot give every soldier his discharge who is guilty of a breach of discipline. If he could the exercise of such power would be a premium instead of a punishment; and would be so considered and acted upon; and yet if the punishments in the power of a commanding officer as stated in my paper are considered it will be seen that in fact none of them can be carried into execution unless some higher and effectual punishment is within the power of the commanding officer if the more moderate one should be resisted.

I believe that a great deal of mischief has been done to discipline already by the discussions on this subject and the course which some commanding officers of regiments have thought it proper in consequence to take. If enquiry is made I believe that it will be found that in some of the battalions of Guards in this town, there are now twice the number of men 'billed up', the battalions being about 600 strong that used to be so punished when the battalions were 1200 strong.

I must say that all the attempts to discover a punishment to substitute for corporal punishment have hitherto failed. Consider what passed lately at Brixton! There are there the means of subjecting the soldiers to hard labour for breaches of discipline, in company with the thieves and pickpockets of the suburbs of the metropolis. But the soldiers mutinied; and it was necessary to force them to submit and to guard them while in the tread mill! Did any man ever hear of a mutiny on account of corporal punishment?

But in other gaols of the kingdom there are no means of enforcing a sentence of hard labour; and I understand that soldiers confined for breaches of discipline are either employed at their trades; or being generally very handy, trustworthy fellows become the servants of the gaolers or the turnkeys of the prison! This is the punishment by means of which the officers of the British army are expected to maintain its discipline, its efficiency; and indeed I must add its harmlessness; for I tell you fairly that as a friend to the King and his authority and safety I infinitely prefer for him to have no army at all to having one which shall not be in a state of discipline and order to be relied upon.

It would be invidious and I will not enter into a discussion of the services which the army has been called upon to perform in the last two years even in Great Britain; but I must say that I see no reason to believe that it will not be called upon again to perform similar services.

I cannot however avoid to call your attention particularly to the army in Ireland. It is very easy to ascertain the number of Irish soldiers generally Roman Catholick, serving in each of the regiments in Ireland. Considering the state of party always existing in Ireland, and the influence and power exercised by the demagogue and priest over every description of the lower orders of the Irish people, it has long been matter of astonishment to persons who do not know what the discipline of the army is that we have continued to enlist Irish soldiers to serve in the regiments in Ireland, notwithstanding the system of influence and intrigue constantly carried on to debauch them from their duty.

Such parties could not in fact have any effect upon the mass of the men. Our discipline is too strong for them. Here and there an individual may be found to neglect his duty; to sell his arms or ammunition or to desert from the service instigated by those who exercise an influence over his mind and conduct. But the mass of soldiers cannot be affected. The influence of the officers and of discipline; and of punishment is too strong for the malignant influence of the demagogue and the priest. But deprive the commanding officer of the regiment of the power of inflicting corporal punishment, and not only will all power and influence of the commanding officer cease in a regiment in Ireland as it will in a regiment in England or any where else, but it will in fact be in the hands of the demagogue and the priest.

These will be the persons upon whose good pleasure will depend whether the commanding officer of the regiment shall or shall not exercise authority, until it will come to their turn and it will be their duty to administer the regular government of the country. They will then find that an army which there is not the power of keeping in order and of governing, can be used only as the instrument of subversion and mischief, even by those who will have corrupted its fidelity and will have thus employed its powers.

Let any man reflect for a moment what will be the consequence in Ireland, if the discipline and fidelity of only a small portion of the army are shaken by these measures. Yet I declare my firm conviction that neither can be maintained if commanding officers of regiments are deprived of the power of inflicting corporal punishment.

I am going out of town and have written to you in a great hurry. *Liberavi animam meam*! I wish that I could rely upon any good result. I refer you to a paper in which I think that I have stated the case fairly; and I intreat you to use your influence to prevent these misfortunes from happening to the country through the degradation of our hitherto honourable profession.

RA 36067–36074. *Copy in Wellington Papers.*

Wellington to George Codd, Town Clerk of Hull, 3 April 1833

London. In conformity with the intention I announced to you in my letter of the 20th March I sent the petition of the Corporation of Hull in which that body expressed its desire that I should be appointed its High Steward to His Majesty's principal Secretary of State to be laid before the King.

In a few days afterwards I received from the Secretary of State an intimation that he had received information that proceedings were likely to be adopted in Hull calling in question the validity of the petition to the King, which I had transmitted to his Lordship, and that his Lordship had in consequence advised the King to delay the completion of the warrant appointing me to be High Steward of Hull until the election shall have been enquired into and ascertained.

I beg to recall to your recollection that I did not seek the honor of being the High Steward of Hull, and I urged the corporation to select for the office a person better qualified than myself by the connection with the town or neighbourhood, those relations which result from such a position, and above all an acquaintance with its interests.

To be appointed to fill an honorary office in a corporation such as Hull by the unanimous voice of its citizens or by a preponderating majority of them is an honor of the value of which I am not insensible. But I must say that I feel that it is not desirable that I a stranger to Hull and its interests, residing in a distant part of the country, and having there important duties to perform, should be the object of a contest at Hull the result of which is so doubtful that the Secretary of State has been under the necessity of delaying to complete the warrant which the King had ordered to be prepared in consequence of the petition of the corporation, which I had transmitted to his Lordship.

I think I ought to have been informed of the nature and state of the election.

But at all events I beg again to mention to the corporation my earnest entreaty that they will select some other person to be their High Steward better qualified than I am who is likely to receive the unanimous support of those whose right and duty it is to elect him, and present him to His Majesty to be appointed to this high office.

The Marquess of Salisbury to Wellington, 3 April 1833

Private. I am sure you will be glad to hear that all the conferences which have followed that in which you left me engaged have terminated in an arrangement by which Dawson stands if the Member cannot and we have agreed to have no canvassing until the writ is issued which will I am afraid be a long time. In other respects the arrangement is satisfactory but I am afraid that we shall not want the services of Charles which you so kindly offered unless Price retires. Pray however have the goodness to leave it open. The committee decided against us by the casting vote of Mr. Bernal. What ill luck to have had such a committee! We must hope for better times but at all events I am equally obliged to you for your great kindness on this occasion.

Undated. Docketed 1833, April 3.

Wellington to John Charles Herries, 3 April 1833

Stratfield Saye. Nothing can be worse than Mr. Marryat's proposed bill. It is like every thing else of the present day a sacrifice of the publick interest and in this case of the safety of lives and properties for the advantage of a few constituents of the Members who put themselves forward upon the subject.

I will immediately put the affair in a train of being opposed in the most energetick manner; and I will take care that the bill shall not pass through a single stage in either House without giving the Government the advantage of hearing of the benefits of the notable system of legislation which they have established in this country.

ADD MS 57368

Wellington to Robert Henry Jenkinson, 3 April 1833

Stratfield Saye. I send you with this a note from Mr. Herries, and the draft of a Bill presented or to be presented by Mr. Marryat for providing additional security to shipping on the coast of the Cinque Ports, that is to say for placing the trade of the country at the mercy of Mr. Marryat, his colleagues, and their supporters in Sandwich, Deal, Dover, etc. In my opinion the pilots and the shipping interest at Lloyds, if the Cinque Port pilots do really give them satisfaction ought to prepare themselves to petition against this Bill and desire to be heard by counsel against its provisions.

As far as I am concerned personally I do not care one pin about the matter. I shall be able to shew and I will shew that I have performed my duty in every case brought before me. I shall oppose the intended new system but as it is founded upon individual interests against those of the publick I should not be surprized if Mr. Marryat was to carry his Bill.

The Earl of Aberdeen to Wellington, 3 April 1833

House of Lords. We have an important piece of intelligence today from Spain. There has been a change of Ministry, entirely in favor of Zea. The three members of the Council supposed to be hostile to him, and at the head of the Liberal party, have been dismissed, and their places supplied by persons devoted to Zea. I think they are the Ministers of Finance, Marine, and Justice. This makes all chance of mischief against Portugal quite impossible on the side of Spain; and must afford an agreable prospect to Stratford Canning!

Wellington to the Earl of Aberdeen, 4 April 1833

Stratfield Saye. I am very happy to hear of Zea's success. I was apprehensive that the King of Spain would proceed in the usual course and that having consented to the departure of the Portuguese princesses and Don Carlos he would have given a blow to Zea.

After I saw you on Tuesday I heard that the Algerine affair was becoming very serious.

ADD MS 43060, f. 86.

Wellington to the Marquess of Salisbury, 4 April 1833

Stratfield Saye. I am very happy to learn that your discussions with your Hertford friends were brought to a conclusion that was satisfactory to you.

It is not very advantageous to any man under existing circumstances to be a Member of Parliament. It may be agreeable to one endowed with parliamentary talents. But a seat in Parliament is positively disadvantageous, and may be very inconvenient to a military officer.

However Charles was ready and I was willing to assist him to come forward to be of use to your interest at Hertford. Both he and I think that it is best for him that he should not be in Parliament; and at the same time that I assure you that he and I will at all times be ready to make every effort to promote your views and interest. I beg you not always and under all circumstances to reckon upon him as a candidate for Hertford; as it may and must happen that he may be so situated in his profession as that if he was in Parliament he might be under the necessity of vacating his seat, and that if he was not it might be absolutely impossible for him to offer himself as a candidate.

My own opinion is that you will have your writ issued at an early period after the recess. According to all accounts there is no case for a disfranchisement of the borough. The object will be to throw a little dirt at you and the aristocracy; and *Tommy* will gain an advantage if he can have the writ issued at the moment you will be off your guard.

Heretofore it would not have been difficult to find a gentleman in the House of Commons to undertake for you the management of such a case. But that is now impossible. You must take your chance of justice being done; and you must be prepared at Hertford for the moment which your opponent will fix upon for the renewed contest.

SALISBURY MSS. *Draft in Wellington Papers.*

Sir Herbert Taylor to Wellington, 4 April 1833

Windsor Castle. Private. I was honored yesterday afternoon with your Grace's very important letter on the subject of the alteration in the Mutiny Act which there appeared reason to apprehend and I am certain that I need not assure you that I took the earliest opportunity of submitting it to the King with the memorandum of the 4th March 1832, for which I had in the mean time sent to Lord Fitzroy Somerset.

That I have at all times felt most sensibly the value and the importance of your Grace's opinions on all questions connected with military regulation and discipline, and been ready to subscribe to them, would be merely acknowledging that deference which is due from every man who feels for the character and credit of the military profession, and which none is more disposed than I am to pay to the individual who has been the distinguished instrument of raising both in this country to their unparalleled height. But I am happy to be able to shew also, by documents which I have the honor to inclose, that I have not been in the situation which I now hold an indifferent or idle observer of the attempts made to destroy the beautiful fabric for the perfection of which the country is indebted chiefly to the unwearied and able exertions of the late Duke of York and of your Grace. These documents, which the King has ordered me to communicate to you, with the assurance of his thanks for the warm and zealous interest which you continue to take in the credit and the welfare of the army and in its influence on the security and prosperity of the State, will prove also how anxiously His Majesty enters into the subject and how decidedly he concurs in your view of it, and in your opinions on the questions more immediately under discussion.

It is impossible indeed not to be forcibly struck with the weight and the justice of every remark which your letter and your memorandum contain, and it is lamentable to think that there should be found any military men, especially of experience in the field and in the command of regiments, who are so misled by prejudice or influenced by popular clamour, as to overlook or to treat lightly the considerations which you urge.

Your Grace will observe in my letter to the Duke of Richmond that even Sir Henry Hardinge was inclined to curtail the power of the commanding officers of regiments, and I assure you that I had considerable difficulty in preventing the introduction of provisions to that effect in his new version of the Mutiny Act.

His Majesty requests your Grace will consider the communication of his own letters to his Ministers to be made to you confidentially and for yourself only. It may be satisfactory to you that I should add that Lord Grey appears quite disposed to enter into our view of the question. In a letter to me of the 28th March, he says that he wishes to avoid, if possible, the agitation of the question of limiting the power of inflicting corporal punishment which, if anything is proposed upon it, requires the greatest caution, and that he has no hesitation in adding, that the change which has been suggested is one to which, as at present advised, he sees very strong objection. In a letter of 29th, he says that, after writing the above, he had read my letter to the Duke of Richmond. That it had confirmed his opinion of the inadmissibility of the proposed alterations in the Mutiny Bill and that he had settled with Lord Althorp that they should not be proposed. That the objection on account of the difference made between foreign and home service, if there were no other, would of itself be quite decisive.

I trust therefore that the communications made this day to Lord Grey[1] and Lord Althorp will have the desired effect.

First enclosure: Sir Herbert Taylor to the Duke of Richmond, 28 March 1833.

Windsor Castle. Private. If our friend Sir Andrew Barnard had not forgotten to deliver to me a message from Lord Frederick FitzClarence on Saturday last I should not have had occasion to trouble your Grace with this letter, but could have communicated its purport verbally during your recent visit to the Castle.

It related to an alteration proposed to be made in the Mutiny Act, of which as yet the King has received no *official* intimation, although, if carried into effect in opposition to the opinions of most military men, and in deference to popular clamour, it would essentially affect the discipline, and might seriously commit the *security*, of the army.

---

[1] Royal Archives 36083.

The proposition as His Majesty has gathered, is, that the power of regimental courts martial to award corporal punishment should be abolished in the army serving within the United Kingdom except as to cases of mutiny *on parade* (I conclude this means under arms) and His Majesty has ordered me to write to you privately on the subject and to put it to you, as an experienced and practical officer, whether this proposition be reconcileable to the principles of discipline, to the feeling which it is desireable to maintain in the service, or to the security of the State.

The subject of corporal punishment in the army has been so often under discussion and the arguments for and against have been so much exhausted that it would be a waste of your time and my own to enter into it at present, otherwise than with reference 'to the proposition *supposed* to be contemplated.

You are aware, I believe, that objections had been taken to some of the alterations introduced by Sir Henry Hardinge in our military code as too greatly abridging the power of commanding officers of regiments, upon whose judgement and discretion must mainly rest the maintenance of discipline and subordination in our service which is one of detachment, and I do not deny that I, as Adjutant General, supported by the opinions and advice of many better qualified by experience and practice than I could be to enter into the subject, strongly contested this point.

But, in adverting to the necessity of preserving to regimental courts the power of awarding, and to commanding officers the power of confirming corporal punishments, greatly limited by successive Acts, I have always had in view the existence of this power, and the soldier's knowledge and sense of its existence rather than such exercise of it as should not be placed under such restrictions and safeguard, as would much circumscribe it, and in support of this assertion, and of the principle to which it applies, I appeal to the orders and regulations issued or enforced in 1829 and 1830 particularly to the order for monthly reports from *all* corps and to the private order or regulation of 25th June 1830 respecting interior discipline and the treatment of minor crimes and offences. To these restrictions and precautions tending so much to the abridgement of punishment by regimental courts, and the prevention of crime and irregularity, may be added the influence of popular feeling and clamour upon the *responsible* officers, upon *judge and jury*, and all this will justify my saying that corporal punishment, as compared with periods not very remote, exists more in name than in reality.

But, to proceed one step further and to abolish altogether the power and the discretion of which the exercise has been thus restricted, may strike at the root of discipline in *our* service and it must not be forgotten that the power could not be restored after discovery of the mistake.

I am aware that there are many officers of high character and experience in the command of regiments, who are advocates for the maintenance of discipline without corporal punishment and who may have *occasionally*, and for *certain periods* succeeded in carrying their theory into practice. But ask them whether they could have done so or whether they would now hope to do so, if it should be known and declared to the soldier that the *power* of awarding and of confirming corporal punishment had been taken from regimental courts martial and commanding officers?

Again I question whether the continuance of the power of awarding corporal punishment to regimental courts be not more essential than to general courts martial, inasmuch as the latter may apply the punishment of transportation and even death to crimes calling for serious and *immediate* notice.

Short of these indeed, and of corporal punishment, the usual sentence is confinement to jails, with or without hard labour, and I again appeal to your Grace, as a practised soldier, whether any be less calculated to reclaim the individual or to further the object of the service.

Lastly, I come to the distinction between home service and foreign service which the proposition is supposed to embrace, and I may be permitted to observe that none can be more objectionable, more inconsistent with the feeling and the principle which ought to govern our service, more hazardous in its effect and operation.

Nearly two thirds of our infantry and a portion of our artillery and cavalry are *constantly* on service. The Austrians and Prussians and other foreign armies *may* draw the line between peace and war, and they may establish a code of discipline for service in the field, contradistinguished from repose in quarters and garrisons. But in our service, whether the period be one of peace or war, there is no such repose or the soldier can enjoy it for three or four years only. He then is embarked again for a colony or other foreign station and, according to the proposition in question, every such change from home to foreign service, and vice versa, places him in a different position, as to discipline and liability to punishment, nay the distinction must be introduced in the separate parts of the same regiment, the service and the reserve companies.

The same commanding officer in whom the power has been vested in one station and the same soldier who has in that station been subject to the exercise of this power, are removed to another, where the commanding officer is known to be deprived of the power, and the soldier is relieved from the apprehension of its exercise. Nor is this the only objection—I have already observed that the greater proportion of our infantry etc. must *at all times* be serving abroad and, as many stations are obnoxious on account of climate, and other objections, it is of the greatest importance that foreign service should not be rendered, in other respects, disadvantageous, and above all that it should not be held out to the soldier as being of less value in point of credit, and character, and yet such must be the impression on the service in general if punishment, deemed or declared ignominious, and partaking of the nature of torture, be reserved for foreign service only, if regiments ordered to India or service companies ordered to other foreign stations, be placed in the condition of what were formerly termed *condemned* corps with reference to corps or detachments stationed within the United Kingdom, including be it observed *Militia* when embodied.

I put it again to your Grace as a practical officer whether any principle or system can be more dangerous in such a service as ours, and whether the establishment of these two distinct codes would not probably occasion frequent mutinies in corps receiving orders to prepare for embarcation.

I am aware that my last objection may be used as an argument for abolishing corporal punishment by regimental court martial abroad as well as at home; but here again I ask what will you substitute for it abroad? and by what means or example will you enforce discipline in stations where regimental courts martial can alone be held, and where the power of confirmation must be vested in the commanding officer of the regiment unless punishment be deferred sine die in cases requiring immediate or early notice?

The conclusion to which I naturally come is that the continued existence of the power actually vested in regimental courts martial and in commanding officers of regiments, is essential to the maintenance of discipline especially abroad and that different codes for home and foreign service would be objectionable in principle and unsafe in practice, and after all, why not let well alone?

Copy.

Second enclosure: Sir Herbert Taylor to the Duke of Richmond, 28 March 1833.
Windsor Castle. Private. In addition to what I was ordered by the King to write with respect to the proposition supposed to be contemplated for an alteration in the Mutiny Act, His Majesty has ordered me to call through you the attention of his Government to the extreme embarrassment and danger which may result from its adoption in the naval service. The alteration must be extended to the Naval Mutiny Act, so far as the marines are concerned, and it is impossible to calculate what may be the effect of it upon the seamen and whether these will not expect also to be relieved from the exercise of the power.

This additional objection has occurred to His Majesty since the dispatch of my letter and forms in his opinion a strong ground for not trying hazardous experiments in deference to clamour and prejudice.

Copy. Dated March 28 1833. 12 at night.

Third enclosure: The Duke of Richmond to Sir Herbert Taylor, 28 March 1833.
House of Lords. Lord Grey desires me to say that he agrees with every thing in your letter, and I need not I trust express the same opinion. I have only time to write this on the table of the House of Lords, but pray assure His Majesty that no such change as the one you allude to could have been decided upon without His Majesty's sanction.

Copy. Dated Seven o'clock P.M. March 28 1833.

Fourth enclosure: The Duke of Richmond to Sir Herbert Taylor, 29 March 1833.
London. I have just received your letter dated last night at 12 o'clock. Before this you will have received my short note from the House of Lords which will I trust have been satisfactory to His Majesty. My opinion respecting punishment in the army has never varied, I have ever been of opinion that the power of inflicting corporal punishment could not be given up without danger to the discipline of the army, and that it was necessary to prevent some of the very bad men who are enlisted into our ranks from disgracing those who deserve so much from their country. But at the same time I have always thought that every

care should be taken by frequent returns etc. to the Horse Guards, that this punishment should never be had recourse to unless necessary. I believe that the attention of the Commander in Chief has been for many years directed to this point, and that there is no instance of the commanding officers and regimental courts martial abusing the power. It appears to me that a strong case was shewn the other day of the absolute necessity of having a strong power over the soldiers. I saw in the police reports that between 30 and 40 of the Guards who were confined in one of the prisons in London refused to go upon the tread-mill and only were induced afterwards to do so by a large party of the police who had been sent for; if these men had been with their regiments and had been ordered to drill, and had refused, if corporal punishment had been abolished, you must have tried the ringleader who must either have been shot or transported. I quite agree with you that it would be very dangerous to permit the soldiers to be subject to one code of laws in England and to another abroad, and I am quite certain that there is no officer who ever served with the army in a campaign who must not remember some instance of the beneficial effect of a drum head court martial, and two dozen lashes inflicted on the culprit within five minutes of the commission of the crime, but I do not think it fair upon you to take up your time, as I agree with every sentiment expressed in your letters of yesterday's date, and I must again repeat that no change of this importance in the Mutiny Bill could have taken place without its having been submitted to His Majesty.

I have read the papers you gave me, and I must say you have made the case quite clear.[1] In a few days I hope to be able to send you some strong facts respecting the military rewards.

Copy.

Wellington to Sir Herbert Taylor, 5 April 1833

Stratfield Saye. When I sent you my letter on Wednesday last I had reason to believe from the report of what Mr. Hume had said in the House of Commons, that he intended again to take the sense of the House upon the subject upon the third reading. I afterwards heard

---

[1] Footnote in pencil, partly in the hand of the copyist and partly in that of Taylor: 'The War Office papers and proposed Minute of Council sent to Lord Grey—of which I pointed out the fallacy and inaccuracy.'

that late at night he had said that he was satisfied with the impression made; and that he would not make another attempt to alter the bill. I then regretted that I had troubled you. But upon the whole I hope that the notice taken of the subject will do good.

I wrote to you as a person well informed on the subject; feeling an interest in it; and enjoying the confidence of those upon whom in fact the decision depends.

Unfortunately in these days Members of Parliament look only to their popularity. It is forgotten that all government is a restraint; and that the protection even of life and property requires restraints upon personal liberty which are more or less unpopular. The moment that the powers of the Crown enter for this race of popularity there is not a law or an institution which can stand. The whole must fall. Each must depend upon the degree of violence with which the press and the popular leaders of the day can attack it and the nerves of those whose duty it is to defend and protect the powers of the Crown and the institutions of the country, to meet the difficulties and disadvantages attending an unpopular cry against them.

In truth we are in a very false position; in which we cannot long remain.

I am in hopes that the Mutiny Bill having passed the House of Commons the danger is over for this year as far as regards the discipline of the army. But we must look to the future.

Kings of England have reigned without the assistance of regular armies. But they possessed neither colonies nor foreign territories; and the country was more easily governed than it could be at present; and there existed powers within it which do not exist at present.

If we are to have an army it must be the best that can be formed; and before those entrusted with the Government allow themselves to give way upon this point of discipline they ought to ascertain beyond the possibility of doubt whether discipline can be maintained, and by what means.

I quite concur in your opinion respecting the impossibility of having one system abroad and another at home; indeed as you will have seen I think that we shall have no army and it is better that we should have none, if we cannot maintain our discipline.

I should infinitely prefer to deprive general courts martial of the power of sentencing corporal punishment than I would regimental courts martial. I have been long enough in the army to recollect the times in which it was a very rare event indeed to assemble a general court martial for the trial of a private soldier. It was done only in cases of appeal by the soldier himself or in cases of very flagrant offence by the soldier; when it was necessary to create an impression by the solemnity of the trial, and for which the court would have been justified in sentencing the prisoner to suffer death. I can't say that discipline has gained by the greater frequency of general and district courts martial. They tend to weaken the hands of the commanding officer of the regiment, who as you say with great truth is the most important individual in the service.

It is a most curious circumstance attending corporal punishment in the army that we have none of us ever heard of a complaint of it from the soldiers. I have heard of many complaints of regulations to maintain discipline and to enforce order and regularity, and to punish breaches thereof by minor punishments; but never of flogging. There is a most curious record in the Horse Guards of a mutiny in a corps commanded by Major Taylor. It occurred when I commanded the army. The corps mutinied I think at Tynemouth: and fired their buttons upon their officers. The cause of the mutiny was incessant teasing, minute regulation, and little punishment with a view to maintain discipline and order without having recourse to corporal punishment. There was some irregularity in some of these punishments. But the object was to prevent the necessity for flogging. Yet the soldiers mutinied.

RA 36084–36087. *Copy in Wellington Papers.*

Sir John Macdonald to Wellington, 5 April 1833

Horse Guards. The subject of corporal punishment has now arrived at an interesting crisis, and I rejoice to find that Lord Grey has recommended to the General Commanding-in-Chief to obtain your Grace's opinion upon the momentous question to which that subject has been brought, and which I understand to be the following, viz. whether notwithstanding the passing of the Mutiny Bill, for the present year, it may not be advisable considering the smallness of the majority on the second reading of the bill, the progress which the dislike to military flogging is supposed to be making in the society of this country, and the probability that the enemies of that punishment will, next year, succeed in limiting its application greatly, if not in abolishing it entirely, the General commanding the army and the military authorities charged with the maintenance of its discipline, under his guidance should, at this crisis of the discussion, anticipate public desire by means of some relaxation or concession, under this head. I am not sure that I have been so fortunate as to state my question with sufficient clearness, yet I think I have put it in such a shape as shall enable your Grace to deal with it. I have stated it from what I recollect of a very curious conversation yesterday with the new Secretary at War who had just seen Lord Grey upon the subject, and as Lord Grey immediately afterwards recommended the question in nearly, if not exactly the above shape, to Lord Hill's consideration, I do not think it possible that I can have materially misstated it or any part of it.

In conversation with Lord Duncannon yesterday afternoon, I collected from him that Sir Francis Burdett had assured him that he (Sir Francis) had no desire to embarrass either the Government or the military authorities or both with regard to the disposal of this subject, and that if any concession was made to public feeling *even in the shape of regulation* (so I understood him to say) he would abstain from pressing the further discussion of it.

Your Grace is, doubtless, aware by this time that Sir Francis has given notice of a motion which, if followed up, will bring the whole subject again to issue in the House of Commons, notwithstanding our having secured the Mutiny Bill upon its former footing for the present year. Thus your Grace will at once perceive that Lord Hill must now finally determine, first, whether he will make any relaxation or concession under this head, and next, the extent to which he will relax or concede if at all. I hope your Grace will believe that, upon a subject so important (indisputably important) to the discipline and general interests of the army, I have never ventured to entertain a shade or shadow of difference of opinion from your Grace. I am perfectly acquainted with your opinions. I saw your detailed memorandum of last year, and am aware of the state of your mind this year, with regard to the proposal of limiting the power of inflicting corporal punishment. I have never intruded my own humble opinions upon that point, although they have been long and maturely formed and recorded, in my own department. There they are, there they may be referred to at any time, and there they will be found to correspond most minutely and faithfully with your Grace's writings, although I had never seen them or heard of them when I committed my own sentiments to writing as the respective dates will distinctly shew.

Your Grace will accordingly I hope do me the justice to believe that I have not and that I do not presume to have any the most remote difference with you, either upon the general subject or upon any consideration arising out of or connected with it. I, however, cannot help foreseeing that Lord Hill will find it difficult if not impossible to maintain his present position beyond the present year, and if you should, upon due reflection, do me the honour to agree with me to that extent, perhaps you will feel disposed to suggest to us what you shall conceive to be the best and safest means of endeavouring to hold what we have under the Mutiny Act and the Articles of War, that henceforth to dispense our powers under new and *stricter* regulations that shall satisfy every caviller that we value the possession of our powers not to mis-apply them wantonly, but on the contrary to hold them from our Sovereign and from our fellow subjects in trust, to apply them for the general good as necessity or expediency shall dictate. I cannot perhaps have a better opportunity of assuring your Grace that although the open and avowed attempts to curtail our powers are confined chiefly to civilians, we have many opponents in our own ranks, amongst whom I am persuaded there are several officers of high rank and long experi-ence, and who therefore find no difficulty in the most patient hearing from a Secretary at War, who happens to be prejudiced and prepossessed against flogging. Sir John Hobhouse stated to me, about a fortnight ago, that I was mistaken if I supposed my brother officers adopted my view of this subject, and that he had received communications from various officers (some of whom he named) against the continuance of corporal punishment. Let us be satisfied with naming one. I know not whether Lord Fitzroy Somerset ever mentioned to your Grace that more than a year ago Sir Hussey Vivian sent him a long essay of several sheets of folio paper, accompanied by a multiplicity of returns and other results (comprizing altogether a voluminous appendix) to prove that every consideration of justice, humanity, policy, and expediency required that the awarding of corporal punishment should henceforth be confined exclusively to general courts martial, and that even they should be empowered to award no more than 300 lashes *in any case*!!! Now, I give you this as a specimen of the state of the queries. Here is an officer unquestionably of high rank, of great experience in the command of troops (for he never was, I believe, on the staff, until he became a general officer, and he was constantly employed) and, I presume, of considerable distinction, and who is at this moment actually in command of far the largest corps of the army that we have in a collected shape—not being prepared to all but entirely abolish corporal punishment but urging its curtailment by every means that his ingenuity can suggest to him.

Can your Grace therefore be surprised that the civil branch of our community should array itself against the military authorities upon this question, and is it not manifest to your Grace that the difficulties experienced throughout the last few years, in maintaining the power of inflicting corporal punishment, are daily becoming more formidable! It has often struck me, when reflecting upon this subject, that even were you in charge of the Government, you would experience the greatest embarrassment whilst upholding this power, against military opinions thus urged behind the curtain upon statesmen, and philanthropists, and patriots, and *schemers* in and out of Parliament.

We may think of Vivian's opinion what we choose, it will have, and it has had, a very powerful effect in other quarters, and it was (naturally enough) the very first that Sir John Hobhouse threw in my teeth, when he sent for me the week before last, to apprize me, for Lord Hill's information, of the new clause which he meant to introduce into the Mutiny Bill to limit the power of regimental courts martial in awarding corporal punishment. Since then Sir Hussey has written to myself to ask what is going on respecting corporal punishment. Moreover, I have for some time known that he was impatient to come over to take a lead in the discussion with the Secretary at War.

There cannot, I think, be a doubt that the key stone of our discipline is the regimental court martial, or that, in proportion to the curtailment of its powers, must be a falling off in our discipline, and a consequent deterioration of our military character. I have taught myself to be so immoveable on this point that I would infinitely prefer yielding a portion of the powers of the superior tribunals than cripple the regimental court martial to any extent, however trivial. Our character is most enforced upon the march. It is there, consequently, that we have most need of power to enable us to maintain our character as an army in public estimation. Cripple the regimental court martial, by confining its power to award corporal punishment, to offences against superior authority (as was proposed in the new clause alluded to), and the soldier will become gradually so licentious that his fellow subjects will dread his approach as he enters their town or village.

Mr. Ellice called yesterday on Lord Hill and having missed his Lordship made me the bearer of a message to the following effect—

'Tell Lord Hill that I have just seen Lord Grey and that he and I are anxious to prevent the further discussion of the corporal punishment subject in Parliament this year if possible, but that we feel that Burdett's motion cannot be stopped unless something is done out of respect for public feeling. Suggest therefore to Lord Hill to prepare a clause that shall suit his own views and that shall embrace distinctly every offence to which he would wish to apply corporal punishment by the award of a regimental court martial, *yielding something* to public opinion.

'By doing this spontaneously it will have the best effect, whereas by refusing all concession your powers will be finally curtailed by Parliament.'

I wish your Grace would turn the matter seriously over in your mind, and suggest to us whether you see any (and what) means by which we can yield something with safety.

If you were in command of the army would you allow me under present circumstances to propose to you to sanction the issue of the accompanying circular letter to commanding officers of regiments? Perhaps something of that sort would be received by the abolitionists of corporal punishment as a satisfactory compromise, yet I very much doubt it.

The tenth clause of the Mutiny Act, and the 79th and 80th Articles of War, are the parts which it was proposed to alter this session.

Sir John Macdonald to Wellington, 6 April 1833

Horse Guards. Private. I wish to trouble your Grace with two words, in reference to the details which I submitted to you by yesterday's mail. Lord Grey has desired Lord Hill to assure you that, upon the general question of corporal punishment, he entirely concurs with the military authorities, and that he is most anxious that our present powers should be preserved to us; but that he feels perfectly satisfied that unless we put the infliction of this punishment upon a milder footing, and under restraints and restrictions that shall evince, upon our parts, a willingness to meet the public wish, we shall displease the House of Commons, and produce some decision in that quarter, the effects of which will prove seriously injurious to our views. Lord Duncannon called on me this morning, and spoke to me precisely to the above effect. He also goes along with us upon the general question, but feels confident that the present House of Commons will not suffer it to remain upon its present footing, and that unless we enable the leader of the House (Lord Althorp) to place upon its table a copy of some very strong restrictive regulation, that shall shew the sincerity of our determination to limit the infliction of corporal punishment to cases of the greatest emergency or of necessity (to be specified to the House as nearly as it may be in our power to specify them), some violent resolution will be moved *and carried* which will cripple us for ever.

It is, therefore, of vital importance to the army that you should, if possible, bring your mind to an admission that Lord Hill must *now* give some earnest proof of his anxiety to defer to the opinion of at least a very large portion of the Commons, if not the majority of them. I enclose a memorandum which Lord Hill gave Lord Grey last week upon the matter expressing a wish to be informed as to the nature and extent of our present checks upon excessive corporal punishment. That memorandum was prepared at five minutes notice, but Lord Grey upon reading it declared himself perfectly satisfied with it. I also enclose an extract of a letter which I had in 1830 from Sir Frederick Ponsonby, and which cannot (coming from such a quarter) be read at this time but with intense interest. His letter was in answer to one which I wrote to him, to entreat that he would not suffer commanding officers to make experiments upon discipline (abolishing corporal punishment entirely and substituting a course of vexatious minor punishments).

PS. Lord Hill has gone into Shropshire for a week or so.

First enclosure: Circular to commanding officers of regiments. April 1833.

Horse Guards. Confidential. I am ordered by the General Commanding-in-chief to impress upon you the importance of limiting the infliction of corporal punishment in the regiment under your command as much as you may find it possible to do so consistently with the due maintenance of discipline and subordination. You cannot but be aware that the wanton and unnecessary infliction of that punishment has ever been deprecated by your Sovereign, and that every succeeding Commander-in-Chief has evinced the utmost anxiety that commanding officers should never resort to it as an auxiliary, but where milder means would be unavailing.

Lord Hill is earnestly desirous to follow up the views and wishes of his predecessors in this respect, and desires me to say that he, upon his part, deprecates nothing more than excessive corporal punishment, and that, whilst it is his settled conviction that neither discipline nor good order nor military subordination can be maintained without the occasional resource to flogging, he is also conscious that the superintending care and vigilance of commanding officers may render the necessity of resorting to it comparatively rare.

His Lordship contemplates few cases in which the infliction of corporal punishment for a *first* offence can be necessary, and even for repeated offences his Lordship would have it applied but sparingly, except where the nature and degree of the offence were calculated to bring obloquy and disgrace upon the character of the soldier.

His Lordship abstains from particularizing every offence now in his contemplation, satisfied that your own military experience and good service cannot fail to suggest them to your mind.

I am, however, commanded to point out to you the leading offences to which corporal punishment is considered applicable in cases of emergency or necessity. These are:

Violence to superiors, by which his Lordship would be understood to mean violence towards non-commissioned officers.

Gross insubordination.
Drunkenness on duty.
Selling necessaries.
Repeated theft.
Outrages against persons or property, more especially when on the march.

Mutinous conduct may be so modified as to be rendered cognizable and punishable by even a regimental court martial, but Lord Hill cannot suffer the comprehensive crime of *mutiny*, the most heinous of military crimes, to be regarded by the soldier as one for which he may atone by the award of any but a general court martial.

I am to add that Lord Hill will scan rigidly the monthly returns of courts martial, and that his Lordship will henceforth consider it one of the most important points of his duty to bring to the notice of His Majesty the extent to which each commanding officer uses the power of inflicting corporal punishment.

In Sir John Macdonald's hand.

Second enclosure: Extract of a letter from a general officer commanding at a foreign station to Major-General Macdonald, dated 3rd December 1830.

I agree most decidedly with you, on the subject of corporal punishment. It is strange to me that people talk so much of the *disgrace* of the *punishment*, and never advert to the disgrace of the *crime*. I have had, during the last six years, two regiments under my command where corporal punishment was not practised. They were not trustworthy out of the barrack yard. More crimes were committed than in other corps; and when I found that the plan had completely failed, the old system was adopted, and they are now in as good a state of discipline as any battalion. I hate the punishment as much as any man; but without it the discipline of the army cannot be maintained. I speak from experience and conviction. By it the punishment of death may be avoided; without it you must have recourse to death to support the discipline of the army.

There is no humbug in this garrison; it is indeed excellent; the men happy and contented, and so they will remain till innovation makes them otherwise.

I have good commanding officers; and this is the great secret for preserving the efficiency of the army.

Copy. Docketed by Macdonald Sir Frederick Ponsonby on corporal punishment.

Wellington to Sir Herbert Taylor, 6 April 1833

Stratfield Saye. When I wrote to you yesterday I was in hopes that we had got rid of the question of corporal punishment for a year. But I learn from a communication from Lord Hill received this morning that Sir Francis Burdett has given notice of a motion upon the subject. Lord Grey has consequently desired Lord Hill to consider of some concession upon the subject in order to satisfy publick opinion; and his Lordship has desired Lord Hill to consult my opinion.

We military men are put in a very curious position on this question. We say that it is our opinion that military discipline cannot be maintained unless this power of inflicting corporal punishment is maintained particularly in regimental courts martial. We think that if the discipline of the army is deteriorated the same confidence cannot be given to its performance of its duty; that is indeed if any such confidence can be placed in its exertions. And we are told in answer make some concession to publick opinion. We have been in fact by our actions conceding to publick opinion for years. I don't know what else can be done.

But might it not be advisable for those who possess the publick confidence to endeavour to enlighten the publick opinion upon this subject?

If we are wrong; if the discipline of the army is unimportant; or it is possible to maintain it sufficiently for all the purposes of government without resorting to this punishment the Government ought to decide this question and ought to alter the law.

But if we are right the Government ought to declare its conviction upon the subject. It ought to endeavour to enlighten the publick mind upon it; and it would very soon be found that but a small proportion of the publick required the change and that the law might and ought to be maintained. As for my part I am ready to declare my opinion whenever it may be called for even in the House of Commons itself, or before any committee or commission of the consequences of this alteration.

I have never seen any man yet who could suggest a mode of insuring the unresisting submission of the soldiers of the British army to subordination and discipline and to the enforcement of both by light military punishments excepting the power in the commanding officer of the regiment who is responsible for its good order to try an offender by regimental court martial and to inflict corporal punishment.

There is the whole question. Of course you will see what I shall write upon the subject.

I have written now only in consequence of the change from what appeared to be probable yesterday.

RA 36109–36112. *Copy in Wellington Papers.*

The Earl of Lauderdale to Wellington, 6 April 1833

Dunbar. In answer to your letter, in which you propose to do something about Mr. Praed, I think I wrote you saying that I found that his conduct was taken up by others in such a way that it was better just leaving it alone.

Yesterday however I received a letter from Mr. Halse, the Member for St. Ives, of which I inclose you a copy: together with my answer to it.

It has placed me in a very disagreeable situation but when I balance betwixt the probability of Praed's having said so, notwithstanding he had never written in answer to my letter, and Halse's having mistaken what he said, I thought the latter more likely and acted accordingly.

When I re-asserted in my second letter to Mr. Praed that without trusting to my own recollection corroborated by that of my sons, I had incontrovertible evidence that I had not been guilty of any misconception, I had before me a letter from our friend Holmes to the following effect.

'I inclose you a letter received this day from Mr. Praed, a very clever and useful member of our House and highly Conservative. Your Lordship will perceive how much you and Lord Maitland can do for him at St. Ives. Mr. Halse played a very shabby part by us, for he not only abandoned us in our utmost need, but at the last dissolution brought in a reformer as his colleague. Mr. Praed's family and connexions have large estates in the neighbourhood of St. Ives, therefore he is neither a stranger nor adventurer among them.'

If this is not a canvassing letter I really do not know what is; it not only recommends the candidate for whom he interferes as agreeing with me in politics, but it runs down his opponent as having behaved ill to those Holmes knew I wished to support.

You will not be surprised that I have lost other letters to the same purport, some of them to my sons, and some of them to myself, in which I am certain by the bye, that both your name and Sir Robert Peel's were used to influence me.

I inclose you however a letter from my son stating his recollection of the application from Harris.

To all these I certainly lent a deaf ear because I did not choose to interfere, and yet, you see how remaining totally neutral I have got attacked.

I think Praed must be wrong in the head, for it is impossible he can conceive that he did make every exertion to secure my interference.

I have written this that you may know exactly how things stand.

Signature only in Lauderdale's hand.

First enclosure: James Halse to the Earl of Lauderdale, 3 April 1833.

London. Mr. Praed and I having casually passed each other in Parliament Street this afternoon, he soon to my surprise returned with a friend, and coming along side asked me in an angry tone whether I had said in the House of Commons that you had represented to me that *he* had applied to your Lordship for your interest in St. Ives? I answered *No*, but that his friends had made the application, and the reply, in a great rage, was that 'If he' (meaning your Lordship) 'had so stated he lies—and I desire you' (meaning me) 'will tell him so', and which I thus do that you may the better appreciate the character of such a man. I must regret on your Lordship's account that your name should be called in question upon such a subject, but as it was not used by me in any way in connexion with the borough, but was exclusively introduced and abused by him I hope I shall stand acquitted by you of all blame in that respect.

Copy.

Second enclosure: The Earl of Lauderdale to James Halse, 6 April 1833.

Dunbar. I have just got your letter which puzzled me very much. After mature deliberation I cannot help thinking that there must be some mistake.

In my first letter to Mr. Praed is the following paragraph.

'But I need not make you aware that numerous applications have been made both to myself and my sons soliciting interference at the last election in favor of Mr. Winthrop Mackworth Praed, by men I too highly respect to doubt the truth of their assertion, that it was at your desire they made the solicitation, some of whom indeed rendered it evident by inclosing your letter on the subject.'

In answer to this he writes—'I beg to correct a misapprehension which appears to exist in your Lordship's mind. I cannot but think that in reference to any letters which I may have written to my friends, may have shown to your Lordship, your Lordship will find that my only request has been that the influence of your Lordship might *not* be exerted in a manner of which it appeared to me impossible that your Lordship could be aware.'

My reply was to the following effect—'Sir, In performing the duty which my habits of civility requires of acknowledging the receipt of yours of the 26th, I have only (after perusing a letter I have fortunately retained in my possession) to re-assert the accuracy of my former statement, as without trusting to my own recollection corroborated by that of my sons, I have now incontrovertible evidence which I have placed in Mr. Vizard's hands, that there is no misconception on my part.'

Now I hold it impossible for any man to read these communications without perceiving that I have asserted and reasserted both on my own part and that of my sons, that we were applied to, to interest ourselves at the St. Ives election in favor of Mr. Praed.

If therefore he had wished to take it up in the way you state, it is impossible that he should not have made that communication to me. I must therefore conceive that you must have made some mistake, for it is not in the nature of things that he should have passed these letters over and refrained from all communication to me till a casual meeting took place in the street with you.

Under this conviction I shall certainly feel bound to take no further notice of what you have stated.

Copy.

Third enclosure: Viscount Maitland to the Earl of Lauderdale, 6 April 1833.

Dunbar. Agreeable to your wish I have endeavoured to tax my memory in regard to the application made to me by Mr. Herries in favour of Mr. Praed and to the best of my recollection Mr. Herries urged me to use my influence and to get you and the captain to use theirs as proprietors of stock in the St. Ives Consols Mine in favour of Mr. Praed as a candidate for that borough. Mr. Herries also inclosed me a letter, at least I think he did, which I remember began with the words 'My dear Fitz', and in that letter Mr. Praed says to his friend 'If I can only get the Maitlands the election is mine' or words to that effect. He also said, 'I am in no way acquainted with any of the family except Lord Maitland, with whom I have had the honor of some communication in the House of Commons.'

I wrote to Mr. Herries that I had no property myself in the St. Ives mines and that I knew Lord Lauderdale had declined in any way interfering in that election.

Dated April 6.

The Bishop of Exeter to Wellington, 6 April 1833

Exeter. I have recently received a letter from Major-General Wulff, asking me to confer on his son a living in my gift, which is now vacant, and grounding his request on your Grace's favourable mention of him to me last year. The very delicate manner, in which your Grace expressed your wishes in this young man's behalf, while it only made me more anxious to gratify these wishes, convinced me that Major-General

Wulff's application to me was without any knowledge of your Grace; and as it is of great importance to me, in the management of my patronage, that I should keep myself quite free from the appearance of being influenced by external application, I have found it necessary to answer in a manner, which, while it cannot offend, will probably much disappoint him.

His application has been most unfortunately ill-timed—for it has arrived exactly at the period, when another living (more valuable than that which he has solicited) which I have long destined for his son, has actually become vacant—and, but for this unlucky contretems, I should have had unmixed pleasure in bestowing it on the young man, and in requesting your Grace to make known to Major-General Wulff that such is its destination. As matters stand, I feel it right to delay the disposal of this living for a short time—but it may be satisfactory to your Grace to know, that I purpose giving it to Mr. Wulff.

I am here for about a fortnight—but I purpose returning to London before the Irish Church Reform Bill can have reached the House of Lords. The more I consider the tendency of that Bill, the more I am satisfied of the dangers with which it is fraught to the cause of the Protestant religion in Ireland. As such, I cannot but give to it my most earnest resistance—and most fervently do I hope, that it may be resisted in quarters of incalculably more importance. I see the danger of displacing this wretched Government. But in a cause, which I conscientiously believe to be the cause of true religion, I cannot but think the duty of all, who so regard it, requires them, at any hazard, to unite in determined hostility to the Bill. If it be indeed God's cause— and such from my heart I dare avouch it to be—no mere prudential considerations ought to make us waver. I would go straight forwards in the discharge of duty, and would humbly, but confidently, rely on God's mercy, that be the path of duty as thickly beset with difficulties and dangers, as it might, it will yet be found to be the path of safety.

Wellington to Sir John Macdonald, 7 April 1833

Stratfield Saye. I have received two letters from you, written by desire of Lord Hill, in consequence of a communication from the King's Ministers. Till I received them, I was in hopes that we should have a respite from the pain of reconsidering the subject of corporal punishment in the army, for a time at least. It appears however that the King's

Ministers desire that Lord Hill should consider immediately of some concession to be made to public opinion upon this subject. Lord Hill knows his own position better than I do. Before I should make a concession upon a point in which a mistake is irretrievable, and may be attended with fatal consequences to all the interests and institutions of the country, I should ask the Government to declare their own opinion; and by their speeches and declarations to make an effort to enlighten, and influence the opinion of the public. But here we are, without a fair discussion on the subject, without one influential person having declared his real opinion upon it (for even Sir J. Hobhouse admitted that my memorandum of March 1832 put the subject in an entirely new light) proceeding to take a most important step from which we can never recede; and the military authorities are the persons called upon themselves to do this mischief. I am quite aware that there are men ready to undertake, or make a concession upon this or any other subject. But can such men be trusted? Can you confide the public interests to their judgement? I deny that there has been any fair experiment of the consequences of the abolition of sentencing corporal punishment by regimental courts martial. Whenever the experiment has been tried it has failed even under the advantageous circumstance that the commanding officer still held in his hand the power of trying and punishing, although he did not think proper to exercise it; till at last he found it necessary, or some superior authority found it necessary, to require him to exercise it. But hereafter the power is no longer to exist; and we might as well pretend to extinguish the lights in our houses or theatres by extinguishers made of paper as to maintain the discipline of the army without such power in the hands of the commanding officer of the regiment. I see enough of what is passing to be convinced that no public man will in these days meet the press, and the political unions, and those who influence public opinion upon this subject. Yet there is no doubt of its importance, and if *we* are right, of which I have as little doubt, there is not an individual in the country who has any thing to lose whose substance is not exposed to spoliation and destruction. You then call upon me to concede to public opinion the power of the commanding officer of a regiment to try by regimental court martial, and to punish by flogging, breaches of good order and discipline. I would much prefer to concede the power of a general court martial, because that does not affect the discipline and the conduct of every day of the man to be made a soldier. The difficulty which

I should have in the plan adopted by you is the impossibility of speci-fying detailed crimes and punishments in the Articles of War instead of the general words 'disorders and neglects'. It is admitted that there can be no difference between the army abroad and the army at home; and I ask any man to look on my articles, and to see whether it is possible to specify crimes and punishments, and if not, whether it is fair to put in the field a British army and not to afford to its officers the means of keeping it in order. But even in peace in their quarters or barracks in London or else where I can shew cases in which the public are most materially interested, and on which there would be loud and vehement complaints if they were not protected; in which the charge against the soldier would be disobedience of the orders of the com-manding officer. I believe that every thing has been done and that every thing is done at this moment to prevent the abuse of the power in the hands of the commanding officers of regiments and that if there is any ground of complaint it is that commanding officers are too much inclined to seek for other means of maintaining discipline besides those allowed by the existing law, and that a great deal of discontent and undiscipline has been the consequence. But if any thing else can be suggested, having for its object to bring under the knowledge and controul of their superiors the conduct of commanding officers of regi-ments in the exercise of their powers I should be the last man to object to it. In all this we must bear in mind that no new expence must be incurred. It has always occurred to me that it would be very desireable that the Commander in Chief should have it in his power at all times to place under the view of the public an accurate state of the discipline and conduct of the army or of any part of it. I would establish at the Horse Guards an office at which should be lodged a copy of the guard report, and defaulters list of every regiment and detachment of the army. This would shew what the state of crime really is, and what it is commanding officers of regiments have to deal with, and how they dispose of these offences. In the same office a copy should be lodged of the proceedings on trial by every regimental court martial; and a report by the commanding officer of the steps taken in consequence thereof; these proceedings should be read with care and attention by the officer at the head of the office, and he should report to the General commanding the army in chief anything deserving notice. This same office would be able by the inspection of the guard reports and de-faulters lists to give an accurate account at any time of the state of crime and of punishment and to answer any enquiry that might be made of Government and Parliament.

If these measures should not be thought sufficient, that which appears to me to be most important is that the Government, Parliament, and the public should be really informed of what they are about to do before they take any step whatever. I would therefore if necessary have an enquiry by military or other commission or a committee of the House of Commons or House of Lords or by some well known course to investigate the whole subject, lay it fairly before the public, let all see the bearings of it, and how far all are interested in the maintenance of discipline and good order of the army, and then if necessary make the alterations or let us keep what we have got. I don't apprehend any danger or inconvenience from the enquiry: for it is a most curious part of this subject that the party that manifests the least anxiety upon the subject is the suffering one. The non-commissioned officers and soldiers of the army have never complained of being flogged. I have served with the army for nearly half a century, and up to this day have never heard of a mutiny or even a complaint from a non-commissioned officer or soldier that he was liable to be flogged, nor in fact is there any difficulty about recruiting the army on the score of punishment: there is much more on account of the restraints of the service and of the severity of the duty and the unwholesomeness of the climates, and the distances at which the man is exposed to serve, and I am certain that it will be found on enquiry that regulations, restraints, and minor punishments have occasioned more discontent than flogging ever did.

You will see then what I recommend is a more detailed knowledge at the Horse Guards of the state of crime and discipline in each regiment and detachment of the army so as to bring the whole in a greater degree under the controul of the General commanding the army in chief: and secondly if necessary a full and fair enquiry into the whole subject. There is one point which does not immediately affect *us*, but which is most important in this enquiry. What is to become of the navy? Mind! that our men are enlisted by voluntary enlistment; they know what will happen before they enlist: not so the seamen of the fleet. They are pressed into the service. I contend justifiably pressed to serve afloat. Yet they are liable to corporal punishment not after trial and sentence by a court composed of their officers on their oaths, but by the decision of the captain alone! Can this system stand if our's does not? Let the question be put to the Admiral who now commands the only squadron we have at sea. To tell you the truth my opinion is that the public opinion and the great cry upon this subject upon which *we* are called upon to make a concession are to be attributed to the desire to break down the discipline and efficiency of the army. I don't mean to insinuate that such men as Sir Francis Burdett and Sir John Hobhouse entertain such views, but they have pledged themselves; their political existence and that of many others depend upon the suffrages of those who do entertain such views; and I say the Government and those in whom they confide [ought] to proceed with the utmost caution and circumspection in a course in which a mistake must be fatal.

The Marquess of Salisbury to Wellington, 7 April 1833

Hatfield. I am fully aware of your very great kindness in allowing Lord Charles to stand for Hertford and I would willingly have endeavoured to avoid trespassing upon it but the fact is that the unaccountable defection of Baron Dimsdale at this particular moment renders it necessary for me to bring forward a candidate not only unexceptionable in every respect but one who bears a name which will carry weight with it. *Your* son is the person of all others who possesses these qualifications and will rally every body to our standard. I have the difficult task not only to bring in the Member whom I recommend but also to prevent the split in our party which will be occasioned by the nomination of Dawson on the part of the Baron. If he fails I am equally embarrassed by the return of Spalding or perhaps Duncombe and the consequent certainty of a contest at every future election. If they succeed it will not be necessary for me to ask more than that you would sacrifice your objection to Lord Charles's being our Member during this Parliament as it shall be clearly understood that he only takes the seat until Ingestre can resume it. There is something in the son of the Duke of Wellington which will *applanir toutes les difficultés* and I can assure you that the general feeling of Hertford requires as I was told by one of the principal inhabitants today something aristocratic for a Member. I must therefore avail myself of your promise and I can assure you I fully appreciate and am truly grateful for the kind feeling which dictated it.

I am very glad to have your opinion of the probability of the issue of the writ and I will take care to be prepared for the event.

PS. I have written by this night's post to Lord Charles.

Sir Robert Wilson to Wellington, 8 April 1833

The date of the renewed assertion of the Duke de Broglie in the Chamber of Deputies and of the declaration made by the Minister of Marine as to the resolve of the French Government gives great importance to the proceeding.

There is a report the French Government proposes to offer Oran to England as a peace offering. Doubtless France would have no objection to make England an accomplice in the plan of spoliation—keeping to herself the lion's share.

Lord Granville is to be here on Wednesday and the Duke of Orleans probably on the same day. Monsieur Mauguin does not exaggerate the value of the settlement to France commercially or politically. Already twelve large ships upon an average enter Algiers weekly.

It does not however envelope [?] half of Clauzel's plan, which *englouties* Tetuan, Ceuta, Tangiers, and the Mina—*an or*—*an pecunia*—*an fraude*.

There are most unfavourable advices from Jamaica. The officers of a militia regiment have been dismissed by Lord Mulgrave and letters prepare for accounts of serious mischief by next packet.

Some *on dits* are circulating that Lord Palmerston is resigning. But perhaps his absence from office this day may have given rise to these.

Young Cobbett stands for Coventry against E. Ellice and Cobbett *père* takes the field as his son's mentor.

I hope your Grace is enjoying health for there is much illness in London.

PS. May I beg care to be taken of the *Journal des Débats* as it is a club property.

Sir John Macdonald to Wellington, 8 April 1833

Horse Guards. Your letter of yesterday is quite unanswerable, and I am glad that you suggest a meeting of the superior authorities (civil and military) that are principally concerned in the discussion of the corporal punishment question, with the view of looking closely into the details of the whole subject, and determining what course to proceed next, with reference to the proposal so strangely urged upon Lord Hill by the Government viz. that some concession should be made to publick feeling, upon the present occasion. I find that there will be abundant time to consider the subject maturely, before Sir Francis Burdett or Mr. Sheil's motion comes on. The new Secretary at War (Mr. Ellice) also has suggested a meeting as nearly as possible upon your Grace's plan, and for the very same purposes, and it strikes me that it cannot fail to have a beneficial effect if it takes place. Lord Fitzroy and I have just had a conference with Mr. Ellice at which he reiterated Lord Grey's concurrence in your opinion, but at the same time reiterated his Lordship's declaration, that, circumstanced as the question is, in Parliament, he believes some concession to be indispensable and inevitable. Mr. Ellice seems to be strangely impressed with the notion that any spontaneous proposal, upon the part of the military authorities, to place this punishment under stricter and (what would be deemed by Parliament) more wholesome regulations, would be very well received by the House of Commons, and, that as the House has so committed itself with us as to sanction (by passing the Mutiny Bill in its former shape) the principle of continuing this punishment in the army, it would readily accept from us any liberal proposal to the above effect. I shall not trouble your Grace with any further communications upon this momentous subject until you come to town, when I hope you will send for me as soon as you can conveniently see me. I had very nearly resolved to intrude myself upon you at Strathfieldsaye tomorrow, but that will be unnecessary, as we have so much time for deliberation, and as Lord Fitzroy goes to Tern Hill on Wednesday for some days we cannot be absent together at this moment. I wrote to your Grace on Friday in such a hurry that I kept no copy of my letter, or of the draft of the proposed circular letter which accompanied it.

Perhaps you would kindly return me these documents to enable me to send copies of them to Lord Hill who has not seen them but might wish to read them in the country. The originals shall be returned to your Grace.

PS. I can put what Mr. Ellice said still stronger. He says that as the minority upon Mr. Hume's motion admitted the principle of continuing to apply corporal punishment to certain offences even they (the minority) are committed to us and in a manner bound to chime in with any fair restrictive regulation we may offer—and, therefore, that to offer one would be wise and proper. His expression was 'that minority are in a scrape, therefore let us take advantage of the dilemma in which they have thus placed themselves'.

Lord FitzGerald to Wellington, 8 April 1833

Dublin. I have for some time past delayed to write to your Grace on the subject on which I take leave to trouble you at present. I had hoped long 'ere now to have had the pleasure of seeing you in England; and I was rather desirous to ascertain, which I thought I might have done from other communications, and without direct application to you, whether any arrangement might have been entered into by your Grace with others, which would prevent my looking for assistance in the matter on which I address you. On the death of Lord Conyngham, some of my friends, attaching perhaps more importance to my being in Parliament, than I am likely myself to ascribe to it, suggested to me to become a candidate for the representation of the Irish peerage.

I was aware that Lord Downes was already a candidate, not only with great prospect of success, but under your Grace's recommendation, and respected by all whom you could influence. I was aware too that these engagements to him were of long standing, and I would not, even had there been any chance of success for me, have stirred a step which might interfere with him.

In point of fact, however, all that I could have looked to for support, were already engaged to him, and on the other side was the Government making, though a tardy and ineffectual, still a very anxious canvass for Lord Lismore. I was myself not qualified to vote. But I solicited others, and I hope not altogether without success, for Lord Downes.

Now that his election is over, I have been urged to look to the next vacancy—and I am told that even amongst those who are not of my opinion in politics, and who voted for Lord Lismore, there is a strong feeling that my election, as the only member of the Irish peerage who has been engaged in active political life, would be creditable to the body to which I belong.

Of course because I should have to encounter the bitter hostility of the Government—and there is a class, I apprehend, in this country, a very *ultra* body, who, I have heard, state their objection to me to be, my having shared in those measures of your Grace's Government, which ended in the Catholic Bill. This objection if felt, only shews what a vain race of politicians they must be, in the present state of Ireland.

Under the circumstances, I have not encouraged any of the suggestions which I have received. I have preferred, before committing myself, to ascertain the feelings of my personal and political friends, and to learn whether any engagements have been taken which might interfere with my success, or which by my standing, might be endangered, in the event of their proposing another candidate to me. It would mortify me to find that they did; after a long life of personal and public sacrifice; and of not undistinguished public service. Yet I shall not complain if such be the case—though I should probably never again look to the object which I have been now led to think of.

I have mentioned the matter to no one but to Sir Robert Peel: and if I have delayed to ask your Grace's advice, and to submit my wishes to you, it has been because knowing your interest for Lord Downes, and not being aware what might be necessary to ensure his success, I was unwilling to trouble you with any request until his election was secure.

It is evident from his victory that there are sufficient means of beating the Government, if all those who oppose them stand together—that a split would be fatal, and a division of interests would ensure the success of their candidate. In me, as one of the lowest in the peerage, I am aware that notwithstanding individual good wishes, there would be little chance, except on the ground of public character, and of my connection with your Government.

It is therefore doubly incumbent on me to take no step without your Grace's approbation, and without the assurance of that support which would alone make success easy, as it would make it more gratifying.

I little thought that I should ever have to seek this accession to Parliament, and it is sufficiently mortifying to find myself in a situation, in which I should have to canvass for a seat in the House of Lords, that it is now the only door which is likely to be opened for my entering either House. I will not trouble your Grace further, but refer all that I have taken the liberty of suggesting to you.

I have been in such miserable health for some time, that I know very little of what is the state of this country beyond what the public prints tell. Yet more deplorable than that state I can conceive nothing—the Lord Lieutenant and Council have proclaimed the county of Kilkenny, but I shall be much surprised if the Act which has been passed be enforced with either vigour or sincerity.

The compromises made in its passing, and the concessions to O'Connell have disgusted people very much—and it is impossible to augur from the appointment of Sir J. Hobhouse, steeped as he has been in factious politics, any principle of administration to which loyal men and Protestants, those anxious to maintain our institutions, can look with confidence or security.

But I need not tire with my speculations.

Lord Plunket's Jury Bill is likely to leave us at the mercy of undutiful and egregious rebels to make our own tribunals, the last hope left to us, useless or fatal.

I beg your pardon for troubling you at such length.

Wellington to Sir John Macdonald, 9 April 1833

Stratfield Saye. I return you the letters which you wished to have. I am very happy to find that you concur in my opinions; but I beg that I may not be misunderstood. If I was the Commander in Chief and I thought that any concession could be made with safety upon this subject, I would make it at once in clear and distinct terms which nobody could misunderstand. I am aware that there is a great deal of tacticks in the management of a question in Parliament but such tacticks will not answer for Lord Hill upon such a question. Nobody must misunderstand Lord Hill, whatever may be the measure upon which the Government may think proper finally to determine. It was with this view that I proposed for your consideration a measure which might be adopted immediately, which would bring to light the whole system of the discipline of the army, would shew the state of crime and of punishment in every corps, would enable the General commanding in chief to check the latter, and would shew the Government and Parliament if it was thought necessary what were the efforts made to check and put an end to corporal punishment in particular corps, and with what success in relation to crime. If the Government should not think this measure calculated to satisfy the objects to which they are looking I would then recommend that before any step is taken, or any communication whatever of future intentions is made to Parliament, a commission or a committee of either House of Parliament should be appointed to consider of the subject, and bring before the public all its details. I should think a commission the preferable mode of proceeding on account of the interest which the King and his Government must have in the maintenance of the discipline of the army and navy. I don't think that the commission should be composed exclusively of military men. The Judge Advocate General either in office or one or two of those who have held that office, the Secretary at War, the Paymaster of the Forces, possibly some officers of the navy might be members of the commission besides officers of the army. I enter into these details because you mention a *meeting* to consider of this question. A meeting is nothing at all.

Wellington to the Marquess of Salisbury, 9 April 1833

Stratfield Saye. I have received your letter respecting your Hertford affairs and Charles has shewn me one which you have written to him. In this last you call upon him to perform his promise; to advertise himself *now* as a candidate for Hertford and to offer himself to defend the interests and rights of the borough against the report of the committee of the House of Commons.

I am quite certain that you don't think that this is what Charles promised to perform or I promised to support him in undertaking.

It involves him as a borough politician in the most serious affair in which a young man could be engaged, and me in an expense of which the amount cannot in any manner be estimated.

I understood that Charles was called upon to decide before five o'clock on a certain day whether he would or not stop a gap at an expense to me of seven hundred pounds. I am not particularly anxious to spend seven hundred pounds at a Hertford election, particularly for Charles to whom it will be a positive disadvantage to be in Parliament. But neither he nor I would refuse that which appeared to be a convenience to you.

Neither if the writ was issued and you wished him to go down and stand for your convenience would he or I refuse; he to undertake the affair nor I to incur the expense to a limited amount. His superiors in the army and every body would clearly understand such a course. But it is quite a different thing for him now to advertise himself as a candidate to represent Hertford in Parliament and to offer to defend their rights. I must extinguish him as an officer of the army looking to his profession as his only object; and I should involve him as a young man in a scene of borough politics, to which if he is to be a politician it is better that he should have nothing to say.

I am very peculiarly circumstanced in relation to my sons. I am under the most strict trusts. I am to form a state for my eldest son.

For the other I must do what I can. He has very little by right. I have always felt that if I could lay out money for electioneering purposes for Charles I should do much better by him to give him and settle upon him the money rather than expend it upon his election to Parliament.

I am not now referring to such a sum as seven hundred pounds, an expense which I would willingly incur to enable him to render you a service. But if the expense was to go farther I should say that I was doing to Charles a great injustice not only in the way to which I have above referred, but in a pecuniary way.

I beg you not to misunderstand me. If when the time of the election approaches you want Charles to stand I entertain no doubt that he will be ready to step forward; and I will support him to the extent specified. But I beg you not to call upon him unnecessarily; or prematurely; or to involve him in the question now pending respecting the rights of the borough.

SALISBURY MSS. *Draft in Wellington Papers.*

Wellington to the Bishop of Exeter, 10 April 1833

Stratfield Saye. I have received your letter of the 6th and you may rely upon it that I will take the course upon the Irish Church Bill which shall appear to me best calculated to maintain the Protestant Church in Ireland.

It is very necessary that in our course upon this subject, we should consider of the state of general politicks and of what is most likely to promote our object of saving the Church of England. I am aware that this language is laughed at and despised by those who think that all ought to be sacrificed in order to bring themselves and their friends into office. There are some indeed who don't look even so far. These are satisfied if there is only a good sharp debate in the House of Lords for their amusement and a division afterwards which will afford topics for the conversation of a day or two to account for the mode of voting of the Lords present and the absence of those not in the House. Neither class reflects upon the imminent peril in which the country is placed, occasioned as I could prove clearly very much by their own intrigues and folly, and of the delicacy and difficulty of managing the House of Lords so as to keep it in a state of useful dignity, and to be able to make use of its legislative powers at the moment at which the country will bear and will require the use of them.

I am very much obliged to you for what you say of Mr. Wulff. I really know nothing of the son, the clergyman, and you must judge whether you ought to prefer him to others. The father is a general officer of the artillery of whom I do not know much. He was a friend of the late Marchioness Dowager of Londonderry, the mother of the present Lord, and was recommended to me strongly by the Marquis Camden when I was Master-General of the Ordnance. He was employed in Ireland where he conducted himself in a respectable manner. He is so far entitled to my aid in doing any thing for his family, if the candidates belonging to it themselves are deserving of preferment. I think you are quite right to keep yourself clear of the imputation of political bias, which however I must say I have never heard made against the bench of bishops. If I had there is no person who could justify the bench so well as yourself.

I was First Lord of the Treasury for three years. I recommended the appointment of the Archbishop of Canterbury, the Bishop of London, Bishop of Chester, Bishop of Oxford, Bishop of Gloucester, Bishop of St. Asaph, Bishop of Bangor and yourself, and excepting from yourself, this act of kindness towards Mr. Wulff, I have never received even an acknowledgement of an act of kindness.

I have a nephew in the Church who was educated in my house, and is one of the finest, best behaved young men that exists. He is an admirable scholar, and is calculated to be a distinguished man in any profession. He is now serving as a curate without salary to my brother the Rector of Wearmouth. I have some patronage of my own, as well as some which I hold by virtue of my office of Constable of the Tower. At the persuasion of the Bishop of London, I appointed a gentleman to be chaplain of the Tower. But his Lordship has never thought it expedient to prefer this gentleman and to leave at my disposal the chaplaincy of the Tower that I might give it to my nephew. There is no man therefore better qualified than I am to defend the bench of bishops from any imputation which may be cast upon them of political bias in the disposal of their patronage.

The Marquess of Salisbury to Wellington, 10 April 1833

Hatfield. Private. Confidential. I ought certainly to have stated explicitly that in making my request that Lord Charles should come forward at the present moment it was to be at my expence and I beg pardon for not having done so but it would have been a request of such extreme indelicacy to ask anyone to support *my* interest upon other terms that I considered it as a matter of course. I am very singularly placed with regard to the approaching election at Hertford. Before the petition was decided I mentioned to my friends my intention to bring forward Price to supply the place of Ingestre. Mahon was to find some one to take his seat. I applied by his desire to Sir Edward Sugden who gave a very unwilling consent requesting that some other person should be found. In the mean time Baron Dimsdale brought forward Dawson. Terms were agreed upon between him and Mahon. A correspondence took place between Mahon and Baron Dimsdale which led to a quarrel and the negotiation was at an end. But I had lost Sir Edward Sugden. I then in conjunction with Mahon applied to you to allow Lord Charles to stand. You were good enough to acquiesce but you also expressed great dislike to it. I therefore again negotiated with Baron Dimsdale and Dawson and by the assistance of Sir Henry Hardinge made satisfactory terms with them. I then wrote to you stating but expressing myself rather doubtfully, that I believed we could dispense with the assistance of Lord Charles. But Lord Charles's name had been mentioned at Hertford and the preference shewn towards him was so great and so decided that my friends told me that although I should probably bring in Price it could not be done without occasioning a split in our party which would end in reestablishing Duncombe and endanger the future return of Mahon. I had therefore first to put it to Price whether he would stand under these circumstances. He very handsomely released me from my pledge to support him. In the mean while Duncombe, Spalding, and Dawson issued addresses and it being necessary that some avowed candidate should do the same on our side I then wrote to you and to Lord Charles. No canvass can by my agreement with Dawson take place until the issue of the writ without our mutual consent but there is nothing to bind Messrs. Duncombe and Spalding. The uncertainty of our candidate is injuring our cause and I may at any moment be forced to commence a canvass which however under existing circumstances is not probable. Our present strength is great, in proof of which an address has been signed to Lord Ingestre and Mahon by 400 out of 650 voters pledging themselves to support them as soon as they are again eligible. I believe I have now troubled you with a full detail of the politics of Hertford and I can only add that I will suffer any inconvenience however great rather than trespass unfairly upon your kindness. The question remains entirely for your decision. When I first asked your consent to Lord Charles's standing it was to occupy Lord Mahon's seat. He paid his own expences and I stated on the present occasion that they would not exceed £700. I have now wished to bring Lord Charles forward in the room of Lord Ingestre whom I have always borne harmless. It is therefore but natural that I should do so for Lord Charles. My letter to him was written without weighing the strength of my expressions. I thought I had his and your consent to his being a candidate and that it must be a matter of indifference to him when he so offered himself that I did not mean to call upon him on the ground of his having entered into an engagement from which a mere act of volition on his part did not release him. I send this to your house with a request that your porter will forward it to you by coach as time presses.

The Earl of Aberdeen to Wellington, 10 April 1833

Priory.[1] You may probably have seen in our newspapers, some allusion to another discussion in the Chamber of Deputies on the subject of Algiers; but if you are not in the habit of reading the French papers you will have a very imperfect notion of what took place on that occasion. The discussion occurred on the 4th of this month, a few days after Lord Grey had informed me that communications were going on between the two Governments; with what success, you will see. I have extracted from the *Journal des Débats* the principal features of the debate, which I have no doubt are substantially correct.

M. Martineau de Chenez, Commissaire du Roi, apologizes for the absence of Marshal Soult, and enters into an examination of the different modes of colonizing Algiers. He says, 'Le Gouvernement ne songe nullement à abandonner la conquête d'Alger, il veut en tirer tout le parti possible pour la France, mais il se présente de graves difficultés à cause de la position du pays et de la nature particulière du sol.'

M. de Rigny, Ministre de la Marine, also discusses the policy to be followed in the administration and government of Algiers. He says, 'Il y avait trois systèmes à suivre à Alger. Le premier, après avoir fait la conquête, après avoir délivré l'Europe du spectacle honteux que nous

---

[1] Bentley Priory, near Stanmore, Middlesex.

présentait ce repaire de brigands en face des états civilisés, le premier parti consistait à détruire toutes les fortifications, combler le port, et abandonner le pays après avoir pris toutes les précautions pour empêcher la piraterie de renaître. Ce moyen n'était pas sans inconvéniens. Le second système était une colonisation complète, dont l'exécution serait difficile. Le troisième système consiste à organiser des milices, à rallier à nous la population musulmane, à fortifier les points principaux du littoral, tels que Bône, Alger, Oran, Bugie, et à lier ces points principaux par des forts détachés; c'est ce que nous avons entrepris, et le Gouvernement persistera dans cette voie.'

M. Mauguin begins by suggesting that some engagement may have been entered into by the Polignac Ministry, but is interrupted by the Duc de Broglie. 'Il n'y a eu aucune espèce d'engagement.' M. Mauguin then continues, and enlarges on the importance of Algiers—insists on the necessity of colonization on a large scale, and looks forward to the establishment of the dominion of France in the Mediterranean. He takes a view of the state of the Levant, of the independence of Egypt, and of Greece, and the necessity of the French power being strong on the African coast, in order to profit by the changes which have taken place, and are in progress. He says there is no danger of their being dispossessed of Algiers in the event of a maritime war, and he gives his reasons. He concludes his speech by saying, 'Vous pouvez donc être intimement convaincus que nous garderons paisiblement Alger. Ne craignez pas l'Angleterre, l'Angleterre a plus besoin de la paix maritime que nous mêmes. Parlez au nom de la France, et la France saura se faire respecter.'

The question related to the vote of some expences in the war budget, which, after a few observations from persons of less consequence, was carried.

I think we are placed in a new situation by the repetition of these assertions and declarations; and that it will be our duty, both with reference to what has passed with the French Government on this subject in our time, and with a view to the future interests of the country, to be silent no longer. I should think the best plan now would be to give notice, on the meeting of Parliament, of a motion for papers explanatory of the subject. It is possible the Government may grant them; but if not, the motion has the advantage of being easily abandoned if necessary, from a consideration of what is due to the publick service. If it should be thought expedient, it might also enable us to bring into view the state of affairs in the Levant, with our position in that quarter, and generally in the Mediterranean.

We may thus avoid pressing the question to a division, with credit to ourselves, while we endeavour to open the eyes of the House, and of the publick, to the conduct of Government, and to the real nature of the situation in which we are placed.

Wellington to George Codd, 10 April 1833

Stratfield Saye. I have had the honor of receiving your letter of the 6th instant.

It is quite clear to me that the impression under which I wrote my answer to the corporation of Hull when they first proposed to me the honor of being their High Steward was the correct one. In truth I am not qualified for the office. There exists no relation whatever between the town of Hull and myself; I did not know that any other person could have pretensions to that office; that any body of inhabitants could desire that that nobleman should be appointed to it; what the right or usual mode of election was; or that there was any doubt respecting the election till the Secretary of State informed me that he had found himself under the necessity of advising the King not to compleat the warrant of appointment which had been solicited by petition of the corporation. It appears now that I stand as the candidate for an office of honour against the pretensions of another noble Lord, the Earl of Durham; the King's Ministers having to decide between the two.

This is certainly a false position for me and one in which I ought not and should not have placed myself if I had acted according to dictates of my first impressions. Every step taken since the first has been erroneous; and I must beg the corporation of Hull to excuse me for declining to accept the appointment of their High Steward; and that they will proceed to elect a nobleman more nearly connected with their town than I am and who must know more of their interests.

Draft, in Wellington's hand.

Wellington to Sir Robert Wilson, 11 April 1833

Stratfield Saye. I return the *Journal des Débats* with many thanks. I conclude that Lord Aberdeen will have another communication with Lord Grey upon the subject of Algiers as soon as Parliament will reassemble.

The state of the Mediterranean is becoming very interesting to this country. But I am much mistaken if it should not soon be found that our interests in all quarters of the world require more attention and exertion to promote them than have been applied to them lately.

It appears from the newspapers that Lord Palmerston has been unwell.

ADD MS 30114, f. 15.

Wellington to the Earl of Lauderdale, 11 April 1833

Stratfield Saye. I received your letter of the 6th and those which accompanied it. Your answer to Mr. Halse is admirable. I envy you for writing it.

A gentleman who wishes to attack a peer for interfering against him in an election must of course come forward with clean hands. He must be able to shew that he did not apply to the same peer or to any other peer for support to himself. But your note takes the exact tone which becomes you.

William Holmes to Wellington, 11 April 1833

Grafton Street. I send your Grace under another cover the copy of a letter received this morning by a friend of mine from a colonel in the Company's service, and a man who has a regiment.[1] I think he appears prepared to mutiny himself. I understand that 15 privates and 10 jemidars of the native horse artillery were blown from the mouths of the guns the day the mutiny was discovered.

The private accounts also state that Lord William Bentinck and Sir Edward Barnes are on the worst possible terms, so much so as not to speak to each other, and that Lord Clare and a General Halkett at Bombay are if possible on worse terms. The Government is in a pretty mess. I can hardly venture to write what I hear of General Halkett's violent proceeding towards Lord Clare.

Edward Ellice left town on Tuesday night (to be re-elected for Coventry) in fear and trembling, not so much for the result of the contest as for his own safety. Young Cobbett is gone down and has got

---

[1] Not printed.

the Radical voters and mob on his side. It is said here that Lord Durham is the writer of the articles of yesterday and this day in *The Times*. From what I could infer from a long conversation with Ellice on Tuesday last, Lord Hill's reign at the Horse Guards is drawing to a close.

Wellington to Lord FitzGerald, 12 April 1833

Stratfield Saye. Private and confidential. I have received a letter from you of the 8th instant which to tell you the truth I have not been able to read throughout but of which I can read enough to see that it relates to a subject on which I had thought a great deal, and on which I had already taken some steps.

The rule according to which Lord Liverpool acted and I acted and every Government ought to act in relation to the Irish representative peerage is to consider residence in Ireland as an indispensable qualification, and as you resided and was the Lord Lieutenant of the county of Clare I certainly considered you as the peer who of all others ought to be preferred upon the last vacancy. I was aware that my friend Downes had got many engagements. I have no vote myself and had made no engagement to him nor to anybody else. I had had some conversation respecting the claims of the Earl of Bandon with his son, Lord Aberdeen, Lord Wicklow, and others. But nothing that could be considered an engagement which indeed I did not think that I had any right to make as I had no vote.

Upon communication with others respecting you however I found so many objected that it would have been impossible to succeed against the Government candidate, and the candidate of the party to whose support I was to look for success, whether that candidate should be Lord Downes or another. I therefore was very glad to have Lord Downes, and to obtain for him all the support which I could.

I think that the success in this election has put these elections on new grounds. I have already heard more than once that Lord Bandon must be our next candidate. I have said nothing as yet. Indeed I have passed the greatest part of the winter in the country, and have never been in town for more than a day. I am now going up however and I will consider of this as well as of other subjects. The first object of all is that we should carry the election. In order to do this we must not split the party. If we do we shall give up the choice to the Whigs. You see from this statement that I was thinking of you long before you was thinking of this object for yourself. You may rely upon it that I will not give it up unnecessarily. But I think that you had much better leave it to my management with the party who have undoubtedly the preponderance in these elections. I do not recommend that you should not quietly make as many friends as you can. Let me know how you are getting on from time to time. I shall then know what chance you would have for the next vacancy. I think that I should be able by good management to insure you for the second vacancy. There is no mode by which I can have any effective influence in carrying one of these elections excepting the assistance of the party which is now opposed to you. I can prevent them from carrying an election and I should enable the Government to carry it. But to do good I must manage this party, and I can manage it only by keeping myself free from all engagements.

I never expected any permanent good in Ireland from the Coercion Bill. I hoped that it would produce a permanent breach between the Radicals and the Government. But the latter are endeavouring to patch up the difference occasioned by the discussions on the Coercion Bill, by every description of dirty concession on every subject.

Wellington to the Earl of Aberdeen, 12 April 1833

Stratfield Saye. Sir Robert Wilson sent me the *Journal des Débats* and it is very obvious that we must take some fresh step respecting the engagements regarding Algiers.

I think that the form of our proceeding depends very much upon what passed with Lord Grey before and upon the contents of his answer in writing to you.

If, as I think I recollect, he said to you that he was in discussion with the French Government upon the subject of what had then recently passed in the Chamber of Deputies, I should think that you ought not to move at all without previous communication with Lord Grey and letting him know what you intend to do and leaving to him to object to your mentioning the subject if he should think proper. This communication I would have in writing. I don't think that you and I can be with justice accused of having made a false statement or of submitting to a contradiction by the French minister as long as the Government tell us we are in negociation with the French Government on the very point which you wish to elucidate by discussion. But if I have misrecollected the purport of Lord Grey's answer to you I should think that you might be justified in giving this form to your proceeding: viz. to ask him on your legs in the House whether it would be inconvenient to him that you should move on a day to be named for the production of a document etc., etc. If he should answer that it would be inconvenient, I would not move for the document. You will have gained by this mode of proceeding so far as that you will have shewn to the world that you are not insensible to the position in which we have been placed by the *dictum* of the French minister, that we think we have the means of shewing that we were justified in saying what we did by what had passed in 1830, and that we refrain from discussing the subject because His Majesty's servant tells us that the discussion will be inconvenient to him.

If Lord Grey should give no answer or an intemperate answer you might then bring the subject forward and in the debate throw upon him the responsibility for the inconvenience which the discussion may occasion.

ADD MS 43060, ff. 88–91. *Copy in Wellington Papers.*

Sir Herbert Taylor to Wellington, 12 April 1833

Windsor Castle. Private. Your Grace will I fear have considered it extraordinary that I should have delayed until this day acknowledging the receipt of your letters of the 5th and 6th instant, which reached me on the 7th and which I immediately submitted to the King, but it was His Majesty's desire that I should learn from communication with the Horse Guards what had been done, or was contemplated on the subject of the apprehended alteration in the Mutiny Act, and the notice given by Sir Francis Burdett and Mr. Sheil of motions respecting corporal punishment, and the expectation of seeing Lord Fitzroy Somerset, who was here yesterday, caused further delay, to which I may add the occurrence of a little indisposition which has rendered application to any serious subject uphill work to me for some days past.

In the mean time I have received from the Adjutant General and submitted to the King his correspondence with your Grace and other documents having reference to the subject, as well as Lord Hill's letter of the 25th ultimo to Sir John Hobhouse (which states clearly, forcibly and ably his objections to any alteration) and I have assisted at an interview, which Lord Fitzroy Somerset had with the King yesterday, and have had further communication with him. The result of all this has been to confirm and strengthen the impressions and opinions which had been received both by His Majesty and myself upon the question of regimental discipline and corporal punishment and which, as they have been already fully stated and as they accord in general with those entertained and expressed by your Grace, I need not here re-state. I will add merely one or two observations, arising out of Sir John Macdonald's communications, the one is, that the returns of men tried by court martial in each year, from 1825 to 1831 both inclusive, and of the punishments awarded and inflicted, shows an encrease of crimes and offences with the diminution of *corporal* punishment in the army, and that Sir Frederick Ponsonby, the kindness of whose nature and humanity are generally acknowledged, states in December 1830 that he has had, during the last 14 years, two regiments under his command where corporal punishment was not practised, that they were not trustworthy out of the barrack yard, more crimes were committed than in other corps, and when he found that the plan had completely failed, the old system was adopted and they were then (December 1830) in as good a state of discipline as any battalion.

I am very sensible of the difficulties under which we labour in maintaining our position, however well supported by facts and experience and common sense, against the effect of prejudice and clamour and the anxiety of Members of Parliament to obtain and preserve popularity. This however is a difficulty which, in these times, is not confined to the agitation or discussion of this question only, but extends to many others, as it has indeed for some years past, has proved and must continue to prove seriously embarrassing to any Government—must as your Grace observes, endanger the existence of all laws and institutions; and experience has unfortunately shown, upon more than one occasion, that the endeavours and exertions of those whose duty it is to defend the powers of the Crown and the institutions of the country have been unable to stem the destructive torrent.

I am perfectly convinced from all that has passed and every communication made by the members of the Government, that they are seriously and anxiously desirous to prevent the introduction of any material change in our military code and system, that they would decidedly and strenuously resist it if they could depend, in the present temper of the House of Commons, on a sufficient majority, and that the measures now contemplated are expedients to obviate that which they cannot wholly prevent, and to render, as far as possible, innoxious the reptile which they cannot crush. I admit that military men, whose declared opinion it is that military discipline cannot be maintained, unless the power of inflicting corporal punishment is preserved, particularly in regimental courts martial, are called upon to introduce or propose, in deference to public opinion, some regulation which is at variance with their declared sentiments, but I conceive the Government to be placed in the same predicament, that it is a common cause, that the greater proportion, if not all its members, share the sentiments and opinions of the military men and would sincerely rejoyce to see them prevail, and that the appeal now made to them is, not for the sake of producing concession, but for the sake of obtaining their aid and cooperation in some arrangement which may have the effect of neutralizing the attempt to prejudice the discipline of the army. It is impossible that the Government can obtain any opinion from the military authorities which shall accord with the sentiments and views of the advocates for the proposed alteration, nor do they wish or expect it. 'They are clearly anxious to resist such proposal and Lord Palmerston opposed it strongly, but doubting whether, in the present state of feeling in the House of Commons, this resistance will be successful, without something to show that every care has been taken to reduce the practice of corporal punishment within the narrowest limits which the *paramount* consideration of the discipline of the army will admit, they have suggested what they conceived to be the best means of insuring this result, apprehensive as they are that, from the want of some further regulation which might be adopted with safety and hardly ought to be called a concession, a vote may be carried against all their efforts to resist it.'

I have transcribed the above passage from Lord Grey's last letter to me on the subject, as stating distinctly the object of the Government, the difficulties under which it is placed, and the aid and cooperation which it seeks from the military authorities. There can be no doubt that it will become the Government to declare its conviction that the military authorities are right in their view and opinion of the question, and there does not appear to me any reason to apprehend from any thing that has passed on the subject, that they will not do so.

I have no hesitation in saying that the more I consider the subject and advert to the opinions of your Grace and other competent authorities, the more I am satisfied of the importance of maintaining the existing powers, especially of regimental courts martial and the existing authority and responsibility of commanding officers of regiments, and having carefully read your Grace's letters to the Adjutant General, I take the liberty of submitting, whether a proposition founded upon your proposal to establish a still more particular scrutiny and investigation and consequent reports and notice of the proceedings of courts martial, of minor punishments, and of defaulters lists than have yet prevailed, and to appoint a competent officer, specially charged with the details of that duty, might not answer the purpose and relieve us from the difficulty. Such proposition, brought forward in the shape of a regulation, for the consideration of the Government and to be submitted to Parliament.

I own that I should greatly prefer this to the appointment of any board or commission of enquiry, upon the results of whose deliberations we could not entirely depend, whereas, in the other case, we keep the view of the question and the steps which it may be advisable to adopt in our own discretion, having acquired a full knowledge of the sentiments of those whose judgement and experience best qualify them to have a voice on the subject. The King, by whose authority I write, who is alive to every part of the question, and who has read all that has been written upon it, has ordered me to convey the above opinion, as one to which His Majesty inclines, and as being in favour of the most simple and most direct course.

The foundation for what your Grace proposes is indeed already laid and the machinery requires mainly some amplification. Reports of all courts martial held in or connected with regiments are now made *monthly* by every corps in the army, to head quarters and to the generals commanding districts. They are carefully examined and any thing calling for attention is noticed and produces special reference to and inspection of the proceedings, instructions for enquiry, reference to the Judge Advocate General, if necessary, reference to the confidential reports of corps in order to compare its state of discipline with the nature and amounts of punishment, and occasionally an order for the production of the defaulter lists, or an instruction to the general officer to inspect them, with reference to the immediate object of notice.

This, which is now done in a general way and as occasion calls might be established more extensively and under special superintendence and report, as proposed by your Grace, and I apprehend that a statement of what has been the practice, of the proposed extension of it, of the encrease of crime and offences shown by the returns in proportion as corporal punishment has been diminished, and a declaration of the decided and concurrent opinion of the officers of the army that the power now vested in regimental courts martial cannot be further diminished without compromising the discipline of the army, etc., that such is the declared opinion of even those officers who had, for certain periods, carried on the command without resorting to the exercise of the power they possessed. If such a statement, I say, were produced, it is to be hoped that it would answer the purpose of the Government and enable it successfully to contest the point.

Wellington to the Marquess of Salisbury, 12 April 1833

Stratfield Saye. You must not be surprized that I should have been alive to the engagement into which in your letter you suggested to Charles to enter. I know well that there is not an attorney or a lawyer in Hertfordshire, probably not one in Westminster Hall, who would not have commenced his calculations of what he could make by such a cause supported by my supposed inexhaustible purse. For no man would suppose that Charles would write such an engagement without my consent; and observe that there was no qualification in the engagement: it went not only to defend and protect the rights of your friends and party, but those of Baron Dimsdale and of whomsoever else could pretend that he had rights and interests.

I never could suspect that you intended that such an engagement should be made. But it would have been made. I should have been bound by it; and should have been enabled to get out of the difficulty only by declaring that I would have nothing to say to the affair and by throwing over you and your party at Hertford. It was for this reason that I wrote to you as I did.

I think that you are quite right in supporting your interest at Hertford; and in incurring a reasonable expense in doing so. But allow me to entreat you to proceed with caution; not to pledge yourself to an unlimited expense; and most particularly not alone while Baron Dimsdale remains aloof from you with a separate independent party. I am certainly very unwilling that Charles should so pledge himself. Nobody will understand that it is your pocket which is to bear the expense; and you will feel the inconvenience of my being supposed to be the holder of the purse strings. It will besides be a serious disadvantage to him to start for this election excepting as *locum tenens* and *stop-gap* for the convenience and interest of a relation. I wish you therefore not to declare him as your candidate till you are certain of the moment of your election.

If he is so situated as then to be able to stand he will do so; and I am ready to defray the expense which was originally stated. But I deprecate his being put forward at the present moment or till that at which the writ will be issued.

SALISBURY MSS. *Draft in Wellington Papers.*

The Marquess of Salisbury to Wellington, 14 April 1833

Hatfield. Very many thanks for your kind letter of the 12th and for the excellent advice which it contains. My purse strings have certainly been very much extended of late but I trust that the worst is over, little or no treating will in future be necessary if we escape disfranchisement and I hope that the Baron will not give me much trouble. Since I last wrote to you a great change has taken place. Duncombe has sold his property to the Baron at an exorbitant price and his address therefore offering himself as a candidate was in all probability to obtain that sum. The idea also that the late Members will stand again has very much gained ground. The people of Hertford universally believe that they will be enabled to do so. All therefore that I have to ask at the present moment is that I may be allowed to state privately to my principal friends that Lord Charles will offer himself to occupy the ground for Lord Ingestre should he be disqualified by the report of the committee as my interest would be impaired by the supposition that I had no person ready to come forward. With regard to your very handsome offer of incurring the expence of £700 I must beg to decline it. When I proposed it my idea was that he should fill Lord Mahon's seat. The case is now different. He would stand in the room of Ingestre whose expences I should always pay and I am sure *besides* that you have already too many calls upon your liberality to justify me in adding to the number.

Wellington to Sir Herbert Taylor, 14 April 1833

Stratfield Saye. I am very happy to learn from your letter of the 12th that you have seen my correspondence with the Adjutant-General regarding the question of corporal punishment; and that His Majesty takes an interest in it.

It appears to me extraordinary that so few persons of consideration on account of their talents and weight in Parliament, should attach importance to this question. I consider it to be a question not whether there shall be more or less of discipline in the army, but whether that body shall be disciplined at all, and in a state of efficiency and order to perform its duty. If it should be decided that the powers of commanding officers of regiments are to be destroyed, I am convinced that it would be better for the King, as well as for those who look to the King for protection for their lives, properties and honour that there should be no regular army at all.

In truth that is the object which those have in view who are raising a clamour to put an end to this description of punishment.

Besides the indifference to this question of men of talent and reputation in Parliament, there are two classes of officers even in the House of Commons upon whom no reliance can be placed. I put out of the question the brawlers for popularity of whom there are some. But there are some respectable men, supporters of Government, who represent populous places, and who are apprehensive of the consequences of speaking out, and of saying what they know and feel upon this subject. The other class, highly respectable, is of men who in the course of their service have seen little of regimental duty; and that little when they were young. These men have but little knowledge of the details of the service of a regiment, and of the manner in which the soldiers must be kept in a state of order and discipline. They and others see the army in a perfect state of discipline and efficiency. They do not consider how it has been brought to, nor by what means it is to be kept in that state; and probably their minds have never adverted to the consequences as well to the Sovereign as to individuals of a serious mutiny of the troops upon a critical occasion.

On the other hand whatever may be the opinion of the King's servants upon this question I have not heard, and possibly it might be imprudent for them to declare positively in Parliament their intentions.

If we had stood where we did in April 1831, and the General commanding in chief, called upon to make a concession to publick opinion, had asked my opinion, I should have answered at once, 'Maintain the established discipline of the army.' I should have been certain that the Government would be supported in that course by Parliament.

But situated as we are and seeing things as they are, I have recommended to the General commanding in chief to endeavour to acquire for himself all the information that can be obtained regarding the state of crime and punishment in the army, in order that he may have it in his power more effectually to check any irregularities; and to convey to Government and to Parliament a knowledge of the real state of the case if such information should be called for.

If when this arrangement should be made the General commanding in chief should still be called upon to make a concession to popular opinion, I have recommended to him that a commission should be appointed to enquire into and report upon the whole case before any step should be taken.

Although I don't think that the enquiry would be attended by inconvenience, I agree with you in thinking that it would be better that such an enquiry should not be made if ulterior concession should not be pressed upon the General commanding in chief.

But in the existing state of things is that probable?

It appears to me to be desirable that before the General commanding in chief is pressed to make such concessions, the respectable Members of Parliament and the publick at large should know what is the real subject for deliberation; what is the object to be attained; and what the consequences to the Sovereign on the throne and to those of the community who look to him for protection.

It is with these views that I wrote to the Adjutant-General the letters which have been laid before you.

PS. Since writing the above, it occurs to me that when you wrote to me on the 12th you had not seen my letter to the Adjutant-General of the 10th.

RA 36160–36162. *Copy in Wellington Papers.*

Wellington to the Marquess of Salisbury, 15 April 1833

London. I think that the retreat of Tom Duncombe from Hertford is a good thing for you and the town. The most probable consequence is that the Government will not endeavour to throw any new electors into the borough. Indeed it is not improbable that Duncombe withdraws because he found that the Ministers were not disposed to put reform any farther in that quarter. Any reform there would certainly eventually be followed by other reforms in other places.

The affair will probably end by the issuing of the writ after some abuse of you in the debate.

In respect to Charles I have no objection to your whispering that he will stand if Ingestre should not. But don't let him advertise till the last moment.

If you bring him into Parliament whether I pay the expense or not I clearly understand that he is your Member; but I think that the question whether you or I ought to pay the expense is one which we ought to leave to a reference. I was quite ready to pay the expense in one expected case. I don't see why I should not in another. I hope however that Ingestre will be able to stand.

SALISBURY MSS. *Draft in Wellington Papers.*

The Rev. Thomas Singleton to Wellington, 15 April 1833

Elsdon Castle, Newcastle-on-Tyne. I have the honor herewith to transmit to your Grace the petition of the Archdeacon and clergy of Northumberland whose names are thereunto subscribed, which they pray your Grace to present to the House of Lords, in deprecation of a Bill now pending in Parliament, under the name of the Irish Church Bill.

The limits of this archdeaconry are very extensive; and neither the personal convenience nor the parochial engagements of the clergy would warrant the convention of a general meeting; but the petition has been circulated from parish to parish, and has been deliberately signed by an immense proportion of our body. Indeed I do not believe that there are ten resident beneficed men who have refused the sanction of their names.

Your Grace will have the goodness to observe, that the petitioners make no reference to the general question of Church reform. They say nothing of the inexpediency of sacrificing a loyal and meritorious order of men to the clamors of a malignant faction—they leave it to political oeconomists to determine how the starving peasant of Ireland is to be relieved by augmenting the remittances of his absentee landlord at the expence of his resident and charitable minister—and they are not even tempted to comment on the whimsical inconsistency of those who propose in one session of Parliament a grant of public money to the Irish clergy because they are so poor, and in the next an oppressive and annual and especial taxation upon them because they are so rich!!

The petitioners, my Lord Duke, confine their remonstrances to the forced alienation of the bishops' lands and revenues and to the imposition of an arbitrary tax upon the parochial clergy of Ireland; measures which they do not scruple to characterize as tyrannical and unjust—as tending immediately to injure and eventually to overthrow the united church of which they are members, and shaking to its very basis the security of all property whether lay or ecclesiastical.

My Lord Duke! The petitioners are very grateful for those exertions of Sir Robert Peel in the House of Commons by which a concession has been extorted in favor of existing interests; but they cannot on this account diminish in the slightest degree their opposition to the ulterior objects of this bill nor consent to any compromise of the indefeasible rights of their successors from any considerations of a personal and selfish nature.

It will be a proud consolation to the petitioners if, in the approaching assault of the sacred establishment in which they serve, they shall find themselves supported by your Grace; and if they shall be permitted to hope that he who above all other men has ennobled this nation by his triumphs in the field, will under Providence protect our violated institutions by his authority in Parliament.

For myself my Lord Duke who am moreover bound to you by ties of personal and private gratitude, I can only add [etc].

PS. I beg to inform your Grace that I go to the college, Worcester, tomorrow, and that such will be my address should your Grace have any commands for me.

The Marquess of Salisbury to Wellington, 19 April 1833

I was extremely sorry to find that you were unwell when I called to thank you for your last letter. There is only one part of it in which I hope you will allow me to differ from you. I must presume in making myself chargeable with the expense of Lord Charles's return. You already make a sufficient sacrifice in affording me the advantage of his services. It is just p[ossible][1] though I do not think it likely that the writ may be issued on Monday. Would you therefore have the goodness to write to Lord Charles to say that if [it] should occur an express will be sent down to him immediately after the division; and that it would be very desirable that he should make his entry into Hertford at nine o'clock the next morning. He cannot come a nearer way than through London and Ingestre would be ready to accompany him down. I am very much afraid [the]re[1] is no chance of the old Members being allowed to start again.

I write this as I fear there is no chance of your coming here today.

Undated. Docketed 19 April 1833.

SALISBURY MSS.

Wellington to the Marquess of Salisbury, 23 April 1833

London. I send you a letter from Charles. It appears that as I expected the affair is put off for some days.

PS. You and I must have a reference on the point on which we differ.

SALISBURY MSS.

Lord FitzGerald to Wellington, 26 April 1833

Dublin. I am unwilling to trouble you so soon again, and am ashamed of having deserved your rebuke for my illegible writing, yet I cannot forbear sending you a few lines, though but to assure you that I am most sensible of the kindness of your last communication, and most grateful for the friendly interest which you have taken on the subject of the representative peerage, with respect to which you had so kindly thought of me, before even I had thought of it for myself.

I will only add that I feel as happy in knowing what your luck had been in my behalf as if I had succeeded in the object itself.

In leaving the whole affair in your friendly hands, I am not unaware that, owing to the feelings of that party who are all to decide the election, there will be no little difficulty in reconciling many of them to accept me, and that except to meet your Grace's wishes they will be very disinclined to give me their support.

Of course I should not, under any circumstances, persevere so as to *split* the party. I feel that the first object is to make it impossible for the Government to nominate. If I am not the choice of the Conservative peers, I shall not complain. If on the contrary, they are content to

---

[1] Page torn.

elect me, I shall be gratified and proud to think that I owe it to your Grace's kindness, to your recommendation of me, and to that friendship of which I have received so many proofs.

PS. The grand jury of the City of Dublin have found bills of indictment against O'Connell's printer, for libel, in publishing his letters on the Coercion Bill.

The Rev. William Barlee to Wellington, 27 April 1833

West Chiltington, Pulborough. Deeply impressed with a sense of the vast injury which must be inflicted on the labouring classes by political unions, if not checked, I venture to write to inform your Grace that they are certainly upon the increase in this county. One was established in the little village where I reside, about a month since, and is rapidly increasing—it is connected with a large one in the neighbouring parish of Billingshurst, which last is a branch of a very violent one at Horsham. No one can calculate to what lengths these people may proceed. But I heard from a most respectable farmer who has better means of information than myself, that it has been already contemplated to use a kind of imperceptible influence to compel the little tradesmen to join them through the fear of losing their custom.

Being of opinion that these things should be known, and yet, from certain circumstances which took place between high members of the present Government and political unions, not wishing to communicate with them upon such a subject, I have ventured to write to your Grace leaving you to form your own conclusions.

I hope that your Grace will pardon the liberty I have taken.

Draft reply 1 May 1833. Compliments. The Duke recommends to him to communicate any positive facts of which he can adduce proofs on the subject which he has referred in his letter to the Duke to the Lord Lieutenant of the county of Sussex or to the Secretary of State for the Home Department.

Bickham Escott to Wellington, 29 April 1833

London. The manner in which former communications of mine have been received by your Grace induces me to trouble you with this. I have heard that the Chancellor of the Exchequer has this evening announced his intention of moving tomorrow in the House of Commons as an amendment to Sir John Key's motion for a repeal of the house and window tax a resolution to the effect that a reduction of half the malt tax and a repeal of the house and window tax would derange the financial condition of the country and make it necessary to inforce a property tax, and would therefore be inexpedient. It appears to me that such a resolution proposed by this Government after the vote of the House of Commons of Friday last affords the best possible opportunity for the party which opposed the Reform Bill to regain that popularity in the country by which alone after the passing of that Bill any party can hold the reins of government; and that it is the duty of that party to take advantage of this opportunity, and make a bold endeavour to rid the nation of a Ministry composed of persons the bare falsehood of whose professions is now apparent to all.

I think if that party wishes for office it cannot hope for a fitter occasion for gratifying that desire. I think if it wishes to do its duty it must firmly and decidedly oppose such conduct as this.

I know it will be said, would the Duke of Wellington or Sir R. Peel or Mr. Manners Sutton have proposed to go on without the malt tax? The answer is no but the Duke of Wellington and Sir R. Peel did not carry the Reform Bill. They did not promise reduction of taxes as its consequence, but that Bill being carried they will not attempt to carry on the Government in direct opposition to the opinions and stedfast hopes of those electors whom the Reform Bill has created, and who will, first or last, have a House of Commons to do their bidding. Instead of engaging in so hopeless a task as this the party which opposed the Reform Bill will I should hope properly expose the fallacious conduct of those persons who having promised the country great relief from the taxation as the consequence of the Reform Bill, are now satisfied with having carried the measure and tell the country they have no relief to give. They will then probably set themselves to consider whether in the present state of this country it be not absolutely necessary to make great legislative changes especially in its finances, and whether bold and decisive measures are not the only prudent and safe ones. And should they decide on the alternative of this proposition they will not hesitate to incur some risk in order to escape greater dangers; always remembering that they are driven to incur the risk, and that the danger and difficulties are none of their creating.

Should the party which opposed the Reform Bill support the Minister tomorrow, the greatest danger which I anticipate will not be in the absence of that popularity and influence which I think they might gain by a contrary course, but in the certain and inevitable loss of warm and ardent friends. The alienation of these will be a great relative addition to the democratical party. Many will join that party. Some will say that the Tories, as they are called, who support the Ministers are as bad as the Ministers themselves; and some of these will join the Ministers. The Ministers will gain nothing by such an alliance in comparison with what they must lose by their false promises bared and detected. Both parties will sink through the absurdity and childishness of such a proceeding. And thus it is plain that the party which alone will really gain both in numbers and moral power will be the democratical party, the consistent reformers, who supported the Reform Bill for its practical advantages, and who not yet having been tried as a governing party have not been proved to be fools or knaves. If I had any doubt that an accession of strength to this party must be the consequence of such support given to the present Ministry it would be removed by observing the manner in which the acute democratical writers (in the *Morning Chronicle* and *Examiner*) for instance argue in support of the present Government in preference to a Government composed of men who opposed the Reform Bill and whom they call Tory. Their desire is to set up the democratical party. These are the means which in their opinion are most likely to attain that end. If these persons thought that the continuance of the present Ministers in office was likely to keep themselves out they would be among the foremost to oppose that continuance.

In conclusion I beg to say that I think some votes already given this session have done much, and that the vote on tomorrow evening may do more to ruin the cause of sound legislation and honorable government in this country, and the hopes of that party of which I consider your Grace to be the head; more indeed than could ever have been effected by the energies of its most bitter enemy.

Wellington to Bickham Escott, 30 April 1833

London. I have had the honor of receiving your letter of last night.

I have no vote or influence in the House of Commons. If I had I should make every exertion in my power to prevent the House from breaking down the existing financial system of the country. It may be very possible to discover a better one. I have not discovered it, nor have I heard of any body who has. Till that better system will be discovered and explained and the publick should be prepared to adopt it, no consideration of popularity, of power or of party shall induce me to give my support if I have it in my power to give any, or my countenance, to any measures which have for their object to deprive the country of its existing resources.

I feel a great respect for your talents and opinions. But begging your pardon I have been in the habit of judging for myself and I cannot adopt a course upon any subject which in my conscience I believe will be injurious to the country.

Wellington to John Charles Herries, 30 April 1833

London. I inclose a correspondence which I have had with the Board of Trade upon certain papers which Lord Auckland put into my hands.

You will see from his letter to me what they are about to do.

Send me back my letter and the answers as I have no copies.

ADD MS 57368.

The Earl of Lauderdale to Wellington, 30 April 1833

Dunbar. I have never received any answer to the letter I wrote to Mr. Halse, a copy of which I sent to you, and I have therefore thought it unnecessary to take any further notice of the information he conveyed.

I write you at present to say that as the Duke of Bedford has now allowed a month to elapse without taking notice of my last letter, I conceive there is an end of our correspondence on the subject of re-moving my bust from what he calls the Temple of Liberty, in which he has distinctly announced that busts of those who take the liberty of differing in opinion with his Grace are not allowed to remain.

On the belief that this correspondence is closed I now send you a copy, which you may shew to Sir Robert Peel, or to any of the members of the late Government whom he has thought proper to libel; but I do not wish to make a general display of the contemptible imbecility he has betrayed.

I trust on reading it you will be of opinion that I have sufficiently repelled the unjustifiable and unprovoked attack upon myself and those with whom I have in principle acted, without being unnecessarily severe upon a man whose weakness I pity.

Ministers appear to me to have received practical proof of the mischief they have inflicted by reducing this once happy country into a state in which in reality no power of governing exists.

Signature only in Lauderdale's hand.

Bickham Escott to Wellington, 2 May 1833

21 Essex Street. Mr. Escott has had the honor of receiving this morning a letter from the Duke of Wellington: he is very reluctant to trouble his Grace again; but he is afraid that some expressions in his letter of the 29th ult. have been misunderstood.

Mr. Escott had not the slightest idea of putting his judgement in competition with the Duke's; nor did he suppose for a moment that the Duke would for the sake of any ulterior object whatever 'adopt a course which in his conscience he believed to be injurious to the country'. He only made the communication, sincerely thinking (though he fears too presumptuously) that the opinions of so humble a person as himself might possibly by such a communication be rendered in some remote degree serviceable to the country. He feels very much obliged by the communication of the Duke's opinion against breaking down the existing financial system: and as he should have been much vexed not to have had the opportunity of setting himself right by this explanation he trusts to his Grace's goodness to excuse it.

The Marquess of Londonderry to Wellington, 5 May 1833

Paris. I doubt, my dear Duke, if I can give you any information from hence, that you will not have from more authentick and better sources. Still it may not be wholly uninteresting to you to receive a report from me as a *voyageur* returning to Paris since the days of July and contemplating it under the new dynasty. I shall first inform you how the capital appears to me to be changed, and next, what I should say was the state of the Government and the country.

In Paris there is an evident revival of commerce. The city seems inundated with capital, new buildings, new shops, new embellishments and new luxuries of all kinds. Strangers of every country, clime, and class make every quarter of the town full and it is difficult if not impossible to get an apartment. Immense funds seem to be laying out while they also are locked up in the country from the great uncertainty that exists of knowing where or how to place them advantageously or with surety elsewhere. The society of the upper class has been entirely broken up and changed since the last revolution. The Faubourg St. Germain, and the adherents of Charles X neither go to court nor mix or frequent the salons of the *corps diplomatique* where they would meet the *juste milieu*, and since the Duchess of Berry's imprisonment this separation of the partisans of the late and reigning family has become more bitter and more marked. Apponyi tells me he has been obliged to shut up his house from the feelings that pervaded. The Duke of Orleans would not meet the old court, and the old court would not associate with the grandees of the new reign. There are no *réunions* therefore now at Paris, except at the theatre or diplomatick dinners and the Ministers' receptions. The theatres are more splendid and better filled than ever.

The Government of the *juste milieu* at this moment is becoming stronger from great divergence of opinion amongst the sections of the Opposition. Louis Philippe has contrived by much shrewdness and dexterity to steer his bark between various contending elements. But he is endured now only because there is a horror of risking further commotion, and his unpopularity is submitted to because there is no hope of any return to the legitimate line, and that this reign is better in the opinion of many than a republick. It is evident however, that Louis Philippe is detested by all parties, and the Liberal party with La Fayette, La Fitte, at their head, to whom he owes his crown, can not contain their indignation. It is impossible to describe how much this man is abused, reviled and disliked, and my own impression is, from what I observe and see, that his career will be cut short by some fatal catastrophe. The blood thirstiness of the republicans is as much as in Robespierre's day, and by the juries not convicting on the late trials there is an encouragement to perpetrate a regicide, and failure brings no condemnation. I must however observe that the prevailing feeling amongst all parties at present is tranquillity and preservation of property. All seem to admit the chances are against its being of long duration. But the wish is to preserve it under a thorough hatred and contempt of the monarch and the acknowledged weakness of the ministry.

The fine guards who used to inspire you with feelings of respect are all vanished and miserable troops appear in their places, little men badly equipped and apparently worse drilled. Still, they tell you the army was never in finer order yet I saw a wretched exhibition of cavalry and infantry yesterday in the Carrousel.

I have had some conversation with Apponyi and Pozzo on our foreign affairs. I learn the very intimate alliance professed between France and England to the repudiation of former understandings is *at bottom very hollow*. The two countries *au fond* are as jealous and watchful of each other as ever. England by her policy is laughed at by Russia, Austria and Prussia, who think their triple alliance strong enough to hold England and France in check, and a great proof of this is that these powers have managed their own game in the east as a set off against Belgium, and England has not had a voice in the Mediterranean and France has only blustered. The French have only three ships and we about the same in those seas, and were we to pass the Dardanelles with a combined squadron to prevent Russia doing just what she pleases at Constantinople Pozzo would ask for his passports and we should have immediate war. But I believe the truth is this Government would submit to any thing rather than have a war. The result however of Lord Grey's foreign policy is that we are separated from the Quadruple Alliance. That France only holds to us to carry her own objects. That the three powers remain in the strictest understanding and that they still look to the hope that the absolute governments by wise counsels and able statesmen will make head against the republican and liberal efforts in the countries of Europe.

I have scratched these few hasty lines, though I am conscious there is little worth your perusal in them. As I stay here, whatever occurs of any moment I will write if you have patience to read.

Things in England seem to me to be approaching a crisis. But it will not be so soon as many seem to expect.

If I can do any thing for you here, pray let me know.

Viscount Strangford to Wellington, 5 May 1833

Harley Street. Private. On conversing yesterday with some of the principal Portugal merchants, I found them unwilling, so long as the game continues to be *undecided* in that country, to sign any petition to Parliament, which they think might commit them with Pedro should he be successful.

There is another course which, with your Grace's approbation, I should like very much to follow, or what would be better still, to see followed by Lord Aberdeen—namely, a motion for a return of all vessels, clearing outwards, or entering inwards, to and from Oporto, for the last two years, with *cargoes and passengers*— distinguishing the years, and including steam vessels.

This would shew the stop which has been put to a most valuable part of the trade of the country, both in imports and exports—as well as the extent of the recruiting system, and to a certain degree, of that of the supply of *munitions de guerre*.

Government could not refuse these papers, so, though we should be able to fire a few shots at them, there would be no necessity for coming to close quarters, in the shape of a division, which I know your Grace does not like, except upon *really* important questions.

If I am well enough to go down to the House tomorrow, perhaps you would have the kindness to intimate to me *there*, your opinion as to the propriety of this motion.

Docketed by Wellington Answer that Lord Aberdeen should move for the number of ships entering inwards to and from Oporto with cargoes and passengers for the last two years.

Wellington to the Earl of Lauderdale, 6 May 1833

London. I am very much obliged to you for the perusal of your correspondence with the Duke of Bedford.

As you say truly it has brought the removal of your bust to the sole crime of having given your aid to prevent your friends and coadjutors, in opposing the Reform Bill, from being excluded from the House of Lords on account of their votes upon that question.

I will shew the correspondence to Sir Robert Peel and to some others who will peruse it with interest.

I am not surprized that you should not have received any further communication from Mr. Halse.

Richard Oastler to Wellington, 7 May 1833

Fixby Hall, near Huddersfield. Do not blame me if I venture once more to occupy your Grace's valuable time for a few moments.

I know that I have no *right* to obtrude my sentiments on your notice; but I am sure you love our country, and you are so placed as to

have the power to help her, in this her hour of danger. I love her too—
but I aspire not to become a leader; I am too happy if her natural
benefactors will permit me to offer the results of my observations to
their notice.

Your Grace is perfectly aware that of late years a cry has been *'got up'*
against the nobles. They have been abused and defamed in the ears of
the people until the people joined in the cry 'Down with them'—
having been convinced, by their masters the *capitalists* and *factory lords*,
that all their troubles were attributable to the tyranny and oppression
of the aristocracy, and by whom has this cry been raised and fostered?
By a set of the most contemptible, low bred, tyrannical wretches who
ever lived—the *capitalists* and *factory lords*. By men who all the time they
are abusing the *real* nobles, are themselves actually *killing*, by excessive
labour, and by low scanty wages, the very slaves whom they persuade
to assist them in crying down the noblest race of Britons! And whilst
they are doing this, they are laying the foundation of destruction for
the aristocracy by amassing large fortunes, and then mortgaging or
buying their estates. This is a true fact, my Lord Duke, and what is
worse, a certain portion of the aristocracy help them to ruin 'their own
order'.

Now if some measures are not adopted to release the people and the
aristocrats too from the power of this *money* and *steam* interest—the
sooner the better we have a regular blow up. It is impossible that
prosperity should ever again shine on this country if *honor, health,* and
life are to continue to be esteemed of *less* value than *money* and *steam*.

Believe me, my Lord Duke, I know what I am saying. I live amongst
these tyrannical, hypocritical wretches, but thank God I fear them not;
I have long watched their operations, they have regularly progressed
as the happiness of the working class has declined; and (rising upon the
fall of the aristocratic influence, and the *actual* slavery of the people)
they have now attained an importance which nothing but a *strong*
Government can controul; and yet Government fosters them!!! I have
faced them and the people, I have exposed their villainy to their teeth—
the people see—and know and *feel* all I say is true—they are ready to
throw off the yoke. But the aristocracy, with very few exceptions, hold
back. Once more I entreat your Grace to help. *Begin* to curb their power
by supporting the *Ten Hours Factory Bill*—release the people from a
tyranny worse than Egyptian. Did your Grace conquer for England
that her sons should be enslaved by plebeian tyrants?

We have just had a committee meeting in Manchester from the factory districts in England and Scotland, among other things it was resolved to present an humble and dutiful address to Her Majesty the Queen on behalf of the poor, industrious, oppressed factory children— and I resolved to ask your Grace *if you would so far oblige the working classes as to present it to Her Majesty.* I feel assured your Grace will pardon me for making so free; and I am convinced Her Majesty could not be offended at the words of the address.

If some plan be not adopted to break the chains by which the *capitalists* bind fast the people—if the good old feeling (which once united in mutual affection the *owners* and the *workers* of the soil) cannot be again introduced—if the aristocrats *will not* take the place nature has assigned them—to lead—to guide—and to cherish the people—why then the plebeian wretch, who happens to be *rich*, will very soon ride roughshod over every other class.

It is to save my country from this calamity, I venture once more to steal a few moments from one who has done more for his country than any other, one whom to name, excites in my mind the liveliest emotions of gratitude—and to have conversed with whom is the proudest boast I e'er shall have.

Excuse me, my Lord Duke, I love my country, or I dare not thus venture to incommode the Duke of Wellington.

Wellington to Robert Henry Jenkinson, 7 May 1833

London. It is understood that Mr. Halcomb had no qualification for Dover and that he will be thrown out by the committee.

It is proposed to set up Captain Gordon who is a sort of *Saint*, who sat in the last Parliament for Dundalk in Ireland.

We might find many better candidates and many worse. I understand that young Fector will not stand.

I confess that I would rather prefer to take no part till we can find a decidedly good candidate.

Let me know what you think upon this subject.

Sir Henry Hardinge to Wellington, 8 May 1833

Mr. Ellice called upon me yesterday and told me he was anxious to consult you not only as the highest military authority but also as colonel of the 1st regiment of Guards, on the expediency of placing the stock-purse of the Guards on a footing which would bear public explanation in the House of Commons.

He admitted the management of the Guards to be excellent and even economical but that it was difficult to satisfy the House who would be influenced by Parnell's statements, that £17,000 of public money was drawn for public purposes of which not more than £6,000 was appropriated to the troops—the remainder being shown in the stock-purse of the officers.

His view was to leave the management with the officers as at present —to give the officers a fair and just equivalent—making in reality no saving—but in principle, placing this expenditure on a footing more capable of a public justification.

Before he addressed you in writing, he wished to converse with your Grace, so as to make his letter correspond with the arrangement which the conversation might produce.

If you write a line to say when you can see him I will forward your note to Mr. Ellice.

He says Parnell has taken this matter up—and he must be prepared to defend the *form* as well as the substance.

Wellington to Sir Henry Hardinge, 9 May 1833

London. Since I wrote to you last night, I have found that I could not get the information to enable me to converse with Mr. Ellice on the subject of the stock-purse of the Guards till late this day.

I therefore propose to postpone my waiting upon him at the War Office till tomorrow morning.

VISCOUNT HARDINGE PAPERS

Wellington to Richard Oastler, 9 May 1833

London. I have received your letter of the 7th. Before I can tell you that I will present to the Queen the address which you desire that I should present to Her Majesty I should wish to see a copy of it.

I must then inform you that I have no opportunity of approaching the Queen excepting to pay my respects to Her Majesty at her drawing room. I could not approach Her Majesty to present an address at any other moment.

Her Majesty has a drawing room this day. She has another to celebrate the King's birthday on the 28 May, and she will have another in June. I don't think that the King's birthday would be deemed a fit occasion to present an address to the Queen. The presentation of the address, if by me, must be postponed till June.

But allow me to submit to you the information that the Queen has attendants of high rank and in official situations. Her Majesty has a Lord Chamberlain through whom all applications are made. His Lordship can approach Her Majesty at any time, and I would beg leave to suggest to you the expediency of sending through his Lordship's hands the address which it is intended to present to the Queen which you had thought of entrusting to me, and which as you will see I should not have an opportunity of presenting till the month of June.

Sir Bethell Codrington to Wellington, 9 May 1833

Dodington, Cirencester. Sir Bethell Codrington presents his compliments to the Duke of Wellington, hoping he shall be pardoned in requesting his Grace to direct the return of the two affidavits which Sir Bethell Codrington took the liberty of sending about a fortnight ago. Sir Bethell Codrington presumes that the Duke of Wellington does not think it advisable to notice them in the House of Lords, but it is thought that publishing them may tend in some degree to shew the value of such anti-slavery petitions as have been lately presented to the two Houses of Parliament.

Wellington to Sir Bethell Codrington, 10 May 1833

The Duke of Wellington presents his compliments to Sir Bethell Codrington.

The Duke returns him the affidavits to which Sir Bethell refers.

The Duke did not make use of them on account of the disinclination which he feels to enter into any discussion so useless as would be one respecting the manner in which the slavery petitions to the House of Lords are got up.

Dated May 10.

Sir Alexander Grant to Wellington, 14 May 1833

I leave a paper which will show you the different dates that you require. That the agreement with the West India body was that they should have twelve years apprenticeship as part of their compensation, and that they were to have £20,000,000 in money as a *gift* for their co-operation here and their exertion of their *influence* with the colonial legislatures. But it was *not* part of the compact that they were not to receive the gift if those legislatures did not yield to that influence.

The abstraction of five years from the apprenticeship is a breach of faith: the making the payment of the £20,000,000 dependent upon the acts of the colonial legislatures is a still grosser one.

In giving your Grace the accounts of the yielding of my property for the year—a *clear income* to me of £9,000—I should have guarded against the product of a particular, and indeed peculiar, estate being taken as a criterion of general West Indian prosperity. If Mr. Stanley were to act up to his *original principle* of ten years purchase of income, I ought to have £90,000 instead of the miserable £15,000 which is now talked of, but by no means assured to me.

Undated. Docketed 1833, May 14.

Enclosure: Income from my Jamaica estate.

Wellington to the Rev. Thomas Singleton, 15 May 1833

London. I have not yet presented the petition from the archdeaconry of Northumberland which you sent me some time ago nor have acknowledged the receipt of it and of your letter upon the subject. Till within these two days I was in hopes that I should have been able to present that petition and others upon the same subject which are in my hands. But upon communication with others I find that it is not considered to be very courteous for a member of the House of Lords to present to that House a petition against a Bill depending in the House of Commons till the measure will have reached the Lords.

I had delayed to present the petitions because I wished to present them at the moment at which some discussion upon them in the House of Lords might be of some use to the cause in the House of Commons. But as you will see I must now delay to present them till the Bill will be in the House of Lords.

We are in a curious state. The truth is that we have a House of Commons all powerful which has no community of interest or feeling with the property, the establishment, the institutions, the commerce, or the policy of the country.

Thomas Duncan to Wellington, 17 May 1833

British Hotel, Jermyn Street. Your condescension and kindness in presenting the Edinburgh petition for the gradual abolition of colonial slavery with a due regard to the interests both of the master and the slave, emboldens me to request the favor of your Grace to present the accompanying petition from the inhabitants of Musselburgh, at such a time and with such remarks as your Grace may deem necessary and proper (in the present crisis of that awful question) to the House of Peers.

Wellington to Thomas Duncan, 17 May 1833

Compliments. The Duke of Wellington returns the petition from Musselburgh which Mr. Duncan has sent him. There are no signatures on the same sheet with the petition; and according to the usual custom it would not be received by the House of Lords in its present form. The Duke will present it when sent back to him with any signature on the sheet with the petition.

Richard Oastler to Wellington, 19 May 1833

Fixby Hall, near Huddersfield. I have had the honor to receive your Grace's kind letter of the 9th inst. for which I am exceedingly obliged.

I called a meeting of the Friends of the Factory Children, which met yesterday. I read your Grace's communication to them, and they desired that I would communicate to your Grace, 'their most heartfelt thanks for your kindness and attention to their business, but as it is very desirable that *no* time should be lost, and as it is impossible your Grace can present the address to Her Majesty the Queen before June, they will with much regret be deprived of your Grace's much wished for and most powerful assistance'.

I sincerely hope your Grace will excuse the trouble I have given you and with the most ardent wishes for your Grace's long life, health and happiness *etc.*

Sir Hudson Lowe to Wellington, 21 May 1833

3 Park Square West. As the subject of slave emancipation appears to have engaged in some degree your Grace's attention, I hope I shall be excused in the liberty I take of sending you a reprint of some proceedings which took place at St. Helena, upon an occasion when the slave holders on that island adopted some measures with a view to a gradual abolition, and which in that confined spot, although the late Mr. Canning declared against the principle which they had adopted, produced, I believe, all the effect that had been anticipated.

Having ventured this intrusion on your Grace, I hope the high interest which still attaches to the question and which is likely to be increased by the Duke of Broglie's speech, will be received as some kind of apology for my forwarding at the same time a privately printed copy of some observations upon another subject to which my attention happens to have been more particularly drawn. Although circumstances have greatly changed since these were first written yet as the general views and principles which they sought to convey have been indulgently considered by some persons of high political experience, I ventured to send a copy of the paper some time since to Earl Grey. In submitting it to your Grace, should you honor it with a perusal, it will pass through the last ordeal to which I could refer it.

In the papers of yesterday I find it stated in a letter from Constantinople that '*Russian officers have been sent to the Dardanelles to put the castles into a state of repair*' or in other words it may be presumed to occupy them. If such be the case, they will have secured the Chersonesus (a more important point than Constantinople itself) or at all events interposed a serious obstacle to its occupancy by any naval power, for which some grounds have at times offered. This however the French may not perhaps so much resent if suffered to establish that ascendancy at which they have been so long aiming in Egypt and the Levant. Indeed one of their leading journals a short time since admitted almost as much. Algiers they might more then regard as secondary. To counteract those designs it would still not appear to me too late, acting even in conformity to *some* of the views expressed in the within paper, though they are not those I fear most likely to meet with favor.

Viscount Arbuthnott to Wellington, 27 May 1833

London. Being obliged to go down to Scotland in the course of this week, I beg to send you my proxy.

Should your Grace consider personal attendance necessary at a later period I hope your Grace will inform me of it, and I shall most readily and instantly return to town.

Draft reply 28 May 1833. Compliments. The Duke will take charge of his proxy; and is much flattered by this mark of his confidence.

The Earl of Airlie to Wellington, 27 May 1833

London. I have the honor of sending your Grace my proxy, as I am obliged to set out for Scotland in the course of the week.

I beg however to assure your Grace that should the necessity arise of my presence I shall most readily again come to town, when your Grace should have the kindness to inform me of it.

Draft reply 28 May 1833. Compliments. The Duke will take charge of his proxy and is much flattered by the proof which it affords that the Duke enjoys his Lordship's confidence.

Wellington to Vice-Admiral Sir George Cockburn, 31 May 1833[1]

London. I am much obliged to you for the turtle which you have sent me. William Wellesley cut his throat and I have every reason to believe that he has reached London in a state fit for the food of good Conservatives.

I am likewise much obliged to you for your kindness to my nephew.

We are going on here very much as we all expected, that is to say destroying as much as we can and doing nothing. I should think that the Government have commenced to discover that the House of Commons has no community of interest or feeling with the wishes, the interests, the establishments or the policy of the country, that it is detested and despised and that it will very soon be incapable of governing the people.

---

[1] In reply to a letter from Cockburn (not printed), Port Royal, Jamaica, 20 April 1833.

But the Ministers are desperate, they are holding their existence by a thread, and they are making a fresh plunge or rather tumble every day to prolong it.

They are now running breast high upon the West Indies question. But I should not be surprised if after all they were to come to a stand-still upon that.

Wellington to the Duke of Buckingham and Chandos, 12 June 1833

London. Mr. Barrett called upon me one day with Mr. Burge and Lord St. Vincent.

I quite concur in his opinion. The cultivation of sugar even during the 12 years is out of the question.

We are about to try the experiment of turning a nation of slaves into first a nation of apprentices for three-fourths of their time and of freed men for the remaining fourth, which no country ever tried before.

The usual course has been to turn slaves into freed men as soon as the progress of civilization and improvement had been found to render the work of freed men cheaper than that of slaves. But we knowing that there is neither civilization nor improvement and not only that the work of freed men is not cheaper than that of slaves but that the work of freed men to cultivate sugar can not be procured at all, are about to pay 20 millions sterling in order to set free 800,000 slaves!

The work of these 800,000 slaves now gives to this country in sugar only not less than 12 millions sterling annually of which five go in mass to the Exchequer. Lord Brougham pretends that the Exchequer will get the revenue upon the sugar even though it should not be produced in our islands and colonies. I joined issue with him upon that point. But whether we get the duty or not, we are going hand over head to ruin the commerce and navigation as well as the colonies of the country by these measures.

Then if the legislatures of the colonies resist and are to be coerced we shall have a civil war between the King, the people of colour and the negro slaves on one hand and the colonial legislatures and resident colonists on the other.

Wellington to the Marquess of Salisbury, 12 June 1833

London. It is not worth corresponding more about; but he does not admit the fact that you was not the first to propose to him to stand for Hertford. Your notion is that the plan was proposed to him by some of the people of Hertford; then to you; and that you acquiesced.

The only reason for which it may be desirable to notice this point is that I think it likely to be one on which his family rely; and it might be expedient to set it right if you are quite certain that your recollection of the transaction is correct.

SALISBURY MSS.

Wellington to John Charles Herries, 13 June 1833

London. I send you the copy of my letter to the Board of Trade on the Cinque Port pilots.

ADD MS 57368.

Enclosure: Wellington to Lord Auckland, 24 April 1833.

London. According to your Lordship's directions I have perused and taken into consideration the papers which your Lordship sent to me on the complaints of the boatmen of Deal and Dover. It is impossible to submit to your Lordship an opinion upon them without at the same time adverting to a bill now on the table of the House of Commons introduced by the honourable Members for Sandwich, the same gentlemen who being candidates to represent Sandwich in Parliament presented to your Lordship the petition from the boatmen of Deal which was the foundation of the subsequent enquiry ordered by your Lordship by three Elder Brethren of the Trinity House.

The institution of Cinque Port pilots has existed as is stated in the Act of Parliament 'time out of mind'; it has frequently been regulated by Parliament, by Orders in Council, and by superintendence, and there is no doubt that it has afforded for centuries the means of a secure access to this metropolis of the commerce of the world by the most intricate and dangerous navigation that exists.

Notwithstanding the acknowledged antiquity and merits of the institution I admit that it is a fair object of enquiry as well in regard to its constitution, the regulations for its conduct, its conduct under those regulations, its expense to the commerce of the country and the result in providing for a secure access to the metropolis.

There may be much ground for enquiry and censure upon all these points. But I beg leave to submit to your Lordship that the distresses of the boatmen of Deal and Dover are a subject quite distinct from such topicks of enquiry.

The measures in contemplation which are effectual only in breaking down the system under which the Cinque Port pilots are regulated under the direction of Parliament, will but partially relieve the distresses of the 400 boatmen said to be at Deal and about as many at Dover.

The bill now depending in Parliament will give to the commerce of the country as pilots from Dungeness, instead of a set of men educated for the service, examined and found qualified to take charge of ships in this dangerous navigation by persons on their oath, capable of judging of their qualifications, and then appointed and licensed by a regular and responsible authority under whose regulation and controul these men serve as pilots and their conduct is liable to be enquired into and their misconduct punished, another set of men who however meritorious, will be volunteers in the service; will not be known to be, and may not be qualified at all, who will be under no regulation or controul and whose misconduct must remain unpunished.

The Act of the 6 Geo. IV c. 125, s.18 requires that eighteen Cinque Port pilots shall at all times cruise between the South Foreland and Dungeness in order to go on board any ship requiring their assistance. This was the law under the 52 Geo. III from the year 1812. The 53 Geo. III enabled the Privy Council to alter this system, which upon repeated applications by the pilots themselves the Privy Council refused.

The system of keeping the pilots in cruising vessels has been established with great difficulty and perseverance by the Lord Warden of the Cinque Ports. I am aware that there have been complaints against the cruising system and that a great deal of the attention of a committee of the House of Commons had been directed to it.

The Act of the 6 Geo. IV 1825 applied the amendments to the system recommended by the committee principally referable to the amount of the 'boarding money' from vessels of the smaller classes and till I received the papers transmitted by your Lordship I had heard of no complaints excepting from the pilots themselves.

I see that some of the persons examined complain that they could not get pilots and that the vessels were not to be found on the cruising station; but these complaints have never to my knowledge been made to the proper authority. If they had they would have been noticed.

From what I know of the litigious spirit existing among the pilots, the eagerness of all and each of them to be employed and their readiness to complain of each other, I cannot but believe that if there was any remissness in the cruisers to keep their station the fact would have come to my knowledge.

It is quite obvious that in the years 1830, '31 and '32, 1729 vessels took in their pilots at Dover and 979 in the Downs, 3170 having taken in their pilots off Dungeness. As the payment of the boarding money is smaller in the Downs than at Dover, and at Dover than at Dungeness, it appears to me to be as probable that the vessels which did not take in their pilots off Dungeness endeavoured to avoid the cruising vessels as that these last endeavoured to avoid those which required pilots. This is quite clear, the 979 vessels which did not receive pilots till in the Downs might have received them off Dover if they had made the signal. Whether the cruising system is right or wrong it will be put an end to by the provisions of the bill now depending in the House of Commons.

That bill enables masters of vessels coming from the westward to employ the first boat or vessel that offers itself to take charge of their vessels respectively and conduct them to a Cinque Port pilot or to the Downs; and such boat or vessel is to receive the remuneration allowed by the Acts of Parliament called the boarding money and is not to be deprived of such employment by any person, boat or vessel whatsoever but shall be paid according to the rates fixed for pilotage, certain distances westward of the Downs.

The cruising vessels having pilots on board under the 6 Geo. IV are bound to cruise between Dungeness and the South Foreland. The boats and vessels referred to in the bill cruise where they please. They must be the first to fall in with every vessel coming from the southward and westward; the consequence must be that the cruising system established at great expense to the pilots themselves, maintained at an expense of three thousand a year for each vessel, must be discontinued.

If no other evil was the consequence, excepting that the lives and properties of His Majesty's subjects would be exposed to navigation from Dungeness to Dover or to the Downs, that evil alone would be sufficient reason for not adopting this bill.

But the next clause of the bill goes to the supercession of the Cinque Port pilots at the will of certain persons called the commissioners of pilotage, an authority not known in the Cinque Ports. This authority is enabled to employ a competent boatman to act as pilot of any vessel who shall not be superceded excepting by order of the commissioners by whom he should have been appointed, and all this notwithstanding the recital of the preamble of all the Acts of Parliament regulating pilotage, and the known fact 'that ships and vessels have frequently been wrecked and many lives and much property have been lost from the ignorance and misconduct of persons taking charge of ships and vessels as pilots'.

I regret exceedingly that when your Lordship thought proper to direct an enquiry into the distresses of the boatmen at Deal and at Dover, you should not have sent your directions to the principal civil and maritime authority in that part of the country. I think that some useful information might have been afforded to your Lordship to which no reference is made in these papers.

It is well known that the boatmen whose distresses have been under consideration were in the habits of making large sums of money by smuggling. These practices have been put an end to by a general reduction of duties upon foreign trade and by other measures adopted by the Government for that purpose. Another mode of employment was the salvage of vessels wrecked upon the coast or upon the Goodwin Sands. This mode of employment still exists in some degree. But fortunately owing to the success of the pilot regulations there is less of it every year. But the boatmen have not yet reconciled themselves to any other mode of employment.

It is a curious circumstance that in flourishing towns such as Deal and Dover, the latter probably the most flourishing in late years of any town of its extent in the kingdom in sea ports, through which particularly the Downs so many vessels pass up or down Channel every day, there should not be employment for four hundred boatmen, if only in the casual supply of the wants of these vessels for the hours or days during which they are at times detained.

But there is another fact of which the notice is omitted in the papers deserving your Lordship's attention.

There are constantly in the Downs fleets of French fishing boats, manned by a body of seamen superior only to those whom we all see idling about the beach in Deal. These boats go out to sea, return, and their crews cure their fish in the Downs, and after the vessels are filled they return to France with their cargoes.

It cannot be denied that the hardy race of boatmen, inhabitants of the beach at Deal would enjoy infinite advantages in this same employment.

The papers which I have the honor of returning to your Lordship refer to other modes of employing the boats and boatmen of Deal upon which I shall make but one observation. They all tend to increase the expense of the navigation of the coasts of this kingdom and particularly of the narrow seas, which expense it has been the policy and the object of the Government for years to diminish.

All the pilot regulations, the construction of harbours, quays etc. still going on, the regulation for the fares of the boats and boatmen have all had this object in view. But if it be true that the right principle is to enable the boatmen of the Downs and Dover to gain what they would deem a reasonable subsistence from the commerce of the narrow seas it would be absolutely necessary to put an end to all our regulations and all the works still carrying on, each of which has for its object to enable ships to navigate and to trade with security and ease without the assistance and the expense of boats.

Wellington to Lord Lyndhurst, 15 June 1833

London. Private and confidential. I hear that Lord Bute is unwilling to vote with us on Monday, and I have heard from more than one noble Lord a desire to avoid a division in that stage of the Judicature Bill.

The Bill is founded upon a report of the commissioners and I have always thought that it would be desirable to answer the Lord Chancellor's speech and thus lay some grounds in argument before we should throw it out upon the principle.

I would recommend therefore that we should not divide on Monday, but let the measure go into a committee and finally throw it out upon the third reading. You will be better supported and the House of Lords will stand better before the publick if this course is taken than if the Bill should be thrown out upon the question of referring the Bill to a committee.

Wellington to the Marchioness of Salisbury, 21 June 1833

London. We have a great affair in the House of Lords on Tuesday which will certainly prevent me from dining with you and may prevent me from attending you to the opera. But I will do the latter if the House should be up in time; and I will dine before I go down.

SALISBURY MSS.

Major-General William Nedham to Wellington, 23 June 1833

Worthing, Sussex. I beg leave to make my acknowledgements for the honor of your Grace's note of the 25th ultimo.

Recently a coincidence of ideas has occurred, strongly illustrative of the sentiments on the emancipation of the negro population, which I had the honor of submitting to the consideration of your Grace in a former letter, that I have thought it right, in justice to myself, to transmit copies thereof to your Grace, which are herewith enclosed.

No. 1 is extracted from a letter, addressed to me by Messrs. Davidson, Barkly and Co., eminent West India merchants, of Lime Street Square. They write on the 15th instant to acquaint me with the arrival of one of their ships, of which some property of mine was included in the cargo.

No. 2, out of a letter from a Mr. Colin Mackenzie of Spanish Town, Jamaica, my principal attorney, of the 28th April, received the 7th instant.

For this final intrusion, I entreat your Grace's acceptance of my apologies, which scarcely the importance of the subject can warrant, not being so fortunate in my career as to have had the honor of being known to your Grace.

In common with all concerned in our West India colonies, I pray that under the auspices of your Grace the House of Lords may be induced to cause justice and protection being administered to us, two essential qualities which are withheld by such numbers of our countrymen.

Docketed Answered. Received.

Enclosure: No. 1   From Messrs. Davidson, Barkly and Co. Lime Street Square. London, 15 June 1833.

Our market has improved 1 to 2 per cent, and God knows it seems wonderful, looking to prospects before us, that it has not advanced at once ten shillings: but our customers for colonial produce nowadays would rather wait till the evil of a want of supply stares them in the face, than by filling their warehouses by times be prepared for the falling off. And the day of a great diminution of supply from our colonies cannot we conceive be far off: for whatever effect the measures of Government may produce, the less timid, the most sanguine, must expect diminution in the cultivation. Assume that the colonial assemblies (of Jamaica for instance) will bury angry feelings, will sincerely and honestly endeavour to carry into execution the plan of emancipation as promulgated. Assume that the whites will have power to restrain 'the liberated' negroes from rising up in insurrection—that no acts of incendiarism be committed—that houses and cornfields will remain unscathed by the lighted torch, admitting all this, for the sake of argument, still it seems contrary to all reasoning upon human nature to believe that the half savage negro, whose idea of 'freedom' is thoroughly ingrained with that of 'idleness', will at once, or soon, or for a very long time, become an industrious peasant, working voluntarily for wages: if not then how is to be supplied the one fourth labor now to be taken from the master? It will not be supplied, and estates, if they can under the new system be managed at all, will give a greatly diminished return. In order to meet this, compensation is justly given, but without entertaining the extreme apprehensions, which many do of the rejection of the measures, when made known in Jamaica, we certainly must say we think a very long time is likely to elapse before laws are passed, sufficiently in conformity with the spirit of the resolutions of the House of Commons, to justify a distribution to the Jamaica proprietors of their share of the twenty millions—even if it should be determined by the country to grant that sum, for we are very sorry to learn that great opposition to so large a grant is to be anticipated when the Bill itself is passing through both Houses of Parliament.

No. 2   From Colin Mackenzie Esq. Spanish Town. April 28 1833. Received June 7 1833.

It is too true that dangers and difficulties are thickening around us day after day—with regard to the colonies, I fear there is now little room left for hope, and their fate may be considered as sealed. What the result is to be God alone knows! But it does not require the gift of prophecy to say that so soon as emancipation is proclaimed these fine islands will become *next to valueless* to the mother country: for the cultivation of sugar *cannot* be carried on with *advantage* under a different system than the present one, which, with a very few and trifling innovations, would be both mild and humane in the extreme. We have now arrived at an awful crisis, and must meet our doom whatever it may be, with fortitude and resignation.

Miss Mary Shute to Wellington, 24 June 1833

2 Park Place, St. James's Square, Bath. In the year 1827 when Lord Bathurst was at the Colonial Office and subsequently when the colonists had the privilege of Sir George Murray's services, I had together with Miss E. B. Threlfall the honor of presenting a case to your Grace of very great hardship, an outline of which I now enclose. I would have sent it through his Grace of Rutland, or through Lord Fitzroy Somerset (to whom if you feel disposed to trouble yourself I beg leave to refer your Grace for reference as to my respectability) but the time fails me, as I see the colonial question is to come before the Lords tomorrow evening. May I entreat your Lordship to further the views of the oppressed *West India proprietors*, with that weight and influence which you possess, to obtain from his Majesty's Ministers a loan, to be worked out by the labour of the negroes instead of the twelve years of apprenticeship proposed by the late resolutions. The disadvantage of the apprenticeship must be apparent, as *all* command over the slaves is by the proposed Bill taken from their masters. This proposal of a part of the slaves' wages being appropriated to the loan fund has been an unanimous feeling amongst all to whom I have spoken on the subject. I pray your Grace's pardon for thus abruptly addressing you upon a subject in which my *all* is involved. I am possessed of from 70 to 75 negroes *unlocated*—I have no friends to maintain them, no estate to place them on as my petition or rather memorial shews. Compensation is so much saved out of the fire for mortgagees, but nothing but a loan from Government can enable the proprietors to give their best aid to work the Bill about to be brought before the House of Peers, and restore confidence in West India affairs.

PS. I am obliged to send my memorial to your Grace in two envelopes— it being too heavy for one. Should your Grace find upon perusal of it that it is an urgent case upon which to ground the petition for a loan perhaps your Grace will present it to Mr. Secretary Stanley—if *not* upon its being returned I will transmit it to him.

Enclosure: The humble memorial of Mary Shute of the city of Bath, spinster. 27 May 1833.

The Marquess of Lothian to Wellington, 24 June 1833

Monteviot, Jedburgh. I have heard *indirectly* that you think in the discussions about to take place in the Lords that as few proxies should be given as possible. Do you think it right that I should come up? I should not have waited to ask you this had I heard that the above was your opinion from anyone to whom you had yourself expressed it.

The Rev. George Robert Gleig to Wellington, 25 June 1833

Ash, near Wingham. I am aware that your Grace possesses all needful sources of information, yet I think it right to forward the inclosed. Whatever your intentions may be on the subject of the Irish Church Bill, it is at least satisfactory to find that the bench of bishops will neither play false to you, nor destroy themselves. As to the country, I don't believe the rejection of such a measure, particularly now that the principle of spoliation has been deserted, would create one moment's feeling, one way or the other.

If I recollect right your Grace desired me, when pilots were last made, to remind you of the case of a man whom Lord Darnley had strongly recommended long ago, but who, by some chance or another, had hitherto failed. His name is Gardener. He is a most respectable person, and would have been made last time, had there been another vacancy. He is again a candidate, and of course very anxious.

The Dean of Ardagh (Richard Murray) to Wellington, 26 June 1833

Deanery House, Edgeworthstown. I take the liberty of enclosing your Grace a copy of the resolutions of the Ardagh clergy. The note appended to these resolutions relate[s] to the reasons why dioceses were united in former times, namely necessity.

The most objectionable part of the Church Reform Bill is the proposed reduction of the number of our bishops, and I'm afraid if this part of the Act should become the law of the land, a very considerable secession from our Church will take place both of clergy and laity. The general opinion is Parliament may interfere with our temporalities but not with the spiritualities or internal regulation of our Church, that she ceases to be apostolical as soon as that interference takes place. The most feasible plan as far as I can judge is to make our four archbishops the permanent imperial peers—the eighteen bishops not to have seats in Parliament, but lords only by courtesy like the Bishop of Sodor and Man. By this means the income of the bishops may be curtailed to whatever extent may be necessary, and the deans and archdeacons in the archiepiscopal dioceses being put on the same footing as in England (with ecclesiastical jurisdiction) would enable our archbishops to give up more of their time than our bishops can do at present to their parliamentary duties. The bishops by this arrangement could give up their entire time to the duties of their respective dioceses and sustain with greater effect their spiritual characters without being connected with politics.

I shall have great pleasure in affording your Grace if necessary any further information on this or any other subject connected with the Church of Ireland.

Draft reply 30 June 1833. Compliments. The Duke has received his letter of the [26 June] and the inclosure for which he begs leave to return his thanks.

Wellington to Miss Mary Shute, 26 June 1833

The Duke of Wellington presents his compliments to Mrs. Shute.

The Duke has received her letter of the 24 June and the inclosed copy of her memorial to the Secretary of State.

The Duke is not in office. He is not even acquainted with Mr. Stanley. He has no power of being of any service to her.

Viscount Saint Vincent to Wellington, 26 June 1833

Upper Grosvenor Street. I cannot resist the feeling which I entertain of your incomparable and unanswerable speech last night, without thanking you as an Englishman and one connected with the colonies and expressing my gratitude and admiration.

Sir Charles Colville to Wellington, 26 June 1833

York Hotel, Albemarle Street. The ready access which it is your Grace's character to grant to persons much less distinguished by your patronage and kindness than I have had the good fortune to be, has made the difficulty I have experienced in obtaining an opportunity of offering you my personal respects, after an absence of five years, the cause (it must be admitted) of a very natural surprise and mortification, and, allow me to add of frequent embarrassments also, on occasion of the enquiries made of me, of when I had seen your Grace, how I thought you looking, etc.

My not having had the honor to be of your Grace's dinner party on the 18th instant has further been noticed by several persons, esteemed I am sure by you, as they are equally my personal friends, and to them I gave the reply I had on prior occasions given—namely that I was neither considered by your Grace or myself 'a Waterloo man', not having immediately shared in the dangers and glories of that day. But to this was offered the presence at the dinner of Sir James Lyon who commanded a brigade under me at the period in question.

The inference therefore drawn was that my not having been invited arose with the knowledge your Grace had obtained that I had not been presented to the King since my return from abroad and that it was contrary to etiquette that an individual should be asked to meet His Majesty under such circumstances.

I consequently determined on not further importuning your Grace until I should be enabled to mention some satisfactory termination of the matters at issue between His Majesty's Ministers and myself respecting my government of Mauritius, and should have abided by that resolution—but for the occurrence of what I must now speak of with equal embarrassment and vexation.

I feel that no man exists who is less addicted than I am, I will not say to intrude, but even without being met half way, to offer himself to the notice, in publick, of his superiors in station but last night while standing by the railing round the throne in the House of Lords, when there was no crowd or pressure, your Grace passed so close to me and looking in my direction, that I could not without an effort which would have been revolting to my nature, avoid making you a respectful bow, but which passed unacknowledged: thus shewing that I must have either fallen out of your Grace's recollection or into your displeasure.

The former would be sufficiently mortifying, but the latter could not be, except through the intervention of mistake or misrepresentation, and which as much out of respect to your Grace as in justice to myself it is my anxious wish to have cleared up; as I am sure you are the last person in the world who would approve of my remaining tonight under such distressing circumstances.

May I therefore intreat some explanation on a subject which makes me most unhappy?

Wellington to the Marquess of Lothian, 28 June 1833

London. I told Lord Courtown from whom I conclude that you heard, and who applied to me to know whether he could go to Ireland, that I thought that circumstances were becoming so critical that noble lords ought to judge for themselves of the course which they ought to follow and not leave the decision solely to me.

I propose as soon as I shall receive the Irish Church Bill to determine upon the course which I shall follow upon it, of which I will inform those at a distance whose proxies I hold; and I will desire them to instruct me specially as to the giving their proxies, or to come up themselves and vote.

This is the only mode in which I can be relieved as I ought to be from the responsibility which now rests upon me to decide what the course is that the House of Lords ought to follow in the critical circumstances in which the House of Lords is placed.

I will write to you and you will determine for yourself what course you will take.

Signed: Ever yours most affectionately.

SRO GD 40/6/194. *Draft in Wellington Papers.*

The Marquess of Chandos to Wellington, 28 June 1833

I inclose you my proposed resolution, and shall feel extremely obliged by your opinion as to its form, and to the expediency of moving it as an instruction to the committee on the Bill or else in Committee of Supply.

I need not add that your opinion will decide the course I shall pursue.

Undated. Docketed 1833, June 28.

That in the present state of the finances and in the distressed condition of a large portion of the people it is expedient that the compensation to the West Indian proprietors on the emancipation of the slaves should be afforded by an adequate reduction of the duties on West Indian produce, whereby relief would be afforded to them without increasing the burdens already borne by the people of this country.

Wellington to the Marquess of Chandos, 28 June 1833

London. I think that you had better consult Sir Robert Peel upon the expediency of making the motion in the House of Commons to which you refer. If the result of the measures now in contemplation should be that any sugar is grown and exported to this country from the colonies, by far the best arrangement for the proprietors of estates would be to lower the duty payable on the import of sugar into this country. It would likewise be the best arrangement for the publick interests.

But I am afraid that it is most probable that no sugar or very little sugar will be grown and exported. The proprietors of estates in the colonies would therefore object to your arrangement. There is one class in particular who would object to your amendment and that is the class of proprietors of slaves who are not proprietors of estates. These would derive no advantage from the low rate of duty upon sugar imported into this country. I think likewise that the class of persons having mortgages on estates in the West Indies would object to your proposal.

Lord Carbery to Wellington, 1 July 1833

Carlton Club. Having received a note from His Royal Highness the Duke of Cumberland last night requesting my attendance at a meeting at His Royal Highness's apartment at two o'clock this day, I felt it to be my duty to attend to His Royal Highness's wishes. The result of the deliberations at that meeting will no doubt be communicated to your Grace. I trouble your Grace with this note to say that I am not among those present who avowed their determination to vote and divide on the second reading division. I distinctly held myself unpledged as to any part of my conduct. Having been present I feared I might be reported as concurring in that plan if I had not thus explained myself to your Grace.

Dated 4 o'clock. *Docketed* 1833, July 1.

Wellington to Edward Ellice, 3 July 1833

London. Private and confidential. I inclose a note which I have received.

I can have no objection to the examination of any officer in the Tower.

But the Tower is the King's palace; and I recommend that you should take and signify the King's pleasure that the officers of the Tower may attend the committee of the House of Commons when called upon.

PS. I beg you to return me the inclosed papers.

Endorsed by Ellice: Written on the occasion of an order being sent from the committee on Army and Navy emoluments to the officer at the Tower to attend to give evidence.

NLS E57, f. 39.

Sir Robert Gardiner to Wellington, 4 July 1833

Claremont. Having forwarded Colonel Macleod's letter to your Grace, I feel it now a duty to submit it in a legible form. I fear I presumed too much in intruding on your Grace's attention, but some of the results defined by him were so distinctly foretold by your Grace, that I ventured to submit it to your perusal. He has had means of thoroughly knowing the present state and prospects in Jamaica from his own experience, and his intimacy with the persons most interested in the manner of effecting emancipation.

Enclosure:

Jamaica. May 13th 1833

We have the expectation of some measure for the negroes—and the violent language and action of the white people here have given them great reason to suppose something in the shape of immediate emancipation is coming out. The consequence is they are particularly well conducted just now—but the reaction will be the greater. This, with the state of the House of Assembly, for the same members have been returned as for the last, and our daily expected visit of the cholera (committing dreadful ravages at Cuba) does not render this a pleasant station. People in England cannot be brought to think that the negro's idea of freedom is absolute idleness, and indeed, a total cessation from work beyond cultivating their own grounds for mere yams etc. Some of the people who have heavy families will undoubtedly remain, and work a certain way; but the young and active will controul, and soon teach them that by industry they injure their future happiness. In *civilized* countries the parents have difficulty enough in making their children believe this; but *here*, where the parents' controul is nothing, who or what can persuade them, or make them see reason? If you attempt by soldiers to make them, they will take to the impenetrable woods: and if in order to bring them back, you destroy their provision grounds, then the work of plunder begins, and those who do remain on the estates must make common cause or starve. When once disorganized, the white managers must fly, for there is no longer safety for them when the negro becomes excited: and then, one wide field of insurrection, and its concomitants, murder and every worse horror, commences, and rages throughout the island. Your Camberwell and Clapham ladies and Buxton and Co. will hug themselves with the idea of having abolished slavery, without having a thought of the miseries they have entailed on the wretched creatures. There is another thing which does not appear to be thought of. When the proprietor has to hire his workmen, can he be expected to keep an hospital for the sick, nurses for the children, or support the old and infirm? and who else will do it? All this is fact—there is not a word overstated in the misery that must take place if emancipation takes place.

Viscount Mahon to Wellington, 5 July 1833

Albemarle Street. According to your wish I have attended this morning to Lord Carrington's proxy. It will be left behind and put into Lord Rosslyn's hands, but Lord Carrington gives it with reserves on the questions of the Bank charter. His opinion on that point is the same as Mr. Baring's.

The Marquess of Lothian to Wellington, 6 July 1833

Monteviot, Jedburgh. Private. I received your letter last night. I can assure you that my application was solely dictated by a desire to know whether in the question that is coming before the House you would prefer my voting in person rather than by proxy and though carrying with it an appearance of a desire to avoid responsibility, yet believe me no such motive in any way influenced me. I shall be ready at any moment to come to London. The person from whom I heard on the subject was one of my sisters who had heard it from Lady Brownlow.

Draft.

SRO GD 40/6/194.

Henry J. Richardson to Wellington, 8 July 1833

Ironmonger Lane. Dramatic Performances Bill. I am requested by the proprietors of the minor theatres to request your Grace would grant them an interview on the subject of this bill (about being introduced into your Grace's house) tomorrow any hour after twelve. I have the pleasure to state that several noble Lords have already acceded to this request and they feel assured your Grace will comply with this request. Your Grace will be good enough to name the hour.

Signed: Henry J. Richardson, solicitor to the proprietors.

Draft reply 9 July 1833. Compliments. The Duke begs leave to decline to receive the proprietors of the minor theatres.

He is desirous of forming his own opinion upon subjects which come under discussion in Parliament without attending to the solicitations of parties.

Wellington to Viscount Mahon, 9 July 1833

London. I am very sorry that you are going; but I confess that I wish that I could go likewise. I would do any thing to be able to quit this unfortunate and unhappy country.

CHEVENING PAPERS 685.

The Earl of Eldon to Wellington, 9 July 1833

Confidential. I will attend where your note mentions tomorrow, unless you inform me that that attendance may do hurt.

The House of Commons has given way upon one material point, in which at present [I] agree with them, unless it shall appear that I misunderstood them.

Upon all vexatious proceedings in collecting Church cess or Church rates, of course such proceedings are to be removed.

With respect, however, to continuing the liability of Catholics to pay Church cess or rates, I cannot agree to discontinuing their obligation to pay them.

I consider the question whether they should be continued or discontinued as involving a question of no less importance than this: 'Whether we ought or ought not to have a national Established Church connected with the State.' If we are to have *such* a Church, I conceive that there must rest an obligation upon *all persons*, members of that State, to contribute to its support—whether the support of its fabric, its buildings, or its Ministers. To this liability all, though not attending upon the service of the Established Church, the national Church, connected with the State—all have purchased their property subject to that liability—all purchasers have had allowances on the price of purchase on that account. If the national Established Church is not to have its fabrics supported by the *nation—the members of that nation*—how is the right of the ministers of that Church to tithes etc. as their means of support *as such ministers* to be vindicated?

I could pursue this point much more but I forbear.

I cannot agree to the demolition of the ten bishopricks—and that too, meditated in a country where I understand there are 27 Roman Catholic bishops.

I don't find fault with the Irish proclamation against processions in Ireland on the 12th of July. Why the Lord-Lieutenant permitted the procession of Roman Catholic bishops, priests, etc. upon the consecration of a Roman Catholic edifice the other day I know not.

If my memory does not deceive me, one reason for the Union and the strong passages in the Act of Union was by making Ireland and England one kingdom and the Churches of both one Church for ever. It was to found and establish in one kingdom one established, national, Protestant Church, with respect to which in the same one kingdom Protestants might be numerically contrasted with Roman Catholics numerically considered.

I think the clause, which is given up for the reason assigned that there is no fund with respect to which the question, whether though arising from property belonging to Protestant establishments, it can be applied to secular purposes, is unfortunately given up. It will be made from year to year the subject of application to Parliament and discussion, till it may after a lapse of several years be a decided subject the wrong way.

I fear if we are beat in committee—indeed if such be the case I think the fate of the whole Bill is probably decided.

I am told there is reason to believe that some of the bishops will fail to oppose, if persons, laymen of influence, give way upon any point of principle.

Dated Tuesday 9th. *Docketed* 1833, July 9.

On the fourth sheet of the above there is another letter by Eldon, dated 9 July 1833, to an unnamed correspondent. On a separate sheet there is the following from Eldon to Wellington:

You will see that I have, by mistake, written the enclosed upon a sheet of paper which I can't destroy without destroying part of what I have taken a great liberty in addressing to you.

Lady Salisbury's diary, 10 July 1833[1]

Met the Duke of Cumberland, Duke of Wellington, Sir R. Peel, Lords Lyndhurst, Wicklow, Mansfield, Londonderry and others of the Tory leaders at Lord Falmouth's at dinner. The Duke appeared much worried—he had previously told me that at a meeting held on the eighth, the Primate of Ireland had declared that if so much of the Irish Church Bill was not passed as provided for the payment of the vestry cess, the Irish Church must fall. In pursuance of this view the Duke wished to allow the second reading of the Bill to pass with a view to amendments in the committee, and a larger meeting including some of the Ultras was assembled on this day (the 10th) to deliberate upon it. He had apparently found them very unmanageable and exclaimed when I heard him speak on the subject in the evening, 'I have but two objects in view—to save this great party from being split, and to secure the Irish Church, and those two are incompatible.'

---

[1] Frances Mary, 1st wife of James Brownlow William Gascoyne-Cecil, 2nd Marquess of Salisbury.

The Bishop of Exeter to Wellington, 11 July 1833

9 Mansfield Street. I venture to submit to your Grace's better judgment a string of resolutions, embodying a scheme both for abolishing vestry cess, and for reform of anomalies in the Church of Ireland.

Hastily as it has been drawn up, it may yet serve as the frame-work, on which a better plan may be constructed. My object has been to meet the evils commonly complained of by reasonable people, without violating any principles of Church government, or of property.

Should your Grace finally resolve to oppose the second reading of the Irish Church Temporalities Bill, perhaps you would deem it not inexpedient to announce at the same time your wish to promote a measure founded on such resolutions, after they shall have been duly corrected and matured.

I have not had time to take a copy of the resolutions which I take the liberty of transmitting to your Grace.

Dated 11 July. *Docketed* 1833, July 11.

Enclosure:

1. That it is expedient that compulsory assessment by vestries in Ireland for the building, rebuilding, and repairing of churches, and other such like purposes, and for providing things necessary for the due performance of divine worship, be abolished; and that in lieu thereof, a charge of not more than $1\frac{1}{2}$ in the pound of annual rent of all lands not now in lease, or not occupied by the lessee, and of all other lands, so soon as any leases on which they are now held, shall determine.
2. That it is expedient that no benefices with cure of souls be in future held in plurality in Ireland.
3. That [it] is expedient that many parishes, now in union with other parishes, be made separate benefices; and that parishes, which are inconveniently large in extent, be divided, and separate ministers appointed to the different parts.
4. That it is expedient that the income of small benefices be augmented, in such manner that none be of less annual value than £200.
5. That it is expedient that the stipends to be assigned to curates in Ireland be raised, according to the rule now established by law in England.
6. That it is expedient that all parsonages, tythes, or portions of

tythes, now appropriated to archbishops, or bishops, be disappropriated, and transferred to the vicars, or other ministers of the parishes, where they accrue, on the next vacancies of such sees—provided that the income of no bishop be thereby reduced below £4000 per annum.

7. That it is expedient that the inducements to translation from one bishopric to another be removed, and therefore that the income of the several bishoprics be brought nearer to an equality.

8. That it is expedient to effect this by enabling the present archbishops and bishops (with such consents and approbation as shall be deemed proper, especially with the consent and approbation of His Majesty) to dispose of such portions of the property of their respective sees, either by giving the same, or parts thereof, by way of augmentation to small livings, or by selling the same, and transferring the proceeds of such sales to the Board of First Fruits, to be applied to the like purposes as Archbishop Boulter's fund is applied to.

9. That the Archbishop of Armagh be in like manner enabled to dispose of portions of the property belonging to his see, in such manner that the income remaining to future incumbents be £10,000 per annum, and the Archbishop of Dublin, so that the income of future incumbents be not less than £7,000 per annum.

10. That on the next avoidance of the archiepiscopal see of Tuam, the archiepiscopal and metropolitan powers over the province of Connaught be transferred to and always thereafter held by the Lord Primate, provided that the Lord Primate, who shall be living at the time of such vacancy, shall choose to accept the same. And in like manner (and on like condition) that the archiepiscopal powers over the province of Munster be transferred to the Archbishop of Dublin.

11. That in contemplation of such transfers the Archbishops of Cashell and Tuam be enabled to dispose of such portions of the property of their sees as shall (with like consents, and for like purposes) assimilate those sees to other bishoprics when they shall cease to be archbishoprics.

12. That an annual tax be levied on all livings in the gift of the Crown, or of any archbishop or bishop, above the value of [1] per annum—such tax to vary according to the different value of such livings, on a scale to be settled hereafter—to accrue after the next avoidance of each living, and to be paid to the Board of Irish Fruits for the augmentation of small livings.

---

[1] Blank in MS.

Wellington to the Bishop of Exeter, 11 July 1833

London. If I had the power of proposing and carrying any measure in relation to the Irish Church, the resolutions which you have sent me might be as good a ground work as any other that could be proposed. But it is obvious that I am not likely to have such power and that such resolutions even if they could be carried could not be carried in the House of Lords or proposed at any time without the certainty of being rejected, and not even mentioned in these times without occasioning the greatest inconvenience and injury. To mention such a plan in debate would only draw the discussion from the mischievous plan of the Government to that which he who should promulgate the new plan should propose.

I never despaired of the publick cause before. It is quite clear to me that the Church of Ireland is gone. I can understand that a bishop cannot vote for destructive principles which may be applied to the Church of England in this country. But I cannot understand statesmen who see the state of the case clearly, who are unable to point out any road of safety to the solution of the difficulties of the times and of the country, should what they call adhere to a principle and see the ruin of the Church in the sister kingdom and do nothing to assist in extricating it from its difficulties. I have done my best and I will continue to perform my duty according to the best of my judgement. But I hope that I shall not be blamed if acting from my own judgement, misfortunes follow for which I shall not be responsible. Those who are taking the course which I deprecate upon this occasion joined with the Whigs to break up the last Government. I believe they have bitterly repented of their conduct. I only hope that they may not have renewed and greater cause to repent the course which they are now about to follow.

The Earl of Jersey to Wellington, 12 July 1833

Berkeley Square. Your note is dated July *11* and you say tomorrow at 12. I have this moment received it—½ past 4—but presuming that you mean tomorrow, Saturday, I shall with pleasure obey your summons.

The question you have to decide is a difficult one: from *numbers* of our friends, I do not mean peers, I have heard an anxious wish that we should not give the country a cause for saying that we will not hear of improvement in ecclesiastical matters. They hold language much in the spirit and tone of the petition presented by the Archbishop of Canterbury yesterday.

Numbers of course are for the principle of any interference or alteration.

The language of the friends of Government as to their retiring is very strong should this Bill be rejected (not that they would retire). How far has Sir R. Peel committed himself by publick approval of any part?

Should we alter it in any material parts this House of Commons will never be brought to pass it.

Should we knock it on the head at once and Ministers take the opportunity of escaping from endless difficulties which surround them, could a Government be formed?

PS. Excuse so long a note in answer to yours.

Dated July 12. *Docketed* 1833, July 12. From Lord Jersey. In answer to the Duke's note begging him to call upon him to consider of the course to be taken by the House of Lords upon the Irish Church Bill.

The Bishop of Exeter to Wellington, 13 July 1833

9 Mansfield Street. Though quite convinced of the necessity and duty of acting as I have already announced, and though I cannot but trust in God that the issue will be favourable, yet I enter deeply and warmly into your Grace's feelings.

I intended to have called on Lord Ellenborough this morning, for the purpose of communicating with him on a matter which, if he concurred in my view, I should have requested him to communicate to your Grace.

By a note which I have just received from him, I find that he is about to go to your Grace; I therefore scruple not to throw my suggestion before you.

It appears to me, that if your Grace should think fit to express yourself as generally ready and desirous to concur in any tolerable mode of settling the question connected with the Irish Church, and if some other leading lay Lord—Lord Harrowby had occurred to me—would give notice that if this Bill should be rejected on the second reading, he would be prepared to move a string of resolutions, embodying a plan of Irish Church reform, and of proposing that if they should have the concurrence of the House of Lords, they should be sent to the other

House of Parliament for their concurrence in order that a Bill or Bills might be brought in, founded upon them—a collision might be avoided, or much mitigated.

Your Grace will, I hope, forgive my obtruding this suggestion.

Dated 13 July. *Docketed* 1833, July 13.

Wellington to the Bishop of Exeter, 13 July 1833

London. If a practicable course is to be founded upon the decision of any man, it is absolutely necessary that that decision should be founded upon a knowledge of all the details bearing upon the case.

You recommend a course which you admit may lead to a collision with the House of Commons, and you recommend a mode of avoiding this evil. That it will occur sooner or later is very probable. But whenever it does occur it is desireable that it should be the House of Commons and not the House of Lords which throws the first stone. Why is it probable that there will be a collision? Because it is in the nature of things since the Reform Bill. Because the House of Commons have already indicated an inclination to such a collision. Because the Government have more than once manifested at least an indifference to the existence of such a misfortune. I make no doubt that many of them deprecate it. All foresee that it is probable and they are determined that occur when it may the blame shall rest with the House of Lords and not with their measures, the House of Commons, or above all themselves.

Am I right in these views of the case? If I am can I recommend to any body a course manifestly on the face of it inconsistent with the known privileges of the Commons, which in the best of times would have been resented by that House, but which in these times would be exaggerated and aggravated into an insult and all its consequences? My dear Lord, we must look, at least I must look, at things as they really are. I cannot recommend to any body the course which you suggest.

Wellington to the Duke of Hamilton, 13 July 1833

London. I send your Grace the inclosed petition which I have received this morning because your Grace's name is mentioned in it.

The course which ought to be followed upon this petition as well as upon others is to present it to the House of Lords if respectfully worded, and it is not inconsistent with the orders of the House. But I cannot present a petition in which your Grace's name is mentioned without communicating it to your Grace in the first instance.

The Duke of Hamilton to Wellington, 13 July 1833

Portman Square. I have the honor to acknowlege the receipt of your Grace's letter of this day, inclosing a petition entrusted to your Grace's care from the town of Hamilton to be presented to the House of Lords.

Nothing can be more handsome nor more obliging than your Grace's conduct, and I beg leave, in saying this, to subjoin many thanks. In regard to the petition, your Grace has been called upon to do a publick duty. In performing that duty your Grace will of course use your own discretion. In permitting me to see the petition before it is made publick, I recognize an additional proof of that candour and delicacy that never fails to distinguish your Grace's conduct. It is my purpose to be in the House of Lords tomorrow and next day; when, if I should feel myself, however reluctantly, compelled to talk of self, I think I shall be able to point out the unreasonableness of the petition in question.

Viscount Hereford to Wellington, 13 July 1833

Tregoyd, Hay. I have been honored with your Grace's letter containing a proxy which I readily return duly signed. Your Grace does me the favor to enquire if I entertain any particular opinion upon the Irish Church Bill. I have no hesitation in expressing my desire to resist all the reforms in Church and State as suggested by His Majesty's present Government, but I must not disguise from your Grace the dread I entertain of the consequences which may result if a collision between the two Houses of Parliament was to occur.

To your Grace I willingly confide the disposal of my proxy, accompanied with an assurance that I hold myself always ready to attend in person if I am honored with an intimation of your wishes to that effect.

The Duke of Buckingham and Chandos to Wellington, 13 July 1833

Buckingham House. Private. I shall attend your meeting tomorrow. But if what I hear is true I shall do so with a heavy heart. Rumour says that you have acquiesced in the advice of those who have expressed an opinion that a division upon the second reading of the Church Bill should not be attempted. *If this be true*, for God's sake reflect that the party will immediately be broken up by such a decision. That a very different result was anticipated by your language in the House of Lords, that in consequence of that language many of your friends have pledged themselves to oppose the principle of the measure, and that they neither can nor will retreat; and that should Sir Robert Peel, influenced by whatever motives, decline to cooperate in Government in the House of Commons, there are many who feel that their duty calls upon them to rescue the country out of the hands in which it is placed, with the least possible delay, although he may shrink from that duty, or not consider it as imperative as I do.

The Marquess of Salisbury to Wellington, c. 13 July 1833
(fragment)

. . . would justify me in offering it as a suggestion.

But there is a greater objection than those to which I have alluded upon which it would be presumptuous in me to offer an opinion. Your Grace deems it nearly impossible to form an Administration if these Ministers resigned, and here I come to the point which induced me to trouble you with these observations.

Upon this rests the question whether or not we are considering our conduct on the Irish Church Bill upon its true basis. It is obvious that the difficulty amounting almost to impossibility of forming an Administration is an argument which equally applies to an opposition to the second and to the third reading of the bill unless we can expect such a change of circumstances in the interval between the two readings as materially to change our position in the country. It is matter of consideration therefore whether the abandonment of the principle of the bill on your Grace's part would have any other result but to weaken the confidence placed in you by the Ultra Tory party, without any corresponding advantage. There can be little doubt now that we should be defeated on the second reading. The bill is not capable of much improvement without interference with its financial part. Improvements such as we *could* make might still be made in committee and we are precluded from throwing it out on the third reading. I would also submit to your Grace that if it be impossible to form a new Administration it might be expedient to place the question in a point of view in which few have hitherto considered it *and* not upon the individual defects and merits of the bill. It might be expedient to explain to the parties most hostile to the bill the full extent of the sacrifice which is to be expected from them as otherwise the divergence of opinion will be carried to an extent . . .

SALISBURY MSS.

Note on the preceding by Wellington

There is some difference in throwing out the bill upon the second or the third reading. I should doubt the expediency of it on either. What I contend for is this. Let him who pretends take care what he is about. He must be prepared to go through with his work even to the extremity of laying his head upon the block. If he is not he is either a traitor to the King; or a fool. But I go farther and say that if I was certain of being able to form a Government tomorrow some parts of this bill or some such bill must pass. I cannot myself nor could I ask others to throw it out on one day; and to vote for another the next.

Then observe that we are in the middle of July! I regret all this as much as any body. It is not my fault.

Let those who have produced these evils reflect well before they have produced others as great in another form; by creating a fresh schism with as little ground as there was heretofore.

SALISBURY MSS.

Lady Salisbury's diary, 13 July 1833

3 o'clock. Lord Salisbury just come back from a meeting at the Duke of Wellington's. Lords Ellenborough, Aberdeen, Rosslyn, the Duke of Buccleuch and ten or twelve others attended. Lord Roden was not summoned but having been appointed to have an audience of the Duke at another hour he called either intentionally or accidentally at the time of the meeting and was admitted. A majority of the meeting

were in favour of passing the second reading. The Duke does not consider himself in any way pledged by his speech of the other night. He did not announce which way he happened to vote himself, but it was decided that no attempt should be made by his party to throw out the Bill on the second reading. Some recommend that he should vote against the second reading directing his friends to vote for it, as a means of conciliating the Ultras, without running the risk of displacing the Ministry, for which the Duke is of opinion the country is not ripe.

We dined at Lord Brownlow's to meet the Duke of Gloucester. I sat next Lord Falmouth who was not aware of what had passed in the morning and seemed anxious to discover from me the Duke's intentions. He at first said that he conceived the Duke to be pledged—I told him I did not believe it was so considered by his friends—he then declared that if it were not so and if the Duke did not oppose the second reading, he would have nothing more to do with it, and should retire into the country—he had always been a Church and King man etc. etc. I assured him I knew nothing of what was to happen and tried to soothe him but in vain. He is a pompous fool: but I am afraid most of his party will have the same feelings. It is enough to drive the Duke mad. The Ultras are honest, but their wrong-headedness has ruined the country once and probably will again.

Earl de la Warr to Wellington, 14 July 1833

Buckhurst Park, East Grinstead. I have this moment heard from authority which I can not doubt that you have come to the determination of not opposing the second reading of the Irish Church Bill, considering all the circumstances of difficulty, present and future, which seem to surround the case.

I am prevented by the very melancholy and wholly unlooked for death of poor Lord Plymouth from personally communicating with you on this subject, and being uncertain what the feelings *now* may be of many of my friends, I shall venture to enclose my proxy *to you* as soon as I receive one from London, with a request that you will have the goodness to consider it as placed at your *entire disposal* upon this question.

PS. I was giving Lord Plymouth's proxy against the Local Courts Bill, at the very moment when he was seized with apoplexy on board his yacht at Deptford.

Viscount Strangford to Wellington, 14 July 1833

Most confidential. You will, I know, forgive me for troubling you, and for appearing to meddle in matters that don't belong to me.

I accompanied Lord Londonderry last night, from Lord Brownlow's, to the Carlton Club. I was very anxious that he should see your Grace before he went to the Duke of Buckingham's, because in his mood of mind I thought it quite requisite that something should be done to prevent him from communicating *his* views to others, and getting them to act upon those views. He was not so fortunate as to see your Grace. We then went to the Duke of Buckingham's where we found the Duke of Cumberland and others. A great deal was said (and not very temperately said) on the same subject as that which formed the Duke of Buckingham's letter to your Grace, which he shewed us. I hope I did some little good, but do not flatter myself that so humble a person could do much. It was settled that *before* your Grace's meeting today certain High Tory peers are to be summoned to meet the Duke of Cumberland at Holdernesse House, where he is to communicate to them his determination to oppose the second reading, to get them to concur in that determination, and to charge the Duke of Buckingham to communicate this intention at the subsequent meeting at Apsley House. I have thought it right that you should know all this in time. The ground they take is, the danger of the breaking up of the party (as if the very step which they are taking did not tend more than any thing else to break it up), and the position in which they allege that they have placed themselves in consequence of your Grace's speech of Thursday night. If something be not done, I fear (from the language held last night) that we shall again witness a *split* worse than that of 1829.

Once more forgive all this, and attribute it solely to my sincere devotion to your Grace—which I will shew, even at the risque of appearing presumptuous.

Dated Sunday evening, 8 o'clock. *Docketed* 1833, July 14.

Lord Downes to Wellington, 14 July 1833

Bert House, Athy. I received yesterday evening your Grace's note of the 11th instant. I fear that I have done very wrong in pairing off with the Duke of Leinster on the Church Reform Bill, but as yet there has been no breach of faith committed which would justify me in declaring off, as Lord Cloncurry had a fair right to give in the Duke's proxy on the Local Jurisdiction Bill, my engagement with him having been confined to the Church Bill. I saw the Duke of Leinster this morning and urged him to let me off the engagement, but I did not succeed in persuading him to do so. He told me that on leaving London he gave his proxy to the Duke of Richmond and that he had acquainted the Duke of Richmond with the circumstance of his having paired off with me on the Church Bill only, and he did not conceive that any mistake could arise. He thinks that Lord Cloncurry is coming over immediately to Ireland, as he had received a letter from him dated Lymington, Warwickshire, but in this the Duke may be mistaken. He also told me that he had just received a letter from Lord Holland about his attending Parliament, in answer to which he told him that he had paired off with me on the question which most interested him.

Under these circumstances I do not think that I can vote on the Church Bill, but if there is any other question likely to come on in the House I shall be ready to set off at an hour's notice, should my presence be required.

Lady Salisbury's diary, 14 July 1833

Another meeting at the Duke's which was attended by some of those who were present at the last—Lord Salisbury among others. The Duke of Buckingham and Lord Londonderry most opposed to the intended plan of action. The latter went so far as to say that it was useless to summon him and his friends there when the line of conduct was already determined upon and asked why it was deemed impossible to form an Administration as he concluded that was the chief objection to throwing out the Bill.

Altogether a most violent attack upon the Duke, who turned red with indignation, an unusual mark of emotion with him, but answered it extremely well and with great dignity. He said that he made no decision for others and assumed no power to himself, that he was there, happy to give his opinion to those noble Lords who did him the honor to ask it—as to forming an Administration he could give no opinion as to the possibility or impossibility of it, until he received the King's commands to do so and there would certainly be great difficulties attending it. There was at all events a great difference between making every effort to extricate the King from an embarrassing situation when he found himself there, and plunging him into it: whoever undertook the latter must be prepared to go through with his work, even to the extremity of laying his head upon the block: if not, he would be either a fool or a traitor. 'It is very well', he added, 'for those who sit still in their rooms to talk of sacrificing everything to principle: I am a practical man, I have always been a practical man, and before I undertake a thing I must be satisfied that it is possible to go through with it.'

With respect to the third reading he gave no positive opinion. In an answer to a memorial Lord Salisbury addressed to him he added the following remarkable words, 'Were I certain of being able to form a Government tomorrow some parts of the bill or some such bill must pass. I could not myself nor could I ask others to throw this out one day and vote for another the next—I regret all this as much as anybody. But it is not *my* fault. Let *those* who have produced these evils reflect well before they produce others as great in another form, by creating a fresh schism with as little ground as there was heretofore.'

Lord Carbery to Wellington, 16 July 1833

As your Grace was understood to be the person to whom the amendments intended to be proposed are to be entrusted, I may be at liberty to suggest one which seems to me of some importance. Assuming first that as many bishoprics as can be spared shall remain, in order as far as possible to preserve the representation of the hierarchy of the Established Church, I am persuaded if the thing be rightly managed four or five or at the most six will be the utmost that will be required. Well then the Bill provides that the residences in all those reduced sees shall be sold. The whole value of them would not produce a very large sum, indeed in such great transaction the amount would be immaterial. But in point of fact it goes a step further in the annihilation of the Protestant Establishment. I would therefore suggest that these residences should not be sold but reserved to the bishops as mansal lands and houses. Where there is only a house as at Waterford some allowance might be made to the bishop for keeping it up, or he might let it on the regulation of manual leases only for his own life. Where there are domains as at Clogher they would be an acquisition to the see, a benefit rather than a disadvantage. But independent of personal consideration it would seem to be good policy to reserve them.

The making this reservation would affect no money clause. It would be only to expunge the clause in the Bill which authorizes the sales.

Already there are hints abroad of three residences being purchased for the Roman Catholic bishops. Of this I am assured, particularly as to Cork, while that see residence was supposed to be transferred to Clogher. Waterford is the next city in magnitude to Cork. Query could not the bishop be required to reside occasionally there?

Dated Tuesday morning 16th. *Docketed* 1833, July 16.

Lord Manners to Wellington, 16 July 1833

Upper Brook Street. I must beg of your Grace to take my proxy into your hands, and as I am very sure that you have well considered the subject in all its bearings I wish you to make that use of it that you think most conducive to the interests of the country.

I am too ill of the gout to attempt being present, but I am very sure that my proxy will be right.

Dated July 16th. *Docketed* 1833, July 16.

Wellington to Viscount Ferrard, 16 July 1833

London. I have received your Lordship's note.

I conclude that the House of Lords will agree to the second reading of the Irish Church Bill and that the Bill will go into a committee. I don't know whether there will be power to alter the Bill in the committee. If there should be such power I will attend to your suggestions.

Wellington to the Bishop of Exeter, 16 July 1833

London. I told you that you should hear from me in case anything should come under discussion in Parliament which should be interesting.

We are likely to have tomorrow the Local Courts Bill. Lord Brougham's speech of December 1830 has not been replied to; and the report of the commisioners of judicial enquiry in favour of the measure has never yet been discussed in the House of Lords. I have recommended to Lord Lyndhurst therefore that tomorrow should be devoted to the purpose of enlightening the publick mind upon the question; that we should not divide to prevent the Bill from being considered by a committee; but that we should after consideration reject it if rejection should be the course determined on upon the report or the third reading. I don't yet know whether he will follow my advice; or whether he or I can prevent the members of the House from dividing. But I recommend to the spiritual lords not to be driven into a division tomorrow; and for this reason I would recommend that they should not attend.

Wellington to the Earl of Harewood, 16 July 1833

London. Since I saw you last night I have seen what I believe to be a correct copy of the resolutions of the House of Commons on the emancipation of negro slaves.

I consider that by far the best mode if not the only mode of executing the purpose of Government is to leave the execution to the colonial legislatures. Any other mode of proceeding will lead to a contest in the legislative colonies, particularly in Jamaica and perhaps Barbadoes, of which no man can in tranquillity contemplate the consequences. I should think that the resolutions point out too minutely the mode of execution. But it is better that they should go in that form rather than in the form of a law.

There will still remain the crown colonies in which the Government must by Order in Council institute the model of the system which they intend should be generally established. Among these is the island of Mauritius. The subject is a most difficult one; and much more likely to be well considered in His Majesty's Council than in Parliament. And considering that the object of it is to change a nation of negro slaves into a nation of free men and apprentices, I should think that it was to be very desirable to leave to those who are to execute the purpose of the Government as much discretion as may be possible. The Government, the West India proprietors, and the House of Commons having agreed to these resolutions and the intention being to refer them for execution to the colonial legislatures, it does not appear to me that the House of Lords can oppose itself to that course of proceeding. Having been in the Cabinet in the year 1830 and having been a party to the Order in Council of March 1830 and having taken part in other discussions upon the subject I must state my opinion of these resolutions, if they should come to the House of Lords. But I don't believe that any party in the House can wish to reject them.

Earl Howe to Wellington, 18 July 1833

Windsor Castle. I go to Cowes for a day or two tomorrow morning but shall come up whenever I am wanted, I suppose on the 15th. I imagine that you are aware that Lord Grey has informed His Majesty *that at his next beating he leaves*! I *know* from the *best* authority he has said so. Whether he will keep to this intention or not is quite another thing. At the same time I thought it right to tell you this. The crisis is rather unpleasant, but perhaps not more than the inevitable *gradual* ruin which now stares us in the face.

Dated Thursday. *Docketed* 1833, July 18.

The Bishop of Oxford (Richard Bagot) to Wellington, 19 July 1833

Canterbury. Private. I trust your Grace will forgive my troubling you with a few lines, but being anxious to be of any use I can, and at the same time being placed in some difficulty as to moving from this place, I wish to be guided by your Grace.

I write under the full impression that the Irish Church Bill has passed the second reading, though I have not yet heard the result of the division.

Inconvenient as it will be to me I will certainly attend the committee if it is desirable I should do so, as I find very few other bishops can remain in London, but I do not think it will be possible for me to be in town before the middle of next week. Perhaps your Grace will have the goodness to let me know when you think I should be most wanted, and to give me as much of next week as can safely be granted.

The Bishop of Durham has placed his proxy in my hands for the third reading.

Sir Robert Peel to Wellington, 20 July 1833

Whitehall. Private. I think you must have misunderstood Lord Grey as to his intention of withdrawing the clause respecting incumbencies in Ireland in which service has not been performed for three years before a given day named in the Bill. There is an article in *The Times* this morning strongly in vindication of that particular clause, which would hardly have appeared if the intention to withdraw the clause had been announced or was entertained.

I am confident (even if you should not agree with me) that you will excuse me for pressing upon your notice the following considerations before you enter upon the committee of the Bill.

First. Is it possible to form a Government which shall command a majority in the present House of Commons—or which shall either in this or in any future House of Commons pass those Bills which are essential for the maintenance of the Church in Ireland? I allude particularly to the provision of a substitute for church cess—and also to the infinitely more important question, the provision of a substitute for tithe. Unless this latter substitute be immediately found, there is an end in my opinion both of tithe and of any equivalent for it.

I mention this the more because I find that some peers, who are most bent on throwing out the Church Bill, have never considered the position of the Irish Church with respect to tithe.

But I will not trouble you with details. I will only mention those points which should I think be well considered before the present Government has a fair cause given to it for escaping from its difficulties by resignation.

Can thirty seats be vacated as they must be to enable the King to form a Government? Can the present Parliament be dissolved without the remaining estimates having been voted, and is there a chance that the present Parliament will vote them?

In case the King should fail in forming a Government, or having formed one that Government should be unable to maintain itself—will not the democratic party in this country be greatly strengthened?

Looking at the influence given to the dissenting interest in elections, is not a Church question, and particularly one connected with the Church in Ireland, a very unfavourable one for a general election?

Does not the present state of the West India question present in itself alone a very serious difficulty in the way of the formation of a Government? Both Houses of Parliament have pledged themselves to resolutions which it is equally difficult now either to enforce or to abandon, and yet the promise of immediate emancipation has gone forth to the West Indies.

I have so strong an opinion on these points, and I differ so much from many of our friends as to the prospect and as to the advantage of gaining the support of Radicals for a Government acting on really

Conservative principles, that I could not help writing to you, though I have little doubt that every thing I have said has already occurred to your own mind.

Wellington to Sir Robert Peel, 23 July 1833

London. I did not write to you yesterday as I had persons here all day upon the amendments of the Church Bill.

We shall not be able to do it much good. But I think that if there should be a serious division in the House of Lords, it will be upon some point of importance on which the Government will be manifestly in the wrong.

The majority in the House of Lords, however, are decidedly against the bill. It is very difficult to restrain them; and they are very much displeased. But it is better to displease them than to increase and aggravate the confusion of the times.

I quite concur in your opinion of the state of the House of Commons, of the consequences of breaking down the Government by a vote of the House of Lords, and of the prospects from a new election. But it is not so easy to make men feel that they are of no consequence in the country who have heretofore had so much weight and still preserve their properties and their stations in society and their seats in the House of Lords. The true sense of their position will be imposed at last; when they will become more manageable.

ADD MS 40309, ff. 264–265.

The Earl of Elgin to Wellington, 23 July 1833

Broom Hall. Availing myself of your kind permission to lay before you any suggestion which may strike me as deserving notice, and especially when, as in the present instance, I request you not to be at the trouble of any reply to me, I beg leave to express a very strong conviction that if the celibacy of the Catholic clergy could be done away with in Great Britain and Ireland (it being not an original doctrine of the Church of Rome, but one more recently introduced, decidedly in a view to the advantage of priestcraft rather than as an injunction of the Gospel)— if this could be effected, the political objections to the Catholic religion would in one material point be lessened, and the tendency removed which now so prejudicially operates on the Catholic clergy to alienate them as a body from the social virtues and interests which they otherways would share with the rest of the community.

I do not pretend to enter into any detail of the considerations by which the influential members of the Catholic body, whether laymen or ecclesiastics, might be reconciled to such a measure: but it may be presumed that since the removal of disabilities has placed every individual of that persuasion essentially on the same footing with his fellow citizens, anything so unnatural, and in itself so objectionable, as the celibacy of our native clergy cannot be sustained as a rational institution, to be upheld after their Church has been so freely sanctioned amongst us.

To Protestants, on the other hand, and to all, on an enlightened view of the best interests of religion in the country, there can be no doubt that the removal of every peculiarity in the machinery of Catholicism, which tends to keep up an esprit de corps in the way of freedom of discussion on its tenets, must be an object of paramount importance if, as it cannot be denied, many of the leading and very obnoxious errors of the Catholic religion arise out of misrepresentations of unquestionable truths.

I take the liberty of offering this suggestion, at the present crisis, because, however ignorant I may be of the proceedings and intentions relative to the Irish Church spoliation bill, still I think circumstances may occur in the progress of that discussion to admit an opening for recommending this measure.

The Archbishop of Cashel (Richard Laurence) to Wellington, 23 July 1833

Cashel. I feel that many apologies are requisite for my troubling your Grace on the present occasion; but I cannot relinquish my feeling respecting the important measure now before the House of Lords, the progress of which through the Commons I have watched with so much anxiety. On one point I am particularly interested. I do not wish either for myself or successors to have the whole diocese of Waterford united to that of Cashel. Waterford ought not to be left without a resident bishop; but as the Bill now stands it is very likely to be left so. But what I am desirous of pointing out to your Grace more particularly is an incongruity in the Bill with respect to other bishopricks. By the

39th section it is enacted that when Ossory and Ferns are united the residence of the bishop shall be in the see house of Ossory, and so also when Cork and Cloyne are united the residence of the bishop shall be at Cork. The reason for this is obvious. But no notice is taken upon a similar principle of *Derry and Raphoe*. When the Bishop of Raphoe dies, the Bishop of Derry will be enabled to make choice of the see house at Raphoe, and give up that at Derry altogether; and this I know he is not only willing but very anxious to do. Ought Derry to be forsaken? It is the only other town residence of a bishop which will be affected by the Bill. May I take the liberty of suggesting to your Grace the propriety of having this case also inserted in the 39th section?

I some time since suggested to Government and also to Sir R. Peel the reduction of *six* only instead of *ten* bishopricks, preserving Waterford, Cloyne, Elphin, and Raphoe. There would then be twelve episcopal and four archiepiscopal turns for the rotation in Parliament, so that the cycle would be still complete. But I have not succeeded; and I fear that Waterford is too fast in the gripe of the revolutionary monster to hope for a rescue. Administration has indeed been kind enough to obviate two of the objections to the first plan, which I made by retaining an episcopal residence at Kilkenny and Cork; but they have forgotten, or will not look, at Derry.

I must confess that some of the defects (may I not say of the iniquities?) of the first Bill are removed. I will not therefore trouble your Grace with any detailed remarks upon it.

It has been urged in favor of the measure that the commissioners will be enabled by it to build churches and glebe houses. I fear however that this power is clogged with such restrictions as will render it generally useless. For no grant is to be made by them for building a church unless *twenty* at least of the inhabitants of the parish will bind themselves to contribute by voluntary subscription *one fourth* of the whole expence (section 76); or for building a glebe house, unless the incumbent enter into a bond *with one or more sufficient sureties* for the execution of the work and the annual repayment of the loan during his whole incumbency (section 83). Your Grace, I doubt not, knows enough of this country to be persuaded that in very few cases indeed twenty subscribing parishioners will ever be procured; and that sureties for the purpose of securing payments etc under the incumbent's bond seem wholly out of the question. But in the last case reference is made to 43 George III, c. 106, section 47 and the words of that Act are

copied into the present Bill, but with the difference of a little addition
to them, and that is the addition of the very words objected to 'with
one or more sufficient sureties'. I am convinced, unless these obstacles
are removed, the powers given to the commissioners will in most
instances prove nugatory.

The Earl Cathcart to Wellington, 25 July 1833

Berbeth, by Ayr. I beseech you to pardon this interruption. But I have
been so urgently solicited that I could not refuse to acquaint you that
the magistrates and council of Glasgow have deputed Mr. Archibald
McLellan, Deacon Convenor of that Royal Borough, and most important and populous city, to deliver to your Grace and to require you to
present to the House of Lords a petition of the burgesses of that city,
stated to be extremely respectably as well as numerously signed, against
the *Royal Burgh Reform Bill*, now waiting for a second reading, 'setting
forth the effect it would have, if passed, upon the community, its large
funds, and extensive and wealthy charities; depriving the burgesses of
the management and benefit of property arising from and vested in
these different institutions to the amount of more than half a million'.
I have no knowledge of my own concerning these allegations except
that I believe them to be true. All I undertake is to take the liberty of
recommending and naming to your Grace this Mr. McLellan as a
person whom I very highly esteem, and who I think most likely to give
a clear, honest and satisfactory answer to any question your Grace
might do him the honor to put concerning the petition and the matter
of it, if you condescend to present it.

Lady Salisbury's diary, 26 July 1833

The Duke called upon me: full of complaints of the Ultras who seem
indeed to have behaved very ill. The other day the Duke of Cumberland
told the Duke he wished to put a question to the Ministers about the
King's letter to the Archbishop of Canterbury. The Duke entreated
him not, upon the ground that any private correspondence which might
pass between the Archbishop and the Head of the Church was not a
subject for public inquiry. The Duke of Cumberland notwithstanding
engaged Lord Winchilsea to make the inquiry and one of the bishops

to answer it. The Duke was apprised of this as he is of most of their proceedings, and took means to prevent its going any further. The question was put but stopped. This and various grievances of the same sort perpetually recurring convinced the Duke that it was impossible for him any longer to undertake the responsibility of being nominal head of a party who acted independently of him. The Duke of Cumberland is at the bottom of all this, unable to meet the Duke or anyone in fair argument he endeavours to establish his power on intrigue. Lord Londonderry and the Duke of Buckingham are the most unreasonable. The latter who has always been open to the highest bidder, looks to nothing but office, and grows impatient at the long possession of the Whigs—in the early part of the year he took offence at the Duke about some trifle, and after sulking a little while sent him a message through some other peer to express a wish to be reconciled and to know if he should be well received. 'I have not time for lovers' quarrels,' said the Duke. 'I know nothing about it and shall be very glad to see him.' In this last committee the Duke of Newcastle, Lord Kenyon, and others were always ready to take an opportunity of attacking the Duke and recurring to the Catholic Question. In addition to all the Ultras have been holding private meetings independent of the Duke, some previous to the 14th, when the chief of them were assembled at his house ostensibly to consult with him on the line of conduct to be pursued. On Wednesday last (the 24th) the Bishop of Exeter met the Duke of Wellington going to the House of Lords and told him that he had just attended *one of their* meetings and nothing could go off more satisfactorily, nothing better than the feeling shewn towards the Duke etc. The Duke was perfectly well informed before, not only of the fact of the meetings but of all that passed there. His reply was to the effect that he was very glad to hear there was a friendly feeling towards him, that he would never quarrel with any of them, but that it was impossible he could any longer consider himself as the leader of a party who put no confidence in him and who held meetings independent of him to decide upon their own course.

Wellington to the Earl of Elgin, 27 July 1833

London. I return you many thanks for your letter. The worst of the Roman Catholic religion is that no law of the State in which it is established can reach it. The State may declare by law that the Roman

Catholic priests may marry, the Pope will answer that they shall not. The Roman Catholic congregations will, that being the case, not listen to a married priest. This is the great disorder resulting from the existence of the Roman Catholic religion, particularly in the regular form in which it exists in Ireland.

I hope that you are quite well. We have had a very fatiguing fight upon the Irish Church Bill, which we have improved in some degree. But it is still a great mischief.

Wellington to the Archbishop of Cashel, 27 July 1833

London. I had the honor of receiving your Grace's letter, and I mentioned last night in the committee of the House of Lords the subject to which you had adverted, viz. the residence of the Bishop of Derry. What I said produced no effect. But I will mention the subject to the Lord Primate of all Ireland and with his concurrence I will make another effort upon the subject upon the report of the Bill on Monday. The Bill has been improved in the committee and I hope that it will be further amended upon the report. But I cannot but think it, although some measure is necessary, the most portentous measure for the Church of Ireland that could be devised. The diminution of the number of bishops, the graduated tax upon the bishops and clergy and the sale of the fee of the bishops' estates will still remain. I cannot but think that these measures will give a severe blow to the Protestant interest in Ireland.

The Marquess of Bute to Wellington, 27 July 1833

Campden Hill. Lord Bute presents his best respects to the Duke of Wellington and takes the liberty of sending to him, enclosed, a copy of a paper which was delivered to Lord Althorp yesterday on the part of himself, Mr. Keith Douglas, and other gentlemen, regarding joint stock deposit banks.

Enclosure: Considerations on the Bank Bill.

After the panic of 1825 it became the general acknowledged opinion of the country that its banking transactions could only be securely conducted by removing the hitherto existing restriction which limited the number of partners carrying on banking business, with the exception of the Bank of England, to six partners.

Since that period by the provision of Parliament joint stock banks have been allowed to join themselves with an unlimited number of partners at a distance of sixty-five miles from London and notwithstanding a very unnecessary restriction was imposed on them of not being permitted to establish any house of agency in connection with them to employ their surplus capital, those establishments have met with great support from the public and have given great accommodation and security to the communities where they have been established.

Notwithstanding that experience has confirmed the advantages of increased security and steady accommodation to the public by the extension of the system of such banks, it is now proposed by His Majesty's Government to renew the Bank charter and impliedly to prevent any joint stock associations from being established in London or within sixty-five miles of it, thus placing the most important district of the kingdom where public credit is the most sensitive in times of difficulty in a state of danger and insecurity during the period to which it is proposed to extend the new charter; and even then the joint stock banks which are established in the country are still subject to the restriction of having no bank under their own management in London.

The first question to be asked is what can be the motive which has induced the Government to restrict more than six persons with the exception of the Bank of England from carrying on business within the prescribed limit? It cannot be from the consideration that although security and facility is afforded to other parts of the country from the establishment of joint stock banks with an unlimited number of partners, that the past history of banking within London and sixty-five miles has proved that more security has been given by private bankers than elsewhere, for if an accurate return could be got of the number of bankruptcies and of suspensions of payment which have afterwards been wound up under trust within the last twenty years within this district it would be found that the amount of capital thus withdrawn from the public has been a very extensive calamity and the public are called upon strenuously to exert themselves to prevent the perpetuation of a similar system with the like consequences for the next twenty years.

No good reason seems to be assigned for drawing a circle of sixty miles round London with a view to the limitation of the issue of no other notes than those of the Bank of England within it.

If it be thought necessary for the prevention of forgery to make a reserved circle, the grounds require to be explained why sixty-five miles is that accurate limit, but this is comparatively a small part of the consideration. No general objection is made to the Bank of England being the only bank that is to have the power of issuing notes within London and a district surrounding it, and to that extent the public is prepared to allow the Bank to have that most important monopoly, but that this monopoly is to be extended and the public deprived of the privilege of being permitted to lodge their money in and to obtain accommodation from secure banking establishments within this district appears to be as preposterous as inexplicable.

It is obvious that a joint stock bank combines all the advantages of a private bank without any of the objections to which the most substantial private bank is exposed.

To depositors a joint stock bank would insure security, the chief of all advantages.

This is an advantage which the best of private banking houses does not afford. The actual capital in each banking house *is not known*. The private debts and expences of each partner and of the members of his family and how they operate upon the banking house purse *is not known*. The private speculations in which each partner may indulge *is not known*. He may be a loser in a speculation and his partners pay up the loss out of the common fund to prevent exposure and how often this is done or may be done *is not known*. The business, other than banking, in which the partnership, tempted by expectation of profit, may engage by common consent easily obtained or by giving way to the powerful and speculating mind of one of their body *is not known*. How the private, real and personal property of each partner ostensibly backing the capital in the concern is incumbered by private debts, engagements, and family arrangements to liquidate which the property is first applicable *is not known*.

Where a private banker has fortune it is usually tied up in lands, in houses or in family settlements. His resources for his business therefore depend upon his deposits and at every period of pressure in the country he is uneasy and unsteady in his transactions with his customers and at such periods as his aid to them would be most essential he is too much busied in protecting himself to afford any protection and assistance to others.

It would be wholly different with a joint stock bank. Not one of the objections stated to private bankers as occasioning to the public a well founded doubt of their perfect security would apply to the joint stock company.

The capital is large and enough to meet the utmost demand upon it at any time made.

This capital is sacredly applicable to the debts and the business of the bank. The speculations of members of the bank, their habits of expence and those of their families, and heavy private debts might all exist yet the bank would not suffer the loss of a shilling nor be shaken in its credit to the twelfth part of that amount. The security of such a bank would be therefore solid and undeniable. From this course credit would be given to it. Never would it stand in danger of a run and always from its stock in trade in deposits and its capital subscribed it could continue to distribute judiciously and equally those accommodations to the public in times whether of quiet or of emergency which are daily and hourly wanted.

All England beyond sixty-five miles from London, the whole of Scotland, and the greater part of Ireland have the security and advantages of such joint stock banks of deposit, and it would be most injurious and unfair to the important community resident within London and sixty-five miles from it if joint stock banks should not be permitted within these limits. Much is justly said of the delay[1] of trade in the port of London. Every means should be used to avert this delay[1] and stop its progress and joint stock banks would in no inconsiderable degree help to revive London commerce from its increasing depression.

The Bank of England has a strong interest in assisting a secure system of joint stock banking in its neighbourhood. This corporation if it attended to its real interest is deeply concerned in the formation of such associations around them as give increased stability to the transactions of the country at all times, for this is the true ground on which their success and that of the proprietors must rest.

The opinion of some of the most eminent lawyers has been taken and it is considered that under the existing law a joint stock bank consisting of more than six persons might be constituted in London or within sixty-five miles subject however to some inconveniences which ought to be removed.

The public therefore feel that they have a right to it, and it is considered that Government ought to relieve them from such inconveniences rather than confirm the existing evil or make it more obnoxious than before.

---

[1] The word is clearly 'delay' but perhaps 'decay' is meant.

Some noblemen and gentlemen who have long viewed this subject as one of great national importance have associated themselves together for the purpose of exposing the injurious and unfair tendency of continuing the present restrictions upon joint stock banking within London and sixty-five miles and of adopting such measures as may afford the advantages of a joint stock bank in London for the purpose of giving increased security and accommodation to the nobility, gentry and shopkeepers and to offer a practical example of the benefits that are likely to arise from a more general formation of such establishments.

The Earl Grey to Wellington, 28 July 1833

Downing Street. Lord Grey presents his compliments to the Duke of Wellington, and has the honour of returning the clause which his Grace put into his hands the other night, with one containing the alterations which, with his Grace's consent, he would propose to make in it.

It has appeared to Lord Grey that the addition to the patronage of Trinity College, of one half of its present amount, would be as much as could be reasonably expected; and that to take more from the suppressed bishopricks would have the effect of reducing the patronage of the bishops in their dioceses too much.

It has also appeared to Lord Grey that it would be expedient to give to the archbishops alternate nominations, rather than joint nominations with an appeal.

The only other material alteration is that for giving to the bishop of the diocese the reversion of the vacant nomination, if no fellow or ex-fellow should be found willing to accept it. To this, when he proposed it in the House of Lords, Lord Grey did not understand the Duke of Wellington to object.

If the clause, thus constructed, should meet with the Duke of Wellington's concurrence, Lord Grey will propose it on the report, or leave it to his Grace to propose it, as he may think fit.

Wellington to the Earl Grey

The Duke of Wellington presents his compliments to Lord Grey. He returns his thanks for the communication of the clause regarding the grant for the benefit of Trinity College of certain benefices to which his Lordship is disposed to agree.

The Duke is satisfied with the clause proposed by his Lordship. He recommends that as the grant is one of benefit, grace and favour to the College the clause should be moved by his Lordship.

Undated.

Lord Monson to Wellington, 31 July 1833

Frankfort-on-Main. Having left Spa just previous to the introduction of the Irish Church Bill into our House, you may suppose with what anxiety I have sought for later news from England. I have yesterday seen the papers of the 24th of July and learn that you consented to pass the second reading of the Bill in hopes of amending it in committee, but I deeply regret to see that your amendment relative to the bishops was negatived by a majority of 14. Although I doubt not the question will be set at rest before you receive this letter yet I feel so strongly upon what I conceive to be the principle on which it is founded that I cannot refrain from sending you a few lines, in the hope, if you have a spare moment to waste on me, of knowing your sentiments on the subject. The two great points which struck me as most objectionable in the measure were the possibility of the appropriation of Church revenues to other than ecclesiastical purposes, and the diminution of the number of bishops. I confess myself to be one of those who consider both these acts to be unconstitutional and contrary to the solemn oath taken by His Majesty. I understand however that the former of these was given up in the House of Commons and all the property of the Church affected by the Bill still preserved to that body. With regard to the latter, as far as I can gather from the newspapers, the most hollow sophistry, the weakest, nay, the most irreligious arguments, have been used in its defence. For my own part I cannot conceive how a man having taken a lawful, voluntary, and unequivocal oath, can consider himself exempted from it whilst the circumstances under which he took it remain the same. That the King's oath should be binding in his executive and not in his legislative capacity or vice versa is to me unintelligible. I find no such distinction in the oath. George IV and the Catholic question is no argument to the purpose, being in no respect a parallel case. I fear you will think what I am going to say rather strong. Of the weakness of the King in yielding his judgement and his conscience so completely into the hands of his responsible advisers I will say nothing, but if the word 'impeachment' is not an empty sound a weightier occasion can never occur for trying its efficacy upon Ministers than at a time when they recommend His Majesty to give his assent to a measure, contrary to the constitution he has *sworn* to maintain, contrary to the rights and interests of that established national religion which he has *sworn* to uphold and protect, and to justify him in gross perjury, cram him with sophisms which would now be rejected by the most Jesuitical college in Spain, Italy or Ireland. This is a serious question. The Irish will doubtless be but the shadow of the English Church Bill— at least in principle. What occasioned the Revolution of 1688? Perjury. Our oath of allegiance to the King and his to the constitution go hand in hand. James II broke his oath by an attack on the Established Church and his people declared themselves absolved from theirs. Should William IV do the same, may not the same consequences ensue? They probably will, but not in the same justifiable manner as before. A spirit of revolution and insubordination is abroad. Our constitution has been dreadfully shaken by the Reform Bill and such an attack upon the Protestant Church of Ireland and *England*, based upon perjury, is flinging wide open the gates to admit a flood of liberalism and infidelity which will soon sweep away all the landmarks of our constitution and our religion, depriving us of both by leaving us a multiplicity of each. I trust we shall be saved from this consummation to which however I fear we are fast hastening—not from alterations and improvements. I am no *Ultra Tory* to refuse to guide the torrent which I cannot arrest. Our present difficulties and dangers are from a disregard of principles in those now in power, a mockery at experience, and a love of theories unfounded on facts, the day dreams of political economists, miscalled march of intellect. I believe that (with God's blessing) you and you only can now stay the present tendency of events. However, you of course best know. Prizing, as I do, the opinions of your Grace, I shall feel it extremely kind if you will let me have ever so few lines from you on these interesting subjects. I am very sorry to find party feeling running so disgracefully high. It is painful to see persons so far forget their own duty and their own dignity as to compromise the interests of their country for the childish gratification of indulging ill feeling towards individuals. Has the Jewish Relief Bill yet come into our House? As a *political* question I see not on what grounds it can be refused them. As a religious question, in which view some I believe regard it, it seems to me to be equally unobjectionable. The Jews respect an oath and may therefore be bound in any way the legislature may think fit. Those who see in the measure danger to our Church and the interests of Christianity had better see if they are not 'straining at a gnat and swallowing a camel'. Let them look at more open and evident attacks against that Church and faith, and in seeing about for a quagmire, mind that they do not fall into the river. I must apologise for giving you so much of my political creed but I feel that the man who undertakes to legislate for his country should keep his eye steadily fixed upon his one great object, should sacrifice all private feelings, passions and prejudices, and legislating for each class with a sole view to the aggregate prosperity of all, should be firm to his principles, his God, his country and his King. Does Lord Grey do so?

We leave here tomorrow and purpose to remain at Lucerne till the 14th of August.

The Rev. John Ellison to Wellington, 2 August 1833

Killymard Glebe, Donegal. Your Grace has proposed as an amendment to one of the clauses in the Irish Church Temporalities Bill that some of the livings now in the gift of the bishops whose bishoprics are to be suppressed should be given in trust to the Archbishops of Armagh and Dublin to be by them conferred upon the junior fellows of Trinity College, Dublin.

Your Grace, in your zeal to benefit the members of that learned college, has overlooked the very serious, nay grievous, injury, which would be inflicted upon the deserving curates of these dioceses, by taking from them the chance of promotion to those benefices which would be thus given to the fellows of the College.

Take for instance the diocese of Raphoe, which by Lord Grey's spoliation bill is to be added to Derry.

In Raphoe the patronage is thus distributed:

Description of benefice	*Patron*
The deanery	The Crown
6 perpetual curacies under the Dean	The Dean
Rectory of Taughboyne	Marquess of Abercorn
1 perpetual curacy under Rector	Rector of Taughboyne

Description of benefice	Patron
Vicarage of Kilbarron	Colonel Conolly
Rectory and Vicarage of Templecrone	Marquess Conyngham
5 rectories	Trinity College, Dublin
15 benefices	Lord Bishop of Raphoe
1 perpetual cure	Rector of Killybegs and Rector of Inniskeel alternately

There are at present 25 curates in the diocese of Raphoe, some of them of long, very long, standing. These all look to the 15 benefices in the bishop's gift as affording them the only chance of promotion, and can your Grace think it would be fair and just to lessen that chance by taking, I will not say a large proportion, but even one single benefice from this diocese of Raphoe to give it to the College of Dublin which has already five of the best livings in it.

Promotion is slow, very slow, in Raphoe. I was twenty-four years rector of a parish little better than £300 a year. About two years and a half ago I was promoted to the one I now hold (£500 a year gross) and there is but one other parish in the bishop's gift better.

I should heartily rejoice at any measure beneficial to the College of Dublin, and not injurious to the just claims and prospects of others. My father was a fellow of Trinity College, Dublin, and I believe personally acquainted with your Grace when in Ireland. I myself was a scholar of the house, and gained many under-graduate honours; and still as an ex-scholar I have a vote for the representatives in Parliament, and feel an honest pride in having given that vote at the last election for our present most valuable Members, Shaw and Lefroy.

Should your Grace have any desire to satisfy yourself that the writer of this letter is the person he represents himself to be, Colonel Conolly and Sir Edmund Hayes, our county Members, can inform you about the Rev. John Ellison, Prebendary and Rector of Killymard.

Your Grace will, I hope, excuse the liberty I take in addressing you on this subject.

Draft reply 7 August 1833. Compliments. The Duke has received his letter. The Duke is most concerned to learn that any proposition made by him in Parliament should prove disadvantageous to him.

The fact is however that the proposition made by the Duke has not been carried out complete.

The Duke did not propose that a living should be taken from each diocese; or any from those in which Trinity College had certain livings at her disposition.

Alfred Bunn to Wellington, 2 August 1833

Theatre Royal, Covent Garden. Apprehensive that your Grace's important avocations will not allow me the honor of an interview, and in the humble hope I have not been too presuming in asking it, I beg most respectfully to state the object I had in view.

The Dramatic Performance Bill is to be read *a second time tonight*. Its object is to rescind His Majesty's prerogative of being the sole arbiter of theatrical grants (defined by the present Lord Chancellor in the accompanying document), to wrest all discretion from the Lord Chamberlain, and throw open as many theatres as are asked for by party.

I have been honored by His Royal Highness the Duke of Cumberland's support, by that of His Royal Highness the Duke of Gloucester (who presented my petition last night), and by many noble Lords—amongst whom the Lord Sidmouth has signified his wish to oppose the Bill.

From the great protection your Grace has given to the vested rights of the Crown and the country, and from the known safety any cause must have your Grace may condescend to advocate, I humbly and respectfully solicit your Grace's vote *this evening* against the Dramatic Performance Bill.

Signed: A. Bunn. Lessee of the two Theatres Royal.

Wellington to the Earl of Aberdeen, 6 August 1833

London. Lord Lansdowne will not be in the House of Lords this day and does not proceed with his committee till tomorrow.

Probably you would postpone till tomorrow the presentation of your petition. Indeed, there will be nobody in the House to notice it. I was thinking of going to Hatfield to dine. But if you determine upon presenting your petition this day I will not go. I shall return in the morning if I should go.

ADD MS 43060, f. 92.

Lady Salisbury's diary, 6 August 1833

Returned with the Duke of Wellington who came to dine and pass the evening. He was in great force and very amusing about the Dukes of Gloucester and Cumberland, describing their sitting on each side of him in the House suggesting their own ideas into each ear (one of which is stone deaf) and totally preventing his attending to the speaker opposite. The Duke of Gloucester especially always proposing some impossible situation. 'And what would your Grace do under *such* a circumstance?' 'For Heaven's sake, Sir, let me just hear one word of the speech that is going on for I have to reply to it.' He told me the Ultras were behaving better and anxious to make it up with him: but he was determined to have no explanations, no *lovers' quarrels*—it would all come right. He seemed to wish Lord Salisbury to remain within reach of London till the end of the session: on that account he has put off his journey to Scotland for the present. The Duke is deserted by almost all his friends already, the session is so late—and it would be too bad to leave him to fight his battles with nothing but empty benches to back him.

Charles Bagot to Wellington, 7 August 1833

5 Arundel Street, Panton Square. I beg leave most respectfully to return my warm thanks to your Grace for the kind attention you have paid to my communication on a subject that so deeply affects the community of Christians to which I belong and in reply to your Grace's letter take the liberty of sending you 'The case of the Separatists' and the copy of a memorial of one of our religious community (a Mr. Chance) to the Lords of His Majesty's Treasury. In case your Grace should think it necessary to inquire into our religious sentiments I send a 'Brief account of the Separatists' which will give you every information on that point.

.But I would beg leave respectfully to draw your Grace's attention in particular to the memorial of Mr. Chance which sets forth the great losses and inconveniences to which the Separatists are exposed from their conscientious inability to swear.

The Separatists have been in existence for thirty years and though they are a small sect yet their case may affect the interests of the public more than that of others, whose numbers are far greater but their disabilities of a different nature. For their inability to give legal evidence has already put the parties engaged in trials in courts of justice to inconveniences and even in some cases to great loss.

I appeal to your Grace whether the indulgence which they seek of having their affirmation allowed instead of an oath, can reasonably be refused, it having already been granted to two sects, the Quakers and Moravians.

The Bill for their relief has passed the House of Commons without receiving any opposition and many honourable Members who knew us in various parts of England and Ireland testified strongly to our good character.

I shall conclude this unwarrantable trespass on your Grace's time by hoping that the bill will receive your support in the House of Lords on Friday next when I hope Lord Gosford will bring it forward.

Draft reply 9 August 1833. Compliments. The Duke has had the honor of receiving his letter and the inclosures.

William Burge to Wellington, 8 August 1833

8 Upper Wimpole Street. The planters and others having property in Jamaica held a meeting yesterday at which they adopted a petition to the House of Lords and respectfully solicit your Grace to present it. I have sent your Grace a close copy that you may be acquainted with its contents. There will be a similar petition from the Jamaica gentlemen at Bristol and Glasgow and which they will also ask the favor of your Grace to present.

Sir Alexander Grant told me that your Grace would let him know at what time it would suit your Grace to see us.

We are waiting for the signatures to the petition before we waited on your Grace with the request of the meeting.

Dated 8th August. *Docketed* 1833, August 8.

Alexander Finlay to Wellington, 13 August 1833

Newton Hall by Haddington, North Britain. Allow me to join in the sentiment of every unfortunate colonist as to the deep debt of gratitude we owe your Grace for your kind, persevering and disinterested exertions in their behalf. Had your prudent and cautious advice been taken as to merely transmitting the resolutions of both Houses to the West Indies, leaving the arrangement of details to the respective legislatures, the evils necessarily attending the *rash* and *headlong* experiment would have been in a great measure averted, for I confess that I fear *the worst* and tremble for the arrival of the next packets.

When Mr. Stanley lately, at the instance of Buxton 'and his tail', reduced the period of apprenticeships from *twelve* years to *seven* and *five*, some Member asked Lord Althorp what additional remuneration was to be given to the planters, in consequence of this infraction of the bargain, on the faith of which the influential colonists agreed to give their assistance and cooperation, without which Mr. Stanley admitted the measure was hopeless—his Lordship however lent a deaf ear to any such suggestion. It strikes me therefore that when the bill goes into committee in the Lords, this breach of agreement should be *strongly urged.* Surely the *honor* and *good faith* of Parliament should not be readily compromised; and if an addition to the grant of twenty millions is declined, Government can scarcely refuse to give the planter *sixty hours* per week of the slaves' labour, instead of *forty-five*, off which is deducted by the bill the time required by the negroe for going to and returning from his provision grounds, as well as for cultivating his vegetables. Should your Grace concur in the reasonableness of this alteration, and condescend to move the same in the upper house, it will add to the many favors for which the West India interest is already your debtor, and insofar lessen the evils attending this unfortunate fruit of the Reform Bill.

Requesting your pardon for this intrusion on your valuable time, and reiterating the thanks of myself and all my colonial friends in Scotland, I have the honor to remain *etc.*

Draft reply 18 August 1833. Compliments. The Duke has received his letter.

He has made every endeavour in his power to prevail upon the House of Lords to modify the Slave Bill.

But the peers have in general left town and the Duke has not been successful.

Wellington to the Marquess of Salisbury, 13 August 1833

London. The farther proceeding on the West India Bill is postponed till tomorrow Wednesday.

But we have this day the Scotch Boroughs Bill; a most infamous measure which the Scotch lords are anxious to fight.

SALISBURY MSS.

The Archbishop of Armagh to Wellington, 14 August 1833

30 Charles Street. I have the honor to enclose a few remarks in reference to a repeal of the laws against Roman Catholic clergymen for celebrating marriages. Mr. Shaw put into the hands of Lord Wynford a full statement of the objections to the Bill, which has been passed by the House of Commons, and I understood his Lordship was to communicate with your Grace on the subject of this bill.

If any further information should be desired by your Grace I shall be happy to attend you at any time that you may appoint.

Lady Salisbury's diary, 21 August 1833

The Duke and Lord Rosslyn visit Hatfield. The Duke is as despairing as ever about the country—so is Lord Rosslyn. They agree in thinking that there will be no blow-up, no bloodshed, that all our ancient institutions will be destroyed by due course of law—that the property of the rich will be attacked in various ways, and that till the tradesmen and manufacturers and those who live on the production of luxuries find the consumption of their goods ruinously diminished, there will not be any danger of commotion. At the same time the Duke thinks there is nothing to be done—that long experience only can disgust the nation and change its feeling, and that till that is the case *we* cannot move.

Wellington to the Earl of Balcarres, 24 August 1833

London. I received your Lordship's letter respecting the amendments which your Lordship wished should be made in the Slavery Bill. Those amendments were made at my suggestion so far as that a proprietor of two or more estates in the same island may with the permission of the *special* magistrate remove the slaves from one to the others. I endeavoured to arrange the matter without the permission of the magistrates. But in that I could not succeed.

Wellington to Lord Monson, 24 August 1833

London. I received your letter some days ago, and I will not allow Lord Warwick to return to you without an answer to it. I should have answered it immediately after I had received it only that I have been much occupied by the business in Parliament, and I was unwilling to trust my answer to a foreign post office.

I quite concur in your opinion upon the Irish Church Temporalities Bill. It is founded upon a false principle, that of relieving the property of the country in general from the charge of maintaining the edifices of the Church and the expence of the performance of divine service therein, for the purpose of loading with those charges the temporalities of the Church. For this there is no excuse or pretext. The people of Ireland are in general Roman Catholicks. But that is no excuse, as in hiring their lands or their houses they do take or ought to take credit with their landlords for the charge for the assessment for the Church as they do for tithe or any other payment out of the produce of the land.

Then if the people cannot or will not pay, there can be no reason why the proprietors of the soil should not be charged with the amount of this assessment. However it appears that the Government proposed and that the Primate of Ireland assented to the proposition that the assessment for Church purposes in Ireland should be charged upon the temporalities of the Church, and that a large body of the clergy of Ireland concurred in that proposition.

The bill passed through the House of Commons, and when it came to the House of Lords it was necessary for me to consider of the course which it was most fit for the House to take. We could have thrown out the bill upon the second reading, and that was the course most consistent with principle. But on the other hand I was obliged to look at the circumstances of the case, and most particularly at the situation of the Church of Ireland. As you are aware the clergy of the Church of Ireland have received no payment of their tithes for the years 1830, 1831, and 1832. They are living upon charity, and the Government had a short time previous to the second reading of the Temporalities

Bill proposed a measure to the House of Commons of a loan of 1,000,000 sterling to be made to the clergy on their tithes for the last two years. On the other hand the bishops by another arrangement of the Government had lost two-thirds of the income of their sees, viz. that part which consisted of fines for the renewal of their leases. The repeal of this arrangement depended upon the passing of this bill.

The consequence of rejecting the bill would have been that there would have been no funds to defray the charge for the edifices of the Church and the performance of divine service, none for the payment of the parochial clergy who must have starved, and even the bishops would have continued to be deprived of two-thirds of their income.

The Government, defeated in their object of carrying the bill, would have retired. If they had not retired it is not to be supposed that they would have proposed or that the House of Commons would have agreed to a less objectionable measure. But if they had retired I really cannot form a judgement of the consequences. The business of the session was in such a state as that Parliament must have continued sitting and not only we should not have been able to aid the Church of Ireland, but even to carry on the common business of the country to the end of the session.

It appeared to me therefore that the wisest course for the House of Lords to take was not to oppose the second reading of the bill; but to allow it to go into a committee and to amend its clauses as far as might be in our power. The charge of the Church assessment is so heavy that it could not be provided for out of the temporalities of the Church without making a sacrifice of some sees. The Primate had originally consented to sacrifice six. The Bill provided for the sacrifice of ten. In truth none are to be sacrificed until they will become vacant and I must add that for many years the charge of the maintenance of the edifices of the Church for the performance of divine service must be defrayed out of the Consolidated Fund.

The principle once adopted of putting down sees to pay this charge, it would have been difficult to contend for one, six or ten.

Upon the whole I believe that the Church of Ireland has got out of its difficulty less damaged in reality than was expected at the commencement of the session. The mischief is, it is true, irretrievable. A severe blow has been given to the Church Establishment and to property. But it is a natural and immediate consequence of the reform of the Parliament. Much worse things have been done since in the same way.

Worse principles have been acted upon, and have so far done much mischief. But this was foreseen and foretold when the Parliament was reformed, and I wish that I could say that I hoped we had seen the worst of the consequences of that ill-fated measure.

Lord Warwick's arrival was quite unexpected. I quite approve of his coming. Pray remember me kindly to Lady Warwick and present my best respects to Lady Monson.

The Archbishop of Armagh to Wellington, 28 August 1833

30 Charles Street. I have addressed a letter to Lord Melbourne on the subject of the 7th clause of the bill. It appears to me to be necessary for the working of the bill to leave out the words 'by the memorialist'. Neither such men as the Duke of Devonshire or Lord Downshire, nor incumbents of uncompounded parishes, who were not appointed until lately, can prove the particulars of the title of the various occupiers for the years 1828, 1829, 1830. There is no use in leaving in those words, for the various points of charge will have to be proved by the oaths of persons duly qualified, and must be subsequently proved by oaths before the assistant barrister and costs awarded against memorialists in failure of proof. His Lordship may do as he pleases but if he leaves in words to prevent the operation of his own bill, he must be responsible for the consequences.

I saw Mr. Goulburn today, and I think we will let Mr. Mahoney and his friends proceed in their course without interruption at present. I am just leaving town.

Dated 28 August. *Docketed* 1833.

The Marquess of Downshire to Wellington, 4 September 1833

Easthampstead Park. I have to thank you for your letter of the 30th which reached me yesterday enclosing Lord Lansdowne's, who appears to have shut his eyes to the details of the Tythe Bill and to the injury which it will entail upon individuals who have property in lay tythes to a very considerable extent, in the hope of purchasing thereby tranquillity in the Roman Catholic districts. The fact is that Mr. O'Hanlon, the lawyer employed by the Irish Office, is a Roman Catholic, much connected with that set and their adherents in Parliament, and the Ministers know very little of the matter, leaving it chiefly to him.

We must make some exertion next session on the subject and your kindness in moving the two clauses and also objecting to the trick which was resorted on the last day, will I expect prove useful in an eminent degree in remedying, *if not too late*, the injury sought to be done.

This property and the estate of Edenderry besides came to my mother by marriage from Sir William Collier's daughter to Sir George Blundell, and the estate is very great. Were it brought to its fair and reasonable value it would hereafter assist me very much in liquidating the heavy family debts which I took upon myself to discharge when I came to my estate.

I am happy to say that Lady Downshire is getting better and we hope soon to go to the sea for her bathing before we undertake the journey to Ireland.

PS. Arthur is at York with the Greys.

Lady Salisbury's diary, 5 September 1833

After describing a visit by the Duke of Cumberland to Hatfield. The Duke of Wellington would not come to Hatfield, he cannot stand the bore of either of the royal dukes, Gloucester and Cumberland.

Winthrop Mackworth Praed to Wellington, 8 September 1833

Bitton. I take the liberty of addressing your Grace in consequence of a note I have received from Mr. Herries. He has been made acquainted with my intention to review the conduct of the Ministry during the late session of Parliament, in a series of papers. I learn from him that he has mentioned this to your Grace; and that your Grace has done me the honor to express an intimation to communicate with me on the subject.

It was my purpose to throw my remarks into the form of letters to the members of the Cabinet and others upon the subjects to which publick attention has been of late principally directed—as for instance:

on the prospects of the Cabinet—to Lord Grey
the working of the Reform Act—Lord John Russell
foreign policy—Lord Palmerston
Ireland—Lord Anglesey

East India question—Mr. C. Grant
West India question—Mr. Stanley
Church—Dr. Maltby
Trade—P. Thomson
tactics of the Government—Mr. C. Wood.

etc. etc.

I have been putting together some part of my materials upon several of these topics; but if I am rightly informed by Mr. Herries that your Grace is disposed to honor me with some suggestions upon the matter, I will proceed no further until, in any way which may be most convenient to your Grace, I may receive your commands.

A note addressed to me at my house in Parliament Place, Westminster, will always be forwarded to me; and I will either attend to any hints your Grace may favor me with, or take the first opportunity of waiting upon your Grace, if you should wish rather to communicate with me personally.

I hope that your Grace will believe that I am very grateful for the flattering terms in which your Grace has on this, as on other occasions, spoken of me.

The Earl of Elgin to Wellington, 9 September 1833

Broom Hall. Being fully satisfied, from living as much as I do in the country, that the general party papers emanating from London are scarcely read, except by their respective friends, so that however gratifying to these individuals attempts thus conveyed for counteracting mischief seldom come in contact with adversaries, and indeed have little effect ever with impartial people, I have frequently felt it might be desirable to circulate pieces of information and influential considerations in the form as it were of *feuilles volantes* or handbills. Short, easy to be read by all classes, but very ably prepared, which, if widely posted up in country towns and places of public resort, would have a fair chance of attracting general notice. If I am at all right in this, no occasion could possibly be better adapted for it than the King's late Speech, which furnishes a singularly eligible opening for a palpable exhibition of a large portion of the maladministration of our present Ministers. For instance, one single page of large print might in one column give the Speech, and on a corresponding one a general review of it. And after this, at a few days interval, the several articles and topicks of it might in the same way be each successively treated, one after the other, in detail. And the series when compleated would put the country in possession of a valuable exposition of the misrule of our leaders; and the fallacy would be exposed that has been practised by putting forth such misrepresentations in the King's mouth at a moment when, from the prorogation of Parliament, no immediate means of detection were to be apprehended.

I am under a strong conviction, not only that this may do much good in the instance alluded to, and supply a desideratum, the want of which is grievously felt at present, but, further, that if judiciously organized and conducted, *in the cause of truth and good government*, such a plan might have a most beneficial tendency to rescue the good sense and the best interests of the country from the baneful influence of an uncontroverted and most reckless press.

I submit these suggestions to your Grace in the persuasion that they are strictly in accordance with your sentiments, and I therefore should be extremely glad if they are found practicable and the execution of them confided to persons well qualified for the task.

Viscount Strangford to Wellington, 10 September 1833

Harley Street. Private. I should wish very much to be governed by your Grace's opinion as to the expediency of *now* answering the pamphlet lately put forth by Government. I have had a great deal of conversation with Sir Edward Sugden on the subject, who, in the event of an answer being determined upon, is willing to undertake the portion relating to law reform, but who agrees with me in thinking (with submission to your Grace's judgment) that it would be better to defer the reply till some little time before the meeting of Parliament. It is indispensable that the King's Speech be *well* done, and it would be better perhaps not to do it at all than to do it weakly or badly, which could undoubtedly be the case if it were done in a hurry. It ought to be the work of several hands, afterwards extracted and *compounded* by one *master*, and scattered as our forces now are, I doubt whether any principle of cooperation and communication could be established among those who would be willing to share the labour. At this season too, it would have few readers. I have written two or three things on foreign policy, which I have sent to the *Herald*, a paper which having lately fallen foul of

The Times, and having behaved very well as on sundry occasions (particularly on the 'swamping' question) deserves some encouragement at our hands. In this way I shall continue to occupy myself. But I cannot help thinking that the full and complete answer to the Government pamphlet ought to be deferred till town fills again.

Mr. FitzGerald tells me that Mr. Praed has probably had some communication with your Grace on this subject. Mr. FitzGerald's idea was that the discussion of the several claims to merit and applause brought forward in the Government pamphlet should be carried on *seriatim* in a set of well-written leading articles in the *Post*, and afterwards combined into one work. To the former part of this plan there does not seem to be any objection, but I think it may be doubted whether a réchauffé of articles from a newspaper, however able, would be the best, most effective, or most creditable way of replying to the Ministers' manifesto.

I hope that your Grace will see nothing in the liberty which I take in troubling you except a sincere proof of my deference to you, and my wish to do nothing and to engage in nothing which has not the sanction of your approbation. Another good thing would I conceive result from delaying the answer. We should, I doubt not, have the advantage of the *failure* of many of the predictions so boldly put forth by Government, particularly with reference to foreign affairs.

Alexander Finlay to Wellington, 11 September 1833

24 Cambray Place, Cheltenham. Confidential. I had the honor, before leaving town, of receiving your Grace's very polite and obliging letter from Strathfieldsaye. I would not have presumed to intrude on your valuable time had I not supposed that from the circumstance of my connection with two sugar estates and a grass-penn or *farm* in Jamaica, I had given much consideration to colonial matters. Having also attentively considered the third edition of the Slavery Bill, namely that of 7th August, several omissions suggested themselves to me. From the kind and disinterested advocacy of your Grace in behalf of the unfortunate holders of West India property, and the condescension I, on several occasions, *personally* experienced in being honored with the correspondence of the Duke of Wellington, I thought it not improbable that the suggestions of even so humble an individual as myself might perhaps be the means of furnishing hints which might be turned to advantage—especially in the hands of one whose opinions so naturally sway a large portion of the Upper House.

I would not so soon again have encroached upon your leisure, had a circumstance not just now occurred which calls upon me to address your Grace.

You may remember that in July 1831, you did me the honor to state your opinions in answer to a letter of mine as to the working of *the Reform* Act in future elections. Finding your ideas so entirely to accord with my own on this matter, and knowing that the influence of your Grace's sentiments could not fail to be powerful in awakening the apathy *then* too prevalent among the Conservative party in Scotland, I, acting upon this notion, got a few copies of your letter privately printed, stating it as addressed to 'a gentleman in Lanarkshire'.

I only communicated copies to five or six gentlemen with whom I was intimate, viz. Mr. Ewing, Member for Glasgow (who is the consignee of our sugars), Sir Thomas Fremantle, whose mother was sister to my late wife, Mr. Horne, the Conservative candidate for Caithness, Mr. Monteith, a neighbour of mine, formerly M.P. for Saltash, and Mr. Fullarton, Stanhope Street, Mayfair, a very old and intimate friend of mine, whom your Grace may have heard of as the writer of three excellent articles (*this he acknowledged to myself*) in the *Quarterly Review* on the reform question. Having sent your Grace a copy, I was deeply concerned to find that you seemed hurt at my having *printed* the letter under the apprehension of its being equivalent to my having *published* it. In consequence of this I applied to such of the gentlemen as might, by possibility, become, though unintentionally, the medium of the letter's reaching the public press and the other copies I committed to the flames. This, you may perhaps remember, I afterwards communicated to your Grace. The copy returned by Mr. Ewing somehow got into the pocket of a writing portfolio and there remained, unseen by me, till Monday last. My nephew, Mr. Connell of Fludyer Street (a solicitor of the house of Richardson and Connell) at whose house in Cleveland Court, St. James's, I stay when in town, accompanied me to see Stowe, having got an introduction from my friend Sir Thomas Fremantle. At Oxford I was surprised and annoyed at perceiving the remaining copy of your Grace's letter at the moment of getting my things packed for immediate departure to Cheltenham to see my sister who resides at no. 24 Cambray Place, from whence I now write. The portfolio was thrown into a box, the key of which was missing, and being therefore only tied down with rope, was, along with my portmanteau etc. conveyed along with myself by the Gloucester coach, I stopping at the Plough Hotel. On reaching this house, I missed the box, and remembering that this unfortunate printed copy of the letter was in it I took immediate means to recover it from Gloucester but hitherto without effect. I still fervently hope that the box may be recovered, for it also contains some documents, the loss of which would prove seriously inconvenient. What however I most fear is that some ill-disposed person may get hold of the letter and hand it to one of the innumerable pests who daily and hourly disseminate their *printed poison* to breed discontent and sedition in the country.

While I entreat your Grace's pardon for giving you the trouble of perusing *this long detail,* I have thought it only due to myself to state candidly and *exactly* the circumstances of the case, should my apprehension be unfortunately realized and with every feeling of respect and gratitude *etc.*

PS. Should I, as I would fain hope, recover the box, I shall not fail instantly to apprize your Grace.

Alexander Finlay to Wellington, 11 September 1833

Cheltenham. I rejoice to say, my Lord Duke, that the box has just been handed to me, and that your Grace may be satisfied as to no risk of the letter getting into the newspapers, I have now the pleasure of inclosing it.

Dated September 11th. *Docketed* 1833, September 11.

Enclosure: (Copy) Letter from the Duke of Wellington to Mr. F., a gentleman of Lanarkshire (Dated) London, July 5th, 1832.

Dear Sir,

I have had the honor of receiving your letter of the 2nd inst.

I quite concur in your opinion of the importance to the British Empire, its establishments and its interests, and to the interests and even the *property* of its subjects, of the next general elections.

The same importance will attach to every renewal of the Parliament under the new system, *if we should ever witness a future renewal.*

But it is very difficult for any man or set of men, to form a judgement of the course which ought to be pursued in circumstances so novel as those in which the country is placed at present. The Ministers and their friends and supporters, in and out of Parliament, have not only formed and carried through a plan of Reform, but have fixed, and in general altered the boundaries of every county, town and borough. No man can form an opinion of what will be the result of any election. This alone is certain—it will be very *expensive*, and it will be so in proportion to the length of time that the candidate will declare himself previous to the election.

We have found that hitherto the gentlemen of the country have not manifested a disposition to come forward as candidates for those towns in which they might be supposed to have an influence, which have therefore been left with representatives under the new system.

It is very true, that great exertions *and large subscriptions* are required. But I am afraid that the exertions made already, in the elections of 1830 and 1831, which have brought the country to the state in which it is, have exhausted the means of *further* exertions, however important these may be to the preservation of all our interests.

> I have the honor to be,
>> Dear Sir,
>>> Your most obedient and faithful servant,
>>> (signed) WELLINGTON

Printed.

The Duke of Cumberland to Wellington, 12 September 1833

St. James's Palace. I write to you these few lines to inform you that after having had a consultation here with the medical men who have attended my son, and calling in Baron Gräfe, the surgeon general of the King of Prussia, who was the person who restored me the blessing of sight again, they all agreed to the proposed treatment the latter advised, and which he says from his experience he has every hope may ultimately succeed, which was to strengthen the nerve of the eye which was damaged by the unfortunate blow he gave his eye last year. I tried every means in my power and gave him carte blanche to name his own terms to induce him to stay on here, but he frankly answered he could not. I therefore had no option left me but decided as the mountain would not come to Mahomet that Mahomet must go to the mountain, and have finally determined to carry him to Berlin. It costs me, I need not say, *much* to take this step, but I feel it a duty I owe my child as a parent, and therefore must submit. I propose therefore carrying the

Duchess and my family to Berlin as soon as I can move them, which as you know is rather more difficult than moving troops, but I trust by the 23rd we may break up. After establishing them there I shall return to my post here and be at your side in the House of Lords when Parliament meets. I yesterday communicated it to my brother, who highly approves the decision, and I trust in God that I may be amply repaid for my trouble. I am to have the pleasure of meeting you on Monday next at *Windsor* where the King has invited me. What do you say to your brother's appointment to Ireland? To me it appears most extraordinary. I passed two very pleasant days last week at Hatfield, plenty of partridges, but as wild as possible, however we bagged 32 brace the second day.

Sir James Willoughby Gordon to Wellington, 12 September 1833

Chelsea. I have with no small difficulty procured a copy of the following work, viz. 'An inquiry into the colonial policy of the European powers', by Henry Brougham junr., F.R.S., 1803, and for which my bookseller says he cannot charge me a less sum than £3 10s. od.

In the first blank leaf of the first volume I find the following manuscript which I give verbatim as a very singular memorandum. The writer I understand was the late Recorder of Oxford.

G. Taunton. Oxford.

'This is a most exceedingly scarce work. Some few years after its publication, a strenuous endeavour was made by the celebrated author of it (for well known reasons) to gather in and buy up all the unsold copies, and it has never been reprinted. I write this in the year 1827. G.T.'

Those are exactly the very words as I have above written them.

I have made the enclosed extract from the last *North American Review*, a work which I have regularly taken in for some years, and which your Grace may find of more than ordinary interest at this juncture.

I am just setting off to join my family in the Isle of Wight.

Enclosure: Extract from the *North American Review* of July 1833.

Of the circumstances that are likely to impede, perhaps defeat, the farther progress of liberal political principles, by far the most threatening is the injudicious zeal of the advocates of the immediate abolition of slavery, especially in this country.

If the question were confined to Great Britain where it affects immediately only a few remote and insignificant colonies, it would be of little moment; and it is accordingly easy to conceive the apparent indifference with which it is brought into view by the British Ministry. In this country the case is different. Here the question involves interests of paramount magnitude; it affects immediately the condition of half the Union; it cannot be agitated without shaking the whole political fabric to its foundation. We have been struck with alarm, we had almost said dismay, at the disposition, recently shewn by some persons of intelligence and high respectability in this quarter, to encourage projects having in view the immediate abolition of slavery.

It is not unnatural that reckless and unprincipled adventurers who can only acquire consequence in times of trouble and confusion, should set such projects on foot; but it is melancholy enough that men who have a large share in the preservation of the public tranquillity, and who act habitually upon full deliberation, and with the best motives, should be so far deluded by a few specious phrases, as to lend them their names and influence. We entreat such persons to consider what they are doing and to change their course, before it is too late. They may rest assured that the formation and activity of a party in this quarter, avowedly bent upon the immediate abolition of slavery, would produce in the southern states a feeling entirely incompatible with the existence of the Union.

A separation of these states, we hardly need to say, would be attended with results infinitely more disastrous to the cause of freedom and humanity, than the continuance of slavery, as it now exists in this country, for a thousand years. But this is not the alternative presented. The institution of slavery contains within itself the principles of its own destruction, and will die a natural death at one time or another. Whether this catastrophe can be much expedited by the use of any artificial expedients, is exceedingly doubtful. That it will not be expedited by the agitation of projects of immediate abolition in the free states, is a point that admits of no doubt, and one which we earnestly recommend to the attention of the real friends of humanity and the country.

Wellington to the Duke of Cumberland, 13 September 1833

Woodford. I had the honor of receiving your Royal Highness's letter this morning. Certainly no father ever had a son who on every account claimed more strongly than Prince George does any sacrifice which his parents can make for his recovery; and even if I was not aware of the affection felt for him by your Royal Highness and by her Royal Highness the Duchess, I should not doubt of your putting yourself to any inconvenience for his sake. It appears to me that no man can doubt, and that all must applaud, the course which your Royal Highness has determined to adopt.

I sincerely hope that your Royal Highness will receive the reward of this sacrifice in the recovery of the sight of your son, whose preservation and prosperity are so interesting to all His Majesty's subjects as well as to your Royal Highness and his family.

I was as much surprised as your Royal Highness could be when I heard of the appointment of Lord Wellesley to be Lord-Lieutenant of Ireland. I believe that Lord Wellesley wished for the office. But I cannot understand what object his appointment to it can attain either in the way of gratifying any party or of acquiring strength for the Government or even of administering the government of Ireland.

It will certainly dissatisfy greatly the Protestants, that is to say the proprietors. But in these times that class of men are put entirely out of the question.

I am very happy to learn that I am to have the honor of seeing your Royal Highness at Windsor.

Wellington to Viscount Strangford, 14 September 1833

Woodford. I have only this morning received your letter of the 10th. I have not yet read the Government pamphlet,[1] excepting a few extracts of it in the newspapers. It appears to me to be a most impudent performance and well deserving a reply and attention.

I agree very much in opinion with you that it ought to be dealt with in both ways. First by the *Morning Post* and next by a regular answer at a later period.

But I besides think that something might be done to draw the attention of the publick generally to these subjects more than they have been. A pamphlet has a few hundred readers. The *Morning Post* a few thousand. But handbills would have hundreds of thousands and it is by such numbers that we ought to act.

---

[1] *The Reform Ministry and the Reformed Parliament.*

I am going to another review at Windsor, and to Walmer Castle on Tuesday. If you have a mind to come there I shall be delighted to see you. I shall be there all this and the next month.

You have only to put yourself in the Margate steam boat any morning at nine. You will be at Margate by three, and at Walmer Castle, fifteen miles, by five.

The Marquess of Downshire to Wellington, 15 September 1833

Hayling Island, Havant. I must thank [you] again for your kind letter of the 7th which has been some days reaching me. I received it on Friday and there was no post yesterday.

The state of affairs is one of perplexity, and no one is a clearer judge of what is passing than yourself.

The observations which you have made upon the Irish Tythe Bill are very true as the principle affects property in general, and if so, it is certainly in a helpless state. However I trust that so great a stake as the three kingdoms will not be thrown away, and as Lord Wellesley is to go to govern *Ireland*, I am *not* without a hope that a firm hand will be used. My brother George I learn is to be continued in the viceregal household as with the late Lord Lieutenant.

Your disposition towards His Majesty's present Government is highly to your honour, allow me to say, from the motives which actuate you as you have explained them to me.

I am happy to say that Lady Downshire has already derived benefit from this air. The place, a new one, will probably be better known. Her Royal Highness has been pleased to give it her countenance. I hope we may next month all get over to Ireland and I heard today one line saying that my agent at Edenderry had succeeded at a tythe meeting in Carbery (near there) and I anxiously await further particulars. In Down there have been some party quarrels, but they are well looked after.

The Earl of Clanwilliam to Wellington, 17 September 1833

Eastbourne. I am just returned from Bohemia, where however I heard so little, that perhaps I had better not trouble you with the scraps—and but scraps—which I brought away with me. The only curious circumstance I have to report, and which is positively true, is that Metternich and the Emperor of Austria did not know what it was that the Emperor Nicholas came all the way to Münchengrätz to say, and the Emperor Francis was much annoyed beforehand at the prospect of a ten days séjour, during which he said he could not conceive what they should find to discuss. Ancillon, on the other hand (and in a minor degree the King) is terribly alarmed, and impressed with the notion that the Emperor's object will be to drive matters on, and to propose declarations or alliances. The King said, the other day: 'Emperor Nicholas has an easy game to play; he is not in the front rank.' But in contrast with this anticipation, they seemed to disapprove of the *expédition* jointly to London and Paris, with explanations, at the last moment, respecting the journey, which were considered as in too apologetical a tone: 'petitio non quaesita' was Ancillon's expression. While the King of Prussia and the different Ministers were at Teplitz, Minto and Bresson both came, the former in virtue of his wife, who used the waters, and the latter in spite of Ancillon who had told him that his Prussian Majesty disliked being followed to Teplitz by the diplomatick body. (Minto is quite a puppet in Bresson's hands, and goes by the name of *le maillot de Bresson*.) Both of them, and General Maison likewise, were quite convinced, up to the last, that Nicholas was not coming at all, and wrote home accordingly.

Metternich's *fatuité*, I think, increases upon him with each succeeding year, and he now thinks he has but to talk to a man, in order to convince and to convict him. In this way, he undertook Bresson and Maison at Teplitz, and Bresson expressed himself afterwards much struck by many things that Metternich said. But among other statements, he said that people were quite wrong to imagine that he was the antagonist, par excellence, of the English Whigs, properly so called— that the misfortune now-a-days was that there were no Whigs—all liberals or radicals. 'Voulez-vous que je vous dire ce que moi j'entends par un vrai Whig anglais? Quand M. Fox entra au gouvernement, il m'envoya tout d'abord un courrier pour me déclarer que rien ne sera changé à la politique d'Angleterre, etc., etc. Voilà un homme qui préférait la gloire de son pays à toutes choses—un Whig du bon tems.' Now unluckily for this statement, every word of which Metternich had invented, he was not Minister for Foreign Affairs till 1809!

The Emperor's wish to see the two sovereigns must be very strong, because, notwithstanding his unquestionable courage, he is much afraid of assassination, and Taticheff stated as much when local police arrangements came to be discussed, for the Emperor's journey and *séjour*. I forget the man's name, but there was a Polish colonel who, on his way to Siberia, wrote a *lettre foudroyante* to the Emperor, saying that he had allowed himself to be taken in the intention to obtain access to his person, that having failed, life was no longer valuable to him, that he was on the point of self destruction, but that he should die content, as he was one of a hundred who had bound themselves, by an oath to rid the earth of such a tyrant. This man did then kill himself, and his letter, in connection with other circumstances, has made a great impression on the Emperor's mind.

I hope soon to have the honour of meeting you somewhere.

PS. My Lady begs her best regards; she is come back quite recovered by the use of the Marienbad mineral waters.

Wellington to the Earl of Clanwilliam, 19 September 1833

Walmer Castle. Your account of things abroad is very curious. I heard that the Emperor of Austria was not pleased with the conduct of his brother of Russia in keeping the Turco-Russian treaty a secret from him. In fact the first accounts which they received of the treaty were from the English and French Ambassadors at Constantinople; who received the intelligence from the disaffected officers of the Grand Signior's Government. I likewise knew that the meeting of the three sovereigns was a surprise upon the two in this part of the world. But I did not know that it was so disagreeable to them as it appears to be. They are quite right to avoid to give cause for offence. They may rely upon it that England would assert herself in any quarrel with them, sufficiently to render France great service and to do them all very great mischief. I do not believe that our Ministers wish to be under the necessity of exerting the resources of this country in a war. But they would be delighted to see the Continental powers engaged in a war with France, in which they would take part with their peace establishment, which alone is sufficient to sweep the seas, and to enable them to cooperate with France in revolutionizing Germany, Italy, and Spain. The person who maintains peace in the world at present is Louis Philippe. But he must not be tried too highly; and I agree with those who think a conference of the sovereigns at present a very serious and a very foolish affair. At the same time an apology for having it is not the best mode of getting out of the difficulty. The Emperor of Russia should reflect that in these degenerate days assassins do not look for their reward in heaven. They expect it on earth. Assassins therefore do not like to risk their own lives. He therefore should always appear in publick as an Emperor. He should have no private haunts, and there take his chance. This is better than any police.

The Duke of Cumberland to Wellington, 25 September 1833

Kew. I was prevented writing to you yesterday, having been detained at a vile coroner's inquest held upon a poor unfortunate servant of mine, who in an act of insanity chose to drown himself on Sunday morning in the river, and in order that there should be no mystery or false reports made I was determined that every circumstance the most minute should be enquired into, and most satisfactorily it went off, but it lasted from *ten* in the morning till near *six* in the afternoon. Your son Charles came and dined here yesterday with us, is gone to Strathfield Saye this morning, and returns this evening back to town, and meets me there tomorrow. Permit me to return you my best thanks for this mark of confidence in trusting this young warrior in my suite, and you may depend upon it that both the Duchess and myself will do *all* in our power to make his stay agreeable to him. I shall through him, as I suppose he will go down to you either Friday or Saturday, write again to you and inform you of *all* that is requisite concerning our arrival at your hospitable mansion, which I believe, unless some unforeseen accident occurs, will be on Tuesday night the 1st October. As far as I possibly have been able to ascertain (for though Government has received *two* separate messengers, the first this day week, the second on Friday last, nothing has transpired and I was told Lord Holland is the *only* Cabinet Minister that has any knowledge of the contents of the despatches). The English *extraordinary* Minister, Lord W. Russell, made proposals to Bourmont to cease hostilities, that Don Pedro would give a duchy to Don Miguel, he relinquishing his claims to title to King. Bourmont is said to have refused all such proposals, declaring that *they were by no means driven to that*, and the people are all flocking to Miguel's standard. Great impatience exists for the messenger's return from Howick. Don Pedro I also hear has demanded military assistance from our Cabinet. If they consent to send troops to his assistance I see *war* staring us in the face *everywhere*.

Wellington to the Earl of Aberdeen, 28 September 1833

Walmer Castle. I will attend to your wish to have a commission in the Grenadier Guards for your son Alexander as soon as it will be in my power. Unfortunately I have a very long list of candidates. But he shall be recommended as soon as it may be possible. I write this day to have his name inserted in the list of candidates. When I shall see you we can talk over the best mode of disposing of his time and of promoting his views till I recommend him for a commission in the Grenadier Guards.

You have not mentioned whether you are likely to move or what your plans are for the autumn.

If you would come here you would be very quiet; and I should be delighted to receive you and we could talk over the system of non-intervention of the day. I shall be obliged to stay here till the end of October.

ADD MS 43060, ff. 93–94.

Wellington to John Wilson Croker, 30 September 1833

Walmer Castle. Private and confidential. I don't know that I could have been of much use to you in grappling with the ministerial pamphlet[1] if I had not made a mistake, as I find I have, of a week in the time at which you was desirous of hearing from me, as I have here no means of obtaining accurate information from documents, and I am aware that in most cases one's memory is not to be trusted. But having looked into the pamphlet and considered the subject generally, I am about to give you my views of the mode in which it ought to be answered.

Although the work is a very flimsy one and is full of exaggerations and falsehoods, it is calculated to make and has made an impression in favour of those who certainly wrote it: I mean the Ministers themselves.

I think that the object of the answer ought to be to shew that the Parliament which has been formed, and the measures which are applauded in the pamphlet are equally the legitimate offspring of the dissolution of the 21st April 1831, and of the King placing himself by that act and by the mode of carrying it into execution at the head of

---

[1] *The Reform Ministry and the Reformed Parliament,* 1833.

the party whose object had been for nearly two centuries to pull down the institutions of the country instead of protecting them. It was with such measures in view that the electors of the empire were called upon to elect members delegated for the purpose of pulling down the ancient constitution and institutions of the monarchy. These measures were to be the reward of the parties in the country which enabled the ministers to attain their purpose.

It is not believed that the ministers had any immediate object in view excepting the legitimate one to party men of keeping their rivals, the Tories, out of power *for ever*. It is extraordinary that the Monarch should not have been sensible of the consequences to himself and his successors of success in the attainment of even this limited object. The Tories are avowedly the great landed, commercial and manufacturing and funded proprietors of the country, the Church almost to a man, the universities, the great majority of the learned professions in the three kingdoms and of the professors of arts and sciences, of the corporations of the empire etc. This is the party to be excluded for ever from power. This was the object of the Ministers, and it is the repeated boast of their pamphlet that they have attained it.

If they have succeeded as they have boasted that they have, what becomes of the King? He is either in their hands for ever; or he is delivered over to the tender mercies of a Radical Administration.

This was the object of my question which will be found in the *Mirror of Parliament*,[1] and more fully developed in subsequent debates in the *Mirror* of the 3rd March 1831, page 617; page 1206, March 28th; page 2682, October 4th. The Ministers pretend that they have effected much in the way of oeconomical reform of the government in all its branches, and particularly in putting down and rendering impossible in future a government by corruption or patronage. My belief is that we have all done too much in the way of oeconomical reform. That we have deprived the King of the power of rewarding those who serve him faithfully, and of relieving the unavoidable distress of the meritorious among his subjects, who by these measures of ours have been thrown upon the bounty of individuals. But they deceive themselves and the publick when they tell us that they have put down corruption in government by patronage. What are these innumerable commissions? What the choice of the commissioners? What is the selection

---

[1] Blank in MS.

of Lord Minto, Lord William Russell, Mr. George Villiers for diplomatick situations? What of Mr. Bowring and Sir Henry Parnell for enquiries at Paris or in the excise or customs, but patronage; and expensive patronage too? It cannot be pretended that there were not in the diplomatic service men capable of serving the publick at Berlin, Lisbon and Madrid, enjoying pensions at home, who ought to be selected for employment instead of those men who must have claims for pensions in their turn when they will be put out! In the same manner it cannot be pretended that there were not men actually in the service capable of performing the duty entrusted to Sir Henry Parnell or Mr. Bowring!

But if we want to know the answers of the Government in respect to all these questions of patronage we ought to look into the enquiry on Sir John Key's case. We shall there see the real object of all these arrangements.

I very much doubt their immediate oeconomy as questions of pounds, shillings and pence; and referable to them only. But when we come to consider of the expenditure only of the measures of the Government I believe that we shall find that they are as far from being cheap as those of any other revolutionary government in the world.

What did the Reform Bill cost the government alone? What have all these enquiries by commissions cost? What the three Irish tithe arrangements? What the West Indies arrangement? What the East Indies arrangement? What the arrangement with the Bank?

But it is not in the view of money only that we must consider of the measures of the Government; it is in the view of the influence with certain parties in the country which these measures have given them, influence at first made use of to carry their bill of reform and afterwards to keep themselves in power, that we must consider their measures, their pamphlet and themselves; and this brings me to the consideration of the several heads into which they have divided their pamphlet.

The first is Ireland.

They started with a Lord-Lieutenant governing by the arts of popularity. I had said in one of the last debates upon the Roman Catholic Bill in 1829 that the measure of concession was then filled; and that if farther demands were made they must be of property and must be met by resistance on the part of government; and that in case those demands should be enforced by conspiracy, by violence or intimidation, I should have no hesitation in going to Parliament and asking for powers to put down such illegal conduct. Sir Henry Hardinge had prepared not less than nineteen (I believe) remedial measures.

Our successors succeeded to our Proclamation Act. Lord Grey was reminded by me in the spring of 1830 that it would expire at the end of the session; and declared his intention of renewing it. It is not true then that the first remedies which they applied in Ireland were such as are described in page 5 and 6 of the pamphlet. While the Lord-Lieutenant was acting the popular he was putting in execution the Proclamation Act. He prosecuted O'Connell, convicted him and this individual was saved from punishment because Parliament was dissolved in April 1831. In the meantime the tithe conspiracy, which commenced with the Government of the Whigs in November 1830 was carried on with impunity, nay was protected by the Government. The convicted criminals were pardoned; those taken up for felonious outrages were bailed by order of the Lord-Lieutenant. The preachers and speakers in favour of the conspiracy against tithes were treated with the confidence and favour of the Lord-Lieutenant, as for instance Dr. Doyle; and O'Connell himself, after being convicted and all but sentenced for a breach of or rather resistance to the Proclamation Act was rewarded by a patent of precedence which placed him above the whole bar of Ireland including Mr. Saurin.

While this conspiracy was actively forming and blood was shed, the delegated Parliament met in June. Were any of these measures of page 5 and 6 proposed or even adverted to? Read the King's Speech to the Parliament assembled in June 1831; and yet it was at this very time that the affair of Captain Graham occurred in the County of Wexford!

It was not till Parliament met in December 1831 that the subject of tithes was adverted to and enquiry directed. Were these or any such then in contemplation? Certainly not. The Government went fishing for measures in the committees of the two Houses of Parliament; and it was not till late in the autumn of 1832 that any measure was proposed.

Nobody can doubt but that it was the duty of Government to give efficient protection to this as to all descriptions of property existing in the country. Did they do so? It cannot be pretended that they did. They omitted the performance of this duty, they protected and favoured those whom they ought to have punished because they wanted their support for their Reform Bill. Their Reform Bill augmented the power of this party instead of demeaning it as the true interests of the empire required. All their measures in reference to the Church of England established in Ireland have the same object in view; that of conciliating the party in Ireland as well as another party in Great Britain, whose object it is to put down the Church of England, and particularly that branch of it established in Ireland. Property in tithes in Ireland is nearly extinct; equally so in the hands of laymen or churchmen; and the laws introduced by the Government which have the semblance of giving relief to the tithe owner do in fact authorize the plunder of the greatest part of his income. The resource then is not to make the occupier of the soil pay that for which he is liable; but to throw the burthen upon the proprietor of the soil; and to bribe him to undertake it by farther plunder of the unfortunate tithe owner. How the Irish landlords or the Irish clergy will bear these measures remains to be seen. If they don't there will be an end in Ireland to that description of property called tithes!

The relief given to the clergy in the way of money is like every other part of the system illusory. The clergyman who takes it forfeits all claims to arrears prior to Christmas 1830; and he must take his relief for the three years from Christmas 1830 to Christmas 1833; and he must collect the tithes for those years, as he can, in order to repay to the government the relief afforded him. The Ministers would not say whether they would or not assist the clergy in recovering the tithes of those three years.

But to shew what chance there is of their having that assistance let us just look at their conduct on the Coercion Bill. Look at the proviso to the fourth clause of the bill which shews clearly the mind of Parliament in respect to tithes in Ireland; and of the clause at the end of the bill which in case it should be necessary to establish a court martial in any county or district in Ireland is to prevent the court martial from giving to the clergy the relief in recovering their tithes which a court of law would have given them if a court of common law could have continued in existence in Ireland.

Then observe that the first effect of the existence of the Coercion Bill was to enable the clergy throughout the country to collect tithes. As soon as this was discovered the fact was denounced in the House of Commons. The Ministers immediately declared that it was not intended to apply the powers of the bill to the collection of tithes (although, mark! that the conspiracy against the payment of tithes was the cause of the disturbed state of Ireland); and that no soldier or policeman should be employed in protecting tithe owners or even the officers of government in the collection of tithes. The Lord-Lieutenant also on his side issued a notice that it was not intended to proceed farther in the collection of tithes under the act of the session of 1831. The consequence of all these measures and declarations has been to put an end entirely to the collection of tithes in Ireland.

It is not necessary to enter upon a discussion of the other measures. They are of the same description and that relating to education upon the same principle. The Irish Church Bill together with the measures above referred to relating to tithes must destroy the Church of England whether in England or in Ireland as a religious establishment only. It promotes and encourages learning among its ministers as well as piety, morality, good manners and civilization. The clergy are composed of the best educated gentry of the country. They owe much of their influence, particularly among the higher classes, to their education and manners. But deprive the Church of its dignities, its honours and emoluments; pay the clergyman no more than is necessary for his bare subsistence and to enable him to rear a family in the cheapest and worst way in which a family can be reared, and we shall soon deprive the Church of those ornaments which have given it strength and efficiency as well as credit.

It remains to be seen whether erudition will exist in the country when deprived of its reward and driven from the Church. This is certain: the Church of England, religion, morality and good manners will suffer.

The next question is the abolition of West Indian slavery.

Nobody doubts that this question has been taken up by the Government solely to obtain for their Reform Bill and their measures the support of a formidable party in this country.

The former Government had done everything that was necessary to carry into execution the resolutions of Parliament of the year 182[5]. The present Administration had only to enforce the regulations ordained by their predecessors. But they issued Orders in Council in 1831 requiring them to be passed as laws by the colonial assemblies, so impracticable, so absurd and so inconsistent with the state of affairs in the colonies and the relations of society there, as that they were under the necessity of recalling them first in relation to the legislative colonies and next in relation to the crown colonies before any one of them had been carried into execution.

These orders were issued to obtain the support of a certain class to the Reform Bill; and they produced that effect. It was quite obvious that the state of the colonies did not require these measures. The colonies had not carried into execution the Orders in Council of March 1830; and it would have been desirable to enforce these before others should be proposed. There was an insurrection of negroes in Jamaica in 1832; but that was occasioned rather by the unnecessary interference of Government than by any want of legislation; and the insurrection was put down and the colonies were quiet at the opening of the session of 1833.

It might have been expected that the Government, having recalled the Orders in Council of 1831 and having quelled the insurrection in Jamaica, and committees of both houses having sat in the end of the session of 1832, would have allowed those committees to reassemble and to compleat their enquiries; and in the meantime would have enforced the Orders in Council of 1830. But a reference to the elections of the reformed Parliament will shew that a formidable party in the country still insisted upon the total and immediate abolition of slavery throughout the British dominions.

It was forgotten that slaves were property; that the labour of slaves was necessary in order to give value to extensive estates in land; that the King was bound by his coronation oath and by various statutes and charters from Magna Charter downwards to protect all his subjects in the enjoyment of their property. His Ministers did not scruple to put themselves at the head of the cry against slavery, and to propose measures to Parliament for its immediate extinction. It was soon found that when the royal authority is exerted for the purpose of depriving the subject of his property instead of being exerted to protect his enjoyment of it, it must be successful in the destruction of the property in question. This was the case in respect to this property as it had been in respect to the Reform Bill. The West Indian proprietors could not even get their case stated in the House of Commons. The Reform Bill had thrown out of Parliament the whole body of them; and the divisions in support of their property did not amount to a tenth of the number of Members in the house.

But the grossest injustice and breach of faith was committed by altering the term of apprenticeship of the slaves in a late stage of the bill after the resolutions had been passed and had been sent by the West Indian Proprietors to the colonies, with their recommendation that they should be carried into execution by laws to be enacted by the colonial legislatures.

The loss to individuals of their property is not the only evil consequence of these measures. The value of the sugar imported from these colonies is not less than twelve millions sterling. Of this sum five millions goes to the exchequer in payment of duties; of the remainder about two millions goes into the pockets of the proprietors in England; the remainder in payment for goods sent out for the supply of the negroes and for the cultivation of the estates; and of freight and charges of merchandise and agency out and home. So that it is the exchequer and [the] British publick that will suffer from this arrangement as well as the proprietors in England and planters and proprietors in the West Indies.

That it will fail is most probable, indeed certain. Indeed it is not easy to explain why the publick are to pay twenty millions sterling unless it be because it is not expected that manumitted negro slaves will labour in agriculture for hire. But I believe that it has been proved that there is no instance of any human creature working for hire within the tropicks at the labour of regular husbandry in the low grounds, excepting under the influence of force and tenor of punishment. The system of *castes* in the East Indies is one in reality of slavery; and there is no other part of the world within the tropicks in which the soil is cultivated excepting by undisguised slaves.

It is most probable therefore that our measure of last session will deprive us of all the advantages derived from our colonies; that the European society therein established will withdraw from them; and the black population will sell each other as slaves to the Spanish, French and Dutch colonies and to the southern states of North America, as they now do at what is called Free Town in Sierra Leone.

The next subject discussed is finance, upon which from the want of documents I am not enabled to give you much information. It appears to me that the Ministers have taken credit for some reductions of expense which were made by their predecessors.

First, we made all the essential reductions effected in the civil list. They have made others, as for instance on pensions, which are prospective. But we made all those first mentioned. Secondly, in the miscellaneous estimates we had already discontinued the expense of building Buckingham House and Windsor Castle. Their great saving is on the naval estimates; of which you know more than I do.

As they take such credit for their enquiries they ought at least to give their predecessors some credit for theirs into the colonial expenditure; which laid the ground for the savings under that head which they have made. But when the sums are added to their expenditure laid out for West Indian slavery; for Irish tithes; for payments to the East India Company on which I shall have to write presently; for the charges of St. Helena taken upon the Government the balance will be found most terribly against them.

In respect of their repeal of taxes I beg to refer you to that of the coal tax; and to remind you that the greatest coal proprietor and importer of coals into London is the Earl of Durham, late Lord Privy Seal and son-in-law of the First Lord of the Treasury. In truth the repeal of the coal duties has not relieved the publick, because all the local abuses as well in London as elsewhere which ought to have been removed before the exchequer was deprived of this resource still exist.

I beg you to observe that the writer of the pamphlet in comparing the contents of the naval storehouses takes for our time one period of the year, for that of the Ministers another.

I believe that the writer has made a mistake in page 19 in respect to the sum on which their reductions of expense have been, and can be made. He states it as fifteen millions. I think that the amount of half-pay and of superannuation allowances, civil and military, ought to be added to the permanent charges of interest and others on the consolidated fund; and that the remainder only is the sum upon which any saving can be made. I don't believe that that sum would exceed eight or nine millions instead of amounting to fifteen millions as stated. We see therefore how small the sum is that can be saved unless there should be a breach of faith towards those who have passed their lives in the service of the country.

The next subject adverted to is the Bank Charter.

The principal point of this arrangement is the breach of faith with the Bank in the last stage in the House of Commons. You know the history as well as I do; and you are more capable than I am of appreciating the value of the legal arguments on the question. It is quite obvious however that during the negociation for the renewal of the charter, and up to the last stage of the discussions on the bill in the House of Commons both parties understood that banks of deposit consisting of more than six partners were not to be established in London.

I don't approve of Bank of England notes being made a legal tender.

I think that the Bank have allowed themselves to be placed in an invidious position in relation to country bankers, who will now have a right to require from them assistance at a moment at which to grant it would not exactly suit the interests and convenience of the Bank. In arguing the question at least in the House of Lords the Ministers did not conceal that the object was to facilitate in the country the operations of credit. The attainment of this object is not very desirable in the existing state of the country. I must observe likewise that the consequence of making bank notes a legal tender of payment will be to establish in the country an agio upon gold.

But this measure is avowedly not yet compleated. The country bankers, still a formidable party in the state, have not given their consent to it. The Ministers did not dare to grapple with them; and that part of the arrangement is postponed till the next session; and the other part will probably be altered. This fact shews to what a state of weakness the Government is in reality reduced in Parliament; and affords another proof of the justice of my observation upon the reform.

The next subject referred to is the East India Charter.

If you will get from the House of Lords my protest upon the East India Bill, it contains the whole of my opinion upon this arrangement.

In respect to the home government the East India Company are powerless whether in relation to the Administration or to Parliament. Of course when powerless at home they cannot command respect abroad either from their servants or the native powers of India.

It is false to assert that the arrangement is founded upon a desire to make the interests of the rulers coincident with the interests of the subject. If the Act is read with attention it will be seen that the nominal rulers, the East India Company, have no power whatever. The board of commissioners have the whole. The interests of the former have nothing to say to the matter.

There are several important *jobs* in the arrangement besides the formation of the new government at Agra. There is a member of the general council who is not one of the company's covenanted servants. There is a board consisting of six gentlemen called a council of legislation which may likewise be composed of persons not covenanted servants of the East India Company. Observe the consequence of the powers given to the board of controul in the nomination to these offices. What is the arrangement but the addition of so many more places placed at the disposal of the Minister of the Crown; and this concealed under the semblance of the appointment being made by the directors of the East India Company.

I think that you should enquire from Peel whether he made the remark attributed to him in page 45.

You will observe in my protest that St. Helena is transferred to the Crown at the expense of 90,000 pounds a year. This sum and the difference between three per cent. and the interest of the day on two millions sterling is the amount of the immediate expense of the arrangement to the publick.

It is impossible to say what it will cost eventually.

The next subject adverted to is *trade*: upon which I have but little to say. Trade in general has certainly taken a spring within the last few months; for which I don't think that anybody can account. I don't think that it can be attributed to the bank arrangement, although the commencement of the two was nearly coeval. I am inclined to believe that there would have been a revival of trade and of confidence in the year 1830 if the glorious days of Paris had not occurred. We had a tolerable harvest in 1831, a very good one in 1832, and a good one this year. The effects of the glorious days are beginning to disappear on the Continent. Industry is reviving in France and in the Netherlands in some degree; and it is not improbable that all this may have produced its effect here. The improvement is certain whatever may be its cause; and notwithstanding that everybody feels the inconvenience and danger to the position in which we are placed.

The next subject adverted to is the law reforms upon which as well as the corporations in England and Scotland you must be a much better judge than I can be.

I confess that I can't see the very great advantage of paying the officers of courts of justice by salaries instead [of] by fees. I believe that the publick have expended large sums, and that their business is not better done since they have paid the clerks in the government offices by salaries instead of by fees. But I am certain that when the business to be done is not for or on behalf of the head of the office, but for the benefit [of] a suitor in the court, the fee is a reward much more likely to expedite the transaction of the business, which is the great object of the suitor, than a salary can be.

The principal of all these law reforms refer to this point. It may be very right to put down sinecure employments in the gift of the Lord Chancellor and Chief Justice, and to give them salaries in lieu thereof.

I confess that I think it doubtful whether the first men at the Bar will be induced to accept even the first situations on the bench, if shorn of all their advantages as well for themselves as for their families. Some of these arrangements, as for instance those for establishing the new system for administering the bankrupt laws, have given the Lord Chancellor more valuable patronage than he had before. God knows that between Reform Bill commissions etc. he had added sufficiently to his patronage since he made that arrangement.

I don't understand his intended plan of modification of the Court of Chancery. But I believe that he means that the Lord Chancellor shall not sit in Westminster Hall; but only in the House of Lords and the Privy Council; and that he should be a Cabinet Minister. This will be a very important constitutional alteration of the nature of the office, having more patronage and power than all the other offices of the Government put together.

It is quite evident that the commissions to enquire into corporations are inconsistent with all former practice, and an invasion of the rights of property in these corporations. You might avail yourself of the example of these commissions to remind the corporations of London of the fate of their brethren of the corporation of Paris. The corporations of London are much more worth plundering than those of Paris were in 1789.

In respect to Scotland the Acts of last session have robbed the corporations of that kingdom of their property and their rights of church patronage etc. in the first instance, while a commission has been appointed to enquire into the question of their affairs. By the Acts of the last session large properties in Glasgow, Edinburgh and other large towns belonging to the burghers of these towns and applicable to charities under their directions have been handed over to the management of the corporations elected by the ten-pound constituency! We are, after doing that, to have an enquiry.

The only observation to be made upon the commission for poor law amendment is that as yet it has produced nothing; not even a report.

The next topick of the pamphlet is the foreign policy of the Government.

The foreign policy of England should be to maintain peace not only for herself, but between the powers of the world. This should be her policy not only because she can have no interest in a change of the state of possession of the several powers; or in any other change whether constitutional or other which could tend to alter their relative strength; but because she has the most extensive commercial relations depending upon peace with each and all the powers of the world, the interruption of which must be injurious to her growing prosperity. There is but one exception to the existence of such commercial relations and that is in our intercourse with France; yet it will be seen that that is the power which the existing Administration has almost exclusively favoured.

There are two modes of preserving peace; the one by maintaining the existing relations between the several powers, supporting the weak against the strong by the aid of the alliances formed at the period of the settlement of Europe in 1814, 1815; the other by submitting to the pretensions and encroachments of revolutionary France, and by rather forming the advanced guard of revolution than checking the propensity of the councils of the Tuileries to embark in such projects.

When the *glorious days* occurred in 1830 the preceding Government very wisely determined that they would recognize the Government of Louis-Philippe; and in him the same rights under existing engagements as had been recognized in Louis XVIII and Charles X. These engagements placed the King of France on the same footing in the great European alliance as the most powerful of the continental sovereigns.

But the right of Louis-Philippe to encourage insurrection or revolutionary attack by the *société propagande* whether in Spain, in Belgium or in Italy was resisted, remonstrated against and prevented by the same Government as it would have been if the same course had been followed by Louis XVIII or Charles X.

This was not the course followed by the existing Government. Before they had been in office a week an immense augmentation was made to the armies of France; and from that time forward the tone of our negociations was altered; and the interests of the ancient allies of the country and those of peace in general were abandoned. This will appear clearly in the subsequent review of the statements in the pamphlet. The first transaction adverted to is Greece. It is useless to enter into a discussion upon that subject. The papers upon it were laid before Parliament early in the year 1830; and notwithstanding the repeated calls for and threats of enquiry, the subject was never alluded to. The arrangement in respect to Greece was made by the three governments England, France and Russia. Its object was to perform the engagements of the country in regard to Greece with as little injury to the Ottoman Porte as possible. There was some discussion respecting the boundaries of the new Greek state, as settled by the three powers, between Prince Leopold and me. I gave him an answer which I think was quite conclusive. It is published among the papers in a memorandum from Prince Leopold.

After Prince Leopold declined to accept the sovereignty of Greece, the affair remained unsettled because the revolution at Paris occurred in a very short time. The three allies did not at that time consider that there was any ground for dissatisfaction with the boundary. It is not known for what reason their opinion was altered; or by what means the Ottoman Porte was prevailed upon to make a farther sacrifice of territory in order to improve the Greek frontier. It would be a curious circumstance if the cession had been obtained by a payment by the Greeks of a part of the money raised by loan guaranteed by the three allied powers; and if it should turn out that this money had been handed over to Russia in part payment of the sums stipulated to be paid by the treaty of peace.

But the Greek affair since the year 1830 is scarcely deserving notice in our foreign transactions. The great affairs are Holland and Portugal. It is perfectly true that the preceding Government had determined that *they* would not *interfere by arms* to restore and maintain the authority of the King of Holland in Belgium. They were sensible that they could not maintain His Majesty's authority without the formation and permanent maintenance in the country of a formidable army; which at that moment of revolutionary excitement might have led to war in which the extreme opinions prevailing in Europe would have been ranged against each other. We therefore, upon the request of the King of Holland, entered into conference with our allies, France included, upon the best means of putting an end to the contest in the Netherlands; and the first act of the conference was to make an arrangement for suspending hostilities between the belligerents taking from each an engagement that the treaty of suspension of hostilities should be carried into execution. It is not true that the late Government declared that 'the two parties should fight no more'; and 'established the principle of *separation*'.

That which the late Government did was to settle an armistice, unlimited in point of time; and as usual the positions to be taken by the troops of each of the belligerents. The principle of the *separation* was not even considered. This is quite clear by the perusal of the first protocol of November 1830. It is most important to Great Britain that Holland should be in a state of security, independence and prosperity. Belgium is not an object of interest to us excepting for the sake of Holland principally; and next for the sake of the north of Europe. It is important that Belgium should be independent of France, not only for the security of Holland and the north of Europe; but because France, even if so disposed, cannot remain at peace if in possession of Belgium. She must extend herself to the Rhine; and when upon the Rhine she would find herself not so secure as she is at present till she should bring her left flank to the ocean.

This is however antiquated stuff in these days. I confess that I was disposed to act upon these principles; and having got France into the conference, and thus under controul, I was disposed to wait till the revolutionary fever in Belgium had subsided and till the King of Holland should have organized the military resources of Holland; and I should then have sought the reunion of Belgium and Holland under a different form; but one which would have equally provided for the security of Holland and the north of Europe, and would have kept Belgium out of the hands of France.

Instead of taking this course our wise rulers having allowed France to arm before they had been a week in office, in less than a month recognized the independence of Belgium by the protocol of the 20th December 1830. They took this course notwithstanding the protest of the Dutch plenipotentiaries, who were upon this occasion turned out of the conference. This last step was a breach of the engagements of the convention of Aix-la-Chapelle.

You will ask why the three continental powers consented thus to injure Holland and their own interests. The answer is this. The interests of Holland in these conferences had always been considered as peculiarly British. It was the duty and the great business of our plenipotentiary to promote and protect them. As soon as the British plenipotentiary not only abandoned the defence of these interests but leagued with France against them the case became the same as that of the King of England leaguing with the reformers, or with the plunderers of West Indian property, or with the conspirators against the Church and priests in Ireland; nobody could give to the interests of Holland a support which was adequate to protect them.

The history of the negociations which will be found in the parliamentary documents will prove the truth of this observation. After having, as I before stated, recognized the independence of Belgium, which ought to have been the price paid for the concessions to be required from Belgium for Holland, and ought to have followed and not have preceded these concessions (supposing the separation to be decided upon), the first step taken was to propose to Holland on the 20th and 27th January 1831 the bases of the separation between Holland and Belgium. The King of Holland accepted these bases; and nothing remained to be done excepting to enforce their acceptance upon Belgium.

In the meantime however the election of a sovereign for Belgium came under consideration. The French endeavoured to obtain the throne for the Duc de Nemours. The Duc de Leuchtenberg and others were started against him. The settlement between Belgium and Holland, of which the bases had been laid, went too fast for the intrigues attending this election. France objected to the bases after her plenipotentiaries had consented to them. The English ministers, apprehensive of the election of the Duc de Nemours, had him set aside; and Leopold elected. But they abandoned the bases of the protocols of January. They thus gave up the interest of Holland; and established in Belgium a supposed English interest in preference to that old and solid one founded upon the security, independence and prosperity of Holland, and the independence of Belgium upon France.

All the rest has been the consequence of these first mistakes and of the submission to or rather of the practice of running before the wishes of France.

As soon as Leopold was sent into Belgium a new plan of separation was proposed to the King of Holland quite different from that of which he had accepted the bases. He refused to accept this proposed plan; and invaded Belgium with his army. Leopold put himself under the protection of France; and the Dutch were under the necessity of retiring from Belgium.

The armistice was then renewed as was insisted upon by the conference for a *limited* term; and it is worthy of observation that the possession of the citadel of Antwerp which had been recognized in more than one negociation as belonging to the King of Holland, remained in his hands under this convention.

The conference then proceeded to consider of a pacification between the belligerents, or rather the powers, Belgium having been created one, and recognized as such. In doing this they established themselves in the character of arbitrators, from being mediators as they were under the convention of Aix-la-Chapelle, and by the request of the King of Holland in conformity therewith.

They proposed in November 1831 a treaty of separation and peace between the two powers which was stated [to] be irrevocable and unchangeable; but which was in fact altered before it was accepted by Leopold. It was however accepted by him, and refused by the King of Holland. It was not ratified by the three continental powers; England and France alone having ratified it. It was declared unchangeable; yet each of the continental powers in ratifying the treaty in the spring of 1832 expressed reserves and exceptions to be made in favour of the King of Holland.

Negociations were then commenced to obtain an alteration of the treaty; and these were proceeding to the desired conclusion when the Belgian ministers at Bruxelles discovered that they had pledged themselves to their Chamber that the treaty of November 1831 should be accepted by the King of Holland, and that before any negociation should be commenced to alter that act the King of Holland must surrender the citadel of Antwerp. This discovery was cooked up at an interview at Compiègne between Leopold and Louis-Philippe; the Belgian ministry was changed; the negociations for the pacification were broken off in a very indecent manner; England consented to a fresh invasion of Belgium and to the siege of the citadel of Antwerp *par la jeune armée*; the blockade etc. which were carried into execution under a special convention between England and France. The continental powers then withdrew their ministers from the conference; again leaving France and England alone.

It is not true then that the citadel of Antwerp was held without the consent of those with whom the first suspension of hostilities was negotiated and concluded. It is not true that it was attacked because the King of Holland was bound to surrender it, because the limited armistice of 1831 authorized his retaining possession of it, which possession had repeatedly been recognized in previous negociations since November 1830. In truth it would have been grossly unjust to deprive [the] King of Holland of the citadel of Antwerp till the Belgians should on their part have performed the convention of the November 1830 for suspending hostilities.

But besides these circumstances the treaty of peace of November 1831 offered to the King of Holland expressly stipulates that each party shall remain in possession of what it holds till fifteen days after the treaty shall be ratified.

The attack of the citadel of Antwerp then was an unprovoked act of war, for the gratification of the war party in France and in Belgium.

It is not true that Prussia coquetted about Venloo. The possession of that place was offered to Prussia to obtain her neutrality. Prussia remained neutral, but refused the possession of Venloo.

The boast of the efficiency of the blockade of the Dutch ports is worthy of observation. The two greatest maritime powers in the world join their forces in the month of November to blockade the ports of Holland; and it is a matter of surprise and boast that they should have succeeded in intercepting the return of the Dutch trade, every ship of which must pass before the ports of one or the other. If the King of Holland had only not retaliated and he could have left to the ships of England and France the liberty to enter and trade in his ports, he would have had more trade than ever during this blockade.

In respect to the effects of the convention of May 1833, that which would be desirable would be to trace from the newspapers the great anxiety of the plenipotentiaries of the belligerents, England and France to get out of the scrape as soon as Antwerp was taken; and the various *twists* and turns that they gave to the negociation in order to put an end to the till then unresisted blockade and attack upon Holland. But it is not true that that convention settles the question of peace or war because it is unlimited. The suspension of hostilities was unlimited in 1830, yet Belgium was attacked in 1831. It was unlimited in 1832 (having been rendered so after having been limited in 1831 after the attack upon Belgium) yet Holland was attacked by England and France in 1832.

The question of peace or war depends not upon a limited or an unlimited armistice, nor upon 'florins, tolls and duties' as Lord Palmerston says, but upon England and France taking a fair view of the interests and security of Holland in the termination of this affair. In the meantime the subjects of King Leopold are becoming as tired of their separation from Holland as it was expected they would be when the subject was first under our consideration in November 1830.

In respect to Portugal we are told that the contest there is drawing to a close; and the Ministers of the King of England tell us 'that British valour has as usual been associated with Portuguese freedom, and Cape St. Vincent has again witnessed the exploits of British heroism'.

In considering the question of Portugal it is my opinion that all questions of right to the Crown, and all questions of personal fitness should be laid out of the case altogether. Whoever might be the sovereign *de jure*, there can be no doubt that Don Miguel was the sovereign *de facto*. We had discontinued our diplomatick relations with his Government, but we had from the commencement of what is termed his usurpation, so far recognized its existence as to continue in communication with it; and to insist, nay to enforce upon him, the performance of the obligations of the treaties between the king and protector's government of England and the kings of Portugal.

When the glorious days of Paris occurred a fresh attempt was made to induce Don Miguel to take such a course as would have enabled our Government to recognize him as King of Portugal. We could not prevail upon him to take that course. Our successors would not have recognized him if he had taken it. Yet nothing appeared more important than to restore to Portugal her place in the society of nations; and thus to ensure to the Peninsula, if possible, continued immunity from the dangers of revolution.

Our Government however again encouraged France in her unjust attacks upon Portugal. In the spring of 1831, the French Government made a most unjust demand upon Portugal in relation to the punishment of certain Frenchmen, naturalized residents of Portugal, who had been guilty of gross offences and were sentenced to be punished by the courts of law. These demands were made not by ministers or by consuls, but by ships of war. Our Government, instead of protesting and protecting Portugal, as ought to have been done considering that we were every day enforcing upon Portugal the execution of our treaties, followed the example of France as soon as the accounts were received in London of the first expedition of the French squadron. This will appear quite clearly upon the examination of the Portuguese correspondence which has been laid before Parliament. We sent out a squadron to make our demands; and succeeded. The French then sent a second squadron under Rabaudy, which not being sufficiently strong they sent a squadron of ships of the line which forced the entrance into the Tagus, levied a contribution upon Lisbon, and carried off the Portuguese fleet under circumstances of breach of faith which will be easily understood by a perusal of the documents of the day. It is positively fact that the peace was signed; and that the fleet was not demanded; on the contrary the treaty contained a stipulation that the ships taken by Rabaudy in his blockade should be restored. In the meantime a steam vessel arrived from Brest; and the fleet was demanded three days after the peace was signed. Because Don Pedro had arrived in Europe; and already meditated the expedition to Portugal; which could not have been undertaken had Portugal not been deprived of her fleet.

Towards the close of 1831, preparations were making for the attack upon Portugal. The revolutionary conquest of the Azores was completed; and forces were publickly levied in London and expeditions of ships fitted out and sent to Belle Isle first and then to the Azores. The Portuguese consul obtained and gave to the Board of Customs positive information of these levies of men, arms, stores, etc. and of their being embarked in the Thames in certain ships named 'The Asia', 'The Fairlie' etc. and the Board had ordered that measures should be taken to prevent their sailing according to the provisions of the Foreign Enlistment Act. But the Government, with the assistance of the law officers of the Crown discovered that the Board of Customs were acting illegally, how is not stated; and the orders given in relation to these ships were countermanded. The commissioners of customs, although specially charged with the execution of the Foreign Enlistment Act, positively refused to receive farther information from the Portuguese consul.

In the meantime the King of Spain, who must naturally feel an interest in the tranquillity of Portugal, and most particularly that that country should not be the seat of a revolutionary contest, was told that he must be neutral. That the consequences of his interference must be the interference in favour of Don Pedro of the forces of His Britannic Majesty. But says the Catholick King 'will you not prevent your subjects from carrying on this revolutionary war?' 'Is Don Miguel and am I eventually to become the object of attack of all the adventurers that can be collected throughout Europe, raised and paid by the resources of England, and commanded by Englishmen?' To these questions he has never received an answer but some fine flowing paragraphs about neutrality; and at last we have our Ministers boasting in this pamphlet that 'Cape St. Vincent has again witnessed the exploits of naval heroism'! We are told also that 'a British minister has again presented himself at the court of the rightful sovereign of Portugal'. The contest is not yet over; and if it should terminate by the establishment of the power of Don Miguel we shall be in the happy state of having recognized as sovereign of Portugal a princess who reigns over about as much of Portugal as she stands upon. How we are to withdraw our recognition when this princess will remove with her armies and fleets [I] don't know.

But if she should succeed we shall be instrumental in having placed in Portugal a revolutionary government which will collect round it a band of revolutionists who will from thence plot and intrigue in safety; and under the protection of England will shake to their foundations every government in Europe including that of France itself. It is then indeed that we shall have the means of 'slipping the dogs of war'.

In respect to Turkey there can be no doubt that the war carried on against the Porte by Mahomet Ali of Egypt was fomented by France. England could have prevented and could have saved the Porte at first only by forbidding Mahomet Ali to make the attack. The predecessors of the present Government prevented him in a similar manner from co-operating in the French attack upon Algiers. But they could have prevented and have stopped the attack if they had only sent a squadron into the Levant instead of keeping their ships in the Tagus to protect the revolutionary attack of Don Pedro upon Portugal, or in the Downs to make the shew of a blockade of the coast of Holland. Neither having been done the Porte was under the necessity of calling for the assistance of Russia; and a Russian army has been in Constantinople and a Russian fleet lying off the Seraglio! This is truly honourable to the British Government and advantageous to the British nation.

But we are told 'that it is the business of the British Government to take care that neither shall return again'. We cannot prevent Mahomet Ali from returning when France pleases. Neither have we it now in our power to prevent the Emperor of Russia from returning when he may choose to attend to the demands of the Grand Signior for assistance; and we may probably then again find that the Dardanelles cannot be forced.

The threat in respect to Poland is like every other part of the pamphlet. It encourages revolution, and revolutionary attempts; at the same time that those who wrote it know well that those attempts can tend only to plunder and the shedding of blood; and to the misery of the countries in which such attempts should be made.

I am not sufficiently aware of the nature of the proceedings in committees in the House of Commons to tell you much about them. It is quite obvious however that the Government was in the hands of committees. I believe that there were not less than five sitting upon the police.

I think that the conduct of the Government in respect to the House of Lords is worthy of observation. See the speech of Lord Palmerston upon the Portuguese affair, when he called the address voted by the House of Lords throwing the first stone.

The conduct of the Ministers towards the Throne deserves attention. Why were the supplies postponed till the second week in August? But really the time is come when if possible we ought to look a little higher and to warn the King of his own danger. The rights of his subjects are violated, their property is plundered, the interests of the commerce of his subjects are neglected; the allies of his crown are abandoned to the attacks of the ancient rivals of this country or of revolutionists; and the influence of this country in Europe is lost. All this is the produce of three years of a government of popularity! I do not recommend that any notice should be taken of the regulations respecting army punishments. This regulation is very injurious to discipline. I believe that if it is discussed it will be discovered that it is more so than it is now supposed to be; and that the explanation of the ambiguities which it contains will render it still worse.

I do not at present recollect other points to be attended to.

I was not able to finish this letter yesterday as the Duke of Cumberland embarked at Dover where I attended him; and I was obliged to return there early to dinner. But I hope that what I have written may be of some use to you.

PS. Since writing the above I observe that there are two points of importance in our foreign affairs which I have not touched. The one is Algiers; the other Ancona.

When Charles X determined to attack Algiers we remonstrated and declined to countenance the operation. We admitted the right to demand satisfaction from the Dey for injuries received. But when we saw the scale of preparation, and observed the tone of the French papers on the subject, and even that of the Commander-in-Chief of the expedition, Bourmont, we desired to have some explanation of the course intended to be pursued in case the expedition should be entirely successful. An explanation not exactly such as it ought to have been was given. Charles X declared that he went upon the expedition without any object of conquest for France; and that if entirely successful he would consult with his allies respecting the future disposition of the conquest.

After the 'glorious days' this subject was mentioned among others to the Government of Louis-Philippe; and even to that King himself. He admitted the existence of and declared he would perform the engagement. The papers are before Parliament. We have had some discussion on the subject in the House of Lords. The Government have not manifested any disposition to defend the French Government from the charge of a breach of faith upon this subject.

In respect to Ancona it happened that shortly after the glorious days there were revolutionary insurrections in the Pope's dominions on the Adriatick. He applied to the Emperor of Austria for assistance to put down the insurgents, which was given notwithstanding the remonstrances of the French Government; which put forward the pretension that they by means of the *société propagande* might revolutionize where they pleased, but that no power should assist another to restore order. After the lapse of a certain time; and I believe the partial restoration of order the Austrian troops were withdrawn.

In some time afterwards the revolutionary insurrection broke out again. Assistance was again required by the Pope from the Emperor of Austria and given. The French Government immediately sent a frigate or a squadron having troops on board from Toulon to Ancona; landed the troops in the night, took possession of the fort and town, as their ambassador at Rome said, *by way of compensation* for the advantage supposed to be acquired by the Austrians in sending their troops to assist the Pope! Thus the Pope was not to call to his assistance the power in whose friendly disposition he could place confidence. But he was to give compensation to France, the power from which he and everybody else knows that he received the injury.

There the French troops remain at the present moment.

Observe that Ancona is the most important point in the Adriatick particularly to ourselves. It is one point of communication by land with our possessions in the Adriatick; with the Levant; and with our dominions in Asia.[1]

ADD MS 38078, ff. 21–62.

---

[1] This letter formed the basis of an article by Croker, 'The Reform Ministry and Parliament', in the *Quarterly Review*, October 1833.

George Arthur to Wellington, 30 September 1833

Government House, Van Diemen's Land. A pamphlet was sent to me a short time since from England containing, in a letter to Earl Grey, the 'Remarks' of the Archbishop of Dublin upon transportation, a punishment which Dr. Whately condemns as an experiment that has failed, and strongly recommends other experiments being tried, more especially the construction of penitentiaries upon the plan of the American prisons, and the employment of criminals at hard labor upon the Irish bogs.

Having very attentively read the Archbishop's pamphlet I can be under no doubt that his Grace labors under the greatest misconceptions respecting the state and condition of convicts in these colonies, and that he sadly errs in referring the increase of crime at home to the inefficiency of the punishment of transportation. I have therefore felt it to be a duty to offer some 'Observations' in reply, in order, as well to divest this important question of all ¦the misrepresentations which have unfortunately been conveyed to the Archbishop, as to place more fully before the public the position of convicts after their deportation, and to shew what transportation actually does effect, and what it may still further effect if it be deemed proper to encrease its severities. I most respectfully request your Grace will suffer me to present a copy of these 'Observations'.

Although the immediate occasion which called forth the remark has escaped my recollection, your Grace has somewhere, I perfectly remember, strongly recommended officers abroad to have some mercy upon their superiors at home by confining themselves to the strict facts of cases, and to write no more than is necessary for the elucidation of their meaning—this excellent rule, I perceive, when too late for correction, I have woefully transgressed. Still I venture to hope, notwithstanding the error into which I have so evidently fallen, the observations of an officer who has had long experience of the results of transportation, and has carefully watched its workings, may be useful at a moment when the subject of secondary punishments is so much engaging the public attention.

Draft reply 2 May 1834. Compliments to Colonel Arthur. The Duke is much obliged to him for his pamphlet upon transportation which he will peruse with much interest.

The Duke of Cumberland to Wellington, 30 September 1833

Kew. Though I am to have the pleasure of seeing you tomorrow, still I feel it incumbent upon me previous to my leaving this country to state for your consideration before we meet the general view I entertain to the system of politics that seems to me should be pursued and for that purpose ought to be well digested previous to Parliament meeting, having but one object in view, which is the salvation of the monarchy and the institutions of the country (if that still be possible) after all that we have seen.

It appears to me that there can be no doubt that the Government remaining in the hands of the present men must inevitably bring utter ruin to every thing, for in fact they, under Whig colours, are legislatively destroying every thing that is most sacred, just as if they were absolute Radicals, and in truth their conduct appears to me (strange as it may sound) even worse and more dangerous than if the absolute Radicals were at the helm, as the country views with apathy measures of the Whigs, whereas if the *Radicals* were actually in power they would create such a feeling of alarm and disgust that they could not stand six weeks.

I know that many persons were alarmed *last session* at the idea of throwing out the present Ministers from the apprehended difficulty of forming a new Government under the present House of Commons elected as it is. I am ready to admit that there may be difficulty to a certain point; but we have but a choice of evils, and let us take the alternative for one moment into our consideration. If we go on in the present system, a quiet revolution under colour and pretence of legislation and by abuse of the King's authority steals gradually and imperceptibly upon us, without our having made a firm and decisive struggle to avert it. That a revolution must ensue in this way I am perfectly satisfied, and whether this be in one, two, three, or four years is as far as the result goes a matter of little consequence. Can then this be still avoided? I hope and really think it may, though no man can pretend to say that there may not be some risk in the attempt. What then are the means to be employed? They appear to me to be the following, namely the principle of a well organized party, founded on the plan of *open* and *decided* opposition to the Government. That plan cannot be carried into execution without a cordial cooperation and a sacrifice (if need be) of any minor differences of opinion. Neither should the system of opposition be too nicely weighed according to the private feelings as to the merits or demerits of any ministerial plan. These were the tactics of the present men when out of office, and there seems *to me* to be this difference, that *then* opposition *obviously* proceeded *only* in faction and not supported by reason, and the results falsified their predictions; whereas the opposition *we* should render will leave (God knows) ample and sufficient ground to stand upon and would be based on loyalty to our Sovereign, reverence for our establishments and true religion, and the maintenance of the real liberties of the country.

Supposing our opposition so conducted to be successful on any given point so as to overthrow the present Cabinet, the next question that arises is what means would *then* exist to form and carry on another Administration? It is to be presumed the King, who I believe to be heartily sick of his present Ministers, would naturally wish for a *Tory* Government, and there can be no doubt that one might be formed, with what prospect of duration would naturally depend upon the measures they brought forward on the onset. A dissolution would probably be necessary. A chance of a Conservative House of Commons will be diminished every year in proportion to the time the present Ministry remains in favour. My reasons for this opinion are the following: firstly, every fresh session under the present system will produce fresh inroads upon the stability of our institutions and will lessen the proper influence which wealth and station ought to have and *still have* on the elections in this country; secondly, *as yet* property has not been subdivided by the abolition of the law of primogeniture, which we are threatened with next session; thirdly, by the extension of the elective franchise on a still more democratical principle than now actually exists. And here permit me to call your attention to a publication which took place at Birmingham of the political union there, addressed to the branch members, stating that the existing 'Reform Bill was good for nothing and that to make it of any use it must be followed up by universal suffrage, vote by ballot, short Parliaments, no qualifications for Members of Parliament, and that the Members themselves ought to be paid for their attendance'. Wild and mad as this may sound, still depend upon it that the present Government to keep their place will blindly submit to such dictation. Nay I have heard that some of the members of Government themselves *also* deplore what has been done, are weak enough to acknowledge that what has been done is bad, but they cannot stop. Are we then to sit quiet and see *all* this going on and not at least try to check it? If then my argument is a sound one, that every session will produce a *worse House of Commons* elected as the present one has been under the influence of the mania of reform, is not my assertion borne out when I recommended to your consideration the necessity of turning out *those men* who have been the sole promoters of this Parliament and are now forced to flatter and obey the dictates of this their own creation in order to maintain their situations? I therefore think that you would have another chance *now* of procuring a more Conservative House of Commons than if this was to take place in a year or two later.

The country looks to you, who have upon so many occasions been its guardian angel, and for God's sake let us rally together before the meeting of Parliament upon a united plan of action, for I fear if this does not take place a supineness will occur and many who feel as I do will not be brought to the field, but will regard every thing as lost. I really feel ashamed at having thus occupied so much of your time, nothing but feeling most deeply the awful crisis I leave my country in would have induced me to have bored you during your relaxation, especially at a time when I myself am so worried at the eve of my journey; but having the most complete respect and confidence in your superior judgement I feel it a duty I owe to you thus candidly to commit to you my sentiments previous to my leaving England. You may be assured that I shall certainly be back before the meeting of Parliament and ready to stand by you on all occasions.

Viscount Mahon to Wellington, 1 October 1833

Deal Castle. I shall be very happy to have the honour of waiting upon your Grace today, and rejoice to hear of your seeming in such excellent health.

On my return through Paris, I saw several times Count Pozzo di Borgo whom I had met last winter at Strathfield-saye. He told me that in case I should see your Grace this autumn and that you should be desirous of learning his views as to the present state of things in France and as to the prospects of peace he wished to communicate them to me in confidence. Accordingly he did so, enjoining me at the same time not to speak of them to any person but yourself.

CHEVENING PAPERS 685.

Wellington to the Marchioness of Salisbury, 2 October 1833

Walmer Castle. I shall be delighted to see you whenever you will come; the sooner the better. But if you cannot come sooner let it be on the 24th.

I am not going to Eglinton Castle. I never thought of such a journey.

I understand that the King did make a sort of anti-Gallican speech I believe in presence of Lord Palmerston as one of a great company. I don't know whether he used the terms mentioned in *John Bull.*

The Duke and Duchess of Cumberland and Prince George have just gone off from Dover. They dined here yesterday; slept here last night; and strange to say I got them to breakfast at eight o'clock; walked the Duchess upon the rampart, shewed her the garden; and embarked her at the moment fixed, ten o'clock in Dover harbour. They will be at Calais at one. I think that was a great feat with a great lady, her servants, etc., etc.

I inclose you the copy of the letter which I wrote to Lord Cowley about the marriage of his son. Send it back to me.

SALISBURY MSS.

Sir Andrew Francis Barnard to Wellington, 6 October 1833

Hôtel d'Artois. I have just learned the following particulars relative to the state of affairs in Spain from Colonel Minuzzi who had them from the Conde de Parsent. Thinking that they may be interesting to you at the present conjuncture I loose no time in transmitting them to you.

As soon as the King died on the night of the 29–30th of September[1] the Duque de San Fernando and Count Florida Blanca saw the Queen, and were in council till three o'clock in the morning when it was determined that they should publish two decrees, the first confirming the existing Ministers, and the second the other employés of government, in their offices. This is however considered as a temporary measure.

The Conde de Parsent received last night a letter from Don Manuel Maria D'Aguilar (who had been chargé d'affaires in Portugal during the last period of the Cortes) written by order of Count Florida Blanca and the Duque de San Fernando, saying that the Apostolicals in many

---

[1] MS: October.

parts of Spain and above all in Vittoria and Guipuscoa would immediately proclaim Don Carlos V, but that measures were taken to repress them and that confidence was entertained in the army and its commanders and above all in Morillo who commands in Madrid. It also states that probably the Duque de San Fernando would be Minister for Foreign Affairs and the head of the Cabinet and Florida Blanca Ambassador to France.

The French Ambassador at Madrid (Rayneval) is in constant communication with the Queen's advisers, and directs all their measures ('*es el alma del consejo*' is the phrase used). The Conde de Parsent has received a letter from him by an extraordinary courier but Minuzzi does not know what it contains.

The French Government dispatched an envoy (immediately on the announcement of the King's death by telegraph) to the Queen of Spain, strongly urging her not to take up the Ultra Liberal party. This was told me by Alava on Friday and he assured me that I might rely upon it. Alava left Paris yesterday for Tours but is going to Valency on the 14th.

Minuzzi shewed me a letter which he had just received from a correspondent[1] at Madrid which states that Bourmont and the French officers who left Don Miguel's army had joined Don Carlos at Abrantes.

The following are the names of the grandees who have formed the private advisers (la camarilla) of the Queen:

the Duque de San Fernando—President and chief
el Conde de Parsent—the Queen's favorite and (cortejo) lover, banished to Paris six months ago
el Conde d'Oñate
el Conde de Florida Blanca
el Marquez de Santa Cruz
el Principe d'Anglona
el Duque de San Lorenzo—banished to Xerez
Duque de San Carlos—do. to France, now in Paris
Conde de Puñan Rostro—now in prison at Pamplona

I have been obliged to take this down in great haste from Minuzzi's Spanish and must apologise for the confused manner in which it is written.

---

[1] The name 'Andrews' has been added in pencil.

Monday 7th

The *bureau d'affranchissement* closes at so early an hour on Sundays that I was unable to send the above by yesterday's post. I have therefore opened the cover to add some further particulars which have been communicated to me this morning.

Morillo commands the army of Galicia but that his name stands on the list as Captain-General of New Castille which includes Madrid.

The Conde de Parsent, who exercises great influence in Valencia and Arragon, assures Minuzzi that in the event of a civil war there are subscribers who have declared themselves ready to come forward with a loan of 50 millions (francs) to the Government—that from this circumstance and two decrees that the Queen Regent is about to promulgate: to abolish the octroi and tithes—that the Apostolicals are expected to be abandoned by many of their partisans.

The letter mentioned to have been received by the Conde de Parsent from the French Ambassador at Madrid contained a congratulation to him upon the new *era* and engaging him to come to Madrid.

These latter circumstances do not appear to correspond exactly with Alava's information. And as to the loan of 50 millions!!!

Dated Sunday 6th October. *Docketed* 1833, October 6.

Sir Andrew Francis Barnard to Wellington, 8 October 1833

Hôtel d'Artois. The Conde de Parsent has sent an official note on the affairs of Spain to the French Government, of which the following are the principal features.

The fear which existed of the party of Don Carlos and the Apostolicals has been greatly diminished by the acknowledgement of the Queen by France and the expectation of the same from England, and that it is hoped in consequence of the countenance of these powers that Russia, Prussia, and Austria will ultimately give way in their opposition to her mounting the throne. That the Queen Regent is not of a character sufficiently decided to act for herself and that she will require the assistance of very steady counsellors to guide her conduct. That Zea Bermudez is for many reasons unfit to be the person—and in this part of the note the Conde remarks that Spain is very deficient in statesmen owing to various causes which are not detailed. That whatever Ministers are chosen the present institutions and system of ruling the country ought to remain the same, but that measures for the encouragement of industry and commerce as well as a just administration of the laws must be adopted. There is also (not mentioned in the note) a project talked of to endeavour to unite parties by proposing to marry the infant Queen to the son of Don Carlos who is now fifteen years old.

It was supposed that this Government were about to reduce the army and it is true that unlimited furloughs had been granted to a large extent but an order has been issued since the news of the death of Ferdinand to call out the conscription of 1832, which amounts to 35,000 men, and it is confidently asserted that a corps of observation is to be immediately formed on the position of the Pyrenees.

Sir Henry Frederick Cooke to Wellington, 8 October 1833

Paris. Perceiving by the papers that your Grace is at Walmer, I venture to say that as I shall land at Dover very early next week (I think Monday or Sunday night) it would give me great pleasure to have the honor of passing a few days again at Walmer.

I will on landing send to know if there is any note for me at the post office.

I have a very important message to deliver from one whose official position renders it too dangerous to write. He represents one of the '*two corporals*' in your dining room.

The influence of France in the Spanish councils should prepare us for civil war *there*. It is the policy of the former Government to do the republican work for the propaganda, and having acknowledged the Queen they are determined to support her by a threatening attitude.

It is for this purpose they are now forming an army of observation on the Spanish frontier, and it is nevertheless a curious fact that although the principle of this Government is Ultra Liberal *at least*, they complain with bitterness that the British Cabinet urge them on to measures which tend to compromise *all monarchies*.

It is the Duke de Broglie who has put Switzerland in a flame.

France is in a state of gradual prosperity. Commerce increases, and the capital seems quite satisfied with the present state of things. But the whole south of France is decidedly *Carlist*. I have just seen an English merchant who has been through the whole wine country of the Garonne and Rhone, who represents the population to a man, except the actual employés, as inimical to the present Government, and as ready to rise at the unfurling the white flag as they were when your Grace's army were on the other side the Pyrenees in 1814.

Very decided measures are now in progress to put down all movement in Germany, and there will be a meeting at Vienna or *Frankfurt* for the purpose of engaging the main German powers in this compact.

There are however *five* or *six* declarations on the part of France and England *of war* in the event of certain circumstances occurring, and as I know your Grace acted upon the policy of *avoiding threats*, I can estimate your opinion of the dangers which menace Europe were it alone from these threats.

John Wilson Croker to Wellington, 9 October 1833

West Molesey, Surrey. You really astonish me; after so many years observation, I am still surprised at the activity of your mind and the precision of your judgement. This last letter from you is the most comprehensive view of our policy that I ever read. I wish I could use it *just as it is.*

I am now pretty certain of leaving town on Saturday by the steam boat, but *they tell me* that as it does not start till 10 o'clock, I cannot possibly be in time for dinner at Walmer; therefore pray put me out of the question—if I come in time, well and good—if not, a plate of the 'potage'.

May I ask your Grace to write to Holmes for a particular account of the case of the borough of *Stafford* last session. It was a most infamous transaction and altogether a *Government one*, but as *our friend Bear Ellice* was the prime mover and as I want to keep up a little *secrecy*, I do not like to ask Holmes myself for an account of this affair which he no doubt knows, but if your Grace were to enquire you would have the whole truth. Baring told me it was the worst thing he had ever known. It ought, therefore, to be exposed.

I know not how your Grace may feel, but I have less hope than ever. I hope and believe that the Government *want to stop*; and I think the Parliament will stand by them in *as much* resistance to revolution as they have pluck to offer, but I fear that will be very little and even if it were much it cannot last long.

The Earl of Lauderdale to Wellington, 12 October 1833

Dunbar House. I have just received your note of the 6th October, with a copy of your protest against the India Bill as inserted in the journal of the House of Lords of the 19th of August.

The sentiments you have expressed throughout the 17 reasons for dissent, thoroughly accord with the opinions on the subject I advanced long ago, when the sum to be annually discharged in Europe was comparatively small, and which I have never seen reason in the smallest degree to alter, as the debt to be discharged in Europe has been uniformly increasing.

Government must indeed be short sighted if they do not perceive that in the state in which the finance of India now stands, in relation to the sums they have undertaken annually to discharge in Europe, the system cannot by possibility fail ere long to come to a crisis, which will exhibit their ignorance and their folly.

It is not the provisions of the bill in themselves which has done the mischief; the present situation of things is owing to an erroneous system that has been long pursued. But the bill is blameable because so far from attempting to parry, or even to mitigate the impending evil, it sanctions the line of conduct which has produced it, whilst it relieves the proprietors of India stock from the consequences of the vicious policy that has been pursued, and takes upon the shoulders of Government the responsibility for all the evils that must inevitably result from that perseverance in it which it directly sanctions.

You have pointed out most distinctly the charges for which this arrangement as it now stands sanctioned by the legislature renders it necessary that funds should be found in this country.

Sum as stated in the third reason of protest
£2,578,000
As stated in the fourth reason of protest
£200,000
Ditto as stated in the fifth reason of protest
£277,000
Ditto as stated in the sixth reason of protest
£667,000
Making a total of £3,722,000

Now this singular situation of one country being made tributary to another to the amount in value of £3,722,000 is an arrangement that must undoubtedly ruin the country that has annually to export commodities to produce that value (if it could be effected for any continuance of time, which I hold to be impossible). But what I maintain to be equally certain is that it would inevitably destroy the industry of the country which by importation of commodity to that amount would appear at first sight to the vulgar eye to benefit by such an arrangement.

The first of these propositions I formerly argued much at length in a tract I published in the year 1809, intituled 'An enquiry into the practical merits of the system for the government of India under the superintendence of the Board of Controul'. You will there find the facts set forth which clearly prove that from the time of the grant of the dewannee which laid the foundations of our territorial possession in India, the trade of India has been a trade of remittance, and the consequence that must ensue in impoverishing a country out of which such remittances are for a length of time forced are clearly displayed.

The second of these propositions I have argued also at great length in a tract which was published in the year 1805, intituled 'Hints to the manufacturers of Great Britain on the system of borrowing in England for the service of Ireland'. I remember Charles Fox, who was always very sceptical about the inferences drawn from reasoning on all questions of political economy, told me that he would deem the argument I used to prove that Ireland's being rendered tributary to England would prove ruinous to the manufacturers in this country[1] conclusive if he could persuade himself that any inference on a question of political economy could be conclusive.

The reasoning used to establish both these propositions is too extensive to be concentrated into the bounds of a letter, but if you could get a hold of these tracts I think it would be worth your while to devote an hour or two to consider the facts I have detailed as bearing on the one and on the other. In particular, you will find the details cited to prove that the extensive tributes paid to Rome from the conquered provinces, which could then only be remitted in grain, had within a few years the effect of destroying the agriculture of Italy extremely curious.

I have been lately so well that I have serious thoughts of taking my seat at the commencement of the session. I do not believe that I can

---

[1] The words 'of England' are added here in Lauderdale's hand.

remain and take an active part, but it will be satisfactory to me to have it in my power to leave my proxy with you.

My friend young Coventry who you was so good as to get into the Rifle Corps has been unwell at Corfu, which makes me very anxious to get him exchanged into the Guards if possible, the money is at all times ready at a call.

Signature only in Lauderdale's hand

Sir Robert Wilson to Wellington, 14 October 1833

Confidential. I had only time to dispatch Mr. Latham's note last night with a minute on the manifesto which I thought most important, but which to my surprise I have not found published in any of the morning papers.

I have not yet seen any of the communications from Lisbon of an official character, but I am told by those who have that the Algarves is lost to Don Pedro, that the Miguelite forces were entrenched close upon the lines of Lisbon, and that a variety of concurrent indications authorized belief that a serious attack was in contemplation. That Oporto was left in a most defenceless state, and unless Don Pedro could make a successful sally and by its results be enabled to reinforce Oporto the city and Villa Nova must be occupied almost *sans coup férir* by the gathering Miguelists. It is positive that Louis Philippe wrote to the British Government that with the advice of his Council who assured him of the right to which he pretended, he had announced to Don Miguel that unless Marshal Bourmont was compelled to quit his service he should send a fleet to the Tagus and land a body of French troops; that he felt justified in taking this step as Marshal Bourmont might achieve success in the Peninsula that would force operations against France, but he added that although he had sent this message he should take no active measure without communication with the British Government. It is however also intimated that the step so announced was instigated by the British Minister.

It certainly does not appear to be impartial dealing however, originating where it may, after the permit given by the French Government to Solignac, and the unfettered latitude of aid advocated by the British Government in Parliament as the evidence of strict neutrality between the belligerents.

Some message of a similar tenor has been communicated to the Queen with the addition that her request for French succour would meet with the most friendly attention. It appears Pozzo di Borgo has written to the Russian Minister at Madrid not to commit himself in any way until direct instructions reach him from the Emperor. 'But at the same time it would be desirable if the Queen would allay the alarm of the Sovereigns by declaring the Spanish Government should maintain the monarchical principle', and the manifesto is perhaps the fruits of that insinuation, as well as of the feeling expressed in favor of Don Carlos and his system.

Mendizabal has returned from Portugal. He is come it is said to get money to supply the Portuguese expedition, and to create a new one for Spanish operations under Don Pedro's auspices, and this I believe to be the fact.

The Sovereigns now style themselves in all their official notes 'the three *allied* powers' and 'the three *allied* monarchs', and several of these confederate notes have been transmitted to the British Foreign Office without any allusion to France or England, as component parts of the alliance, so that it is presumed separate treaties of union amongst themselves have been formed recently.

It is added however that Count Schwarzenberg brought strong admonitions to the King of Holland against hazarding the peace of Europe, and that he has been recommended to apply to the Diet for sanction to dispossess himself of Luxembourg, Austria and Prussia promising their votes.

At Vienna there has been much squabbling between Metternich and Sir F. Lamb, the former having become the panegyrist of the Emperor Nicholas on the Turkish transaction and on approval of the treaty. Some high language is reported to have been held, and Sir F. Lamb imagines the division of Turkey has been settled between the three allied powers when the knell of the Sultan is rung.

Lord Ponsonby writes there must be revolution in Constantinople at the approach of winter when the Russians will return, and he wishes to know if he is to remain Minister in a Russian province for so European Turkey will become. To this repeated enquiry no answer has been sent.

The Belgian Minister has been sending to England in great alarm for protection against the intended change of garrison in Maestricht by a prohibited route. The Dutch insist upon going over a bridge in the shortest line of march. The Belgians refuse passage but offer communication and transit by Meerssen on the Meuse where there is a ferry. They pretend that passage by the other route would bring the advancing and retiring garrisons into contact with Belgian troops, cantoned on that line, and that conflict would be inevitable, since the Dutch have not granted the right of water way on the Meuse as promised, and they conclude by affirming that if the Dutch go by the bridge road they must go disarmed.

Lord Palmerston and the French chargé d'affaires here under great alarm dispatched a letter to the King stating that as the troops are not moving with artillery, they can very well go over the ferry, and interdicting force. The *fit via vi* will not be permitted but some uneasiness is felt lest the remonstrance and note may arrive too late to prevent the march being attempted.

Louis Philippe himself writes that in his late tour he has been encouraging the doctrine of free trade and making converts and reiterates ceaselessly that in all things he is solicitous to conform to the wishes of England, and that he will ever endeavour to check for that end *'le soif des français pour la gloire'*.

Portuguese scrip has declined nearly 2 per cent this day and there is a rise of nearly 4 per cent in the Miguelite loan as last quoted on the Paris *bourse*.

I hope tomorrow to get at promised particulars for I am satisfied we do not yet know the whole information that has been received.

PS. Tomorrow I shall provide myself with a copperplate writing pen.

First enclosure: Private and confidential.—Memoranda.

Les trois cours alliées—les trois puissances continentales have announced *aux deux Cabinets maritimes* the instructions conveyed by Count Schwarzenberg and the communications of their opinions to the King of Holland as friends and sovereigns.

These communications were generally satisfactory to the British Government but in one of the communications it is observed that the tranquillity of Europe does not depend on the Cabinet of The Hague and the solution of the Belgian question, but on circumstances totally distinct. These circumstances are however not explained.

Two ships of the line are sent off to the Mediterranean, one in four hours notice, and it is proposed to Lord Grey to send also the *Salamander*. This reinforcement no doubt is connected with the statement of Lord Ponsonby that events at Constantinople will bring back the Russians during the winter, 45,000 of whom are kept ready at Odessa and environs for embarkation etc., whilst the greatest maritime efforts are making both in the Russian and Turkish arsenals to encrease the naval force.

Sir Frederick Lamb is ordered to Italy to ascertain the force of Austria and her proceedings. It is supposed this mission is in concurrence with the French Government whose agency in Italy is not so able to gain information.

Captain Napier wrote by last mail that various Spaniards had joined Don Miguel's army and that if the British Government did not take measures to resent this breach of neutrality, and protect the Queen from further prejudice, *he*, *Napier*, would go and blockade Cadiz etc. and that he had the means to carry his threat into execution.

He received for answer that the British Government would regret to see an officer who had so distinguished himself in the service of the Queen adopt measures at variance with the interests and policy of his own country, but if he did act, as he threatened, Spain would no doubt march an army into Portugal and that she would have a right to make reprisals.

Absence from town from an early hour has prevented attention to the occurrences of the day but no intelligence has been in circulation.

Second enclosure: Private. Colonel Evans, who has just returned from Lisbon, reports that the lines are remarkably well drawn and made. That Don Pedro has about 9,000 regulars and 7 irre[gulars] with which he might act out of the lines. That the service is but laxly executed, that no detachments or patrols are sent out, so that Don Miguel's troops are left in undisturbed possession of the country, that there are about 80,000 inhabitants in Lisbon including Galegos who are neutral, and that the majority of the natives in Lisbon may be said to be in favor of Liberalism, but the whole country is adverse, so much so that if it could be overrun it could not be kept down without an army of occupation. It is however his, Colonel Evans, opinion that if Don Miguel's forces be conducted by an energetick and at the same time cautious officer, the country could be held forever against Don Pedro and all the means he could bring into cooperation.

That Don Miguel's army is contained and concentrated in three villages—Lumiar, Campo Grande, and another [my] informant could not recollect, and all his regulars, about 11,000, are kept in the centre.

That there have been no desertions from the main army, only some few runaways from the scattered corps chiefly on the south bank. That since Marshal Bourmont's presumed departure there has been no apparent diminution of discipline, but on the contrary more appearance of vigilance and regularity. That Don Miguel has fortified Santarem and Abrantes and provisioned Elvas but that he wants guns in his works before Lisbon whilst the Lisbon lines bristle with 230 heavy ordnance. That there seems no probability of an early termination to the conflict but Don Pedro hopes he may one night surprise and cut off one of the flank cantonments as it is thought the range is too extensive and that there are too many impediments in the way of prompt succour from the centre.

Oporto was still in great jeopardy and General Stubbs had written that if the troops sent for were withdrawn he would not answer for the safety of the place.

Inspection of a written memorandum drawn up by Colonel Evans is promised.

A proclamation against the anti-assessed taxes associations is preparing and Lord Grey is expected in town for the purpose—of course Lord Brougham must also attend the Cabinet.

The circular of Lord Shelburne it is said has only emboldened the associators.

The accounts from Ireland are most unfavourable—even payment of rents is being refused.

Ministerial opinion predicts the downfall of the Queen of Spain if Monsieur Zea remains her Minister one fortnight.

Mendizabal sends off *tomorrow* £25,000 sterling in dollars for Lisbon.

The silver provider is the informant.

It is quite *positive* and *official* that Bourmont was ordered by the French Government to withdraw under the penalties stated in the memorandum of this day. It is also certain France is endeavouring to find a pretext of some kind for interfering in the Spanish quarrel but Lord W. Russell wrote that Marshal Bourmont when last heard of was at Seville with a few officers and about to leave Spain. The greater portion of the French officers under the former command of the Marshal had remained in Portugal under the advice, or as it is called the hint, of the Marshal given before his departure.

Toledo was certainly *up* and a letter states Toledo was the telegraph signal for the army of General Sarsfield to proclaim Don Carlos and to move on Madrid with the King.

Celerity can alone prevent civil and foreign war.

The Diet has refused to make any regulations for the civil administration of Luxembourg, after such regulations had been promised as is said. They refer Mr. Cartwright and Baron d'Aller, i.e. England and France, to the King of Holland.

Captain Ross who is on way home is said to have been enclosed in his ship for eleven months in the ice of Davis's straits.

October 16 1833

Parliament is prorogued in Council this day to Thursday, 12th December.

Third enclosure: In the *Morning Herald* of this day, a Paris correspondent invokes the sneers, laughter, and ridicule of mankind, if that which he was about to predict was not verified—namely, and it is printed in large italic letters, '*In the course of twelve months Don Pedro of Portugal—if he plays his cards well—will be Emperor of the Spanish and Portuguese peninsula*'.

The writer of this prophecy is certainly one of the initiated who invited Don Pedro from the Brazils for the execution of that project, than which none is more fraught with consequences of graver interest to every government in Europe.

The machinery for the operation is now in active progress, and the unfettered latitude of neutrality as expounded by the English and practised by the French Government assures the supplies required to ignite the combustibles.

It will be easy henceforth to trace the signs of confederate progress.

There is no event communicated this day in any Peninsula intelligence but it is certain the fermentation was encreasing in Spain, and that great apprehensions were being entertained for the maintenance of the Queen's authority in any city or camp.

A well informed and neutral communicant arrived in last packet from Lisbon states the lines of Lisbon were well traced and would be well manned in a short time, that Don Pedro's fighting force amounts to 12,000, that the town of Lisbon generally is much inconvenienced for want of water and all other supplies, that Donna Gloria's popularity did not continue beyond two days, and that Don Pedro was rendering himself obnoxious to the Liberal party by his *absolute* proceedings. That the country was overrun by guerillas who devoured worse than locusts all the subsistence of the population and made Portugal one of the most wretched countries in the whole world.

Don Miguel was in force and in well fortified position and Oporto was in extreme jeopardy from the reduced amount of its garrison and the augmenting Miguelite troops in the immediate neighbourhood.

October 15 1833.

The Lord Provost of Glasgow (James Ewing) to Wellington, 15 October 1833

Glasgow. I have the honour to acquaint your Grace that, at a full meeting of the magistrates and Council of this City, in Council assembled, they unanimously voted their thanks to your Grace for your zealous, able and efficient support in the House of Lords, to the modifications of the Royal Burghs of Scotland Reform Bill; and for the concession which has just been obtained, so much to the benefit of the municipal constitution.

Alexander Finlay to Wellington, 16 October 1833

7 Marine Parade, Brighton. After having the honor of hearing from your Grace at Cheltenham I paid a visit to my friend Sir Thomas Fremantle in Buckinghamshire, where I heard so much of the benefits of *shampooing* for a strain by the Indian Mahomet here, that I came down to try the efficacy of removing the effects of a fall from a horse in Scotland.

I have this morning heard from my correspondent Mr. Ewing, the Member for Glasgow, who tells me that '320 to 330 of the first in rank, wealth and respectability attended, while Mr. Oswald's Radical dinner consisted of no more than 200 persons whom nobody knew and who were pressed into the service from the *high ways and hedges*'. As Mr. Ewing sent me the Glasgow paper containing the account of the dinner, your Grace may like to see the state of political feeling in the great Scottish Tyre, which is evidently becoming Conservative. Mr. Ewing's speech is of a neutral description, but I know him to be *safe*. After perusal, your Grace may perhaps take the trouble to forward it under cover to *Sir Thomas Fremantle, Swanbourne, Winslow, Bucks.*

While in Cheltenham I met with Mr. Dacre, a respectable gentleman who left Jamaica *in June*. I wrote him from Swanbourne, and received the enclosed answer which your Grace may appreciate as the opinion of a *practical* man, who had been in the island twenty years. His simile of the schoolmaster is rather apposite.

Should your Grace continue at Walmer Castle, I would be happy could you honour me with a *personal* interview, as I rather think I could give you some *practical* information regarding the colonial question, to which you have so kindly dedicated your valuable time. I shall leave this for town on my return to Scotland in a few days, and can either have an audience in town or country, as may best suit your Grace's convenience.

Mrs. Finlay's father was Secretary of Jamaica for many years, and I have learned much from him.

PS. The part of the chain pier composing the third arch was struck down by lightning last night, but no lives lost.

Enclosure: James Dacre to Alexander Finlay, 14 October 1833.

7 Clarence Street, Cheltenham. I had the pleasure of receiving your favour of the 2nd instant, with its enclosure which I lost no time in forwarding to Cambray Place.

I received no letters by the packet from Jamaica. I heard, however, from one of my friends there, by a late merchant vessel. He seemed to think that the negroes were extremely dissatisfied at the idea of being apprenticed; from which he feared a great deal of trouble would arise. For my own part, I don't see how the new system is to work now the *right* of coercion by the masters has been taken away, and no substitute left in *their* hands; for to say that the paid magistrates will answer that purpose, every one acquainted with the management of negroes knows to be ridiculous.

What would the people here think of a proposition to vest in a magistrate the power which a schoolmaster has over his scholars? and yet the two cases are not very dissimilar. The *new* mode may possibly answer by and bye; but in the meantime something between that and the *old right* ought to have been fixed on.

I quite agree with you in thinking that Government will allow great modifications to take place in framing the local bills; but I am afraid the former power of the master, even in a limited degree, will never be again allowed.

However, a very short time will shew the effect of these changes; and it will soon be discovered whether land can be cultivated cheaper by *free* than *slave* labour. If it can, the abolition of slavery will prove a blessing to the colonies. If not, their total ruin; for the planters will no longer have the same motive for holding property affording little or no return as they had when slaves formed a part of it.

The House of Assembly you perhaps know was to meet on the 27th August. We may therefore look for news every day.

You say nothing of your shampooing experiment. I trust you mean to try it and hope it will answer.

Wellington to Sir Robert Wilson, 17 October 1833

Walmer Castle. I am very much obliged for all the intelligence that you have sent me. I will not comment upon it.

The most important of all is that from Ireland. If that be true I hope that it may prove to be *le commencement de la fin*.

I have had Cooke, Herries and Barnard here. But I don't think that they have more news than you have picked up in London.

ADD MS 30114, f. 20.

The Duke of Cumberland to Wellington, 22 October 1833

Berlin. Your son Charles has already informed you of our *safe* arrival at this place. I deferred writing till I had seen some of the principal and leading people to learn a little *what* the feelings of the Government are. I yesterday had a long conversation both with Witzleben in the morning and in the afternoon with Ancillon, and I should say an untruth was I not to state that their language was precisely that I should have expected from them, execrating and deploring *our line* of policy, our truly degraded position with France, and that this is too true, there is no denying, and this I understand is so publick and notorious that every one both at Frankfurt as well as at this place knew that neither Mr. Cartwright there, or Lord Minto here present any note or write any dispatch unless under the *influence* of the French Minister. Lord Minto seems to be in no great favour here. I have not seen him, for the very day I was to receive him he started for Teplitz to see his wife. I do not break my heart at this, but it was the foolishest thing he could possibly do as it appears to every one he did it to avoid me, for in fact it was his *duty*, considering who I am, to have been here on my arrival. From all I can learn the meeting at Münchengrätz went off perfectly well, and after the two Emperors had separated Nesselrode and the Austrian Ambassador, Ficquelmont, at Petersburg, both came here and here they remained a full fortnight to conclude their treaty. These three powers seem perfectly to be aware of the absolute necessity of putting a stop to the revolutionary spirit that is afloat, and I understand that a congress of Ministers is immediately to be assembled purely to consider the state of Germany and to enforce the decrees of the Diet of Frankfurt which it published last year but never had till now insisted on. They appear to me to feel perfectly the necessity of giving no further way to the demands of France. What I saw of the French troops in the different garrisons I passed through, and especially at *St. Omer*, near which there was a camp of fifteen to twenty thousand men, I must say I never saw a more miserable looking set of men, very short, very weak, and many almost children, but active and in constant motion, the streets at Calais, etc., crowded with them. It was quite funny to hear the contempt with which they spoke of their dear friends the Belgians. As to appearance, these are better looking men, but so completely dressed as the French soldiers that there is hardly knowing the difference. Don Pedro I hear has debauched a prodigious number of them, and in one regiment alone, the 2nd *Chasseurs à pied*, 300 deserted with bag and baggage. A more thorough Jacobin and Radical spirit I never yet witnessed as I did even in that small part of Belgium I was under the necessity of passing. I slept one night at Mons, and was obliged to stop the following night at Namur, having been driven so slowly that it was near eight o'clock before we reached that place, so that the idea of getting to Liège was out of the question, and I was afraid Monsieur Leopold might meantime have thrown himself into our way, which would have been very unpleasant. Nothing could exceed the kindness and friendship with which His Majesty here received us, and he enquired most particularly after you and desired Charles when he wrote to you to remember him to you. I heard one anecdote yesterday of Talleyrand, that on his return to Paris he had said to Pozzo di Borgo, speaking of England, *Qu'il n'y avait qu'un homme qui pouvait sauver l'Angleterre, et c'est le duc de Wellington*, and considering that he has had Lords Grey, Palmerston, and company in his pocket so long, it is a most curious declaration. I hear that the conduct of Palmerston and his dispatches are of a nature that one must think he must be half mad and so violent and intemperate that it offends all the Cabinets, and when he is called to an explanation his only refuge is denying all he has authorised his *sous ordonnances* to express, thus it is that Johnny Bligh has been sacrificed. They seem to know nothing for certain here either from Spain or Portugal. The French Minister it is said had received yesterday a courier from Paris, stating that Bourmont had joined Don Carlos and that that Prince had been proclaimed King in the province of Biscaya. Never has any Ministry made a prettier kettle of fish for themselves than Lord Grey has done, and here he cannot run to *Stanley and company* for advice and explanation if demanded by him. Pray do let me know of all that is going on for we were never in such a crisis as at the present moment and it must soon come to a blow up. Your son is in high trust and a favourite with us all. He has taken his first German lesson this morning. The Duchess and George desire to be most kindly remembered to you.

Lady Salisbury's diary, 25 October 1833

A conversation with the Duke at Deal Castle. He told me Peel was going abroad, to winter at Rome. I observed that I could not comprehend what game he was playing—'Nothing but weakness', he replied, 'he is afraid—afraid of everything.' The Duke was consulted by Croker about the article on the Reform pamphlet in this month's *Quarterly Review* which was written by the latter. Croker requested the Duke to send him 'some sense' for it. The Duke would not put it in the form of a discussion but wrote Croker a letter upon the subject. It appears however that Croker did not write it exactly as the Duke advised. Praed also came down here to consult the Duke upon writing an answer to the same pamphlet. I asked the Duke if he thought Peel's absence would conduce to the good of our cause or not. He said, 'Yes, it might give an opportunity to others more decided opponents of the Whigs to come forward.'

He repeated his opinion that the country was doomed to revolution, revolution 'in due course of law'. Should it however terminate in a contest of arms he thinks that Napier (of the Peninsular War) is the only man who has military talent for a leader of the democrats—'he is twelve or fifteen years younger than I am', said the Duke, 'but he has no health.' 'In case of such a struggle the Brunswicks will be sent to the dogs, but it is all their own folly.' 'If I am applied to', said he, 'to take the command I shall tell the King I cannot trust these Ministers for a moment—they cannot be depended upon—I shall demand the strictest written instructions, and I will not do the slightest thing upon my own responsibility. They have no honor.' The Duke of Cumberland wrote to the Duke before he went abroad, requesting him to lay down a plan for the Opposition in the next session—the Duke replied it was impossible to concert a plan of opposition till it was seen what Ministers would do—that he should recommend great moderation and no decided hostility unless their measures were such as to force it.

Speaking of the foreign ambassadors he said they were now afraid of frequenting the houses of the Conservatives, so great was the indignation it drew down upon them from the Ministers—van Zuylen was recalled because he held intercourse with the Duke. The King never asks the Duke now to meet any foreign princes etc. who may be in this country, 'and', added the Duke, 'I am a natural person to ask—I happen to be Field Marshal in most of the countries in Europe.' He does not think it would be possible now to make a Tory Ministry. This however he rather contradicted in the evening, when he gave it as his opinion that there was still energy enough left in the country to save it if the King had common firmness: but that a change of Ministry proceeding merely from his (the Duke's) measures could do no good—it must proceed from the King himself, and be his own determination. As to Peel 'if he will not come forward and sacrifice himself for the public good, we must make it without him.'

Lady Salisbury's diary, 26 October 1833

Speaking of poets the Duke said, 'I hate the whole race—I have the worst opinion of them—there is no believing a word they say: your professional poets I mean—there never existed a more worthless set than Byron and his friends for example—poets praise fine sentiments and never practise them, their praise of virtue and fine feeling is entirely from the imagination, if they describe a fine action they quote some other author from whom they have taken the idea, to prove that it is in nature. There was no blemish in Scott's character but his reserving from his creditors a settlement for his children when he entered into the bookselling speculation: nothing else can be said against him:—but *he* was not a professional poet.'

Viscount Strangford to Wellington, 26 October 1833

Carlton Club. Mr. Walton, whom your Grace knows, at least by name, has written me the enclosed letter, covering Sir John Campbell's account of his present situation and sufferings.

The case seems an atrocious one, but I am not aware that any thing can be done [about] it, and therefore I only send it that your Grace may know how the matter now stands. I have shewn it to Sir Henry Hardinge, who is just come up to town. He tells me that in all parts of the country where he has been, there is but *one* feeling—that of disgust and hatred towards the Whigs—but still as yet there are no symptoms of a *good* feeling towards *us*.

Dated Saturday evening. *Docketed* 1833, October 26.

Enclosure: Sir John Campbell's case.

Wellington to Viscount Strangford, 27 October 1833

Walmer Castle. The only mode of dealing with Sir John Campbell's paper is to keep it quiet till Parliament will meet. I don't think that any step that we could take could be of any use to Sir John Campbell. On the contrary I believe that the more we should urge Lord Palmerston the less he would do in his favour.

To tell you the truth I don't like the case. I thought that Sir John Campbell was serving regularly in Portugal by permission of His Majesty or in virtue of his position as a Portuguese subject. He was neither. He was as much guilty of a breach of the Foreign Enlistment Act as Napier or any other adventurer.

I may find fault with the Government for having interfered with Don Miguel in favour of others, and for not interfering with Don Pedro in favour of Sir John Campbell. But I cannot find fault with them on other grounds.

Henry Unwin Addington to Wellington, 29 October 1833

29 Albemarle Street. Private. Had I known, on my arrival at Dover, that you were at Walmer I would have gone over there to have greeted you, especially as I had a few words to say to you about the Soto de Roma, which matter, although eternally pressed by me, I grieve to think was not finished before the King's death. I do not accuse Zea of want of good will towards you, for good will he possesses abundantly, but he has the strange propensity of never being able to say the proper word at the proper time. One urgent and directed word with the King would have settled the whole business in five minutes; but that word I could never get that *pig-headed*, but generally honest, man to utter. He has however certainly the merit of entertaining a sincere respect and regard for your Grace.

I have returned under jury-masts from the mission which I owe to your kindness. But on reflecting well, and, as far as I can, impartially, I feel that I have no ground for self-reproach, and I have no doubt that those whose opinions I most value, will do me justice. The public will also do me justice one day, although I shall give myself no trouble in laying my conduct before them.

Circumstances, and especially the King of Spain's death, and his daughter's succession, have now accomplished that which a dictatorial tone failed, and always would have failed, to achieve—the acknowledgment of the Queen of Portugal by Spain.

It now remains to be seen whether Don Pedro will give us trouble or not, and whether he aims at placing himself on his daughter's throne or not.

Spain has done wisely in not delaying her acknowledgment of Dona Maria. In my last conversation with Zea, three days before the King's death, I perceived clearly that he was preparing to put about ship, and sail before the wind, since he found that he could no longer make head against it.

He does not want character, but he much wants tact and intimate knowledge of the Spanish character. But it must be admitted that he has had, and has, a difficult game to play.

In my opinion the Queen has great chances in her favour; but to secure those chances will require a great sagacity as well as great energy on her part.

'Othello's occupation' being now gone, I shall probably avail myself in no long time of the absence of further public duties to visit countries which I have not yet seen, having just paid a few visits to friends in various parts of England, for which purpose I shall leave London in three or four days.

Before I again pass the Channel however, I shall hope to have the great pleasure of shaking your Grace by the hand, and offering you the renewed tribute of my sincere respect and gratitude.

The Marquess of Salisbury to Wellington, c 2 November 1833

I avail myself of your kindness to send you the opinion of Serjeant Andrews and Mr. Rose upon my libel case and I also inclose two notes from my solicitors on the same subject. The only new fact that appears is that Duncombe may move to have a verdict recorded for him, and that this point cannot be decided until Monday when the verdict will be entered for me unopposed, as a matter of course. I shall be entirely guided by your advice. We got to town in very good time for the play on Thursday. You cannot conceive the difference in the atmosphere of Walmer and London.

SALISBURY MSS.

Wellington to the Marquess of Salisbury, 5 November 1833

Walmer Castle. I return Mr. Nicholson's letter.

It is my opinion that you should call for judgment as soon as you can after Thursday. Baron Bailey's whispered opinions ought not to weigh with you. Your counsel ought to make use of the reports of the debate at Hertford as an aggravation. Of course they must be able to prove that the words were spoken.

You cannot submit to the system of bullying adopted by Mr. Thomas Duncombe. The only means of resistance at your disposal are the means in your power by the verdict of the jury.

If the court or the Government should not perform their duty, you will have the satisfaction of reflecting that you did all in your power to resist.

I am glad that you arrived in time for the play.

We have had bad weather since you went.

SALISBURY MSS.

Charles Arbuthnot to Wellington, 10 November 1833

Apethorpe. I wish you to read a letter I have received from Herries, and a copy of my answer to him.

You saw the letters which before passed on the same subject, and you approved of my caution.

I hope you will equally approve of what I now write, and of my declining to make myself a party to a transaction from which I have kept free.

I think Herries had better not have introduced the man to me, but from the man's own acknowledgment he gained no points with me. I fear that Herries and others were indiscreet; and that promises, not fulfilled, were made. I never was in the confidence of any of them upon the subject of the press. At least they did not communicate with me about it.

If *Charles Street* should come into a court of justice it will be most injurious. It is on this account that I urge Herries to lose no time in consulting Scarlett.

Lord Westmorland is remarkably well, but he complains of a weakness in the foot, though I understand there is nothing discernible.

PS. I don't let Herries know that I communicate with you, but I am very anxious to have your advice and guidance. I would not willingly act unkindly by him, but I think you will approve of my not allowing myself to be drawn into a very unpleasant affair with which the man himself owns I have no concern.

Wellington to the Marquess of Salisbury, 12 November 1833

Stratfield Saye. I shall be anxious to learn your decision about Duncombe.

I shall be very much obliged to you if you will let me know what is the exact nature of your relation with Mr. Hardwick. Is he in your service? What do you pay him? on what footing? Give the inclosed to Lady Salisbury; it is about a pony.

SALISBURY MSS.

The Marquess of Salisbury to Wellington, 15 November 1833

London. On the receipt of your letter last week I desired my solicitor to take the necessary steps to bring up Mr. Duncombe for judgment. On going with the brief to Serjeant Andrews, he expressed a strong wish to see me, again entered into his objections to the proceedings, and added that at all events he should not like to lead in the case but recommended me to apply to Scarlett. I only received this intimation yesterday and came up to town this morning. I requested Sir Henry

Hardinge to go with me to Sir James Scarlett. His opinion coincided with that of Andrews, that it would not be prudent under the circumstances to press for judgment unless something could be brought in aggravation, that I ran the chance of losing the advantage I have got in obtaining a verdict and that I must be prepared to go to a new trial. He also told me that the judges had stated that they would only give judgment on Saturday next, that I was too late to give notice to Duncombe for that day (tomorrow), that if I gave him notice for this term when there was little or no chance of bringing him up for judgment it would be thought that I acted with a view of annoying and persecuting him, and that my case would not be the least damaged by waiting till next term, while the suspension of the judgment would not give him the least power of boasting that I did not dare to bring him up as I might at any moment ask for judgment.

From him I went to Serjeant Andrews and I inclose the summary of this conversation which I took down in his presence. I also send the verdict and the third count without which the whole of it would not be very intelligible. I have under these opinions suspended the notice to Duncombe for the present. The verdict is recorded and it will remain for you to decide if you will have the great kindness to do so whether I shall call him up for judgment or not next term.

I hope you will think I have done right as far as I have gone.

Hardwick is the manager of my London property. I pay him £100 per annum. He puts a value upon such of my houses as fall out of lease. He treats with the tenants for renewals, directs the repairs to be done by them, and certifies that they have been properly executed before I grant any lease. He also charges the tenants with the expence of his survey, besides the £100 he receives from me. I cannot tell you at what rate but I believe rather too high. He and his father have been long engaged on the property and he has always discharged his office, which is one of great responsibility, exceedingly well to me. If ever I entered into new terms with a manager I should certainly fix the rate of his charge to the tenants, but I have no wish to disturb my existing arrangement.

Mr. Hardwick likewise manages the property of the Goldsmiths' Company and I believe of Bethlehem Hospital and of some part of the Merchant Tailors. He is the surveyor of St. Katherine's Docks and a good deal employed as an architect by different persons. I should of course consider him in the same light as I should any other architect.

I believe I have answered every query: and I can only add that I think very well of him indeed.

Pray excuse all the trouble I am giving you with this very long letter.

PS. I need hardly add that I did not tell Serjeant Andrews to whom I meant to refer the decision of my line of conduct.

Enclosure: Verdict of the jury.

Not guilty on the first and second counts—guilty of so much of the third count as relates to the composing and publishing the placard dated the 22 December containing reflections on the character of the Marquess of Salisbury. N.B. The judge said he could not take such a verdict and ultimately it was thus recorded: guilty on the third count, with the written verdict attached to the record.[1]

Third count of indictment. That the said Thomas Slingsby Duncombe further contriving and intending as aforesaid to wit on the 22nd day of December in the year 1832 at the parish aforesaid etc. *unlawfully wickedly and maliciously* did compose and publish and cause and procure to be composed and published a certain other address by him the said Thomas S. Duncombe to the electors of the borough of Hertford containing therein among other things the false scandalous malicious defamatory and libellous matters following of and concerning the said Marquess (here follows the libel) to the great scandal and distress of the said Marquess in contempt etc.

Wellington to the Marquess of Salisbury, 16 November 1833

London. I believe that the word *no* ought to be at the end of the first or at the beginning of the second page of the inclosed paper.

It is impossible for you to proceed contrary to the opinions of all your counsel.

However it is quite obvious that you have done every thing that depended upon you. I should prefer to go on, if there was any mode by which a farther progress would not prove injurious to you. But if ever you are reproached for not going on you can shew that two sets of distinguished advocates advised you to remain quiet.

I am much obliged to you for your account of Mr. Hardwick.

SALISBURY MSS.

---

[1] This sentence was added in Salisbury's hand.

Lord Cowley to Wellington, 19 November 1833

Grosvenor Street. I see that the Tory newspapers have espoused the cause of Don Carlos. I cannot think that his success would be advantageous to Spain in any point of view. His government would be worse than Ferdinand's and would probably occasion another revolution in the course of a very few years.

If the Queen conducts herself prudently, if she does not throw herself into the arms of the Constitutionalists, and maintains a party in the clergy, she will probably struggle through her difficulties and succeed in establishing her government. I fear however that she may give too much encouragement to the Liberals. I see that she has issued a decree manifesting a disposition to make some concessions in favor of the liberty of the press and appointing a commission to examine and report upon that question, of which Quintana (a dangerous fellow whom you must have seen at Cadiz) is one of the members.

I hear that Anguillas and other Spaniards included in the amnesty are furious that it has not been extended to Mina and others of his stamp, and talk of not availing themselves of it unless it is extended to the others. This shews how difficult it will be to manage these people when they return to Spain.

My object in writing to you is to learn your opinion respecting the contending parties in Spain, as I should be sorry to hold a language upon the subject different from yours. The Duke of Gloucester who called upon me yesterday has adopted the opinions of the Tory newspapers, and is violent in favor of Don Carlos.

I have suffered much lately from my leg but hope I am now getting well.

Dated Tuesday. *Docketed* 1833, November 19.

Addressed My dear Arthur.

Lord Fitzroy Somerset to Wellington, 21 November 1833

Horse Guards. I am much obliged to you for letting me see Alava's letter of the 13th with its inclosure. I had already prepared a copy of his of the 9th and should have sent it to you two days ago had I not been unusually occupied. I now send it with some observations which I have made on difficult parts of it. I will write him a line by M. de Bacourt's courier today and will suggest to him 'till otherwise advised by you to do nothing about his pension until he sees what he has got to live upon, and I shall be glad to hear that you approve of what I have stated on that part of his letter. I will mention to him the great kindness you intend him, in the event of the failure of his other resources.

He means to take the armistice very properly. It is viewed in the same light by Ruiz de la Vega, who is the only Spaniard to whom I have spoken since it was published; but many of the refugees here instead of being grateful are indignant; and among these is the impracticable Acquelles. He says that the exclusion of some, and the admission of others, is calculated to place the latter in a state of suspicion and they will be supposed to have intrigued for their recall. A few of the Deputies it is believed were omitted by mistake but probably the exceptions were in most cases made from Zea's knowledge of the conduct of individuals during his residence here as Minister. I knew he espioned them and he more than once told me, that he knew that such and such persons were conducting themselves very properly and that others were conspiring against the Spanish Government. I am not surprised at Mina's being omitted in the amnesty. You may remember that he entered Spain in 1830 at the head of a Constitutional force and was defeated and abandoned on the heights of Vera. Having therefore so lately made war against Ferdinand he can hardly have a right to complain of being treated differently from those who have lived quietly in exile for the last ten years.

You have not returned the list of candidates for the Guards or informed me whom you propose to recommend in succession to Lord John Scott.

PS. I send you a copy of the letter from Algiers [*sic*] and a pretty tough job it was to make it.

Enclosure: copy of a letter (in Spanish) from General Miguel Ricardo de Alava, Valencey, 9 November 1833, to Lord Fitzroy Somerset, with comments (in pencil) in Somerset's hand.

Lord Francis Egerton to Wellington, 10 September and 22 November 1833

Castiglione. You may perhaps be amused with what I shall be able to tell you of the state of the Austrian army in this quarter, after three days hard fighting on the Mincio. They have been able after leaving ample forces for the security of their garrisons and the Piedmontese frontier to bring together in this neighbourhood 60,000 men *bien comptés*, and the infantry of all classes the finest in appearance I ever saw or could imagine. The artillery appears to me the part of their force which would the least well stand comparison with that of other nations, and compared to our own in particular, in movement as well as construction, is what a diligence is to a stage coach. This is a wretched country for cavalry and they only produced four regiments. Two crack regiments of Hussars appeared to me moderate enough, the others cuirassiers and dragoons better mounted, but none I think remarkable for manoeuvering. The manoeuvre which is just concluded lasted three days and involved some very heavy marches. I was told previously that the troops had been well exercised, but could hardly have believed it possible that any troops could go through what they did in respect of marching with so little appearance of fatigue or ill humour. Many of their movements were performed at a tremendous pace in a very broken country and their Croats in particular, of which they have a very large force, seem to possess every quality which can make light infantry formidable and to be admirably drilled. They have I believe a very heavy force in the provinces adjacent to the eastern frontier of Italy, and altogether as far as numbers and discipline are concerned they are in fine condition for a stand up fight with the French. In other quite as important respects I am afraid they are in a less advantageous position; and I believe that your observations to me on the principal difficulties of these great military powers are in a rapid process of verification. It is difficult to produce a general and extensive national excitement in the Austrian empire and nothing but such a feeling against the French could enable it to go to war. Bohemia in particular is in a state of ferment under its burthens which nothing but the personal popularity of the Emperor prevents from explosion, and of Italy it is unnecessary to speak, for you well know that, however little expensive or really oppressive their rule may be as compared with that of the French, they have not found the secret of making it acceptable to the upper, nor I believe to the middle, classes. The lower, who are oppressed by the former, have I believe little share in the political discontent and would certainly gain little by such a change as the *possidenti* require, for the great grievance of the nobles is that they have not the aristocratic privileges, exemption from service etc., enjoyed by the nobles in Bohemia and other parts of the Empire. They are rich, spend nothing, grumble, and from time to time enter into the most rash and ill concocted conspiracies; the first person arrested immediately makes an ample confession, shews up every body, and a certain number of persons of substance and family find themselves in a prison and a greater number escape without passports. Ninety went off in this manner a few days since; having hit upon the design of taking the vice-regal palace at Milan in the teeth and mustachios of the Hungarian grenadiers. A good deal depends upon the state of Piedmont; if any thing *éclates* there they will certainly occupy it, and *reste à savoir* what the French will do on their frontier. In the mean time we have been playing at soldiers with great success upon the ground so often fought over by Napoleon between this and Peschiera. The civility and profuse hospitality of the officers here from the general in chief, Radetzky, downwards, exceeds what I can describe and makes me almost ashamed to receive it. They give us artillery horses to take our carriages from quarter to quarter, and every stranger who comes with a uniform has a troop horse and an orderly from the Liechtenstein hussars at his disposal for the whole manoeuvre, added to which we have been billeted like princes, though the place *fourmilles* with real ones. The Archduke himself is as civil and hospitable as his subordinates, and we have made our campaign, with as little hardship as danger; in all other respects I presume it would be impossible to produce a better image of the reality. The hussar saddles which are simply two boards and a sheepskin are certainly less agreeable than English ones, but are both promoters of appetite and preservatives from tumbling. I believe a whole squadron of the Liechtenstein regiment has been dismounted to supply a quantity of strangers idle and curious, and many of them unrecommended in any way. No French officer has appeared among us but I dare say there are plenty *en bourgeois*. The Archduchess is handsome, represents well and is remarkably agreable in conversation. There is as little *ton de garrison* or military ostentation among the officers as in any society I ever saw, and more frankness and cordiality. I wish you could pay them a visit, not that a manoeuvre would be as absolute a novelty or excitement to you as to myself, but because it would please them.

Oatlands. November 22nd.

I was interrupted in the above by letters which called me back to England, and have had since no opportunity of sending it. I have since been through Paris, where I was a second time struck by the unfavourable to us comparison which I am compelled to draw between the situation of that country and my own. They have a strong Government which I believe looks with as much contempt and aversion at ours as any Tory of us all. I saw few people and heard little politics. My impression was that they were puzzled and vexed to death by Spain, and that all parties were reluctant to interfere with force, and *de se mettre dans ce brasier là,* as Pozzo called it. I saw the garrison of Paris reviewed. The infantry are the most dwarfish race of men I ever saw in any country. The artillery superb to look at, the horses being of the best French quality, and the guns burnished and kept like toys. They complain of their great deficiency of cavalry in case of a war with the great powers. I think that Louis Philippe understands that the military chances of a great struggle would be against France, unless she could Jacobinize the dominions of her opponents, in which case his own must reundergo the same process. I am going when my books come from Paris to send you one by a Pole on the Russian army, which seems to me curious, very much so if true.

Lord Farnborough to Wellington, 22 November 1833

Bromley Hill. Finding there was no memorial of Mr. Pitt at his own college at Cambridge, I employed Mr. Chantrey to make a bust of him, from the different likenesses either of bust or painting which we could collect of him, as he appeared in his younger days at college. He has succeeded as he always does in these things remarkably well. He undertook also to superintend the casting of a *very few* busts which I intend for those of his friends whom he most esteemed and admired.

I know no person in whom he had more confidence and of whom he had a higher opinion than yourself, and which have been so fully and so gloriously confirmed by achievements which have occurred subsequent to his death. I beg your acceptance of one of these busts, which I have ordered to be sent to your house.

Wellington to Viscount Mahon, 24 November 1833

Stratfield Saye. I'll send you to London by the coach tomorrow the work upon the French constitutions published by the *Gazette de France.*

I am not sufficiently good historian to be able to decide. But I suspect that the facts have been distorted in order to prove the truth of the theory with which the author starts. At all events he does not prove that universal suffrage ever existed in France. Neither do I think that the author proves that the dissatisfaction with former Governments was to be attributed to the want of a representative system. I think that there was enough to dissatisfy any nation with the latter end of the government of Louis XIV and the whole government of the Regent, and that of Louis XV, and even that of Louis XVI without calling in aid the want of a representative constitution.

I am afraid that the trial of universal suffrage even with all the proposed stages between the voter in the commune and the representative would be found a very dangerous one for the monarchy. It is very probable that it would not be more dangerous than that system now under trial: viz. voters paying not eight pounds rent, but eight pounds in direct contributions to the State.

To tell you the truth I am very much afraid that our experiment will go to prove that there is no safety for governors and no security for property under any of these representative systems. They are terribly gone out of fashion in Europe.

Nothing can be more curious than the facility with which this author writes of changes of the constitution of the State; and of establishing a representative system founded upon universal suffrage in a despotick State. He loses sight altogether of the fact that if the experiment does not answer the Sovereign may be under the necessity of conquering over again his State; or that he may perish upon a scaffold. At all events the interests, the habits, the wishes and the wants of the people, particularly of those possessing property are entirely laid out of the question.

However I was very much entertained by the work; and I am much obliged to you for having allowed me to peruse it. There are many very interesting and new observations in it. I have kept it longer than I wished; but in truth I could not commence to read it till I came here.

CHEVENING PAPERS 685.

William John Bankes to Wellington, 27 November 1833

Old Palace Yard. The sanction of your good opinion is of such high value before the British public, and above all to one who has had the honor of being personally known and noticed by you during several years, that I have only been deterred from making application to you sooner, first by the feeling that it might seem a sort of presumption in me, and next from a little misgiving that in these days of party spirit and of slander, a coincidence of political sentiment might afford some handle for deprecating testimony given as to character, in a case where party spirit was sufficiently shown at the outset by the part which the press took.

Several friends however quite opposed to me in politics have readily and cheerfully come forward, and the little weight therefore that was perhaps due to the last consideration is *quite* done away. The full advantage therefore of your appearance among those who give this testimony to my character is now felt by my legal advisers, and by myself, and though it is with extreme reluctance that I take the liberty of requesting so great and inconvenient an act of kindness, as to appear in court on the trial, I yet *most earnestly* venture to do so. It is fixed for this next Monday, the 2nd of December.[1]

Should your Grace kindly accede to my wish, since it is considered necessary that my solicitor should have a few moments of previous interview with each individual who may be called, that my counsel may know the extent of his evidence, I am desired to add that the favor will be increased, if you can name any where in town or country where my solicitor, Mr. Faulkner, 1 Bedford Row, could have the honor of speaking with you before Monday.

If I have not made all the apologies that are due for so great a liberty, and so inconvenient and disagreable a request, I am sure that your Grace will impute it to the true cause, the insufficiency of all expressions on such a subject, and the harassed state of the mind of *etc.*

Viscount Mahon to Wellington, 28 November 1833

Albemarle Street. The day before yesterday I had the honour of receiving my French book and yesterday your Grace's letter, and I beg to offer you my sincerest thanks for having so kindly given me in the second a most interesting and valuable commentary on the first. The way in

---

[1] William Bankes M.P. and Thomas Fowler, a private in the army, were brought before the court of the King's Bench on 2 December 1833 on a charge of homosexual behaviour. They were acquitted.

which I have heard the scheme of universal suffrage and two degrees
of election, for France, defended by some of the new school of Royalists
in that country, is by supposing that in every village and country district,
the *seigneur du lieu* or the most respectable resident neighbour would be
chosen as elector, and that these gentlemen meeting together as a body of
constituents would in fact produce as aristocratic a result, though by
the most popular means, as if in the first instance the elective franchise
were limited to men of considerable property; thus combining what
recent times have shown to be so very often jarring, the gratification
of the multitude, and the ascendancy of the landed interest. They also
allege that under the present rate of the elective franchise, the real
representation is monopolised by one class, namely the smallest tax-
payers (of £8 yearly) who in France are to a great extent the present
owners of the Church or emigrants' estates which were seized and
parcelled out for sale during the Revolution and who are therefore in
general attached by interest to the principles of that period. As a remarkable instance of the manner in which both the upper and the lower
classes in France are misrepresented under the present system they
mention that M. Manuel—perhaps the most *exalté* of all the deputies
under the Bourbons and at last expelled the Chamber for some words
that seemed to justify regicide—sat as a member for no other than that
most eminently loyal province, La Vendée!

Yet, although these arguments do not appear devoid of a certain
degree of plausibility, and although the present grievance is certainly
very real, I quite concur with your Grace in thinking that the sub-
stitution of universal suffrage would be a highly dangerous and doubtful experiment. It seems to me also that the author has failed in proving
that such a system was ever established in France. Some facts there
undoubtedly are in support of that notion. But the truth is that during
the middle ages governments were so uncertain and varying—so
constantly looking to particular emergencies instead of rules and
systems—so often moulded anew by convulsion and civil war—that
instances may be drawn from them of every possible sort of popular
assembly. And it is evident that any theory as to those governments
will appear to be well-founded if you merely pick out and marshal
together all the instances in its favour and carefully omit all mention
of the others.

One remarkable thing in this work which I think must have struck
your Grace is that Henry the Fourth who has hitherto been held up

as the main-stay and hero of the Bourbons is rather disparaged and thrown over, his government by *assemblées des notables* not suiting the author's system.

Your old acquaintance at Vittoria, Marshal Jourdan, died last Saturday morning at Paris.

I hope your Grace will not think me troublesome if I take this opportunity of reminding you how very highly gratified I should be some time or other by the perusal of the memorial on the Russian campaign, which you once had the kindness to say that you would show me.

The other day at the Carlton Club, I found Sir Alexander Grant and some others talking of the different lines on Spanish politics which have lately been taken by the *Morning Post* and the *Guardian* and seeming very doubtful which of the two your Grace would consider preferable. The *Morning Post* has been rather attacking M. Zea and the *Guardian* supporting him. There appeared to be a feeling that it might be better if the same line on that subject were taken by both.

I left Lord and Lady Salisbury alone on Tuesday and am going again on Monday when they expect the Duke of Gloucester and a large party. On that day I am also to give evidence on W. Bankes's trial as to his character in society; his solicitor told me that he would have nearly a hundred witnesses.

Wellington to the Earl Bathurst, 28 November 1833

Stratfield Saye. Some time ago Lord Sidmouth communicated to me the desire of the Conservative party of the University of Oxford that I should be their Chancellor.

I answered that I had not received an university education; that I knew no more of Greek or Latin than an Eton boy in the remove; that these facts were perfectly well known; and that I must be considered incapable and unfit.

I earnestly recommended to them to think of others; and I named the Duke of Beaufort, yourself, Lord Mansfield, Lord Sidmouth, and Lord Talbot.

I received this morning the enclosed letter and the gentlemen named have been with me.

I repeated to them what I had told Lord Sidmouth and again recommended to them to look to others. They answered that they had applied to Lord Mansfield who had positively refused. That they had considered of proposing the office to yourself and to Lord Sidmouth, but that both being of the same standing with Lord Grenville they were apprehensive that you might both be considered too old; and that Lord Talbot was not sufficiently known as a publick man; and that the Duke of Beaufort laboured under the same disadvantage with this addition that he had never been in publick office, however respectable in private life and in his county.

I then urged them to consider whether it was absolutely necessary that the Chancellor should be a peer. They answered positively now more than ever, and one constantly in the habit of attending the House of Lords.

I told them that I could not alter my opinion upon the subject adopted from the first impression and that I was convinced that it would occur to every body that I was an example of success in life without academical education and an example to be avoided, rather than an example for the university to hold forth to the youth of the country. I said that they would find themselves in the awkward position of a publick body having to make an excuse for their act.

I entreated them to reconsider the subject and whether Lord Bathurst or Lord Sidmouth would not either of them be a candidate acceptable to the university whose election would answer the temporary purpose equally with the election of myself.

I said that I was convinced that I was right in declining. That I was very sensible of the distinction which they proposed to confer upon me; and that moreover I felt that if the election should be unfavourable the defeat would be theirs and not mine, while they would have to bear the odium of having selected an improper person if the election should be successful.

They answered that they had no doubt of the result if I would allow that they should propose me.

I then said that in all cases of this kind I considered myself as an instrument to be used by the publick when it was deemed necessary. However that in a case of this kind in which personal feelings might have an influence I wished to have the opinions of others.

I named yourself as one that I should consult. I requested that in the mean time they would consider what I had stated and whether they could not find another noble Lord better qualified than myself. It appears that from delicacy towards Lord Grenville they do not propose to make any publick nomination of a candidate to succeed him so long as he will be alive.

Dated November 28. *Docketed* 1833, November 28.

Wellington to Sir Henry Hardinge, 28 November 1833

Stratfield Saye. Your Oxford friends have been here with your letter of the 27th. We parted very much as I did with Lord Sidmouth some months ago.

I should be highly honoured by the appointment; and I don't think that I should be damaged by being rejected upon the election, as I don't seek the appointment. The blame would fall upon the university for making a bad appointment if the selection should succeed; the ridicule if it should fail. My opinion is that it would succeed, as the Whigs are so cordially detested by every thing in the shape of a gentleman or a man of education unless he should be one of their own majority in Parliament.

I am going on Monday to attend Bankes's trial. I shall come back here immediately afterwards. I wish that you and Lady Emily and your boy would come down to pay me a visit: fix your own time previous to about Christmas when I must go northward. I have a good account of the pheasants. Cooke and Croker were talking of coming.

I would take your boy out hunting.

I asked your friends whether it was necessary that their Chancellor should be a peer, meaning to recommend to them to select Sir Robert Peel. They answered positively; and one in the habit of attending Parliament constantly. They gave a very good reason: viz. that they had two Members for the university in the House of Commons who could speak for them. They had nobody in the Lords excepting their Chancellor.

VISCOUNT HARDINGE PAPERS

Wellington to Viscount Mahon, 29 November 1833

Stratfield Saye. The plan of French reform of the *Gazette de France* is not to give a vote to every proprietor, but to every payer of taxes.

I am aware that the payer of taxes of eight pounds a year is in France a revolutionist. This fact shews to what a degree local circumstances influence such questions. A payer of direct taxes (for that is the description of tax) of eight pounds a year would in England be a considerable person. He is in France a man of 100 to 150 pounds a year. I must say that I know enough of the internal situation of France to be able to decide that no confidence can be placed in the support of any representative Chamber in a conservative system of policy.

What I wished for Spain was if possible to avoid a civil war. Now that we have got the war, there is nothing to wish for excepting to have peace as soon as possible; and that the operations of the war should be limited in respect to space.

Our newspapers are like our publick men; each going his own way. The *Standard* objects to Don Carlos because he is Roman Catholick! The *Guardian* takes up the cause of the Queen for no reason at all; while the *Morning Post* supports sometimes the one and sometimes the other. We are at least impartial!

I am summoned to attend Bankes's trial.

CHEVENING PAPERS 685.

The Earl Bathurst to Wellington, 30 November 1833

Cirencester. I have no acquaintance with either of the gentlemen who have been with you. The first I have heard mentioned as a distinguished member of the university, and I make no doubt that they are both very influential people, but I wish that they had not been *both* of St. John's College; for though St. John's is a powerful college in the university, and has I understand of late much cultivated influence generally in it, there are other great colleges who are jealous of their respective powers, particularly Christ Church, Magdalen, University, and Queen's, and are each much in the habit of not dividing their influence, but go bodily in support of whatever candidate the heads of each college or the most influential men in them may be disposed to favor. The great majority of electors are non-residents, and the majority of those non-residents are inclined to go with their respective colleges. The gentlemen who have been with you may be fully convinced and justly too that the majority of those with whom they *converse* will be in your favor, but unless they have told you that the heads, or the most influential members of many of the colleges I have mentioned are prepared to answer for their respective colleges, I do not think that they are at present prepared to make such a proposal to you as you in your peculiar situation ought to accept, without further inquiry.

I do not think that your not having had an university education an objection which will be much felt, though the friends of the opposing candidate would try to make it avail. Your Oxford sins of carrying the Roman Catholic question, and the having then taken your sons from Oxford to place them in Cambridge, are the two which will be also brought against you: the latter even more than the former. But the gentlemen whom you have seen must be aware of this, and I presume know that these sins have been pardoned, or at least will not be much remembered against you.

Lord Carlisle will I am afraid be rather a formidable opponent. His high rank and family connections and his having been of Christ Church together with his *reputed* moderation in politics would I think have given him a very good chance, if the Government to which he belongs were not actually engaged in attacking the Church, and even now there may be some who will persuade themselves or persuade others that by voting for him they will mitigate the hostility of Government in their measures against the Church establishment: not foreseeing that by electing Lord Carlisle they would give the impression that the university had declared itself in favor of Church reform.

Of course all the friends of Government would be active in his cause. Probably Dr. Shuttleworth, the head of New College (sufficiently inclined politically that way) would be so disposed: and if so, would I believe prove an influential man. He has already so far taken the lead as to make the offer to the Archbishop of Canterbury, who has declined on the ground that at such a time, when the Church is looked upon with so much jealousy, it is more prudent not to accept a high station, which has been almost exclusively filled by distinguished laymen. Dr. Shuttleworth may therefore now exert himself in favor of Lord Carlisle without appearing to do so, solely on political motives.

The Dean of Christ Church is a man of very retired habits, and little inclined to take any part, and so little popular as not to have much influence even in his own college, and still less out of it, neither do I believe that there are any in the chapter or among the tutors who are generally considered; it is possible therefore that Christ Church would have less influence than usual in the election, and that they might not even go as bodily together as usual. But you should ascertain what University College and Magdalen and Queen's are likely to do. I take it for granted that in some way or other the offer has been made to Lord Eldon, for though I do not imagine that at his time of life he would accept, I am sure he would like the compliment, and be even hurt at its not having been made.

Your failing would be a great blow to the cause, and there is no exertion which the Government could make which would not be made against you. Ascertain therefore before you agree, what assurances the gentlemen whom you have seen can give you that some of the leading colleges, besides St. John's, will support you as a body.

It is possible that they may have entered into these particulars, though you have not mentioned them, but as you are not acquainted with Oxford politics, you probably may not have directed your inquiries into those particulars which from the little I have heard of these subjects on the occasion of university elections I know to be material.

I have accounts from time to time from Dropmore of the state of my poor old friend. They are any thing but consolatory, but there is no immediate apprehension. Four and twenty hours however may bring it to a conclusion at any time.

We propose migrating sometime in January. If you should happen to be at Stratfield Saye about that time, we shall be happy to accept your invitation.

Apsley had intended to offer himself to you any time after next week, [if] you would have the goodness to admit him. I have told him that I was writing to you, and would make his proposal. Let him have a line to fix the time you will receive him.

Sir Henry Hardinge to Wellington, 30 November 1833

Wildernesse. I think the result of the application from the university will end in their forcing their honors upon you in spite of your reluctance —and as this feeling on your part is known to be most sincere, and not liable to any insinuations of secret management, I hope as a matter of personal gratification to myself, that to your military and political services we may be able to add that of defender of the Protestant establishment.

Brecknock is going to town and I send this note by him.

Lady Emily and myself should be most happy to pay your Grace a visit from the 10th to the 14th or 15th or from the 11th or 12th for three or four days as may best suit your convenience. Charles will be proud of the honour of accepting your kind recollection of him and we are very grateful for it.

Wellington to the Rev. Thomas Wintle, 30 November 1833

Stratfield Saye. It has this day been stated to me that Lord Talbot having first declined to allow himself to be put in nomination as a candidate to be elected Chancellor of the University of Oxford had subsequently signified his assent to the proposition which had been made to him. I am inclined to believe that there is some truth in the report; as the gentleman who mentioned it to me stated with tolerable accuracy the details of the conversation which I had with you on Thursday.

If the offer has been made to Lord Talbot and he has accepted, or if his Lordship is likely to accept if the offer should be made to him, I am convinced that you ought to elect him. He is highly respectable; and in every way qualified; and the election of him will not require explanation, or be considered a matter of necessity.

I beg you then to allow me to consider that I am no longer in your thoughts for this honour, if it be true that Lord Talbot is willing to become a candidate to fill the office.

The Earl Bathurst to Wellington, 1 December 1833

Cirencester. Since writing my letter of yesterday's date, I find that Oriel and Brazennose Colleges are to the full as numerous in votes as any of those which I mentioned, excepting always Christ Church. Queen's College owes its weight in all elections to the rule which they strictly observe, much more than other colleges, of always going together.

This however makes no difference in what I suggested to you yesterday, viz. that you must not depend upon general dispositions in your favour, and that you ought not to allow your name to be committed, until you shall have been assured of the solid support of some of the great influential colleges, in addition to that of St. John's. There are many who will mean you well, but yet when the time comes be unwilling to go against their own college.

All this must be well known by the gentlemen whom you have seen, but they may be too sanguine, and I am unwilling that you should embark in this business without having substantial grounds for expecting success. I am at the same time quite aware that much may be lost by indecision. I hope therefore that your Oxford friends will be able soon to furnish you with a statement which will justify your accepting their proposition.

Explanation respecting Lord Talbot's acceptance of the office of Chancellor of the university[1]

At a second meeting, held on Monday, December 2nd, of those members of Convocation, who lately had the honour of communicating with his Grace the Duke of Wellington, through the Rev. Thomas Wintle, Fellow of St. John's College, a letter from his Grace, dated November 30th, was read. It was the opinion of all present that the following statement of facts ought, without delay, to be in the most respectful manner submitted to his Grace's attention.

In the prospect of an early vacancy of the office of Chancellor of the university, a formal application was, in the first instance, made by the Dean of Christ Church to Lord Mansfield, who was requested to allow himself to be named as a candidate; but who declined the offer. A similar application was in the next place made to Lord Talbot, from whom a negative answer was received on Monday, November 25th. On the same day, it was signified from Christ Church that no third candidate was likely to be proposed by that college; and in consequence, the meeting, of which the Duke of Wellington has already been informed, took place at Mr. Wintle's rooms, on Tuesday, November 26th. The result of the meeting was made known at Christ Church where acquiescence seemed to be expressed; and it was distinctly understood that no measures would be adopted by that society, before the arrival of an answer from the Duke of Wellington. In the evening of Tuesday, one of Lord Talbot's sons (himself a member of Christ Church) reached Oxford from London; and stated to his friends that he had come, without the sanction of his father but with the intention of asking for an opportunity of reconsidering the decision, which, in his opinion, Lord Talbot had somewhat hastily formed and announced. Mr. Talbot was clearly told that he had come too late, but whilst some of his Christ Church friends advised him to return at once to London, others detained him in Oxford during the evening and attempted, although without any success, to delay or modify the communication,

---

[1] Docket, in Wellington's hand.

which in the morning of the same day it had been determined to forward to the Duke of Wellington. Mr. Talbot proceeded to his father's residence on Wednesday morning, whilst Mr. Wintle was on his way to Strathfieldsay; and before the return of the latter to Oxford on Thursday, November 28th, intelligence was brought to Christ Church that Lord Talbot had altered his purpose and was now become willing to listen to a renewal of the former proposal, if it should be made. In the course of Friday morning, Mr. Wintle was astonished by the receipt of a written document, purporting to come from the chapter and common room of Christ Church and conveying an opinion that Mr. Wintle ought, in his interview with the Duke of Wellington, to have stated the probability of Lord Talbot's allowing himself to be nominated—a probability, which Mr. Wintle at that time was not authorised to regard as any ground of proceeding; and which, if he had so regarded it, would have precluded all possibility of such an application as he had the honour, in behalf of his friends, of making to the Duke of Wellington.

It is hoped that a mere statement of these facts may suffice to vindicate those members of Convocation, who have on this important occasion presumed to address themselves to the Duke of Wellington, from the charge, which would otherwise lie against them, of paying to his Grace an unmeaning compliment; and that it may farther serve to show that Mr. Wintle, whom they are most happy to employ once more as their organ, was the faithful interpreter of their views and wishes. Lord Talbot has in fact never been in their contemplation as a candidate, since Monday, the 25th ult. when his refusal transpired; nor can they conceive that his Lordship will by any motives be induced to divide the university under existing circumstances. At all events it is their fixed purpose to put his Lordship in possession of the facts above stated.

Mr. Wintle will have the goodness to explain the details of this written document. It only remains for the members of Convocation now assembled (whose names are withheld from feelings of delicacy already mentioned by Mr. Wintle) to express the deep sense of gratitude, which they must always cherish, to the noble and generous devotion to the cause of the university manifested in this instance by the Duke of Wellington; and their earnest hope and entreaty that his Grace will regard the proposal, made to him, on Thursday last, the 28th ult. as still awaiting his final determination.

Wellington to Sir Henry Hardinge, 2 December 1833

London. I have come to town as an evidence to character in Bankes's trial.

Since I wrote to you I heard on Saturday not only that an offer had been made to Lord Talbot of the office of Chancellor of the university, bu. that [he] had accepted after having previously declined.

I consequently wrote to Mr. Wintle to desire that every thing that had passed with me might be considered *non avenu*.

I am certain that if any Conservative with a tolerable character will stand it is better that I should not. Indeed I will not unless it should be found that there is nobody who will stand the election who has any claim to the distinction.

I shall be delighted to see you on the 10th.

VISCOUNT HARDINGE PAPERS. *Copy in Wellington Papers.*

Sir Henry Hardinge to Wellington, 3 December 1833

Carlton Club. Mr. Bankes the father was at this club today, and the family are of course greatly relieved by the verdict.

Mr. Peach told me Denman's charge was unfavourable—and that William Bankes's friends in the county of Dorset will not be satisfied until he delegates a committee to inquire into certain reports confined to persons within the county. However the great point has been gained, and for the rest he must trust to time and prudence.

Macaulay's £10,000 a year appointment is confirmed, and is a monstrous specimen of East Indian reform. The Leeds patriot was bought because he was troublesome as a subordinate member of the Government, a very bad man of business, and a most insufferable member of the Board to any body who approached him.

Mr. Henry Ellis (Lord Goderich's half-brother) is appointed to be the chief officer at Canton, £7,000 a year—and there can be no doubt that the jobbing in India will flourish and multiply in an increased ratio under Whig management.

I saw Peel and delivered your message. He told me he heard you had been admirably received by the court yesterday when you entered and were the most popular man in the country.

He thinks the Government in a great scrape in the prosecution of the pilot, where exclusive of other considerations the Government caused every Catholic to be struck off the jury list save *one*, in a case where the accused was a Catholic, when in a few weeks, the 1st January, the new law of the jury ballot will be in operation and render it impossible to procure right or wrong a Government conviction against a Catholic.

PS. I am going to take the liberty of begging to be allowed to substitute Walter James instead of Charles.

The visit will be much more *useful* to the young Oxonian than to the Etonian, and he can sleep in my dressing room or any where—and in any thing that is very agreable I always treat Walter as the eldest son.

Dated December 3rd. *Docketed* 1833, December 3.

The Duke of Cumberland to Wellington, 3 December 1833

Berlin. I had the pleasure of receiving a few days back your kind letter and if there is a stagnation of all news in England a fortiori it is so *here*, however the little I have been able to collect I will inform you of. The congress of Ministers on the German business is, I believe, to assemble the first days in January. It was originally intended that Prague should have been the place for their assembling, but why or wherefore it is now decided that Vienna is to be the rendezvous. I must say according to my humble opinion it would have been more prudent and adviseable to have taken any other town in the Austrian dominions than Vienna, as there they cannot prevent the interference either directly or indirectly of the *corps diplomatique.* Now as the topics to be treated there are purely concerning the interests of the various German states, it would have been as well to have prevented *all* exterior influence. That this will more or less be the case *now* there can be little or no doubt, from the line of conduct pursued by the Ministers of France and Great Britain at *Frankfurt*, the British there just as here being totally under the guidance of the Frenchman. This is as notorious here as the sun at noonday, and Lord Minto never writes a note or pays a visit to Ancillon without first consulting Monsieur Bresson. I saw a leading man a few days ago who called on me, when we talked over the present state of European politicks and lamented all the *faux pas* that had taken place. This person said, having been more or less privy to all that has been going on in the political world for the last twenty years, at that time all our *faith* and *confidence* were placed in Great Britain and its

Cabinet. They were the saviours of Europe and its dearest interests, and now, alas, what a change! England has disgraced itself by becoming the most humble servant of and slave to France, and to conceive that she now encourages anything that tends to revolutionize and disorganize all other states! A curious question was put to me, and that too *privately*, whether Palmerston had ever been *mad*? or if that malady existed in his family? for that some of the dispatches he had written were couched in such language, so confused and *violent*, that nothing but a malady of that sort could excuse them. I had also some curious anecdotes of Durham during his stay here. At first he was very reserved and wanted to appear very mild, but unfortunately the proclamation from the Diet of Frankfurt had just come out. This so kindled his rage and violence that it broke out and he shewed to the perfect conviction of all that he had only been disguising his real character. They also told me that he shewed the most inexcusable ignorance of the most trifling and the most ordinary courtesies of Germany. Now if this *soi-disant lumen mundi*, the grand *faiseur* of his father-in-law's Cabinet, is, as I have heard him described, we cannot then not be surprized at the total incapacity of our representative here. There is a great mystery about Felix Schwarzenberg's mission, for the manner in which the King of the Netherlands has taken it proves that there must be some *dessous des cartes*, some secret article that was not publickly known or avowed, but *none* here acknowledge this. From all I can learn the last ministerial visit at Brighton has not afforded, I believe, much gratification to either party. I hear Lord Grey looked wretchedly ill, worn down by *cares and thoughts. These* are the words used in the letter I saw. No wonder, for he must *now* see to what state he and his theoretical plans have reduced our unhappy country, and with his eyes open he finds he is so urged on he cannot stop or retreat. Durham's speech at Gateshead I should think must enrage him and *frighten* him as he seems to hoist the flag of rebellion to his father-in-law's Cabinet, putting himself at the head of the movement party in the House of Lords. Have you had any intimation from the Bishop of Exeter or any of the right reverend bench what are the plans these fellows mean to propose against the Church? *Various* reports I have heard but *none* that I can depend upon. Now *really* it is absolutely necessary that the Archbishop should not injure the matter, or with false delicacy keep *concealed from us till too late* all he knows, for this is a matter that does not merely concern the Church, as *Church alone*, but the State at *large*, and if the one *falls* the other follows instantly. Pray, pray, lose not sight of this, I beseech you, as it is of the most vital consequence to *all*.

Thank God I am able to say my beloved boy is now surely recovered from his late bilious attack and his eye has not suffered in the slightest way. Both he and the Duchess beg to be most kindly remembered to you.

PS. Your account of the *chasses* makes my mouth water.

December 8th

I have opened my letter again to add a few lines, having had this morning a very long conversation with an *officer* of high consideration in the army here, and who has been sent on an official situation to Petersburg last spring and is to return there this very evening. He and I had a good hour's conversation respecting the Russian army and its actual state. He says, knowing it more or less now for the last twenty years, and having attended His Majesty the Emperor during all his inspections last year, I am able to form a pretty accurate idea of its present state, and I must say that the present Emperor has since the last Turkish war done much to cure it of many of its great abuses; and he has as it were remodelled the whole army. He has reduced both in cavalry and infantry the *numbers* of regiments, but added to their strength and efficiency. The Guards Corps remaining the same, their ranks are composed of three battalions, two of which are to march and the third remains as a depot. The cavalry of the Guards have six squadrons per regiment, *five* march, the sixth remains as depot. There are seven corps of army of the line. These other regiments have *six battalions* each, four are to march, and the other *two* are to form the depot. Each army corps is composed of one division of cavalry of four regiments, each regiment having eight squadrons, six are to march, *two* remain in depot. Therefore, there being seven corps of army, they will have seven divisions of cavalry attached to their corps, consisting of one *brigade* of hussars or sixteen squadrons nominally, but *twelve* in fact, and two brigades of lancers, the lancer strength *twenty-four* squadrons actually in the field.

Then they have three corps of cavalry of reserve, consisting each of two divisions or *eight* regiments at six squadrons each, forty-eight squadrons, composed first division cuirassiers, second division lancers. The third corps of reserve corps has been remodelled. It consisted of mounted riflemen, and these he has now formed into dragoons, and they are also *eight* squadrons and to them he has added *two squadrons* of lancers each and it appears from there being besides this attached to them a battery of twelve pounders and two batteries of six that His Majesty considers them as mounted infantry, which he can with greater celerity transport to any distance, for there are also two squadrons of mounted pioneers added to this third corps. All this they are now proceeding with, and that too with great alacrity. So that should any thing *occur here* on the instant they can march certainly a corps of *two hundred thousand* men, and when the number *two hundred thousand* is given, in *real* fact that number *now* and not nominal as formerly, for His Majesty has found it necessary to put an end to *all* false returns, etc., to send eternally his A.D.C. to the different divisions in order to inspect them and make their *special* report to himself so that he keeps them *now* to their duty. I thought this might interest you and therefore I have added this. Probably we shall after *tomorrow* learn when it is likely we shall be called together again.

Wellington to Sir Henry Hardinge, 4 December 1833

Stratfield Saye. I am just now come in from hunting; and have only time before the post goes to tell you that I shall be delighted to see Walter James as well as Charles.

I have plenty of room.

VISCOUNT HARDINGE PAPERS.

Princess Lieven to Wellington, 4 December 1833

Londres. Je m'empresse de vous dire en réponse à votre aimable billet, M. le Duc, que nous sommes à vos ordres et enchantés que vous veuilliez nous y mettre. Commandez, depuis lundi le 9, nous sommes à votre disposition et tout ce que vous choisirez nous conviendra.

Je me réjouis extrêmement d'aller chez vous, cela me rapellera de bien bons tems. Ceux ci n'y ressemblent guère.

L'affaire turque dont vous me parliez l'autre jour dans une lettre est une affaire bien simple d'une part, bien étrange de l'autre. Nous en causerons. En général que de choses sur les quelles causer et s'étonner! Attendons Stratfield Saye. Faites moi savoir vos volontés, M. le Duc, parce que je n'accepterai rien à droite ou à gauche avant de connaître vos intentions.

Adieu et milles amitiés fidèles.

PS. Je suis ravie de connaître l'état du thermomètre chez vous et je n'ai plus d'autre ambition que de ce que ma chambre à coucher soit aussi bien traitée que le vestibule. 64 degrés—c'est charmant et tous les Csars de Russie par dessus le marché!

Sir Henry Hardinge to Wellington, 5 December 1833

Whitehall Place. We are much obliged to you for your Grace's kindness to Walter. Your notice will act as a useful stimulus to both our boys, and they will be delighted to be under your roof.

Lady Brownlow dined with us yesterday. I find from her that the King expected six of his Cabinet to the Council held at Windsor, but that ten came down—the chief object to force Lord Durham into the Cabinet. The King positively refused to consent—Lords Lansdowne and Melbourne declaring that they would resign if the measure were persevered in. The King during the dinner almost turned his back on Lord Grey, addressing his conversation to Lord Lansdowne, and after dinner pretended to fall asleep until Lord Grey retired.

The news from Mr. Booth from Dublin is that the Government are alarmed at the tone taken by *The Times* reprobating their pilot prosecution, and still more alarmed at the trades unions, which have assumed so fearful an attitude that the merchants and traders have called a meeting in the hope of devising some measures to put down an evil more formidable than any which has yet sprung up from the seed of reform. If persevered in (and there is every reason to believe that a constant correspondence is kept up with the London, Birmingham and Leeds unions with those in Ireland) it must end not only in the ruin of trade, but in the forcible seizure of the Government and power of the country by a set of dissolute workmen. The several trades combine their operations by delegates and no business is allowed to be carried on but on terms which shall in the first instance meet with their approval. In this instance the middling classes who have so delighted in reform begin to feel the blessings of democracy.

Captain Elliott of the Navy has just returned from Santarem, having traversed Portugal and embarked at Vigo. Mr. G. Elder, who has seen him, says he gives a good account of Don Miguel's army, and that they intend shortly to resume the offensive: but I presume the first step of the *mediators* will be to have a suspension of hostilities.

The only private gossip I hear is that Stanley treats his wife ill, and that his temper is intolerable. The Duke of Richmond, having the inconvenience at home of a shrew, consoles himself with Mrs. Stanley, and the kind friends of the parties prophesy a fracas. This is believed at Brighton, but is probably much over-charged.

Dated 5 December. *Docketed* 1833, December 5.

The Earl Bathurst to Wellington, 5 December 1833

Cirencester. If one set of Conservatives have been making an offer to Lord Talbot, while another was making a similar one to you, it shews how loosely they are acting, and that they cannot have made such an examination of the disposition of the influential colleges as to make it prudent in you to commit yourself.

As for Lord Talbot, he is a very worthy honest gentleman, and very ill-used, I am sorry to say, by Lord Liverpool's Government, but if he is to be the Conservative candidate, depend upon it, Lord Carlisle will carry it in an hard canter. I am not in the way of knowing, but I suspect that if no offer be made to old Eldon, many of his friends will be out of humour.

Bankes's business ended triumphantly. I was apprehensive, I confess, that prejudice and something of party ill-will would have made his acquittal (for conviction I think was not probable) coupled with something like a stain behind it.

Apsley will write to you, when he proposes to go to you, and desires me to thank you very much for your readiness to receive him. I rather think it will end in his postponing it until you return to Stratfield Say after Christmas. We propose being with you about the middle of that month.

PS. The account which I had from Dropmore since I wrote last to you, was somewhat more favourable, and he was about to try a new medicine.

Lady Maryborough to Wellington, 8 December 1833

I send you this piece of a letter as it pleases me and it shows what right feeling there is in this country could it be brought in use to save us.

Dated Sunday. *Docketed* 1833, December 7th. (*which was a Saturday*).

Enclosure: Extract from a letter from Michael Bruce to Lady Maryborough, 7 December 1833.

Foreign Office. There are various rumours in circulation respecting changes in the Ministry to none of which do I give any credence. I heard the other day from very good authority that Lord Grey had made up his mind to remain at the head of the Government till the end of the ensuing session. In the meantime his colleagues will see whether any arrangements can be made which will enable them to carry it on without his assistance. It is said that they are unanimous on one point, viz., not to allow Brougham to be his successor. The Chancellor is certainly at a great discount, and I strongly suspect that his sun is set never to rise again. There is a most pungent joke now in circulation respecting him in Westminster Hall. It is by some attributed to Sugden but whoever the author may be it is worthy of being recorded. It is a pity, they say, that the Chancellor does not know a little of law, for then he would have a smattering of every thing. A propos of Westminster Hall, I had the pleasure of seeing the Duke of Wellington there on Monday last and he appeared to be in perfect health. I cannot refrain from telling you (because I know it will afford gratification both to you and Lord Maryborough) that when he came into court the whole Bar rose to salute him. This was a spontaneous tribute of respect and is a proof of the high estimation in which he is held by all who are capable of appreciating true merit. His life indeed is most precious. I look upon him as the man destined by Providence to rescue us from the fear of anarchy. Pray pardon all this gossip. I am not yet an old man, but I fear that I have all the garrulity of age. Remember me very kindly to Lord Maryborough and Miss Bagot.

Wellington to the Marquess of Salisbury, 10 December 1833

Stratfield Saye. I consider Bankes as he is described by the verdict; and if I had a party of persons at my house with whom he had been on terms of intimacy I should ask him to meet them.

If Bankes is wise however he will not expose himself to the world for some time. He might be formally or coldly received by some; which would make a lasting impression upon him. The example might be followed by others.

A little patience will set everything right.

SALISBURY MSS.

Viscount Mahon to Wellington, 10 December 1833

Hatfield House. Some time since I met with a little play of Kotzebue (the best comic writer of Germany, or perhaps of Europe since Molière), which has for its subject one of your Grace's coats! Thinking it might amuse you I have bestowed a few idle hours in a literal translation of it, which I now take the liberty to inclose, and I shall be very glad if it should afford your Grace any entertainment and obtain a place among your curiosities.

Mr. Lockhart is going to send to Southey the book of the *Gazette de France* for the purpose of having it reviewed in the *Quarterly.*

Sir Robert and Lady Peel arrived here yesterday. The party here is now very large, amounting to nearly thirty.

CHEVENING PAPERS 685.

The Earl Bathurst to Wellington, 10 December 1833

Cirencester. I am very glad you have had a second interview with the two gentlemen who came from Oxford, and that on hearing what had passed with Lord Talbot (who had at last accepted) you had decided on declining, and advised them to unite and co-operate in favor of Lord Talbot. It is clearly the best course for you to take as the business has gone too far to change. I confess I doubted whether your writing your letter before you had this second interview might not possibly have been rather premature.

The account I have this morning from Dropmore is so far consolatory that he thinks himself better, and can express himself with less difficulty, and this shews, but shews perhaps little more, that he suffers less.

The Princess [Lieven] must think herself very strong in Downing Street, or desperately ill there, to venture on a visit to Stratfield Saye.

After all it may be an imposter who is with you, for according to a paragraph in a Gloucester paper which I annex, it is I who have the honor of receiving the Russian embassy.

Rev. Thomas Wintle to Wellington, 12 December 1833

St. John's. Lord Talbot's name being now withdrawn by Christ Church, it was resolved at a numerous meeting of members of Convocation representing the sentiments more or less of fourteen colleges respectfully to request that his Grace the Duke of Wellington will allow himself to be put in nomination for the Chancellorship of the University of Oxford, whenever a vacancy may occur.

Wellington to the Rev. Thomas Wintle, 14 December 1833

Stratfield Saye. The Duke of Wellington has been highly flattered by the wish expressed by certain members of the Convocation of the University of Oxford that he should be the Chancellor of the university in case the illness of the distinguished person who fills that office shall deprive the university of the benefit of his services.

The Duke has felt his want of qualifications to entitle him to the suffrages of the Convocation at large; and he has more than once stated verbally and in writing that if Lord Talbot would consent to be put in nomination as a candidate for the office, the Duke earnestly recommended to the gentlemen who communicated with him to concur with others to accept his services; and he positively declined to consent that his own name should be put forward as a candidate.

It appears now that Lord Talbot has declined, because he could not allow that his pretensions should be put in competition with those of the Duke of Wellington. The Duke has no pretensions to fill the office of Chancellor of the University of Oxford.

It is his opinion that the heads of the principal colleges of Oxford such as Christ Church, St. John's, Queen's College, University College, BrazenNose, Oriel, Magdalen and the leading members of the Convocation residing at Oxford should agree among themselves as to the person whom they should think proper to elect to be the Chancellor of the university; and then make known their wishes as a body to that person.

The Duke earnestly recommends to the university to elect a person who has been educated at the university.

Wellington to the Earl of Aberdeen, 15 December 1833

Stratfield Saye. Some time has elapsed since I have written to you. But the session of Parliament is approaching and it is desirable that you should be made acquainted with what I know of the state of our foreign affairs. I have had the foreign ministers here and I am positively informed about some of the points upon which I am about to write to you.

In respect to the Netherlands, I believe that the Government are still far from a settlement. The question of the Duchy of Luxembourgh is still unsettled in the Diet. Upon what point it rests I am not informed. There are besides several important points unarranged in the settlement between Holland and Belgium. Dedel says that he regrets these difficulties because he foresees that Belgium would be unable to pay the arrears of the instalments of interest of the debt from 1830 to the now apparently distant period of the final settlement of the treaty. It is obvious that he expects that a demand will be made by France and England of a renunciation by Holland of a part of the amount. I see some symptoms in the newspapers of the existence of this intention. It is quite certain, however, from this view of Dedel's and these statements in the newspapers that the whole question is one of terms, in which our Government mean to do all the mischief they can to Holland.

With respect to Portugal, you'll have seen that the Spanish government had consented to make a joint proposition with England of a mediation between the Braganza brothers founded upon a suspension of hostilities, against which Zea had so stoutly contended in his negotiations with Sir Stratford Canning. I think that Zea can find a pretence for his conduct, but I am apprehensive that it will be attributed to other motives. He is supposed to [be] leagued with Aquado and with other *afrancesados* under the influence of Soult and the French Government and that this is the real cause of his unpopularity.

It appears that Pedro had accepted the proposed mediation and that Miguel had refused. It does not yet appear what is to be the result. Spain cannot enforce the mediation by arms. Will England send an army to Portugal? That is all that England can do that has not been done already. It is difficult to know in what state the war in Portugal really is. It is generally supposed that the foreigners in Don Pedro's [army] are becoming tired of him and mutinous. If that is the case he is gone.

The affair which now excites most attention in the *corps diplomatique* is the Russo-Turkish affair. It appears to be quite certain that at a very early period in the autum of the year 1832 the Russian Government drew the attention of the King's servants to the dangers by which the Porte was menaced, in consequence of the attacks of Mehemet Ali, the Pasha of Egypt. In their communications the Russian Government offered to act in concert with His Majesty's Government, in protecting the Porte. No attention was paid to the earnest solicitations of the Russian ministers upon the subject. None to those of the Turkish plenipotentiary who was sent here in the commencement of this year. In the mean time military event after event occurred, each of them threatening the destruction of the Ottoman Government, and at length the Emperor of Russia listened to the repeated pressing demands of the Sultan for assistance. The first demand was for the assistance of a fleet and of troops, and orders were given that both' should be placed at the disposition of the Ottoman Government. Roussin's interference and negotiations induced the Porte to hesitate and to recede from these demands. His negotiations for peace, however, failed; another battle was lost in Asia Minor, and the demand on behalf of the Ottoman Government for assistance was renewed and granted. A fleet was sent with troops on board, and a *corps d'armée* was sent to Constantinople from the Principalities.

During this period it is stated that the utmost anxiety was expressed by our Government, particularly by Lord Grey, for the arrival of the Russian fleet and troops at Constantinople!

The peace was then negociated and concluded, upon terms certainly as little calculated to secure the permanent tranquillity of the Ottoman Empire and the future security of the Government of the Ottomans as any that could be devised.

In the meantime Orloff was sent to Constantinople. The Russian account is that the Porte proposed to him the treaty of defensive alliance, which was signed. Other accounts state that Orloff brought in his pocket the *projet* of the treaty.

The patent treaty is a simple one of defensive alliance between the parties for eight years, stipulating in six articles that the party requiring assistance shall not pay for more than for the provisions (*approvision-nemens*—which may mean more) required for the troops employed.

The secret article states that it is not intended by the contracting parties that the Turkish Government should be called upon to defend the Russian dominions, if attacked. All that is required is that the Porte shall prevent the passage through the Dardanelles of the ships of any of the enemies of His Imperial Majesty.

This is the purport of the treaty. Upon this treaty the allied governments, France and England, have presented at Petersburgh and Constantinople a joint note signed by the French and English ministers at each court, stating in very abrupt and I should say, improper terms, that in case Russia should interfere in the internal concerns of the Turkish Empire, France and England would take the course most consistent with their own views and interests at the moment, notwithstanding the treaty. To this note the Russian Government has sent an answer *identique* to each court, stating that in case it should be called upon to assist the Ottoman Government in consequence of the treaty, the assistance would be given notwithstanding the joint note!! There we stand. It is upon these transactions and notes that have been founded the articles in *The Times* and *Globe* that you will have seen.

I think that the article in *The Times* has been written by an over-zealous friend, who has overstated the grievance which he was directed to write up. The *Globe* is more cautious, and the perusal of that article has convinced that there is no intention of going to war at present.

In the meantime the allies, Russia in particular, cannot be on worse terms than they are with France and England. There is no communication whatever upon publick subjects with Lieven. The note was presented, and the answer given at St. Petersburgh. The treaty between Russia and the Porte has never been communicated by Russia. The pretence is that it was a treaty made at the request of the Porte, and that out of delicacy to the Porte it was left to that power to communicate it. The Porte has not communicated an exact copy of the secret article. It is obvious, however, that France and England are acquainted with the contents of the treaty.

I think that you will be of opinion that I have given you an account of a most serious state of affairs. France has got in Asia Minor the Pasha of Egypt, and during the period that her alliance with England lasts she can take advantage of any state of affairs in Europe to force the Emperor of Russia to employ half of his army in the defence of the Government of the Ottomans. The Austrian attention to the amount of one third of their army must be drawn to the same quarter under the same circumstances. The Emperor of Russia might perhaps have attained his purpose in a different manner and in less objectionable terms. But when it is avowed that the object of France and England is to establish an Egypto-Arabian Moslem government at Constantinople instead of an Ottoman Moslem government, because the former can contend with the Emperor of Russia which the latter cannot, the Emperor is justified in guarding by every means in his power against the dangers by which he is menaced. The only astonishing circumstance is that he did not at once strike at Ibrahim Pasha last spring, and force him to quit Asia Minor, instead of leaving him there as he is an instrument to be used by France and England, and a thorn in his side.

But we must look a little farther presently at the advantages to be derived from this Egyptian position in Asia Minor, and consider how it will affect the question of peace or war.

It appears that after the meeting at Münchengrätz the three northern courts presented simultaneous notes to France, each in very different, but all in civil terms but very decided, calling upon France to put down the secret political *sociétés propagandistes* of persons belonging to foreign nations, which assembled in different parts of France for the purpose of disturbing the peace of other nations. These powers at the same time declare that they don't admit the pretensions of France that no power, although legally called upon by a third power, can give assistance to such power to quell internal insurrection, without giving to France a claim to compensation. The French government received these notes, and gave to each an answer qualified according to the terms of the note to which theirs was an answer. Both the British and French governments as allies have presented joint notes to different minor courts of Europe to put them on their guard respecting what is called the mischievous system of interference of the northern courts. But nearly three months have elapsed since the original notes were presented, and nothing has occurred which can tend to manifest anything like hostility.

It appears that there are armaments going on at Toulon, and they say that we could have nine or ten sail of the line in the Mediterranean in a short time. I suspect that the armaments at Toulon are destined to extend the French conquests in Africa *nommément* to Constantine.

But let us look a little at the question of peace or war in relation to the interests of Louis-Philippe, and to his advantages in Asia Minor. I put England out of the question altogether excepting as wishing for war, and having in her hands the naval preponderance.

We'll suppose that Louis-Philippe excites the Pasha of Egypt to renew the attack upon the Porte; and sends 20,000 men to his assistance with an English and a French fleet. Is it certain that the Turks cannot or will not defend the forts on the Bosphorus and in the Dardanelles? That the French fleet and troops will necessarily arrive before the Russians will? That Constantinople must fall into the hands of Louis-Philippe and his allies?

If these are not certainties, that which is certain is that this attack upon Constantinople will occasion a general war on the continent of Europe.

But we'll suppose that the attack upon Constantinople succeeds, and that an Egypto-Moslem government is established by the aid of French arms at Constantinople. It is obvious that the influence over that Government must be maritime. It must be British then and not French. British established at the risk and expense of France but by the defeat of two of the allies of Great Britain; and to the injury and weakness of one, in particular Russia, to whose unbroken strength Europe must look as to a bulwark against the increasing dangers of revolutionary war.

I don't give our Government the credit of seeing thus far; but I do to Louis-Philippe; and I firmly believe that he will prefer to keep Ibrahim Pasha to be used as he may require to use him for his own defence rather than to revolutionize the Government of Constantinople, for the advantage of Great Britain. My opinion therefore is that we shall not have war.

ADD MS 43060, ff. 95–100.

The Rev. Thomas Singleton to Wellington, 17 December 1833

Eldon Castle, Newcastle-on-Tyne. The Church in this hour of need has I hope many friends—but as is often the case in friendship, there is perhaps rather more zeal than discretion in some of those who have the best dispositions towards her. Your Grace has hitherto, and will I am sure hereafter, defend us with both qualities. Condescend to bear with me then for a moment, whilst I briefly touch upon a projected measure which I should be glad to hear, if it be persevered in, has your Grace's concurrence and approval—for in that case I shall distrust and abandon my own opinion.

Your Grace will have heard that an address to the Archbishop of Canterbury has been prepared and circulated amongst the clergy, wherein they express their attachment to the Established Church, and their confidence in his Grace as their superior. The measure has been attended with great success. For it has proved what was most desireable to prove—the union of the profession, and their becoming deference to their spiritual ruler. It is now however proposed to go further; and I yesterday received a letter from Oxford calling upon me to circulate a nearly similar address amongst the laity of this county. Here I confess I hesitate. First, because whatever the laity think it right to do they should do it entirely of themselves; and secondly, because I do not see why the laity should address the Archbishop. It is well for us who are ministers to address the chief functionary of our ministration, but surely the laity if they move at all should approach the Throne with petition and if need be with remonstrance. Moreover, will it be wise to put our interest to the poll as it were, and to the decision of the signatures of the multitude? Will not the unions and clubs and the Dissenters beat us in this warfare, where they have had so much practice and have been so little scrupulous? When we fairly calculate on those whom party politics, the feverish love of change, perhaps an honest but not well ascertained desire of improvement, personal pique, avarice, and envy may keep back, even amongst those who still consider themselves and are considered by our enemies as Churchmen, it is much to be feared that we shall not obtain signatures in any proportion to the numbers of the population. And then the obvious inference will be— although they who sign may be for the Church, they who do not sign are against it. We shall have called for a division and we shall appear in a minority. If corporate bodies, counties, universities, cities, towns, parishes, if any defined society of people would petition for us it would be of the greatest service, but so extensive a field as the laity of England and Wales is too vast for our friends to occupy with advantage.

Now my Lord Duke! if your Grace should happen to see the matter in this point of view, would it be impossible for you to see the Duke of Rutland and Lord Chandos, who are reported to favour the plan. Could it be stopped? If it has gone too far, can it be changed to a petition to the Throne?

I implore your Grace to pardon me for the liberty I take in presuming to address you, but I think I see that a false step is likely to be taken, and if any man can put it right it will be your Grace, or if we are right your approbation will confirm us in our course.

Lieutenant-Colonel Sir John Woodford to Wellington, 18 December 1833

Brighton. I do myself the honor of writing to your Grace in consequence of the notice taken by some of the newspapers of an admonitory order respecting temperance in the Grenadier Guards. Your Grace remembers the enquiry you were pleased to make at Windsor, on the occasion of the King's reviewing the 1st battalion, about the existence of temperance societies among the soldiers. The observations which your Grace was further pleased to make on the advantage which the army could derive from the introduction, if it could be effected, of temperate habits, did not fail to make an impression on my mind.

I have always considered it my duty to give the regiment the benefit of every suggestion emanating from your Grace, as far as I am competent to do so. I reflected on the hint then given, to the utmost of my ability, and came to the conclusion, which I earnestly hope will have been conformable to your Grace's views, that it was incumbent upon me to profit by the opportunity of conveying to the soldiers an admonition with regard to temperance under such high authority. I felt convinced that the influence of your Grace's name would effect more than I could possibly hope to accomplish by ordinary means. After the most mature consideration it appeared to me impossible that temperance societies, if they should spring up spontaneously in companies or battalions, could have any but a beneficial result.

Many men become habituated to drinking, solely from the example and society of others. The recruits, on first joining, are seldom drunkards. It seems therefore a suitable plan to give the sober men a rallying point, that they may not think meanly of themselves for being averse to intemperance, or be subject to derision from their comrades. I was aware too that the conversation which your Grace was pleased to address to me at the review must have been partly within the hearing of the men of the right company of the battalion, and would doubtless be communicated, so that my silence or inaction afterwards would have been liable to misinterpretation.

It was not however until late in October that I took final measures, and I felt that I should be culpably dilatory if I postponed doing so any longer. The communication which I made to the regiment, having been alluded to in newspapers, though only, as far as I have seen, with the view apparently of circulating more widely your Grace's recommendation, I think it right to enclose a copy of it, and I trust that your Grace will not disapprove of what I have done.

In conducting the details of management of the regiment which has the honor and advantage of being commanded by your Grace, my humble efforts are invariably directed to the observance of the principles established under your Grace's orders at various times, or sanctioned by your Grace's opinion.

I flatter myself that a very conspicuous improvement will be effected by persevering efforts to check intemperance under your Grace's authority, and principally by that influence.

Enclosure: Grenadier Guards—Regimental Orders October, 1833

The Commanding Officer thinks it right to inform the soldiers of the Grenadier Guards, that his Grace the Duke of Wellington has inquired whether any temperance societies exist among them; and his Grace has expressed his opinion of the great advantage which might result from the adoption of systematic measures to repress habits of intemperance, and to encourage sobriety.

His Grace considers that nothing would be wanting in the character of the English soldier, if the prevalent vice of drinking to excess could be eradicated.

There can be no doubt that a great deal of good may be effected by earnest and persevering efforts on the part of all concerned, and the Commanding Officer thinks too well of the general good feeling and spirit of the regiment not to believe, when his Grace the Duke of Wellington manifests so much interest in their welfare and character, that the men will themselves take pride in conforming to his Grace's views and wishes, and that many now addicted to excessive drinking, will seriously endeavour to break themselves of a habit constantly exposing them to the risk of committing some violent offence against discipline, which must necessarily be visited with severe punishment.

On this account, the Commanding Officer especially advises the men to avoid drinking at the canteen in barracks, where there is more danger than any where else of their being misled into some act of insubordination.

The offence of drinking to intoxication, even when not followed by insubordination, is aggravated by being deliberately committed in the barracks, in defiance of the discipline ordered to be maintained there.

The Commanding Officer, in obedience to the suggestions of his Grace the Duke of Wellington will institute inquiries in the three battalions, and adopt such measures from time to time as may appear likely to effect the object of checking intemperance; but he relies chiefly on the good sense of individuals to restrain them from degrading themselves in character, and destroying their health, by frequent intoxication.

The men are particularly advised to refrain from drinking spirits.

They are also warned that those who become unfit for the service will receive little or no pension upon examination at Chelsea, if their disability shall be traced to habits of excessive drinking.

Such a distinction must be made in justice to the good and steady soldier, who preserves his health, and serves the proper time.

Charles Manners Sutton to Wellington, 19 December 1833

Palace Yard. I have this morning had a long interview with Sir Robert Inglis and Sir William Heathcote, and the result of our communication was that I should take upon myself to lay before your Grace the enclosed, with the request that you will have the goodness to express your opinions upon it. If you concur in its substance, and see no objection to the public feeling being tried upon it, would you suffer such concurrence to be stated at the meeting they are to have of the framers and active promoters of the address? I understand the address, as more directly referring to the doctrines, discipline, and ecclesiastical government of the Church, than having any reference to its temporalities. And I have stated my most cordial and conscientious agreement in every sentiment it contains. Sir Robert Inglis and Sir William Heathcote were down at Cambridge for three days last week on a visit to the Vice-Chancellor, the Master of Queens, a layman, and there the plan was arranged, at least as far as it has proceeded.

I know your Grace will pardon the liberty I have taken; and trusting the importance of the subject, and the high respect I have for your Grace, will be taken as my apology, I have the honor to be *etc.*

Enclosure: To his Grace the Lord Archbishop of Canterbury.
May it please your Grace

We, the undersigned, lay members of the Church over which, by Divine Providence, your Grace, as Primate of All England, most worthily presides, approach you with the assurance of our respectful and dutiful confidence, at a period when that Church is attacked with more than usual violence, and by efforts more than ever combined.

We desire to assure your Grace that in upholding in all their integrity the institutions of our venerable and apostolical establishment, your Grace and the several rulers of the Church (who, in their respective orders, may be associated with your Grace in the maintenance of our ecclesiastical polity) will be supported by our cordial and zealous exertions. We are attached, alike from conviction and from feeling, to the Church of England; we believe it to have been the great and distinguishing blessing of this country; and, as laymen, we feel that in the preservation of that Church we have an interest not less real and not less direct than its more immediate ministers.

While we are not insensible to the possibility of advantage to be derived to all its members from such revived exercise of discipline and superintendence on the part of its bishops, priests, and deacons, as may be sanctioned by the competent authority within the Church, we desire to uphold unimpaired its doctrines as set forth in its creeds and in its articles, and to preserve 'that venerable liturgy in which is embodied, in the language of ancient piety, the orthodox and primitive faith'.

Our earnest hope and our humble prayer is that God may still bless all the labours of the friends of the Church; may overthrow the designs of all its enemies; may cause Kings still to be its nursing fathers, and Queens to be its nursing mothers; and may render it, from age to age, the means of promoting His Glory, and the advancement of His Kingdom upon earth.

The Duke of Cumberland to Wellington, 20 December 1833

Berlin. Private. I hope you will excuse my employing your son Charles's handwriting instead of my own upon this occasion, but the fact is that ever since I wrote to you last, which is now upwards of three weeks ago, I have been confined to my bed from severe illness, but of which, thank God, I am now fast recovering: so much so that I hope to be able to start from hence between the 8th and 10th of next month, so as to arrive in London by the 20th January, which is according to my promise a fortnight before the meeting of Parliament, and I have written to Sir Henry Wheatley to procure me a Government steamer for the 20th at Calais. The object of my writing to you now is to inform you that I have received a letter from a person on whose *veracity* I can depend, and who from his particular situation I know is fully capable of knowing what I am going to tell you, viz. that it having been represented to the Bishop of London that there was a strong impression in the minds of his clergy that his Lordship had been consulted by His Majesty's Government upon the English Church Reform Bill, and thereby was supposed by them to be a party concerned: his Lordship flew out into a violent expostulation, and declared not only that this was *false*, but that he had not only had no communication with them on the subject, but he knew nothing at all about it, and was indignant at the very idea.

Not only did his Lordship do this, but as my informant tells me, he has stated the very same in three or four letters to the archdeacons. Now my dear Duke I certainly should not have ventured to have stated this to you was I not perfectly confident of the *fact*: you being upon the spot, may perhaps be able to learn more, if you already know it excuse my informing you of it, but it seemed to me of such consequence that I would not omit letting you know it. I look upon this as of the greatest consequence and will make our game the easier, and it strikes me that no time should be lost in the bench of bishops, dignitaries of the Church, chapters, the two universities, and all the sound supporters of the Church being prepared with petitions for the two Houses of Parliament, when they meet. I trust and hope that every exertion will be made on our part for a full attendance of our friends on the day of the meeting of Parliament. I have also heard, but mind it is not from such undoubted authority, that there has been, and may still be for aught I know, a division in the Cabinet upon this said Reform Bill, and that the Duke of Richmond, Lansdowne, Stanley, and Graham have refused to go all the lengths of the movement party: that Lord Grey in the beginning was likewise of the same way of thinking, but as usual had been overawed and intimidated by his own precious family, Durham and company. This I only give you as I have heard, the other I can depend upon.

The meeting of the congress of Ministers is fixed for the eighth of next month at Vienna and many of the Ministers of the German Courts have passed through here on their way to Vienna. Ancillon was to have left this place on the 29th, but has been laid up ever since Wednesday last, with a violent boil produced from a blister that he had between his shoulders, and which had the appearance of being a carbuncle: he has suffered prodigiously but informs me that he is better: it will be impossible however for him to leave Berlin for the next five or six days, even if he then can. I heard that Bresson, the French Minister here, is stated to have said that his Court had replied to the three northern powers, respecting their decision at Königgrätz, in the following manner. 'Nous avons répondus à la Russie avec énergie, à l'Autriche froidement, et à la Prusse avec bienveillance.' Now from all that I can learn, from those persons who either were present at Königgrätz, or knew all that did take place there, there is the most perfect good understanding between these three Courts.

I saw last Thursday William of Orange who passed here two days on his road to Petersburgh. He came and sat an hour with me by my bedside. I cannot say how much satisfied I was with his conversation, and I never saw a young man more altered to his advantage than he has been since I saw him. His language was perfectly mild and temperate but determined, and I am happy to say that the greatest *unanimity* seems to exist between the King his father and the two sons. I understand that according to what had been settled by the three northern powers, the King of the Netherlands had applied to the Diet at Frankfurt for leave to exchange that part of Luxemburg which they wished with Belgium, but that the majority of the German princes had till now positively refused their consent. This is the whole budget of my news that I can give you and I think for a *prisoner*, as I have been for the last three weeks, is much. The moment I arrive in town I will inform you. You will be glad to hear that our dear little boy is perfectly well and we have now certain and clear proofs that the medicaments that Graefe has recommended for him have begun to take the proper effect upon his eye, and that the nerve was so much strengthened by it that in spite of a very severe attack of bile and a bad cold that he had about six weeks ago his eye had never suffered in the least. The Duchess has been laid up for more than a week with a violent feverish cold, and rheumatic attack in her head brought on from her own anxiety in nursing me during my illness, so that though we both live in the same house, she living above stairs and I below, we have not seen each other for a full week. However she has sent me word that she is much better today, and I trust my doctor will permit me to go up stairs and see her in the course of the day. There never has been known so sickly a time as the present, and one hears of nothing but typhus fever, inflammation of the lungs, etc., and many a worthy man has paid the tribute to nature. The moment I arrive I shall write to you. Excuse the length of this epistle but as it is the last I shall write to you from hence, I thought it right to tell you all I knew.

Signature only in Cumberland's hand.

Lord Charles Wellesley to Wellington, 21 December 1833

Berlin. The Duke of Cumberland is so unwell that he cannot write himself. He has therefore desired me to beg you will find out from the Archbishop what are his intentions respecting the Irish Church Bill, as he considers that no time is to be lost in forming the plans to be followed next session. At present it is his intention to start for England about the 12th or 14th of January at the latest, but his illness has been so serious that I do not think he will be strong enough to quit Berlin so soon.

I have procured the only book I can hear of here on the organization of the Prussian army. It consists of a number of orders of the Cabinet, respecting its formation, arranged and published by the Secretary of the Minister of War, through whose hands the whole thing passes. On the other points mentioned in your letter, which are not contained in this book, I obtain as much information as I want from the officers of the army.

PS. I have seen the Duke of Cumberland this morning. He is much better and desires me to open my letter to tell you that he hopes to have a day's shooting at Kew. He has ordered a steamer to meet him at Calais on the 20th so that he will arrive in plenty of time for some sport. He now intends starting about the 8th or 10th, and proceeding by easy stages to Calais, as he is not well enough to stand the sea voyage from Hamburg or Rotterdam.

Wellington to Lieutenant-Colonel Sir John Woodford, 21 December 1833

London. I have received your letter of the 18th respecting temperance societies.

The rule according to which I have invariably acted since I have been Colonel of the Grenadier Guards has been to refrain entirely from all interference in the internal discipline of the regiment. I do this upon principle.

First, I know that as Colonel I ought to perform all the duties of Commanding Officer if I was to attempt any excepting the mere honorary duties in relation to His Majesty. Secondly, I know that my other avocations would prevent my performing all the duties of the Commanding Officer.

It is not fair towards the actual Commanding Officer to interfere with him unless in a case of absolute necessity if the Colonel does not intend himself to perform all the detailed duties of the command of the regiment. At the same time I am always ready to give my advice and opinion, and as my mind generally reflects upon the military questions of the day I doubtless very frequently converse upon them with those with whom I may associate without any intention whatever of introducing upon them my opinions, or of interfering with their duties.

I do not recollect the conversation I had with you upon temperance societies though I dare say that it occurred. I certainly never intended to suggest to you an order upon the subject.

It is my opinion that a most desirable result would be produced if we could introduce temperance into the army. I could not in a note of this kind pretend to enumerate the good consequences of such a result not only to the publick interests and to the character of the army but to the individual soldiers themselves.

Whether it is to be done by an order, by example, by care, by remonstrance, or by discipline, or by the united efforts of these modes of influencing the conduct of the soldier must depend upon circumstances. This is however certain that the object is a most desirable one and if attained in every regiment and particularly in one so distinguished in every respect as the Grenadier Guards, the example must be followed in others, and I must add that a great service will be rendered.

PS. I confess that I have always considered that the principal motive to our soldiers to enlist is the propensity of the class from which we take them to drink and the desire to gratify that propensity and other irregular habits. But that is no reason why we should not endeavour to get the better of propensities and habits which certainly deteriorate the quality of the man and the soldier. I am very certain however that this is not to be done by what are called temperance societies or any regimental associations. If such should produce temperance, which is not certain, they will produce other evils, and they would soon establish an authority in the regiment too strong for that of the Commanding Officer. I observe that your order does not authorize temperance societies. It recommends temperance which is certainly desirable.

William Holmes to Wellington, 21 December 1833

I met this morning Edward Ellice who sent this evening to Sir John Hobhouse and goes tomorrow to Mr. Le Fevre, your neighbour, and from what fell from him I am inclined to think he meditates calling on your Grace on Monday. I therefore venture to tell you what I hear are the present intentions of the Government. The treasurership of the Ordnance is to be handed over to Lord John Russell at the Pay Office, the commissariat branch of the Ordnance as well as the commissariat branch of the Treasury to be transferred to the Secretary at War, and the other departments of the Ordnance not to be touched for a year or rather till they see how the partial change works. The store branch in Tooley Street to be abolished, the Comptroller of Army Accounts to be also abolished and their duties performed at the Secretary at War. The Ordnance Board will be abolished and the duties of it carried on under a mixed board of the Commander-in-Chief, the Secretary at War, the Paymaster of the Forces, and a lieutenant-general of the staff who will have charge for the present of the military branch of the Ordnance. I am afraid you will see terrible cutting and slashing when Parliament meets. A plan is in preparation to relieve all persons except Protestants from Church rates or cess. Tithes they are puzzled about and that subject is postponed for the present. The recruiting your Grace knows is put a stop to, and letters were issued this day from the Secretary at War for putting down whole recruiting establishments. The staff officers so employed to be put on half pay. The regimental officers to join their regiments and the staff serjeants to be pensioned. I fear also that some plan for an alteration in the Corn Laws is in progress. I go this evening to Brighton where Lady Stronge is on account of her health.

The Earl Talbot to Wellington, 22 December 1833

Ingestre, Lichfield. I must thank you for your most obliging letters, and for the trouble which you have taken in sending me the communications enclosed in them.

394

It may perhaps be adviseable that I should state to your Grace all that has passed, in which I have had any concern, with reference to the probable vacancy in the Chancellorship of the University of Oxford.

On the 22nd of November I received a letter from the Dean of Christ Church, conveying to me the wish of the resident members of the chapter and common room to be informed whether, in the event of a vacancy, I would consent to be put in nomination as a candidate for that office. At that time I was alike ignorant of any former application made by that body, and of any difficulty which might exist as to supplying the place of the present Chancellor. Considering therefore only my own qualifications for the office, I replied that my habits of life were such as induced me to wish not to be put forward.

On the 27th November my son John Talbot, who had come through Oxford, informed me that an application (he thought a second) to your Grace from certain members of the Convocation was then in progress; but that the resident members of Christ Church would be glad, in the event of your Grace's declining, if I would consent to reconsider my former decision, and allow myself to be put in nomination. I was induced to do so, upon a distinct understanding which John Talbot at my desire expressed in writing to certain members of the college, that I would not come in competition with any one of my own political principles, least of all with the Duke of Wellington.

On the 4th of December the Rev. Mr. Clough of Jesus College waited upon me from Oxford, at the desire, as he stated, of a numerous party of Convocation, to put in my hands a paper (a copy of one which he informed me had been sent to your Grace) the purport of which I collected to be, that the authors of it hoped that I should not by coming forward throw any impediment in the way of your Grace's doing so. I stated to this gentleman, that my feelings were so far in accordance with the sentiment of which he was the bearer, that I considered your Grace's claims paramount, but that I was in the hands of my friends. I heard no more of the matter until the 7th of December when a second letter from the Dean was delivered to me by a member of Christ Church repeating the enquiry from the college, whether I would consent to be put in nomination? The tenor of my reply was in conformity with all my previous declarations, that no consideration should induce me to become an obstacle in the way of your Grace's election.

I have not heard any thing more on the subject, except accidentally that the Dean had communicated my letter to Mr. Wintle. And thus the matter rests.

It is needless that I should explain to your Grace all the motives which induced me in the first instance to decline the honor which was proposed to me, but I will mention that my want of experience as an active member of Parliament, formed in my opinion a very substantial objection to my being appointed to the office of Chancellor of the University of Oxford in these very critical times. It is very obvious that no such remark can apply to your Grace, and any general comparison between our respective pretentions as public men would be absurd.

However, if the heads of the university adopting your Grace's suggestions contained in your letter of the 14th, should concur in making me any further proposal, I shall then give it my best consideration, bearing in mind what you have been good enough to say upon the subject.

But I beg you to believe that when I say this, I am not influenced by any patent wish to become the object of their choice.

Lady Salisbury's diary, 22 December 1833

A conversation with the Duke at Hatfield. I think he sees a change of government is approaching: he said the present state of things could not continue—that we must return to the ancient constitution 'whether by legal means or by force I cannot tell'. 'If this Administration is succeeded by a more Radical one our way will be long and painful before we come to that result, and there will probably be a considerable change in respect to property—but that we *shall* come to that result, I do not doubt.' 'Peel never knows his own mind, he is conscious of that defect, and therefore afraid of committing himself: his opinions are only to be gathered from what he accidentally lets fall.'

The Duke told Peel some time ago that the ancient order of things must eventually be restored. 'You must bear in mind,' said Peel, 'at all events that it must be by *legal* means.' Since that conversation another person expressed the same opinion to Peel, adding 'You will see that these military men if they have the settling of affairs will bring back Old Sarum, Gatton and the whole system.' 'They must reserve a representation for the large towns,' observed Peel, 'or I cannot be a party to it'—thereby indicating what the Duke calls 'a progress in his ideas' and that the horror he felt at the idea of military interference was much diminished. It is evident the Duke feels he cannot do without him, though he never can entirely depend upon him.

He thinks Lord Holland one of the worst among the Whigs—'A *bad man*', utterly selfish and unprincipled, and popular from the effect of manner only. Lord Londonderry not to be trusted, wicked and deceitful in the highest degree.

Princess Lieven to Wellington, 24 December 1833

Londres. Je ne saurais assez vous remercier, M. le Duc, de votre petit mot intéressant de Hatfield d'hier. Je ne saurais non plus vous dire assez combien j'ai été contente du résultat de votre volonté. Cela m'a procuré deux matinées très satisfaisantes. Je vois d'après cela qu'il y aura la plus grande utilité à mettre entre des mains aussi habiles le travail très complet qui vient de m'être fourni. Il sera prêt à être livré demain ou après demain. Auriez-vous la bonté de me faire savoir l'adresse à laquelle je pourrais le faire tenir; il y serait porté par une main sûre.

Je suis enchantée pour mon ami le chasseur qu'il aie l'honneur de vous rencontrer. Je vous supplie de l'entretenir de *tout*, cela nous sera fort utile. J'y inclus le sujet de notre dernier sujet de conversation à Stratfield Saye. Encore une fois, M. le Duc, mille grâces de votre bonté et de votre active bienveillance.

M. de Talleyrand nous est revenu parfaitement pacifique. Il a deux mots à la bouche, le status quo et la paix. Nous ne voulons pas autre chose. Nous verrons si ses pensées domineront ici. Je crois son Cabinet un peu divisé et que tout le monde n'est pas pour la paix autant que lui. Je crois aussi que son retour n'a pas fait à votre Ministre des Affaires Étrangères autant de plaisir qu'à d'autres.

La conduite de Don Pedro continue à mécontenter fort votre gouvernement et celle de Zea à lui donner la plus grande satisfaction. Voilà les vicissitudes de la politique.

Le discours du Roi des Français reçu à l'instant me parait convenable.

Dated Mardi soir, 24 décembre. *Docketed* 1833, December 24.

Wellington to William Holmes, 25 December 1833

Woodford. I have received your letter of the 21st. I am very sorry not to be at Stratfield Saye when Mr. Ellice was likely to pay me a visit.

I am very sorry to learn that there is truth in the report that the Government intend to destroy the Ordnance department.

This department has shewn itself to be most efficient during war which we *certainly* never shall have again. Since the war it has been revised. Several other departments have been put under its management. It has managed them so successfully and economically that committees of Parliament have approved of all that has been done and have held out the Ordnance as a model to others; and that even this Government have endeavoured to follow this model in their new arrangements of the Admiralty and yet we are now going to destroy our model.

However I have nothing to say to it all. What I should wish is to see something put clean out of hand; upon which we could rely as likely to last for a little time.

I am sorry to learn that Lady Stronge still suffers. I have not seen your son for some time but I conclude he has been to Brighton with his mother.

Wellington to Lord Francis Egerton, 25 December 1833

Woodford. I return the work upon the Russian army which you was so kind as [to] lend me. It is a very remarkable one. The writer has had good sources of intelligence of which he has known how to make use. Indeed it is impossible that he or those who have assisted him should not have got their information from the *Etat Major Général*. I think however that he has exaggerated some evils; that he has misrepresented some circumstances; and that in the latter part of the work in which he recommends the remedy, he has forgotten or has lost sight of the circumstances of the country which he had detailed with great truth and interest in its commencement.

What I observed in that part of Russia which I visited when I was there in 1826 was the absolute impossibility of invading that country with a force at all adequate to command success. The extent is immense in proportion to its population, its fertility and its produce. There are few or no towns. I believe none on the northern road except Mitau not fortified. The communications were infamously bad, even the great post road scarcely practicable, through a country covered with pine forests or morasses. I believe that the whole country is nearly the same or in some parts more difficult or impracticable on account of the swamps, excepting immediately in the neighbourhood of Moscow. Indeed the author so represents it; and he explains clearly the difficulties which the Emperor of Russia would experience in a war or invasion against his neighbours, owing to the nature of the country in which he must assemble his army, and from which he must take his departure. He forgets these difficulties however when he comes to recommend a plan of operations for the combined powers of Europe against Russia.

All that he says in respect to the difficulties of recruiting the Russian army is perfectly true; nay I think that he has understated them. I don't think that the basis of the recruiting is so large as he says it is. Indeed it cannot be so. He has likewise omitted to enumerate among the difficulties of augmenting the army the immense distances which the recruit must march. I saw at St. Petersburg a recruit just arrived who had come by the regular *étape* and who had been a year en route.

In respect to the Russian soldier's pay it was originally a rouble a month; that is to say a silver rouble or four shillings. If that pay is compared with that of any troops in Europe, even with our own, it will not be found insufficient. Besides this pay he has his food and every thing found for him.

That which renders the pay insufficient is the paper money system. The soldier still receives his rouble [a] month; but it is a rouble in paper instead of a rouble in silver; that is to say ten pence instead of four shillings. He receives the rouble a month in silver when he passes the Russian frontier. I don't think that the author has traced very accurately the period at which the different allowances of food etc. were made to the Russian soldier; most probably not in the time of Peter the Great or till the art of paper money was discovered; and the discovery applied to the payment of the troops.

It is certain however that it is the foundation of most of the evils of which the author complains. It is quite clear that the corruptions of the army which are the undoubted consequences of the paper money system absorb one half of its effective force. It would not be easy for the Emperor of Russia to discharge one half of his army. But I firmly believe that he would find that he could pay one half of the number in silver at the rate of expence now incurred for the whole in paper, and get rid in the operation of all the corruptions and abuses complained of.

But it is necessary for him to make up his mind in the first instance to have the reputation of being a sovereign with 400,000 men instead of being one with 800,000 men in his service.

If you will look at the pay of the officers of the Russian army in the same view of the discontinuance of paper you will see that they would be well paid in comparison even with our own; and that the Emperor might put an end to all exactions.

All that the author says about the military colonies, about the system of discipline of the army, about the life of the officers in their cantonments, is true. I think that the Emperor has lately rather extended the cantonments of his army (when he can keep them in cantonments) in order to prevent their communication with each other, and the discussion and excitement of political questions during the long repose and cessation from military exercises and duties of the Russian winter. I know that a strong feeling existed when I was in Russia of the necessity for keeping the army either united in large corps under the eye of the general officers, or so separated in cantonments as that the officers could not communicate and cabal.

All that he says respecting the education of the officers of the army is true. It is likewise true that the youth of the first Russian families are but very ill educated. Their education is entirely a matter of chance. A French, English or German tutor is introduced into the family; generally a Frenchman. He may be equal to the task which he undertakes. But he is generally a hairdresser or a dancing master or an adventurer of some kind or other, and the scholar turns out accordingly.

I believe the author's description of the mode of action of the Russian troops in the field is quite correct; and I concur in his sentence upon the stupid pedantry of Diebitsch's orders. Upon the whole I consider this a very valuable military work and I send to Paris for a copy of it. I would recommend to our Ministers however to avoid to quarrel with Russia as allies of France.

PS. When the expence of clothing, arming and equipping and feeding 400,000 men is deducted from the present expence of the army and the vast number of horses proportionately reduced as they might be, my belief is that the Emperor of Russia would gain by keeping only one half of his army, and paying it in silver instead of in paper. He would certainly be really stronger in a military point of view.

The Earl of Aberdeen to Wellington, 26 December 1833

Haddo House. Many thanks, my dear Duke, for your very full account of the present state of our foreign matters, respecting which I knew but little; and over which there is still much obscurity.

The Portuguese and Dutch questions, which have occupied us so long, appear to be pretty much in their former state; or at least, are as far from a final settlement as ever. Complicated as these questions were, and scandalous as the conduct of our Ministers was in both of them, their importance was practically diminished, from the fact of neither of them being likely to terminate in war. We have now two new questions, the pacifick result of either of which is by no means so certain. The evils of the state of Spain have arisen entirely from the unfortunate change of the succession effected by Ferdinand. It was perhaps not unnatural that he should have wished to see his daughter recognized as Queen; and we must recollect that he took measures to accomplish this, before the French revolution. Had that event not taken place, it is probable that the Princess would have succeeded her father without much difficulty; and I think that we must do Ferdinand the justice to believe that he would not have attempted to make the change, had the French revolution been completed at the birth of his daughter. I cannot comprehend Zea's position, and think it must be impossible for him to maintain it. Of all the difficulties which a Minister ever had to encounter, his appear to be the greatest. The progress of revolution in Spain has always been regarded by the Austrians as tending very much to produce an effect in Italy; and in this view, it may lead to important consequences. I presume that if Zea should not be able to maintain himself, all chance of anything like a monarchical government in Spain will be gone.

The most important, and most urgent question for us now to consider, is without doubt, our position in the Levant with respect to Russia. This question, which we touched very lightly in Parliament last session, always appeared to me to display the incapacity and misconduct of our Ministers in a more striking manner than all their other exhibitions. I observe that you think we shall still contrive to avoid war, and you may very probably be right; but your opinion is principally founded on the prudence of Louis Philippe; now, I would ask whether, in the event of our Government being desirous of war, the French King is in a condition to decline acting with us? Is his situation, even at home, such as to leave him perfectly free to act in the most prudent manner, in the case supposed? I am almost inclined to think that if our Government are determined to go to war, they will find means to draw Louis Philippe into the concern; and there are many ways in which the French may hope to derive advantage from such a course. The inclination for war is obvious in our Ministers; but as yet, an assignable cause is wanting. At least I have seen no pretext which could be admitted for an instant; unless abuse of the Emperor, and of Russia, may be taken as good grounds of war. A cause however, will doubtless be found when it is wanted.

I perceive that Mme. de Lieven, who writes to me sometimes, appears to think that we shall arrive at this result at last; although she professes to be of opinion that they must be very ingenious if they contrive to find any cause of quarrel that will bear to be stated. At all events, the situation of affairs is very serious, whatever may be the result. War would be likely to influence very extensively our domestick position.

Unless anything should be decided respecting a parliamentary course, which should make attendance indispensable, I have no intention of leaving this part of the country in time for the meeting of Parliament. You will easily appreciate my motives, without the necessity of my entering more fully on the subject. I may probably hear from you again in the course of the next month.

It has given me the most sincere pleasure to learn from various quarters, of your good health, and remarkably improved appearance. I need not say that there is nothing I more ardently desire than that this should continue.

Wellington to Viscount Mahon, 26 December 1833

Woodford. I did not answer your kind note upon the communication of Maréchal Wellington's coat, as I received at the same time one from Mrs. Arbuthnot in which she told me that you had desired that she should see it; and she charged me not to read it till I should come here.

I read it with her yesterday before dinner and was delighted with it. I don't know that I was ever more entertained.

I have not seen you for some time. The Duke of Gloucester is coming to Stratfield Saye on Monday the 20th of January. Will you come and meet him and some of my friends?

I have seen the King of France's speech which I think excellent. It is the best king's speech that I have seen for three years at least.

The King of France is taking our place in the world much faster than those like, who contributed a little to put this nation in it.

CHEVENING PAPERS 685.

William Holmes to Wellington, 27 December 1833

Brighton. I this morning received your Grace's letter of the 25th. The Duke of Richmond came down here on the 17th instant and submitted his plans to the King for the abolition of the Ordnance department, and after he went to Goodwood Sir Herbert Taylor wrote by the King's command to Sir James Kempt who came down on Saturday and remained till Monday. The result has been that a stop has been put to all further proceedings as connected with the Ordnance department. Sir Herbert Taylor spoke to me of the contemplated changes as most mischievous and fraught with danger both to the navy and army. I was quite surprised to hear *him* speak in the manner he did. Sir Stratford Canning was here on Tuesday last. He told me that *he* was not going to Petersburgh. I shortly afterwards met the Duke of Gloucester who informed me that the Emperor refused to receive him, and that he has in consequence of this resigned the appointment in order to relieve Lord Palmerston from the embarrassment he was placed in. Mr. Bligh is to remain there. I never saw such a scene of confusion as the Pavilion exhibits. Young children crawling over the house, nurses running about with saucepans in their hands, and I believe there is cooking going on in every room in the house, at least the smell of the kitchen is perceivable in every part of the house. Mr. Marsh told me that the guests now at the Pavilion and their attendants occupied last night 241 beds, this of course including the whole establishment. Lord Maryborough is here and looking remarkably well. It is reported here this morning that Mrs. Fitzherbert is dead. I had a letter dated the 15th instant from Mr. Jelf, written by order of the Duke of Cumberland who was too unwell to write himself. He had been confined to his bed for a week before. I yesterday saw a letter from Lord Combermere who is at Naples, giving a most deplorable account of Lord Hertford's state of health. He cannot last long. Lord Lowther is now with him.

The Duke of Gordon to Wellington, 28 December 1833

Gordon Castle. At this season when our mind naturally surveys the events of the past year, and casts our kindest thoughts on our friends, there is none to whom my heart turns with more regard and friendship than to you and I fondly hope you may enjoy many happy years in spite of the reformers and Radicals. Do let me know if it is your intention to collect your force at the meeting of Parliament, as my health is again perfectly re-established and equal to meet the enemy, and the sooner we have the fight the better.

Henry Goulburn to Wellington, 29 December 1833

Cambridge. Private. On the day before I left London I received from Sir R. Inglis a copy of an address to the Archbishop of Canterbury which he as a member of a committee at Oxford proposed to circulate with a view to its general signature by the lay members of the Church of England. It appeared to me so objectionable in many particulars, as to the quarter to which it was addressed, as to the topics to which it was confined, as to the probability of its giving rise to controversy and division among the friends of the Church, and as to the time selected for its promulgation that I (not having an opportunity of seeing Sir R. Inglis) wrote him on Friday morning a statement of the reasons which induced me to consider such an address inexpedient at the present time. On coming here I found among the lay members of the university and among the clerical also a general feeling analogous to that which I had expressed as to this particular address and from what I hear this morning I believe that it has been abandoned. There still however prevails a general opinion that some declaration of attachment to the Church as by law established on the part of the lay members of her communion is advisable. Nor am I prepared altogether to differ from that opinion provided that the declaration or address to the King (for those are the two modes of proceeding now considered the most eligible) be drawn up so as to comprize the property and privileges of the Church as well as its doctrines and not to exclude such reforms as all reasonable men may deem necessary for advancing the real objects of the establishment. What may be ultimately done upon this subject I cannot say but as I learn from the Speaker that he had been in communication with you on the subject of the former address I thought you would like to hear in what situation the affair now stood. Whatever may be done the important point is as it appears to me to secure first the means of having the declaration most extensively signed and to avoid giving it at its outset the character of a measure of opposition to the Government.

I received your kind note this morning and in reply to your enquiries am happy to say that I am so much better as to give me reason to believe that I may yet be fit for service in time of need.

Viscount Mahon to Wellington, 29 December 1833

Dover Street. I am extremely obliged by your Grace's kind remembrance and shall have the greatest pleasure in waiting upon you at Stratfield Saye on the 20th day of next month.

I am also very glad to find that the German play entertained you as I thought it would.

The King of the French is now taking a line at home which in many respects might serve as a lesson to Princes with a better title. In his foreign relations I hear on good authority that contrary to the common opinion, he looks to the present Government of England with suspicion and contempt and that he is withheld from the course which he otherwise would pursue in his Continental policy from an unwillingness to lean upon the feebleness and folly which now direct the counsels of his chief ally.

In reference to his late speech and especially to its phrase 'mettre un terme aux révolutions', I see the *Gazette de France* observes: 'Pour mettre un terme aux révolutions il ne faut pas que la révolution soit sur le Trône.' Must it not be admitted that there is considerable force in that objection?

As to parties; the *Gazette* and the other leaders of the old Royalists still adhere closely to their scheme of extended suffrage and more popular elections, but have determined to change their policy in one other important particular. They had for the most part carefully kept aloof from the elections since 1830; they are now to try their strength at the next and endeavour to carry as many Deputies as possible. They feel, or at least affect to feel, quite confident of finally prevailing. Yet surely it must be a very disheartening thing to have to strive for a family which like the Bourbons has done so little for itself—or rather so much against itself. It reminds me of a passage in Lord Bolingbroke's correspondence which I met with the other day, where he speaks of the conduct of the house of Austria in his time and compares it to 'the image of a man braiding a rope of hay, while his ass bites it off at the other end!'

Wellington to Henry Goulburn,[1] 31 December 1833

Apethorpe. I have this morning received your letter of the 29th instant.

I take very nearly the same view that you do of the proposed address to the Archbishop of Canterbury. An address to his Grace from the clergy of the Church of England expressing their confidence in his Grace may be very proper.

But if the laity address at all they ought to address the King: and they ought to intreat His Majesty to protect the rights, privileges and property of the clergy, as well as the doctrine and discipline of the Church.

I know nothing of reasonable reforms in the Church. I should be unwilling to sign any address which should recognize that such were necessary.

However in my letter upon the subject to the Speaker I expressed my doubts of the expediency of any address. We know of no intended reforms in Church government excepting from certain flying paragraphs in seditious newspapers. We should do the Church very serious mischief if we should strike the first blow. There would be undoubtedly meetings all over the north of England, and possibly in Scotland and Ireland. The indifferent of our own opinions would stand aloof; the feeble would be intimidated; the numbers would appear to be on the other side. The Government would triumph; and their success would be attributed possibly with truth to the false step which we should have taken.

GOULBURN PAPERS ACC 319/II/12.

Wellington to the Duke of Cumberland, 1 January 1834

Apethorpe. I have had the honor of receiving your Royal Highness's letter. Your Royal Highness may rely upon my readiness to consult with those who wish to consult with me upon the course which ought to be followed in Parliament in these critical times.

I am not at all disposed to oppose myself to the assembly of large bodies for that purpose. I must observe however that I never knew that any benefit resulted from such consultations excepting possibly the gratification of the persons called to participate in them. They occasion

---

[1] Wellington always spelt the name 'Goldburne'.

great loss of time, they seldom lead to any decision, never to a wise or discreet one, they prevent all secrecy even from the opponent, and they expose the party to ridicule on account of what passes in discussion at such meetings. However if others wish to have such consultations I shall not oppose myself to them.

I must say of consultations of general that unless they are under the necessity of acting as a Cabinet are, or upon some occasions as Members of Parliament are on a particular debate, I can't see much use in them. Some have their doubts, others their difficulties, all some objection or other, and the consultation generally breaks up without coming to any decision. This was very much the case with the meetings which took place in the years 31 and 32 of Members of the House of Commons to consult upon the measures which they should pursue. In truth so much depends upon the course followed by the Government and hereafter so much will depend upon the course to be followed by the Radicals that it will be impossible for us to decide beforehand what we will do.

These are my thoughts upon the perusal of your Royal Highness's letter, stating at the same time my readiness to do whatever may be thought most adviseable.

We are in a most critical situation. The Conservative party have a majority in the House of Lords. The royal mind will be with them. The royal authority, the Administration, the majority of the House of Commons, and the decided sense of the country against them. At the same time we know now to a certainty that the Conservative party consists of the infinite majority of the landed proprietors and the great commercial and manufacturing capitalists throughout the three kingdoms.

We must be very cautious in our measures. A false step might do the greatest injury to the institutions and interests of all descriptions which it is our duty as well as our object and our inclination to support and maintain.

We must never forget that in times of revolution such as those we have the misfortune of witnessing, the passions of individuals have an influence upon publick affairs which in ordinary times they have not, and that it is the duty of those who wish to preserve what exists not to excite those passions unnecessarily, at the same time that they steadily persevere in their course, making no compromise of principle or of any interest.

I think it very improbable that there will be any desire on the part of those who have the power of the country in their hands to share it with their rivals and those who entertain opinions so different from their own. I think that they are much more likely to find themselves under the necessity of making further concessions to the democratick side of the question and of forming a closer union with the Radicals. It is my opinion that that is the tendency of the policy of the day, and in my view of the situation of the country the chances of the junction of the Whigs with the Radicals greatly increase the difficulties and embarrass all our proceedings.

PS. I observe that I have written part of this letter upon half a sheet of paper which I hope that your Royal Highness will excuse.

Wellington to Winthrop Mackworth Praed, 3 January 1834

Apethorpe. I expect to be able on Sunday or Monday to let you know that something had been sent. I observe [*sic*] has taken the usual course of the Government, that is to throw upon me the blame of the state in which the Turkish empire is. I was the negociator of the Greek convention of April 1826 with the Emperor of Russia. Any body who can read and understand will see the difference between this convention and that of 1827 negociated by Mr. Canning with Russia and France, which occasioned or rather gave the opportunity for the battle of Navarino. I did not negociate that convention. I did all that I could to induce Mr. Canning not to conclude it. I was not in office when it was concluded.

I returned to office in January 1828; and I did every thing I could to settle the Greek affair (the object of the convention of 1827 which I was bound as the King's Minister to carry into execution) with as little injury to the Turkish government as was possible. Lord Palmerston and Mr. C. Grant, were in office till the end of May 1828 and are responsible if I am so for the destruction of Turkey. But they are not responsible for such loss. We did all that we could to prevent the Russian war; which certainly originated in the feelings excited by the unjustifiable battle of Navarino.

The Greek papers will shew all this very clearly. If I should find them at Belvoir Castle I will send you a memorandum upon them. But if not, I will as soon as I return to town. I should think that in the columns of *The Times* in the first six months of 1828 will be found some pretty strong abuse of the Government of that day for not joining the Russians in the attack of the Turks. That was the Liberal cant of the day. See Lord Holland's speeches etc.

Dated January 3 1833. *Docketed* 1834, January 3.

William Burge to Wellington, 4 January 1834

Lincoln's Inn. I should fail in evincing my respect for your Grace, and my sense of the interest you take in the welfare of our colonial possessions, and my gratitude for the invaluable assistance you rendered the people of Jamaica, if I did not give your Grace the earliest information of the proceedings of their Assembly. They have passed with scarcely any opposition and have sent to the Colonial Office and to me a copy of their Slavery Abolition Act. It adopts all the enactments of the British Act, without any deviation from the emancipation plan of the Government. The regulations which it makes for the new state of society are borrowed from Lord Howick's scheme. This implicit adherence to the Government plan is to be attributed to their perfect conviction of its impracticability, and their determination that the entire responsibility shall rest with the Government; that no responsibility shall be incurred by them and that it shall not be in the power of the Government to impute its failure to them. They pass their Bill under a strong protest expressing these sentiments, and renouncing the responsibility and claiming from the Government indemnity. I was desired to convey these statements to the Government in the most explicit and unreserved manner.

I believe the Government did not expect and I doubt whether they wished that Jamaica should pass the Act quite as soon, or quite so much in conformity with the British Act. They would have liked a deviation which might have afforded a pretext for withholding the King's assent to the Jamaica Act or at all events enabled them to make the Jamaica legislature a party to the plan finally adopted and therefore equally responsible for its failure and all the consequences it might involve.

Jamaica has preceded every other colony in its legislation on this measure. Its example will be followed by every other colonial legislature and by the end of February all the colonial legislatures will have transmitted home Acts of such a nature as to ensure their receiving the King's assent. Strong objections were entertained to the apprenticeship and the Assembly if it had consulted and acted on its own opinions would have preferred immediate emancipation. Lord Mulgrave seems with his usual precipitancy and rashness to have hurried on the measure, although he had not received his instructions as to the extent of the deviations which the Assembly might make from the Government plan. The packet which conveyed them did not arrive until the 24th of November, when the Bill had been reported from a committee of the whole House and ordered to be engrossed. The people of Cuba are speculating on the advantages which await them from the convulsion which they anticipate must take place in Jamaica, or at all events from the certain diminution of its cultivation.

The Bill will not be objected to here and those who look at this measure with reference only to the share of Jamaica in the twenty millions will congratulate themselves on the implicit adoption by that colony of the Government plan. But I confess I see in it an unequivocal proof of the utter despair in which it has been passed and a determination to incur no part of the responsibility attending it. If I had seen some deviations and alterations I should have believed that the assembly had been satisfied that the Act of Parliament contained elements on which they might have constructed a more safe and practicable plan. But the Bill they have passed and the language held by those who compose the House prove the contrary.

Henry Goulburn to Wellington, 8 January 1834

Betchworth. When I last wrote to you on the subject of the address from the lay members of the Church of England I believe that I mentioned that although all reasonable men concurred in rejecting the proposed address to the Archbishop there was nevertheless a strong feeling to declare the opinion of the laity in favor of the Established Church. The enclosed has been prepared by a committee of gentlemen as the declaration to which they think it advisable to procure signatures. The committee consists of sincere and reasonable men and they have adopted the form of a declaration instead of an address (either to the Archbishop or the King) as calculated best to obviate the objections which have reached them from various quarters. They state further that the feeling for an immediate expression of opinion is such that they find it impossible to controul it and have therefore been anxious to direct it in the best channel.

The declaration is undoubtedly a great improvement upon the address previously submitted to us. It refers to the preservation of the Church's rights and to her union with the State as essential points and it has omitted all that reference to the exercise of ecclesiastical power over the laity which would have made the former address alarming to many, while at the same time it does not exclude the possibility of such regulation and reform as may be for the improvement of discipline or the advancement of real religion. To those also who like your Grace and myself thought it better to postpone any declaration till the measures of our adversaries were promulgated, it offers less objection since a declaration of this nature being a general reply to the declarations made either openly or covertly by various Dissenters and others has less appearance of striking the first blow.

From the communication which has been made to me I do not believe that even this declaration has been positively decided on. But as a copy has been sent to me by the Master of Trinity, Cambridge, I thought you would like to have the earliest intimation of what was going on.

Enclosure: A declaration of the laity of the Church of England.

At a time when the clergy of England and Wales have felt it their duty to address their Primate with an expression of unshaken adherence to the doctrine and discipline of the Church of which they are ministers, we, the undersigned, as lay members of the same, are not less anxious to record our firm attachment to her pure faith and worship and her apostolic form of government.

We further find ourselves called upon by the events which are daily passing around us to declare our firm conviction that the consecration of the State by the public maintenance of the Christian religion is the first and paramount duty of a Christian people: and that the Church established in these realms by carrying its sacred and beneficial influences through all orders and degrees and into every corner of the land has for many ages been the great and distinguishing blessing of this country and not less the means under Divine Providence of national prosperity than of individual piety. For the preservation therefore of this our national Church in the integrity of her rights and privileges and in her alliance with the State, we feel that we have an interest no less real and no less direct than her immediate ministers. And we accordingly avow our firm determination to do all that in us lies in our several stations to uphold unimpaired in security and efficiency that establishment which we have received as the richest legacy of our forefathers and desire to hand down as the best inheritance of our posterity.

    Name   Residence   Designation

In Goulburn's hand.

Wellington to William Burge, 10 January 1834

Stratfield Saye. I am very much obliged to you for your interesting letter of the 4th which I received when at Belvoir Castle.

I hope that the course pursued by the legislature of Jamaica may prove to be the correct one. But I confess that I doubt it.

Houses of Parliament and colonial legislatures are become manoeuvring bodies instead of pursuing a direct course towards a legitimate object. I admit that this is an inconvenient and destructive consequence of the false position in which we are all placed, that is to say the Crown by its Ministers being leagued with those whose object it is to destroy property instead of endeavouring to protect it. But I think that those who take the course taken by the legislature of Jamaica are mistaken. They can never retrace their steps. Their enemies, the King's Ministers and their adherents, will laugh at them and at their complaints of the failure of the plan. They will tell them with truth that it rested with them to amend it, and that they (the Ministers) had instructed the Governor General to admit of amendments.

Wellington to Henry Goulburn, 10 January 1834

Stratfield Saye. I received last night upon my arrival in London your letter of the 8th instant. I don't know of any questions that are so difficult or so disagreeable to decide upon as is one of this description, whether a party is or is not to deliver its sentiments upon an important question not regularly under its consideration and what language it shall utter. There are no facts upon which any man can found an opinion excepting that the question is a most important one interesting to the whole community.

My opinion has not changed. I think that we ought to be silent. We do not know from any authority that any mischief to the Church is intended. Even the reform of the Church establishments has not been mentioned by authority.

You may rely upon it that when such men as you and I begin to talk others will also. All the enemies of the Church will be loud. The Whigs, the Radicals, the indifferent, the idle, will say nothing, and will be supposed to be the enemies of the Church. I have recently been in the hunting countries, and seeing in what manner gentlemen pass their time there, I don't see how it would be possible to procure even half a dozen signatures; or to find leisure to explain the object of the declaration or the necessity for it.

A publick meeting in any county is out of the question. Such a one would be attended by the whole rabble, each of whom whether Churchman or Dissenter would scream against the declaration because it would be supported by such men as you and me. Then we must not conceal from ourselves that there are many well meaning men, friends and adherents of the Church of England, who wish for its reform, others, although Churchmen and Church frequenters, think that some of the advantages of tithes would be very comfortable in their own pockets.

I confess that I infinitely prefer for the Church to combat the injustice and harshness of the proposition of the Government and to produce an effect upon the publick mind in that way, and by making them feel that all classes and sects are interested in upholding the Church of England than to make any previous declaration. At all events I should be very unwilling to sign the declaration which you have inclosed.

It appears to me that it would be said that we intentionally and ostentatiously avoided to speak out on any one of the interesting topicks connected with the question.

The Marquess of Londonderry to Wellington, 10 January 1834

Wynyard Park. I have received the enclosures from that strange man Sir Harcourt Lees. Two things occur to me to solicit your opinion and advice upon:

1. Is it wise to take any notice whatever or what notice of Mr. O'Connell's most flagrant falsehoods, which almost appear upon the face of his statement?

2. Would it be wise to allude to it in the House of Lords in any manner?

I have received today your obliging invitation. If attendance is useful or desired, rather than my proxy which you have, I will certainly turn up. Although to tell you the honest truth the affairs of our coal trade are in so critical and embarrassing a state, I am afraid to be away from the spot until we can at all see our way. Lord Durham I believe feels this equally, as he was going to Paris but has anchored here.

Docketed From Lord Londonderry. Sending a letter from Sir Harcourt Lees calling upon the Duke (according to his promise) to move the repeal of the Roman Catholic Bill. Distressed state of the coal trade.

Viscount Strangford to Wellington, 10 January 1834

Alnwick Castle. Confidential. I am requested by my noble host (who, I am sorry to say, suffers very much from gout) to express his regret that he cannot have the honour of waiting on you on the 3rd. He does not mean to be in town so early—unless there be a *pressing political necessity* for it, in which case he desires me to tell you that you cannot doubt that he would be in his place. A full personal attendance is, of course, always *desirable*—the only question is, whether on this occasion, it be necessary. If so, the Bishop of Carlisle, who is here, and I am desired also to say, the Bishop of Durham, would make it a point to attend on the first day of the session. (*Private.*) I must confess that I am made very uneasy by some letters which I have received within the last week, from a friend of our's in these northern parts.[1] His affairs seem to be in a state of scarcely retrievable ruin, and his tone of despondency is (*under all circumstances, and connected with certain recollections*) quite *alarming*—frightful allusions to the 'quiet of the tomb', to the difficulty of 'tolerating the burthen of life, when position in rank and society is lost', to the 'prospect of rejoining his brother in a better world', etc. etc. It is impossible to read these passages without feeling the deepest anxiety and apprehension. He is making every effort to meet his embarrassments—he tells me that he means to part with his Correggios and with the Cottage and to sell or let Holdernesse House. I mention all this to you in confidence, because I know the effect and influence

[1] The Marquess of Londonderry.

which a kind word from your Grace always has on his mind, and because I think that *this hint* may perhaps regulate the tone of any letter which you may have occasion to write to him. Of course, it is a subject to which I should [not] venture to allude to any other person in the world.

Princess Lieven to Wellington, 10 January 1834

Londres. Voici, Monsieur le Duc, une partie du travail, celle qui se rapporte à la question en instance, le reste, qui au fond forme le commencement et comme l'introduction à l'ouvrage ne pourra vous être envoyé que ce soir ou demain matin. Dans mon opinion le tout ne devrait servir que de *mémoire à consulter* pour la personne qui serait disposée à en tirer parti dans des publications successives. Mais vous en jugerez. Matousewicz m'a rendu compte des intéressans entretiens qu'il a eus avec vous. Vous sentez de quel poids il sont pour nous! Il y a quelque radoucissement dans les rapports de nos cabinets, et tandis que vos Ministres faisaient à mon mari des avances convenables, l'Empereur de son côté a parlé avec Mr. Bligh pour énoncer franchement et fermement sa pensée du procédé de l'Angleterre, en même tems que sa politique droite et résolue à l'égard de la Turquie. Bligh a envoyé un courrier pour en rendre compte ici. Ces messieurs n'en ont rien dit à mon mari, mais nous savons que cela a produit un effet satisfaisant. Je ne réponds point qu'il dure, car on ne peut répondre de rien avec eux.

PS. Quand venez vous à Londres pour rester?

The Earl of Roden to Wellington, 13 January 1834

Tollymore Park. I received your kind card of invitation for Monday the 3rd, but it is not my intention to go over to the meeting unless you wish it or have something for me to do, as it appears to me if matters are to go on as they did last session there cannot be much occasion for our attendance. I am however entirely at your disposal and desire to be guided by your wishes. You would oblige me much if you would inform me whether your views are in any way altered as to publick concerns or publick prospects since I last had the pleasure of conversing with you. This country is perfectly quiet but the people are all armed and ready at any moment for a conflict whenever any popular topic may call it forth. The repeal question is generally if not universally adopted amongst the Romanists but I trust our Protestant strength is firm.

Wellington to the Marquess of Londonderry, 14 January 1834

Stratfield Saye. I return Sir Harcourt Lees's letter. You did not send me the newspaper and I cannot tell whether it is worth while to notice its contents. In general it is not. I dare say that they will be as easily contradicted as I contradict the contents of this madman's letter. I did not say that I would move for the repeal of the Roman Catholic Bill. I said that that Bill being passed there was an end of concession. That from that time forwards if concession was made it must be of property and that I should have no hesitation in coming to Parliament and requiring powers to put down by force conspiracy and agitation to obtain such concession. This is the sense, if not the very words I made use of. But a lie suits the purpose of a day or of an hour or even of a minute and is sure to be told. You are quite right not to come up to Parliament. Your business is to set your affairs to rights. The task is difficult but not impossible to execute. A man may shew himself and acquire as much credit in adversity as he had in prosperity. You have talents and abilities to enable you to retrieve your affairs as well as for anything else. I would recommend to you to shut up all your houses but one, that is, keep them clean and water tight and well aired. I would keep my post in that one till you should have set all your affairs to rights. I recommend you not to withdraw upon any account.

Wellington to Princess Lieven, 14 January 1834

Stratfield Saye. Je vous renvois [ce] que vous m'avez prêté à lire; dont le contenu est parfait. J'ai lu aussi depuis mon arrivée ici le discours de Monsieur Bignon et les deux répliques de Monsieur le Duc de Broglie.

Il m'est clair que la paix est pour le moment assurée; et je suis d'avis que malgré qu'il soit très important à l'Empereur et à la Russie de concilier l'opinion de la classe de gens bien pensans de ce pays ci, il vaut mieux saisir les occasions opportunes de le faire avec modération que d'imiter les Ministres en sacrifiant le moment actuel.

Je ne sais pas si les versions des notes passées à St. Petersburgh entre le Comte de Nesselrode et le Ministre de France que j'ai vu ce matin dans le *Guardian* sont véritables. Elles sont calculées à imiter les Ministres de ce pays-ci, malgré que le fond en soit le même que celles passées entre le Comte de Nesselrode et Monsieur Bligh. Mais les formes, les explications, les détails en font des pièces bien différentes. Ces messieurs doivent s'en apercevoir; et une imitation au moins inutile pouvoit s'en venir et gâter une affaire qu'on espère être terminée.

Sir Henry Hardinge to Wellington, 16 January 1834

Carlton Club. Lord Grey has this morning gone down to Brighton, and as I understand (in confidence from Gordon) to take the King's pleasure on the measure of sending British troops to Portugal. I also understand that great *doubts* pervade the Cabinet—that Lord Palmerston and Lord Grey concur in their view—but I have not heard the names of those who are stated to be adverse to this line of policy.

Lord Grey will return tomorrow. An expedition to Portugal will not sound well in the King's speech, and I hear on other matters, such as pensions, tythes, and taxes, they profess to be in a great state of alarm.

Gordon and Kempt have been instructed to be in readiness, and I presume the decision will be known tomorrow night or Saturday morning.

PS. I say nothing on the Oxford nomination because I presume you are already in communication with the authorities of the university.

The enclosed is from Merton College, the head of which is a Whig.

When those who are non-resident and are now in town know your wishes, they purpose to sign a declaration supporting you. But until more is known, it is perhaps more prudent for them to wait a day.

I hear from Ross that very few men have signed the requisition to Peel—and those chiefly Whigs.

Bruce (Lavalette) tells me that Lord Palmerston's voice at Lord Althorp's was so loud and angry on the subject of Portugal, that a serious altercation is known to have taken place yesterday which confirms Gordon's hint that serious differences exist in the Cabinet.

Dated 16th January. *Docketed* 1834, January 16.

William Holmes to Wellington, 16 January 1834

Brighton. I was greatly surprised at meeting Edward Ellice here this day at two o'clock, particularly as I knew from himself that he was ordered to go down to Holkham for the benefit of his health. He told me that Lord Grey had suddenly taken it into his head to come down here this day and that he agreed to accompany him. He said Lord Grey wished to submit to the King the draft of the speech for the 4th of February. They drove in the first instance to the Albion and they are now at the Pavilion. This visit was quite unexpected at the Pavilion. There was a large evening party last night to celebrate the Duke of Gloster's birthday. The King had in the morning requested that all the dinner party should be punctual but just before dinner the messenger arrived and His Majesty did not make his appearance for nearly an hour, and when he did he appeared greatly agitated and remained in bad spirits all the evening. This circumstance with Lord Grey's sudden arrival has set all the politicians at work in speculations. Lord Maryborough is here and very well.

Dated Thursday. *Docketed (incorrectly)* 6 January. *The correct date is indicated by the Duke of Gloucester's birthday, which in 1834 was on Wednesday, 15 January.*

Wellington to the Earl of Aberdeen, 17 January 1834

Stratfield Saye. The session is approaching; and you will be anxious to hear from me again, if only for the purpose of assisting you to make up your mind whether you will or not come up for its commencement.

Since I wrote to you last the Russo-Turkish affair has taken a very curious turn. At the time I wrote to you the foreign ministers had gone or were going upon a party to Broadlands, Lord Palmerston's place in this county. Lieven was there among others. It appears that he and Lieven communicated there upon publick affairs, and had some explanation. I understand that it was quite obvious from that explanation that Lord Palmerston had no knowledge of the text of the treaty of alliance; particularly not of the secret article. After his return to town, he wrote a dispatch to Mr. Bligh at St. Petersburg, partly giving and in part requiring explanations quite in a different tone from that of the note; and in short there was every reason to expect that the mighty pretty quarrel might be settled without a duel.

Then came the King of France's speech which I think will have tended to convince you that I was not mistaken in respect to that king's interests and intentions. The King of England in the best of times never made a better king's speech. That speech has been followed by Monsieur de Bignon's speech, and by Monsieur de Broglie's two explanations or replies. It was obvious that the object of Bignon and the war party, which is now the English party, wanted to pledge the Chamber of Deputies to a war with Russia. No man could justify the Russian-Turkish treaty better than the Duke de Broglie. Indeed, so well that he has been sick ever since. I therefore now consider all chance of war on the score of that treaty as entirely at an end.

I conclude that you have seen in the newspapers a copy of the note of Lagréné, the French minister at St. Petersburg, and of the Russian answer. That which Lieven shewed me here was a joint note and an answer from Nesselrode to both ministers. The note and the reply were more laconical and less civil than those published in the *Augsburg Gazette*, from which our newspapers have published a translation. It is possible that I may be mistaken (but not probable) and that which I saw was the note to Mr. Bligh; and that the note from Monsieur Lagréné and that to that minister were in less pointed terms. If this be true, nothing can prove more strongly the state of degradation and of detestation in which this country is held in Europe.

It is said that the Dutch affair will be finished by the meeting of Parliament. I cannot tell you positively how it stands.

In respect to Spain, the civil war continues in the northern provinces. It has not yet extended to the southward. But it is said that the dislike of the new system is general. There was a report that a General Llander of Barcelona had written to the Queen in a revolutionary sense. If she happens to give way to revolutionary measures, God knows what will be the result.

The war is nearly in the same state in Portugal. I think that Don Pedro has rather gone backwards. But I heard this morning that Lord Grey had gone yesterday to Brighton, after long and stormy discussions in the Cabinet, to take His Majesty's pleasure upon the measure of sending a body of His Majesty's troops to Portugal to support the cause of Donna Maria. It is said that the condition of this sending is to be that Don Pedro is to come away. There is non-interference for you! It is impossible to form a judgement what the King will do. I think it most probable that Lord Frederick FitzClarence will be appointed

Adjutant-General or Quartermaster or something General; and that the King will consent.

There is a good deal of alarm about the Church, principally among the dignified clergy; and the politicians of the world. My friends the hunting gentlemen don't seem to me to think much about that or anything else excepting their horses and foxes.

I shall go up for Parliament and I think that I shall make some noise upon foreign affairs, Ireland and home upon the King's Speech and Address. The West Indian legislatures have I believe adopted the Government measure. That of Jamaica has protested strongly; but it adopts the measure, thinking that it will fail and that Government will be responsible. They forget that they will be ruined in the meantime.

ADD MS 43060, ff. 101–103. *Copy in Wellington Papers.*

Sir Henry Hardinge to Wellington, 17 January 1834

Lord Grey has returned and report is that *he is out of office*. It is further said that this report proceeds from Edward Ellice, who if he is correct must have preceded Lord Grey from Brighton, for the latter has not been in town an hour.

If any thing more definite can be traced, I will write an hour later.

We are all delighted here that you have accepted the Oxford requisition. The *Globe* of this evening says the requisition is so powerfully signed that no opposition will start.

Lady Lyndhurst died at Paris two days ago and the courier who brought the intelligence called Lord Lyndhurst from the bench at two this day.

Dated 17 January, 5 o'clock. *Docketed (incorrectly)* 1833.

Wellington to Sir Henry Hardinge, 17 January 1834

Stratfield Saye. I am very much obliged to you for your intelligence.

The measure in contemplation is worthy of every thing else that has been done.

The gentlemen from Oxford went to Hatfield to seek for me; returned to Apsley House; thence here and arrived about half an hour after I was gone hunting. I did not see them till I returned home; and in fact did not know of their resolution consequent upon Lord Grenville's death till the hour at which it was published in the *Standard* in London.

I have answered in the same tone as before; but in consideration of the number and respectability of the resident members of the Convocation who signed the resolution, and understanding that the Dean of Christ Church when he saw the resolution observed 'that he could not sign it *yet*', I have thought it but fair to them, after urging them to reconsider their resolution, and to see whether such reconsideration would not lead to an unanimous and satisfactory choice, to tell them that if I should be the object of such a choice I would not decline to attend to the call of the university.

The three gentlemen who were with me thought it most probable that my answer would put an end to the question.

I urged them again to elect Sir Robert Peel; and pointed out to them the advantage of putting him forward as it were officially in the affairs of the Church.

They declared positively that it was impossible to carry the election either for him or for Lord Talbot.

VISCOUNT HARDINGE PAPERS.

Wellington to the Duke of Cumberland, 17 January 1834

Stratfield Saye. I received your Royal Highness's letter of the [20 December] and nearly at the same time one from Charles in which he assured me that your Royal Highness would certainly cross on the 20th of January. It was therefore useless for me to write to your Royal Highness. Indeed I could inform you of nothing. I have only slept in London on my way to the north and again on returning a week ago; and I saw nobody who could give me any positive information on the affair of the Church on which your Royal Highness expresses so much anxiety.

The clergy have signed an address to the Archbishop expressing their confidence in whatever he should agree to. I was desired to sign a similar one on the part of the laity. It occurred [to me] that if the laity did anything it ought to do more. That some of us have nearly as much to do with alteration in the Church as the Archbishop has; and that if we spoke at all it ought to be to the King. I confess that I doubt the expediency of speaking at all. It must be observed that up to this moment we know nothing of Church reform excepting from squibs in the newspapers and such authorities; although I entertain no doubt that such a one will be proposed. We may rely upon it that the moment we shall speak the question will be started; and every Dissenter, Whig, and Radical in the kingdom will become an ardent Church reformer. We should have the reputation and the odium of having started the question which it is as well to avoid. It appears that the quarrel upon the Russo-Turkish treaty is at an end.

I have heard this day that Lord Grey had gone to Brighton yesterday to take His Majesty's pleasure upon sending a body of His Majesty's troops to Portugal to promote the cause of Donna Maria.

I hope that your Royal Highness will have landed in England quite recovered from your recent indisposition; and that you left Her Royal Highness the Duchess and Prince George quite well.

Wellington to the Earl of Roden, 17 January 1834

Stratfield Saye. It is impossible for me to tell what will be the course of events in Parliament. From the moment that the word 'reform' was mentioned in Parliament I never doubted of the consequences which must follow from it. We have not half done with them yet.

My opinion has been invariably that we ought to descend from our high station by the most gradual road, in order to avoid any great shock to our complicated machine and that we might each of us take our station in the new system according to which it has pleased gentlemen to be governed. I therefore have done and will do all that I can to prevent any sudden or general mischief.

People are telling me every day that noblemen and gentlemen like to be consulted, and to know the opinions of each other. I thought that I could not adopt of better mode of consulting than to invite to dine with me on the day preceding the meeting of Parliament every nobleman in the habit of speaking in the House of Lords or whose opinion was likely to have weight with others. I have invited as many as fifty. From some I am sorry to say that I have not received very civil answers. Many have not answered at all, some have excused themselves for not attending, very few have said that they will attend. I confess that I should find it difficult to give a reason for having sent these invitations. If a meeting was desireable, those who should wish it might have met at a club or at the house of any other noble Lord.

I will let you know if I should hear of anything that is deserving your attention that is not in the newspapers.

William Holmes to Wellington, 17 January 1834

Metropolitan Road Office. I came up from Brighton this morning to attend a meeting of our Metropolitan Roads Commission and to sit for Lord Lowther. I return this evening. I understand that the differences in the Cabinet relate to Portugal. Lord Grey and Ellice are not yet returned from Brighton. I have just heard that Lord Lyndhurst was called out of court about an hour since in consequence of the death of his wife in child bed. I hope it may not be true but I fear it is from the quarter through which I received my information.

The Marquess of Salisbury to Wellington, [ante 18 January 1834]

I am really quite ashamed of trespassing so often upon your kindness, more especially on the same subject but it is one of so much importance to myself that I trust you will excuse me and give me your advice.

The inclosed letters are from Mr. Duncombe's solicitors to mine, Nicholson and Longmore. To No. 1 Nicholson replied with my consent that he had received no instructions to proceed but that he would communicate with Duncombe's solicitors when he did receive them. This has brought a rejoinder No. 2 which I also inclose. It arrived this morning at Hertford, and I purpose delaying any reply until I have an answer from you, which I calculate may reach me if you will have the goodness to send by the coach to my house in London on Monday, in time for Nicholson to write by that night's post. If [I] do not receive it I shall call in Grafton Street for it in my way to you on Monday.

There appears [*sic*] [to] me three modes in which the letter may be answered: by stating openly that it is not my present intention to call up Duncombe for judgment; by saying that I shall consult my counsel and act by their advice; or thirdly by bringing him up in defiance of my counsel's opinion and standing the chance of the sentence. I confess my own feeling is in favour of the last alternative. The first is no doubt the most direct mode of proceeding, and the second has only in its recommendation that it will keep the rod suspended over Duncombe which evidently annoys him. Pray have the great kindness to suggest some better course or direct me which I shall adopt of those I have stated. I will not make more excuses for the trouble I am giving you.

Undated.

Wellington to the Marquess of Salisbury, 18 January 1834

Stratfield Saye. My opinion is that you should say that you intended to act in every respect according to the opinion of your counsel which is tantamount to giving no answer at all.

You must expect to hear from Duncombe upon the subject; and the answer must then be that you request to have no communication with him excepting through his attorney.

PS. You will come through London of course on Monday and I will write to you there if any thing should occur to me.

Princess Lieven to Wellington, 18 January 1834

Londres. J'ai exactement reçu, Monsieur le Duc, votre paquet et votre lettre de l'autre jour. Il me reste à vous envoyer le travail sur la question de la Pologne et celle qui traite individuellement de l'Empereur. C'est bien volumineux, mais peut-être trouverez vous cependant le moment de le parcourir. Votre opinion est la loi pour nous. Ainsi je me range à votre avis de ne point encore faire usage de ce que vous avez lu. Cependant me permettrez vous de vous observer que comme tout ce travail n'a que pour objet de nous défendre et d'éclairer l'opinion sur la politique de la Russie je ne vois pas d'inconvénient à ce que cet effet s'opère dans un moment où votre gouvernement a pris une ligne pacifique à notre égard. N'est ce pas servir cette politique que de détruire les préventions et la haine qui existent contre nous dans le public? Voilà une réflexion que j'ose vous soumettre. Tout s'est beaucoup adouci entre nos deux gouvernements; et je crois avec vous que le danger est écarté pour le moment. Les bruits de Londres vous seront parvenus. Il est parfaitement clair que le Cabinet est divisé sur la question de l'envoi de troupes en Portugal; que Lord Grey qui veut cette expédition est en minorité dans le Conseil et que la demande de sa démission a été une conséquence de ce désaccord. Si je suis bien informée, Lord Grey reste, mais l'envoi de troupes en Portugal ne se fait pas.

Adieu, Monsieur le Duc. Comme vous me dîtes que vous serez en ville vers la fin du mois voulez vous nous faire l'honneur de venir dîner chez nous le 31 janvier ou le 1er février, selon que cela vous arrangera le mieux. Vous me direz le jour.

William Holmes to Wellington, 19 January 1834

Brighton. I did not go to my own house on Friday when I was occupied at the Metropolitan Road Office the whole day, and I returned here by the evening coach. I have therefore only this day received your Grace's letter. I shall leave this early tomorrow morning and find my way to Stratfield Saye tomorrow evening or early on Tuesday. I believe the Cabinet breeze has blown over. The King is quiet and more calm than he was on Thursday and Friday. He says no troops shall be sent to Portugal. I received a letter this morning from Lord Lowther. Lord Hertford is much better. The letter was dated the 3rd January at Naples. The English Government had purchased at Naples 25,000 quarters of wheat to be sent to Malta. The price was paid for it in French money. He says there are 28,000 troops assembled at Toulon.

I find by the papers that my letter written in a hurry to your Grace on Friday last was too correct as to Lady Lyndhurst's death. No person who takes an interest in Lord Lyndhurst's fame or good character can regret the event though we may lament the suddenness of the occurrence.

Dated Sunday. *Docketed* (*incorrectly*) 1834, January 7.

John Wilson Croker to Wellington, 20 January 1834

West Molesey, Surrey. I have a letter from Lord Hertford of the 31st December written in good spirits and giving a good account of himself.

He desires me to let your Grace know that the Toulon armament is certainly going to the Dardanelles to take the castles in the rear, while we support by our naval force. He also says your Grace may be glad to know that 'a British agent came lately from Malta to Naples and bought 100,000 tomoli of wheat, about I think 20,000 quarters, and other provisions, and instead of paying in bills on London paid in

French coin—proving that we are only cats' paws'. So says Lord Hertford. I doubt the inferences which he draws from his facts. I believe well enough that the French would be glad and perhaps mean to *ascionize* Salonika or Gallipoli, but I cannot believe that *we* are yet mad enough to help them.

I suppose your Grace knows all about this late Cabinet brangle. I know nothing, having been at Baring's till Saturday, and since that here, whither no *news* ever makes its way under a week—but I happen to *know* one of the preliminary incidents. Palmerston and Althorp had a meeting on Wednesday evening (whether after a Cabinet dinner or not, I have not heard) but they had a meeting, which prolonged itself into the night and whatever passed it was so serious that at two o'clock in the morning some others of the Ministers were sent for, knocked up out of bed and brought down to Downing Street, where they remained till near daylight. Althorp did not go to bed at all. This much, I think, is certain: but I know little or nothing else. The *on dit* was that Palmerston wanted to send troops to Portugal, and that Althorp said he could not stand the expence—I *doubt*. The *expence* of ending that war for the moment would not be £100,000, nor half the money I believe; so that I must suspect that there was something else at bottom. An expedition to the Dardanelles would probably cost more—twice or thrice as much —but still not enough to break up a Government about. Nor do I believe that Governments, *otherwise cordial*, are ever broken up on such details—particularly as the Ministers boast of having a large surplus. But why trouble you with my *rêves creux* when you no doubt know the truth?

I go to town tomorrow for two days and if by any accident your Grace should have occasion to write to me, my address is 50 Albemarle Street. I shall call at Apsley House for the chance of meeting you though I believe you are at Stratfield Saye.

Sir Henry Hardinge to Wellington, 20 January 1834

The Ministerial papers are like the Cabinet—very equally divided on the subject of sending or not sending troops to Portugal.

The *Courier* advocated the measure—the *Globe* denies that any orders were actually given or preparations made and is against the measure.

The Times is again very warlike and insists that the policy ought to have been to have sent the troops, and ends by an indirect hint to Palmerston to resign.

The *Chronicle* is quite convinced that the Ministers and King did right not to send the troops.

Then I hear Lord Grey, having in the autumn assented to the measure, supported Palmerston but feebly, convinced by Edward Ellice that the measure would have a fatal effect on the Ministry in the House of Commons. Lord Holland furiously for it. Charles Grant equally so—and Brougham suspected of being so from the line adopted by *The Times*.

Stanley and Graham, Duke of Richmond, Lord Lansdowne and Melbourne against it. Lord J. Russell and Ripon are not quoted.

The anxiety of the Foreign Minister to interfere by force at a critical moment of Portuguese affairs and his inability to carry his own departmental measures into effect, place Palmerston in an awkward predicament.

He has a worthy colleague in the Duc de Broglie, whose conduct has done more to humiliate his country than I thought it possible for the folly of any individual's tongue to do.

PS. By the bye there is a *printed* prospectus of your Grace's correspondence, commencing with India and closing in the year 1828—being as it were a life of the Duke of Wellington by our friend Gurwood.

I hear it stated that your Grace has consented to review what is to be given to the public. I am probably mis-informed on the latter point, but as some of your friends are most anxious on this subject and doubt not the zeal but the capacity of the editor, I have ventured to draw your attention to it.

Lord Stuart de Rothesay shewed me the prospectus.

Dated 20th January. *Docketed* 1834, January 20th.

Lord Cowley to Wellington, 20 January 1834

Grosvenor Street. I enclose a letter which I have just received from the Rev. Mr. Richards, who acted as chaplain to my embassy at Vienna during the absence of Mr. Bradford. When I came home he requested me to appoint him my chaplain, which I did. I have written to thank him for his votes, and told him I should send his letter to you who I was sure would be equally sensible of his kindness.

You have of course received from various persons accounts of the late dissensions in the Cabinet. The result seems to be that the expedition to Portugal is not to take place, but the Ministers are to keep their places. Lord Grey is said to have returned from his interview with the King in high dudgeon.

What a condition our Ministers are in: bullied by Russia, their favourite ambassador rejected by the Emperor; their ally Louis-Philippe acting the conservative and Lord Grey defeated in an important measure by his own Cabinet!! To say nothing of the session that awaits them which is likely to be more stormy than the last.

I conclude that you will have no competitor at Oxford.

Sir Henry Hardinge to Wellington, 21 January 1834

After the late breeze we have a dead calm.

Croker, who came to town this morning, says he knows from undoubted authority that on Wednesday night Palmerston remained at Lord Althorp's in very animated discussion till two o'clock, and then they sent for another Cabinet Minister who joined them at three, and that it is supposed the third person was Lord Grey. This trio it is said had very angry voices, and that the papers or statements were prepared during the night, the party having met after the Cabinet broke up. In short, every clerk in the Foreign Office on Thursday knew as well as the messengers at Lord Althorp's that the night had been spent in wrangling.

Edward Ellice is very angry that he should be quoted as the author of the report, and I hear the Mayor of Bristol like a goose posted up a private letter in the newsroom of Bristol, stating on the writer's authority, Serjeant Ludlow, that Lord Grey had resigned.

I think Ellice will thus let the matter rest—it won't do for him to set himself up as a man of very sensitive feeling in matters of political reports.

Dated 21st January. *Docketed* 1834, January 21.

The Rev. William Hayward Cox to Wellington, 21 January 1834

11 Beaumont Road, Oxford. I had the honour of receiving your Grace's letter of the eighteenth instant by this morning's post, and in reply to your very condescending explanation of the circumstances under which your Grace acceded to the nomination, I trust I may be permitted to say that the reasons you assign for declining to withdraw are most satisfactory ones. At the same time I cannot conceal from myself that the candour and fairness which distinguishes your Grace have been very imperfectly imitated by those gentlemen to whom you entrusted the task of reconsideration and of endeavouring to effect an unanimous choice. The circumstances however of Sir Robert Peel's having absolutely declined to come forward renders further canvass of the merits of the case unnecessary, and it becomes my duty therefore, in common with that of his other supporters, to abstain from observations prejudicial to good feeling. Allow me then, my Lord, in conclusion to repeat the strong obligation under which I feel myself placed by your Grace's liberal attention to my letter, and to congratulate you as well as the university on the prospect of your succeeding without opposition to that high office, to which you are invited by an array of names which I must confess are, as you justly observe, most respectable and influential.

Dated Tuesday evening. *Postmark* January 22 1834.

The Rev. Thomas Wintle to Wellington, 22 January 1834

Committee room, St. John's College. When I wrote my letter of yesterday I was not aware that I should so soon have the gratification of conveying to your Grace the decisive proof, to which I now have the honor of directing your attention, that all probability of a contest is over. The Vice-Chancellor evidently well satisfied that such is the case, has deemed delay inexpedient, and has, this morning, circulated the customary form of notice, in which he fixes the hour of twelve on Wednesday next the 29th instant as the time of proceeding to the election of Chancellor. Immediately after the convocation, which will be then held, and which will not last more than an hour, an official messenger carrying intelligence of the result to your Grace, will be dispatched by the Vice-Chancellor. May I request that your Grace will in the meantime do me the favor to intimate where you are likely to be in the afternoon of that day, in order that I may inform the Vice-Chancellor how you may be most readily approached?

I will not lose the present opportunity of signifying to your Grace that the statutable forms of the installation of a newly elected Chancellor are usually observed on an early day after the election and at his own house. It will be for your Grace to appoint both the time and the place of this ceremony. When your pleasure on these points shall have been communicated to the Vice-Chancellor, he will be accompanied by such deputies as are indispensably necessary to represent the university, and will hold a convocation in your house. The number of the deputation will probably be between twenty and thirty. A minute detail of all the proceedings will of course be submitted beforehand to your Grace. I will therefore for the present content myself with saying that the Latin language will be employed, and that a brief reply from your Grace to an address that will be made to you will be expected to be in the same language. A copy of the address will be placed in your hands in time to allow full consideration of the terms of your answer. Your Grace will permit me to state that it is a matter of difficulty for the Vice-Chancellor and other officers of the university to withdraw themselves from Oxford in full term. I have reason to believe that the Vice-Chancellor entertains some hope that it may suit your Grace's convenience to name a day between February 3rd and February 8th for the reception of the university, because that week happens to be one comparatively free from academical engagements. I beg however that your Grace will not consider this suggestion as coming from the Vice-Chancellor. I respectfully offer it as my own, and as one on which your Grace may not have it in your power to act. The Vice-Chancellor will undoubtedly, as soon as the election shall be over and he can officially address your Grace, refer to yourself on the subject and will do his utmost to comply with any wishes which you may express.

I will not this evening forward the day's list of additional signatures. Neither however will I withhold from myself the pleasure of reporting that they have come in and are still coming in, as on former days. It affords high satisfaction to your Grace's friends to reflect that the numerous names which we have received are so many voluntary testimonies in your favor, and have been furnished, not in consequence of anything like a canvass for votes, but with the design of shewing the prevalence and strength of Conservative sentiments among the members of Convocation and thus of preventing a contest.

Charles Ross to Wellington, 23 January 1834

60 Portland Place. You are of course aware that the election is fixed for Wednesday, and it adds considerably to the gratification all your friends must feel at the result that it will be unattended with a contest. Some additional names are daily adding to the list in London. Among others the clergyman of Lord Winchilsea's parish, Mr. Chisholm, sent in his adhesion today. I had a letter from Lord Delawarr, but he tells me he had previously written to your Grace.

The East India Company and the Government have had a serious dispute. The latter, in consequence of a pledge exacted it is said from Lord Grey by Lord Wellesley, previous to his departure for Ireland, insist upon the entire payment of Mr. Prendergast's claim, with which I have no doubt you are acquainted, and which every Board of Control till the present has uniformly rejected. The Court of Directors have peremptorily refused to send all the necessary dispatches, and a mandamus is to be sued out to compel them. This I heard today from Colonel Lushington, one of the directors.

The Earl of Falmouth to Wellington, 23 January 1834

Tregothnan, Truro. I regret that the business which will detain me here for some little time after the meeting of Parliament must also prevent my having the pleasure of waiting upon your Grace at dinner on the 3rd of February. I know not if any report has been recently sent you of the state of public feeling in these parts, and in this ignorance I take the opportunity of adding a few words upon that subject, which I hope may not be considered obtrusive or officious. Your Grace I am sure has perceived how much the tide of opinion among the educated and middle classes has turned, if not in favour of the Tories, at least against the Whig Government, in other parts of the country. It is so here, and the more remarkably, because nowhere, from the circumstances of our numerous boroughs having peculiarly excited the envy and dislike of those who being near had no share in them, was the reform cry more violent during the progress of the bill. But unfortunately by the deep artifice of that bill, the chief power is not in the hands of those who would gladly correct the effects of their delusion—of the landowners, the town *gentry*, or even the honest tradesmen—it is with the little low shopkeepers and the journeymen, and consequently with their leaders sent from the Radical focus's in London. It is extended by the unions and is deeply rooted at the beer shops. Thus it appears to me that although another Parliament would probably be a better one as regarding the counties and some of the corporate towns, it can promise

431

little as to the borough Members generally (which are as more than three to one in the whole representation) so long as property and education are sacrificed to numbers, so long in short as the reform law in its present monstrous shape shall endure. Of one thing I will venture to express to your Grace my strong conviction. I hear that the offering to be made the revolutionists this year is to be the destruction of, at least, the *borough* corporations, the great majority of which will be found to be Conservative bodies, and even where connected with Whig patrons, as Bedford etc., must necessarily have an indirect conservative tendency.

If this plan should succeed, if these bodies should be made elective by the commonalties or otherwise merged in them, it appears to me quite obvious that the only anchor upon which constitutional aristocracy can yet have the smallest chance of riding out the storm will be irrecoverably gone. After the visit of the corporation inquisitors, whose course here by the bye was one continued round of compliments paid to all the corporate officers after seeing their books and papers almost without exception, I thought it a good moment for doing all we could to revive the spirit of these bodies and restore them as far as possible to the favor of those who really had been deluded by the libels against them. Many others thought the same, and the good that has been thus done, in the chief places around me, has more than ever confirmed my estimate of their immense importance as clogs to the revolutionary wheel. If *they* go, I confess to your Grace that all further attempts on the part of those who may now usefully guide them appear to me utterly vain and futile. The Church may live out a year or two—it is evident the Radical portion of the Government (Radical par excellence) is beat upon that point—but beyond that it will not stand (I mean of course the establishment) without the corporations—nor can property stand upon any principle that this precedent will not at once destroy, the property of corporations being to all intents and purposes as the property of individuals in the eye of the law, and the throwing it open or taking it away precisely the same, in principle, as the cutting up for others or robbery of Stratfield Saye or Tregothnan. All this however your Grace can tell me with far more knowledge and experience, and I feel that I ought to apologise for occupying your time with it. My sole desire is to be of all the use I can under the present deplorable circumstances of the country, and if I am obtrusive in writing so much I entreat that it may be attributed to that desire alone. If your

432

Grace can in any way redress the balance of the State or prevent further evil I rest assured that you will do so. If my proxy can be of the least use, it will be at your disposal. I most heartily wish that any good may come out of the ensuing session.

The Earl of Aberdeen to Wellington, 24 January 1834

Haddo House. Your last account of the state of our foreign matters is curious indeed; and is sufficiently inviting for any one who may be disposed to indulge in a little criticism on the Address to be proposed in answer to the King's Speech. I hope, and believe, that if you had thought my attendance at all essential, you would have told me so. In this, as in all other publick matters, I hold myself at your disposal; and of course I cannot pretend to be ignorant that in the discussion of foreign questions, I am likely to be of more use to you than most of our friends who may be at your side. I am quite ready to make any motion, or to support any motion, if made, which you may think desirable; or, without any such specifick object, if the general course of your proceedings makes you wish to have me with you, this will be quite sufficient to govern my conduct; because I know how considerate you are on these occasions. But if I am to follow my own inclinations at present, I should prefer remaining here for some time longer. The debate on the Address, I take for granted, is not likely to lead to any consequences; and your general view of foreign affairs, as well as domestick, will be made with much more effect, and have much greater weight than anything which could fall from me. In the absence of any positive wish on your part, I have therefore determined to remain here for the present. Indeed, it is no easy matter for me to say, if left entirely to myself, when I should be disposed to follow a different course. In case of any sudden and unforeseen emergency, I shall send my proxy to Abercorn, and have recommended Lord Morton to do so too. He will be in the neighbourhood of London, and ready to obey any summons which he may receive from you. I have now said quite enough upon this subject; and, again referring to what I have already stated, I will only express a hope that you have known me long enough to feel that you may have implicit confidence in my declaration, and that you may take it precisely au pied de la lettre.

Your anticipations of the pacifick policy of the French Government are perfectly correct; but am I so far wrong in doubting the power of that Government to give effect to this policy? The recantation of M. de Broglie is but a sorry security, after all; and in the pacifick speech of M. Thiers there is a good deal of warlike matter. Besides, have we not seen very pacifick Governments do very warlike things? Indeed, we have lately seen war actually made, in order to preserve peace! It is very likely that Lord Grey may be as pacifick as Louis Philippe himself; so far at least as an open and avowed state of war is concerned; but there are those about them both who entertain other notions; and we must not forget that Bob Acres himself was at last spirited up to take the field. I do not say it is very probable; but it would not at all surprize me if either, or both of these pacifick Governments, should find itself engaged in war.

Of home questions, the state of the Church is one of the most interesting and important. The alarm in this country is greater than in England; and if the Government did not feel that the example must be followed in England, sooner or later, there is reason to suppose that they would be willing to sacrifice the Church of Scotland to the clamour of those who oppose the system of lay patronage, as it exists at present, and who desire to introduce something in the nature of a popular election. As it is, the danger is imminent. It is a curious fact that the Scotch Church, which has so long been the object of admiration with all those who were hostile to the Church of England, of all religious denominations or of no religion at all, appears to be now in the greatest danger of the two. Indeed, from all I hear, I am very sanguine in believing that the Church of England will prove too strong for its enemies, should the attack really be made.

PS. I forgot to tell you how much you had charmed Mme. de Lieven when at Stratfield Saye. She writes to me, 'J'ai eu le plus grand plaisir à voir la bonne mine, la bonne santé, et la bonne humeur du Duc de Wellington. Je ne l'ai pas connu aussi bien depuis avant Vérone.'

James Amphlett to Wellington, 24 January 1834

Peel's Coffee House, Fleet Street. Though I am aware that your Grace has a poor opinion of the newspaper press of the country, which its general character is but too well calculated to justify; yet a circumstance has come accidentally to my knowledge, on the subject, which I venture to suggest to you.

I have formerly troubled your Grace with some communications from Lincolnshire and Stafford. In the former county I sunk some hundreds in a Conservative journal; but a long company shareholding journal being established there with a capital of £5,000, professing Conservative principles, and supported by persons who had professed to support myself, was in the end lowered to a sort of *juste milieu* grade of writing, that only betrayed the cause; I left the country, and have since resided in Stafford on a small independency.

Being in town for a few days, I have learnt that a sort of shadowy journal, on Conservative principles, is got up in London *for Dover*: part printed in one place and part in another; but having a circulation in Dover of 500, with a quarto page of good advertisements.

If a meagre establishment of this kind can do so much, a well-conducted paper, printed wholly at Dover, on sound Conservative principles, would do more than double the business.

Your Grace is known, and you have an interest in the district. If you think that any service could be rendered by such an establishment, I would willingly go down and make the necessary enquiries; but I am totally unknown to all parties there. If your Grace could apprise me of the names of any influential persons in the neighbourhood, who were likely to take an interest in the thing, the chances of my journey on such a purpose would be improved.

Few persons have had more experience with the press than I have; and I only desire to render the remaining days of my life useful and honorable in a good cause.

PS. My address after tomorrow the 25th will be at Stafford.

Draft reply 26 January 1834. Compliments. The Duke must beg leave to decline to interfere in any manner with the affairs of the public press.

The Duke of Cumberland to Wellington, 24 January 1834

St. James's Palace. I found a letter from you on my table on my arrival here and should have replied to it ere this had I not been prevented from so many persons calling on me. I do most fully agree with you in your observation that if *we* were to address any one it ought to be the *King* and not the Archbishop; but I cannot exactly agree that we ought not to do something, for it is *not* from mere newspapers that we are informed of a projected Church reform in this country as the immediate servants, I may call them, of the Crown have openly avowed this to be the intention, viz. Lord John Russell himself, a Cabinet Minister, in a speech at a public meeting in Devonshire when he stated 'that *great* alterations were contemplated by Ministers in the Church'. Secondly, Mr. P. Thomson stated at a public meeting 'that Ministers meant to abolish Church rates and establish a new system of registration for baptisms, marriages, and burials'; and thirdly, Dr. Lushington declared at a public meeting at London Tavern 'that Ministers intended a complete and radical reform of the Church'. Now surely *this* is strong enough. But add to this what has taken place in various parts of the kingdom, the great meetings of Dissenters and their resolutions published in which they declare 'that they will pay no more Church rates or tithes, that they will not register their births, marriages, or burials but in their own way, and that they will insist on burial grounds of their own, also that every Dissenter should be allowed to study at Oxford and Cambridge and take their degrees, in fine that the Church must and shall be separated from the State'. Is *this* not declaring at once war to the Established Church? Now if the point of Church rates is carried which I understand Ministers certainly mean to propose and support, I say that the Established Church is gone, and *that* principle once admitted from that moment I consider that the Church is in fact separated from the State and there will be no resisting then either the intended alterations in the liturgy or the expulsion of bishops from the House of Peers or any other *radical* or distinctive measure. Excuse my laying thus before you my view of the subject, but it presses itself so strongly on my mind that I cannot forbear laying it before you.

I received a very kind invitation to go to Brighton tomorrow where I probably shall remain till Monday. I hope your son Charles [is] looking very well. I can assure you I parted with him with great regret. However the row may be made up at present in the Cabinet *Grey* is done for, he is virtually no more Minister of this country.

Sir Robert William Gardiner to Wellington, 24 January 1834

Melbourne Lodge, Claremont. I send your Grace the enclosed, from its shewing the state of the island at a very recent date.

Enclosure: Jamaica. 21 December 1833.

. . . and the question with the negroes is whether they will suffer six years of apprenticeship, or 'take arms' and burn the plantations. This is the state of the island, to be determined in the short period of a fortnight—it is therefore a momentous period in the destiny of the colony; and although I do not apprehend any general outbreak, still I look at it with a degree of uncertainty. As in all similar cases, there are of course great alarmists, and others expressing a way of thinking that there is not the slightest apprehension: yet these latter are to the full as anxious for the troops as the former, thereby belying their opinion. Now there is undoubtedly a strong idea among the negroes that after New Year's Day they are to be free; and all the explanation of the King's proclamation cannot get rid of this feeling among some of them. Your 'whereas' and 'nevertheless' and 'notwithstanding' are words not understood by them; and keeping the only one point in view, you cannot make them see they have a sort of primary ordeal to go through. In consequence, the language held by many estates is that they are free—and 'no work more than they like after Christmas'. It will require the greatest firmness, and at the same time temper, in such a case; for the old system of driving will no longer do. If frightened, they will take to the woods; and there is no knowing how far it may spread, or to what extremity. The Governor is going round the island in a steamboat—reviewing the militia, with the intention also of explaining to the negroes on the estates he may visit. I am left in command on the south side—and besides numerous detachments, the 22nd regiment complete, and part of the 8th and 50th, in hand to work with; whereas where they are, I don't think that more than 200 men could be moved in a body at once. If an enemy was expected, this would be an enviable situation, but war against these poor devils however well conducted is but inglorious work. I hope the weather may be favourable, as our rivers being principally mountain streams are difficult to pass, and having no bridges except the few kept on the main communications.

My last letter you will remember was written when there was no idea of compensation; and therefore the feeling of all proprietors was against the bill. It is another thing when he finds he is to be paid for his property; and hence my different view now of *immediate consequences*— not of the bill, remember.

The Bishop of Exeter to Wellington, 24 January 1834

Exeter. If I have been tardy in expressing the great gratification with which I have heard of the assured election of your Grace to the Chancellorship of the University of Oxford, my delay has not been caused by indifference to the event. As an Oxford man, knowing well the high tone of sentiment and principle which actuates the university in its elections, I have always been in the habit of regarding its choice of any individual as its head as the highest, because I verily believe it the purest civil honour which England can bestow. Although, therefore, no body of men can confer honour on your Grace, yet I rejoice to see Oxford do what it can to testify its sense of achievements, both in war and peace, which it is unable to reward.

I know not that I should now obtrude my feelings on this subject were there not another which I am anxious to bring to your Grace's attention. What the intention of Government may be in its plan of Church reform, I have no means of knowing. But if, as is highly probable, it is of an extensive nature, it appears to me of the utmost importance that the Government be called upon to bring it forwards, either by bill in the House of *Lords* or by resolutions simultaneously in both houses. If it be embodied in a bill introduced first into the House of Commons, it will receive its form and character from the enemies of the Church, and the Lords will be threatened with extinction or with a resignation of the Ministers, if in any important particular they presume to alter the ministerial plan thus sanctioned by the other house.

The reason for insisting on the Lords having a voice in devising the measure is obvious. They are the body in which the estate of the clergy, one of the three estates of the realm, sits and deliberates. No clergyman can sit in the other house. For that other house, therefore, to be made by Government the authors of a plan of change affecting the Church in its highest interests, preferably to the house in which the representatives of the clergy sit, would be an act of injustice and wrong, which it would be scarcely possible for Ministers to perpetrate, if timely precaution be taken to prevent it.

I therefore venture to submit to your Grace whether it might not be of great moment if Church reform be, as must be expected, one of the matters of the King's Speech; that Ministers should, on the first night, be asked in which house the bill will be introduced; and that they be urged to do so in the House of Lords. If your Grace should concur in this view of the matter, I venture to hope that you would feel no objection to your being the individual to urge the point. From you, above all men, it would come with the greatest weight.

Wellington to the Duke of Cumberland, 25 January 1834

Stratfield Saye. I have had the honor of receiving your Royal Highness's letter. I entertain no doubt whatever of the intention of making some movement in Church reform in this year. But I believe it will be very difficult to say what is to be done. If I am not mistaken the Ministers laid aside the consideration of the subject in November last, not having been able to agree upon it, and they had not considered it when I heard last.

Then we are to be called upon to make a declaration or to address the Crown. Upon what? Not upon Church reform generally because if I mistake not the Archbishop had in Parliament two bills upon Church reform for two or three sessions, which Parliament did not pass; but they passed the House of Lords.

Not upon Lord John Russell's or Mr. Poulett Thomson's or Dr. Lushington's speeches, or the declaration of the Dissenters. Yet that is all that we have. Nothing can be more painful to me than arguments upon a subject which can lead to no result.

We are to sign the declaration or address in order to produce an impression on the publick mind. What impression? That the Church is in danger? Is that desirable at the present moment? Is that the course proposed? I must say that it is not at all clear that if we begin with these declarations and addresses we shall not be in a minority. I have been a good deal in the interior of the country and I know that men in general were not disposed to come forward upon this subject. I certainly should not think it wise to force them.

However, Sir, I decide only for myself. I intreat that others will do what they think proper. I intreat that if they should wish to have declarations and addresses that they should have them. Of this they may be certain, that whenever I shall think that I can do anything to promote the benefit or the safety of the Church I shall not be found backward whether to sign papers or any other act that may be beneficial.

Wellington to the Bishop of Exeter, 26 January 1834

Stratfield Saye. I am very much flattered by your congratulations on the honour conferred upon me by the University of Oxford.

There is no man who feels more sensibly than I do my want of qualifications to fill that office. I did everything in my power to induce the university to select one less disqualified, but in vain; and I am flattered by their favour in proportion as I feel that I am not qualified for the office.

I quite agree in opinion with you that it would be desirable to induce the Government to bring in the Church Bill to the House of Lords, and if there should be an opportunity on the first day of the session I will urge them to adopt this course.

I do not think that they dare to do so, much less that they dare to propose their measure in the shape of resolutions simultaneously in the House of Lords with the production of the bill in the Commons. That is no reason why the course should not be strongly urged upon their consideration.

You don't mention whether you propose to come up for the meeting of Parliament.

The Duke of Buckingham and Chandos to Wellington, 29 January 1834

Avington. I had fully intended attending your dinner on the 3rd of February. But the unseasonable and tempestuous weather which we so long have had has kept up such a guerilla warfare of gout in my constitution that I really do not dare take a journey up to town at this moment. I hope therefore that you will excuse me for not dining with you on the 3rd of February.

I see but little hope in our political prospects. I fully expect that the present Ministers will split. The shell will burst, but the fragments will do infinite mischief in falling. I consider it however so essential to the safety of what remains to us that the present Ministers should not be allowed to continue to misgovern the country that there is no sacrifice that I would not make to attend Parliament if I could but see a chance of an *united effort* to achieve the object of their overthrow. I therefore hold myself in readiness to attend your summons should such an effort be determined upon. I don't see how they are to provide their money, as it is clear that they will be beat out of their turn. What appears to me more likely is that in order to keep their places they will join in some popular outcry at the expense of our institutions, of the public creditor and of public faith.

One only point remains to me to trouble you upon. I sincerely congratulate the country and the Church upon what is going on respecting the chancellorship of the University of Oxford. My feelings are deeply interested in this matter, and it is a great consolation to me for the loss of one whom I dearly loved to see the honour which he most valued fall upon one whom I honor and respect and esteem as much as I do you.

The Earl of Rosslyn to Wellington, 30 January 1834

St. James's Square. Private. I wish you joy of your election for Oxford, which as Wilson tells me was announced to you last night.

I have seen no one but Ellenborough, who is extremely anxious to see your Grace before your dinner on Monday. I am inclined to believe that he will state in writing the views he has taken of the course which it would be expedient to adopt even at the opening of the session. If he should do so the little I have to add may be taken as *non avenu*, but it appears to me that it may otherwise be convenient that you should be apprised of the outline of his purpose.

He thinks it most advantageous for the party that even on the first day there should be a declaration of *principles* upon which you mean to act, and by which you will be pledged to abide upon the great leading measures to be brought forward, and more especially those affecting the Church in tythes and temporalities or spirituals. He seemed to think the foreign policy must come under discussion, but he seemed to dwell less upon that.

I could not help observing that all such declarations appeared to me to be premature and that those important and interesting questions must be debated under great disadvantage if discussed in the abstract in total ignorance of the nature and extent of the measures to be proposed. And that it would be more prudent to reserve all declaration and attack till you were in possession of a full knowledge of the Ministers' plans and were enabled to take all the advantages in argument which a disclosure of their projects and an exposition of the details might probably afford.

Ellenborough seems always afraid that the High Tory party will be dissatisfied with anything like reasonable prudence.

Of moderation and caution the Gloucestershire Tory squires are I fear incapable.

I will not trouble you with anything more. James Loch told General Arbuthnot that the Poor Law Bill was ready.

Wellington to the Earl of Aberdeen, 31 January 1834

Stratfield Saye. I received your letter of the 24th but too late to urge you to come up to town for the discussion on the Address. I do not ask you to come for any ulterior discussion, because, unless circumstances are much altered in the House of Commons since last year, I don't think that it would be advisable to originate any discussion in the House of Lords. Besides I am rather inclined to think, in foreign affairs at least, those whose cause we should wish to promote would prefer that *we* should not bring their affairs under discussion.

I have heard nothing lately that is interesting.

I am going to London, where I understand that our zealous friends are very unreasonable; and I shall have some trouble with them.

You will have heard that I have been elected Chancellor of Oxford unanimously. That is as extraordinary a revolution as the conversion of Madame de Lieven. I did everything in my power to prevail upon them to take Sir Robert Peel, but in vain.

ADD MS 43060, ff. 104–105. *Copy in Wellington Papers.*

Wellington to the Duke of Buckingham and Chandos, 31 January 1834

Stratfield Saye. I am highly flattered by your congratulations upon the honour recently conferred upon me.

I am very sorry that I shall not have the pleasure of seeing you on Monday; and particularly that you will not be in your place in the House of Lords on Tuesday.

The discussion of the Address affords an opportunity of discussing the topicks of the day which the course of business in the House of Lords will not otherwise give us. I confess that I see little chance of bringing any question forward with advantage. Matters appear to me to remain in the House of Commons very much as they did.

We might carry in the Lords a question upon a point of foreign or of home policy. Everybody would admit the truth and justice of our proceeding, would peruse our debate with interest, and abuse the Ministers. But the House of Commons, the King and his Ministers would join in a censure of the majority of the House of Lords as they did in the last session of Parliament; and not a soul in the Commons would venture to utter a word in our favour, or in support of the cause which we should have espoused.

I concur in your opinion that as long as this Administration lasts the mischief continues. I don't think that they will split. My opinion founded upon long observation is that they are under some engagement to each other not to split upon trifles; but to continue to act together in office although they should not approve of the principle or the detail of what is doing.

I don't think that their retirement from office would improve the state of our affairs; unless it should be followed by an universal persuasion that all that they have been doing for the last three years requires revision. The truth is that all government in this country is impossible under existing circumstances. I don't care whether it is called monarchy, oligarchy, aristocracy, democracy or what they please, the government of the country, the protection of the lives, privileges and properties of its subjects and the regulation of the thousand matters which require regulation in our advanced and artificial state of society are impracticable as long as such a deliberative assembly exists as the House of Commons, with all the powers and privileges which it has amassed in the course of the last two hundred years.

The Duke of Northumberland to Wellington, 1 February 1834

Alnwick Castle. I have herein enclosed my brother's and my own proxy vote in case any question of moment should come on in the House of Lords before I arrive in London, so that your Grace may have them entered in case you should consider it desirable.

I must congratulate you, my dear Duke, which I do most sincerely on your election, unanimously, to the honorable office of Chancellor to the University of Oxford.

The conduct of all the parties concerned appears to have been admirable, and I am the more gratified, as I feel confident that the selection of your Grace at this moment unanimously as champion of the university will produce the best effect through the different countries of Europe.

In these good wishes the Duchess and a large party of friends unite.

The Earl of Balcarres to Wellington, 6 February 1834

Haigh Hall. I have the honor to forward to your Grace my proxy, which I request may be used for your support and that of your political friends.

Draft reply 8 February 1834. Compliments to Lord Balcarres. The Duke is much flattered by his Lordship's confidence in entrusting him with his proxy.

The Head Master of Eton College (the Rev. John Keate) to Wellington, 7 February 1834

Eton College. The great kindness and attention which I have always experienced from your Grace induce me to think that you will pardon this intrusion, and receive favourably the application which I now make, as Master of Eton, to the most distinguished of her sons, upon a subject of vital importance to the school. The fact is that we are threatened to be hemmed in by two railways, the one a branch of the Bristol railway (which itself, if carried in Parliament, will be too near Eton not to interfere with its discipline), the other, a distinct road from Windsor to London. Both these are proposed to be in our immediate neighbourhood, indeed to be carried through the grounds and gardens of the college, and must necessarily interfere with the discipline of the school, with the studies and amusements of the boys, and be injurious in their consequences to the health of the inhabitants, and even endanger the lives of those who from the curiosity and adventurous spirit of youth will constantly be endeavouring to pass over these roads. But the plan, which I take the liberty to enclose, will shew your Grace the lines which these roads are intended to traverse; and the accompanying statement will point out the consequences which we dread in the event of the measures being carried. We earnestly request your Grace's attention

444

to these points, and hope that, if not inconsistent with your general sentiments upon these subjects, we may count upon your Grace's powerful opposition to these bills, if they ever come into the House of Lords.

I hope I may be allowed to congratulate your Grace, or rather the University of Oxford, on your Grace's election as Chancellor.

First enclosure: Printed broadsheet, Opposition to the Great Western and Windsor railways, *Eton, January 1834.*

Second enclosure: Map of Eton, showing the proposed course of the railways.

Wellington to the Duke of Richmond, 7 February 1834

London. Private and confidential. In consequence of the conversation with you on Wednesday I have seen Sir Robert Peel and he and I have agreed that it is desireable to endeavour to prevail upon Lord Lowther to refrain from renewing the notice of his motion upon the Post Office. I don't believe that Lord Lowther will return as soon as you expect he will. But I leave in town a letter to be delivered to him on his arrival to request him not to renew his notice till I shall have seen him, or if I should be out of town till Sir Robert Peel will have spoken to him.

It is very desireable that it should not be known that Sir Robert Peel or I intend to mention the subject to Lord Lowther till one of us will have communicated with him.

Wellington to Princess Lieven, 9 February 1834

Stratfield Saye. Je suis venu ici hier au soir, et j'ai avec moi vos deux pièces. Il me paroît que la publication de ces pièces, ou l'usage qu'on pouvoit faire des faits et du raisonnement qu'elles contiennent pour éclairer l'esprit publique ne feroit aucun mal dans le moment actuel, si ce n'est aux relations entre le Ministre de Russie et l'Ambassade de Sa Majesté Impériale et éventuellement entre les deux gouvernements. C'est à vous à juger si vous devez risquer ce résultat. Je dirois, Risquez tout pour éclairer l'opinion publique de ce pays-ci si dans le moment c'étoit nécessaire. Mais dans le moment je n'en vois pas la nécessité.

Je vous suppose assurée de la paix. Il n'y a aucune question à discuter au Parlement dans le moment où la Russie se trouveroit directement intéressée. Je crois donc qu'en publiant ces pièces dans le moment ou en faisant des extraits des faits importans qui s'y trouvent vous pouviez publier *your case before [you] should be attacked*; et quand le moment d'attaque arriveroit vous n'auriez rien à dire qui n'eut déjà été sous les yeux du publique, et attaqué, commenté, calomnié, comme est la pratique ordinaire des factions ici. Mon conseil donc est de ne rien publier dans le moment. Mais je peux me tromper et je vous prie de décider. Je vous donne mes raisons; vous voyez qu'elles sont fondées sur le fait qu'il n'y a rien qui dure ici plus que neuf jours. On oublieroit tous vos faits et vos raisonnemens; on en écouteroit plutôt les réponses quelques mensongères qu'elles puissent être si vous les donniez au publique à un moment qui ne fut pas l'opportun.

Princess Lieven to Wellington, 11 February 1834

Londres. J'ai reçu votre lettre, Monseur le Duc, et je m'empresse de vous dire que je me soumets entièrement à votre opinion et que je ne puis qu'approuver tout à fait les raisonnemens sur lesquels vous l'établissez. Nous attendrons le moment opportun; et tout ce que je désire c'est que cette opportunité ne se présente jamais. Les apparences sont assez bonnes aujourd'huy. J'espère que le fond y répond, mais ni vous ni moi ne pouvons répondre de ce qu'amène le lendemain.

Wellington to Viscount Melbourne, 15 February 1834

Stratfield Saye. I have this morning received your letter of the 11th instant which I have lost no time in communicating to the authorities at Oxford. As it appears to me that the proposed clause in the charter to be granted to the London University does not attain the objects in view in the communications made to your Lordship by my lamented predecessor on the 8th and 26th of February 1831, I hope that your Lordship will allow time to the authorities of the University of Oxford to consider of this clause before the proposed charter will be granted to the institution called the London University.

Wellington to the Vice-Chancellor of Oxford (the Rev. George Rowley), 15 February 1834

Stratfield Saye. I inclose the copy of a letter, and copies of its inclosures which I have received from the Secretary of State this day. I have perused the correspondence between his Lordship and my lamented predecessor, which I do not send you, as I conclude that you possess copies at Oxford.

It appears to me that the proposed clause in the charter to be granted to the London University does not attain the objects in view in the communication made to the late Lord Grenville by the Vice-Chancellor on the 25th of February 1831, communicated to Lord Melbourne on the 26th of February 1831; and that the Secretary of State has taken no notice of that part of the same communication which refers to the *title, University*, by which the institution in London is called, nor to a letter from the Vice-Chancellor to Lord Grenville, dated the 21st of January 1831, upon the same subject and communicated by Lord Grenville to Lord Melbourne on the 3rd February 1831. I beg you to submit these documents to the heads of houses, and to call their attention particularly to the points above referred to.

Lord Francis Egerton to Wellington, 16 February 1834

Oatlands, Esher. I shall probably go up to London on Tuesday or Wednesday for the purpose, as I hope and trust, of bringing to a final conclusion the legal part of my arrangements for the management of my property. As you mention the very agreeable possibility of your coming here, I will take my chance of getting a morning out of you as well as as an evening by mentioning that the Surrey hounds draw this place on *Friday* the 21st. The local is pretty and I believe there is a fox on St. George's Hills. For the rest our chances of sport are not so good as you would have at home but I can lodge your horses if you could be tempted to send them here overnight. I shall probably be back here in any case by that day, but can make it certain if you can answer this favourably to Bridgwater House. Perhaps you could come Thursday evening.

I have had a letter from Hardinge about Mr. Scarlett's views on this county, and I write to him today to inform him of some reasons I have for thinking that the speculation is a bad one, which I can explain to you if we meet. Of course anything that I can do in this neighbourhood will be at your disposal. My horse's eyes are well, and he is at least as fit to hunt as the Duke of Cumberland whom I met yesterday on Moulsey Hurst looking for a stag which he lost there a week ago.

If you cannot do precisely what I propose, we shall be equally happy to see you whenever you can come after my return from town where I shall stay not a minute longer than I can help.

Baron Smith and Sheil's cases sufficiently shew, as seems to me, that if the Ministers were to commit forgery or arson tomorrow they would be equally sure of their majorities in the House. Out of it their characters must suffer by both transactions, and I see *The Times* even takes up the Baron. He is mad, and this will either kill or drive him madder. He is one of the most singular men I ever met with.

The Rev. George Rowley to Wellington, 18 February 1834

Oxford. At the request of our weekly board I have the honor of transmitting to your Grace under a separate cover a copy of the clause drawn up by Sir Charles Wetherell when the subject of the London University was before under consideration. It was then thought desirable, and on this point our opinion remains unchanged, that either this or a similar form of words should be proposed for insertion in the new charter. Your Grace may be assured that we neither wish, nor indeed ought, to oppose the London University in their scheme of conferring honors and titles of distinction on persons educated in their institution. Independently of theology, our objection is to their adopting the same names or titles for their degrees in arts as hitherto have belonged by law to the ancient universities of the realm, inasmuch as ecclesiastical privileges and advantages might be enjoyed in virtue of such degrees by persons belonging to a university which gives no religious instruction whatever and disavows all connexion with the Established Church. I beg also to suggest to your Grace that the M.A. degree is a necessary qualification for the mastership of many of our endowed schools, the superintendence of which it is very desirable to confine to members of the Establishment.

The Rev. George Rowley to Wellington, 18 February 1834

Oxford. I have communicated your Grace's note with its inclosures to the board of heads of houses and proctors and am requested to say that they retain unaltered the opinion which they expressed when their attention was, on a former occasion, called to the draft of a charter for the London University. I have also to state their anxious wish that the accompanying clauses, or something equivalent to them, should be inserted in the proposed instrument.

Enclosure: Proposed clause for insertion in the London University charter.

Further we declare it to be our royal will and pleasure, notwithstanding we have by this our charter constituted the persons herein before named and referred to a body politic and corporate by the name of the University of London, that the said university shall not have power or authority by virtue of this our charter, or by any resolution, order or by-law or otherwise howsoever, to grant to or confer upon any person or persons any degree or degrees whatsoever in divinity or theology or any degree or degrees in arts bearing the same name or names with the degree or degrees in arts conferred by the existing universities of the realm; and if any degree or degrees in arts bearing the same name or names with the degree or degrees in arts conferred by the existing universities of the realm shall be attempted to be conferred or granted in any manner or upon any pretence whatsoever, the same shall be utterly void and of no effect.

Lastly we declare it to be our royal will and pleasure that nothing in this our charter contained shall entitle or be construed to entitle any graduate of the said University of London to any office, place, privilege, benefit or advantage in any ecclesiastical court, or to hold or enjoy by dispensation or otherwise any preferment, office, place, right, privilege, benefit, emolument or advantage in the united Church of England and Ireland by law established.

Wellington to John Gurwood, 19 February 1834

Stratfield Saye. I return your last papers. I have altered a few words in your introduction and likewise in the précis. They are principally errors which any body might make. As for instance *Prime Minister.* We don't know such an office. The First Lord of the Treasury is generally *primus inter pares.*

Baron Capelle to Wellington, 20 February 1834

Londres. Le voyageur de confiance qui étoit chargé de la lettre que j'ai eu dernièrement l'honneur de vous remettre, est de retour à

Londres d'où il doit repartir dans très peu de jours, pour rejoindre son Prince. Je seroit heureux de pouvoir dire qu'il a vu votre Grâce et d'être porteur d'une réponse écrite ou seulement verbale. S'il convient à votre Grâce de lui assigner un jour, je m'empresserai de l'en informer; son nom est *St. Silvain*.

The Provost of Eton College (the Rev. Joseph Goodall) to Wellington, 21 February 1834

Cloisters, Windsor Castle. I can not refrain from expressing the satisfaction which I feel in being able to avail myself of my privilege of according to the Etonians a whole holiday without exercise in the language of the place (or as the Duchess of Oldenburg phrased it, 'a free day for the children') on the event of your Grace being unanimously elected Chancellor of the University of Oxford. Proud as we were of your predecessor, and highly as we esteemed him for his personal worth, and respected him for his character, as a statesman, and second to none of his Etonian contemporaries but to a Wellesley in classical reputation, we must congratulate our alma mater that to a worthy son has succeeded a no less worthy. The merits of the departed may be allowably praised to their full extent, but convinced as I am of the truth of the maxim *nihil est inverecundus quam coram in os laudate* (an ex-schoolmaster may be forgiven a little Latin) I will not act against conviction: but I should be indeed inexcusable if I did not in my own name, and in that of the whole establishment, over which by the partial kindness of your Grace's brother who was most instrumental in obtaining my appointment, I have the happiness to preside, acknowledge the ready condescension with which our petition against the impending horrors of a double railroad was received, and not only aid and protection promised, but that promise rendered more valuable by the advice with which it was accompanied.

With the truest gratitude as an individual, as an Etonian, and as an Englishman I have the honor to be *etc.*

Wellington to Baron Capelle, 21 February 1834

Londres. J'ai eu l'honneur de recevoir la lettre de Votre Excellence.

Vous m'avez apporté une lettre de la part de Sa Majesté Charles X; et je vous ai toujours reçu et écouté avec toutes les attentions dues à la position de ce Prince; qui comportent avec mes sentimens de respect et d'attachement pour sa personne.

A la dernière occasion que j'ai eu l'honneur de vous voir, vous m'avez présenté une lettre de la part de l'Infante Don Carlos. J'ai lu cette lettre; et je vous ai témoigné tout l'intérêt, le chagrin même, que me causoit l'existence d'une guerre civile en Espagne et la position de Don Carlos.

Vous me demandez à présent une réponse pour Don Carlos.

Monsieur le Baron, je me trouve dans une position toute particulière pour un individu. Immiscé dans les affaires publiques de presque toutes les nations de l'Europe, et surtout de mon propre pays pendant une carrière qui a duré plusieurs années, j'en suis à présent éloigné.

J'ai des relations avec l'Espagne aussi bien qu'avec d'autres pays en Europe. Le Gouvernement de Sa Majesté Britannique en a aussi. Me convient-il dans ma position publique et politique dans ce pays-ci et en Europe d'entretenir des relations secrètes avec un Prince quelconque? Me convient-il d'en entretenir avec l'Infante Don Carlos dans la position actuelle des affaires en Espagne, et des relations de Sa Majesté Britannique avec le Gouvernement de fait, qui existe?

Monsieur le Baron, permettez moi de vous dire que m'approchant comme serviteur du Roi Charles X vous auriez du éviter de me présenter une lettre de la part de l'Infante Don Carlos; et que vous ne servirez pas la cause du Roi Charles X dans ce pays-ci, en vous chargeant des correspondences de l'Infante Don Carlos.

Wellington to Sir Henry Hardinge, 22 February 1834

London. I have been all day at the Charterhouse; and have only now returned home.

I send you an order for £53. 3s. od. The three pounds three are for the subscription for the notices.

The £50 as my subscription for the other subject of your secret committee.

I am however so tired of and disgusted with every thing relating to the gentlemen of the press, and particularly of the daily press; I know so much of their proceedings and I know that they are so little to be depended on and that there is so little of secrecy in any of these secret committees, that I request that my name may not be entered on your lists or proceedings.

To tell you the truth I would not subscribe at all as I know the risks which all subscribers, particularly those of my station in life, incur by so becoming, only that you mentioned the names of some highly meritorious individuals whom I wish to encourage and assist. But I intreat that my request may be attended to that my name may not be entered on any list; and that my share in this transaction shall be entirely confidential between you and me.

VISCOUNT HARDINGE PAPERS. *Copy in Wellington Papers.*

Thomas Collinson to Wellington, 23 February 1834

Wirksworth. My unfeigned loyalty to the Established Church has induced me to state my sentiments which can be little more than a drop in the ocean of evidence that will occupy your Lordship's consideration.

I shall endeavor to describe the genius and motives of that large portion of inhabitants emphatically called Dissenters without touching on what they ask of the legislature, that will be obvious to everyone as their claims will be heard from one end of the island to the other; but however humbly they may implore and however modestly they may ask, their ambition will not be satisfied till they have divested the Establishment of all its emoluments and beheld its structures in the utmost dilapidation.

My Lord, all the sectarians in Britain look with a jaundiced eye on the dignity of our Church Establishment and every religious dissenter looks at our beautiful churches and at the Gothic architecture of our venerable and sublime cathedrals with mingled emotions of envy and contempt, notwithstanding I have no doubt that the energies of the sectarians have been the means that religion and morality have been promoted and in our mixed and extensive community good order has been produced, and I feel no hesitation in asserting that there are many estimable characters among them but I conceive all are tainted with some degree of bigotry and disloyalty.

My Lord, in Mr. Wesley's time the Dissenters were comparatively a small band of unassuming pious enthusiasts. They now form the greater part of the inhabitants of our crowded cities and populous towns. Their costly places of worship mark their ambition and they only want to *graduate* in our universities to vie with the Establishment in learning as they certainly outvie it in popularity. I shall conclude these brief remarks by imploring your Lordship to pause before you give your potent influence to increase the power of the Dissenters or lessen that of the Church Establishment and every person of loyalty and good feeling will rejoice.

Docketed by Wellington Compliments. Received. *Docketed by secretary* Done. February 27.

Lord Wynford to Wellington, 25 February 1834

House of Lords. Wishing to have a few minutes conversation with your Grace I sent to Apsley House this morning and found that your Grace was gone to Stratfield Saye. I entirely concur in the opinion delivered by your Grace at Apsley House on the third of February that the Conservative party should entirely abstain from all opposition that can be considered factious and that we should avoid as much as possible every thing likely to bring the two Houses into collision. But if it be possible to prevent the country from forgetting that there is a House of Lords without incurring the charge of faction or the risque of dangerous collision with the Commons we should attempt to do something that will have this effect. The proper position of the House of Lords is at [the] head of the landed interest. By supporting that interest that House most effectually supports Conservative principles and supports the Church and the other institutions. Whatever difference of opinion might have prevailed three years ago as to the state of the landed interest no man can now doubt that unless something can be done to relieve it it must shortly be entirely ruined and that it will bring down with it in its fall every interest and every order in the State. The relief to the land from commutation of tithes or from an amendment of the poor laws is very doubtful but at all events it is so remote that all the mischief to be expected will have happened before either of those remedies will have produced any effect. Lord Chandos's plan will be attended with immediate benefit. The encouragement that it will give to agriculture and industry hitherto I must say neglected by the legislature will operate more powerfully than the increased rate of the produce of the land from the diminution of its price. After the division in the House of Commons on this subject, a majority in our House in favour of a similar motion to that moved by Lord Chandos might produce a collision with the Ministry but not with the House of Commons, for if the Ministry had not opposed to this motion their whole strength it would have been adopted by the House of Commons. A majority in the Lords will give confidence to our party in the Commons and induce them to renew the attempt lately made by bringing the case on again in some other shape. But I will not limit the benefit of such a motion (if followed with success) to relief from the burthen of taxation to which the land has so much stronger a claim than any other interest. I think an alteration may be made in the law by which farmers might borrow money on the security of the stock of their farms and take them out of the hands of the corn factors who now take advantage of their distress and contrive to obtain from them the profits made from any rise in the price of corn. But the greatest advantage that I expect from our taking up this subject is the restoration of that weight which we have unfortunately lost by attaching to us not only the owners and occupiers of land but all that are dependent on agriculture and enable us to make that stand which it is our duty at all hazards to make against the innovations which are leading us fast to destruction. I thought it my duty to suggest this to your Grace for your opinion. I shall not stir unless sanctioned by your Grace. Indeed I had rather if your Grace views this subject as I do that it was taken up by your Grace than by so humble an individual as myself. I cannot conclude without mentioning to you what the Duke of Cumberland has told me, namely that he has received a letter from Sir H. Lees informing his Royal Highness of a widely extended conspiracy that is likely soon to burst out into revolution. I should think nothing of Sir H. Lees's information if it were not confirmed by accounts that Lord Eldon has received from Dorsetshire and that I have also received from three different [*paper torn*] of that county. The Duke was pressed [*paper torn*] Sir H. Lees to bring that business before the House this evening. From this I took the liberty to dissuade His Royal Highness and recommended him instead of speaking of it publickly to mention it to Lord Melbourne in private. The House is now up and Lord Melbourne has not been here.

Wellington to Lord Wynford, 26 February 1834

Stratfield Saye. I am very sorry that I should have gone out of town without seeing you at a time when you wished to see me. I had been in London from Thursday and finding that there was no dinner for the celebration of the Queen's birthday I came here after the drawing room on Monday.

It does not appear to me that any Lord is precluded from what passed at my house on the 3rd of February from taking any course that he may think proper on any question. I would recommend noble Lords not to stir questions in the House of Lords unnecessarily, but that is a matter of opinion upon which it is more probable that I am wrong than the noble Lord would be who should propose to make such proposition. I think however that the Reform Bill has nearly extinguished in the country the political influence of property.

The House of Lords as a body must feel the consequences of this degradation of the influence of property, and it is much the wisest course for the House of Lords not to use the power which it undoubtedly possesses in cases in which it must be brought into fruitless collision with the House of Commons, but that it should keep itself in reserve for occasions in which its opinions must be attended to, and must affect the measures which the Government bring up or the other House of Parliament send up for their consideration.

In this very case of Lord Chandos's, I suspect that an opinion given by the House of Lords would not be very favourably received by the House of Commons and Lord Chandos might find himself not in quite so good a division upon the following occasion as he was on the last.

But upon the whole of this subject of agriculture the question is what do we want? You mention a power to the farmer to borrow money upon the stock on his farm. I am afraid that you would find many who would object to such a measure. The first lien upon the stock of the farm is the rent of the landlord, and although hundreds and thousands might consent to allow their tenant to give their stock as security few would like to see themselves deprived of their security by Act of Parliament.

But Lord Chandos's plan is as I understand a repeal of certain taxes supposed to bear upon the landed interest, or other arrangements of that description which must according to the ordinary course originate in the House of Commons. These are measures upon which of all others the House of Lords ought to avoid to touch till regularly brought under its consideration in the ordinary course of business.

I tell you fairly that my belief is that the cause of the agricultural distress is now beyond our reach. We have no government in England. We are not able if we are willing to protect them in the enjoyment of their property and in their bargains with their labourers for their labour. The consequence is that the latter are paid much more than the value of their labour. They *will* be so paid. They will burn, plunder, and destroy till they are so paid and the Government will not, possibly cannot, now protect the gentlemen and farmers in resistance to these demands. To talk of the lowness of the price of corn or of any other article is under these circumstances futile. The English labourer receives for his labour more than it is worth. He *will* receive that reward whether the price of corn is high or low and consequently agriculture must be distressed.

I have heard nothing of conspiracies in Ireland or elsewhere. I don't doubt however that they exist. It appears to me that it is not a wise course to denounce conspiracy in the House of Lords unless the proof of it should be quite clear and the Government after information of it should decline to take any steps.

Lord Fitzroy Somerset to Wellington, 3 March 1834

Horse Guards. I have just got a letter from Alava announcing his apprehension that Don Alexo Guillen (the Salamanca correspondent) has been shot by Quesada. It appears that Guillen, who was prior of the cathedral (an appointment which he obtained on your recommendation) left Salamanca and placed himself at the head of a party of guerrillas in the interest of Don Carlos. A few days afterwards the whole were taken by the peasants and brought into Salamanca. Quesada's directions were solicited, and he immediately ordered that he should be shot. Such is the substance of what Alava says on the subject. Tomorrow I will send you a copy of his letter which it is difficult to decipher.

You may remember giving me an opinion upon what you denominated Whittingham's dream. I allowed Macdonald to shew the papers to Mr. Charles Grant, who by the inclosed appears anxious to have a copy of your letter. You probably have no objection. I send you a copy in case you should wish to refer to it, and shall be glad to have it back.

Enclosure: Copy of a letter from Wellington to Lord Fitzroy Somerset, Apethorpe, 29 December 1833.

It is useless to consider of and write upon a scheme which it is quite impossible to carry into execution.

Whittingham proposes to seize the kingdom of Oude, and to attack

Runjeet Sing and seize the Punjab; establish ourselves upon the Indus; and ally ourselves with the kingdom of Cabul.

These measures contrary to law, either of which must involve us in all the risks and consequences of war, must be attained by increasing the British infantry in the army on the frontier to 20,000 men, the cavalry and the native army and the artillery in proportion.

Whittingham has been out of England during all the painful discussions on the formation of the military establishments of the country. He is not aware that every increase of the European army in India requires a corresponding increase for reliefs of the army at home, as well as I can recollect to the amount of one fourth for the increase in India. Thus then an increase of 20,000 men would require an addition to the army here not only of the 20,000 men, but of 5,000 men here to relieve the additional number in India.

Lord Hill has only to ask the Secretary at War whether he could obtain such a vote.

Mr. Charles Grant will tell him whether he will authorize orders to seize the kingdom of Oude and the Punjab.

This is a dream of Whittingham's. I don't recommend that it should be attended to. I think that there is much to be said against the scheme, even if there were, as there never can be, means of carrying it into execution.

I believe that if ever we are to come to blows with the Russians in India we must rely upon our sepoys, as we have in all our wars there with European as well as with native powers. These with our superior knowledge of the art of war in that country and our superior equipment, founded upon our knowledge of the resources of the seat of the war, the character of the natives and other circumstances, will give us advantages which will more than counter balance the supposed inferiority of our troops.

At all events the Bengal sepoys are as good as the Hanoverian militia with the aid of which we fought for the world at the battle of Waterloo; and better than the Spanish infantry with which we fought for many a field in Spain and in the south of France.

Together with this is 'Extract of a letter from General Alava to Lord Fitzroy Somerset, 28 February 1834, Paris' (in Spanish).

Benjamin Disraeli to Wellington, 3 March 1834

Bradenham House, Wycombe. Being about to publish the first part of an epic poem, devoted to the celebration of those mighty wars terminated by your victorious sword, and of those antagonist principles of government, which may yet call upon you to unsheathe it, I am desirous of inscribing this work to your immortal name. And as such inscription, without your Grace's permission, might be considered a liberty, that permission is now solicited by one, who has the honor to subscribe himself, *etc.*

The Dean of Ferns (Henry Newland) to Wellington, 4 March 1834

Bannow Glebe, Taghmon. I have taken the liberty to order a copy of the *Dublin University Magazine* to be sent to your Grace, in the hope that you would condescend to read a dialogue on the 'Popular objections against the Established Church'.

I know not what apology to offer for presuming to engage one moment of your Grace's attention, if I should not find one in the interest which you have ever exhibited for the preservation of the Protestant Church, and in the calm and truly philosophic spirit, with which your Grace distinguishes your patronage of the established religion.

Draft reply 13 March 1834. Compliments. The Duke has received his note of the [4 March] but not the work to which he refers.

Samuel Lock to Wellington, 4 March 1834

Shipdham. In the present distressed situation of the agricultural classes they find themselves compelled to take such steps as may possibly have a tendency to alleviate their condition. Impressed with these views the inhabitants of the fifty parishes comprising the hundreds of Mitford and Launditch in the county of Norfolk have prepared and signed petitions to the legislature, praying for the repeal of the tax on malt, which bears with disproportionate severity upon them as cultivators of the soil, by diminishing to an immense extent the consumption of one of the staple productions of that soil. Their petitions have been disregarded by the House of Commons; nay more, they can but feel that insult is also heaped upon them, as that remission of taxes which their distressed situation rendered necessary, and which from the tenor of

458

His Majesty's Speech they had reason to expect would be accorded to them, has been given to other classes of the community who are described as being in a flourishing condition. Under these circumstances their only remaining hope that attention will be paid to their well founded complaints, and relief afforded to their distresses is centred in the House of Lords; and the committee acting for the said parishes have directed me to forward their petitions to members of your Grace's House, with the request that they will do them the honour of presenting the same. I hope your Grace will excuse the liberty I take in addressing those from the parishes of Mattishall, Mattishall Burgh, Reymerston, Shipdham, Hardingham, Swanton Morley, Gressenhall, Elmham North, Great Dunham, Little Dunham, Scarning and Hoe to you, confident that if your Grace will condescend to take charge of them they will be certain of commanding the attention of the House. I can assure your Grace that the petitions convey the sense of all the middle and lower classes connected with agriculture, and they have been signed by much more than half the adult male population. Our parishes are some of them very small, but we considered that, scattered as are the inhabitants of the country, we could in no way so well obtain their real sentiments as by appealing to them in their parishes. Although our hopes have been most materially, and I must say most cruelly depressed, still we cannot believe that the most important interest in the kingdom will be entirely disregarded, and ruin and pauperism be allowed to spread among us, without a single effort being made to ameliorate our condition.

I beg my Lord Duke that you will excuse the presumption of an entire and obscure stranger encroaching upon your valuable time, and that you will allow me to subscribe myself, *etc.*

Draft reply 6 March 1834. Compliments. The Duke has received his letter of the 4th instant and the several petitions which [he] has sent to him to present to the House of Lords. The Duke will peruse these petitions and will present them to the House of Lords on the first day that he will be in that House.

Wellington to the Rev. George Rowley, 6 March 1834

Stratfield Saye. I inclose you the copy of a letter which I received this morning from Lord Melbourne; and the copy of my answer. I beg you to peruse the reports of the discussion in the House of Lords on the 4th instant. I had not sent to Lord Melbourne the purport of your answer to my communication of the 15th, because I was in communication with Sir Charles Wetherell upon the import of the title, London University, conferred by the charter; and I wished to be certain upon that point before I should write to his Lordship. But finding that the Lord Chancellor stated in the House of Lords that the antient universities objected to the grant of a charter to the London University, and that the Secretary of State who communicated to me the correspondence with my predecessor did not set his Lordship right, I thought it proper to lose no time in calling his Lordship's attention to the real state of the question.

I think it not unlikely that the University of Oxford will after all find itself under the necessity of petitioning the King upon this subject; and I recommend to you to consider of such a petition without loss of time. The difference between the University of Oxford and the patrons of the London University, however important, is a very short case. There is no doubt about the grant of degrees in divinity. Upon that part of the subject the question turns upon the terms to be used in the reservation. The difficulty consists in the grant of the right to confer degrees in arts of the same names and titles as the degrees granted by the antient universities; and I must say that I think that the objections of the University of Oxford are so reasonable and that they are founded upon such solid grounds that the university ought to proceed to all extremities in order to attain the proposed reservation in the charter. I cannot believe that the Government will allow this question to come to an extremity. But I am convinced that if they entertain any doubts the manifestation of the determination of the university not to submit quietly to the infliction of such an injury would bring them to more moderate views.

Captain Stevenson to Wellington, 6 March 1834

Royal Crescent, Bath. Captain Stevenson, late A.D.C. to the Earl of Carnwath presents his compliments to his Grace the Duke of Wellington, and has the honor to enclose his Grace an *Address to the Working Classes of Weymouth, Portland etc.*, and if by so doing Captain Stevenson has stepped out of propriety and line, he hopes that his Grace will kindly permit *loyalty* and *truth* to plead his apology.

Captain Stevenson is happy to find that the address has already produced good, (his *reward* for trouble and expense) as his Weymouth correspondent writes as follows, 'Never was a paper more admired by all *classes* from the *highest* to the *lowest*—even our *violent* Radicals can say nothing against it. The bills are in the villages and those placarded on the walls are not in the slightest degree *defaced*. Several gentlemen have asked for them to carry to different parts of the kingdom and the working classes say there is nothing but real truth in it. Politics are much changed here I assure you sir.' Weymouth, 26 February 1834.

Docketed by Wellington Compliments. The Duke is much obliged to him for the communication for [*sic*] his address to the working classes; which the Duke thinks calculated to produce a good effect. *Docketed by secretary* Done. March 11.

Wellington to Viscount Melbourne, 6 March 1834

Stratfield Saye. I had the honor of receiving this morning your Lordship's letter, dated the 3rd inst., in which your Lordship informs me that by His Majesty's command, the whole of the documents relating to the proposed charter for the London University have been transmitted for the consideration of the Lords of His Majesty's Privy Council.

I have twice perused the report of a discussion on the 4th inst. in the House of Lords upon the same subject; from which it appears to me that as far as regards the University of Oxford His Majesty's servants labour under a mistake.

The object of the correspondence between your Lordship and my lamented predecessor was not to object on the part of the University of Oxford to the grant of a charter by His Majesty to the institution in London styled the London University; but to render such grant consistent with the publick interests by the amendments suggested by the University of Oxford; and thus to avoid the necessity of appealing by petition to the King; and of putting the affair in a course of judicial discussion before the Privy Council.

The University of Oxford have never expressed any wish to prevent the grant of a charter to the London University to enable that institution to confer honours and titles of distinction on persons there educated, excepting degrees in divinity and theology, and degrees in arts by the same names or titles as have hitherto been used by law in granting degrees by the antient universities of the realm.

The reasons for these exceptions are obvious; and are fully stated in the correspondence of my predecessor with your Lordship.

I have only requested your Lordship in a letter of the 15 February to afford time to the University to consider of the clause proposed to be inserted in the charter as communicated by your Lordship in a letter dated the 11th February received on that morning; which clause I informed your Lordship in my letter of the 15 February did not appear to me to attain the objects in view in the communications addressed to your Lordship by my predecessor in office of the 8 and 26 January [?] 1831.

I understood that your Lordship intended to comply with my request.

My judgement upon the subject of the proposed clause is not erroneous; as I have since received from the Vice-Chancellor the opinion of the board of heads of houses, and proctors; and their resolution that they retain unaltered the opinion which they expressed when their attention was on a former occasion drawn to the draft of a charter for the London University and the expression of their anxious wish that the following clauses, or something equivalent to them, should be inserted in the proposed instrument (here enter the clauses as the annexed paper) in the letter from the Vice-Chancellor of the 18 February.

Your Lordship will see therefore that no objection is stated at Oxford to the grant of a charter to the London institution provided that it contains the clauses above recited.

Draft.

Viscount Melbourne to Wellington, 7 March 1834

Whitehall. I have the honor of acknowledging your Grace's letter of the 6th instant, which I have received this morning.

It is possible that the material distinction to which your Grace adverts may not have been clearly pointed out in the very short debate which took place upon this subject in the House of Lords on the 4th instant, but the objection of the University of Oxford has always been understood to be as your Grace states it: not absolutely to the grant of a charter, but to the grant of a charter not containing the prohibitory clauses transcribed in your Grace's letter.

Upon referring to my letter of the 18th February, I find I have to apologize to your Grace for not having given you previous notice of my intention to advise the transmission of the petition of the institution called the London University for a charter, with all the documents relating thereto to the Privy Council; but I trust your Grace will believe that this omission arose entirely from inadvertence, and that you will also feel that no inconvenience or injustice can arise therefrom, inasmuch as the question is still open to accommodation between the parties, and as the Privy Council will of course not proceed in the matter, except with due caution and full and sufficient notice to all the parties interested.

Signature only in Melbourne's hand.

Wellington to the Rev. George Rowley, 7 March 1834

I was very much struck by Sir Charles Wetherell's opinion on the title, *University*, assumed by the London institution; which is now to be confirmed by the charter to be granted by the Crown; and I wrote and spoke to Sir Charles Wetherell on the subject.

He was anxious to see his first opinion when I conversed with him in London; which he has since received from Oxford and has sent to me, with the enclosed letter received this morning.

I think that if the University of Oxford should petition the King they ought to advert to this assumed title; and to the apprehended consequences of the confirmation by the charter from His Majesty.

Wellington to Benjamin Disraeli, 7 March 1834

Stratfield Saye. I am really much flattered by your desire to dedicate to me by permission your epic poem.

Unfortunately I found myself under the necessity twenty years ago of determining that I would never give a formal permission that any work should be dedicated to me. I will not trouble you with the reasons for this determination. They were founded upon a sense of the necessity for this course; or for the adoption of another; viz. that I should peruse every work which it was wished that I should give permission that it should be dedicated to me before I should grant the required permission.

This last alternative was impracticable; and I have found myself under the painful necessity in many instances as in this of declining to give such formal permission.

If however you should think proper to dedicate your poem to me without such formal permission, you are at full liberty to take that course; assuring you at the same time that I feel greatly flattered by the expression of your desire that I should permit it.

HUGHENDEN PAPERS B/xxi/w/156. *Copy in Wellington Papers.*

Wellington to Viscount Melbourne, 8 March 1834

Stratfield Saye. I have had the honour of receiving your Lordship's letter of the 7th instant, and I am very sensible of your Lordship's courtesy in recollecting that your Lordship had intended to give me previous notice of any farther step being taken upon the subject of the grant of a charter to the institution called the London University. I trust that your Lordship will excuse me for troubling you again with my observations upon the position of the University of Oxford in this discussion. It appears from the correspondence that early in 1831 an application was made by the institution called the London University for a charter. It does not appear that any application was made for the power to grant degrees. It is concluded that that power will be inherent in the title, University, assumed by the institution and to be confirmed by His Majesty's charter. The consequence of the grant of the charter was noticed by the University of Oxford, and they submitted to your Lordship their request that its inconveniences might be provided against.

Their interest in the question is that of the Church of England and of the publick; they desire that it shall be provided first that this institution shall not confer degrees in divinity or theology, because it gives no religious instruction whatever and disavows all connection with the Church of England; and next that it shall not confer degrees in arts of the same names or titles as the degrees conferred by the antient universities, because the graduates of the antient universities are prepared for their degrees in arts by attendance at theological lectures and examinations, as well as by the discipline of the several colleges in the universities; and as Masters of Arts they become entitled to certain advantages conferred upon them by law, as well when in orders as when pleading in the ecclesiastical courts.

The Church of England and the publick are interested that the persons enjoying these advantages should have received a disciplined education, of which religious instruction should form a part, and in an institution which does not disavow all connection with the Church of England.

The University of Oxford appealed to your Lordship to protect the interests of the Church of England and of the publick upon these subjects.

They have refrained and have been desirous to avoid to put themselves forward as a party by petition to the King, for reasons which are obvious.

I am convinced that your Lordship will feel that it is desirable that if possible they should adhere to that course.

The Rev. George Rowley to Wellington, 8 March 1834

Oxford. In reply to your Grace's communication dated the 6th instant I have the honor to inform you that, having consulted the board of heads of houses and proctors, I find that they fully concur in the expediency of your Grace's valuable suggestion, and the draft of a petition will in consequence be immediately prepared.

As it may, however, be requisite to take some legal measures while the question is before the Privy Council, I shall write to Sir Charles Wetherell as the university counsel, to request that he will have the goodness to afford us his advice and assistance. Some little doubt also arises respecting the mode in which, under the circumstances of the case, our petition should be presented to the King.

Wellington to the Rev. George Rowley, 8 March 1834

Stratfield Saye. I enclose the copy of an answer which I have received from the Secretary of State to my letter of the 6th.

I have marked a few words in this letter, upon which in justice to the university and the cause I must observe in my reply, of which I will send you a copy.

Wellington to the Rev. George Rowley, 10 March 1834

Stratfield Saye. I have received your letter of the 8th. Those which I have sent you since I wrote to you on the 6th will have shewn you how

465

the question stands; and you and the gentlemen of the university must be as well able to judge of the course to be pursued as I can be.

My opinion is that the Government are anxious to avoid to decide upon the charter of the London institution *quasi* Government. They refer the case therefore to the Privy Council, where, as you will have seen, it will be decided judicially, according to Lord Melbourne's letter of the 7th.

It is impossible for me to say where the judicial power for decision rests! I believe that neither of the universities has presented a petition; and you will have seen the ground (not that I have taken for you, but which) I pointed out that you had taken for yourselves.

Whatever may be the result, whether we are to come to a judicial decision or not, it will always be an advantage that you should have been forced to petition. You are quite right in preparing your petition. If possible I still think that it would be desirable to avoid to present one to the King. But if you should be under the necessity of presenting one, you should do it in the most formal manner; and you should recite in the petition all the steps that you had taken to avoid that course; and state clearly and distinctly the evils which must result, the frauds which must be practised, if graduates from the new institution should not be distinguishable from those from the antient universities.

Alexander Finlay to Wellington, 10 March 1834

6 Dean Terrace, Edinburgh. Since I had the honor of visiting your Grace at Walmer Castle in the end of October, I have had various letters from Jamaica, both from my manager and others. They concur in stating that although the Slave Act is in many respects extremely exceptionable, the planters deemed it more for their interest to refrain from opposition, in the fear that by doing so they might run considerable risk of losing their portion of the twenty millions. The Assembly of the Island, however, did not consider that they were thence debarred from addressing His Majesty with a view of getting Parliament still to make such modifications in the Act as may tend to render its present provisions less injurious. This address may possibly have already met your Grace's eye, but in case it should not have done so, among your numerous avocations, I now take the liberty of inclosing it, as I cannot help thinking it worthy of perusal by one who has proved himself so steady and true a friend, at once to the West India interest and to his country.

Before leaving town in December last I availed myself of some agricultural acquaintance with Lord Althorp to have a pretty full conference with him on such parts of the Act as I thought objectionable. I at that time threw out a suggestion that interest should be payable on the twenty millions *from the 1st August next*, that being the period when slavery is declared to cease, and when the apprenticeship commences. Though his Lordship did not seem to think this unreasonable, he was not then prepared to pledge himself to its being acceded to. However I am glad to find that this is now distinctly arranged at the Treasury.

I was in hopes that before this, Lord Wynford would have brought forward his promised motion as to the prohibition of sugar *produced by slave labour* being imported after the 1st of August. I endeavoured to elicit from Lord Althorp whether ministry would be likely to concur in this, but he seemed rather to fear that it would make sugar too dear. He allowed, however, that Mr. Buxton and his party would be obliged, in consistency, to support such a measure, seeing that it must necessarily tend to check the slave-trade still extensively carried on, in spite of the immense sums this country paid to Spain and Portugal to abolish the traffic. As Lord Althorp very candidly admitted, that during the *first* two years of the apprentice system it can scarcely fail to operate against the planters by a considerable *decrease* in the crops, it appears only fair to meet this defalcation by any advantage in price to be gained through the exclusion of sugar made by *slaves*.

Your Grace will probably learn whether Lord Wynford still thinks of bringing forward his motion, and as it seems too much to be feared from recent discussions in the House of Commons, that the duties on East and West India sugar will 'ere long be equalized (which would compleat the ruin of the unfortunate colonists) there is the more reason for presently urging the justness of Lord Wynford's proposal. Were your Grace to originate the motion, I am persuaded it would meet with powerful support, for I really cannot anticipate any forcible argument against it.

Begging to reiterate my thanks on the part of the colonists in this part of the country, as well as from myself individually, I have the honor to remain, with the highest consideration, *etc.*

PS. Had your Grace's proposal been fortunately adopted, of merely sending out to the colonies the resolutions of Parliament, leaving it to the local governments to legislate, the measure would have been more gracious, and the details in all probability more calculated to meet the existing circumstances of the black population, from their knowledge and experience of the negro character.

Enclosure: Newspaper cutting containing the address of the Assembly of Jamaica to the King. 12 December 1833.

Draft reply 18 March 1834. Compliments. The Duke has received his letter and the copy inclosed of the address from Jamaica to His Majesty for which he returns his thanks.

The Rev. James Dean to Wellington, 10 March 1834

Derby. As an individual somewhat concerned in stirring up this part of the country to petition the legislature on the subject of the church establishment of this country, a number of petitions have been forwarded to me without any directions as to the further disposal of them. And in the absence from their place in Parliament of those noble lords who reside in this county, I transmitted such as had reached me last week to his Grace of Rutland and Earl Howe, both of whom are connected with the county. The former, from whom I have before me a polite and obliging answer to my request, will not be in town for *some* time. Anxious not to burthen the latter with all our petitions, and desirous of obtaining for him some cordial co-operation and support, I have taken the liberty of forwarding to your Grace's address at the House of Lords five petitions: from Aston 248 householder signatures, Breaston 47, Risley 53, Quorndon 54, Kniveton 75, all in Derbyshire and villages. To these I add one from the town of Derby, with 948 signatures, comprizing almost all the respectable inhabitants. A few of these (30) have been placed on the first sheet, shewing at once to anyone acquainted with the town the leading inhabitants, and of all political creeds. Of these 30, 17 had been affixed on their respective parochial sheets, but were repeated on the head sheet for the above reason, and to fill it up. The whole of the corporate body have signed except one, who from age now declines all signature of his name to petitions, but, as he expressed himself, even his heart is with us. Exclusive of these repetitions, the signatures are 948. They might have been doubled, but for the great trouble in collecting them from house to house; some streets have not been visited, owing to another cause: the great indifference to all petitions on the part of a class of householders, who are now connected with the Trades Union and consequently very suspicious. But your Grace may be assured of a very great reaction here within the last six months. Men's minds are much more in favor of order and old established institutions and principles.

Your Grace will find the petitions alike. The one from Derby will be sufficient for your own information. It expresses a conviction of the necessity of a Christian government providing for the establishment and maintenance of a Christian form of worship. And while the petitioners would gladly see certain changes and improvements introduced into the Church, which may confirm her stability and increase her efficiency, they conclude with a prayer that her spiritualities may be held inviolate, that no alteration affecting them may be entertained except they proceed from those in whom they are constitutionally vested.

Being personally a perfect stranger to your Grace, it will be needful that I refer you for my own character to Earl Howe, and to Mr. Wagner, who will remember me at Eton as the tutor of Lord Scarsdale's sons; and to allege, as the grounds of forwarding these petitions to your Grace (and that must be my apology) your Grace's public character and well known attachment to our church establishment. May I add that the Chancellor of my 'alma mater' will naturally expect the honors of the office to be connected with some of these respectful intrusions and liabilities to trouble, and to excuse them. The petitioners are anxious not to have their petitions classed as reform, but church, petitions.

PS. There are very few signatures under the age of twenty-one.

Draft reply 14 March 1834. Compliments. The Duke received his note and the petitions to which he refers, which he will present to the House of Lords on the first day that he will attend: he believes on Friday the 14th [*sic*] instant.

Wellington to the Marquess of Salisbury, 11 March 1834

Stratfield Saye. You will have seen that the Warwick Bill is coming up to the House of Lords, which we may rely upon it will be made a precedent for others.

I shall be in the House on Friday. In the mean time I have written to Lord Ellenborough about the Warwick Bill; and have requested him to consult with you and others and to take care that the second reading should not be carried by *coup de main*. I rather believe that the preamble ought first to be proved.

Will you be so kind as to see Lord Ellenborough on the subject.

PS. I hope that Lady Salisbury is well. I will go to see her when I shall be in London.

SALISBURY MSS.

Viscount Melbourne to Wellington, 11 March 1834

Whitehall. I have the honour of acknowledging your Grace's letter of the 8th instant.

The statement which it contains of the measures taken, and the language held by the University of Oxford upon the subject of the charter petitioned for by the institution called the London University, appears to me to be perfectly correct.

I have to assure your Grace that I will take care that the whole of the correspondence which has taken place in relation to this application, between the late Chancellor of the University of Oxford, and also between your Grace and this office, shall be submitted to the Privy Council and brought under their consideration.

Signature only in Melbourne's hand.

Wellington to the Rev. George Rowley, 12 March 1834

Stratfield Saye. I inclose the answer which I have received from the Secretary of State to the last letter which I addressed to his Lordship.

I am going to London tomorrow and shall probably see Lord Melbourne in the House of Lords on Friday.

I will endeavour to learn which course the Government propose to follow in the Privy Council and at what time. I recommend to the university not to allow the question to be considered by the Judicial Committee of the Privy Council without a petition from themselves; and desiring to be heard by their counsel.

I will let you know exactly what I shall lean upon when I shall be in London.

I shall return here early in the week.

The Rev. George Rowley to Wellington, 13 March 1834

Oxford. I have the honor to inclose a copy of my letter sent to Sir Charles Wetherell on the 8th and to forward, in a separate cover, a copy of his reply received this morning. The draft of a petition will, in accordance with his suggestion, be conveyed to him by tonight's post, and being addressed to the King in Council, will not, we conceive, require a delegacy for its presentation. We have indeed a precedent on this point in the petition from Cambridge on the same subject in 1831. When received back from Sir Charles it will be prepared for convocation and I will take care to communicate the form of it to your Grace without loss of time.

First enclosure: The Rev. George Rowley to Sir Charles Wetherell, 8 March 1834.

Oxford. I yesterday received a letter from his Grace the Duke of Wellington in which he recommends us to be prepared without loss of time with a petition to the King on the subject of the charter for the so called London University; and the form of a petition is accordingly now under consideration. This morning's post, however, brought me your last communication to his Grace, in which you express a doubt how far the clauses formerly proposed for insertion in the charter would be sufficient to secure the object in view; and from this I judge that it may be expedient to say in the petition that, though such clauses had been proposed, we were now advised that if a charter were granted conferring the title of University, such exceptions in regard to degrees might be legally invalid; and we therefore feel ourselves compelled to petition against the charter itself. Something equivalent to this will I conceive be requisite, and I hope that you will have the goodness to say if I am correct in this idea.

We presume also that some measures may be necessary with regard to the Privy Council; and, as we are ignorant on these points, it is requested by the board of heads of houses and proctors that, as counsel for the university, you will, at your own discretion, put in train any legal proceedings which may be immediately requisite, and favor us with any suggestions which you may judge expedient for our guidance here.

Second enclosure: Sir Charles Wetherell to the Rev. George Rowley, [12 March] 1834.

Being out of town yesterday, I did not get your letter till this morning, or I should have answered it by return of post. After I wrote my opinions in 1831, I was not informed what course was taken. I presume, however, *that* in some communication from the University of Oxford the clauses prohibiting degrees being conferred in *theology* and *arts* were then *proposed* on their part. The difficulty which I expressed in my second opinion, dated 23 February 1831, still continues and I renewed it in my late observations to the Duke of Wellington, which are now before you. It arises from a legal principle whether the restriction might not be deemed void, as inconsistent with the constitution of an university. I will not trouble you with going into the subject at large. I perfectly concur with you in thinking that the petition ought to be against the *charter itself*, and that a passage ought to be introduced to the effect that upon full consideration you were advised that so many difficulties might arise, both of legal and practical nature, as to the operation and effect of clauses prohibiting the conferring degrees, as might endanger the fulfilment of the prohibition and even render it wholly inoperative. When the draft of the petition to the King has been prepared, if you think I can be useful in perusing it, and suggesting any remarks upon it, any assistance I can give is at your service. A copy of it might be sent to me and be returned by the post, for I think the step should be taken *immediately*. The petition should pray that you may be heard by your counsel against the charter. At present I have only to add that I should feel myself gratified and indeed most materially assisted if any gentlemen in the university who have considered this subject would throw together whatever has occurred to them respecting it. This would be of great service to me in my argument before the Privy Council.

Undated.

Wellington to the Rev. George Rowley, 14 March 1834

London. I have just returned from the House of Lords. I did not meet there Lord Melbourne; but I saw and spoke with the Lord President, Lord Lansdowne.

The result of the conversation is an impression upon my mind that the University of Oxford ought to petition the King without loss of time. I have not time at present to enter into details. But I will write to you from London tomorrow.

The Rev. George Rowley to Wellington, 15 March 1834

Oxford. In obedience to your Grace's suggestion, we have lost no time in preparing the draft of a petition to the King, praying to be heard by our counsel before the committee of the Privy Council. I have this morning received it back from Sir Charles Wetherell, to whom it was submitted for his remarks, and a notice has been issued that it will be proposed in a Convocation to be holden on Tuesday next at two o'clock.

I have the honor to inclose a copy of the draft and will forward the petition itself, so soon as it shall have received the university seal.

Enclosure: To the King's most excellent Majesty in Council, the humble petition of the Chancellor, masters and scholars of the University of Oxford.
Sheweth,

That your petitioners have been informed that the council of a literary and scientific institution lately founded in London have renewed their solicitation for a charter of incorporation under the title of '*The University of London*' which, your petitioners are advised, may enable that body to confer degrees in the manner of the ancient universities of the realm, notwithstanding the insertion of any prohibitory clauses whatsoever.

That these universities studiously educate the youth entrusted to their care in the principles of Christianity after the doctrine and discipline of the Church of England; and that accordingly their degrees in arts and civil law, as well as in divinity, have been recognised as qualifications for many offices both ecclesiastical and civil.

That Your Majesty's petitioners anticipate with alarm serious injury to numerous ancient institutions of the land, and much consequent evil to the public, if similar privileges shall be conferred by a royal grant, either expressly or by implication, upon a society disavowing all connexion with the Established Church, and educating its members in no system of religion whatever.

That your petitioners by no means desire that an institution formed for the promotion of literature and science should be restricted from conferring suitable marks of distinction on its members; but they at the same time, with all humility, submit that such marks of distinction in the faculties of arts and civil law as well as theology should not bear the same titles as those which for a long series of years have been conferred by the Universities of Oxford and Cambridge.

Your petitioners therefore earnestly implore Your Majesty to take these matters into Your Majesty's most gracious consideration, and to withhold your royal sanction from a charter, in its proposed form, fraught with danger to principles and establishments, which, under the blessing of God, have essentially contributed to the welfare of our country. And they further pray that they may be heard by their counsel touching the matters aforesaid.

Wellington to the Rev. George Rowley, 15 March 1834

London. I send with this another letter which you will see is quite unreserved; and which I hope that the members of the weekly board will consider as *confidential*. It would be impossible for me to explain to you and the board how the important question under consideration stands, if I did not write facts and opinions in an unreserved manner. It cannot be expected that I should do so, if such communications should not be considered confidential.

Wellington to the Rev. George Rowley, 15 March 1834

London. I wrote to you last night after the adjournment of the House of Lords; and had seen the President of the Council, Lord Lansdowne. I asked his Lordship to inform me, as Lord Melbourne was absent, what course it was intended to follow in respect to the question of granting a charter to the London University. His Lordship said that the papers on the subject including the letters from me had been received in the office I think on that day, and that it would be taken into consideration by a committee. I asked him whether it would be taken into consideration in the Judicial Committee or if in any other, whether the University of Oxford would be permitted to have counsel to state their case. His Lordship answered that the subject would not be considered in the Judicial Committee, but that some petitions had already been presented to the King in Council which in the usual course had been referred to a committee; which committee would consider, and report upon the whole subject. That he believed that some of the petitioners had desired to be heard by counsel; and that although he did not admit that it was a right of a petitioner to the King in Council to be heard by counsel, he thought that in this case the committee would not object to the petitioners being so heard, as his Lordship said he believed the practice was not unusual. I observed that the case was one of the exercise of the royal prerogative, and I thought it extraordinary that it should be referred to the Judicial Committee of the Privy Council. His Lordship answered, 'Yes! of the royal prerogative and of expediency'. I then asked his Lordship whether the case would be referred to that committee called the Cabinet, or to a larger committee: his Lordship said he believed to a larger committee: but he added afterwards, 'all the members of the Cabinet would be summoned'. I stated to his Lordship that Lord Melbourne had given me reason to believe that nothing would be done till the University of Oxford should have time to consider of the course which they should follow, and that I hoped that time would be given to the university. His Lordship answered that the Council might meet, and the papers might be referred to a committee, which might meet to consider of the course to be pursued; but that nothing would be done till the University of Oxford should have time to consider of the course which they would take. This is nearly *verbatim* the report of the conversation which I had with the Lord President. The question for His Majesty to decide on in this case is one of the expediency or policy of the exercise of his prerogative; there is no occasion for the assistance of the Judicial Committee or of any other committee of the Privy Council to advise His Majesty in deciding it excepting the committee called the Cabinet. That committee however do not choose to decide it, and they refer it to the consideration of a more numerous committee of which the members will be summoned by the Cabinet: that is to say the patrons of the institution called the London University. This committee so summoned and the members of the Cabinet are to consider upon and report upon this subject to the King in Council. The pleading of counsel and the judicial forms adopted by this committee will relieve its members whether belonging to the Cabinet or not from all responsibility. I have considered it my duty to the university to let you know how this matter stands. I earnestly recommend therefore the university to petition the King; to explain clearly the ground on which the university stand in this question; to point out the fraud which will be committed upon the public, and upon the Church of England if the institution in London should be allowed to confer degrees in theology or divinity, or degrees in arts bearing the same designations or titles as those granted by the University of Oxford, and to entreat His Majesty to take measures which shall prove effectual to protect his subjects and the Church of England from these frauds. I do not recommend that the petition should contain a prayer that the university should be heard by counsel, because that prayer will give their sanction to the act of adopting a judicial form in the committee of the Privy Council, upon a question which is purely political. It is probable that if the committee should hear any counsel they will desire the University of Oxford to state whether they wish to be heard. The university will then decide whether they will employ counsel or not.

Wellington to the Rev. George Rowley, 15 March 1834

London. Since I wrote my other letters of this day's date I have received yours of the 13th inclosing your correspondence with Sir Charles Wetherell.

I refer to my other letters for my opinion on your petition. My opinion [is] that it ought to be put into the King's hands and that the object of it should be clearly understood by His Majesty. It will not be easy to induce His Majesty to believe that a committee of the Privy Council aided by a judge and having heard counsel could decide erroneously upon petitions from the universities of the contents of which His Majesty should have no knowledge. The King might view the matter in a different manner if he should be made acquainted with the contents of the petition of the university as he ought to be.

The Rev. George Rowley to Wellington, 16 March 1834

Oxford. I have the honor to acknowledge the receipt of your Grace's letter dated March 15; and as I must today write to your Grace without communicating with the other authorities of the university, I may perhaps take the liberty of mentioning, as from myself, the deep feeling of gratitude which has been expressed at our board, for the very anxious and efficient solicitude evinced by your Grace for our interests. Your note dated March 12 induced us to think that our petition to the King should contain a request to be heard by our counsel before the committee of the Privy Council, and that there should be no delay in adopting this measure. With this view, the necessary steps were immediately taken, and a copy of the petition was forwarded to your Grace by last night's post. I regret therefore to find that your conversation with Lord Lansdowne, as detailed in your Grace's letter received this morning, has caused some doubt as to the expediency of this mode of proceeding. The petition having been approved at the weekly board, and notice issued for proposing it in Convocation on Tuesday, it is now open for the inspection of the members of that assembly; and it cannot therefore be statutably withdrawn without the exercise of a power very rarely called into use, nor altered without a subsequent reference to the board of heads of houses and proctors. For it may, perhaps, be right to apprise your Grace that our Chancellor or his deputy is vested with an absolute veto on all questions submitted to Convocation. Should your Grace, therefore, under the circumstances of the case still think that we ought in the first instance to make our petition to the King, without praying to be heard by counsel, I shall be ready to interpose this veto on Tuesday; otherwise I will allow the matter to take its ordinary course. It is also to be observed that our petitions to the King (when not in Council) are presented to His Majesty on the throne, with an attendance of delegates, etc., etc. May it not, therefore, be questionable whether, with a Government probably adverse to our wishes, obstacles may not be thrown in the way of such presentation, and the petition, even if presented, fail to secure the desired attention?

Wellington to the Rev. George Rowley

It is perfectly true that my views of the course which the university ought to pursue have altered, as the circumstances have altered; and as the alteration has come to my knowledge.

I at first thought that you ought not to petition. That opinion was altered when I found that the Government intended to refer the case for consideration to the Privy Council; and as I concluded that it would be to the Judicial Committee of the Privy Council that the case would be referred I recommended that you should petition to be heard by counsel. I found upon enquiry that the case is to be referred to a committee of the Privy Council as described in my letter of the 15th March. That committee will be stated to be a judicial committee inasmuch as a judge will probably be summoned as a member; and the parties will be heard before it by counsel.

But it is obvious that it will not be the *Judicial Committee* of the Privy Council. It will however partake so much of the appearance of the judicial character as to relieve its members from all responsibility even in reputation for the advice which they will give their sovereign.

When I found that this was the case I thought it best to omit to recommend that the university should in the first instance pray to be heard by counsel.

There is in fact no law in the case; and it is very desirable that they should not themselves by applying to be heard by counsel give their sanction to the measure which is about to be adopted.

My opinion has been invariable that if you should petition it should be to the King himself; and you should take care that His Majesty receives and sees your petition.

I was very much struck by Sir Charles Wetherell's opinion upon the consequences of the assumption of the title London University; and it *may* be necessary to take some steps to secure the antient universities against the pretensions arising from that title.

That might be the subject of a supplementary petition.

But I should be very sorry to see in the first instance the ground abandoned which was first assumed by the University of Oxford; viz. that they do not object to the grant of degrees, not being degrees in divinity, by the new institution, provided they do not bear the same titles or names as those granted by the antient universities.

You must judge for yourselves which course it is best for the university to follow under the circumstances of the case; assuring you that in whatever course you may follow you shall have all the assistance I can give you.

I have not yet received the copy of your proposed petition.

Undated.

Richard Oastler to Wellington, 17 March 1834

Fixby Hall, Huddersfield. I have to thank your Grace for your favor of 26 November last. I have no doubt I could prove to satisfaction that our present system of commerce is *certain* to reduce our labourers to paupers, and to destroy the property of the aristocracy. I am as sure as I am of my existence that we shall, if we proceed, either have anarchy and then despotism, or we shall shortly see all the property of the country in the hands of the fund holders and the money changers. I fear to trouble your Grace with my arguments, but I am certain no class has half so much to fear from the present system as the noble order, of which your Grace is the ornament. All must give way to the goldocracy. They are now raising the cry against the Church and the Corn Laws, just to keep the people's eyes off their own tyranny and rapacity.

I cannot refrain enclosing for your Grace the addresses of the clergy in these parts. I do hope the Church may be saved, but really our great men seem to me to be so fast asleep, that I fear the greedy wolves will have their own way. I quite agree with your Grace, about our wanting a Government. This has long been our want. I knew, when your Grace yielded to the clamour out of doors, we might in vain look for a Government.

But our present ministers actually mounted to office by the cry of 'we will pay no taxes', and by insulting the King and the Queen; nay, their partisans in Yorkshire, at the instigation of the son of the present member for Leeds (Baines) actually gave three groans for the Queen of England. Men who have waded through treason to the Cabinet can never govern; they have no power to stay the outcry they have raised. Would that some person in whom the country can confide, someone who is honest and has the nerve which the occasion requires, might now come forward and save this nation.

These Whigs have bargained for the destruction of every institution, and although they see their error, they have no power to resist. Do excuse me, my Lord Duke; I do love my country, and I want her nobles to save her.

Docketed From Mr. Oastler, March 17th. Respecting the oppression of workmen.

The Rev. George Rowley to Wellington, 18 March 1834

Oxford. I have the honor to inform you that I have negatived the petition to the King in Council, and that another is being prepared in accordance with your Grace's opinion. This will be laid before our board tomorrow, and proposed in Convocation on Friday. It is very desirable that the petition should be voted in term time, and to effect this we have not a day to lose. Our statutable forms, however well contrived for ordinary proceedings, are sometimes inconvenient on occasions like the present. Your Grace will perceive that our objection is extended to law degrees. They give privileges in the ecclesiastical courts, etc.; and as, in Sir Charles Wetherell's opinion, any restrictive clause might be invalid, it does not appear that there is any other safe course to be pursued.

Wellington to the Rev. George Rowley, 18 March 1834

Stratfield Saye. Since I wrote to you yesterday by your messenger I have received your note of the 15th inclosing the copy of your petition to the King. I consider that that part relating to the title assumed, 'University of London', is exceedingly judiciously done; and connected with the fourth paragraph removes all my objections to the insertion in this petition of any observations upon that branch of the subject.

The effect of the grant by charter of the title *University* is certainly a question of law; and the including this branch of the subject in the petition may justify the leave to be heard by counsel. However I still feel strongly the inconvenience and disadvantage of inserting that passage in this petition for the reasons which I stated in former letters.

I will not trouble you with a repetition of them; and I assure you that I will give every assistance to promote the objects of the petition, whether it should or not contain this passage when finally adopted by the Convocation.

The Rev. George Rowley to Wellington, 19 March 1834

Oxford. I have the honor to transmit to your Grace a copy of the petition agreed to this day by the board of heads of houses and proctors; addresses and petitions from this university are received by the King on the throne, and should the one in question be passed in Convocation on Friday next, it will become my duty to request that your Grace, as our Chancellor, would have the goodness to take the necessary steps for fixing the time when it may be presented. Hoping that the terms in which it is now drawn up may meet with your Grace's approbation, *etc.*

Enclosure: To the King's most excellent Majesty, the humble petition of the Chancellor, masters and scholars of the University of Oxford. Sheweth,

That Your Majesty's petitioners have been informed that the council of a literary and scientifick institution lately founded in London have renewed their solicitation for a charter of incorporation under the title of the University of London.

That on the occasion of a similar application formerly made the insertion of certain clauses was suggested restricting the said institution from conferring degrees in arts and theology bearing the same names and titles with those conferred by the Universities of Oxford and

Cambridge; and likewise providing that no graduate of such institution should be enabled to practice in the ecclesiastical courts or enjoy sundry other privileges now appertaining to graduates of the existing universities.

Your Majesty's petitioners however have since been advised that a body incorporated under such title may thereby be enabled to confer degrees in the manner of the antient universities, notwithstanding any prohibitory clauses whatsoever.

Under these circumstances your petitioners venture dutifully to represent to Your Majesty:

That the existing universities studiously educate the youth entrusted to their care in the principles of Christianity after the doctrine and discipline of the Church of England; and that accordingly their degrees in arts and civil law as well as in theology have been recognized as qualifications for many offices both ecclesiastical and civil.

That Your Majesty's petitioners anticipate with alarm serious injury to numerous antient institutions of the land and much consequent evil to the public if similar privileges shall be conferred by a royal grant either expressly or by implication upon a society disavowing all connection with the Established Church, and educating its members in no system of religion whatever.

That your petitioners by no means desire that an institution formed for the promotion of literature and science should be restricted from bestowing suitable marks of distinction on its members; but they at the same time with all humility submit that such marks of distinction in the faculties of arts and civil law as well as of theology should not bear the same titles as those which for a long series of years have been conferred by the Universities of Oxford and Cambridge.

Your petitioners therefore earnestly implore Your Majesty to take these matters into Your Majesty's gracious consideration, and to withhold your royal sanction from a charter in its proposed form fraught with danger to principles and establishments which under the blessing of God have essentially contributed to the welfare and happiness of our country.

Nathaniel Howard to Wellington, 19 March 1834

Ashton-under-Lyne. In compliance with the wish of the committee appointed to arrange and forward a petition of the laity of the Established Church resident in this borough, and its immediate vicinity, to both Houses of Parliament, I beg leave to inform your Grace that the petition to the House of Lords (a copy of which is on the other side) will be transmitted by this evening's mail to the Right Honorable Earl Grey for *immediate* presentation, and that the committee are exceedingly wishful that I should earnestly solicit your Grace to be most graciously pleased to support its prayer, believing that your Grace will be so condescending and obliging as to comply with their solicitation in case your Grace should find it convenient to be in the House on the presentation.

The Right Honorable Lord Kenyon will also be requested to support the prayer of the petition.

I conceive that it is almost superfluous for me to say how very grateful and thankful the committee will feel for any assistance your Grace may be pleased to render upon this occasion.

Draft reply 24 March 1834. Compliments. The Duke has received his letter and the petition from Ashton-under-Lyne to the House of Lords. The Duke attended the House yesterday when the Earl Grey presented the said petition.

The Rev. George Rowley to Wellington, 21 March 1834

Oxford. I have the honor to inform your Grace that our petition, in the form last transmitted, was passed this day in a very full Convocation, with only one dissentient vote. The parchment itself may, of course, remain here till it is wanted. I shall be most careful in attending to any directions which I may receive from your Grace with regard to its presentation, *etc.*

Wellington to the Rev. George Rowley, 22 March 1834

Stratfield Saye. I was in the neighbourhood of Hungerford on Wednesday; and went to London yesterday to attend the House of Lords on the discussion of a petition presented by Lord Grey upon the admission of Dissenters to take degrees in the University of Cambridge; and I did not receive your letter of the 19th and its inclosure till I returned here last night. I quite concur in the pet[ition][1] to be proposed to the

---

[1] Paper torn.

Convocation. As soon as I shall hear from you that it has been adopted by the Convocation; and that it is their wish to present it in the usual manner I will make application accordingly in the usual manner.

The Rev. George Rowley to Wellington, 22 March 1834

Oxford. In writing to your Grace yesterday it did not occur to me to mention that the proctors for the ensuing year are to be admitted into office on Wednesday the 9th of April, and should that day be appointed for presenting the petition it would involve us in great statutable difficulty. It will, therefore, be highly expedient to avoid such a contingency if possible.

Wellington to Rev. George Rowley, 23 March 1834

Stratfield Saye. I have received this day your letter of the 21st; and I write to the Secretary of State to request that he will prevail upon the King to fix a time at which His Majesty will be graciously pleased to receive the petition of the University of Oxford.

I should think that it would not be convenient to the university to attend His Majesty on Wednesday next, the 26th instant, and this is moreover Passion Week. It is probable therefore that His Majesty will fix either Wednesday the 2nd of April or Wednesday the 9th of April for the reception of the petition of the university.

Wellington to Viscount Melbourne, 23 March 1834

Stratfield Saye. The University of Oxford in Convocation assembled on Friday the 21 instant resolved to present a petition to the King on the subject under consideration of the grant of a charter to the institution called the London University.

I request your Lordship to prevail upon His Majesty to afford to the University of Oxford an opportunity of presenting in the usual manner the petition in question of which I inclose your Lordship a copy.

Wellington to the Bishop of Exeter, 23 March 1834

Stratfield Saye. I left London on the rising of the House of Lords on

Friday. I did not write to you, because I was certain that the newspapers would give you a sufficiently accurate report of what passed.

The Duke of Gloucester was not present and I was obliged to take the cudgels for the University of Cambridge. It was fortunate that I had seen you as I knew little enough about Oxford and nothing about Cambridge. However with the information given to me by you, and the strength of the case as it occured to me upon the statement by Lord Grey, I made a tolerable good battle for them. There was no occasion to say a word about the University of Oxford and I thought it best not to mention that body.

Nobody supported me. Lord Ellenborough took a different course. It is obvious that he does not understand the question even as affecting the University of Cambridge. He does not suspect even how little our friends at Oxford would relish his notions. I hope that you are better and particularly that your health has not suffered from your exertions to assist and instruct me.

The Rev. Philip Bliss, Registrar of the University of Oxford, to Wellington, 24 March 1834

Oxford. I take the liberty of requesting your Grace's signature to the usual Act letter, dispensing with certain forms and exercises which have been dispensed with, in like manner, for the last century. As it is read in Convocation on the first day of next term, I shall be glad to receive it at your Grace's convenience.

Private. As my office and my private studies lead me often to an investigation of the university annals, I may be permitted to remark on a strange mistake made (according to the newspaper reports) by Lord Grey in his Lordship's speech on the petition from certain individuals at Cambridge. His Lordship is made to say that the first imposition of signature or assent to any articles at admission to the universities was in the time of King James the first. His Lordship appears to have confounded the three articles in the XXXVIth canon (which were doubtless first so commanded by King James) with the XXXIX Articles, the latter having been assented to and subscribed by all persons upon matriculation in the reign of Queen Elizabeth. I have before me, from the university archives, a copy of the Thirty-nine Articles printed by the Queen's printer, appended to which are 174 folios of closely written signatures made by individuals entering at the university in 1571 and the following years to 1605.

It appears to me strange that the persons who (as an argument for the admission of Dissenters) urge that religious tests are, comparatively, of recent introduction, forget that till the Reformation there was no need of such a precaution. When the whole country was Roman Catholic and of course the universities were the same, there was no dissent, and consequently no need of test civil or religious. But no sooner had the Reformation taken root, and Protestantism become the religion of the State, than all Dissenters (meaning the Roman Catholics for there were none other) were excluded, and, with the exception of their re-introduction during Queen Mary's reign, so continued in the universities, the subscription to the Articles first, and to the three articles in the thirty-sixth canon afterwards, only becoming necessary as the number and the various sects of Dissenters gradually became more formidable.

It is false in history therefore to say that the Articles were first subscribed to by the universities in the reign of King James: and it is absurd to argue on the impropriety of tests on the ground that they cannot be traced farther back than to the only period at which they could be useful.

I cannot sufficiently apologize to your Grace for the liberty I have taken in writing thus freely to you, but the zeal, the ability, the discretion and the earnestness with which you have pleaded our cause induce me to hope that you will forgive me.

Wellington to Viscount Melbourne, 24 March 1834

Stratfield Saye. When I addressed your Lordship yesterday I considered myself authorized to state that the university were anxious to present a petition to His Majesty on any day that His Majesty might name. I have this morning received a letter from the Vice-Chancellor in which he states that the university are anxious that the King should not fix Wednesday the 9th of April as the day on [which] they should have the honor of attending His Majesty, as it was the day on which the proctors were to be admitted to office.

I have thought it better to inform your Lordship of this circumstance without loss of time than to run the chance of the King naming the 9th of April and then to request His Majesty to name another day.

The Bishop of Exeter to Wellington, 24 March 1834

London. I thank your Grace very much for your kind enquiries after me; I am proceeding towards recovery, but slowly. My physician is anxious that I should not, as I intended, go to my diocese during the recess, but should avoid all business and should therefore stay in and near London, going for a day or two occasionally for change of air into the country.

I have wrung from him his consent to my going to the House of Lords tomorrow. It appears to me very important that some *bishop* should say something, before the House breaks up, on the claim of the Dissenters to be admitted to the Universities, especially to Oxford. I fully hoped that the Archbishop of Canterbury would have been present on Friday, and would have spoken. Unfortunately he is confined by illness, not, I trust of a dangerous, though of a distressing, kind.

I read with much pleasure the manly speech of your Grace, asserting sound principles in your own energetic and impressive manner.

Lord Ellenborough to Wellington, 25 March 1834

St. James's Place. I was obliged to give notice of a motion for the 15th on the papers relative to Prendergast's claim, as the 19th is the Queen's drawing room and the mandamus will probably be before the King's Bench on the 18th. I shall be in town on the 14th, if not before.

I should be glad to have the two reports of the Committee of correspondence before that, as I wish to refer to them again, and I likewise wish to know your opinion as to the form of motion.

The Chancellor has admitted to me that the letter ought not to be sent as the direction it gives to the Governor-General is not sufficiently distinct. He had no idea *force* was intended. He had never read the letter, nor did he know the interpretation put upon it by the court. Lord Grey told me he knew nothing about the matter.

I go to Southam tomorrow.

The Earl of Carnarvon to Wellington, 25 March 1834

Grosvenor Square. I have just found on my return from the Continent a letter from your Grace containing a card of invitation for the 3rd of February. I regret extremely that my absence from England at that time (being then in Italy) should have prevented my having had the honor of waiting on you on that day and am equally grieved to perceive by the date that the invitation with which you honored me has remained so long unanswered. I rejoice to hear by enquiry at Apsley House that your Grace is perfectly well.

Dated Tuesday. *Docketed* 1834. March.

Wellington to the Earl of Carnarvon, 26 March 1834

Stratfield Saye. I regretted much that I had not the honor of receiving you on the day previous to the meeting of Parliament. The object of the meeting on that day at my house was to discuss and fix the course which we should take upon the Address, and that which we would recommend to our friends, members of the House, and to the House to take during the session. The former is not now deserving your attention. In respect to the latter we settled that we would forbear from bringing forward questions that would be likely to embarrass the Government or to bring the majority of the House of Lords into collision with the Government, or the majority of the House of Commons, unless on occasions on which it would appear that such course was absolutely necessary for the publick interests; that we would wait till Government should bring forward their measures and that we would then take such course upon each of them as should appear to be required by the publick interests and the character and consistency of the members of the House of Lords. We have hitherto adhered to this course. I have been in the House of Lords only twice during the session; the first time to present a petition, the last within these few days to be present at the presentation of a petition by Lord Grey. I think that your Lordship will be of opinion that the course which we have followed is the best upon the whole. After the Easter holidays we shall have to consider of the course to be taken upon the measures which the Government will propose and I hope that your Lordship will allow me to have the advantage of receiving your opinion.

Wellington to Sir Robert Wilson, 28 March 1834

Stratfield Saye. Many thanks, my dear Sir Robert, for your note. The independence of Portugal of Spain has always been an object to England.

If Portugal is not entirely independent she cannot be allied with England. England then is no longer certain of the Tagus.

Putting aside all the other objects of the alliance out of the question, I should think that there is enough in the present times to convince those who are not determined that they will not see that a friendly Tagus is important to this country.

I don't understand what is meant by the Dutch demonstration. Are they acting upon any understanding that King Louis-Philippe will not move?

ADD MS 30114, f. 21.

The Earl of Carnarvon to Wellington, 30 March 1834 [?]

Grosvenor Square. Being out of town on the Saturday morning I had not the honor of receiving your Grace's letter till the evening but I cannot allow another post to go out without expressing my sense of your kindness in communicating to me the general line of proceeding determined upon at the commencement of the session. I feel also highly gratified by the permission, which your Grace so kindly grants me of expressing to you occasionally my opinion on public measures. May I venture to add how fully I concur in the very judicious course which your Grace has adopted and which in my humble judgment appears to me to have been the best calculated to avert the embarrassment that might have arisen from a collision between the House of Lords and the Government and the most likely to promote in the public mind a return to a more healthy state of feeling than has latterly prevailed. I am going into the country almost immediately and, being my poor father's executor, a great mass of complicated business may detain me there beyond the reassembling of Parliament, but should that be the case, my proxy is in the hands of a warm adherent of your Grace and should any occasion arise on which proxies cannot be used, I would come up to town at the shortest notice.

Dated Sunday evening. *Docketed* 1834. April.

Joseph Planta to Wellington, 31 March 1834

Warren's Hotel, Regent Street. I feel extremely obliged to your Grace for your great kindness in giving me your opinion as to the possible effect of my address at Hastings, but as it appears by the last accounts from thence (a little abstract of which I venture to send to your Grace) that the object we have in view has been attained, and that Mr. Warre has decided at once not to accept the Lordship of the Treasury and not to vacate his seat, it is perhaps unnecessary for me now to trouble your Grace with any further discussion of the matter. Hardinge is delighted with the result and Sir Robert Peel seems also much pleased. I have finished my part in this business with another short address, a copy of which I send to your Grace. I hope it may lay good ground for the future.

Enclosure: Hastings, 29 March 1834. The Planta address has this day had the effect desired. Warre has decided on keeping his seat warm. Elphinstone (the Radical candidate he is, J.P.) has published a notification accordingly this afternoon after he received the news. I heartily congratulate you on this success. Many were sorry they had already pledged themselves, but their promises I consider now at an end, and not binding for any future election.

Another letter dated the 30th March:

'Warre yesterday afternoon published an address to say that he would not vacate his seat, so that no election is to take place and your end is answered. After Warre's determination was made known, the Radical party brought forward their band and played what I understood to be the "Rogue's March". It proceeded with a large mob to the Albion, where Elphinstone is staying, where he was *cheered*, Warre hissed as a *runaway coward*, Planta *an honest man*. Such were the sentiments of the sovereign people. There is talk now of a petition to Warre, to say that as he has just canvassed the place and finds he represents only a minority, he is expected to give up his seat. To this, however, he will of course not listen.'

Donald Bain to Wellington, 31 March 1834

1 Gayfield Place, Edinburgh. Mr. Bain had the honor of receiving the Duke of Wellington's note, in answer to a request of the Duke's patronage of a then intended publication on the subject of the protection of agriculture, and from the tenor of that note it is obvious that the request or the terms were displeasing.

Mr. Bain can only regret if this was the case. The publication having now been made, a copy is herewith submitted that the Duke may see for what his favor was requested. The importance of the subject alone excuses this trouble and it is hoped the publication may be found not altogether unworthy of the subject.

Farther, should the [directions] be reproached as *old*, the author is of opinion that they are *safe*, to the existing people and the existing institutions of this country; and he thinks that Britain can only exist by a factitious population, and a factious [*sic*] population be supported only by artificial means.

The Earl of Elgin to Wellington, 1 April 1834

Broomhall. I feel that I may ask the favor of your Grace to look at a speech which my second son has made (his first attempt in public) on the occasion, last Thursday, of the institution of an agricultural association in this county. Being called upon a few days before to move one of the resolutions, he investigated the subject as far as in his power; but he put nothing on paper, and I happen to know that the topicks which he had selected as best suited to the point assigned to him were anticipated at the meeting, before his turn came. Still the views which he did enter on were so encouraged and his progress throughout so cheered, that with the most unhesitating command of excellent language and by interspersing some local allusions that were impressively managed, he was enabled to sustain universal attention during an hour to a closely argumentative and powerful support of his cause.

In indulging thus the personal gratification I derive from such an exhibition of my son's abilities, I may add from what passes around me that besides the tendency to bring this momentous question to its legitimate merits, the discussion of it, in this way, by persons respected in the country, men of education and talent, cannot fail to produce a benign influence in counteraction of the mischief and misrepresentation which the press and low demagogues so industriously disseminate.

I send the newspaper containing the speech.

Wellington to Viscount Melbourne, 1 April 1834

London. In the existing state of Ireland I could not think myself justified in omitting to communicate the inclosed letter to your Lordship.

I know nothing of the writer. He is probably a clergyman of the Church of England, and must know some facts on which he founds the opinion which his letter contains, which he would probably state to any office of Government who should communicate with him.

I don't at all doubt of the state of preparation for action whenever any leader offers himself.

Melbourne's reply, Whitehall. 1 April 1834: I have the honour of acknowledging your Grace's letter of the 1st instant enclosing a communication from Mr. Ryan of Rathcore Glebe, to which due attention shall be paid without delay.

Wellington to Viscount Melbourne, 1 April 1834

London. In reference to the letter which I addressed your Lordship on the 22nd [*sic*] March in which I inclosed the copy of a petition which the University of Oxford was anxious to have an opportunity of presenting to the King and in order that time may not be lost in conveying to the university His Majesty's pleasure regarding the time at which His Majesty would receive the petition, I write to inform your Lordship that I am going into the Cinque Ports; and to request you to send to my house in London any intimation of His Majesty's pleasure which your Lordship may think to make to me on this subject.

Lord Francis Egerton to Wellington, 3 April 1834

Paris. I have got your books and will send them by the first opportunity. I sat up till three this morning and read Bérard through at a stretch. If Croker reviews it pray let him do it in company with Bertrand and Raton. I know nothing of the author's real character, but will try to find it out. I expected from it more illustration than it contains of the author's views on the departure from liberal policy of which he accuses the King. The Government has had a slight *secousse* in the American affair but I do not think it will be of much public consequence, and I think Broglie himself evidently makes it an excuse for retiring from a post which has long been irksome to him and unsuited to his silent and studious habits. Soult will be glad to get rid of him. The Chamber has acted with childish vacillation, first by affectation of oeconomy, putting the army into a state of discontent, and then in a fright giving Soult all he wants. Ellice abuses them heartily and treats France as a republic. He says England may be saved or ruined by the peers, that this House of Commons and the next may be managed with ease if not *heurtés* on such points as the admission of Dissenters to the universities. He *affiches* unbounded respect for yourself. I have this all at second hand, as I do not love the man nor he me. He talks to the right and left. The journals are of course busy with Durham. The republicans treat it as nothing at all. I believe that a principal incidental object is to raise Bowring by attentions above the *niveau* to which his vulgarity and offensive manners have hitherto condemned him. He, J. Bowring, dines perpetually at Lord Granville's, I suspect for the same purpose. He is full of activity and instruction, and is an instance how much, even in this country, where a Frenchman told me this morning there were but two gentlemen and one grand seigneur, in the Duke of Orleans, Broglie, and Talleyrand, the absence of gentlemanlike breeding may mar a clever man's utility for serving his own party, for good or evil.

I write in great distress on account of Lady Francis who has been suffering torture for five days with an earache and as yet shows small symptoms of decided amendment but is rather easier today. Many thanks for your enquiries about my boy. He is going on very well, there is reasonable prospect of a cure, and the remaining treatment involves neither risk, pain, nor apprehension, but it must be slow. Lady Francis's condition has left me little spirits for society lately, or through Alava and others I could tell you more of the gossip of the day, and will do so if I find the means.

PS. Ellice had undertaken to forward the books by his bag so I send this the same way.

Sir John Macdonald to Wellington, 5 April 1834

Horse Guards. I find that the clothing of the Grenadier Guards is still in the regimental stores, and has not yet been served out to the men, so that we must forego, for the present, the advantage of shewing it to your Grace.

When you settle in town after the meeting of Parliament, I shall take leave to trouble your Grace again upon the subject. I take this occasion to send your Grace an interesting extract of a letter which has just been received from an artillery officer in the Mauritius.

I, at the same time, take the liberty to enclose for your Grace's perusal a note which I have just received from Mr. Robert Grant upon the delicate and important subject of which perhaps your Grace will have the kindness to favour me with an opinion. It appears to Lord Fitzroy and to me (in Lord Hill's absence) that it becomes matter for grave consideration how far the introduction of a body of priests into India for the purpose here contemplated would be compatible with the maintenance of a military superiority in that country. I must mention to your Grace that Mr. Ellice, last year, suggested the notion of giving pecuniary compensation to the Irish priests (as in the cases of the clergy of the Established Church) for officiating to the soldiery of their own persuasion, but that, upon talking the matter over here, he was induced to suspend whatever scheme he might have had in contemplation for the payment of the Catholic clergy.

Viscount Melbourne to Wellington, 5 April 1834

Whitehall. I have the honour of acquainting your Grace that His Majesty has been graciously pleased to appoint Wednesday the 16th instant, at one o'clock, for receiving the petition of the University of Oxford in the usual manner and I have the honour to remain, *etc.*

Lord Francis Egerton to Wellington, 6 April 1834

Paris. I think my former letter sent in company with your books may, unless corrected by more solid correspondence than mine, give you an erroneous notion of the extent of the embarrassment produced to this Government by their recent defeat in the Chamber. Whether their Cabinet be patched up at the moment I write I do not know, but the difficulty of doing so has been great and the process *orageux*. Soult had a scene at the Council yesterday with Humann and D'Argout. The former replied to some observation by the term *voleur* and said he could prove it by half an hour's reference to the papers of the army finance, alluding to the item of £60,000 which Soult is universally supposed to have made by the remount of the cavalry last year. Barthe's office was disposed of without his knowledge and he threw up the office offered in its stead with indignation. Duchâtel also declined taking office previous to the new elections. I do not of course answer for the truth of all this

493

but my authorities are female, and you know that information and influence too are more diffused among that class here than in England. In fact the plots of vaudevilles and *romans* turning on that influence are realized every moment in the bureaux here. The husbands are seldom spoken of or to, and the influence of their wives is frequently exercised to procure them the best possible appointments at the greatest possible distance from Paris. I fell in last night with the American secretary of legation. His talk was violent. He spoke of an immediate vote for the increase of their navy, a law of non-intercourse, the ruin of French commerce, without disguise or reserve, and treated the idea of a composition or abatement with contempt. He disavowed all gratitude or good feeling for French assistance in the War of Independence and said that the arrogance of this nation and the tone of superiority and protection they had lately assumed would never be lowered till the Americans *had flogged them.* It is said that Louis-Philippe, for the first time, lost his head and temper at the Council yesterday and laid about him without discretion. His moral courage has stood some severe tests; he was the only individual who retained it at the period of the trial of the ministers of Charles X, when Montalivet, the boldest of them, pleaded guilty to *des maux intestins,* and when he gives way the cause must be violent. I confess I regret it all, and am anxious for the stability of any Government here, short of a republic, but despair of it. I dare say you know ten times as much as I do about Madame de Vaudémont's papers, but I will run the risk of repeating what may be familiar to you. A friend of mine had a conversation two days ago with an old Mr. Cauchois, the compiler of Madame de Créqui's memoirs. He gave out that the papers, firstly *accaparés* by her *dame de compagnie,* who was left after twenty years service without a shilling, were offered to him and that he had seen an *échantillon* of twenty-four of them including some private notes from T[alleyran]d to Madame Adelaïde which the Princess had perhaps not delivered. Among them was also the passage, of which you have of course heard, respecting yourself, in which you are described as the only man who knows the state of Europe and can save it or France. One of the notes to Madame Adelaïde concerns the education of the Duke of Orleans to this purpose. *Il faut le former, lui donner des bonnes manières, ne pas l'entourer de ces pékins de militaires et d'aidecamps. Il faut lui donner des femmes, beaucoup de femmes, mais des femmes comme il faut.* Another to Madame de Vaudémont, herself, is still more entertaining. *C'est étonnant chère Princesse que, vue la longue amitié qui a existé entre nous, je ne vous ai jamais eue.* Another contains a criticism on Madame de Créqui's first volume. T[alleyran]d is very indignant as to the attacks on his family, its antiquity etc., but adverting to his own letter published on it, in which he interferes to procure the canonization of some female fanatic, he says, *pour cela il y avait quelque chose.* Other letters detail the whole Belgian affair and are so diffuse upon it that the report of the King of Holland having offered *only* 30,000 francs for them is treated with derision. It is now said that they have been bought in Germany. Query: Metternich.

One feature of all that has taken place in the Chamber and the Council is the demonstration of the great necessity of Soult. There is no one to replace him with the army and he knows it. Humann's apostrophe to him certainly comes under Pope's definition of true wit: 'What oft was thought, but ne'er so well expressed'! but hard words cannot break the bones of the old brigand. Much as he has done for the army, I do not believe it is what it was. The conduct of the officers in one of the Algiers affairs lately has been suppressed by all possible means by the Government, but is well known to have been disgraceful to their aims. *Contrebandiste* was the word used by Soult to Humann.

April 6. The ministry is arranged, and is, I apprehend, calculated to please our Government, for Duchâtel is supposed to be more favourable to a commercial arrangement than Thiers, who never would have anything to say to Bowring. You will see however that in office he neither can nor will do anything. Dupin speaks confidently of the late events producing no unfavourable effect on the elections.

Alava leaves us today for Tours. He desires me to say everything that can be said of remembrance to you. He is furious with his nephew, Floridablanca, for having been seduced to see Soult's pictures and has refused Soult's advances, who sent Harispe and others to him on pretext of consulting him on some military question or point of history.

Adieu, my dear Duke. I wish you all success in the struggle which I fear awaits you. You will think me Durhamized if I say I wish you may be able to avoid extremities. His deportment is, for some purpose or other, conciliatory and he has even condescended to pay me a visit after we had accidentally met, but I have seen him but once. With Ellice I have conversed at length.

PS. The elections for the National Guard have gone off so as to satisfy the Government.

Wellington to Lord Ellenborough, 6 April 1834

London. I have to apologize for having so long kept your papers, but I have had other affairs to attend to; and Lord Rosslyn informed me that he had postponed your motion, and I have perused them only this day. Before I write an observation or two upon your motion I request you to allow it to be postponed from the 25th to the 28th of October [*sic*], as I am engaged on the 25th to dine with the Duke of Gloucester, where I am to have the honour of meeting His Majesty.

In reference to your resolutions I would recommend to you to omit the first altogether.

I have not by me the papers presented in this session of Parliament, but as well as I recollect Lord Cornwallis's letter of 1787 to the Nabob Vizier is not before the House of Lords.

I believe that your last resolution might be strengthened.

Since it is contrary to the customs of civilized states and the laws of nations to go to war to enforce payment of a debt to an individual at all; must we without proper examination and enquiry into the justice on account of the claim?

Draft in pencil.

Wellington to the Rev. George Rowley, 7 April 1834

London. I write you one line to tell you that I returned to London on Friday. I have not yet received from the Secretary of State any notice of the petition from the University of Oxford. It may be desirable that you should examine your records to see whether there is any instance of the refusal or delay to receive a petition from the university.

Wellington to Donald Bain, 8 April 1834

Compliments. The Duke has received his letter and returns thanks for his publication which the Duke will peruse at the first moment of leisure that he has.

The Duke has no recollection of having written to him before upon this subject.

The Duke certainly receives more letters and applications than any man that now exists. There is not a gentleman or lady or a child who publishes a work, whether in verse or prose, in whatever language, or a drawing or an etching or engraving or needlework or sculpture, who does not write to the Duke to require his patronage as it is called of such work; which work is not infrequently left at his house without his consent; and then those who write are much displeased if they do not receive further answer of compliance with the requisition made.

If the Duke had two days of leisure where other men have one he would not have time to answer even these claims upon his leisure.

But besides this he must say that large as his houses are he has not house room for all the articles which he is required to receive and to patronize.

It is not extraordinary that he should be anxious to be allowed to purchase those works which he wishes to peruse, as other men are.

Draft.

The Mayor of Cork (Charles Perry) to Wellington, 10 April 1834

Mansion House, Cork. By the desire of the common council of this city, I take the liberty to address your Grace.

In consequence of the prevailing opinion that the Reform Acts were to undergo revision, the common council of Cork considered it their duty to avail themselves of so critical an opportunity in order to make known those defects in the Irish Act which have been ascertained by experience.

With this view a statement has been prepared, under their direction, and I take leave to transmit a copy to your Grace. They are fully aware of the numerous claims upon your Lordship's time, but being under the impression that the future well-being of Ireland may be materially effected by the changes that shall be made in the Irish Reform Act, they are induced to hope that your Lordship will excuse them for thus trespassing upon you.

The imperfect construction of the Irish Reform Act will appear manifest in its results upon the constituency of this city as detailed in the accompanying document.

The common council of Cork direct me respectfully to solicit your Grace's attention to the subject and your aid for the attainment of the objects sought, so far as they shall appear to merit your support.

Lord Francis Egerton to Wellington, 11 April 1834

Paris. I made a mistake in my last in telling you that the American *secretary* had held strong language to me about the treaty. The individual in question was employed here but is no longer so. His sentiments must therefore be taken as those of a *particulier* only. The last accounts I got at Madame de Flahault's last night were that the workmen had again entrenched themselves in the narrow streets at Lyons, and that the troops were just marching upon them. The former had failed in an attempt on the telegraph. My informant, who was formerly Casimir Périer's private secretary, told me that the commandant, who is said to be an excellent man for the business, has not above 7,000 men disposable. This I can hardly believe. The Government seems to have been well satisfied with the conduct of the troops in the first affair. They must be well blooded by this time as the nature of the service is exasperating. I could get at no account whatever of the amount of the slaughter.

Ellice was abusing the high Tories the other day, but added: I will have nothing to do with them, nor with *Durham* either. He seems to dread and deprecate the rôle which Durham may be able and inclined to support as much as anyone. He treats the idea of Peel or Stanley forming an Administration as futile and says that the latter has no hold on the country. I think he looks to Althorp as eventual minister, and says he has a larger following than anybody.

I believe the troops at Lyons are increased to about 15,000 men. I have just been over the *dépôt de guerre* where they shewed us everything, maps, dispatches etc. with great civility. They have immense materials for the history of Napoleon's wars and those of the revolution and admirably arranged.

Viscount Melville to Wellington, 12 April 1834

Melville Castle. I had intended writing to you or Lord Rosslyn as to whether any business was likely to come before the House of Lords during the present session which would indispensably require everyone to attend; but I feel that going on, year after year, waiting for some such collision, is neither proper nor very decent, however convenient and agreeable my stay in this country may be to me in other respects. Under those circumstances, and also feeling very irksome at being so long apart from yourself and other friends whom I may hope to meet in London, I am going to pass our Northern Rubicon, the Tweed, about the 24th instant, and I expect to be in London (with Lady Melville and my daughters) on the 28th.

James Amphlett to Wellington, 13 April 1834

Stafford. I have taken the liberty to enclose to your Grace a statement of the available constituency of this borough, in case it should be deemed advisable to disfranchise the old freemen.

The design to disfranchise, or to subject to a pro-Whig and Catholic sway, was premeditated from the first; and though the origin of the bribe money of one candidate may not be traced, there is no possible doubt that through Mr. Wood of the Treasury it was a ministerial project.

If the House of Lords should do the borough the common justice of testing the evidence on oath, it will admit of proof that out of the 1049 burgesses alleged to be bribed, more than 800 were personally unimplicated: that is, their names were inserted in different lists without their knowledge or consent, and after the election the dole of bribery was sent to, or taken for them by a few profligate leaders, through whose hands the money was dispensed in the usual mystified way, as the great majority of the burgesses would have voted just as they, without reference to any payment for their votes, which they neither contracted for nor required. I know this, personally, to be a fact, from having gone round with two respectable manufacturers, during the progress of the Indemnity Bill, in order to ascertain the extent of the corruption among the lower classes of freemen. To practise thus on the temper and necessities of the poor, under the pretence that money so given does not constitute bribery, and then to deprive them of their liberties on account of their ignorance is another way of legislating *for the poor*, à la Brougham, worthy of the new school.

Docketed by Wellington Compliments. Received. *Docketed by secretary* Done. April 17th.

Enclosure: Reasons why the borough of Stafford should not be totally disfranchised.

Lord Francis Egerton to Wellington, 13 April 1834

Paris. We are just relieved from the greatest anxiety here by the news from Lyons announcing the suppression of the *émeute*. I do not yet know what terms were granted to the rebels but I presume something passed of the nature of a capitulation. The ministers had an uneasy 24 hours while the communications were interrupted. My uncle began to lose a little of his optimism and Pozzo, who loathes *émeutes*, looked very uneasy. There was in fact a strong disposition here last night to *attroupement*, only checked by the knowledge of the good disposition of the National Guard. I sat up late watching the movements of the *état-major* close to my hotel in the Place Vendôme. There were patroles, and non-commissioned officers in disguise etc. coming in every five minutes, guards doubled etc, etc. The crisis being over, as I presume it to be, the Government will probably have gained temporary strength, but they have shewn alarm amounting to cowardice, and both Thiers and Rigny made an hash of it in their explanations to the Chamber, to the great increase of the public alarm. They will have gained little if they do not found upon all this something like the *ordonnances* of Charles X, for if the *Tribune*, the *National* and other papers are to go on undisturbed in their systematic attempts to debauch the army, Soult himself will not be able to keep it sound. I am very glad the present attempt is put down, for the example of Lyons might be fatal in our own manufacturing towns.

Monday 14th. The above shews the vanity of speculations on the present state of affairs. I do not believe that the *émeute* at Lyons was finally quelled, as the official notice concludes with the expression that the *anarchistes* were in a state of the *greatest disorder*. It appears also that the *fauxbourgs had* been in possession of the said anarchists, as it had been necessary to retake them. Next as to Paris: while I was writing yesterday at about half-past six G. Dawson came up to tell me that there was fighting in the Place de Grève, and that barricades had been thrown up in that neighbourhood. I was just sitting down to dinner with Lady Francis who does not yet leave her room, but at eight o'clock I went out with D. Dawson to reconnoitre. The drums in the mean time were beating the *appel* for the National Guard which appears to have answered with great alacrity. Two squadrons and two companies of infantry drew up before the Ministère de Justice, Persil's, in the Place Vendôme, not without reason, for he is looked upon as the Jeffreys of

France by the Republicans. We passed through the Carrousel, which as you may imagine was well stocked with troops of all arms. Here, as everywhere else, the National Guard was largely mixed up with the troops and it was impossible not to admire their order and equipment. They also give much less trouble than the line as to keeping them from the wine shops, which drew off of necessity a great number of sentries from the latter along the quays. I saw one or two cases of men serving without uniform, which must be inconvenient in these *échauffourés*. They let us pass everywhere without notice and I followed the quays to the Place de Grève, which I found filled with troops and artillery, but after going into cafés and questioning wherever I could venture I could not *constater* that anyone had heard a *coup de fusil*, or that anything had been killed but one horse of a gensdarme. I turned back to the Place de Châtelet, and finding a cabriolet, told the driver to take me to the Boulevard through the Rue Saint Martin. He told me he thought it impossible, for he had been already turned back, but that he would try and he turned at once into the thick of it through one of those streets which admit only one carriage. The *reverbères* were all unlighted, whether by order of the police I do not know, and the small streets were quite dark, but the larger very sufficiently lighted from the windows. There was also a moon in the last quarter and the night was mild and fine. He got us into the Rue Saint Martin and as far as the corner of the Rue Aubry Boucher, where we were pulled up by a strong post of the Grenadiers of the National Guard. They made us get out and *fouiller'd* us for *poignards* etc. Nothing could exceed their civility in the operation and they made a thousand excuses. However they could not let us go on further as they said we were close to the barricades, but advised us to turn down the Aubry Boucher to the Marché des Innocens. We were stopped and searched two or three times always with the same civility, but walked through the Rue Saint Denis to the Boulevard without interruption. It was tolerably full of people who were merely made to pass on by the patroles, and I returned home by the Boulevard. I have been unable to ascertain this morning that the contest has been renewed, or that there was at any period much fighting yesterday. Some barricades erected before nightfall were carried, but I do not believe that any shots were fired after the time that I was on the spot. Troops have poured in this morning and it really appears too insane for even the *jeunes gens* of this accursed country to attempt anything against a force so overwhelming, unless they rely on corrupting the troops, which their journals unceasingly endeavour to do, but in which they have hitherto failed. I heard that a colonel of the National Guard had been wounded and an officer of the staff killed, but even this is uncertain.

Two o'clock. Since writing the above I have heard that the barricades, after having been blockaded as I left them all night, were this morning at six o'clock attacked and carried by the Duke of Orleans in person, attended by Lobau. The resistance appears to have been insane as usual. Three officers of the 35ᵉ were killed and a colonel of Lancers wounded, amputated, and since dead. Some say the Duke of Orleans was fired on from two houses, others doubt it. It is certain, however, that two houses, from which the fire was kept up, were stormed and every living thing in them put to death and flung out of the windows, including, I believe, many wretched people who had no part in the transaction. The *gamins* as usual distinguished themselves: an officer was killed by one of 12 years old, another such was arrested with a cuirass round him of pasteboard. He said he wore it for the rheumatism. The loss of the rebels is variously stated at from 200 to 1000. Several of the leaders have been arrested, as well as all the editors etc. of the *Tribune*. All this may lead you to conclude that I was an idiot for going where I had no business last night. I knew, however, that there is always *relâche* in these things after nightfall, and I calculated that even if the Republicans persevered, which I own I thought impossible, the thing would take the course it has. If I had been silly enough, as many people are on such occasions, to have put a pistol in my pocket, I should have been arrested, perhaps maltreated. As it was, they did nothing but make apologies, saying *il ne faut pas vous fâcher; nous avons arrêtés plusieurs qui étaient armés*, and shook hands with me. The National Guard are said to have fought quite as well as the line, particularly the seventh legion, which was doubted. They boast much of the skill of Soult's dispositions. He has called into Paris every disposable man, the National Guard of the *banlieue* etc. and I have no doubt that 100,000 men were under arms this morning, including the National Guard.

Lord Francis Egerton to Wellington, 15 April 1834

Paris. I continue my letters thinking that as they require no answer you may be not unwilling to have a diary of what passes here at a moment which will be of great historical interest. The Government has in my judgement, and I have been of the same opinion from the commencement, committed a capital error in making the law of association permanent. They might have got it for ten years without a murmur; as it is, nothing but the temporary horror and disgust of all persons of property against the authors of the last *émeute* prevents a great explosion against the law, and the necessity which the Government is now under of ulterior measures against the press will aggravate its difficulties and excite an opposition far more dangerous than that of a few desperadoes. There is also a general feeling against the present administration as incompetent, temporizing, and Russian in its inclinations, and I think it very probable that the King will soon be hurried onward to measures which will produce a general war in Europe. The King reviewed the regiments lately arrived yesterday, soon after the affair of the barricades was over. The people received him with a *morne* silence. The late attempt was certainly of the lowest and most contemptible description, but it was more widely spread than was at first supposed. It now appears that it extended to the other side of the river, and that barricades were attempted in the Porte Saint Michel and other parts near ₜhe Luxemburgh, at one of which one of the officers who fell was killed. I believe the fact to be that one only of the sections of the *droits d'homme* determined to move in defiance of the resolutions of the others in favour of delay. The mode of proceeding was worthy of the cause and its supporters. A *sous-officier* was wounded and left in a shop while his comrades went for a surgeon. They found him on their return with his throat cut from ear to ear; the people of the place said that three *jeunes gens*, probably young surgeons, had entered and done this with their penknives or *bistouries*. A national guard on his way to answer the *rappel* was stabbed by three others in the street. No wonder that the bodies which lay in the houses yesterday exhibited no bayonet wounds apiece. It is, however, said that the troops made a mistake as to one house and killed the innocent proprietor, the maid servants and the children, circumstances which at least have not yet been denied, and will be made great use of by the two extreme parties against the Duke of Orleans, to revenge whom these horrors were perpetrated, if they really took place. I believe fifty-four people were killed in one house and forty-two in another. Fourteen of the gensdarmerie who led the attack were killed. This is nothing to Lyons where 1,700 of the soldiers and six or seven thousand of the people have fallen. The ministers have

I think purposely underrated the number of the troops employed at Lyons (which they say has never exceeded 10,000 men), in order to facilitate the vote of 50,000 men which Soult has today got from the Chamber which a few days since risked a mutiny by courting popularity with petty oeconomies. I am writing at night and after the Chamber has received from the ministers the project of their laws of repression. They have, after much deliberation, shrunk from meddling with the press in any shape, and have contented themselves with the trifling measures of deportation against the possession, carrying etc. of arms, and the punishment of death against that which is capital in all civilized societies: viz. using them against the Government. I have just had a long conversation with Ellice; he has more means of judging and informing himself and more capacity to boot than I have and his opinion exactly coincides with that which I have not ceased to entertain from the moment of the commencement of these troubles: viz. that war is inevitable, and that Europe must once more be scourged with it, because France wants depletion. Is it to be endured that the civilized world must thus be tormented for the vices of this accursed country? I speak of it, as every Frenchman I have seen speaks of it, as a country in which morality in any shape, religious or otherwise, is an unknown thing. The language of men of all classes, from the entourage of the Duke of Orleans to the bourgeoisie, is now become the same; that *la gloire*, and we all know what that means, is the only cure for the radical evils which render it impossible for this country to be governed in peace. I do believe that Louis Philippe, from a wise view of the interests of his own dynasty, has done what man could do to avoid this, and that he has failed and must swim with the stream; and that a pretext will soon be found in Neufchâtel, Switzerland, it matters not where, for advancing to the Rhine. God send we may live to see them with the Vosges for their frontier, but they are secure from the opposition of England and fear nothing. I should doubt that the manufacturing prosperity of Lyons would ever recover the shock which must inevitably drive its capitalists to Switzerland or wherever they can look for security. The trials of the rebels are committed to the Chamber of Peers, a queer tribunal according to our notions.

Lady Francis is gradually recovering and I hope I shall be able to start for England on Monday, which nothing but her illness has prevented me from doing sooner, as I am impatient to get to work in the neighbourhood of Manchester where I think I can be of use. Durham goes about like a spoiled child with a tutor, and has made a fool of himself with a foolish woman, but is tame in his language and demeanour. Yarmouth, whom they have courted and found at first very shy, has condescended to make his acquaintance for the purpose of quizzing him, which he has done with his usual gravity and to the great delight of the bystanders. He is one of the cleverest men I ever met with.

April 17. I went over the scene of action yesterday by daylight and made all the enquiries I could among the neighbours. It appears that the horrors related of one house: no. 12 Rue Transnonains, in which a dozen perfectly innocent people were put to death, really took place, but I could not discover that anything like 50 or 40 persons had in any instance perished in one house as was related in all the newspapers. The headquarter [*sic*] had been established in an hotel of some consequence, full of various establishments, lodgers, magazins etc.: these were spared, but eleven of the insurgents were killed *blottis* together in the porter's lodge; the court retained traces of the blood coagulated between the stones. The news today would be very alarming from Grenoble, Dijon and other places if the victory had not been gained at Lyons; General Aymard certainly at one period contemplated retiring. The action appears for many hours to have been one of artillery and of heavy pieces on the part of the troops. The proclamation of the Lyonnese is remarkable as singling out two persons: Barthe, the renegade, and Persil, *le pourvoyeur d'échafauds*. The elevation of Barthe, an ex-carbonaro of the worst character, has been as offensive to respectable people as that of Persil is to the republicans. A son of Bourmont and I believe others of that party have been taken at Lyons and are I suppose shot by this time. I can conceive little advantage to the Bourbon interests in their connection with an enterprise so sanguinary and with a party which has declared the republic. It has been insinuated that the King of Holland has supplied funds to the insurgents. The great fear of the Government now, and I think a just one, is that of assassination. The turn which events have taken and the character and relative situation of the parties concerned certainly make such attempts very probable. Altogether I think worse of the position of the King and the prospects of the country than I have done at any period since the revolution. I think the vulgarest and most despicable of the men who have worked themselves into power here on the shoulders of the rabble and kicked away their ladder is Dupin. He could think of no better subject the other day than abuse of the Poles at a dinner where Czartoryzki was present, who meekly observed *qu'il faut excuser au malheur*, that he remembered the French emigrants were very troublesome at one period in Poland. At Rothschilds yesterday Dupin fell openly upon Soult and his 50,000 men, saying that he did not see that more horses were wanted to enable the artillery to fire on the people. Soult is not unlikely to have the opportunity, and assuredly will not in such case want the will, to hang the lawyer. The news from Marseilles this evening is very alarming. It is said to swarm with refugees whom Austria, Switzerland and all neighbouring countries seem alike anxious to toss over to the care of France and England. Ellice talks almost seriously of getting the Treasury to propose a vote for sharing with France the expence of transporting them to America.

I have just seen a man who has a mercantile friend arrived from Lyons. He is an Englishman and I should think a Radical. His version is that the *ouvriers* engaged were probably few, and that the insurgents were nearly all Carlists who did not belong to the place and refugees from all countries.

Wellington to Viscount Melville, 15 April 1834

London. I have received your note and shall be delighted to see you and Lady Melville again.

We have, up to this moment, avoided to give the Government any trouble in the House of Lords and I propose to persevere in this course if I can prevail upon our friends to act upon it till the Government will bring forward some questions upon which we must oppose them.

I am inclined to think, however, that the session will be very short, as they are not prepared with any measure upon which they would like to risk the continuance of the Administration. God send that this may be the case, as there is nobody who wishes more than I do that they may exist till they will have experienced the effects of their handywork.

Sir John Dillon to Wellington, 18 April 1834

72 Quadrant. Sir John Dillon has the honor of enclosing to his Grace, the Duke of Wellington, his treatise on the state of the marriage law regarding the marriages of Catholics and Dissenters (as he conceives it to stand even at present) and respecting the principle on which he conceives any new enactment should proceed.

In the course of the discussion Sir John Dillon has introduced (at a passage marked) a vindication of the rights which he conceives to appertain to the bishops of the Church of England both as to their property and as to Parliament; also in a long English note at the end much diplomatic matter connected with the settlement of Ireland.

Draft reply 23 April 1834. Compliments to Sir John Dillon. The Duke has received Sir John Dillon's note and his work. He will peruse the latter with much interest at his first leisure moment.

Wellington to the Rev. George Rowley, 18 April 1834

London. I have just now seen Sir Charles Wetherell; and have had a conversation with him regarding the question in which we are interested. The King in his answer to the petition of the university has informed them that he has referred the case for the consideration of his Privy Council. I think that it would be desirable that the University of Oxford should prepare a petition to the King in Council to desire to be heard by counsel before that board. That petition once prepared you might retain it till I should let you know that it is desirable that it should be sent up; or you might transmit it to me if you should trust to me to fix the time at which I should present it if it is to be presented at all.

Wellington to the Rev. George Rowley, 19 April 1834

London. Since I wrote to you yesterday I have heard that the Privy Council are to meet next week to take into consideration the several petitions regarding the grant of a charter to the London University. To tell you the truth I don't think that any thing that can be said will be of much use. However Sir Charles Wetherell has considered the subject, and is fully prepared with much valuable information; and it might be expedient that the university should have him instructed to attend the Privy Council on their behalf, when it should meet to consider of this subject. This is the more desirable as I confess that I am not well satisfied with the selection made by the University of Cambridge of the counsel to appear on their behalf.

The Rev. Edward Cardwell to Wellington, 19 April 1834

St. Albans Hall, Oxford. I regret that I had not the good fortune to be able to offer my sincere acknowledgments to your Grace in person on Thursday last.

I have abstained from writing to your Grace during the progress of the recent discussions, because I knew that the Vice-Chancellor was in constant communication with your Grace, and I had reason to believe that no information was omitted by him which could be considered of importance.

Another question however is now arising; and your Grace will probably wish to know whether any desire has been, or is likely to be, expressed by any members of Convocation, corresponding with the petition lately presented to the two Houses of Parliament from certain resident members of the Senate at Cambridge. The question of the admission of Dissenters into the university has never been brought before Convocation, and from what I know of the prevailing sentiments of the place I am confident that, were it confined to the resident members of that body, it would be almost unanimously rejected. But a question nearly allied to it was actually considered by the board of heads of houses a few months since. It was proposed that the test, of subscription to the Thirty-Nine Articles, should not be required on matriculation, with the view of substituting some direct declaration in the place of it. This proposition was negatived by fourteen against seven; but of the minority I much doubt whether more than one would be in favour of the admission of Dissenters. I conceive that the rest were desirous of substituting a declaration, such as 'I declare that I am bona fide a member of the Church of England', on the ground that young men of the age of seventeen are not commonly acquainted with the Thirty-Nine Articles, and are not in practice required to have considered them.

Wellington to Mr. Pollock,[1] 19 April 1834

London. I have received your letter of the 18th instant. I will with great satisfaction present to the House of Lords the petition of the under-

---

[1] Possibly William Frederick Pollock, matriculated Trinity 1832, B.A. 1836.

graduates of the University of Cambridge described by you if you should think proper to send it to me after receiving this letter. The Chancellor of the University of Cambridge, His Royal Highness the Duke of Gloucester, has given notice of his intention to present a petition to the House of Lords on Monday from the resident members of the Senate upon the same subject, and I would suggest to you the expediency of entrusting to His Royal Highness the petition referred to in your letter.

If however you should be desirous that I should present it, I recommend to you to transmit it so that I may receive it before the House will meet on Monday in order that I may present it in the same day that His Royal Highness will present the petition from the members of the Senate.

The Rev. Richard Jenkyns to Wellington, 20 April 1834

Balliol College. Acting in behalf of the Vice-Chancellor during his absence from Oxford; I have had the honour of receiving both of your Grace's letters addressed to him, and respectively dated the 18th and 19th of April.

Had there been any mail to London last night, I should not have failed to acknowledge the former of these; and I should [have] taken the opportunity of informing your Grace of the steps which we had previously deemed it advisable to take.

Our solicitor's agents in town having intimated to us the meeting of the committee of the Privy Council on Thursday the 24th, when we might be heard by our counsel, we immediately gave instructions to our solicitor to retain Sir Charles Wetherell in our behalf.

In order also to put him, without delay, in possession of our sentiments, we desired a copy of our late petition to be delivered to him.

Your Grace's letter therefore of the 19th is most gratifying in the assurance it affords of the propriety of our proceedings; though it unhappily confirms our own sad forebodings respecting the fate of a question most important to the interests of the ancient universities, the Church, and of the public at large. We had indeed some doubts whether a previous petition for leave to be heard by counsel might not be necessary. We have since been told that no such form will be requisite. It will however be prudent to be prepared in case we may have been misinformed.

I must avail myself of this opportunity to express the deep sense of obligation which in common with many others I feel for the very able, kind, and zealous manner in which your Grace has been pleased to advocate our cause.

It is on such occasions, and under circumstances of no ordinary alarm and danger to ancient establishments, that we derive both comfort and hope from the reflection that we are under the protection of a chancellor both willing and able to assist us in our difficulties.

Lord Francis Egerton to Wellington, 20 April 1834

Paris. I hope to be in London nearly as soon [as] this letter but as I may not see you immediately I write a few lines to give you the last of my visit here. Nothing, as I have already told you, could have behaved better than the National Guard here on the last occasion, but I have reason to believe that the Government are not satisfied with the *amount* of their muster which some say did not exceed five or six thousand men. Others hold that there are 25,000 to be depended upon in an emergency. Something like that number certainly appeared at the review last autumn when every endeavour was made to procure a thin attendance. All this is important because there is a prevalent notion that the troops will not fight unless supported by at least a decent proportion of the National Guard. I heard today, though not on authority, that it was true Bourmont's son had been arrested at Lyons, but that it was before the affair, and that he was discharged in the absence of all ground of accusation. I have just received a letter from Mr. Arbuthnot with enquiries after Lady Francis: our setting off tomorrow will be the best answer as to her improvement, though she is not yet free from the remains of cough. The weather has undergone so complete a change that I have little apprehension and much hope from the change of air.

Ellice, who left us on Friday, in his conversations with me and others rather took the tone of suffering innocence, saying that the King's Speech had been framed in as conciliatory a spirit as possible but that both yourself and Peel had attacked the Government, and that they were hampered in their conservative views etc. etc.

Donald Bain to Wellington, 21 April 1834

1 Gayfield Place, Edinburgh. Mr. Bain received in due course the very long note the Duke of Wellington took the trouble to write to him on the 8th instant, and regrets extremely that the Duke should be so intruded upon by correspondents upon every trifling subject which, till the receipt of the Duke's note, he could not have conceived.

The subjects upon which Mr. Bain has ventured to trouble the Duke since his retirement from office have been, 1st tithes; 2nd the Bank of England Charter; and 3rd and last the protection of agriculture in Britain. It need not be stated that these are subjects of great importance, and Mr. Bain has transmitted the papers he has written upon them to the Duke of Wellington, as to a leading statesman, to whom it appeared to him especially desirable that the sentiments expressed in these papers should be known (if of any value), and to whom they were not likely to be known unless thus directly imparted.

But only in regard to the last paper, to wit that on the protection of agriculture, did Mr. Bain express any anxiety for concurrence and assistance, and he did this, not because he has personally the slightest interest in the matter, but because it appears of signal importance to the state of which he is a member and almost the opinion of *the nation* is to be changed. This is not likely to be effected by a writer as yet unknown, but if those more immediately interested do not see his opinion to be worth seconding, he cannot help it.

Ignorant as every one must be of the real value of his own opinions, Mr. Bain can only, when he in future takes the trouble to give his, leave them to their fate with the public in general. But he cannot help saying that *so left*, even the talents of the Duke of Wellington himself might have remained unappreciated and undeveloped, for the *public* cannot judge of such matters till a period when their judgement is of little value. Mr. Bain has in the paper last alluded to attempted to place the subject treated of upon *principle*. It is the first in that spirit, as he believes. The sentiments of a few men in power might make it (if correct) the opinion of the country; and, however correct, if not so supported it will never be heard of. But Mr. Bain has no claim on the Duke of Wellington, and has only made this explanation that he may stand fairly in the Duke's opinion, if such is his due; and if he ought not to have intruded he apologises.

Docketed by Wellington Compliments. The Duke has received Mr.

Bain's note of the 8th April. *Docketed by secretary* Done. April 25th, 1834.

Wellington to the Rev. Edward Cardwell, 22 April 1834

London. I have received your letter, and am very sorry that I had not an opportunity of conversing with you when you were in London.

I am very much obliged to you for the information which you have given me regarding the sentiments of the board of heads of houses upon the subject of the subscription to the Thirty-Nine Articles in matriculation. If I was now to sit down and frame rules for the admission of young men to the university, I should not propose that they should subscribe the Thirty-Nine Articles as a proof that they were members of the Church of England. But that proof having been required, and having been given for nearly three centuries without inconvenience and with manifest advantage to religion and morality as well as to the State, I should be unwilling to see it altered for another at this moment; which other I might prefer if I was now considering of a mode of admitting to the university members of the Church of England only. The difficulty attending the proof now given on matriculation consists in the abstruse nature of the Thirty-Nine Articles, and it is difficult to make a public assembly consisting of many not friendly to the universities understand the difference between a formal subscription by a youth upon matriculation and the subscription of the Articles required from others of a more mature age. The University of Oxford require the candidates for degrees to subscribe something more than the Articles. But the subscription of the Articles themselves is sufficient for some other objects; and it is not easy to make the unwilling understand the difference between that subscription and the other formal one, or made out of respect for superior authority.

The Rev. John Sharpe to Wellington, 22 April 1834

Vicarage, Doncaster. At a meeting of the clergy resident within the deanery of Doncaster lately held in this place it was determined to present petitions to both Houses of Parliament on the present existing critical state of our church establishment. That to the House of Lords was, of course, forwarded to our excellent diocesan, the Archbishop of York, for presentation; but I was, I beg to state to your Grace, at the same time requested by my brethren most respectfully to entreat your Grace to support it whenever it may be convenient for the Archbishop to present it to the House.

That your Grace may long be spared to hold the distinguished situation in which the University of Oxford has so deservedly placed your Grace is, I beg to assure your Grace, the very sincere prayer of, *etc.*

Draft reply 23 April 1834. The Duke of Wellington presents his compliments to [Mr. Sharpe]. He will have great pleasure in attending the presentation of the petition from Doncaster to the House of Lords to be presented by the Archbishop of York.

Wellington to the Mayor of Cork, 22 April 1834

Compliments. The Duke has received the letter of the Mayor of Cork and the paper sent therewith upon the Irish Reform Act. The Duke is perfectly aware of the mischiefs effected by the Reform Acts. But he has not heard of any intention of altering them; nor, indeed, does he believe that it is in the power of any set of men to make an alteration even if so disposed.

The Rev. Edward Burton to Wellington, 24 April 1834

Oxford. I should not have taken the liberty of adding anything to the printed declaration which I have the honor to enclose, but having acted as chairman of the committee, to whom the publication of the declaration was entrusted, I was requested to state to your Grace that it has been signed almost unanimously by the tutors and other persons 'immediately connected with the instruction and discipline of the place'. There are really not above seven or eight persons who have declined signing it, and I never remember any occasion on which so strong or unanimous a feeling has been shewn in Oxford. No application was made to the heads of houses, because it rests with them to prepare a petition to the legislature, and it was thought best that the declaration should be signed only by those who are practically concerned in tuition. I may add that our declaration has been adopted by the members of Convocation generally, who are now signing it rapidly.

Wellington to the Rev. Edward Burton, 25 April 1834

London. I have received your letter of the 24th instant and I quite concur in all the principles of the declaration which you have sent me so shortly, so ably, and so distinctly expressed. I quite concur likewise in the opinion which you express of the consequences of a departure from the system hitherto pursued at Oxford.

I don't mean to censure the declaration when I state that I should not have recommended its adoption at the present moment. My feeling may be formed in some degree in the fact that I am not, as you and the subscribers are, involved in the consequences which possibly may attend this declaration, excepting in the same degree with the rest of the public. It may likewise be influenced a little by notions regarding parliamentary tactics. But I must add that the declaration does honor to the University of Oxford, whatever may be its consequences.

The Rev. George Rowley to Wellington, 25 April 1834

Oxford. I have the honor to inform you that we are preparing petitions to both Houses of Parliament against the bill for removing obstacles to the admission of Dissenters into the universities. The form will, I expect, be agreed on tomorrow, and I will forward it to your Grace. The petitions themselves will be proposed in Convocation on Tuesday next, and on their passing, I will transmit that for the Lords, in hopes that your Grace will have the goodness to present it at such time as you may judge expedient. I have seen the Dean of Christ Church, and beg leave to suggest that it would facilitate arrangements, if your Grace's proposed communication to him were made without longer delay. I have also secured the requisite accommodation for the horses etc.

Wellington to the Rev. George Rowley, 26 April 1834

London. I have this morning received your letter of the 25th instant. I do not know whether a bill has yet been presented to the House of Commons in consequence of the motion made by Mr. Wood as an amendment to the resolution moved by another member, and carried. If such bill has been entertained by the House of Commons, I don't think that it is customary, nay I believe that it is contrary to order for the House of Lords to receive a petition against the enactments of such bill, till it will have passed the House of Commons, and will have been sent to the House of Lords for their concurrence. There [are] undoubtedly numerous, nay daily departures from such a course; but I should doubt the expediency of exposing a petition from such a corporation as the University of Oxford to the observation that the reception of the petition would be a breach of order. This statement however only refers to my own conduct and course in respect to the presentation of the petition. There can be no doubt of the expediency of a petition to the House of Lords from the university upon this subject, and with the permission of the university I will present it at the moment at which it will be most advisable.

Wellington to the Marquess of Londonderry, 27 April 1834

London. I think that it appears that Sir John Campbell, having been dismissed from the service of the King of Portugal by the Cortes and having returned to Portugal after six years absence in 1830, was no longer and did not consider himself in the Portuguese service at his return. It cannot be said, however, that he did not carry arms in the service of Don Miguel. He certainly took part in the war, as many others did, and he is therefore guilty of a breach of the Foreign Enlistment Act. This is a venial offence in the eyes of Government, but I cannot consider it so. Whether venial or otherwise, however, it is one in his quality of British subject and the Government are bound to protect him so far as to take care that justice is fairly administered towards him in any trial to which the Portuguese Government should think proper that he should be subjected, on account of having served against them, that it should not be delayed and that the punishment whatever it may be should be moderate. I do not think that the cause of Sir John Campbell will be promoted by bringing forward that subject in the House of Lords. Indeed those who think as I do upon the Foreign Enlistment Act must blame his conduct, although they may think and express the opinion that Government ought to endeavour to have justice done to him.

However you must do as you may think proper; if you should bring forward the subject, I will take my station in the discussion if necessary.

The Rev. George Rowley to Wellington, 28 April 1834

Oxford. I was not able to fulfil my promise of forwarding a draft of the petition by last night's post, as the form was not finally settled till this morning. It will be proposed in Convocation tomorrow, and I hope to forward the document itself to be presented whenever your Grace may judge it expedient.

Wellington to the Rev. George Rowley

I have received your letter and the copy of the petition to the House of Lords intended to be proposed in Convocation. I quite concur in it.

Send it to me when convenient to you. But it cannot be presented to the House of Lords till the bill will come up from the House of Commons.

Undated.

The Rev. George Rowley to Wellington, 29 April 1834

Oxford. I have the honor to inform your Grace that the petition passed this morning in a very full Convocation with one dissentient vote, and I shall forward it by this night's post.

We shall of course feel obliged by your Grace's determining the proper time for presenting it to the House of Lords.

Wellington to Lord Wharncliffe, 29 April 1834

London. I write to you one line upon the course which you are about to take on Thursday. I will do everything in my power to insure a full attendance. Would it be desirable to enter the proxies on that occasion? You laid upon the table yesterday some petitions which it appears to me impossible that the House should not take into consideration and attend to in the committee and I conclude that the forms of the House will allow of counsel being heard in favour of these petitions in that stage of the bill, supposing that it should pass through the second reading. I cannot be so good a judge of this case as you who have attended to it. But it appears to me that the bill being one of pains and penalties, the House of Lords ought not to read it a second time without proof of the charges recited in the preamble, and that to consider even of the second reading without having such proof is a departure from principle which may become a dangerous precedent. I admit that it may be very inconvenient and expensive to the parties to defend themselves against the charge at the bar of the House of Lords, particularly if they or their friends have reason to believe that the case against them is so feeble that the House will, upon the argument, reject the bill upon the second reading. But I don't think that that consideration ought to influence the course of the House itself which, seeing upon the first reading that the bill is one of pains and penalties, ought before it proceeds to consider of the enactments of the bill in the second reading insist upon the proof of the recital in the preamble.

Frederick Augustus Carrington to Wellington, 29 April 1834

15 Clifford's Inn. As the Poor Law Bill brought in by Lord Althorp will produce a very considerable effect against the landed interest perhaps a few facts showing some of the defects of it may be not unacceptable to your Grace.

I will not trouble your Grace with any observations on those parts of the measure in which I have no practical knowledge but will advert to the proposed alterations in the law of settlement.

It is proposed to make birth the only settlement after the age of 16 except in married women. The obvious effect of this will be to throw an immense additional burden on the agricultural parishes and off the great manufacturing towns because there are thousands born in country parishes who go, and pass the best part of their lives in the great towns and become paupers in their old age, and I should say hardly units who being born in a manufacturing town become paupers in an agricultural parish.

If your Grace were to have a return of the paupers in any workhouse of a large London parish, you would find, I have no doubt, a great number of country born paupers, but if a similar return was made from the workhouses of a hundred agricultural parishes, you would probably not find one London born pauper and if that be so it is manifest that the great town will rid itself of a number of those whom it is bound to maintain under the present law of settlement (by hiring and service renting etc.) and send them to the various agricultural parishes in which they were born.

This settlement by birth will, it is said, cost the parishes a good deal of law expenses in appeals; I doubt the fact. What is more likely to be disputed and uncertain than where an obscure individual of some considerable age was born? It is the only material fact connected with his life of which he can have no personal knowledge and what he has been told by anyone else is not legal evidence nor is the parish register of baptisms; indeed if the latter was so it would lead to innumerable frauds.

To try to remedy the difficulty the bill provides that where the pauper is first known to be shall be taken to be the place of his birth. Is not this a good field for contradictory evidence?

However, I would take it, for the sake of argument, that there would be some saving in the amount paid for parish appeals; but is your Grace aware how very small the expense of parish appeals is in the agricultural parishes? A parish appeal costs each parish engaged in it from £20 to £30, depending on the distance which the witnesses have to travel to the town where the sessions are held, and the number of them.

As to the frequency of appeals I would instance the county of Gloucester, which is a large county partly agricultural and partly manufacturing. In that county there are, if I mistake not, 370 parishes and places maintaining their own poor and the number of parish appeals heard there is about 30 in a year, which is not one appeal a year to every ten parishes taking them one with another, and as the manufacturing places have so great a proportion of the paupers and consequently of the appeals I have little doubt that the agricultural parishes would not have an appeal each above once in every ten or fifteen years, and perhaps some of them not so often as that. In Berkshire the appeals touching the settlement of paupers are also a dozen a year among all the parishes in the county.

Perhaps I here ought to guard your Grace against an error that you may fall into respecting the number of appeals before stated. It may be said that at the last Berkshire sessions there were more than twenty appeals in the list. True; but of those the greater part are never tried and are therefore only entered on the list at the expense of a few shillings. Your Grace may perhaps ask why enter an appeal in the list if it is not to be tried. The reason is this: the order of magistrates removing a pauper is conclusively binding on the parish he is removed to as to the settlement of that pauper and of everyone having a derivation settlement under him, unless it be appealed against. Not to be thus concluded the parish to which a pauper is removed wish to make enquiries and as the appeal *must* be entered at the *next* sessions they enter it in the list and get an order to postpone the hearing of it to the following sessions which costs very little. Between the one sessions and the other enquiries are made and, if the parish removed to are satisfied, they give notice to the other party that they shall not prosecute the appeal and no further expense is incurred, or perhaps they convince the other parish officers that the removal was improper and they consent to abandon the order.

Another proposed alteration is to make the unsuccessful parish pay the costs of the appeal to the successful parish *at all events*. This is decidedly impolitic; at present whether the losing party shall pay costs to the other party or whether each party shall pay their own costs is in the discretion of the court of quarter sessions and this discretion is most beneficially exercised at present in preventing vexatious conduct in the parish officers and attornies.

I will mention two cases within my own knowledge. In the first the bench divided thirteen to fifteen on the question as to which party ought to succeed in the appeal. Of course the fifteen carried it but all were unanimously of opinion that the losing party ought not to pay the costs of the other as so large a portion of the bench thought that the losing party ought to have succeeded in the appeal.

The other case was one in which it was necessary to give evidence of a written agreement which had been signed in the presence of a subscribing witness. By law it was necessary (if insisted on) that the subscribing witness should attend the hearing of the appeal and prove that he saw the agreement signed; however, as the appeal was to be heard at Newbury and the witness was in Cumberland the opposite party were desired to consent to the agreement being given in evidence without the attendance of the witness. This was not acceded to and the witness came from Cumberland but the court of quarter sessions thought that this was so very vexatious that they fixed the parish that would not dispense with the witness's attendance with all the costs of the appeal.

Wellington to J. C. Richards, 1 May 1834

London. I have had the honor of receiving your letter and I have communicated with the Duke of Gloucester upon the subject of the presentation to the King of the petition to which you refer.

His Royal Highness will present to His Majesty the petition intended for the King in his closet as is his Royal Highness's invariable custom. But if his Royal Highness was to present it in any other manner it could not be presented as you propose without a breach of His Majesty's commands stating the mode in which he would receive the petitions of his subjects and even the law of the country.

I will take care to attend in the House of Lords the presentation of the petition by the Duke of Gloucester, but that cannot be received in the House of Lords till the bill which is the object of its prayer will have passed the House of Commons and will be on the table of the House of Lords.

Addressed to: J. C. Richards, Bristol.

Wellington to Don Ramon Luis Escobedo, [2] May 1834

I am much gratified by the receipt of your letter and happy that the circumstances of your country are such as to enable you to return to it.

Since the unfortunate occurrences in Spain in the years from 1820 to the year 1823 I have done everything in my power whether as an individual or in my official capacity as the King's Minister to relieve the Spaniards who were the sufferers.

They were so numerous that the resources even of this state could not afford to give relief to all. To none was there given more than what would have been insufficient even for bare subsistence for any but men inured to habits of oeconomy and temperance; and who were here only because the performance of what they considered their duty had obliged them to quit their native country.

It gives me great satisfaction to learn from you that you think that I performed my duty in the efforts which I made to obtain for and to protect the Spaniards in the enjoyment of the bounty of His Majesty up to the period at which I quitted office in the year 1830. I must do them the justice to say in reply to your letter that the Spaniards have conducted themselves in the most exemplary manner in this country; and that they have in every respect merited the good opinion and the esteem of all.

Undated. Lord Fitzroy Somerset's letter enclosing a Spanish translation of the above is dated 3 May.

Wellington to William Ward, 2 May 1834

London. I am very sorry that I was not at home when you did me the favour of calling yesterday.

The orders of the House of Lords prevent the presentation of a petition against a bill which is under discussion in the House of Commons. But if the bill for the admission of Dissenters to degrees in the universities should come under discussion in the House of Lords I will present the petition of the Bachelors of Arts and undergraduates with great satisfaction.

The Rev. George Rowley to Wellington, 2 May 1834

Oxford. I have the honor to forward a copy of a declaration which we have just issued.

First enclosure: (1) Printed paper, declarations of members of the University of Oxford, and of heads of houses and proctors, against the bill for the admission of Dissenters to degrees in the universities.

Second enclosure: Manuscript copy of declaration of heads of houses and proctors, as above.

The Rev. Vaughan Thomas to Wellington, 2 May 1834

Committee room. I do not present myself before your Grace as a public functionary of your Grace's university, but as one who during forty-two years' residence in Oxford has been variously connected with it by the different academic offices, tutorial or disciplinarian which he has held during that time. Neither do I now state these particulars for any other purpose than to give some degree of weight to my present communication.

The Declaration of Approval and Concurrence which has been so extensively patronized, may be said to have arisen out of an honest impetuosity of purpose overstepping the rules and usages of the place, but producing effects the most surprising upon the feelings and opinions of the academic body in and out of this place: even the utmost universal attestation of their censure and indignation against the tyrannical provisions of the bill.

My object in addressing your Grace is simply and shortly to state the results of the communications made to me by letter or otherwise from absent members of Convocation touching their wishes to have their names subscribed to the Oxford declaration. As chairman of this committee I have by proxy signed the names of 521 out of the 690 names which have been transmitted from the country for signature. The general results this day, Friday, 4 o'clock, stand thus:

Heads of colleges	20
The two proctors	2
Educational and disciplinarian members of the university	88
Approving and concurring members of Convocation and bachelors of civil law	690
	800

Thus 800 academics in one week from April 24th to May 2nd have declared under their hands their feelings and opinions upon this iniquitous measure.

I ought to add that the declaration of the heads of houses is signed by all in Oxford; the Provost of Worcester College is absent, being in residence on his deanery of Exeter; the Warden of New College and the Warden of All Souls are both out of Oxford; and the Rectorship of Lincoln is now vacant by the recent decease of Dr. Tatham.

Draft reply 3 May 1834. Compliments. The Duke has received his letter and returns his thanks for the interesting information which it contains.

Francis Ewart to Wellington, 3 May 1834

87 Jermyn Street, St. James's. Lord Londonderry having given notice that he intends to ask an explanation from Ministers on the subject of the incarceration of Sir John Campbell at Lisbon and which will, I presume, lead to some observations on the policy pursued by Government towards Portugal, I take the liberty of conveying to your Grace a few remarks upon the decree lately issued at Lisbon by Don Pedro.

Your Grace can well appreciate the advantages which England has enjoyed since her intimate alliance with Portugal, advantages to which she probably was well intitled, derived under the custom laws of that country, by which British goods were admitted at an ad valorem duty of *fifteen per cent.*, whilst the goods of all other nations excepting Brazil paid an ad valorem duty of *thirty per cent.*

Now I think that it cannot be denied that this was a most *valuable* advantage and that we have in consequence enjoyed a monopoly of trade, this country having almost totally supplied the Portuguese with manufactures.

Without loading this question by entering into the merits of the contest at present devastating that unhappy country, I will proceed as briefly as possible to point out to your Lordship the consequences likely to be produced by the decree, the effect of which is to place all other countries on the same footing as ourselves.

It would be a waste of time to attempt to shew how much the commerce of England will suffer. I will content myself with *asserting* that the trade of this country with Portugal will suffer materially in consequence of this decree, and few will be bold enough to deny this assertion.

This decree then reduces the duty upon the productions of other nations fifteen per cent. ad valorem while it gives no equivalent to England or in other words *to increase the duty on British goods fifteen per cent.* ad valorem without imposing a corresponding increase upon the productions of other countries.

If then this decree has a tendency to promote the commerce of other nations it follows that it must be detrimental to ours; and, if not intended to promote the commerce of other nations, why issue the decree? Some deep diplomacy has been at work: *it is* intended to promote the commerce of other nations at the expence of England's. Oh! Ingratitude art thou to be found concealed in the bosom of kings and princes? Where would Don Pedro have been if he had not been supplied with men and stores by England? if he had not been supplied with money from England? if he had not had the countenance and co-operation of the British Government? He would not have been in a situation to strike a blow at British interests by an audacious decree. Foster a snake in thy bosom and he will sting thee.

I cannot suppose that the Government will not notice this infamous, not less infamous than ungrateful and not less ungrateful than impolitic proceeding on the part of the Portuguese Government. Surely the manufacturing interest of this country is already in a sufficiently depressed state and can ill support the additional burthen which this decree will inevitably inflict: and it is not the manufacturing interest only that will suffer by this *act of gratitude*, but also the agricultural, for it is a principle of political economy clearly defined that the manufacturing and agricultural interests are inseparable. What affects the one will also affect the other.

It appears to me that it is either an inducement held out to Russia, Prussia and Austria to acknowledge the Government of Donna Maria, or that it is the effect of French intrigue, in either case evincing a *disposition* to sacrifice the interests of England at the shrine of expediency. The Treaty of Constantinople ought to teach those whose duty it is to watch over the commercial interests of this country to be wary.

PS. Since writing the inclosed I have read the article in *The Times* of today upon this subject and think that your Grace will have little difficulty in defining the motives which seem to have actuated the writer. Commercial men are not to be gulled by such sophistry; the arguments might be somewhat more applicable if the two countries were situated alike, but in the present case the one is supported and propped by the other. It ought not to be forgotten that England has been mainly instrumental in establishing the power which now directs its decree against her commercial interests.

Draft reply 5 May 1834. Compliments. The Duke has received Mr. Ewart's letter upon the subject of Portugal for which he returns his thanks.

Wellington to the Rev. George Rowley, 3 May 1834

London. I am much obliged to you for your letter of the 2nd, which I have received. You will probably have seen my letter to Dr. Burton upon the declaration of the members of the university etc. If not I will send you a copy. I quite concur in the declaration of the heads of houses.

Lord Fitzroy Somerset to Wellington, 3 May 1834

Stanhope Street. I send you a Spanish translation of your letter to Don Ramon Luis Escobedo. I have not been in the habit of troubling you with the letters of the Spaniards, but in justice to them I ought to mention that hardly one of them has taken his departure without expressing his thanks for the kindness he has received in this country and without mentioning in a peculiar manner his sense of the support and protection for which they are indebted to you. Several of the letters are addressed to you and were kept with other papers on the subject.

The Rev. George Rowley to Wellington, 4 May 1834

Oxford. I have this morning called on Dr. Burton, who shewed me your Grace's note. The declaration of tutors etc. was first put forward (mainly, I believe, by Dr. B.) without any communication with the weekly board, the more influential members of which, as well as myself, had we been consulted, would probably have disapproved. It was not, however, judged expedient to express any dissent under circumstances which could not then be controlled, and we were, therefore, compelled to proceed with as great an appearance of unanimity as possible. I should doubtless incur much blame in various quarters, were it known that I make this communication to your Grace; it must, therefore, be considered as quite confidential. But it ought to be understood that the heads of houses, generally, are answerable for nothing but their own declaration, the necessity of which was imposed upon them by the proceedings of others.

Mr. Hughes Hughes is to move tomorrow for a return of the monies received and paid by the Treasury (during the three last years) on account of the universities. The payments from this place, and I believe also from Cambridge, are as I think some what more than double the salaries voted to the professors. The object is to negative the assertion of Mr. Roebuck.

The Dean of Ripon (James Webber) to Wellington, 5 May 1834

Deanery, Ripon. I have taken the liberty to direct a memorial to His Majesty to be sent to your Grace's care by this day's post. It is signed by all the members of the two universities, the magistracy and almost every respectable person in this town and neighbourhood.

The purport of it is the earnest request of those who sign it that His Majesty will be graciously pleased to listen to their prayer and reject the bill which is now passing through the House of Commons to enable Dissenters to graduate at either of our universities.

It was thought advisable to express ourselves by a memorial rather than by a declaration and we respectfully beg to leave it to your Grace's judgement when it should be presented to His Majesty.

We have sent also to the committee in London the declaration of the laity in this town and neighbourhood of attachment to the Established Church.

It is signed by 3,446 persons of great respectability.

Draft reply 7 May 1834. Compliments. The Duke has received his letter and the memorial which the Dean has sent him. The Duke will present the latter to the King this day at the levee.

Wellington to Sir Henry Hardinge, 6 May 1834

London. My agents have mentioned to me that Mr. Walter of *The Times* and certain other Radicals are about to oppose on the Hampshire committee, of which you are a member, the Kingsclere enclosure bill in which I am interested.

The committee meet tomorrow and I shall be very much obliged to you if you will attend. Of course I desire nothing but what may be just.

PS. Lord Norreys, Mr. Herbert, Goulburn are members as well as you.

I have spoken to Lord Chandos and Conolly; and have written to W. Bankes.

VISCOUNT HARDINGE PAPERS

Wellington to the Rev. George Rowley, 7 May 1834

London. I have received your letter of the 4th, of which I consider the contents to be confidential. The principal objection which I feel to the declaration is that it places the two universities on different grounds, nay on grounds opposed to each other; of which the enemies of the Church will take advantage in discussion. Indeed the difference between the two had been noticed already in debate; and its continuance stated to be unnecessary. However the declaration is already making a great impression in the country; and is producing a good effect.

The Rev. Thomas Turton to Wellington, 10 May 1834

Cambridge. I have taken the liberty of forwarding to your Grace a few copies of a pamphlet on the admission of Dissenters to degrees in our universities. Before it was sent to the printer, I read it to a person in whose judgement I have the greatest confidence; and he was of opinion that it would do good in the present emergency.

Draft reply 11 May 1834. Compliments. The Duke has received his letter and his pamphlet which he will peruse with much interest.

The Rev. John Manby to Wellington, 11 May 1834

Vicarage, Lancaster. Speaking only as an Oxford man, I beg with all deference to assure your Grace I should not have presumed to have troubled you with the petition going by the same post as this, had you not been lately chosen the Chancellor of our university. In that dignified character, therefore, it is that I humbly intreat your Grace to present the same to your right honorable house the first favorable opportunity, together with numberless others, which no doubt you will be entrusted with, all tending to the same point. And may our united prayers have the desired effect is the sincere wish of, *etc.*

Docketed by Wellington Compliments to Mr. Manby. The Duke has received his note and the petition of the inhabitants of Lancaster. . . . the same as the letter to Knighton. *Docketed by secretary* Done. May 13th 1834.

The Rev. Thomas Collins to Wellington, 11 May 1834

Knaresborough. Your Grace will receive by the same post as takes this a petition of the inhabitants of this town and neighbourhood against the admission of Dissenters to the universities, which your Grace will have the goodness to present to the House of Lords at some fit opportunity.

In obtaining signatures to it I have purposely abstained from soliciting any but educated persons.

Docketed by Wellington Compliments to Mr Collins. The same as to Mr. Manby. *Docketed by secretary* Done. May 13th.

Brisco Owen to Wellington, May 1834

Beaumaris. I take the liberty of forwarding to your Grace by this day's post a petition signed by the most respectable inhabitants of the parish of Beaumaris, against the proposed bill for the admission of Dissenters into the universities with a request that your Grace will be pleased to present the same in the House of Lords and support its prayer.

Docketed by Wellington Compliments to Mr. Brisco Owen. The same as to Mr. Manby. *Docketed by secretary* Done. May 13th 1834.

Lady Salisbury's diary, 11 May 1834

Peel told Lord Aberdeen in whom he has great confidence, the other day, that he preferred his present situation, occupying an elevated position and enjoying great influence in the House of Commons independent of any party, to any that he could possess as part of a ministry, and that his own personal inclination was to remain there. Lord Aberdeen replied that he ought to consider that however personally agreeable to himself, such a situation could not be permanent, nor was it desirable for the country that it should. On my replying to the Duke that this was only one proof more that notwithstanding his great many talents and valuable qualities Peel's leading motive was *self*, he said that no one could suppose that if he or Peel consulted their own convenience they should wish to take the government under the present circumstances, that patronage and what one called the 'sweets of office' had ceased to exist, and that difficult as was the position of a minister three years ago, the difficulties, and chances of failure, were now at least trebled:—therefore nothing but a sense of duty could lead him or any Conservative to undertake the Administration. I regretted that Sir G. Murray had been led to make such concessions to the sentiments of the Dissenters in his speeches at the Perthshire election. It is a great pity, said the Duke, and bad policy. No man ever profits by disguising his real sentiments in the end.

He told me that at the levee the other day Peel passed by all the deputation from the University of Oxford who were attending the Duke without taking the least notice of them, with one exception, that of the provost of Merton, a strong Whig, but who happened to be the man who proposed Peel as a candidate for the chancellorship. If it was an accident it was an odd one, if not, it was a curious proof of the *cotton twist.* But it is evident to me that some influence is at work to make the worst of all Peel does in the eyes of the Duke and to persuade him that he intends to slight or neglect him in trifles where I am sure no such intention exists. I suspect it is the Arbuthnots. Hardinge has begged of us to ask Peel and the Duke to meet each other: but one is so accustomed to be courted, and the other has so much sensitiveness and plebian pride that they are easily led to take mutual offence. However Peel is daily of more importance in the country and its fate in a great measure must rest in his hands. The Duke seems to think, as do many others, that the battle will be fought on the ground between the Church and the Dissenters: the latter have at least played their game most imprudently and discovered their real views much too soon.

The Rev. Walter Posthumus Powell to Wellington, 12 May 1834

Grammar School, Evesham. By this post I transmit to your Grace a petition from the parish of Great and Little Hampton, of which I am incumbent, against the admission of Dissenters to the universities. I only trouble your Grace because the names are few. The parish is small and *every* payer to Church and poor has signed it with two exceptions: the one a Roman Catholic, who was unasked; the other a half-pay officer, who declined on that account himself but ordered his son to sign it.

Docketed by Wellington Compliments to Mr. Powell. The same as to Mr. Manby. *Docketed by secretary* Done. May 13th 1834.

The Rev. Edward Barnard to Wellington, 12 May 1834

Rectory House, Alverstoke. Mr. Barnard presents his respectful compliments to his Grace the Duke of Wellington, and will be much obliged to his Grace if he will have the goodness to present the enclosed petition to the house of peers.

Docketed by Wellington Compliments to Mr. Barnard. The same as to Mr. Manby. *Docketed by secretary* Done. May 13th.

John Cobb to Wellington, 13 May 1834

Hawkhurst. I am desired to transmit to your Grace the inclosed petition from this parish against the bill now pending in Parliament for the admission of Dissenters to the universities and to request that your Grace will do the petitioners the honor to present the same to the House of Lords.

I beg to assure your Grace that the petitioners are all persons of great respectability and intelligence and that it contains the signatures of (with but few exceptions) all those in the parish who are capable of understanding the subject.

Docketed by Wellington The same answer as to the others. *Docketed by secretary* Done. May 17th 1834.

The Rev. Edward Grevile Ruddock to Wellington, 13 May 1834

Westbury, Wells, Somerset. I take the liberty of forwarding to your Grace, as Chancellor of the University of Oxford, and a firm supporter of existing institutions, a petition from the inhabitants of Westbury, Somerset, against the admission of Dissenters to the universities, which the petitioners will feel obliged by your presenting and supporting in the House of Lords.

Signed: Edward G. Ruddock, curate of Westbury.

Docketed by Wellington The same as Mr. Manby. *Docketed by secretary* Done. May 14th.

The Rev. Richard Cutler to Wellington, 13 May 1834

Dorchester. The gentlemen whose names are attached to the petitions which will be forwarded to you by the mail this evening request the favour of your presenting them in the House of Lords, either separately or as the general petition from the county of Dorset of gentlemen formerly educated at the English universities, according as your Grace thinks most advisable. I cannot state the exact amount of the signatures as the sheets lie in different districts, and will be sent direct to London; but from my correspondence with the managers of the petition in the different parts of the county, I am happy to say the feeling against admitting Dissenters is unanimous.

Docketed by Wellington The same as Mr. Manby. *Docketed by secretary* Done. May 14th 1834.

The Rev. Edward Pellew to Wellington, 13 May 1834

Great Yarmouth. I take the liberty of sending to your Grace a petition of the clergy in and about the town of Great Yarmouth, in the county of Norfolk, against the admission of Dissenters to the privilege of obtaining degrees at either of our universities. We trust your Grace will take an early opportunity of presenting it in the House of Lords.

If your Grace would be kind enough to add the following names which could not be obtained in time to send off the petition, so as to be presented by Mr. Goulburn in the House of Commons on Wednesday next, and which I have received full permission to affix; and therefore of course, your Grace, I think I may venture to say the petition will be *unanimously* as well as *most respectably* signed by the clergy in this archdeaconry, though in consequence of its being rather a sudden thought the formality of the archdeacon regularly convening a meeting was obliged to be dispensed with.

PS. Rev. William Colby, M.A.; rector of Clippesby.
Rev. Richard Aldous Arnold; rector of Ellough.
Rev. Thomas Ellison; rector of Toft Monks and Haddiscoe.
Rev. Edward Barker Frere; curate of St. Lawrence.
Rev. Thomas Bewicke, M.A.; of Bungay.
Rev. James Safford, A.B.; vicar of Mettingham.
Rev. Bartholomew Ritson, M.A.; of Lowestoft.
Rev. James Symonds, A.B.; curate of Ormesby.
Rev. Edward Thurlow; rector of Lound.
Rev. N. Thomas Orgill Leman; rector of Worlingham.
Rev. George Orgill Leman; curate of Stoven.
Rev. James Carlos; vicar of Frostenden.

Docketed by Wellington The same as to Mr. Manby. *Docketed by secretary* Done. May 14th.

The Rev. Charles Abel Heurtley to Wellington, 13 May 1834

Corpus Christi College, Oxford. I take the liberty of sending to your Grace a petition from some of the inhabitants of the parish of Cropredy, Oxfordshire, with the request that your Grace will be pleased to present it to the House of Lords, at such time as you shall judge convenient.

I ought perhaps to mention that none of the signatures attached are those of persons belonging to the labouring classes. It was thought better not to apply to such persons in a question, of the merits of which they perhaps could not so readily be expected to judge. Of those who were applied to, I believe that not more than two or three declined to sign.

Signed: C. A. Heurtley, curate.

Docketed by Wellington The same as Mr. Manby. *Docketed by secretary* Done. May 14th.

Thomas Dashwood to Wellington, 13 May 1834

Sturminster Newton. I have the honor to send your Grace by this post a petition signed by gentlemen educated at Oxford and Cambridge, residing in this town and neighbourhood, against the admission of Dissenters to the universities and also a similar petition signed by persons who were not educated at either of those universities and I beg to inform your Grace that the petitioners will be obliged by your Grace's presenting the petitions and supporting the prayer thereof.

Docketed by Wellington The same as Mr. Manby. *Docketed by secretary* Done. May 14th, 1834.

The Rev. John Richard Rushton to Wellington, 13 May 1834

Banbury. A petition having been signed by nearly 200 members of the Established Church resident in the parish of Banbury, praying that the bill for the admission of Dissenters to the universities of England may not pass into a law, I have taken the liberty of forwarding it by this evening's post to your Grace, in the confidence that you will not refuse to gratify the petitioners by presenting it (at whatever time may appear to your Grace most seasonable) to the right honourable House to which it is addressed. Among the petitioners are men of almost every variety of political opinion. Persons who, during the ferment and excitement of the last two or three years, were furiously opposed to each other have on the present occasion united in a very remarkable and (to me) very gratifying manner in petitioning the legislature against a measure fraught, as they conceive, with the most fatal consequences to the venerable establishment of which they are members, and to the interests of sound religion generally. A similar petition to the House of Commons was sent to Sir Robert H. Inglis last week.

Upon your Grace, under Divine Providence, are chiefly fixed the hopes and dependence of the friends of our yet remaining establishments in the present season of gloom and peril. With my hearty and fervent prayers that you may long live to enjoy the fame of your unrivalled achievements over the enemies of your country in foreign lands, and to be the champion and bulwark of our best and most sacred institutions against the attempts of the noisy and designing levellers at home, permit me to subscribe myself, *etc.*

Docketed by Wellington The same as Mr. Manby. *Docketed by secretary* Done. May 14th 1834.

Thomas Dashwood to Wellington, 14 May 1834

Sturminster. I have again the honor to send your Grace the petition from the town of Stalbridge and its neighbourhood against the admission of Dissenters to the universities; your Grace's presenting the petition and supporting the prayer thereof will be esteemed a favor.

Docketed by Wellington The same as Mr. Manby. *Docketed by secretary* Done. May 16th.

George Whieldon to Wellington, 14 May 1834

Wilton Place, near Daventry. The friends of the Church in Daventry and various neighbouring parishes in this part of the county of Northampton are anxious to testify their zeal in supporting its chief bulwarks by petitioning the legislature that the two universities of Oxford and Cambridge may be protected from the fatal measures now sought for by the Dissenters and their hostile coadjutors of every denomination and on behalf of the inhabitants of the parish of Welton who have signed the petition to the House of Lords, I take the liberty of transmitting that document to your Grace as a distinguished champion of our once glorious constitution in Church and State, for presentation to the Houses—and I have written to the Earl of Winchilsea to request his Lordship will support its prayers.

Docketed by Wellington The same as Mr Manby. *Docketed by secretary* Done. May 16th, 1834.

The Rev. Daniel Tremlett to Wellington, 14 May 1834

Rodney Stoke, Somersetshire. As the clergyman of Rodney Stoke I have taken the liberty of forwarding to your Grace a petition signed by all the yeomanry in the parish and nearly all the signatures are of persons who have votes for the county. Some few of the names are from the parish of Wookey where they have no petition but were desirous of expressing their sentiments on the bill before the House of Commons.

There is a slight informality I fear in putting 'The humble petition' etc. before 'The Right Hon. the Lords' etc. but not sufficient I trust to cause the rejection of the petition.

The influence your Grace possesses both in the House and out of it and your sentiments on the subject will I hope be a sufficient apology for the liberty I take in requesting your Grace to have the goodness to take charge of it and present it whenever your Grace may think best. A similar petition to the Commons I have requested our county Member Mr. Miles to present.

69 *signatures.*

Docketed by Wellington The same as Mr. Manby. *Docketed by secretary* Done. May 16th 1834.

The committee of management of the London and Southampton Railway Company to Wellington, 14 May 1834

King's Arms Hotel, Palace Yard. A deputation from the committee of management of the London and Southampton Railway Company consisting of:
The honourable P. B. de Blaquiere
Lieutenant-Colonel Henderson
Captain Stephens, R.N.
to wait upon his Grace the Duke of Wellington and to request his Grace will be pleased, as Lord Lieutenant of the County of Hampshire, to move the second reading of their bill in the House of Lords.

Wellington to the committee of management of the London and Southampton Railway Company, 14 May 1834

Compliments. The Duke will not give the deputation from the committee of management of the London and Southampton Railway the trouble of calling upon him.

The Duke feels that he cannot take upon himself to move the second reading of the Southampton Railway Bill in the House of Lords and it would be unpardonable in him to give the gentlemen the trouble of calling upon him.

Wellington to the Earl of Aberdeen, 16 May 1834

London. I am inclined to believe that Don Pedro has consented to ratify the Quadruple Treaty; but that the ratifications were delayed in order that some form might be gone through in the Council of State. That is what I heard yesterday.

I made enquiries respecting the form of communication to Parliament. The papers will be laid on the tables of the two houses printed and by command of the King without motion. A motion must be made if any discussion upon the treaty should be desired.

I should think it very desirable for us to avoid to call upon the House of Lords to give any opinion upon the treaty; but we might have a discussion upon the subject without calling upon the House for an opinion: that is, by moving for a paper.

It remains to be considered whether it is desirable to take that course, in which I am ready to embark if you should think it desirable. This will involve the whole policy of the Government in respect to the Peninsula.

Let me know what you think upon it. I think that it will not be difficult to shew that their course has been inconsistent and erroneous, and has led to the existing evils, without pledging oneself, much less the House, to an alteration of whatever may be found to be settled.

ADD MS 43060, ff. 106, 107. *Copy in Wellington Papers.*

The Earl of Aberdeen to Wellington, 18 May 1834

Leamington. If the Quadruple Treaty should be ratified by Don Pedro, and laid on the table of the House, which now appears probable, it may certainly be proper to consider in what manner we ought to deal with it. The great objection to discussing a question of this nature, on a motion for some paper remotely connected with it, seems to me, that we neither do justice to the importance of the subject, nor to our own sincerity. If

535

we say what we think of the transaction, and are really sincere in what we express, we ought naturally to do something more than move for some insignificant paper, to the production of which there is no objection. I recollect some time ago, moving for some papers relating to certain proceedings at Terceira and the Western Islands, but meaning to discuss the whole situation of Portugal; and I thought that it gave Lord Grey great advantage in the debate. It is true that, with respect to such a treaty as that which has recently been signed, it is the duty of the Government, and would formerly have been their practice, to call upon the House to address the King; but we cannot compel them to do this, and they will take good care to be silent until they come for assistance to execute its provisions.

If it should be unwise for us to call upon the House for a vote respecting the merits of the treaty itself, which I am far from denying, I am inclined to think that, with the present indifference of the publick to these matters, we shall not gain much by opening the discussion in the manner proposed. Rather than express the strong opinions we must entertain, under the cover of some unmeaning motion made merely as a peg on which to hang a speech, I should prefer to touch the subject quite incidentally; or even in dealing with a question of real importance, although not immediately connected with it. For instance, in making a substantive motion for papers respecting the result of the Algiers negociation, we might shortly and strongly advert to those which they had laid on the table. The treaty is an additional concession to France; and doubly so, as far as regards Spain, in consequence of the present state of the African coast. In fact, I have always thought that the fate of Algiers was very nearly connected with the interests of the Peninsula.

We may have time to talk further on this subject, as I propose to be in town on Friday evening, and I believe that I am to meet you at dinner on Saturday. The treaty cannot be produced before Thursday or Friday.

The Rev. George Rowley to Wellington, 19 May 1834

Oxford. It appears to me that I cannot fulfil the wishes of the board of heads of houses and proctors in a better way than by transmitting a copy of the resolution passed this morning. I therefore do myself the honor of inclosing it to your Grace.

Enclosure: At a meeting of heads of houses and proctors in the delegates room, May 19, 1834.

Agreed

That the members of this board, under a strong sense of their obligation to the Chancellor of the University for the talent, the energy, and the zeal with which his Grace has recently advocated the cause of our academical institutions, and maintained the vital union between religion and learning, request the Vice-Chancellor to convey, in the most respectful manner, to the Chancellor their unanimous thanks for his exertions in their behalf in a season of peculiar difficulty and danger.

Wellington to the Earl of Aberdeen, 20 May 1834

London. The Government will certainly present their treaty without making any explanation of it.

It is erroneous in policy, and infamous in principle. But I doubt whether we could contend against the policy, at least in relation to the succession of Spain, or pledge ourselves in discussion not to carry into execution the treaty.

It may be a question, therefore, whether we ought to move at all. But I think that the principle is so bad, the interference so monstrous and calculated to lead to such dangers, that it is possible to rouse the publick attention to the subject. I confess, however, that I am very doubtful; and it may possibly be true that there are dangers nearer home upon which a discussion might be more useful.

We did a great deal of good upon the Oude discussion; and we might do some upon this subject.

The mode in which I would propose to proceed would be to ask whether the Ministers intended to make any motion upon the treaty or to give any explanation of it, its policy etc. If answered in the negative, I would then give notice of a motion for explanatory papers.

ADD MS 43060, ff. 108–109.

Don Martin Serrano to Wellington, 20 May 1834

3 Maitland Place, Clapton. When the political events of 1823 hurried me out of Spain, I found under the British laws that protection and personal security which was denied me by my country. On that occasion the noble and generous mind of your Grace was not satisfied with the bare asylum granted by His Majesty's Government to those of my countrymen who like myself were sacrificed to the resentment of the victorious party, but thanks to the powerful intercession and energetic exertions of your Grace, I found that assistance which the ruin of my fortune and future prospects in life compelled me to accept.

Amnestied by Her Majesty the Queen Regent of Spain, I am about to return to my country, but cannot quit these hospitable shores without expressing to your Grace the deep feelings of gratitude and respect I do and must ever entertain.

The Rev. John King to Wellington, 20 May 1834

Leeds. About five years ago when your Grace enjoyed all power and had all the preferment of the Church at your disposal, I wrote to you as an old schoolfellow to give me a small living: such a one as you would hardly think worth the acceptance of any other man. I have now nearly compleated my seventy-third year, and have out-preached all my strength and all my spirits, that retirement and something to retire on would be a great boon and a great relief. But now you have neither power nor patronage: nothing to give, nothing to promise. In the answer you returned to my former application you say, 'The Duke regrets much that he cannot prefer Mr. King in the Church.' I presume these words meant something, though they were scarcely applicable to the time at which they were written, because you could have preferred me if you had been so disposed. I am not such a novice in life, but to know well that a man in the situation you then were could not prefer one in ten that confidently looked up to you for preferment. But I think it is a thousand to one, if another, circumstanced as I was, could have passed before you, old, out of health, labouring, at the moment under great affliction, whose whole life had been spent in extreme labour, hardship and difficulty, without a friend or the prospect of help from anyone. But what is the purport of all this, since whatever you might have done, now you have nothing you can do? Yes, you can do this: *keep me in remembrance*; you will soon be in power again. The present state of things cannot continue; all the common natural relations of life are broken up. Mr. Sadler, of this town, told me the other day in his common confident way of speaking, 'The people of this kingdom will never endure another Tory Administration.' I know they will, and a very short moment will abundantly prove it; extremes meet and the present Administration are working themselves out. Not one single thing have they done but they have done ignorantly and wildly. They thought it right to give more power to the people; they had more than enough before, for their own interest and the peace of society. The angry elements of human nature like the throes that precede an earthquake were always at work, and occasionally something was thrust to the surface sufficient to disturb and annoy us, and very often to frighten and appal us. They (the Ministers) have made a vent and helped forward those throes, and which of God's creatures acquainted with history, his own heart and the prospects before us, but must tremble. We have in this town as kind and compassionate a set of masters as any upon earth, but four thousand of their servants have at this moment refused to work for them, have arrayed themselves with a determined front to insult them, by proclaiming to every ear that will listen to them that they are a set of robbers, oppressors and tyrants. This is the natural growth of the new power given to the mob. Lord Grey was a reader of Roman and Grecian story; from which of these or from what other source of human story did he learn that power was safely to be lodged with the people? It was natural enough when out of office and ambitious to get in that he should prose on this subject, but how he should dare to act upon it is amazing. But he is reaping the bitter fruits and I am mistaken if his grey hairs do not go down with sorrow to the grave. I say again the present order of things cannot long continue. *I* can't make an Administration certainly—and I almost doubt if you can. But I would put you first and Sir Robert Peel second. I suspect his taste does not run after finance; but he ought to be the Chancellor of the Exchequer, because that officer should be the Leader of the House and there certainly is no other man qualified to be one—not your late Chancellor, not indeed one that I am at present aware of in the opposition.

Docketed No answer.

Wellington to the Rev. George Rowley, 21 May 1834

Stratfield Saye. I have received your letter of the 19th and the copy of the resolution of the board of heads of houses inclosed. It gives me great satisfaction to learn that the board approve the course which I have hitherto pursued in relation to the questions under discussion, in which the interests of religion and learning are involved. I hope that we shall bring these discussions to a satisfactory termination.

Wellington to Don Martin Serrano, 21 May 1834

Stratfield Saye. I have had the honor of receiving your letter of the 20th instant and I sincerely congratulate you upon your return to Spain.

When the misfortunes occurred in your country which rendered necessary the departure from thence of yourself, and of many other valuable men, and you sought an asylum in England, it gave me sincere satisfaction to become the instrument in the hands of the late King and his Government to afford to those gentlemen the aid which the resources at His Majesty's disposition could enable him to give.

I wish that that aid could have been larger; or that the number of the gentlemen whose misfortunes required that they should participate of it had been smaller. But small as was the amount to each individual the good order and economy and temperance of your countrymen rendered it sufficient, and gave to these concerned in obtaining this aid the satisfaction of reflecting that they had been instrumental in relieving the misfortunes of men for whom they entertained so much respect.

During a great portion of the time that you have passed in England I was either a member of the Government, or was the King's Minister; and I add with pleasure that during that period I never heard a complaint against one of your countrymen although there were so many of them in London in distressed circumstances.

AUTOGRAPH COLLECTION OF OLIVER WILLIAMS, ESQ.

The Earl of Aberdeen to Wellington, 22 May 1834

Leamington. I do not find by the papers that the ratification is yet arrived from Lisbon; at all events, it is not likely that Lord Grey can lay the treaty on the table of the House before tomorrow. In this case, I would suggest the propriety of saying nothing until you had seen and read the treaty. At present, we are not bound to know anything of its contents. This would give time for some consideration before Monday;

and for a little conversation on the subject, which I should be very glad to have. I am the more desirous of this delay, as my return to town tomorrow is very uncertain, having been so unwell since I came here, that the doctor is by no means disposed to let me out of his hands.

In the event of any motion being made, and a discussion taking place, I apprehend there is no question about the execution of the treaty which can arise in any such discussion. Even if stigmatized by a positive vote of the House, its execution need not be at all affected. We have precedent for this.

The motion, if made by you, whatever may be its terms, must necessarily be important—and may be so in its consequences. Might it not be as well for us to have some conversation with Peel, before the final move?

The impolicy and injustice of the treaty are, no doubt, obvious; but in these times policy and justice are not much considered; and we must not forget that, notwithstanding the principle on which we act, we shall practically be fighting for the unpopular cause of Don Carlos and Don Miguel.

Wellington to the Earl of Aberdeen, 23 May 1834

London. I am very sorry that you are unwell.

No evil can result from waiting to see the treaty before we move upon it; and I am certain that the more consideration that is given to the subject the better. I think it very desirable that you should communicate with Sir Robert Peel. But I have had no communication with him for some time upon any subjects, excepting the mere forms of society; and I don't think that he would like either to advise a proceeding in the House of Lords, at least through me, or that I should advise one in the House of Commons. I believe that the best course would be that we should try the ground in the House of Lords; and that the same course should be followed in the House of Commons or not according as we should find the feeling of the publick after our proceeding.

You will have heard of Lieven's recall. I think that this is the commencement of a course of *Coventry* in which this country is about to be placed. I believe that the Government are a good deal annoyed at this recall; and that, having had some previous intimation of it, they had thought of sending to Petersburg immediately Lord Minto. They certainly thought of sending Lord Minto if they have not ordered him to go.

ADD MS 43060, ff. 110, 111. *Copy in Wellington Papers.*

Anonymous to Wellington, 23 May 1834

The following suggestions, relating to a desirable improvement in the University of Oxford, are respectfully submitted to his Grace the Duke of Wellington by a member of the Convocation. Hs is persuaded that the Duke will not neglect them, if he believes them to be founded on truth and good sense.

1.   Most of the colleges were intended as places of support to indigent and deserving scholars, and possess funds for that purpose; the mis-application of those resources has contributed to fill the ranks of the Dissenters, and to deprive the Church of her due supply of learned and industrious ministers.

2.   Several colleges have thrown open their exhibitions to free competition; and the consequences of that measure have been highly beneficial.

3.   It is very desirable that the same principle should be adopted by *all* the colleges.

4.   There is no individual, who by his influence, both personal and official, is more likely to promote this object, than the present Chancellor of that university.

5.   Nor is there any object more worthy of the application of his talents: the welfare of the Church is intimately concerned in its attainment.

6.   It will be expedient to secure the concurrence of the visitors of the several colleges, and of the most influential resident members of the university, in any such improvement as that which is here suggested.

7.   The objects, at which his Grace may at present discreetly aim, are first a *more conscientious interpretation* of the existing statutes; and secondly a *voluntary* revision of the statutes by consent of the visitor and members of each college, in cases where such revision is desirable.

8.   If no serious objection be made by the judicious and influential resident members of the university, a *public requisition* to the foregoing effect, made by his Grace in his capacity of Chancellor, would much conduce to the attainment of the object in view.

9.   A *compulsory* alteration of the statutes is at present liable to almost insurmountable objections.

The writer most respectfully entreats his Grace, on behalf of the Church, to make minute enquiries on the subject of this paper.

The Rev. Benjamin Cheese to Wellington, 23 May 1834

Tendring Rectory, near Colchester. I venture to request your Grace, in the name of my parishioners as well as of myself, to present to the House of Lords the enclosed petition in favour of the Established Church.

Your Grace will, also, allow me, I hope, to take advantage of this opportunity to express the heartfelt pleasure which I experience, as a member of Convocation, in knowing that Oxford has a Chancellor so able and so willing to defend, at this awful crisis, every institution which is really venerable in Church and State.

Draft reply 25 May 1834. Compliments. The Duke will present to the House of Lords on Monday the petition which accompanies his letter.

Viscount Mahon to Wellington, 26 May 1834

Dover Street. I take the liberty of communicating to you a secret, with which, as it is of an entirely personal nature, I should not presume to trouble your Grace, if I were not emboldened by the constant kindness you have been pleased to show me.

I am going to be married to the second daughter of Sir Edward Kerrison. Of the young lady herself I will restrain myself from saying anything since your Grace would no doubt suspect the exaggeration of a lover. In other respects I may observe that she has a considerable fortune and that I have reason to believe that her family interest will be the means of replacing me in Parliament very speedily. The latter point I mention to your Grace in the strictest confidence; as to the marriage itself it is kept secret until my father's answer shall arrive from the Continent. My mother is much pleased with it; it was settled only today.

Wellington to Viscount Mahon, 27 May 1834

London. I did not venture to tell you last night how sincerely I rejoiced at the account I had just before received from you of your approaching marriage and of the expectation of happiness which it held out to you, least I should be overheard by the surrounding crowd.

I have long known and respected Sir Edward Kerrison, and I must say that there does not exist a more honorable gentleman or one who has availed himself to a greater degree than he has of opportunities of distinguishing himself in the service.

As I have not been much in the world lately, I am not much acquainted with the young ladies; but as far as I have seen of them, I think you very fortunate in obtaining either of them and I sincerely congratulate you.

Copy in Lord Mahon's hand. Endorsed by him: The original I presented to Lady Kerrison in 1840.

CHEVENING PAPERS 685.

The Rev. James Blatch to Wellington, 27 May 1834

Basingstoke. A petition to the House of Lords from members of the Church of England inhabitants of Basingstoke and parishes in its vicinity against certain claims of the Dissenters is forwarded by this night's post directed to your Grace at Apsley House. I am commissioned to request that your Grace will have the kindness to present it to their Lordship's house.

A similar petition to the House of Commons is forwarded to Sir Robert Inglis, on the supposition that Mr. Lefevre is at this time absent from London.

The petition though not coming officially from the Corporation of Basingstoke has received the signatures of the mayor and all the magistrates of that town and several other members of the corporation. The signatures, about 218 in number, are all of them highly respectable.

Signed: James Blatch, vicar of Basingstoke.

Draft reply 31 May 1834. Compliments. The Duke will present to the House of Lords the petition from Basingstoke upon the first occasion that shall offer.

Wellington to the Earl of Aberdeen, 29 May 1834

London. I have been just now informed by a person who had seen

Lord Palmerston that his Lordship had told him that he had received the Portuguese ratifications of the treaty.

But I conclude that in the existing state of their affairs, the Government will not exchange them.

ADD MS 43060, f. 112.

The Marquess of Londonderry to Wellington, 29 May 1834

Holdernesse House. I have received your memorandum and Prince Lieven was with me this morning. I flatter myself you will both do me the justice to believe that whatever my own opinions might be, I should bow to your sentiments and the wishes expressed by the Russian Ambassador on this occasion.

You may be perfectly sure, therefore, I shall back out of my notice in the best manner I can, and perhaps you will advise me how best to achieve this purpose.

I consider the unfortunate perseverance of Lord Palmerston in Sir Stratford Canning's nomination has been the cause of our not being represented by an ambassador at Saint Petersbourg; you know that court too well not to admit the advantages we should have had by a clever man having direct intercourse with the Emperor during these late anxious times. Our embassy at Constantinople was for a long time equally neglected, and I think there are fair grounds here for a charge against the Government. However, I have no doubt I am wrong and I am not aware that whenever you have given me any very decided opinion that I have had the stupid vanity to follow my own in preference. I regret you should have had the trouble to write on this subject, as a few words to me at any time will always operate to dissuade me from anything you conceived objectionable, in my conduct, to the party, in the House of Lords.

I own I was very desirous of some publick expression, feeling and sentiment for Lieven, from the friendship I know my brother so long entertained for him, and in this I have succeeded and remain more than satisfied.

The Rev. Edward Harper Wainwright to Wellington, 30 May 1834

Dudley. I have the honour of forwarding to your Grace, by this day's mail, a petition from the members of the Established Church, in this town and parish, against a bill now before Parliament 'for relieving the Dissenters from disabilities' which prevent them from resorting to the universities, or taking degrees there. I have also to request that your Grace will have the kindness to present it to the House of Lords.

Draft reply 31 May 1834. Compliments. The Duke will present the petition to which he refers in his note as soon as the orders of the House permit.

The Rev. Edward Andrew Daubeny to Wellington, 30 May 1834

Ampney, Cirencester. I hope your Grace will permit me to have the honor of laying before you a petition from several parishes in the rural deanery of Cirencester, Gloucestershire, against admitting the Dissenters into the universities of Oxford and Cambridge, which I trust your Grace will present before your Lordship's honourable house.

Signed: Edward Andrew Daubeny, rural dean.

Docketed by Wellington The same as to Mr. Wainwright. *Docketed by secretary* Done. May 31st 1834.

The Rev. George Francis Blakiston to Wellington, 30 May 1834

I have the honour of forwarding to you by this day's post a petition from the inhabitants of the parishes of Bellbroughton and Pedmore in the county of Worcester against the claims of the Dissenters of a right of admission to our two English universities; and also against their claim of exemption from church rates, and of a right to officiate by their own ministers in our churchyards; and to request your Grace to present the same to the House of Lords. They are induced to trouble you with this request from a conviction that it could not be entrusted to any one so likely to secure attention to it either as an individual member of that house or as Chancellor of the University of Oxford.

The petition is signed by almost every one in the parish who is capable of affixing his signature to it.

Signed: G. F. Blakiston, rector of Bellbroughton.

Docketed by Wellington The same as to Mr. Wainwright. *Docketed by secretary* Done. May 31st 1834.

The Rev. Thomas Parry to Wellington, 30 May 1834

Cirencester. With this same post I have transmitted to your Grace a petition from the members of the Church of England in Cirencester and its neighbourhood against the bill now before Parliament, 'To remove certain disabilities which prevent some classes of His Majesty's subjects from resorting to the universities of England and proceeding to degrees thereto', and beg the favor of your Grace's presenting the same, to the House of Lords, at such time as may be deemed most convenient.

Signed: Thomas Parry, curate of Cirencester.

Docketed by Wellington The same as to Mr. Wainwright. *Docketed by secretary* Answered. May 31st.

The Earl of Roden to Wellington, 31 May 1834

Tollymore Park. Things seem coming closer to a crisis and it appears to me that the House of Lords will now be forced to take a part which it never has yet done, in stopping the progress of destruction. You know I have been waiting here ready at a moment's warning to answer your call whenever you think I can be of any use in the House of Lords and I now trouble you again to remind you of my position and to repeat how ready I am and how thankful I shall be to meet your wishes or follow your directions whenever you are kind enough to express yourself to me on the subject. I have had a great deal of leisure this year to attend to my private concerns in this country and to cultivate the good feeling and consolidate the energies of our Protestant population in case of any necessity arising, and I do not think anything that has as yet taken place in the House of Lords should make me regret my absence. But I am aware that a time may very soon arrive when every man ought to be at his post there, and I trust you will not think me too bold in hoping for your counsel or even the expression of your opinion on the subject. I am ready to start on a moment's warning. This country is apparently quiet but the least excitement would fan it into a flame on either side.

Wellington to Viscount Strangford, 31 May 1834

London. Without any reason that I know of I am *servus servorum*; and whenever any noble lord chooses to make a motion in the House of

547

Lords *nolens volens* I must attend although possibly as last night one of four or five. I should be happy if anyone else would undertake the office of *servus servorum*. I don't concur in opinion of the benefit to be derived from your motion, or from such motions in general. However as I have said that I would attend I will do so, and will send my excuse to Sir Wathen Waller.

I must beg leave to be excused however for declining to ask anybody else to attend. Others must take upon themselves that duty.

George Crossley to Wellington, [May 1834]

The Dissenters having of late so stoutly proclaimed their numbers as far exceeding those of the Established Church in this neighbourhood, the Committee appointed for the purpose of obtaining signatures to the address to the King and petitions to both Houses of Parliament have taken great pains to ascertain the fact, and the annexed table shewing the result may be depended upon.

Undated. Signed: George Crossley, Secretary to the committee.

Enclosure: A statement of all the churches and chapels in Manchester and Salford with the number of sittings in each and average attendance (exclusive of Sunday school children).

Independents	*Sittings*	*Attendance*
Grosvenor Street	1100	700
Mosley Street	1200	1000
Cannon Street	700	450
Hulme	300	150
Windsor Bridge	300	150
Rusholme	900	400
Chapel Street	900	600
Gartside Street	500	300
Baptists		
York Street	800	500
St. George's Road	800	500
George Street	600	350
Oak Street	250	100
Mount Street	200	100
Thorniley Brow	100	50

	Sittings	Attendance
Unitarians		
Mosley Street	500	250
Chapel Walks	1000	500
Greengate	400	250
Whole No. of United Dissenters so termed:	10550	6350
Roman Catholics		
Rook Street	400	400
Mulberry Street	1000	1000
Granby Row	1400	1400
Livesey Street	800	800
	3600	3600
New Connexion Methodists		
Oldham Street	700	400
Mount Street	250	150
Pendleton	400	200
Tent Methodists		
Canal Street	1200	200
Primitive Methodists		
Jersey Street	250	150
Hulme	200	120
Independent Methodists		
Millar's Lane	250	150
Salford	200	100
Independent Wesleyans		
Lees Street	300	150
Calvinist Methodists		
Cooper Street	800	300
Swedenborgians		
Peter Street	700	200
Bolton Street	400	200

	Sittings	Attendance
Quakers		
Peter Street	800	500
Scotch Secession		
Lloyd Street	800	450
Cowardites (now led by Joseph Brotherton, M.P. for Salford)		
Christ Church, King Street	400	200
Christ Church, Hulme	300	100
Christ Church, Every Street	400	200
Minor sects:	8350	3770
Wesleyan Methodists		
Oldham Street	1700	1400
Oldham Road	800	350
Ancoats	800	300
Oxford Road	1000	600
Grosvenor Street	1100	700
Bridgewater Street	800	450
Hulme	250	150
Irwell Street	1000	600
Gravel Lane	1200	800
Brunswick Street	600	350
Parliament Street	300	150
Chancery Lane	200	150
	9750	6000
United Dissenters	10550	6350
Minor sects	8350	3770
Roman Catholics	3600	3600
Wesleyan Methods	9750	6000
	32250	19720
Churches		
Collegiate	3000	2500
St. Ann's	1000	500

	Sittings	Attendance
St. Mary's	1000	500
St. Paul's	1500	1200
St. John's	1000	700
St. Michael's	1200	800
St. Peter's	800	500
St. George's	1000	700
Trinity	800	400
St. Stephen's	1400	1000
St. Clement's	1500	1200
St. James	1500	500
St. Thomas	1400	1200
St. Luke's	900	600
All Saints	1600	1300
St. Andrew's	1800	400
St. Matthew's	1600	500
St. George's, Hulme	1600	500
St. Philip's	1500	900
Christ Church	1600	1300
St. Thomas, Pendleton	1200	700
St. Mark's	800	400
St. Andrew's Scotch	1000	750
	30700	19050
Churches	30700	19050

Isaac Lyon Goldsmid to Wellington, [2] June 1834

20 St. James Square. I have been repeatedly requested by those who are interested in the question of the removal of the disabilities of the Jews to solicit your Grace to grant to a deputation from the committee of the Jewish Association for obtaining Civil Rights and Privileges the honor of an interview.

From what passed last year in the House of Lords it appears to them that misapprehensions exist on several points connected with the subject and they think if they were favored with a short conversation they should be able to afford with respect to these, satisfactory explanation. I can assure your Grace that the Jews deeply feel that if you should see fit to give support to their claims they would owe a great debt of gratitude to your Grace for being freed from the degrading restrictions to which they are now subject.

Docketed 2 June 1834.

Wellington to the Earl of Roden, 3 June 1834

London. I don't think that any opportunity has yet offered for the House of Lords to act. It cannot act with efficiency by resolution against the Government and the House of Commons. It can only act in its legislative capacity; and although we hear a good deal of bad laws and their progress elsewhere, none have yet reached the House of Lords. We have witnessed in the last week a ministerial crisis of which I confess I do not yet know the cause. There was a debate in the House of Commons last night which may have made it known: but I have not seen the reports thereof and am still in the dark. The subject was the Irish Church; which it is intended by one party to plunder, but I don't know why the other party should have separated at the commencement of last week. I believe that the Ministry has been botched up; and I confess I see no reason why it should not go on as well without as it did with the aid of the talents of Mr. Stanley and Sir James Graham. In these times it is not talents that enable men to carry on the public business, much less character, but insolence, blustering and above all humbug. I think that you are quite right for remaining where you are: I did not come to town till the 14th of April, and I don't know of any occasion for the presence of anybody in the House of Lords for some time to come. But I dare say that late in the session, and particularly in the last week we shall have plenty of business; and we shall not want for instances of the infirmity of the tempers of some and the insolence of others.

Wellington to Isaac Lyon Goldsmid, 5 June 1834

Compliments. The Duke's time is really much occupied by business and he will be out of town during the whole of the next week.

He is always ready to receive any gentlemen who wish to call upon him; but he cannot see that any advantage is likely to result from an interview with Mr. Goldsmid and the gentlemen who propose to call upon him.

Sir Thomas Troubridge to Wellington, 7 June 1834

29 Albemarle Street. A fortnight having elapsed since I had the honor of laying before your Grace the draft of a bill intended to be brought into the House of Commons, I think it right to inform your Grace that I consider it my duty to introduce the bill immediately and to move its second reading as early as the business of the House will admit.

Wellington to Sir Thomas Troubridge, 8 June 1834

London. I have just now received your letter of the 7th instant.

On the very day that you communicated to me the copy of the bill which you intended to present to the House of Commons I referred to certain officers of the Cinque Ports for information on some of the points to which the bill related.

I received the answers yesterday. I am under the necessity of going out of town on a public duty tomorrow, and I shall be detained at a distance from London till Saturday the 14th. I intended therefore to postpone to make any communication to you on the subject of the proposed bill till the following week.

It is impossible for me to ask you to postpone the introduction of your measure because a public duty requires that I should be absent myself from London.

If Parliament should think proper to entertain the bill I must adopt other modes of making known the opinion I may entertain of its provisions, without putting you to the inconvenience of any delay.

John Foster to Wellington, 8 June 1834

1 Vincent Square, Westminster. Thanks to the peers for the old English spirit displayed on Friday evening; but as one expression fell from Earl Grey which may alarm some timid mind, permit me to remark upon it, as no man knows the feeling that pervades the country better than myself.

The expression I allude to was this—'they must march with the spirit of the age'—which in plain English means—that the Church of England must be destroyed, to gratify the greedy and long faced, rapacious, puritanical devils amongst the Baptists and Calvinists, Shakers and Quakers, Arians and Unitarians, Armenians and Socinians,

the Wesleyans and new Wesleyans, Muggletonians and Southcotto-
nians, and one hundred other mongrel sects, all hating each other as
the Devil hates holy water, but all joining in concert and union in the
hope of the plunder of the Church falling into their separate hands.

This then my Lord Duke is the secret—the hope of plunder of the
Church. 'Spirit of the age indeed'!!! I suppose the reign of brickbats
and bludgeons (conjured up by Lord Brougham and his man Joseph
Parkes late of Birmingham, but now his Lordship's representative in the
Morning Chronicle, with a snug £2,000 a year besides, as Secretary to the
Corporation commissioners) is to be tried to be conjured up again.
But it cannot be done—'the spirit of the age' is disgust at the hypocrisy
and quackery of the last two years, and depend upon it my Lord Duke,
were you Minister tomorrow, and to dissolve the Parliament, using
only the natural and common influence of administration there would
be a *less Whig* House of Commons than has been seen for two centuries,
whilst the Radicals would support the Tories out of pure resentment at
the treachery of the Whigs. Rely my Lord Duke on the correctness of
my information; I once before ventured to address your Grace on the
state of the country, and events have proved the correctness of my
views; and on all occasions I shall be proud to render your Grace every
service in my power.

Docketed by Wellington Compliments. Received. *Docketed by secretary*
Done. June 15th.

John Charles Herries to Wellington, 10 June 1834

Albemarle Street. Sir Thomas Troubridge spoke to me yesterday about his
bill. He said he had been informed by a message from you that you
would not be able to attend to it before the end of the week. But, *as
his friends intimated to him* that the close of the session was likely to be
accelerated, he was anxious to lose no time, lest his bill should not pass
this year. Whereupon he asked my opinion whether he should be
wanting in respect to you if he brought in the bill now, with the intention of delaying the second reading until he should have received some
communication from you.

I told him that as I had not heard from you, and had not seen his
bill, I could give no opinion, beyond stating that I conceived the bill
to be entirely his and that I did not think that you were likely to be a

party to the bringing of it in at all, because I had not heard you state that you thought any new bill on the subject necessary. It appeared to me when he left me that he was resolved to bring in the bill; and I must confess that I think it better that he should bring it in upon his own responsibility than affect to be doing it in some kind of concert with you.

There is some strong reason which induces him and Marjoribanks and the Board of Trade to press this measure. Poulett Thomson spoke to me about it also and was very desirous of impressing upon me that the shipping interest required it. I told him I was very well aware of the real interests intended to be conciliated by the proposed changes.

The accounts received from Spring Rice *by his friends* today are not sanguine; but rather more hopeful than they were yesterday. From Sugden the reports are full of confidence.

Abercromby is gone to Edinburgh as Master of the Mint and a Cabinet Minister. There is, of course, no chance of an opposition to him. The appointment is considered here as being likely to be useful to the new Government by drawing Radical favour towards them.

PS. I am going to Harwich for two days. I return to London at the end of the week and will then call at Apsley House.

Wellington to John Charles Herries, 11 June 1834

Oxford. Many thanks for your letter my dear Herries. I wrote to Sir Thomas Troubridge to tell him that I should be here till Saturday; and that I could not ask him to postpone to bring in his bill. I added that I should adopt some other mode of stating my objections to it.

Lord Auckland spoke to me about it. But I hope to throw it out in the Lords. At all events they shall hear of this job.

ADD MS 57368.

The Earl of Glengall to Wellington, 12 June 1834

34 rue Chantereine, Paris. Lord Clanricarde has again introduced the bill for destroying the theatres of Covent Garden and Drury Lane, and substituting a heap of minor theatres in their place. A deputation of those whose property to a monstrous amount is invested on the faith of these patents, will wait on your Grace for the purpose of obtaining your assistance.

It is (when understood) the most decided attack on private property ever made—and this also in the teeth of Lord Brougham's decision, of the year 1831, he being assisted by two common law judges and the Vice-Chancellor, without which I should have thought nothing of it; *he voted*, as you perhaps recollect, in the very teeth of that, his own decision, which was also addressed in a letter to the King.

It is, also, a decided attack on the prerogative. I am quite sure that if your Grace has time to make yourself acquainted with the subject, you will never allow a bill of this flagrant nature to pass the Lords.

Lord Francis Egerton to Wellington, 13 June 1834

I should be glad that you could find time to run over the enclosed. The subject is one which you must be anxious to consider in all its bearings. I do not know to what extent the writer will find others of his own profession agree with him. He is himself a man of attainment, an excellent clergyman who has kept for many years dissent out of a large parish in the immediate neighbourhood of which it prevails to a great extent, and a very high churchman.

I had myself thought a good deal on the matriculation text before I had any communication with him upon it, and had arrived pretty nearly to the conclusion that it was desirable not to do away with but to alter it.

The admission of Dissenters to the universities I hold to be identical with the destruction of the Church establishment, and I will never consent to the one till I am prepared to vote the other the same evening. It does however seem to me that it would be very possible to devise a form which should give ample security against Dissent without demanding subscription to the Articles which those who now give it have seldom read, if they come straight from school have perhaps not heard of. It seems to me that what is wanted is some form which would give security that the party is, *as far as instructed*, a member of the Church of England, and willing, and able without injury to his conscience, to submit to that instruction which will make him acquainted with its peculiar dogmas, as well as with those general doctrines which he has probably learnt from the pulpit of his parish church, if nowhere else. I am aware, well aware, that alterations in these matters are not to be lightly even advocated, much less adopted, but I take a deep interest in the subject, and have some right to address you upon it. In the first place I have some stake in the country, and am deliberately prepared to peril it for the maintenance of the Church. I have also passed through the process of the matriculation test and know that it leads to scandal. I subscribed the articles without having read them. The person who followed me was an Irishman, who excused himself in the evening from all sense of obligation in the matter by alleging that he had kissed his thumb instead of the Testament.

No one has a greater respect for the Bishop of Exeter than I have, but I think his exposition of this matter has given more satisfaction to the enemies than the friends of the Church.

You will think that the doctor's gown which I wear by your favour has communicated some theological infection, but the fact is I look upon you as the head of the Church, no offence to His Majesty, and only regret that you cannot be Dean of Christ Church for a few months.

I have been reading an Oxford pamphlet by a Mr. Moberly on the admission of Dissenters. It has little to do with this branch of the question, in which he would probably disagree with me, but I think it best on the main question I have seen. A Mr. Sewell's I do not like so well, thinking his zeal impedes his powers of persuasion.

Enclosure: Thomas Butt to the committee on the Oxford Declaration

I have received and seriously considered the Declaration of Approval and Concurrence to which my signature is requested, and am happy to find that the clause respecting 'the admission of persons who dissent from the Church of England' is so worded as not, by necessary inference, to involve an approbation of the *method* by which that exclusion is effected. I have long earnestly wished that subscription to the Articles of religion before the Vice-Chancellor was not required from young men at the time of matriculation, nor indeed till they were candidates for a degree; and my opinion of its impropriety remains unchanged by the arguments and analogies lately urged in support of it.

I cannot identify this formal approbation of truths *not necessary to salvation* with professing the *essential dogmas of Christianity* in public worship or by children when they repeat the Catechism—neither can I assimilate the unavoidable process of sound education by which the *infant* mind is gradually imbued with prejudices on the side of truth with a broad avowal of opinion and by the very same process which the law has constituted a test of the first importance, *after the understanding is unfolded,* and without requiring preliminary instruction and study.

To make no difference between subscription to the Articles and an avowal of Church membership may, by a converse argument be transformed into an assertion that no one is a member of the Church who hesitates to subscribe to the Articles. Yet we are not prepared to repel from our communion every layman who scruples to assent to all the propositions which they convey. It follows then that in our estimation subscription is *something more* than an avowal of Church membership.

If the committee interpret our signatures as involving an approbation of this early subscription and a desire for its continuance, I must, but with great reluctance, decline adding mine to the many names which would honour it by the association; but if no such approbation is meant to be inferred, I most willingly authorize the addition of my name to theirs, as I cordially unite with them in the great object they have in view.

Copy. Undated.

Wellington to the Rev. George Rowley, 14 June 1834

I have considered of the expediency of my signing at Oxford the address proposed to be presented to the King. Such signature must be liable to be considered as official; and in that case the address to which it should be affixed ought to be presented to the King on the throne. I cannot think it desirable that the university should be exposed to the risk of losing its privilege by a supposed voluntary relinquishment of it by myself; or to the charge of having abused it by presenting to the King on the throne an address founded upon a speech of His Majesty to the archbishops and bishops at St. James's on the 28th May, of which there is no recorded copy, and which His Majesty's Minister declared in his place in the House of Lords, that he had not advised.[1]

I entertain great objection to affixing my signature to that address either in London or elsewhere, where I might be supposed to act in my private capacity.

The Sovereign made a speech on the 28th May, of which there is no record; but a copy has reached the publick which has given general satisfaction.

I should have participated of that satisfaction if His Majesty had not

---

[1] See Appendix.

on the same day accepted the resignation of four of his Ministers, as the publick have reason to believe, because they would not concur with their colleagues in the issue of a commission under the Great Seal to enquire into the state of the Church of England in Ireland, as the first step towards carrying into execution a resolution that the Protestant Episcopal Establishment in Ireland exceeds the spiritual wants of the Protestant population and that the temporal possessions of the Church in Ireland ought to be reduced.

One of these Ministers so resigning was the Lord Privy Seal and a special warrant under the sign manual must have been granted by the King for the application of the Great Seal to this commission.

It is impossible for me to found any act upon the personal feelings, opinions and words of the King in contradistinction from his royal sanction of the acts of his Government; or to address His Majesty in terms of congratulation upon a speech, or any part of it, of which there is no record; at the moment that I see that a measure has been adopted by His Majesty's special authority which has for its object to take the first step and must tend to the destruction of the Church of England in Ireland.

As far as I am individually concerned therefore I do not propose to sign any address to the King which contains any reference to His Majesty's speech to the bishops on the 28 May.

Wellington to the Earl of Glengall, 15 June 1834

I will certainly oppose the theatres' bill, but without your assistance I am afraid that my opposition will be of little avail.

I have written to Mr. Bunn to request him to give me all the information in his power, and I will give every attention to the subject, and all the opposition that I can give to the bill.

Alexander Lamb to Wellington, 16 June 1834

Marford Cottage, St. Albans. Having formerly witnessed the loss of two men of war in Tor Bay and some fatal accidents on the south coast of England circumstances drew my attention to Portland Roads as a harbour of rendezvous for the Navy as well as for commercial shipping passing up and down the English Channel, and several years since, after causing the necessary surveys and examinations to be made, I took some pains to satisfy Government of not only the peculiar facilities existing in the Island of Portland for carrying the plan into execution but to demonstrate to them the advantages the public would inevitably derive from the adoption of it.

After having matured my plan for the construction of the harbour I turned my attention to the possibility of an improved road to it and from thence to the great naval arsenal at Devonport, the line of which your Grace will find marked as far as Bridport in the inclosed sketch, and which line I was glad to see was, to a certain extent, adopted by the projectors of the London and Southampton Railway, tending, if carried into effect, to promote my objects; for which reason, I, without any other interest, became anxious for the success of their undertaking; although I felt it due to both the subscribers and my own character to apprise them of the possibility of their work being interfered with by one, which I considered of more value to the public: this induced me to present a short petition to the House of Commons praying for the clause contained in the inclosed reasons, but which, being objected to by the projectors, the committee of the House of Commons refused to admit.

Without any further interest than above stated in either the success or failure of the London and Southampton Railway, I have occasionally attended the committee rooms of both Houses, and have been surprized to find how purely technical the arguments have been both in support of and in opposition to the measure, for I cannot help thinking that the adoption of extensive lines of railway involves a great national question; and the more profitable to the shareholders the projectors shew their proposed works to be, the more deserving are they of serious consideration, especially when I hear them confidently advance as an argument in support of such works that troops, in case of internal commotion, may be moved with great rapidity from one part of the kingdom to another. I hope the peace of society will never depend on means so precarious and so easily defeated.

If this mode of conveyance is really so profitable to the proprietors and so oeconomical to the public as it has been represented, it must necessarily in a great degree supersede all others; coachmasters will convert their horses into steam-engines; turnpike roads, comparatively speaking deserted, will get out of repair; and the important operations of this mighty country become in a measure dependent on a piece of iron being kept firmly in its place which a common laborer can with a pickaxe or a crowbar remove in a minute; thus their success as measures of general use is more to be deprecated than their failure: yet, notwithstanding the golden harvest promised to the shareholders, failure is possible, and the chance of it ought not to be entirely lost sight of; and in case of failure it would both serve the shareholders and benefit the public if in all such bills a clause was introduced compelling the managers to lay yearly an account in detail before Parliament. Without such a clause it's almost impossible for the shareholders to expose the manoeuvres or detect the tricks resorted to occasionally by directors to conceal mismanagement and sometimes fraud; to enhance or depreciate shares in the market; or for the shareholders to ascertain whichever dividends are paid from profits or from capital; in short directors may in all such concerns be considered as irresponsible bodies and it would save many a dupe from ruin if they were compelled to lay their accounts annually before Parliament to which, when amenable, they would necessarily be responsible.

If there is anything of value in the above suggestions I have the satisfaction of knowing they have been submitted to one who is not only capable of appreciating but of giving effect to them; if they are valueless I trust your Grace's kindness will excuse the intrusion of an old man of seventy who is not likely to offend again.

Docketed by Wellington Compliments. Received. *Docketed by secretary* Done. June 18.

First enclosure: Sketch map of a proposed road, by Weymouth, from London to Bridport, designed by Alexander Lamb for the purpose of illustrating suggestions for converting Portland Roads into a harbour.

Second enclosure: Printed broadsheet re London and Southampton Railway; argument for introducing into the bill a clause for the protection of interests in the west of England.

Third enclosure: Printed broadsheet. Observations on Railways.

Wellington to the Marquess of Londonderry, 17 June 1834

London. I return the Duke of Buckingham's letter. It is really necessary that the Duke should come to town and decide for himself what course he will take. My conviction is that this Government cannot be broken down as the last was by a combination of parties of all opinions against it for that purpose; and being convinced that the formation of any Government which we might hope would conduct public affairs on better, or on any principles, is impossible, and that the ruin of which the seeds were sown in the end of the year 1830 would be compleated, I cannot be a party to any combination of discontented Whigs, Radicals or others to promote that object; nor vote for measures which I should consider destructive, and could not carry into execution if the object was attained. I also am for a fair *stand up fight*. Such has always been my practice. It is not that of the Duke. In the last session of Parliament I fought several fair stand up fights throughout the dog-days, and till the end of August, with the support of not more than ten or a dozen peers, upon questions of the greatest public and personal interest even to the Duke of Buckingham himself, but I do not recollect that I had the advantage of the Duke's support on any one of these occasions. I will follow this course again this year. But I decline to make the Poor Law Bill a party question; or to oppose any provision in it, of which when I see it I shall approve. I likewise decline to move abstract questions upon the Irish Church Commission for this reason. Contradictory propositions will be moved and carried in the House of Commons. I do not choose to be the person to excite a quarrel between the two Houses of Parliament. This quarrel will occur in its time, and the House of Lords will probably be overwhelmed; but it shall not be attributed to me with truth at least. The country is in a most serious state. A man like the Duke of Buckingham with his stake in it should come to town and see with his own eyes, and hear with his own ears what is passing, and give his assistance to prevent the progress of mischief. Much may be done by the House of Lords in its legitimate legislative capacity, and I must add that I can be a party only to such measures.

Viscount Mahon to Wellington, 17 June 1834

Dover Street. I believe that your Grace is already aware of Colonel Gurwood's arrival and will have the goodness to send the corrected proof-sheets to him in the same manner as before his departure.

There is one point, however, to which I would take the liberty of calling your attention. There is a letter to Major Graham dated April 11, 1804 and inserted at page 194 which relates to the relief of the famine at Ahmednuggur but which applies in a most striking and remarkable manner to the present state of the Poor Laws in England and to the plan brought forward by the Government for their amendment. Would your Grace have any objection that for the information of the public mind on this great question, that letter should be given in the *Morning Post* or *Standard* without awaiting the publication of the second volume?

Wellington's letter of 1804, relating to famine in Ahmednuggur, Major-General the Hon. Arthur Wellesley to Major Graham. 11 April 1804

Bombay. I have taken into consideration the various reports which I have received from you, of the miserable state of the lower classes of the inhabitants of Ahmednuggur, in consequence of the dreadful scarcity of provisions in that part of the country; and I proceed to give you my sentiments on that subject, and directions regarding the mode of providing for their relief.

The delivery of the provisions gratis, is, in my opinion, a very defective mode of providing against the effects of famine.

It is liable to abuses in all parts of the world, but particularly in India; and at Ahmednuggur, the consequence of its adoption would be that crowds of people would be drawn there from other parts of the country, in which the distress is equally felt, and they would increase the distress at Ahmednuggur to such a degree as to render all the efforts to remove it from its immediate inhabitants entirely fruitless, and it might at last reach our own troops and establishments. The principle, therefore, of the mode in which I propose to relieve the distresses of the inhabitants, is not to give grain or money in charity.

Those who suffer from famine may properly be divided into two classes: those who can, and those who cannot work. In the latter class may be included old persons, children, and the sick women, who from their former situation in life, have been unaccustomed to labour and are weakened by the effects of famine.

The former, viz. those of both sexes who can work, ought to be employed by the public; and in the course of this letter I shall point out the work on which I should wish that they might be employed, and in what manner paid. The latter, viz. those who cannot work, ought to be taken into an hospital and fed, and receive medical aid and medicine at the expense of the public.

According to this mode of proceeding, subsistence will be provided for all; the public will receive some benefit from the expense which will be incurred; and above all, it will be certain that no able-bodied person will apply for relief, unless he should be willing to work for his subsistence; that none will apply, who are not able to work, who are not real objects of charity; and that none will come to Ahmednuggur for the purpose of partaking of the food which must be procured by their labour, or to obtain which they must submit to the restraint of an hospital.

I enclose a memorandum of the work which I should wish to have performed at Ahmednuggur. This work must be carried on under the superintendence of the engineer, by the persons whom you will send to him who may be desirous of partaking of the subsistence which, according to this plan, will be afforded to them. You ought to have a sufficient number of persons to attend the engineer, and to ascertain the number of people who go to work; and each person ought to receive for the day's labour, half a seer of grain and two pice, to be issued daily.

I wish you to provide a building in the pettah of Ahmednuggur, for the reception of those who cannot work. Objects of this description suffering from want, ought to be removed immediately to this building, where they will be attended by a medical gentleman. This gentleman shall provide them with the necessary quantity of food to be drawn from you; and he shall be paid for his trouble at the rate of fifty pagodas per month.

The next point to be considered is the mode in which grain is to be procured for the subsistence of these people. There is at present, at Ahmednuggur, a quantity of damaged jowarry but which I take to be by no means sufficient to enable you to carry on this plan for any considerable length of time. It will answer, however, for a certain space of time, till you will be enabled to procure additional quantities from the districts of the Subah of the Deccan. You will exert yourself to the utmost to procure the grain required; and in the mean time, orders will be sent to Ahmednuggur to place the jowarry at your disposal. From this grain, and from what you will purchase, you will supply the surgeon with what he may require for the hospital ordered to be established by this letter.

You will pay the surgeon for his attendance upon this hospital, and you will keep a separate account of the expense of the whole establishment; whether for labour, or for food for the infirm, or for attendance and medicines for the hospital.

Orders conformable to this plan will be sent to the proper officers at Ahmednuggur.

CHEVENING PAPERS 685. *The Dispatches of Field-Marshal the Duke of Wellington*, edited by John Gurwood, ii. 202–204, 1st edition (1834–1839).

Wellington to Viscount Mahon, 17 June 1834

London. I observed and was much struck by the letter on the relief of the famine at Ahmednuggur.

It is for the relief of a famine in a particular district in a country in which famine prevailed; and not for the permanent relief of the poor. It is very curious that I who had never then heard of poor or Poor Laws should have struck upon that plan; which appears so easy and practicable.

But I should doubt the expediency of now publishing the letter. It would be better to wait till the second volume comes out.

CHEVENING PAPERS 685.

The Rev. John Browne to Wellington, 17 June 1834

Milton, Christchurch, Hampshire. I feel assured that no apology is necessary for thus intruding upon your Grace to solicit the honor and favor of your presentation of the enclosed petition to the House of Lords against the alleged claims of the Dissenters, since your Grace is well known to be the most zealous advocate and supporter of that Church of which the said document is the subject.

The petition includes the names of every respectable individual in this parish but five, four of which are Dissenters.

Signed: J. Browne. Minister of Milton.

Draft reply 18 June 1834. Compliments. The Duke will present to the House of Lords the petition which he has sent to him.

Richard Oastler to Wellington, 17 June 1834

Fixby Hall. Circumstances, which time will explain, induce me to enclose your Grace's letter of November 26th, 1833. If it should so happen that the wave which threatens me should overwhelm me, then my papers might fall into other hands than mine and I feel sure your Grace will not blame me for returning this into your hands. I could certainly have destroyed it, but I hope I shall never disgrace myself so far as to *destroy* one of the Duke of Wellington's autograph letters. I am a marked man, whom the 'march of intellect', 'Liberal', *fools* and *tyrants* hate—and I expect to fall. But I do hope to see, when I am ruined, the 'order' of the English aristocracy under better protection than that of *Lord Grey*!! I want to see the aristocracy and the people friends. I'll tell your Grace who it is that keeps them enemies; Messrs. Rothschild, Louis-Philippe, Morrison and Co. It is the company of cold-blooded capitalists, who now command the destinies of the world, and if they are not stopped they will swamp the aristocracy and the people. Why, in the name of conscience, should land and labour be taxed and capital be free? 'Oh', say some, 'if we tax it, it will leave our shores.' 'Then let it go' say I; 'it's a cursed master; if it won't remain to *serve*, let it go.' I know land and hands can make more. Say what we may, and do what we will, if *capital* is not restrained, the *land* of the aristocrats will all be mortgaged, and the *profit* of the farmer, tradesman and manufacturer all be swamped, and the *wages* of the labourer will be destroyed.

We are beginning to 'confiscate' already: look at the accursed 'commission' to Ireland. Then look at the result of the Poor Law 'Commission'.—(Oh, I do hate governing by 'commissions'.) The Poor Law Bill just confiscates £7,000,000 a year, and the landlords seem to be foolish enough to fancy they shall gain by it!! This little township (Fixby) joins Huddersfield; here our rates are about five shillings per acre. We may be 'united' to Huddersfield by these 'commissioners' and a meeting where our voice will never be heard among so many thousands. Then Mr. Thornhill's little township of Fixby will be saddled with £750 a year tax to save the capitalists and millowners of Huddersfield who always throw all their losses on the land. Now I ask in the name of Blackstone, why or where can any Government find themselves authorised to appoint three men to go round the country to make laws to execute those already made by absolutely robbing a prudent individual of £750 a year to give to these wretches who live on the vitals of the country and call themselves Liberal?

Draft reply 20 June 1834. Compliments. The Duke has received his letter and inclosure.

He shall have back the latter when he pleases. The Duke would have no objection to publish it at the market-cross.

Mary Young to Wellington, 17 June 1834

Clapton, Middlesex. May it please your Grace to pardon the intrusion of a stranger who begs your attention for an hour or two only to peruse the accompanying discourses on the subject of our excellent Church; they point out (I think) clearly the blessings derived from a national Church, and the unreasonableness, as well as the unscriptural feelings of those who refuse to pay, or wish to defraud the Church and her ministers of whatever money or lands that have been left to them for ages past by our good and pious forefathers.

Where are we the loyal subjects of our good King and Queen to look for defenders to sustain the Church in all its purity and authority, but to those heroes who have fought and bled for their native land.

On the day that these heroes meet to commemorate the glorious victory over their foreign enemies, I trust they will not think it beneath their dignity to adopt means to gain a moral victory over domestic enemies to our God and his Church.

O! may they now put forth their hearts as well as their heads to stem the wicked tide of party and prejudice against her, and consequently the happiness and peace of this country.

Man must use the means and God will assuredly bless those means for his glory.

Docketed by Wellington Compliments. Received. *Docketed by secretary* Answered. June 18th.

Joseph Woollams to Wellington, 17 June 1834

Wells, Somerset. I have the honor of transmitting to your Grace by the mail of this day an address to His Most Gracious Majesty from the loyal city of Wells, and to request that your Grace, in company with the Marquess of Bath, the truly worthy and much esteemed Lord

Lieutenant of this county—or that your Grace alone, should not the noble Marquess be at the levee, will be pleased to greatly favour and gratify the subscribers of the address by presenting it to our highly revered Sovereign.

That the address is signed by *all* the resident gentry and clergy, by a decided majority of the professional gentlemen now in Wells and by nearly every tradesman and mechanic is a circumstance most gratifying to us; and as it emanated entirely from the laity, it cannot be depreciated, as might have been attempted had it been the work of the clergy: and though it purports to be the address of the inhabitants of Wells and its *vicinity*, it has been almost exclusively confined to residents within the borough.

Draft reply 18 June 1834. Compliments. The Duke has received his letter. When the Duke will receive the address mentioned therein, he will present it to His Majesty.

The Marquess of Londonderry to Wellington, 19 June 1834

Holdernesse House. It certainly is not very comfortable to be the channel of another person's political sentiments. And I do assure you I have not volunteered nor shewn you half the letters I have received from the Duke of Buckingham. However as he urged me, I could not avoid submitting to you his last communication and I conceived your answer to me was *meant* for his perusal. This morning's post has brought the enclosed which his Grace desires should be shewn to you. You can return it to me in the House of Lords today. And I am rather anxious as far as my good offices are concerned not to be imprudent in these delicate explanations, if I can avoid it.

Enclosure: The Duke of Buckingham and Chandos to the Marquess of Londonderry, 15 June 1834.

Avington. You are very kind to interest yourself in my political well-being, and I consider it a strong proof of your friendship. I leave it to you to express my sentiments to the parties referred to in my last letter, in the manner you think best. But my opinions remain unaltered. Sir Robert Peel is a necessary *portion* of any Conservative Administration which may be composed, *provided he and the Duke of Wellington form it.* But my confidence is not placed in Sir Robert Peel singly or unconnected in government with the Duke. But I am very gloomy and dissatisfied with all that is going on unless what passed at Oxford instils political courage into the minds of those, who *if* they manage well have the game at their feet. I quite agree with Sir Charles Wetherell that it is not necessary to go along with *any* of the Ministers to Hounslow in the way to Windsor.

Pray let me know whether there is to be any *fight* at all upon the Poor Bill, which is become a very serious subject, or upon the Commission, which ought to be well dusted out? Upon the first there ought to be many divisions, and upon the latter, especially if I could be sure of a good *stand up fight*. Pray give me the earliest intimation if there be any such intention; but mind I will not come up to attend merely a parade.

Your doings at Oxford must have been glorious. I should like to have attended them, had the necessary and decorous consideration of my poor uncle's memory permitted me to have done so. I quite agree with the Duke that it may be dangerous to press the House too hard, as Grey will move heaven and earth to bully him into a backing out of, or a diluting of his declaration.

How long will the session last, and what becomes of you after it?

PS. We have a Hampshire meeting on Thursday.

Copy.

Wellington to the Marquess of Londonderry, 19 June 1834

London. If I am to carry on a warfare with the Duke of Buckingham by letter he must write legibly. I can scarcely read one word of his letter, indeed not one word beyond the first page.

In answer to that page I assert that I was left almost alone to fight the battle in the House of Lords in the last session of Parliament. We consequently lost many questions. Most particularly we lost one, by the loss of which the Church of Scotland is now in the progress of destruction.

To talk of my being leader of a party or anything but the slave of a party, or in other words the person whom any other may *bore* with his letters or his visits upon publick subjects when he pleases is just what I call *stuff*. I beg therefore to have no more of the Duke's letters. If he has anything to say to me let him write to me direct. I cannot see any advantage in corresponding through a third person.

569

Wellington to John Charles Herries, 20 June 1834

London. I send you a letter from Mr. Payne and a copy of Sir Thomas Troubridge's bill with the amendments which he proposes should be made to it.

He wishes and so do I that it should be thrown out altogether. I believe that the ship-owners are now quite satisfied with the improvements of the pilot system within the last three years. First we have improved the courts of enquiry into complaints of the conduct of the pilots by requiring at them the attendance of the members of the Court of Load Manage.

Secondly we have improved the cruising system by making it one of competition between the cruisers off Dungeness.

Thirdly we have by improvements in the regulations regarding signals and the keeping of the logs in each schooner insured the attention of each schooner; or the discovery of the fault if there should be any inattention.

Fourthly we have improved the system of examination of the qualifications of individuals proposed to be appointed pilots; and supernumeraries have been named so as to secure at all times the full number for duty required by the Act of Parliament.

There can be no doubt but that the enactments of the bill will put an end to the cruising system; and at length to the Cinque Ports pilots. Just to shew you the consequences of all this I mention that at the last Court of Load Manage Sir Thomas Troubridge recommended two Deal boatmen for examination as pilots. These men I learnt had been selected by their companions as the most competent of the whole number.

They were both rejected upon examination.

Observe that the shipping will have to depend upon this class alone as soon as the Cinque Ports pilot system will be done up.

ADD MS 57368.

L. Percy to Wellington, 20 June 1834

Mountjoy Square, Dublin. As the comparative numbers of the Protestants with those of the Roman Catholics of this part of the empire is now the subject of enquiry, I beg to submit to your Grace as a distinguished supporter of the former class that it is unfair to argue as if Ireland was a separate kingdom, for the case is quite the reverse; it has been made since the conquest a part of England and subject to her laws, it has been made by the Act of the Legislative Union an integral part of the empire, and if the Protestant population is now to be ascertained, let it be of the united kingdoms: it will then appear that an immense plurality of Protestants will be the result.

From the best sources of information that could be obtained the comparative numbers in Ireland stand thus: as $3\frac{1}{9}$ to 1: that is $3\frac{1}{9}$ Roman Catholics to 1 Protestant.

In England and Wales the numbers are: as 59 Protestants to 2 Roman Catholics, so that taking England and Ireland together the numbers will stand thus: 60 Protestants to $5\frac{1}{9}$ Roman Catholics.

I take it to be that all that are not Roman Catholics are Protestants, all equally protesting against the mummery and buffoonery of popery.

If by the enemies to good order it is objected that Ireland is still unconquered, in God's name let it now be conquered; the Protestants of Ireland (not withstanding the great emigration) are yet fully equal to the task; let them only have a clear stage, they require no favor.

The present state of things cannot remain, for as they now stand a Protestant is certain of nothing here but of having his throat cut at the *beck* of a demagogue or a priest.

The Protestants confidently look to your Grace as their chief support.

Docketed by Wellington Compliments. Received. *Docketed by secretary* Done. June 24th, 1834.

Lord Bayning to Wellington, 20 June 1834

17 Suffolk Street. Lord Bayning presents his compliments to the Duke of Wellington, and would be very much obliged to him to present to the House of Lords the petitions herewith sent, from the ministers, church-wardens and inhabitants of the parishes of Dickleburgh, Redenhall with Harleston, Mattishall, Hockering with Mattishall Burgh, and Honingham with Tuddenham in the county of Norfolk against the claims of the Dissenters.

Lord Bayning is personally acquainted with the ministers of the above named parishes, and he believes that all the marks as well as the signatures were freely and willingly affixed; and Lord Bayning trusts that the extreme importance of the matters referred to in these petitions will justify him in troubling the Duke of Wellington with this request.

Draft reply 20 June 1834. Compliments to Lord Bayning. The Duke will present to the House of Lords the petitions to which his Lordship refers.

The Mayor of Leeds (Benjamin Sadler) to Wellington, 21 June 1834

Leeds. I beg to inform your Grace that I transmitted through the post office on Monday last a packet addressed to your Grace, containing an address to His Majesty, unanimously adopted by the corporation of this borough, on the necessity of preserving inviolate the Established Church, with a request that your Grace would take an early opportunity of presenting the same to the King. I have this day been informed by the town clerk who sent the packet to the post office that the person who delivered it asked if any charge would be made upon it as he was ordered to pay it, and was answered that it would go free; upon enquiry, however, I find from the head clerk at the post office that the packet was charged twelve or fourteen shillings! in consequence of which the town clerk has written to Sir Francis Freeling desiring that the packet may be delivered to your Grace without delay free, and the charge will be paid at the post office here. I hope your Grace will excuse this long explanation.

Draft reply 24 June 1834. Compliments. The Duke has received the address from the town of Leeds to the King, which the Duke will present to His Majesty upon the first occasion that may offer.

The clerks at Somerset House to Wellington, 23 June 1834

Somerset House. The undersigned, upon reading in the debates of the House of Lords on Friday night that your Grace intends making some observations in the committee upon the Civil Pensions Bill, take the liberty of humbly soliciting your Grace's kind consideration to their peculiar case as affected by that bill.

The lords of the Treasury by minute dated the 4th August, 1829 directed an abatement at the rate of five per cent. to be made from the salaries (above £100) of all persons who might be appointed after that date to meet the expense of their superannuation.

The parties subjected to this minute indulged the hope that in consideration of the abatement therein directed they would be allowed to participate in the advantages of the scale of retiring allowances *which existed* when they were appointed to their present situations, they therefore view with feelings of deep disappointment that after having held their situations for nearly five years, the ninth clause of this bill proposes to apply a new and much lower scale of superannuation in their cases.

They cannot but look upon this clause as partial in as much as while it affects their interests it is retrospective in its operation and they venture to hope that your Grace may take the same view and so far befriend them as to suggest that the new scale be applied only to such persons as may enter the service after the passing of the bill.

In conclusion they beg to observe that as the appointments since 1829 have been few, and in many cases the vacancies have been filled by persons who held situations prior to that period and consequently will not be subjected to this bill, the extra charge will be very trifling if they be allowed the benefit of the old scale.

Signed by the following clerks in the Admiralty office: W. Anderson, J. Martin, Robert Atkinson, James Bowden, Joseph Saul, Edward Cahill, Robert Thompson, Thomas James, John Matson, C. E. Lang, William Eden.

Signed by the following clerks in the Navy pay office; G. J. Pound, H. Sadler, Henry Morgan, W. J. Eyre, H. A. Reid.

The Rev. George Jenkinson to Wellington, 23 June 1834

Lowick. I am requested by the inhabitants of the chapelry of Lowick, in the county of Northumberland and diocese of Durham to entreat of your Grace to do them the honor to present the accompanying petition signed by 150.

Signed: George Jenkinson, perpetual curate of Lowick.

Draft reply 26 June 1834. Compliments. The Duke will present to the House of Lords the petition to which he refers in his note.

573

The Rev. George Rowley to Wellington, 23 June 1834

Oxford. It has been determined at our weekly meeting held this morning that it would be expedient to put matters in train for presenting an address to the King against the bill for admitting Dissenters into the universities, with as little delay as possible after it shall have passed the House of Commons. Should your Grace be inclined to favor us with any suggestions on the subject, I will take the earliest opportunity of submitting them to the board of heads of houses and proctors.

Wellington to the Rev. George Rowley, 24 June 1834

London. I have no objection to the university presenting a petition on the subject of the bill now depending in Parliament to admit Dissenters to the universities, provided it is to the King on the throne.

It is quite certain that the bill will pass through the House of Commons; with what provisions is not clear; it appears to me quite certain that it will be thrown out in the House of Lords whatever may be its provisions.

Under these circumstances you will judge for yourselves whether you will petition, or only prepare a petition to be presented in case I should be mistaken in my expectation of the course which the House of Lords will take in respect to the bill.

I have not much confidence in the moderation or discretion of the existing Administration, and I should not be surprised if they were to insert in the King's answer to your petition expressions of reproach that you objected to admit Dissenters to your University, while your council objected to the grant of a charter to an university established by the Dissenters. However I don't think that the apprehension of such an answer ought to prevent you from presenting a petition, if such a course should be desirable.

Viscount Strangford to Wellington, 24 June 1834

Brighton. I think it right not to withhold from your Grace the part of the enclosed letter which relates to you. It comes from the head of the principal house in England connected with the silk manufacture, and it is very satisfactory to find that these people are content with what we did the other night and that they think we acted properly in not going further. All this shews that your Grace is always in the right, and (what is just as little surprising) that *I* am very often in the wrong. I do confess, however, that I should have liked to have beaten our opposite neighbours in the House, and to have forced them to *re-beat* us, by their proxies. However, I have no doubt that the course we took was the proper one.

So, Lord Clanricarde has got out of the boat! I have long suspected that such would be the case. The real cause of complaint is Lord Grey having assured him when he applied for an Irish peerage for Sir John Burke (his uncle) that he (Lord Grey) did not mean, for the present, to make any Irish peers. In six weeks afterwards, my Lord Carew was gazetted! All this I learned yesterday from Sir John Burke himself.

I shall be in town on Thursday, and in the meantime have left my proxy with the Duke of Gloucester.

Draft reply 25 June, 1834. Many thanks, my dear Lord Strangford, for your note and letter inclosed, which I return.

It is quite provoking to be in the right so often!!

Wellington to the Bishop of London, 24 June 1834

London. I have had the honor of receiving your Lordship's letter regarding a passage by the Tower wharf to the ship moored in the river, for the purpose of affording to the seamen and others residing in that part of the town an opportunity of attending divine service. It is very desirable to avoid to impose restrictions upon a communication with the river, from the Tower and its wharf. But the Tower contains large quantities of gunpowder and other stores under the charge of the Ordnance which are at times in the course of embarkation or dis-embarkation at the wharfs. It is besides necessary to take care of these stores, and of the works of the Tower as a fortress; and it is difficult to form an arrangement which shall provide for these duties at the same time that it shall give permission to seamen and others to resort to the wharf for the purpose or under the pretence on going on board a vessel to attend divine service. Under these circumstances and referring to what has passed heretofore upon this same subject I am concerned that I cannot give my consent as Constable of the Tower to the proposition made by your Lordship.

John Charles Herries to Wellington, 24 June 1834

Albemarle Street. I send you a memorandum of votes last year and in the present at the instigation of private parties who have solicited the House of Commons and have obtained favor either in spite of the opposition of the Minister, or with a reluctant assent on his part. In Marshall's case the Government were divided. Lord John Russell supported him and Poulett Thomson opposed him.

But I am bound to state that *I* do not think it was an unfair grant, although most of our friends are of a different opinion.

It must be observed however that all of these claims have been preferred on the *ground* of justice.

The committee on Bode and on Buckingham have not yet reported.

It will be said that they will obtain nothing except a clear foundation of claim [to] be made out. Codrington's vote is yet to be discussed in a committee of the whole House. But the discussion will relate more to the amount than to the propriety of the grant.

Docketed Incloses list of grants in contemplation in the House of Commons. Pensions granted instead of sinecure places.

First enclosure:

1832–3.
Marshall—

500—	Services in compiling accounts.
2,625—	For purchase of his statistical work.

1834.

Baron de Bode—	A committee of his own choosing to investigate his claims.
Buckingham—	A committee of his own choosing to investigate his claims.
Captain Ross—	5,000—granted.
Codrington—	Resolution passed to consider of a grant in committee.

Second enclosure: Printed paper entitled 'Accounts respecting offices abolished or regulated under Acts passed for the regulating public offices'.

Annotated in Herries's hand.

The Bishop of Worcester (Robert James Carr) to Wellington, 24 June 1834

Hartlebury Castle, near Stourport. The Bishop of Worcester presents his respectful compliments to the Duke of Wellington, and requests the favor of his Grace to present a petition to the House of Lords from the inhabitants of the parish of Claines in the County of Worcester, against the admission of Dissenters into our universities. It is most correctly worded and respectably signed.

PS. The petition is directed to his Grace, at the House of Lords.

Draft reply 25 June 1834. Compliments. The Duke has received his Lordship's note.

He will present to the House of Lords the petition to which his Lordship refers on the first occasion that will offer consistently with the orders of the House.

The Bishop of Exeter to Wellington, 25 June 1834

9 Mansfield Street. Taking into account the declarations of the King's Ministers in the House of Commons on Monday night, I do not think it possible that the bishops can forbear to address His Majesty, either beseeching him to revoke the commission, or in some other way expressing our sense of the dangers, which beset the Church, and calling on him to do what he has so recently pledged himself to do. The awful rite, in which we joined with him on Sunday last, adds to our obligation not to sit still and see him, whether wilfully or recklessly, sacrifice the best interests of religion, without raising our voice against his proceedings. Duty to the King himself, to our own character, and, above all, to our heavenly master, seem to me to demand this of us.

If, indeed, our taking such a step would embarrass the course, which your Grace and the other friends of the Church think it most wise to pursue, we ought to pause, or to modify our procedure. I venture, therefore, to entreat your Grace to say whether you think that we should embarrass you or others by addressing His Majesty.

To my poor judgment it would seem likely that such a step might be serviceable. It would afford the King a plea for resisting his Ministers, if he is inclined to resist them, and might be the foundation for an appeal to the people, in the name of the King, and in the cause of religion. It would also avoid the mischief of involving the House of Lords in an aggressive conflict with the House of Commons. That House would thus be what it is peculiarly fitted to be, the auxiliary of the King in defending the best and most sacred institutions of the country.

We bishops should, indeed, be committed. But we must be content to be so. For those interests which are especially entrusted to our guardianship and fidelity are openly assailed, and we are bound to defend them at any hazard to ourselves. This consideration does not forbid, on the contrary it enjoins, our having recourse to all the expedients of genuine prudence; and therefore it is, that I venture to seek the counsel of one whose wisdom has with me the highest authority on all occasions.

Wellington to the Bishop of Exeter, 25 June 1834

London. When an important body, such as the bishops of the Church of England, are to be put in motion, we must be quite certain of our ground and must see clearly our object.

The ground is the trickery of the Ministers on the subject of their intentions in relation to the disposal of the property of the Church in Ireland.

Nobody can have doubted that this ground has existed since they have been in office. In plain terms, Lord Brougham is in opposition to Mr. Ellice and Lord John Russell. But they will act together to plunder the Irish Church and to give the spoil to the Roman Catholicks, and both parties will prove, each in his separate House of Parliament, that he has been consistent. But these tricks are not grounds on which the bishops can found a proceeding. Ought they to do so on the commission itself? They can scarcely take this course without reminding the King of his speech. Supposing they omit the speech in their representation excepting by general reference to His Majesty's solemn oaths and his declarations, what would be the object of their representation? What its consequences? They should represent to the King the illegality of the commission; the right of every individual to refuse to swear or to answer to such enquiries. They should point out the avowed object of the enquiries as declared in the House of Commons, and they should call upon His Majesty, in conformity with his oaths and promises, to cancel this commission, and to declare his determination to maintain the Church of England in Ireland. These would be your objects, your course and your language.

The answer would be that of the King's Ministers. It would contain a specious defence of their own measures, an accusation of the measures of former reigns and a positive denial of the just inferences, which you would have drawn from their speeches and their measures in your address to the King. Those who never doubted of the real meaning of the speech of the 28th May would receive from all this only a confirmation of the truth of their opinion.

Those who had confided in the King's declarations then made will begin to hesitate and doubt. They will see that all is not right. They will not know exactly how it happens that it was all right on the 28 May and all wrong on the 28 June. In these hesitations and doubts the innocent and least powerful party, the bishops, will not have a full measure of justice.

The least that they will be accused of will be imprudence in relying upon and publishing the King's speech of the 28 May and thus exciting the hopes of the publick, and then in addressing the Monarch in such manner as to draw an answer from him in direct contradiction with the declarations of the speech but consistent with the actions of the 28 May.

I doubt the prudence of this proceeding.

In such times as these, in which falsehood is the principal instrument used I cannot decide what to advise, excepting that such a body as the bishops should be quite certain of the ground on which they stand and of the object of any proceeding.

Dated (incorrectly) June 24, 1834. *Docketed* June 25.

Thomas Morgan to Wellington, 25 June 1834

Burgh Heath. It is supposed that you and your friends are favorable to the cause of Don Carlos, and it may not have occurred to you that he could very easily possess himself of the Canary Islands, if he took a small force there before the Spanish troops were unoccupied by the troubles in Spain; for at present the Court of Madrid certainly cannot attend to transmarine dangers.

It would be a very desirable circumstance for England, if those islands became a separate state, as we should not only have the principal trade therewith, but might therefrom trade to the interior of Africa, through the desert, by means of those very Arabs who now interrupt all intercourse.

Those islands could maintain a militia of 20,000 men, and would become a more powerful and wealthy State than Brabant or Piedmont; that is, if Don Carlos had sufficient knowledge of mankind to allow every man the liberty to do what he pleased, so that he did not interfere with the comfort of any other man. For that proviso includes all the real difference between English ideas of liberty and European continental ideas thereof.

You may recollect my wish to induce your administration to colonise Bulola territory. It would be easy to fit out one large vessel with five hundred men for that purpose, which Don Carlos and his officers could join at sea; and they could surprise Teneriffe, like Lord Nelson did, and then a sensible proclamation would make all the militia friends to him, instead of being foes, as they were to Lord Nelson.

It should promise that all the population should be armed, and that the workmen should have a house of representatives and the upper classes another, and that there should not be any law whatever without the concurrence of both houses.

Thus might your friends establish a far more liberal government than any in Europe, and attain for the Tories an unexampled popularity here. Thus would Don Carlos secure a valuable kingdom, instead of being an outcast, a kingdom which might open his way to the throne of Spain. Thus could England have a new vent for her manufactures and thus should I be able to effect my purpose at Bulola; which last consequence would certainly be the means of increasing British trade to double its present amount and of reducing the national debt at least one fourth, within two years, by the gold-mines of Boori.

In case the Prince succeeded at Teneriffe, there would not be any occasion for the ruinous expense of a naval armament to keep up the intercourse with the other islands. He need only proclaim that all English steamers carrying twelve or more cannon and ammunition sufficient to defend themselves well should have free trade between the islands, and from them to the African coast; and also a very favored trade between Teneriffe and the British islands, for Teneriffe must be the centre of strength and of trade.

There is finer fruit in the Canaries than in the Azores, and it ripens much earlier; and steamers would reach London sooner from the former, than the orange vessels reach it now from the latter. I've tasted

Canary wine, like Tokay; and the wheat is transparent like *amber*, the Hesperides being its original country, and thence came the *ambrosia*. Much more could be suggested by me, if the subject is esteemed worthy of consideration.

The Rev. William Greene to Wellington, 26 June 1834

Ballymoney, County Antrim, Ireland. Apprehending as I do, with other ministers of the Church establishment in Ireland, the serious consequences which must inevitably follow the present clergy, if visited with the severe and extraordinary enactments of Mr. Littleton's Tithe Bill, I hope I may be excused the liberty I thus take in addressing your Grace.

In the first place, my Lord, it appears by the bill that the income of the present rectors of the Church is to be reduced fifteen per cent. per annum for the next three years, and after that period a further deduction of twenty-two and a half per cent. more is to be charged, thereby deducting thirty-seven and half pounds from every hundred pounds of their income; which must oblige them to give up the life insurances they have made, as a future support for their families.

In the next place, their present credit and respectability will, by so serious a deduction of income, be irrevocably shaken, and many of them thrown into great difficulties. Added to which—I speak from a communication I lately had with several of my brethren upon the subject—an almost general disengagement with their respective assistant curates must follow, leaving those gentlemen, who have devoted the greater part of their lives to the sacred call of their profession, almost without support.

These, my Lord, are distressing and alarming hardships, which, it is presumed, should not under any innovation, in justice, affect the clergy of the present day; and which they humbly hope, should the bill not be thrown out altogether, your Grace and the supporters of the Church will endeavour to avert.

Signed: William Greene, rector of the parish of Ballymoney, County Antrim, Ireland.

Docketed by Wellington Compliments. The Duke has received his letter. *Docketed by secretary* Done. July 4.

Wellington to Sir George Murray, 27 June 1834

London. I return the two letters which you have sent me. I have no acquaintance at Rome at present; although I am supposed to possess an influence there.

I don't think that I could venture to address a letter to Cardinal Bernetti such as is mentioned by Mr. Stewart. But possibly I may be able to obtain for him a letter of recommendation from an influential person in which my name may be mentioned as the person who has applied for it. If I should be able to obtain such a one I will send it to you.

NLS ADV MS 46.8.6, ff. 155, 156.

Sir John Rae Reid to Wellington, 27 June 1834

Pall Mall. With reference to the conversation I had the pleasure of holding with your Grace upon the subject of the Cinque Ports Pilots Bill, if you will have the kindness to fix any day and hour next week, Sir Thomas Troubridge, Mr. Marryat, Mr. Young, Mr. Marjoribanks and myself will have the honor of waiting upon your Grace in the hope that some plan may be proposed, by which the interests of all parties may be considered.

Sir Thomas Troubridge will postpone the second reading of the bill, which was fixed *for this night.*

Dated Friday morning. *Docketed* 27 June 1834.

Wellington to Sir John Rae Reid, 27 June 1834

London. If Sir Thomas Troubridge wishes to converse with me on the subject of his bill, I will request Mr. Herries and Mr. Jenkinson to come here on any day at 12 o'clock that he will appoint.

I confess that excepting upon publick grounds it is a matter of indifference to me what becomes of the bill.

All that I desire is that somebody shall be responsible in character at least for the alterations to be made in this ancient establishment, which I conceive to be an affair of government.

Wellington to Thomas Morgan, 27 June 1834

The Duke of Wellington presents his compliments to Mr. Thomas Morgan.

The Duke is a faithful subject of the King of Great Britain and Ireland; and he obeys and respects the laws of the country.

The Duke cannot be a party to any counsel given to Don Carlos to attack the dominions of Spain, a country in alliance with His Majesty; much less can he be a party to the formation or execution of any plan of attack upon the dominions of Spain by adventurers from this country with a view to the extension of British commerce.

The Rev. Thomas Sutton to Wellington, 28 June 1834

Sheffield Vicarage. Will your Grace do us the honour to present the accompanying petition, against the admission of Dissenters to our universities, to the House of Lords? I have done myself the honour of sending it to your Grace as the Chancellor of my own university.

To myself the first sheet, as emanating from a provincial town, is rather interesting, inasmuch as it contains the signatures of twenty-three gentlemen, lay and clerical, who have been educated at our universities; and of seven others, who have incurred the expense, or are incurring it, of educating sons or near relatives there. One of the latter class had a son brought up in our national school, who afterwards entered at Cambridge, and was Senior Wrangler and first Smith's prizeman.

Draft reply 6 July 1834. Compliments. The Duke will present to the House of Lords on the first occasion that will offer consistently with the orders of the House the petition from Sheffield to which he refers after it will reach him.

The Earl of Carnarvon to Wellington, 29 June 1834

Highclere. At the late Hampshire meeting of lay members of the Church a resolution, as your Grace is perhaps aware, was carried that the address enclosed in another letter be adopted and that your Grace be respectfully requested to present the same to His Majesty. I have only this moment received a copy of the address and make no delay in forwarding it, assuring you at the same [time] of the earnest and unanimous hope expressed that you would be so good as to present the address to the King. The address will, I trust, be ready in a few days and will be sent to your Grace as soon as the signatures are affixed.

The address and petitions were drawn up in a very general way and the discussion was for the most part of a very general nature as some apprehension existed lest a difference of opinion should appear and destroy the apparent unanimity of the meeting, particularly as it was known that the two Whig members for Winchester intended to be present and therefore the ground was felt to be rather ticklish. For this reason some of the most objectionable claims put forward by the Dissenters, such as their admission into the universities etc., were scarcely alluded to. There was, however, in fact only one attempt made to interrupt the harmony of the meeting (by a Radical attorney, I believe) and this attempt was unsupported by the general sense of the meeting and quite unsuccessful. The general feeling evinced by those who attended the meeting was excellent and I may perhaps be permitted to add that your Grace's name was received with very great and very gratifying enthusiasm.

The clergy of Winchester have done me the very undeserved honor of publishing the few remarks I made. As they have done so, I have taken the liberty of desiring a copy to be forwarded to your Grace.

I have just received the invitation for the 2nd of July which you have been so good as to send Lady Carnarvon and me. We regret extremely that our absence in the country which is still unavoidably protracted (though but, I trust, for a few days longer) will prevent our having the honor of waiting on you on that day. I rejoice to hear that your Grace is perfectly well.

Robert Henry Jenkinson to Wellington, 30 June 1834

Norbiton. Mr. Pain informs me that your Grace has appointed to see Sir Thomas Troubridge at Apsley House on Wednesday. I am sorry it will not be in my power to attend, as I leave this early tomorrow morning for Dover, to hold the Court there on Wednesday, for which day it has been summoned according to the arrangement I made with your Grace when I last had the honor of waiting upon you. I hope to be at home again on Thursday evening; Mr. Pain will however attend your Grace on Wednesday, and I have desired him to summon any of the wardens or pilots should their assistance or opinion be required.

With reference to Sir Thomas Troubridge's proposed bill I have already submitted to your Grace the objections to it in Mr. Pain's report thereupon, and of which I have desired him to furnish your Grace with a copy, as you may have given the original paper to Mr. Herries. But I learn from Mr. Pain that there is another bill which may prove even more injurious to the interests of the pilots than that which Sir Thomas Troubridge is about to bring forward, and which is to be brought in by Mr. Young, to exempt all vessels not exceeding 200 tons, and being British, from taking pilots, sailing from ports between Boulogne and the Schaw to London. This if adopted will include *all* British vessels trading from those ports, the pilotage of which constitutes so large a proportion of the employment of pilots at Ramsgate and Margate that they could not exist in those places. Upon reference to Mr. Pain's letter I see that the above proposal of Mr. Young's is not to form a separate bill, but to be inserted in committee, as a clause in Sir Thomas Troubridge's bill; thus I fear that during the proceedings upon this bill other clauses materially interfering with the present system will be attempted to be introduced, and that a constant attention will be necessary on the part of our friends to maintain and uphold it.

Wellington to Sir Henry Hardinge, 1 July 1834

London. Private and confidential. I have heard that the gentlemen of the *Morning Post* think of leaving their editor in custody; and that they will not petition.

The rule of the House is that no person can be released from custody without petitioning. From custody the course is to send the culprit to Newgate.

It would be very harsh towards this individual to expose him to this punishment upon a point of party vanity; or in hopes which I understand that some wisemen entertain that the House of Commons will interfere in favour of the liberty of the subject.

The House of Commons will see the *Morning Post* and the House of Lords at the devil before they will interfere.

I intreat you to give a hint to any of our friends who may have influence in these proceedings that they may urge the gentlemen of the *Post* to take effectual measures to get out of this scrape as soon as possible.

PS. I am going to the [*Messiah*] which is the reason for my troubling you.

VISCOUNT HARDINGE PAPERS.

Frederick Augustus Carrington to Wellington, 1 July 1834

Abingdon. I sometime since had the honor of mentioning to your Grace my idea that sending paupers to the place of their birth and having no other species of settlement would send a great number of paupers from the large town to the country parishes and very few from the country parishes to the large towns.

I have since made enquiries on the subject and from all the information I can get I find that that idea is correct.

I am informed by one of the select vestry of a large Westminster parish that a considerable number of the paupers of that parish were country-born and I find on enquiring of several overseers of country parishes that they have not any pauper who was born either in London or in any large town.

A few days ago I saw by the papers that a discussion had occurred in the House of Commons as to whether General Moreno could be tried here for an alleged murder of Mr. Boyd in Spain in which there was certainly no great display of legal knowledge and as the matter may probably be debated in the House of Lords, your Grace may like to know that till the year 1828 murders committed on land abroad were triable under the statutes 33 Hen. 8, c. 23 and 43 Geo. 3, c. 113.

By the statute 9 Geo. 4, c. 31 both those statutes are wholly repealed and under the statute 9 Geo. 4, c. 31 s. 7 murders committed on land abroad must be committed *by His Majesty's subjects* or they are not triable here and in the case of Captain Helsham (which is reported in 4th Carrington and Payne's reports, page 394) it was decided by Mr. Justice Bayley and Mr. Justice Bosanquet that an indictment for a murder committed at Boulogne must state the prisoner to be a British subject and that it must be proved to the satisfaction of the jury that he in fact is so.

Docketed by Wellington Compliments. Received. The Duke is much obliged to him. *Docketed by secretary* Done. July 2.

Lady Salisbury's diary, 1 July 1834

The Duke of Cumberland dined here. I never can ask the Duke to meet either Cumberland or Gloucester, as he has a horror of it: and their surprise at *never* meeting him here increases every time they come. It is

586

difficult sometimes to find an answer to their very pointed questions on the subject.

James Edward Devereux to Wellington, 2 July 1834

Chapter Coffee House, St. Paul's. You will see in the Dublin *Evening Post* and in the London *Morning Post* of this day a prospectus of a bank set up by Mr. O'Connell signed by twenty persons of whom fourteen [are] Members of Parliament and of the fourteen, nine are of Daniel's tail.

Not being master of the subject I cannot say whether this scheme will succeed or not, but I hear from tolerable authority that it will, and do not think that that financier, Sir John Parnell, would have allowed his brother-in-law, who is at the head of the list and a man of large fortune and great private worth (Evans of Portren, M.P. for the County Dublin) to have gotten into the affair was it not one worth attending to: there is besides the name of Roche of Limerick, M.P., of Lynch, M.P. and both gentlemen of steadiness, judgment and property. All this tends to persuade me that the thing will succeed.

Now what I wish to submit to your Grace's more serious consideration is this, that Mr. O'Connell is at the moment, and has been for some time past, actively engaged in inducing his partisans in every corner of Ireland to take shares in this bank (in which you will see by the prospectus all his family are concerned) in order that not a farmer or shopkeeper throughout Ireland shall get a bill discounted except more or less according to the *liberator's* pleasure, so that by means of this power he will convert the towns and counties of Ireland into so many rotten boroughs to be wielded for his profit.

Under these circumstances I humbly presume to give my opinion that it would be more advisable that the friends to the peace of Ireland and of the welfare of the empire, and consequently the enemies of demagogues and agitators, should in every town and county in Ireland either take shares in this bank or set up another bank on the same general principle, otherwise the joints of Dan's tail will be tripled next election.

PS. In a letter I had the honor of addressing to your Grace in 1829, I distinctly shewed with what ease the Paris bankers commanded the elections throughout France, etc., etc.

Draft reply 4 July 1834. Compliments. Received. The Duke does not know how he is to prevent Mr. O'Connell from setting up a bank, or to prevail upon others to set up one, unless he should himself set the example, which he certainly will not do.

Wellington to the Earl of Carnarvon, 3 July 1834

London. I have had the honor of receiving your letter of the 29 June and the address from the county of Hampshire, which I will present to the King the first opportunity that I shall have of approaching His Majesty.

I sincerely wish that His Majesty may be able to fulfil the expectations of his people founded upon the speech referred to.

The Rev. Henry John Todd to Wellington, 4 July 1834

Settrington, Malton. On your Grace's benignity to pardon the present trespass on your valuable time I beg most respectfully to express my reliance.

The occasion is this: the clergy of the archdeaconry of Cleveland, in the diocese and county of York agreed in last week at Stokesley, Thirsk and Malton, that an address should be offered to the King on account of His Majesty's late gracious declaration in favour of the Established Church; and a petition to the House of Lords against the admission of Dissenters to our two famous universities and their respective privileges. It was my duty, and it was a great pleasure, to forward these memorials to our diocesan, who, however, as a bishop, cannot (his Grace has been pleased to inform me) present the address, as it distinctly refers to the royal speech delivered in *private* to the *prelates*, which therefore by *them* is not thus to be recognized as a *public* document. The Archbishop has added that either the address might be altered, so as that a prelate might present it; or a lay-peer might present it unaltered.

The former method, my Lord, could not easily be adopted, as the clergy of a very long and wide district might not readily be assembled again to sign another document. In thinking, therefore, of the latter method, I could not but call to mind your Grace and your repeated declarations of attachment to the Established Church. Accordingly I presume thus humbly and earnestly to entreat your Grace to do that for us which our diocesan, but for the reason assigned, would have done.

I have communicated to the Archbishop what I have now written; and he will send to your Grace the address, if you have the goodness and condescension to grant my request.

Signed: Henry John Todd, Archdeacon of Cleveland.

Sir Robert Peel to Wellington, 4 July 1834

Whitehall. Mr. Shaw, the Member for Dublin, came to me yesterday with a message from the Primate of Ireland, asking my opinion as to the policy of the Irish bishops presenting an address to the King respecting the Irish Church, and as to the tenor of the address in case an address was thought desirable.

I told Mr. Shaw that I for one saw no object in the bishops addressing the King at this moment; that if they had full confidence in his determination to support the Church, an address was unnecessary; that if they had not full confidence, to assure the King they had it (which was the purport of the address) could be of no advantage, and that the result of their proceeding would probably be that the Ministers would compel the King to deliver a formal official answer, perhaps at variance with, certainly confirming the purport of his former answer to the English bishops.

I strongly dissuaded the presentation of the address, but if you should see the matter in a different point of view, I would make a further communication to the Primate.

I saw Sir James Graham yesterday on the Irish Tithe Bill. He and Stanley will warmly support the principle of the original bill, which the Government will propose materially to alter.

Wellington to Sir Robert Peel, 5 July 1834

London. I entirely concur in the advice which you have given to the Irish bishops. One of the English bishops wrote to me some days ago upon the same subject. He wished that the English bench should address the King. I recommended that they should not do so for nearly the same reasons stated in your note. The bishops knowing that Mr. Stanley and his friends had retired from the Government on the day previous to that on which his Majesty had addressed them, and that the King had accepted their resignations and had formed a new ministry on the principle against which Mr. Stanley and his friends had protested and had resigned their offices, ought not to have published the King's speech. And they ought not to have attended the King at the Chapel Royal on the 22nd of June; at which time they must have been well aware of the course which the Government was taking, notwithstanding the King's declarations.

The publick in England as well as in Ireland have been deceived. It is impossible to undeceive them without exposing the origin of the deception.

I believe that there is nothing that people care so much about as the Church, excepting always their own properties. But I doubt the wisdom of letting them know that they have been deceived by a speech of the King published by the bishops themselves, at the very moment that they knew that the course taken by the King and his newly-formed Government was the reverse of that indicated and promised in the speech.

ADD MS 40309, ff. 268, 269. *Draft in Wellington Papers.*

Richard Oastler to Wellington, 5 July 1834

33 Perceval Street, Northampton Square. Allow me to thank your Grace for the honor you have done me by admitting me to your Grace's presence and to your correspondence.

When I inform your Grace that fear has ever been a stranger to my nature; that I have only one motive, the good of my country; and that I am always most happy when I am overcoming difficulties; nay, that I am never so certain of success as when others would exclaim, 'there is no hope, no chance'. When I see despair darkening the brows of other men, I am wont to smile and patiently to persevere.

Hence, my Lord Duke, I gained confidence yesterday when most men would have shrunk in despair, fancying there was 'no hope'. My Lord I do hope I am not wanting in respect, nay in veneration for your Grace's character; charge me not with vanity and impertinence if I *once* more attempt to do that which your Grace declared to be impossible: to convince your Grace that my views are sound, practicable and above all *constitutional*.

My Lord, the *people* of England are not, as a body, disaffected in heart! They have been deluded, deceived and betrayed; but, my Lord, by whom have they been seduced? By certain members of your Grace's own 'order', aided by the servile portion of the press. They have been taught to hate the King, to insult and groan at the Queen and to despise the House of Lords. Nay, one of the members of your Lordship's house (whose father, by the by, was chiefly influential in *forcing* Mr. Pitt into the expences of the French war) has, in his *own person*, set the *people* the example of 'refusing to pay taxes', and he has never been arraigned at your Lordship's bar! Blame not the *people* then my Lord Duke; but blame those *nobles* (?) who have misled the *people*; aye and that house which has neglected to punish a treasonable guilty peer.

There can be no doubt that *just now* we have *no Government*. And why? —because the hearts of the people have been estranged from the authority of law by those very persons who now *pretend* to govern the country, because the people have been taught *by these very men* to despise the King, the Lords and the law! and because the people discover, in every measure proposed by *these men*, cruelty, tyranny and hypocrisy. Every measure they propose is calculated to advance the *aristocracy of wealth*, but to destroy the aristocracy of worth and of blood, and to sink the working classes to the condition of slaves and criminals. My Lord, this is all *true*! The people know it is true, and they are now fast destroying the magic power of party names in politics, and are at this moment, from every corner of the empire, looking to the House of Lords (whom they have been taught to insult and despise) to save them from the crucible of capital.

The Poor Law Bill, my Lord Duke, is a direct attack on the *constitution*, on the magistracy, on the land, on the rights of private* property

---

* What greater legal and constitutional *right* can be given to compel a parish, which has managed its affairs carefully and prudently, and has thereby prevented the increase of its 'poor rates', to pay towards the expences of another parish, which has increased its rates by improvidence and mismanagement, than there is a legal and constitutional right to compel your Grace to sacrifice your private property towards the liquidation of the debts of those East India merchants, who have just failed by wholesale? Or what right can there be to 'commission' *your* Grace's property, because *they* have ruined theirs? I apprehend there is no right whatever; I am sure there ought to be none. Your Grace may answer, 'the consent of the "guardian" must be obtained'. But why should the property of the parish be subjected by law to the will of the 'guardian', any more than your Grace's private property should be subjected to the will and caprice of your Grace's steward? I must say I cannot separate the cases; the parish is someone's private property, and I humbly suggest that if the East India merchants

and on the last remaining hopes of industrious poverty. It removes from the protection of law £7,000,000 a year! It legalises poverty as a crime!! And is intended to *force* the bravest peasantry in the world, to seek a home in foreign climes, pretending there are too many of them here! Good God! is this possible? Of what use is all the property in the land, or the capital either, when the sound, healthy industrious labourers are transported, and the sickly, weak, lame, helpless invalids are left behind? Men can neither eat gold nor land. The bare idea that we have more healthy labourers than we want is an insult to the Deity himself. We have room and work and food enough for them all, *if we would but protect their labour.*

I was struck with horror, when your Grace assured me that the state of labourers in the south was infinitely worse than that in the north. In the north it is bad enough; hundreds and thousands are there living on a *short allowance* of water porridge and potatoes, *never tasting flesh meat,* save when charity, at very distant intervals, visits their desolate homes. *This is true.* But these men are not idle, not vicious, not tumultuous, no, they labour from morn to night to obtain their scanty fare. Aye, and they are in England too, the pride of the manufacturing world!—making clothes for all the world, themselves clothed in rags! I am not here speaking of *un*employed labourers. Now, if employed labourers in the south are worse then these, I ask, is it not time to enquire the cause, and to administer a remedy? 'We want a strong Government.' So we do; strong in *good measures* to insure the reverence of the people; not strong in delusion and deceit and tyranny, as our present Government is; nor strong in steel and lead, as a military Government would be. But strong in sound constitutional measures, protecting, as our much despised and traduced forefathers did, the labour of industrious workmen. Why, in the name of common sense, should aristocracy and honest industry be any longer prostrated under the monster, capital! Why should the hearts of these classes be estranged from each other, by the delusions and lies of the mere money-scraping, money-keeping capitalist? The aristocracy were wont to

---

have mismanaged their affairs, it would be unjust and unconstitutional to pass a law that your Grace's private property should be confiscated to provide for their deficiencies; and I am sure it is equally unjust and unconstitutional that any parish or *any part of a parish* should by an Act of Parliament be confiscated, for the purpose of paying the debts of another parish, without the consent of the owner or owners thereof. R. O.

rejoice in the happy jollity of the labourer; the labourer, in former days, boasted of the generosity and benevolence of the nobles; but the money-scraper (in the hope of circumventing both) has poured poison in the ears of each and made them believe they are each others enemies! God intended they should be friends.

Does the capitalist threaten to take his money away, if you interfere with it? Then let it go, we can make more if we want it; only let us have our hardy labourers, our engineers, mechanics and our soil, with a good Government *strong* in the hearts of the people, and we will laugh as he leaves our shores in the *vain* hope of profiting in other places more than in old England.

My Lord Duke, we have all been slaves to capital long enough; it was the secret working of this power which compelled your Grace's resignation. It is the self-same power, which empties the cottage of all its comforts. The *un*controlled power of capital will soon, very soon, hurl the King from his throne and the nobles from their mansions. How many of the estates of our ancient nobility have already been spindle-ized? Aye, my Lord Duke, you may smile, but these men know how to spin parchment, signed by the noblest hands in Britain, into yarn, as well as my poor factory-children's sinews and bones.* What charm is there in the capitalist, that he alone should be unrestricted and untaxed? I confess I know of none he possesses over the nobles of the land or over the creators of his capital.

Oh! what a beautiful ship was England once: well built, well manned, well commanded, well rigged; all were merry, cheerful and happy on board. She *then* cared not if all the world frowned; she *was* a world in herself. But *now* if a petty German state says 'bow-wow-wow', her commander unburdens himself of his sword, takes off his hat,

* Last year I had occasion to be in Manchester on business with an eminent land-agent and valuer; he told me that 'about thirty years ago a certain nobleman, with whom he was transacting business in Manchester, expressed a desire to go into a mill'. (There were not many then, it was Mr. Peel's mill they visited.) As they were returning, the nobleman observed, 'Well A——, I see very clearly what is going on here: these *spindles* will in two generations draw all the parchment in Lancashire to Manchester.' My friend added, 'His Lordship's prediction is now fast in the course of fulfilment, for it is astonishing how many of the estates of Lancashire and Cheshire have their title deeds lodged in Manchester.' My informant is himself a large millowner, as well as a land-agent, and no-one knows more about these matters than he does. R. O.

apologises and steers another course! But if *France* says 'fight', then straight he goes to war!!

My Lord Duke, the canker worm of England is unrestricted capital! So long as Messrs. Rothschild, Morrison, Marshall and Co., are allowed to '*do what they like with their own*'; it is in vain that the Duke of Wellington conquered the world! It cannot be said he has saved England, so long as she bleeds at every pore under the pressure of the unrestricted capitalist, so long as she trembles at the frown of any foreign state, so long as *France* is her corporal, and can command her to the right or the left!

Excuse me, my Lord Duke, I feel excruciatingly on this subject. I feel for the constitution: I cannot see her dismantled, without using every effort to save her.

True, she lost her rudder by the Emancipation Bill. Her keel was destroyed by the Reform Bill. Sir Robert Peel's bill removed her cargo from the hold and placed it on the decks.

The Poor Law Bill will confine her officers and crew in irons below (but they will make very unsteady ballast in a storm). A few *piratical* 'commissioners', to be sure, may for a short season, in very fair weather, proudly and impudently strut along her quarter deck. But 'what will *they* do in the end thereof'. The storms will rise and great will be *their* dismay. Oh! that the nobles would now take their proper places, nor suffer capital to 'commission' every institution until he has 'commissioned' the King, the nobles and the people from their proper places, until a triumvirate of 'commissioners' be appointed to 'commission' all the 'commissioners', and there shall be no law in England, but *their* sovereign will!

I do hope your Grace will excuse me; I must write freely, I do write truly: I seek for nothing but the good of my country, which I believe can only be attained by a strong Government, ruling *as in former* times for the good, and in the hearts, of the people.

If this Poor Law Bill passes, the constitution will be destroyed, and he will be the greatest patriot who can produce the greatest dissatisfaction.

True, the present poor laws are very intricate, very voluminous and in some cases very bad, and generally badly administered, in consequence of their intricacy.* But surely this forms no ground for the

---

* If you wish to simplify the poor laws, repeal at once all the 'improving' innovations on the poor laws made in the last thirty years. You will then

destruction of the constitution! The whole thing will soon break to pieces, under the operation of this accursed bill.

It is high time the nation protested to a man against this new-fangled, bewhigged, pettifogging, expensive, delaying, deluding, patronage-making, unconstitutional, plundering system of 'commissioning'; if it be allowed to proceed, in a little time the King's head will tumble into a 'commission' tub'.

We were given to understand, when the Reform Bill should be passed, we should have such a wise, well-informed, well-intentioned House of Commons that all would be righted in a twink. But lo! as soon as they get to work, they declare they know nothing, and appoint 'commissions' for everything that is important; meanwhile occupying themselves in the House and in their select committees (as an honourable and learned Member told me this week) in ascertaining and endeavouring to prove 'that a man might actually get drunk in less time by drinking "dry brandy", than by taking cold water!'

Really, my Lord Duke, England should not be thus trifled with; she is after all worth one more tug. I cannot help looking to your Grace. You saved her from the power of capital, supported by 'commissions', fraud and treason.

PS. The great object I have in view is to save this country from anarchy and civil war by uniting the people and the aristocracy. Their interests are one and the same. As to the capitalist, I know he is pushing on his own ruin by trampling on the aristocracy and the people. But I have no hope of convincing him. His god is his gold, and his god blinds him. R.O.

Docketed by Wellington Compliments. Received. *Docketed by secretary* Done. July 6.

---

seek in vain for 'the immense and general maladministration of the poor laws through every parish in England', of which your Grace with great justice complained yesterday. At present every parish officer should be a serjeant-at-law; nay, even then there would be various and perpetual maladministration, for the lawyers themselves can never agree upon what is, and what is not law about the poor. This is a good reason for simplifying these laws, but it *forms no ground* for the confiscation of private property, for the suspension of the constitution or for the degradation, insult and punishment of poverty. Simplify the laws and welcome, but retain the spirit of the constitution and the rights of property and poverty; England cannot, will not, ought not to submit to this 'commissioning' system of these tyrannical, ignorant 'innovators' calling themselves 'Liberals'. R. O.

Wellington to the Archbishop of Armagh, 5 July 1834

London. The time is approaching at which we may expect that the Irish Tithe Bill will be sent up to the House of Lords. It is now in that stage in the House of Commons at which it would be desirable that the Church should consider what course it would be ultimately expedient for them to take.

The first question is whether the Church in Ireland can bear the rejection of the bill.

The second, if it can: what will be the most expedient mode of making or causing the rejection?

I confess that I feel great objection to voting on any measure of which the principle is that the Church in Ireland shall be even for a limited time a stipendiary Church; and I should not be sorry if it should turn out that we can at once reject the bill.

But if that cannot be attempted, can we venture to amend the bill in the House of Lords by the introduction of the clauses recently struck out? It will then be thrown out in the House of Commons.

I could wait upon your Grace upon this whenever it would suit your convenience. The bill will be in a committee of the House of Commons on Tuesday.

Wellington to Sir Herbert Taylor, 5 July 1834

London. I cannot but think that petitions and addresses to the King founded upon His Majesty's speech to the bishops on the 28 May must be very disagreeable to His Majesty. They are not very regular, inasmuch as there is no authentic copy of the speech in question, and his Majesty's Minister declared in his place in Parliament that he had not advised it. Some events occurred simultaneously with the speech or have occurred since; and some measures have since been proposed in Parliament, all of which render it very possible that the expectations founded upon it will be disappointed. However, the writers of these addresses as the King's subjects have a fair claim to have their petitions presented to His Majesty; and I should not trouble you if they were not so bulky as to render it impossible for me to present them to the King in the usual manner, as pointed out in the regulations of His Majesty's Court. On the other hand, I don't think it quite proper for any peer to ask His Majesty to grant him an audience in order that he may present petitions to His Majesty.

Under these circumstances I send you the petitions and addresses of which I inclose the list; and I request you to be so kind as to lay them before the King.

List appended by Wellington: The members of the Church of England inhabiting the borough of Leeds; the inhabitants of Shackerstone; the inhabitants of Hemwall in Lancashire; Midsomer Norton in Somerset; the borough of Ipswich; Upton in the county of Worcester, two from Upton upon Severn in the county of Worcester; parish of St. Mary's in Maldon in Essex.

Sir Herbert Taylor to Wellington, 5 July 1834

St. James's Palace. I have the honor to acknowledge the receipt of your Grace's letter of this day and of the accompanying petitions and addresses to the King, founded upon His Majesty's speech to the bishops on the 28th of May, which you have been requested to present to His Majesty—namely:

From the members of the Church of England inhabiting
the borough of Leeds;
The inhabitants of Shackerstone;
The inhabitants of Hemwall in Lancashire;
The inhabitants of Midsomer Norton in Somerset;
The borough of Ipswich;
Two from Upton upon Severn in the county of Worcester;
From the parish of St. Mary's in Maldon in Essex.

The King has honored me with his commands to convey his thanks to your Grace for the consideration which you have shewn with respect to the presentation of addresses, which appear to His Majesty, as they do to you, liable to the objection of not being very regular, the speech in question, although delivered by His Majesty, agreably to long and invariable usage, not having been advised by his Minister. To which the King orders me to add that he believes this to be the first instance in which His Majesty's answer to the private address of the bishops has been published and that its publication was not authorized by him.

Misdated 5 February 1834.

The Earl Grey to Wellington, 8 July 1834

Downing Street. Circumstances have occurred which will prevent my moving the second reading of the Poor Law Bill this evening. I shall also put off the report of the Coercion Bill till tomorrow.

I have thought it right to make this communication to your Grace thinking that it might be convenient to you to be apprised of my intention before the House meets.

Sir Herbert Taylor to Wellington. 9 July 1834

St. James's Palace. I have had the honor to receive and to submit to the King your Grace's letter of this day and the accompanying petitions and addresses upon His Majesty's speech to the archbishops and bishops on the 28th of May, which you had been requested to present to His Majesty, and which are described in your letter. And I have received His Majesty's command to thank your Grace for the transmission of these addresses.

Henry Hobhouse to Wellington, 9 July 1834

Hadspen, Wincanton. A few days since I presided at a meeting of the principal persons of this part of the county of Somerset, at which, on the motion of Sir Alexander Hood, were voted an address to the King thanking him for his recent declaration in favour of the Church, and a petition to each House of Parliament against the passing of any bill tending to endanger or weaken the Established Church. These documents have been most cheerfully and numerously signed, and are now ready to be presented. It was the wish of the meeting that the petition to the House of Lords should be presented by our Lord Lieutenant, the Marquess of Bath. But his Lordship being out of town, I have been desired by the leading gentlemen to request that your Grace will do us the honour of presenting our petition to the upper house, on which our hopes are mainly fixed.

Upon learning that your Grace will condescend to accede to our request, the petition shall be forwarded without delay.

Draft reply 10 July 1834. Compliments. When the Duke will [have] received the address to which he refers he will present it to His Majesty. *Corrected by his secretary:* Petition to the House of Lords.

Henry Hobhouse to Wellington, 11 July 1834

Hadspen. I have directed the original address, of which I enclose a printed copy, to be left at the House of Lords, directed to your Grace. It is most respectably signed by above 2,000 persons, and will I hope be found in all respects conformable to the orders of the House of Lords and worthy to be presented by your Grace to their Lordships, according to the promise contained in your Grace's note to me of the 10th instant.

Draft reply 16 July 1834. Compliments. The Duke received yesterday at the House of Lords his letter and the petition referred to therein, which he will present to the House this day.

Wellington to the Rev. Francis Swan, 11 July 1834

London. I have received a large pacquet of petitions to be presented to the House of Lords from several parishes in the town and diocese of Lincoln, and a list thereof at the head of which is one from the parish of which you are perpetual curate, and I therefore trouble you upon the subject of these petitions. There is an order in the House of Lords, indeed I believe in both Houses of Parliament, which prevents the reception of a petition unless it should contain the word 'humble', or the word 'humbly'. I have looked over most of these petitions and find that they are drawn upon the same model, and that, however respectful to the House, the word required by its order is not used. I return the petitions to you therefore in a pacquet by the Lincoln mail of this night and I request you to have them altered and sent back to me or to any other noble lord whom the petitioners may think proper to select to present their petitions.

Addressed to: The Rev. Francis Swan, St. Benedicts, Lincoln.

Wellington to Viscount Melbourne, 11 July 1834

London. I have had the honor of receiving your Lordship's letter of this day; together with the copy of the communication from your Lordship to the King which His Majesty had desired should be sent to me.[1]

---

[1] *Memoirs of Sir Robert Peel*, ii, 1–6.

I beg that your Lordship will convey to His Majesty my grateful acknowledgements for his most gracious consideration upon this occasion.

I do not understand that it is His Majesty's wish or intention that I should make any observations upon the paper sent to me by your Lordship.

R.A. MELBOURNE PAPERS.

Charles Baker to Wellington, 12 July 1834

Yorkshire Institution for the deaf and dumb, Eastfield, Doncaster. Having seen it announced that your Grace intends to support the new Poor Law Bill about to be submitted to the consideration of the House of Lords, I take the liberty of addressing you to suggest that a clause be introduced into it to provide for the board and instruction of the deaf and dumb poor throughout the kingdom. In England alone such class of persons (including all ages) amounts to 8,000.

The institution with which I have the honor to be connected requires 2/6 per week from each pupil towards their maintenance and education. Since its establishment, a period of little more than four years, *twenty* pupils, in every other respect qualified, have been rejected because their parents refused to support them in the Institution for a few years. The short-sighted policy of many parish officers prevents them from seeing if they endeavour to raise their deaf and dumb poor to a level with the rest of mankind, such persons will be less liable to be chargeable to them in future years, than if left untaught.

Signed: Charles Baker (Headmaster of the Yorkshire Institution).

Docketed by Wellington Compliments. Received. *Docketed by secretary* Done. July 14.

Robert K. Cobbold to Wellington, 12 July 1834

Eye. I once took the liberty of addressing your Grace, and the result has fully satisfied me that I did not then take an erroneous view of the subject; I now again take the liberty because I was sorry to see your Grace reported as pledged to the furtherance of the views of His Majesty's Ministers in supporting the Poor Law Bill now pending the decision of the honorable and noble House of Lords, a bill fraught with more danger than any measure that has been introduced to the notice of Parliament in any late period and yet equal to the danger is the difficulty. May it please your Grace to consider this matter, and upon enquiry it will be discovered that the said bill is not popular with any class of His Majesty's subjects, while to the majority it is odious and if this be made evident to your Grace, as I doubt not it may, I shall hope to see that once again your Grace's full powers may be called into operation as a shield to the united empire. May I suggest that a labor rate bill, accompanied by a modified version of the Poor Law Bill and passed for a limited period would have more influence in the improvement of the agricultural population, both in mental and physical renovation, than any other measures, and would enable the rulers to carry into effect beneficial improvements, while the sudden abrogation of the poor man's resource against despotic oppression may raise a storm that will shake to its foundation the whole fabric of social policy. One ruling master mind may prevent this and I trust that ruling mind will be your Grace's.

My apology for this remark uncalled for from so humble an individual is first your Grace's condescension and next the desire to see the vessel clear the dangerous quicksands.

Docketed by Wellington Compliments. Received. *Docketed by secretary* Done. July 14.

Francis Rawdon Chesney to Wellington, 12 July 1834

3 Down Street. I did myself the honor of calling at Apsley House some days ago to mention the progress of the Indian Steam Committee which has been occupied with that question about five weeks.

I think it may interest your Grace to learn that they came to a resolution yesterday afternoon to open both the Red Sea and Euphrates routes experimentally; and dwelling upon the political, commercial and other advantages of the line through Arabia, which, after remaining suspended for more than twenty months, is now to be put into operation with all possible speed.

Docketed by Wellington Compliments. Received. *Docketed by secretary* Done. July 12.

Viscount Melbourne to Wellington, 12 July 1834

South Street. Upon receiving your Grace's reply to my communication of yesterday, I lost no time in laying it before His Majesty, and I am now directed by His Majesty to acquaint your Grace that it was His Majesty's wish and intention that your Grace should make such observations as you should think fit upon the paper sent to you, and that this wish had been repeated upon reading your Grace's letter.

Permit me to add that I should be desirous, if it be convenient to your Grace, of receiving your wishes either this evening or tomorrow in the forenoon, as I am commanded to attend His Majesty at Windsor at two.

Wellington to the King, 12 July 1834

London. The Duke of Wellington presents his humble duty to Your Majesty; and having just received from Viscount Melbourne an intimation of Your Majesty's commands that he should make such observations as he should think fit upon the paper transmitted to him by Viscount Melbourne yesterday, he begs leave to submit to Your Majesty that that paper contains a part of a communication made by Your Majesty to Viscount Melbourne, directing his Lordship to communicate with the Duke of Wellington and other gentlemen; that his Lordship should endeavour 'to bring them together; and to establish a community of purpose'.

Your Majesty was further pleased to declare that you could not 'disguise from yourself the difficulty of the task imposed upon Viscount Melbourne', nor the 'objections which his Lordship might possibly feel to take an active part in the endeavour to carry it into effect'.

In answer to this most gracious communication from your Majesty, Viscount Melbourne has informed Your Majesty that after the most careful deliberation his Lordship feels himself compelled to declare that 'the difficulty which Your Majesty had anticipated appeared to his Lordship to be insurmountable'; 'and the objections to Lord Melbourne's personally undertaking the task were so great as to render the successful termination of such an attempt utterly hopeless'.

This answer of Lord Melbourne and the reasoning upon which it is founded appeared to the Duke to render unnecessary all observations on his part; and he limited his answer to Viscount Melbourne to the expression of his grateful acknowledgements to Your Majesty for Your Majesty's consideration for himself.

The Duke has served Your Majesty's predecessors and Your Majesty too long and he has been too much engaged in the affairs of government not to wish them success be they in whose hands they may. His opposition in Parliament to the measures of Your Majesty's Ministers has been founded upon his views of the constitution of the country; of the necessity for the maintenance of the authority of the Crown; of the privilege of both houses of Parliament; of the Church of England and its privileges as established by law, particularly in Ireland; and of the rights and property of all corporations and of all descriptions of Your Majesty's subjects in all parts of the world.

In foreign affairs the Duke has been anxious to maintain the ancient system of policy of the kings of Great Britain and those alliances which enabled His late Majesty to bring the wars occasioned by the French Revolution to an honourable termination, and which had in the year 1830 preserved the peace of Europe for fifteen years.

The Duke of Wellington has no personal objection to any individual; and he would be too happy to give his support in Parliament to any Administration which, possessing Your Majesty's confidence, should conduct its measures on the principles to which he has above referred.

Although the Duke considers himself bound, and had even been prepared to serve Your Majesty or any of your royal family in any capacity in which his services could be deemed *necessary*, he has long been desirous of avoiding to serve in Your Majesty's councils.

The Viscount Melbourne has referred in his letter to Your Majesty of the 10th instant to the details of an audience with which Your Majesty had honoured him on the 9th, in which his Lordship states that he had ventured to lay before Your Majesty those general objections which pressed forcibly upon his mind to unions and coalitions of opposing parties.

Such coalitions have been supposed to be founded upon views of private interest, which certainly cannot exist at present, although it would be difficult to convince the publick of this truth. But it must be obvious that the union of publick men in Your Majesty's council who appear not to concur in any one principle of the policy of this country, whether foreign or domestick, cannot promote Your Majesty's service, cannot conciliate the confidence of the publick or acquire the support of Parliament, and must lead to the most disastrous results. It can scarcely be deemed *necessary* for Your Majesty's service that the Duke of Wellington should be one of a council composed of men, however able and respectable, whose opinions should be so discordant.

He concurs with the opinion given to Your Majesty by Viscount Melbourne, on the 9th instant, as recited in his Lordship's letter of the 10th; and he begs leave most respectfully to submit to Your Majesty that a review of the events in this country of the last three months would afford a practical example of the consequences to be expected from the union in council of men with the best intentions entertaining a difference of opinion upon points on which it would be their duty to advise their sovereign and to guide the legislature of their country.

Wellington to Viscount Melbourne, 13 July 1834

London. I enclose a letter for the King written in obedience to His Majesty's commands conveyed by Your Lordship in your letter of yesterday.

I have left it open, as it might be convenient to your Lordship to know its contents before you should leave London.

Henry Alworth Merewether to Wellington, 13 July 1834

7 Whitehall Place. May I be excused for intimating to your Grace the possibility of promoting with advantage at the present moment a measure which would have the effect of concentrating the increasing disposition to order and good government, and of uniting the towns in the preservation and administration of the law, by restoring the ancient institutions of the country, and securing municipal government under the charters of the Crown.

Such a measure may, I conceive, be effected during this autumn under the existing law, without legislative interference; and be the means of warding off the meditated attack on corporations; and may eventually lead to a practical correction of some of the evils resulting from the Reform Act. I may also add that such a measure is already partially contemplated in some places.

Your Grace will be the best judge whether these matters are worthy consideration. It is sufficient for me to suggest them, and to add that if any further explanation on the subject might be desirable I shall be promptly ready at any moment to wait upon your Grace to that purpose.

Wellington to Henry Alworth Merewether, 13 July 1834

London. I have received your note, and will avail myself of an early opportunity of conversing with you on the subject of it. There is no occasion for haste as it does not appear to be necessary to adopt, or to prevent any measures from being adopted in Parliament.

Admiral Sir Edward Owen to Wellington, 13 July 1834

Windlesham, Bagshot. The enclosed letter reached me yesterday with a request that I would forward it to your Grace if I declined to offer myself a candidate for Deal and Sandwich in the event of a dissolution of the present Parliament or send it back if I determined so to offer.

So circumstanced, I think it right to send the letter to your Grace and to explain that holding myself free to be governed wholly by the circumstances under which a dissolution may at any time take place, I have been desirous to avoid those pledges or communications which might serve to keep alive a party feeling or bind me to the pursuit of an expensive and perhaps inexpedient contest.

Taking that course, I can have no right to expect my friends to forbear in any other step they may think needful and I owe your Grace this explanation at the present moment, *etc.*

Wellington to Sir Edward Owen, 14 July 1834

London. I have received your note of the 13th and that of Mr. Smith of Deal inclosed.

Such a ministerial crisis as exists at present sets in motion every individual in the country who speculates upon a change. I think men would be quite right to prepare themselves by registry and all other measures to enable them and their friends to exercise their franchises in order that they may take advantage of events. But I cannot recommend to you or to anybody else to step forward as a candidate for Deal or any other place. Such recommendation would occasion serious expenses and other inconveniences which I am convinced cannot be too cautiously avoided.

I do not believe that the ministry will be essentially changed or that any dissolution of Parliament will take place. However, I am writing to you in as compleat ignorance upon the subject as any other individual in the community.

J. E. P. Robertson to Wellington, 14 July 1834

21 Beaufort Row, Chelsea. I am persuaded that my intention in writing on this occasion will be accepted as a sufficient excuse for the liberty I, an entire stranger, take in addressing myself to your Grace.

It seems to be admitted that considerable difficulty exists to the formation of any Administration: on the supposition that a Conservative one is to be formed I will proceed to state how, in my humble opinion, those difficulties may to some extent be obviated with which such an administration must in the outset be surrounded.

It is evident that nothing can be done with the present House of Commons; the question then is, how is a dissolution to be managed and a majority professing Conservative principles to be insured on a new return.

On looking to the present condition of Ireland it would appear that scarcely a moment is to be lost. I assume that Sir Robert Peel takes office, that a new writ is issued for Tamworth and that he is *forthwith* returned. Were that right honourable baronet to make a motion, on the *first* night he resumes his seat, touching the free-trade question and in his *reply* to say 'the points for consideration are in fact whether the manufacturing interests in this country are to remain in their present depressed state or whether they are to be improved, whether we are to take off the *window tax* by taxing foreign manufactures or whether things are to remain as they are'; the effect of this would I think be great in the country. If in addition to this, he could let drop anything about the repeal of the malt tax (that is, if the prospect of increase in the customs or in any other quarter can be fairly calculated on to enable him so to do) so much the better. On the division of course there would be a great majority against the Minister: the following day, therefore, dissolve the Parliament, issue the writs for the new election with the quickest dispatch possible and get the elections over, in Ireland at least, before the Coercion Bill expires. The Irish agitator will undoubtedly influence the greater part of the elections in that country; this evil will, however, be compensated for by the great bulk of Government supporters returned for Great Britain.

The bare mention of the repeal of the *window tax* will be attended with prodigious effect; it will prove a *sop* which must be universally relished. The *philosophers* may at some places try their luck at their darling system, free-trade as they call it; but give, my Lord Duke, John Bull and his brother t'other side of the Tweed the choice between it and the repeal of the window tax, and it will require no witch to foretell the result.

It seems to me that in order to save *time, trouble* and *expense* it is not desirable that anyone now in the House of Commons should be understood to accept office but Sir Robert Peel *until* the dissolution took place which your Grace will see I have fixed for the very day following that on which Sir Robert may resume his seat as a Minister; so that there will be but one night's debate, and in that debate the country will be allowed to see through the intention of Government on a point which interests almost everyone: the repealing of the window tax, provided the country supports Ministers as it ought to do.

The desire I have not to lose a moment in forwarding these thoughts, in the hope they may not be considered altogether unworthy of attention, must stand as an excuse for the abrupt and unpolished style of this letter, which, however, I trust I have written intelligibly.

Draft reply 16 July 1834. Compliments. Received. He will see that the Ministry has been formed again nearly as before.

The King to Wellington, 14 July 1834

Windsor Castle. The King would not do justice to his sense of the manner in which the Duke of Wellington has received and replied to the communication which he desired Viscount Melbourne to make to him, if he were to omit expressing his acknowledgements for it.

His Majesty too highly appreciates the Duke of Wellington's eminent and distinguished services and his character not to have felt desirous that the views and the feeling which produced that communication should be correctly understood by him. It would be idle to deny that, in the present state of the country, he attached great importance to the object which he had contemplated, but he candidly admits that the reasons which have been urged against his views have convinced His Majesty of their impracticability.

Wellington to the Rev. Henry John Todd, 16 July 1834

Compliments to Mr. Todd.

The Duke will present the petition to which he refers. The Duke, however, must add that he feels great objections to the presentation to the King of petitions and addresses founded on His Majesty's speech to the archbishops and bishops; seeing that there is no authentick record of that speech, that the Minister of the Crown stated in his place in Parliament that he had not advised it; and that some events took place at the time and others have since, and measures have been proposed by His Majesty's servants to Parliament which prove that the expectations of the publick founded upon the speech will be disappointed.

Sir Herbert Taylor to Wellington, 17 July 1834

Windsor Castle. I had the honor of receiving at St. James's yesterday your Grace's letter of that date and the accompanying addresses and petitions of which you took the trouble of adding a list; and I did not delay submitting them to the King, but, owing to incessant hurry and interruption, I was unable, before I left town, to obey His Majesty's commands that I should convey his thanks to your Grace for the transmission of them.

The Archdeacon of Richmond (John Headlam) to Wellington, 19 July 1834

Rectory, Birkby, Northallerton, Yorkshire. At the request of the clergy of the archdeaconry of Richmond (in which I beg leave to join) I write to solicit your Grace to do us the honor to present an address to the King expressive of our attachment to his person and of our thanks for his repeated assurances to protect the Established Church of which we are members. I am directed at the same time to convey to your Grace the grateful sense we entertain of your Grace's repeated declarations in Parliament of your attachment to that Church and your resolution to use your utmost endeavors to maintain it in all its legitimate rights and privileges. Should your Grace be pleased to comply with our request and will do me the favor to acquaint me by letter of the same, I will forward the address to Apsley House to be presented to His Majesty at your Grace's earliest convenience.

Draft reply 23 July 1834. The Duke of Wellington presents his compliments to Mr. Headlam. The Duke will take charge of the address to the King of the clergy of the archdeaconry of Richmond.

The Rev. George Rowley to Wellington, 19 July 1834

Oxford. When the heads of houses and proctors proposed to address the King on the Dissenters admission bill, they expected that it would be carried through the House of Commons without delay. Finding, however, that its progress was so slow, I called a meeting a short time since, and suggested the inexpediency, under all the circumstances, of presenting such an address; and obtained their consent for setting it aside altogether, should such a determination meet with your Grace's concurrence. The recent ministerial movements prevented me from troubling your Grace with any communication on the subject, as the bill appeared not unlikely to die a natural death. But as it is now fixed that it shall be brought forward again on Wednesday next, I think it my duty no longer to withhold the statement above given.

Wellington to the Rev. George Rowley, 21 July 1834

London. The derangement of the Ministry has postponed all business in both houses of Parliament and I do not know exactly how the bill stands for the admission of Dissenters to the universities. I believe that there are still two more stages through which it must pass in the House of Commons.

I entertain no doubt that it will pass through these stages and that we shall have it in the House of Lords. I propose to take the discussion of it upon the second reading and then to move that the bill be rejected. I think that that motion will be carried by a considerable majority. If it should not, the University of Oxford will still have time to address the King to use his prerogative to protect them from the injury which will be inflicted upon them by this measure.

As soon as the bill will be sent up from the House of Commons, you had better prepare your address, which can pass if it should be necessary and then be presented.

I confess that I don't think it will be necessary, and if not necessary I don't think it desirable that you should address the King again upon this subject.

I have mislaid the copy which I had of your last address to His Majesty. I shall be much obliged to you if you will send me another.

I have hundreds of petitions to present against the Dissenters admission bill, the presentation of which I have delayed till the bill should be brought to the House of Lords.

The Dean of St. Patrick's (Henry Richard Dawson) to Wellington, 21 July 1834

Deanery House. I have been commissioned by the chapter of St. Patrick's Cathedral, Dublin, to request that your Grace would kindly undertake the presentation of the accompanying petition to the House of Lords on the first favorable opportunity.

Draft reply 28 July 1834. Compliments to the Dean of St. Patrick's. The Duke will present to the House of Lords the petition which he has sent him as soon as the Tithe Bill be brought into that house.

The Rev. Henry John Todd to Wellington, 22 July 1834

Settrington, Malton. I have to acknowledge myself greatly honoured and obliged, as the rest of the Cleveland clergy are, by the communication from your Grace that our petition, through your kindness and condescension, would be presented to the House of Lords.

The frank statement of your Grace's objections in regard to the address to His Majesty forbids me to press your presentation of that memorial; and if no subsequent consideration may have removed these objections, I entreat the favour of your Grace to direct that the address may be sent to Mr. Harcourt (the Member for Oxfordshire) at Archbishop of York's in Grosvenor Square, who will then apply to the Earl of Harewood, who has presented to the King the similar address of the West Riding clergy.

Permit me to repeat, my Lord, how sensible I am of your goodness in presenting our petition to the House of Lords.

Draft reply 24 July 1834. Compliments. The Duke has presented the address to which he refers.

The Rev. George Rowley to Wellington, 22 July 1834

Oxford. I have the honor to forward a copy of our last petition to the King.[1] Mr. West's case is a very common one: a profligate spendthrift gets into difficulties, and then thinks himself ill used because his creditors endeavour to recover from him what is justly their due. I need not trouble your Grace with any of the particulars.

Sir Herbert Taylor to Wellington, 23 July 1834

Windsor Castle. It had been suggested to the King that General Count Wallmoden of the Austrian service would be very much gratified by being promoted from a Commander to a Grand Cross of the Bath, and His Majesty has ordered me to mention the circumstance to your Grace and to request that you will favor him with your opinion whether Count Wallmoden's wish may be met without shewing a preference which might prove embarrassing to His Majesty.

Independently of the high rank which Count Wallmoden holds in the Austrian service, he is a lieutenant-general in His Majesty's and was in command of a successful corps of Hanoverians early in 1814. In his command at Milan he has been particularly attentive to English travellers and has in a manner kept open house for them.

Wellington to Sir Herbert Taylor, 23 July 1834

I have just now received your letter of this day.

General Wallmoden is a highly distinguished officer of the Austrian army. He is a Hanoverian and lieutenant-general in His Majesty's Hanoverian service; and he distinguished himself in the war in the command of a body of these troops. Being the son of old Count Wallmoden he stands in a peculiar relation towards His Majesty's family.

All these are facts which deserve His Majesty's consideration and would probably induce His Majesty to distinguish General Wallmoden.

But the Order of the Bath is one of the orders of honour of this country; and I would humbly submit to His Majesty that he should consult his Minister upon the subject before he should determine upon conferring it as suggested.

---

[1] See above, Rowley to Wellington, 19 March 1834.

Sir Herbert Taylor to Wellington, 24 July 1834

Windsor Castle. I have had the honor to receive and to submit to the King both your Grace's letters of yesterday: the first accompanying some further addresses and petitions addressed to His Majesty upon the subject of His Majesty's speech to the bishops, which I have not failed to convey to His Majesty; the second replying to the communication with which I troubled your Grace by his order respecting Lieutenant-General Count Wallmoden.

The King is aware, from the number and the character of the addresses which he has received, of the impression which has been made by the expression of his sentiments upon the subject of the Established Church, and His Majesty trusts that the confidence which they evince in his attachment to it will eventually not be disappointed.

His Majesty orders me to thank your Grace for the opinion you have given to him upon the question of promoting Count Wallmoden to the highest class of the Order of the Bath, and to acquaint you that he will act upon your suggestion, of which he readily admits the propriety.

James P. Mayers to Wellington, 24 July 1834

60 St. James's Street. I have the honor to transmit to your Grace a copy of a petition from the legislature of Barbados to the House of Lords, complaining of the hardship and injustice of that part of the Act of Parliament for abolishing slavery which relates to the distribution of the twenty millions granted as a compensation to the planters for the loss of their property in slaves, and praying for an amendment of that part of the Act, and also for protection for the produce of the British colonies from a competition in the markets of the United Kingdom with articles, the produce of slave labour; which petition the legislature, under a grateful sense of your Grace's powerful advocacy of the colonial interest on many occasions, have instructed me to request you to present and honor, and honour [*sic*] with your support. This request I now take the liberty of submitting and, should your Grace be so obliging as to comply with the wishes of my constituents, I shall be glad if you will appoint a time for allowing me the honor of waiting on you with the petition and offering a few remarks on subjects connected with the prayer of it. I also enclose a copy of a memorial exhibiting the injustice of the principle proposed for the distribution of the parliamentary grant which was presented to the Secretary of State for the Colonies in September last, and an extract from the minutes of the general assembly of May 5th.

Signed: J. P. Mayers, colonial agent for Barbados.

First enclosure: Barbados: Extract from the minutes of the General Assembly, 5th May 1834.

'Resolved: that the agent of the island be instructed to request his Grace, the Duke of Wellington, to present the address and petition to the Lords.'

A true extract. John Mayers, clerk of the General Assembly.

Second enclosure: A memorial exhibiting the injustice of the principle proposed for the distribution of the parliamentary grant of £20,000,000. The Legislature of Barbados having passed certain resolutions, pledging that body to co-operate with His Majesty's Government in effecting the extinction of negro slavery in this colony, upon the condition that justice be done to their constituents in the apportionment of the £20,000,000 vested by Parliament in furtherance of this object, it becomes the duty of the legislature to show that the principle proposed for the distribution of this grant will be most unjust in its operation upon the proprietors of Barbados. Were the amount of export an accurate measure of the profit of slave labor in the colonies, a ratio compounded of exports and number of slaves in each colony respectively would no doubt be an equitable principle of distribution. But if it can be shown that an estate exporting 100 hogsheads of sugar from one colony gives a net income to the proprietor equivalent to that which would be derived from an estate in other colonies exporting 250 hogsheads, the fallacy of the principle must at once be admitted, and that this is about the rate of profit upon exports from Barbados as compared with most other colonies, not excepting Demerara, has long been notorious.

Extraordinary, and almost incredible as this fact may appear to persons unacquainted with the internal economy of a Barbados plantation and with the local peculiarities of the colony, it can, nevertheless, be satisfactorily explained. A Barbados estate sells more things and buys fewer things than an estate in any other colony.

It is well known that it has always been the practice of the Barbados planter to raise all the food required for the support of his slaves; but it is not so generally known that many planters derive a considerable revenue from the sale of food.

Not quite half the number of slaves in this island are attached to the plantations; the remaining forty odd thousand however, as well as the thirty odd thousand free inhabitants and the large garrison constantly kept at headquarters, are all fed out of the produce of the land. It must be obvious what a large demand this mass of consumers must create for yams, potatoes, green vegetables, poultry, butcher's meat etc., all of which are the produce of slave labor, not indicated by the table of exports. And it would not be more untrue to assert that agriculture is utterly unproductive in England, because all the fruits of agriculture are consumed in England, and do not furnish an article for exportation, than it is to estimate the profit of agricultural labor in Barbados simply by the amount of exports. There is also a large quantity of food annually sent from this to the neighbouring islands.

In estimating exports it should not be forgotten that Barbados sugar is of a superior quality, and perhaps averages one fourth more than sugar sent from most other colonies, and twice as much as that which goes from many of them. Moreover, a very considerable quantity of the sugar produced here is not exported but sold to the numerous domestic consumers, which the dense population, large garrison and shipping furnish.

In most of the West India colonies a large part of the value of the sugar exported is returned in the shape of provisions and other supplies, which in Barbados are not purchased at all, or if purchased, are paid for out of funds raised by domestic sales. One fact may be mentioned illustrative of the extent and value of the home market here, and of the amount of revenue which the planter draws from it: the whole crop of rum produced in the island is consumed by the inhabitants, absolutely none is exported. This may serve as *instar omnium*, to shew how fallacious it would be to assume the amount of exports, as the criterion of the profit of slave labor, without reference to local circumstances. The influence which one dense population exercises upon the value of slaves is most extensive. The number of families here being tenfold greater than in any other colony, there is consequently a corresponding number of slaves employed as domestics about their establishments. The wages of servants being from £15 to £30 currency per annum, the services of this class of slaves must be estimated at that rate. Many families are supported chiefly by wages received for servants hired by officers, professional gentlemen, English merchants, and other strangers. The number of slave artisans is also very great, and they afford a large revenue to that numerous class of slave owners who have no land independently of the tradesmen attached to the plantations and save to their owners [the] greatest part of the expense of erecting and repairing buildings, no small item in the outlay of an estate. Almost every set of sugar works was destroyed by the hurricane in the month of August, and they were all restored in time to reap the following crop, by the carpenters and masons belonging to the respective plantations.

A review of the foregoing facts cannot fail to convince His Majesty's Government that the amount of exports affords no criterion of the actual bona fide profit upon the capital invested in slaves in Barbados and that therefore, to make exports the chief element in a calculation of the value of that description of property, must necessarily lead to a most erroneous result.

It appears however that another standard of the value of slaves in the different colonies has been set up, equally plausible but not less fallacious, namely the selling price of slaves at the present day.

Most of the slaves who have been sold very low at marshals' sales are not agricultural laborers, but town negroes, not accustomed to work. In many instances slaves have been sold upon these occasions at a mere nominal price when the slave has wished to purchase himself, nobody being willing to bid over him in such a case. But it is true that agricultural labourers do sell much lower in Barbados than in Demerara, because the estates here being generally abundantly furnished with slaves and the low price of sugar restricting the planters to the purchase of such things as are indispensable, there is in this country absolutely no demand for slaves. It is this total absence of demand which has degraded the selling price so low, and their value is now to be judged by this circumstance, for many a proprietor who would not encumber himself with an addition to his present sufficient stock, even at £20 per head, would not at the same time sell off the slaves attached to his estate and necessary to its cultivation at £120 per head.

Another great source of fallacy in comparing the value of slaves in Barbados and Demerara arises from the different practice which prevails in the two colonies as to the mode of appraising plantations. In Barbadoes it is the custom to set a large part of the value of the whole property upon the land and buildings; whereas in Demerara almost the whole value is put upon the negroes, and the land is rated at little or nothing. And it would perhaps be as near an approximation to the truth to assert that Demerara land is really of less value, because being plenty it is the custom to rate it at less per acre there than here, as it is to say that slaves in Barbados are not worth half as much as in Demerara, because there being no buyers of slaves here, their selling price is low. The true and sound test of value is the net profit of slave labor per head; tried by this standard Barbados will be found to belong to the very first class. Hence it is that there are more unincumbered estates in Barbadoes than in any other colony in the West Indies, although properties here being generally of a comparatively moderate size there are few large fortunes.

But has Barbados no higher claim to the liberal consideration of His Majesty's Government than she can derive from an exhibition of net clearances? Is there no merit in a system of treatment which has been attended with a rapid increase of the slave population here, while there has been a constant decrease almost everywhere around us? Or can it be supposed that this object has been attained without some sacrifice of income? Is it not obvious that the liberal indulgencies, the lenient discipline and abundant feeding, which alone could have produced a result so different from other examples, and so honorable to the Barbados proprietors, must have been attended with a diminution of crops? And is it for this that Barbadoes is to be, as it were, insulted with an award of £15 per head, while Demerara is to be rewarded at the rate of £51 per head? How this result has been brought out even upon the wrong principle which it is the object of this paper to refute, the legislature of Barbados cannot conjecture, for by a return of reports, certified by the accountant of the financial department and the deputy Colonial Secretary, for the years 1828, 1829 and 1830 (the latest the legislature can produce) it appears that in the first named year Demerara and Essequibo exported 84,996,251 lbs. of sugar, in the second year 91,652,331 lbs. and in the latter year 88,612,177 lbs., making 146,367 hogsheads for the three years, equal on an average to 48,789 hogsheads per annum at an average of 1800 lbs. neat. The following table exhibits the number of hogsheads shipped from Barbadoes from 1823 to 1833 inclusive.

	Hogsheads		Tierces
1823	24,257		5,884
1824	20,256		4,081

	Hogsheads		Tierces
1825	22,590		3,332
1826	20,220		2,401
1827	17,010		1,813
1828	26,789		2,664
1829	22,545		1,668
1830	25,111		1,755
1831	26,096		2,256
1832	18,757		1,281
1833			

There are more slaves actually employed in sugar cultivation in Demerara than in Barbadoes; the produce as appears by the foregoing table, is not at the rate of 2 to 1 and yet, according to the proposed scale which has been cited above, the Demarara planter is to receive at the rate of nearly $3\frac{1}{2}$ to 1 as compared with the Barbados planter. Now our argument founded on facts exhibited on this paper is that taking into account the superior quality of the general crop of sugar of Barbadoes and the much smaller cost of production, the twenty odd thousand hogsheads of this island will give greater net proceeds than the forty odd thousand hogsheads of Demerara.

This calculation does not embrace the exports of coffee and cotton because it has reference exclusively to that number of slaves which are actually engaged in the raising of sugar, from which it is clear that Barbados will not have justice unless their compensation is to the full extent as much per head as that of Demerara and therefore it cannot be expected that the legislature of Barbadoes will co-operate with His Majesty's Government in the accomplishment of this important measure, unless their claims be duly appreciated and faithfully satisfied.

Barbados, 2nd August 1833.

Culling Charles Smith to Wellington, 26 July 1834

56 Jermyn Street. I am anxious to explain to you the proceedings which have led us to the point of presenting a petition to the House of Commons for a restitution of our salaries. I will call again on Tuesday, should I not find you at home, when I call to leave a copy of our petition.

Docketed Sends a memorandum to the House of Commons from the commissioners of customs.

Enclosure: To the honorable, the House of Commons.

The humble petition of the undersigned commissioners of His Majesty's customs humbly sheweth,

That your petitioners were severally appointed by patent to their situations as commissioners of customs at the salary of £1,400 per annum.

That in the year 1830 the Lords of the Treasury, with a view to every practicable reduction of the expenditure of the country, were pleased to direct the board of customs (amongst other public departments) to lay before their lordships a revised scale of salaries of the several officers upon the establishment with the least possible charge to the public with reference to the duties performed.

That pending the enquiries which the board proceeded to make in pursuance of the above directions, their lordships, by their minute of the 19th of February 1830 directed that the salaries of the commissioners of customs (with others) should be reduced from £1,400 to £1,200 per annum, but prospectively only, and as vacancies should occur.

That in the year 1831 the Lords of the Treasury, by their minute of the 12th April, directed that all reductions which had been made prospective only, and as vacancies should occur, should take effect immediately and the salaries of your petitioners with many other officers were reduced; those of your petitioners from £1,400 to £1,200, and the salaries of the others in proportion. Their lordships were however subsequently pleased by their minute of the 19th of February 1833 to rescind that part of their minute of April 1831, whereby the salaries of the officers in question were directed to be immediately reduced, in favor of all the officers upon the establishment, so as to secure to them the full enjoyment of their salaries for the period during which they remained in the service: thus leaving your petitioners the only parties who suffered an immediate reduction of salary.

Your humble petitioners, relying upon the justice of their case, have ventured to address your honorable house in the confident hope that, when the circumstances of their case shall be made known to your honorable house, you will in your wisdom and sense of justice afford your petitioners that relief which they seek, viz. to be placed in the receipt of the salaries respectively enjoyed by them until the operation of the treasury minute of April 1831.

Your petitioners would here beg humbly to state that prior to the consolidation of the three several boards of England, Scotland and Ireland, the total number of commissioners of customs in the United Kingdom amounted to 19, that is to say:

For England
- chairman 2,000
- deputy chairman 1,700
- seven other commissioners at £1,400 each 9,800

13,500

For Scotland
- chairman 1,500
- four other commissioners at £1,000 each 4,000

5,500

For Ireland
- chairman 1,200
- deputy chairman 1,100
- three other commissioners at £1,000 each 3,000

5,300

Total: £24,300.

That by the consolidation of the boards in the year 1823 the number of commissioners for the United Kingdom was reduced to seventeen, which included two local commissioners for Scotland and two for Ireland, and since that period the Irish and Scotch boards have been wholly abolished and a further reduction of four members of the general board has been effected; and at the present period the business which was originally performed by nineteen commissioners, and subsequently by thirteen together with four local commissioners, is performed by nine members only. And with this reduction of number and augmentation of duties, all that your petitioners humbly ask is merely to be reinstated in the receipt of the salaries conferred upon them by patent by which a permanent interest, during good behaviour, has ever been considered to be conferred.

That in humbly addressing your honorable house, your petitioners have the fullest confidence in the justice of the Board of Treasury and are fully impressed with the belief that the Government would have been disposed to have acceded to their claims, had not the provisions of the treasury minute of April 1831 been notified to your honorable house.

Your petitioners would humbly set forth that in all the recent regulations in the Court of Exchequer of England and in the great law departments Parliament has amply recognized the principle of saving existing interests. By the 57 Geo. 3, c. 60, it was enacted that the duties, emoluments and establishments of certain offices in the Court of Exchequer should be regulated by the Lords of the Treasury upon the termination of the then existing interests in the offices, and as vacancies might occur. By the 1 Wm. 4, c. 58, for regulating the receipt and future appropriation of fees and emoluments receivable by officers of the superior courts of common law, all persons who held office on the 24th May 1830 were to be compensated for the loss of their emoluments. And by the 1 Wm. 4, c. 70, persons affected by the abolition of the courts of justice in Wales and Chester were also to be compensated for the losses which they might sustain. And your petitioners firmly believe that they are correct in stating that the same principle has been uniformly admitted by Parliament of keeping faith with existing interests. And that in carrying into effect all great measures of retrenchment and regulation every just consideration has been had to present holders.

That your petitioners humbly trust that in every regulation for the retrenchment of establishments in their department they have done their duty faithfully and zealously; and they confidently appeal to His Majesty's Government to bear testimony to their exertions in this respect: in elucidation of which they beg to state that during the space of the fourteen years terminating with the year 1833, 3,048 offices have been abolished and the salaries and charges of their department have been reduced to the extent of £304,000 per annum.

Under these circumstances, and impressed as your petitioners are with the conviction that it is not consistent with reason and justice that your petitioners should be the only individuals in the department in whose cases a reduction of salary should be other than prospective, they humbly pray that for the period during which they may continue to hold their respective offices they may not be deprived of the salary which they had enjoyed prior to the operation of the treasury minute of April 1831; but be reinstated in the enjoyment of that granted to them by patent on their appointment.

19th July 1834

John Horsley Palmer to Wellington, 29 July 1834

Carlton Club. I hope your Grace will excuse the liberty I am taking upon the present occasion, which nothing but the urgency of the case could have prompted me to do. My object is to solicit your Grace's protection for the inclosed bill, which passes the Commons this day. It is only to its real and intrinsic merits that I ask your Grace's attention, being a bill to afford relief to the unfortunate members of *every one* of the old Calcutta house of agency, who are unable under the present India Insolvent Act to get their release, from the peculiar conditions which that Act imposes, and which it has been found impossible to comply with. This can be better explained by the solicitor who has drawn the bill, if your Grace will name any time for his calling at Apsley House for that purpose. The bill was framed under the advice of Mr. Serjeant Spankie, and has been approved by the law officers of the Crown; I trust therefore that your Grace will not think me intrusive in requesting your protection to such a measure. The distress which has been felt by every part of the population on the Bengal side of India has been excessive, the whole of which would have been obviated, I conscientiously believe, had Lord William Bentinck been at the presidency in January 1833. Unfortunately that was not the case, and not only have twenty millions sterling of property been cruelly depreciated, and almost every civil and military servant of the company seriously affected, but all the members of the once flourishing establishments of Calcutta agency have been brought to the ground, without the power of recovering their lost fortunes, unless this bill can be passed for their relief.

If your Grace will allow me to wait upon you with the solicitor, I shall make a point of attending any appointment of time and place, which you may have the goodness to name.

First enclosure: A Bill to amend the Law relating to insolvent Debtors in India. *Printed Paper.*

Second enclosure: Clause added in committee in the Commons to a bill to amend the law relating to insolvent debtors in India.

And whereas by the said recited Act of the ninth year of the reign of His late Majesty, King George the fourth, it is enacted that all such insolvent debtors as therein mentioned shall within the time also therein mentioned deliver into the court a schedule containing a full and true account of their debts, estates and effects as therein mentioned and which schedule is thereby directed to be forthwith filed in the said court:

And whereas it is expedient that the creditors of such insolvent debtors residing out of the limits of the said company's charter should have the means of inspecting such schedule with equal facility with the creditors of such insolvent debtors residing within the limits of the said charter;

Be it therefore enacted that the principal officer of the said respective courts for the relief of insolvent debtors shall without delay transmit to the court of directors of the said company by different ships two or more copies of each such schedule and the said court shall retain the same and permit any person or persons being a creditor or creditors of any such insolvent debtor to inspect and examine at all seasonable times such schedule and shall upon the request and at the reasonable costs and charges of any such creditor or creditors (such cost and charges to be regulated by the said court) provide for him or them a copy or copies of any such schedule.

The Rev. William Spry to Wellington, 30 July 1834

Rectory, Botus Fleming, Saltash, Cornwall. When your protégé our bishop, opened his political battery of blandishments on that *imperium in imperio*, the Wesleyan Methodists, I who knew them better than he did said they will beat the bishop. The object was to prevent them adding their numbers and influence to the rest of the Dissenters in their exertions to separate Church and State and to effect other political purposes; and then—'Methodists, as you were'. The bishop, though a clever man, forgot that long wars make good soldiers, he mistook veterans in plain clothes for raw recruits; he left out of his calculation that they are a political as well as a religious body, and that their ultimate object is to supersede and occupy the plan of the present establishment. Their feelers in conference to establish bishops and compel their congregations to use their prayer book, to the exclusion of extempore prayer, are proofs of my assertion. I shall never forget what a rich banker of the name of Carne at Penzance, who from his influence and liberality is called there Bishop Carne, said some years since of his sect, 'We shall eat the bowels of the Church out.' When told of the liberality of the sentiments in the bishop's charge, their suppressed titter said, 'He who thinks us fools makes a small mistake.' To the point, Jabez

Bunting and other influential Methodists have had interviews and communications with Lord Althorp, who has been playing Bishop Phillpotts number two, and has only very partially succeeded in his object, as a large body of Methodists will not be controlled in the expression of their political sentiments by their soi-disant leaders. Now look to Lord Althorp's items of intended reduction of taxation: £3,000 per annum, arising he says from the duty on saddle horses used by clergymen and dissenting ministers whose incomes do not exceed £120. I wish Lord Althorp would name one such person, a man who with that income has bought and keeps a saddle horse. Why a saddle horse cannot be kept, in any town at least, under £40 per annum. Why, his Lordship would say, the Methodist preachers have very few of them more than £120, and they are both obliged to, and do actually keep them. If the Methodists have told his Lordship this, they have told him an *infamous falsehood*. Each circuit *provides, keeps, pays tax for* and, if *disabled, procures* a *horse* or *horses* as the case may be for the preachers of that circuit who, except the use of the animal, have no interest whatever in it, so that this, my Lord, is a boon of £3,000 per annum given to the Methodist body. Now have they not outgeneralled the Chancellor and the bishop, as sure as we are alive? Their intention, as Beverley says, is to preach and pray themselves up the steps of the throne and then sit above it. Their next probable step will be to get the taxes, and perhaps the rates taken off the preachers' houses attached to their chapels; and then they are above us, for our glebe houses pay both. Why, my Lord, they now rank in pecuniary advantages with the higher order of beneficed clergy. At what sum they begin with the salaries of their preachers I do not know, but call the average, as the statement of Lord Althorp would warrant us, at £120. Then are superadded the trifling advantages of house, furniture and coals, horse, travelling expenses paid; no rates or taxes, even their servants' wages paid; if popular many handsome presents; ten pounds per annum for every child, and as soon as that child is eight years, I believe, old, maintained and instructed at their public schools, assisted by the connexion to be put out in life, and if orphans, set up wholly by them; the preachers always visiting so that their housekeeping is a trifle; so that clothes is almost their principal expense. I call their situation fully equal to a beneficed clergyman of £400 per annum gross income; nay, when you consider all anxiety for their children is taken away, very superior. With all this, as a legislator, you have nothing to do; but when it is proposed to give a religious sect a boon of £3,000 per annum, your Grace will probably feel it a duty to inquire into it. The boon professes to be given to all teachers of religion, but in reality is given to one sect of Dissenters; to have been just it should have said to all religious teachers under £500 per annum. As it is, is your Grace prepared to sanction the principle that large bodies of men, circuits as they are called, with of course very large aggregate incomes, shall be exonerated from the tax paid on saddle horses provided and kept by them for the use of their religious teachers? If two parishes served by a poor curate at £120 had the kindness to keep a horse for his use, would the surveyor of taxes allow the duty? I do myself the honour to address you as the great Tory head and also because I have observed in all your public conduct such straightforward, manly behaviour, and when I tell you that I myself am a decided Radical,—I mean an advocate to do away with all corruption in Church and State, you will not suspect me of flattery. Depend upon it, my Lord Duke, but a short time [is] remaining for your Tories to take the reins, reforming all abuses, and giving the people the free election of their own house, or to convulsion, revolution and probably a republic. The Whigs are pulling down as fast as they can, and fearful to think, the lower classes estranged from the higher, stand waiting the signal which is to convulse the kingdom. I must insist on not taxing your politeness in noticing this, as I have already drawn too deeply on you to get through this scrawl; I merely wish to draw your attention to this Methodist manoeuvre, and this I have effected.

Docketed by Wellington Compliments. Received. *Docketed by secretary* Done. August 4.

Sir Herbert Taylor to Wellington, 31 July 1834

Windsor Castle. I had the honor to receive at St. James's Palace yesterday your Grace's letter and the accompanying addresses upon the subject of the King's speech to the archbishops and bishops which I took the earliest opportunity of submitting to His Majesty.

John Griffiths to Wellington, 31 July 1834

Leatherhead. The accompanying papers contain some information respecting the Oxford declarations against the proposed plan for the admission of Dissenters into the universities, and may perhaps be of service if your Grace should deem it advisable to allude to those declarations in the House of Lords.

If they are useful, they sufficiently explain themselves; and of their usefulness your Grace is the best judge. I shall therefore make no further remarks upon them.

But as it must at first sight appear very presumptuous that an individual, utterly unknown to your Grace, should venture without introduction to address himself to you immediately on this or any other subject, I will add that the charge of examining and watching over the signatures has been committed entirely to me, that consequently no other person can vouch so positively for their authenticity and accuracy, and that Mr. Vaughan Thomas, by whose activity the signatures were chiefly obtained, and whose station and character in the university would better entitle him to communicate with your Grace, is at too great a distance to allow of my consulting him.

Your Grace would not have been troubled with these papers, if the bill had not passed the House of Commons; and the early day named for the second reading in the House of Lords will, I trust, be my excuse for troubling you now.

Signed: John Griffiths, MA, fellow and tutor of Wadham College.

Draft reply 3 August 1834. Compliments. The Duke returns his thanks for the information which his letter contains.

Thomas Frankland Lewis to Wellington, [1 August 1834]

28 Park Street, Grosvenor Square. I have been suddenly and unexpectedly pressed by Lord Melbourne to suffer my name to [be] placed at the head of the Poor Law Commission, and before I decide one way or another on the subject, it would be extremely gratifying to me to know your Grace's impressions as to what it will be right for me to do.

As the proposal has the appearance at least of being made to me on publick grounds, I feel bound to decide on it in the same spirit, and to set aside as far as possible all personal considerations.

The poor law subject is one in which I have long taken an anxious interest. The measure itself has my approval and, notwithstanding the difficulties which surround the undertaking, there is no publick object to which with a view to its importance I would more willingly devote my time and attention than the amendment of the pauper system. Still I have hesitated in assenting to the proposal; my doing so involves the necessity of going out of Parliament and deprives me of the opportunity which my vote gives me of aiding in that which I most earnestly wish to see, the return of your Grace and your friends to power. Although nearly all the leading interests in Radnorshire are of Tory politicks, still it is uncertain who would succeed.

Your Grace would add one to many obligations by permitting [me] either to see or hear from you on this subject.

Undated. Docketed 1 August 1834.

Lord Francis Egerton to Wellington, 1 August 1834

Oatlands, Esher. I have to acknowledge your letter of yesterday, suggesting to me the possibility of my undertaking to fill the vacancy likely to occur in the representation of Gloucester. In consequence of some communications which I have recently had with gentlemen connected with south Lancashire I could hardly consider myself at liberty to entertain, without their consent, views of coming into Parliament for any other representation, and with regard to that I am most anxious to postpone if possible my views over next year on grounds connected with the present state of my health. I have stated to them that nothing but compulsion would induce me to come forward at present, and that I only included in that term such circumstances as would make my so coming forward the only reasonable chance of supplanting a Whig or a Radical in that important representation. Under these circumstances I am confident you will see that I am justified in declining the proposal, which, were I anxious to come now into Parliament, would doubtless have been a very advantageous one, and for which as such I have to thank you. I have alarms of my old complaint at this moment, and I really believe that a week's abandonment of my eremitical life and regimen would at present make me most inefficient either as candidate or Member for any place.

The Earl Somers to Wellington, 1 August 1834

Eastnor Castle. Having successively entrusted my proxy to the Earl of St. Germans and the Earl Brownlow, who have both quitted the seat of Parliament, and understanding that in a very few days the great question of admission or non-admission of Dissenters into the universities of Oxford and Cambridge is to come on in the House of Lords, I am decidedly adverse to such admission, as a most ruinous measure; and not knowing what Conservative peers, who hold not at present two proxies, are still in London, I take the liberty of enclosing my proxy to your Grace, requesting you will entrust it to, and have it filled up with the name of any peer you may select for giving my vote against the ruinous admission I have alluded to and deprecate, or against any other measure of a similar stamp.

John Bate Cardale to Wellington, 1 August 1834

Bedford Row. I have been entrusted with a petition to the King signed by 171 of the most respectable inhabitants of Rugby, Newbold-on-Avon, Clifton on Dunsmore, and Brownsover in the county of Warwick, humbly thanking His Majesty for his gracious declaration recently made to uphold in her privileges and efficiency our national Church. I have been desired respectfully to solicit your Grace that if your engagements would permit, you would present it on their behalf to His Majesty.

I do myself the honor to request of your Grace an interview, when I might give you fuller particulars as to the character and station of the parties signing the petition, or such instructions as may enable me further to acquit myself of my charge; and, if you will consent to present the petition, to convey it to your Grace.

William Whitmore to Wellington, 1 August 1834

1 Dorset Street, Manchester Square. Mr. William Whitmore presents his compliments to the Duke of Wellington and would feel greatly obliged to his Grace to grant him an interview of a few minutes in reference to the project of which Mr. Whitmore encloses a prospectus. The object is to establish a colony in South Australia and promote emigration on a plan whereby the great expenses attending upon it will be borne by proceeds arising from the sale of land in the colonies. The bill now before the House of Commons will probably pass this that house early in next week [*sic*] and the provisional committee, of which Mr. Whitmore is chairman, are anxious to explain their object to some of the more influential members of the House of Lords. Mr. Whitmore therefore hopes that the Duke of Wellington will not charge him with presumption in the request he now makes. Mr. Whitmore will wait upon his Grace at any time he may appoint in the course of the next four days.

Wellington to William Whitmore, 2 August 1834

The Duke of Wellington presents his compliments to Mr. Whitmore. The Duke will not be in town till Monday. But he [will] be happy to receive Mr. Whitmore on that day at 12 at noon.

Wellington to John Bate Cardale, 2 August 1834

The Duke of Wellington presents his compliments to Mr. Cardale. The Duke will receive Mr. Cardale whenever he thinks proper to call upon him; at the same time he begs leave to suggest to Mr. Cardale that the Duke's time and Mr. Cardale's time and trouble would be saved if Mr. Cardale would send him the address which it is his wish that the Duke should present to the King.

Wellington to the Earl Somers, 2 August 1834

London. I have received this morning your Lordship's letter and your proxy to be used upon the Dissenters Admission Bill, and 'any other measure of a similar stamp'.

The Dissenters Admission Bill was rejected last night by a majority of 102 and I request your Lordship to send me your directions respecting the measure in which your proxy is to be used in future.

The Earl of Home to Wellington, 2 August 1834

The Hirsel [*Berwickshire*]. At the request of the Duke of Buccleuch I have the honor to transmit my proxy to your Grace.

Draft reply 6 August 1834. Compliments to Lord Home. The Duke has received his proxy and is much flattered by the confidence reposed in the Duke by his Lordship.

The Marquess of Downshire to Wellington, 4 August 1834

Hillsborough. The success which appears from the newspaper account to attend the dangerous views and plans of the Irish agitation in the House of Commons by the late division on the Tithe Bill induces me to ask you to take charge of my proxy in the approaching debates upon that measure in the House of Lords. I shall enclose a proxy in this note, *but* am not quite sure if the rules of the House will permit my object being carried into effect for the following reason. Before I left London I gave my proxy to Lord Aylesbury to be used against the Western Railway which has been thrown out, and Lord Aylesbury still retains it, though without my authority to use it again. As I believe he still remains in town, I shall, to prevent disappointment, take the liberty of enclosing a letter to him to explain the matter, and knowing his political feelings I have no doubt he will attend on the day of discussion to vote, in case the enclosed proxy should be useless. I have a thousand excuses to make to you for so long a history which I hope you will forgive.

PS. Hillsborough sends his best respects. Everything in this part of Ireland seems to prosper. The crops were never finer.

The Earl Somers to Wellington, 4 August 1834

Eastnor Castle. Lord Somers presents his compliments to his Grace the Duke of Wellington, regrets his proxy came too late and rejoices at the division. He is not aware of any measure likely to come on in the House of Lords at this late period of the session, on which he would wish his proxy to be used, but should there be a division on the Irish Tithe Bill desires to leave it at the disposal of the Duke.

The Earl of Carnarvon to Wellington, 4 August 1834

Grosvenor Square. I was unwilling the other day when you were much engaged to allude to a subject on which I was anxious to speak to you. I have received letters from persons connected with the projected railway from London to Bath by Basing, requesting me to become one of the provisional committee.

The project is extremely popular in all that part of the country with which I am immediately connected and some of the gentlemen near Highclere have written to me about it.

I believe it will divide one of my farms, without however doing me any very essential mischief and I feel very greatly disposed to add my name to the list; but understanding that it is likely to pass either through your property or very near it and not knowing how it may affect it I have been unwilling to give any sanction to the project till I hear from your Grace whether it is or is not unpleasing to you.

PS. I hope your Grace has received in safety the Hampshire address. I have received the petition, which I am thinking of presenting this evening, if an opportunity occurred.

The Rev. Henry Beaufort to Wellington, 6 August 1834

Harrogate. I do not know whether I am not taking a very unwarrantable liberty in addressing your Grace and obtruding on your attention observations of mine on a subject with which I doubt not your Grace is far better acquainted than myself: I mean the Irish Tithe Bill, about to come before the House of Lords. I humbly trust however for pardon to your Grace's kindness, which I have already on some similar occasions experienced.

I do not advert to the fundamental objections in principle that it violates the constitutional security of property, in opening a channel for diverting that of the Church from its proper object and that it saps or cuts off the original prescriptive *title* of the Church to her property and so endangers her independence if not her stability. On these higher matters I should more becomingly perhaps learn from your Grace; but possibly your Grace may not have scrutinized so closely as to observe smaller matters of detail. For instance the whole system of permitting, or rather inviting and courting a revision and alteration of bargains long since made for the composition of tithes is calculated to undo that which has given satisfaction, and create a new ground of variance. And it is an idle pretence to say, as is said in Parliament, that compositions have been raised above the value. I venture to say that it is not so in one case among an hundred; and that in very many cases (in my own in a small degree and in those of some within my own knowledge to a greater degree) a sacrifice of income was made for the sake of peace. This subject occupies ten clauses: from V to XIV inclusive; and among its least objections is the heavy expense created by the number of barristers to be appointed for the purpose. But clause VIII (in the Commons Bill printed as amended on recommitment, August 1), in the 'rules to be observed in the revision of compositions', seems to me to be filled with gross injustice, as firstly (at the top of page 11) it excludes (on such revision) from the calculation of the amount of such composition 'all sums calculated on the evidence of adjudications' (pursuant to the Act) *made in default of the appearance of the party against whom*, etc. Now it is well known that it has been a constant practice with tithe payers, merely to gain time, to postpone paying until compelled by some process at law; in such cases they make no defence and therefore no appearance; and such are at the least nineteen-twentieths, if not a much larger proportion, of all the *adjudications* made: to exclude them therefore is to cut off claims for the future, grounded on the surest evidence as to the past. The bill says secondly, 'so much as *shall not be shewn* to have been justly due'; but how can a man *now* shew that not to be justly due which then he did not think it worth while to dispute, or if he think fit to pretend to do so, how can such allegation be rebutted at the distance of eight or ten years [as] it may be? Such documents are not preserved after adjudications and payments. Again (*line 10*) 'should a smaller sum have been received in discharge of a promissory note for a larger', the tithe owner is to be entitled only to that smaller sum; and so for ever mulcted to the amount of the balance, for having been moderate in his demand or compassionate to the debtor, whose poverty at the time of payment of his note is no impeachment of the justness of his debt. Surely this is not equitable.

Again (line 16 to 25), if a man making such promissory note should be found to have been insolvent, its amount is to be excluded; and because the tithe owner was cheated five or six years ago into taking bad security, he is not only to suffer the loss thereby incurred, but to undergo the same, himself and his successors, ever after.

Again (line 30), 'when agreement with a vestry shall not have been carried into effect by reason of the dissent of the bishop, and a larger amount afterwards adopted, that rejected smaller one shall be substituted.' The bishop's assent was required to prevent collusion, to the prejudice of a successor, by which it might happen that an incumbent being interested as a landowner in the parish, or by money offered to him, or being of an indolent and easy temper, or being wealthy, etc., etc. might deteriorate the value of that of which he is virtual trustee. Such a case I well remember in which a collusive fraud was defeated by the dissent of the bishop. The effect of this clause will be to give effect to such frauds, and thus add one more to the many ways which have [been] so ingeniously and perseveringly invented for robbing the Protestant clergy.

In page 12 (line 2 and 3), such alterations are left almost to the arbitrary will of the presiding barristers and there is not even the restraint of impending costs and recognizance, etc. upon the litigious complainant. It seems by the repetition of these invitations in Act after Act to be the earnest desire of those who legislate for us, to stimulate the people to such complaints and to create disunion.

I shall not occupy your Grace's time, upon which I have so much trespassed already, with any further continuation of these objections, of which however many more may be pointed out; but humbly beg your Grace's kind indulgence for which I have already done.

I would only suggest the question, whether, if the whole of the redemption clauses be not restored (which would in a great degree remove or lessen the *danger* of this bill), there might not be an option given to proprietors of land to redeem for land if they should think fit: either by purchase at twenty years the amount to be invested in land; or by exchange for land of value equivalent to the rent charge. I have said twenty years because, though tithes have been valued at sixteen only, that depreciation has been owing to their uncertainty and fluctuating nature; when reduced to a certainty there is no reason why they should be worth less than any other perpetuity. Indeed rent charges in perpetuity, from the natural desire to get rid of them, will fetch a much higher price: up twenty-five or thirty years and upwards.

I am really at a loss to know how to apologize for my intrusive freedom and can only plead the great importance of the case which rouses even ignorant persons to think with anxiety, and the deep confidence which we have been taught to place in your Grace's upright, unbiassed principles of attachment to the Protestant constitution of this country in Church and State; and with this plea, throw myself on your Grace's kind and indulgent forbearance.

Signed: Henry Beaufort, a prebendary of Cork.

Docketed by Wellington Compliments. Received. *Docketed by secretary* Done. August 12.

John Howell to Wellington, 7 August 1834

1 Leadenhall St., City. During the progress of the Poor Law Amendment Bill I have watched in vain for the suggestion of an idea which I now respectfully offer to the consideration of your Grace. I had no intention of doing this until I experienced the pleasure I felt this afternoon in hearing from below the bar of the House of Lords the observations made by your Grace on introducing the clauses drawn up by Lord Wharncliffe. If I understood rightly your Grace's remarks they amounted to this, that some concession ought to be made to the strong public feeling on the subject of the proposed changes in the bastardy laws, whose severity towards females you admitted it would be desirable to soften. It appears to me this desired object would be attained by introducing my long cherished plan, viz., 'Make the father of an illegitimate child responsible for its maintenance after birth, provided it be the first illegitimate offspring of the mother, but make the mother in all instances exclusively liable for the maintenance of the second and every subsequent child she may have by the same or any other man, or in any other parish.'

This is a simple and practicable distinction, the good effects of which I am the more thoroughly convinced of the more thoroughly I consider it. It would be easy to expatiate on the score of feeling on this proposal, but I abstain from addressing to you, my Lord Duke, any other sentiments than those which in my very humble opinion legislative wisdom alone dictates. The advantages of this plan are: first, that it would prove a very material check upon the unbridled licentious dispositions of bad men: this is a benefit all parties admit but which the promoters of the bill have abandoned for the sake of the more full exercise of the principle of punishing the woman exclusively. This would shield the chastity of the females of the country in a great degree from the encreased attack to which they will be more subject from the proposed change of the law. Secondly, it gives to the unfortunate victims of seduction an opportunity of saving themselves from the ruin almost necessarily consequent on the maintenance of a child; the disgrace and inconvenience will be a sufficient punishment for the first offence and the door left open to the chance of recovering station and character. Thirdly, it will induce men who have thus injured such females to repair the wrong by marrying them: this is a principle of religion. Fourthly, it will decrease the temptation to commit infanticide; and fifthly, it will not very materially interfere with the principle of the bill, for the penalty imposed upon the woman of maintaining her illegitimate children is not so much directed against the young, confiding and betrayed girl, but against the shameless, lewd or perjured woman, who makes a trade of her vice. The law ought to be directed against the habitual profligacy and calculating wickedness, and not against the weakness and misfortunes of that sex to whom the great philosopher of the human heart has given the very name 'frailty'. It must be admitted that every woman before marriage feels an instinctive pride in preserving her chastity inviolate, and human laws and habits tend perpetually to strengthen this natural feeling. Whether the proposed change of the law will arm the woman against the arts, the unblushing and responsible arts of men more effectually than the sacred feeling alluded to I will not stop to enquire. But it should be remembered by the legislature that woman in early life is affectionate, credulous, and confiding; 'love is her whole existence'; and I venture to assert that mere gross animal appetite rarely renders a woman the victim of seduction; personal attachment to the man, a reposing confidence in his character are the concomitants of her first misfortune. The man, with his flattering arts, professes devoted affection, pretends to greater wealth than he really possesses, often promises marriage, and always protection, on which the female heart is prone to dwell with the greatest fondness and confidence; the consequences of her indiscretion are always distant, and she indulges in the delusive hope of escaping shame. See, my Lord Duke, the incongruity of the law, for a rape a man is hanged; for wily seduction (a rape without force) he escapes with impunity. What reckless designing round about profligacy in men will not this encourage? The charity I claim for the poor seduced girl, I ask not for the abandoned woman who has neglected the opportunity of returning to the paths of virtue, and renouncing respectability gives herself up to habitual vice. The change of the law as applicable to this class of women is wholesome in the highest degree; it will prove the most beneficial check upon profligacy and perjury.

My Lord Duke, I am a most humble individual, but in the sphere in which I move (the merchants and traders of the City) the opposition to the measure is expressed in the strongest terms; but I venture to assert that the opposition arises entirely from a compassionate feeling for the situation of the poor seduced female, who retains a sense of shame and delicacy. The hardened woman who is insensible to feminine propriety shares none of this humane sympathy so generally expressed by the public.

Respectfully and humbly apologizing for intruding these opinions thus hastily written on the attention of your Grace, whose legislative abilities are my constant admiration, *etc.*

Docketed by Wellington Compliments. Received. *Docketed by secretary* Done. August 10.

Sir Herbert Taylor to Wellington, 8 August 1834

Windsor Castle. I have the honor to acknowledge the receipt of your Grace's letter of the 6th instant, transmitting sundry addresses, of which a list is annexed to your letter, upon the King's speech on his birthday to the archbishops and bishops which I have not delayed to submit to His Majesty, and I have received the King's commands to thank your Grace for the trouble you have taken to forward them to His Majesty.

Wellington to John Charles Herries, 13 August 1834

London. You will see that Lord Auckland withdrew the pilot bill after discussion. We had a majority; and they could not carry it.

I return Frankland Lewis's letter.[1] I have given him my opinion that he ought to accept.

ADD MS 57368.

The Bishop of Hereford (the Hon. Edward Grey) to Wellington, 14 August 1834

Parliament Street. I take the liberty of sending to your Grace, together with the inclosed address to His Majesty, a letter which I have received this morning and which will account for my thus intruding myself on your Grace's attention. I think it right, by way of explanation, to add that I declined to present the address to His Majesty on the ground that His Majesty's declaration therein alluded to was made to the bishops privately, and in a strictly confidential manner, and ought not to have been brought before the public, and that therefore I did not feel myself at liberty, as one of the persons to whom that confidential

---

[1] See above, p. 625.

declaration was addressed, to approach His Majesty with any observations of others founded thereupon. Your Grace will pardon me for thus explaining how I happen to be commissioned to place the inclosed address in your Grace's hands.

Wellington to the Bishop of Hereford, 14 August 1834

London. I have received your Lordship's letter.

I feel as you do respecting the King's speech to the archbishops and bishops, and the impropriety of considering that speech as the foundation on which His Majesty should be addressed in terms of congratulation.

I have felt this the more particularly as I have thought that the expectations of those who signed these addresses would be disappointed.

I have however presented many addresses to the King upon this subject, because in fact it is not easy to state the objections to such addresses to those who have signed them without doing mischief.

I would accordingly present that which your Lordship has inclosed, if I was not going out of town. As it is I request your Lordship to ask Mr. Jenkins to excuse me for declining to undertake to present the address in question.

Henry Alworth Merewether to Wellington, 18 August 1834

7 Whitehall Place. In the note which I had before the honor of addressing to your Grace I omitted to mention that the most expedient and legitimate mode of effecting the measure I venture to recommend would be at courts to be held in the ordinary course at the close of the next month; and as some preliminary steps would be necessary, as well as probably communications with many individuals, the intervening time might not be longer than would be requisite for those purposes.

I therefore trust that your Grace will excuse the liberty I take in adding this to my former communication.

Wellington to the Earl of Roden, 19 August 1834

London. I have received your letter of the 16th. I sincerely wish that your meeting in Dublin may produce all the benefit that you expect from it. It would be very desirable if the Protestant gentlemen in Ireland would associate, and pledge themselves to each other and to the publick to protect each other and their neighbours and dependants of all classes in all their rights and property and most particularly the clergy of the Church of England in Ireland in whom they should pledge themselves not only to pay what is their due, but to assist and protect them in recovering the same from others by all legal means.

Something of this kind generally signed and acted upon would have an immense effect in Ireland; would enable the clergy to oppose themselves to the persecution which awaits them; and would tend to excite a kindred feeling in this country in their favour.

Wellington to the Earl of Roden, 20 August 1834

London. I have long intended to communicate with you respecting the representative peerage of Ireland. I believe that there are several persons who are anxious that Lord Bandon should be the next elected. Indeed this was mentioned to me at the period of the last election; and I feel so anxious that there should be no difference of opinion among us that I would assist him, knowing it to be the decided wish of the peers of Ireland, our friends, even if I had not heard of his pretensions and qualifications.

But there is a candidate to whose pretensions and qualifications I am anxious to draw the attention of yourself and your friends upon the next succeeding vacancy: that is Lord FitzGerald. There is not a man in Parliament more capable than he is of taking an useful part in debate; and I am convinced that he would be eminently useful in all the Irish questions likely to come under discussion in the next and in future sessions.

I am aware of the feelings which might operate against him, but on the other hand it must not be forgotten that there are a large number of persons who would be disposed to promote his views, to whose wishes some attention ought to be paid in their turn; and that nothing would be more fatal to the attainment of the object of the Irish peers (that is the return of a Conservative) than that the Conservatives should divide. I earnestly intreat you then to consider of the claims of Lord FitzGerald for the vacancy after that for which Lord Bandon will be elected; and to concert the matter with your friends.

Alexander Bowker to Wellington, 23 August 1834

Lynn. Knowing the great interest your Grace takes upon all occasions in whatever regards the welfare of agriculture of this kingdom, I am induced to take the liberty of handing the annexed extract of a letter from Danzig, by which your Grace will perceive considerable importations of foreign grain are likely to take place to the islands of Guernsey and Jersey, no doubt with the view of ultimately being surreptitiously sent to this country as the produce of those islands and which has already taken place to some extent not withstanding Mr. Poulett Thomson's assertion in the House of Commons to the contrary and which malpractice also still exists through the Isle of Man. I am credibly informed a gentleman recently witnessed (within the last two or three weeks) half-a-dozen foreign vessels discharging at one time their cargoes of wheat and flour into English vessels which when completed proceeded to Liverpool, Whitehaven and other ports. I hope your Grace may see it desirable to take immediate steps in the proper quarter to endeavour to put an end to this nefarious traffick.

PS. I have recently heard of Mr. Hoseason's safe arrival in India and of his being appointed chief magistrate of Calcutta, which [I] think your Grace will be pleased to learn.

Enclosure: Danzig, 3rd August 1834.

The Hamburg mail has just arrived with accounts relative to the grain market there: the holders were anxiously looking for the news of the state of the English market before they sold.

In the last eight days of last month thirty-eight cargoes of grain had passed the sound, of which six only were bound to British ports; there had also passed the sound four ships laden with corn for Guernsey and Jersey and this circumstance, recollecting that many vessels have already been freighted at Hamburg for the same places, has induced the belief that foreign corn is still extensively imported into England from the islands as the produce of those places.

Draft reply 29 August 1834. Compliments. The Duke has really nothing to say to the Board to Trade.

He earnestly recommends to Mr. [Bowker] to give the information which his letter contains to some noble lord who has.

Wellington to the Earl of Aberdeen, 23 August 1834

Walmer Castle. I did not see you in the last days of the session; and various events have occurred since, which, as well as those of the session, are worthy of observation.

The Government appear to bear very tranquilly our majority on the Tithe Bill; which indeed they knew would have been larger if we had allowed the bill to go to the third reading. The Duke of Richmond, Lord Ripon, Lord Chichester and Lord Darnley declared that they would have voted against it. It is said that Lord Howden had made the same declaration; and that the Duke of Sutherland had declared the same. We were unlucky in the absence of some certain friends such as Lord Limerick and Lord Tenterden, each with two proxies. So that upon the whole the Government must see clearly that in their legislation at least they must reckon with the House of Lords. I consider the destruction of the House of Lords to be now out of the question; and that we have only now to follow a plain course with moderation and dignity in order to attain very great, if not a preponderating influence over the affairs of the country. We defeated in the last session three important measures supported by the Government: the Jew Bill, the University Bill and the Irish Tithe Bill; and two others of less importance, but highly revolutionary: the Theatrical Bill and the Cinque Ports Pilots Bill; and we made important alterations in many others which tended to prevent their mischief. If Lord Lyndhurst could have attended instead of Lord Wynford we should have done more good.

In respect to foreign policy, I think that you was not present on the day that Lord Londonderry made his motion. We brought Lord Melbourne to the declaration that the object of the Quadripartite Treaty has been attained by the expulsion of Don Carlos and Don Miguel from Portugal. I contended that the object of the treaty had been attained before it was ratified; that the Spanish troops had been in Portugal before it was thought of; and that if an irregularity had not been committed in the exchange of the ratifications, they never need have been exchanged. I see that the Ministers have made the King contradict me in his Speech from the Throne. But the *Standard* of yesterday has brought me a positive contradiction of the King's Speech. Martinez de la Rosa in his speech of the 8th and 9th August, after giving an account of the operations of the Spanish troops in Portugal and saying that they 'co-operated in the prompt and speedy issue of that tedious conflict', goes on to say, 'Thus ended the contest even before the Treaty of London was duly ratified.' In these times of general revolution, that which is above all things necessary for Governments and Ministers is always to speak the truth. The lie is sure to be discovered at last. Towards the last day of the session Lord Londonderry asked a question which enabled the Government to give him an answer, from which it would have appeared that the objects of the Quadripartite Treaty were not considered as attained, notwithstanding what had been stated in the former debate. I set that matter right, however; and we stand now with the objects of that treaty attained.

In the meantime, however, I had learnt that our Government were straining every nerve to induce that of France to apply its stipulations to the contest in Spain; or at all events to concur in a new treaty, and to make corresponding exertions of interference in the contest in Spain. When I last heard upon the subject, Louis-Philippe had positively refused to send French troops into Spain, whether at his own expense or at the expense of Spain. He likewise refused to employ his ships in a blockade of the coasts of Spain for fear of being involved thereby in questions with neutral powers; and to give to the Regent's Government assistance in arms or money. All that he consented to do was to maintain a strict land blockade to prevent any succours from France to either party; and to allow a corps called *La Légion Etrangère* in the service of France to pass into that of the Queen of Spain at her exclusive expense. This corps is composed of Poles and blackguard refugees from all nations; and I believe that the offer of its services will be declined if there is any Spanish feeling, a feeling for the honour and safety of their country in any individual in the service of the Queen.

That was the last I heard of these negociations; and as Talleyrand left London near a week ago, I conclude that they were broken off. I doubt very much his return. He complains of Lord Palmerston in particular as they all do; but very much likewise of the march of the Government in the internal concerns as well as in the foreign relations of the country. It is curious enough that during the reign of Louis-Philippe the example of England should be dangerous to France; and that England should push France forward in a course of Jacobin foreign policy; and that Talleyrand should be the person to complain thereof.

Lord Palmerston has certainly behaved very ill to him, ever since the foolish affair of Don Carlos's escape.

Bülow is going. So that we have neither ambassador nor minister plenipotentiary from any of the great courts. I should not be surprised if the smaller ones, Sardinia, Naples, Bavaria, Denmark, Sweden and Würtemberg were to follow the example.

I don't think that it will signify one pin. John Bull cares about nothing excepting pulling down the ancient institutions of the country; and getting some plunder from the Church or any other that may come to his hand.

It appears from a paper received from Vienna that the Austrian Government have spoken out very frankly upon the conduct of England and France in the Levant; and have stated their opinion that that conduct has been the cause of the recent Russian measures at Constantinople. They have stated the course which they propose to take in various hypotheses arising out of the state of affairs in the Levant and war being the consequence; and particularly that in case war in the west of Europe should be the consequence of war in the east, they, the Austrians, will consider the west the most interesting point for them to attend to.

Our papers pretend, God knows upon what authority, that Don Carlos is upon his march to Madrid. I think that his officers appear to have outmanoeuvred Rodil; and to have got out of the mountains unhurt. God knows what will be the result. In the meantime if we are to be the allies of the Queen, I think that we ought to endeavour to humanize the war. Rodil's last proclamation is infamous. It is quite curious how little notice is taken of it in any of our newspapers. Yet one would have thought that humanity was a topick which could not fail to be listened to in England. But in truth nothing is listened to, but what tends to revolution, either at home or abroad.

I have not heard from Sir Robert Peel since he left London. I heard of him that he is going abroad at the conclusion of his son's holidays to stay till the meeting of Parliament. I understand that he means to go to Italy, and even to Naples.

It was reported that the King had objected to any mention in the Speech of the fate of the Tithe Bill, or any matter of differences between the houses. This is the reason given for the Speech containing so little. I believe that I have told you all that I know or have heard. I hope that you are better.

ADD MS 43060, ff. 113–120. *Copy in Wellington Papers.*

641

The Duke of Cumberland to Wellington, 23 August 1834

St. James's Palace. Just two lines to bid you farewell, as I leave this early tomorrow (Sunday morning) morning [*sic*]; I embark at Deptford and hope, if the weather remains fair, to be by Tuesday evening safely landed at Hamburg. I was at Windsor on Thursday and found the Queen *well* as to health, but no means pleased with all that has been done and is going on. I have learned the secret of the *row* which I told you I had reason to believe had taken place the day of the prorogation, when I saw my brother after his audience with Brougham. They had put in a *philippic* against the House of Lords for our having thrown out the Dissenters and Irish Tithe Bills, but *His Majesty positively* refused delivering it, and all Brougham's bullying or persuasion would not bring *him* to *this*. This you may depend upon, and fully explains to me the having left out *all* allusion to Ireland which must strike everyone as extraordinary. I saw Lyndhurst this day; he starts in a few days to make a six weeks tour to Italy, and will *en passant* pay you a visit at Walmer. I have begged him to consider well our *two* points: the commission and the threatened attack on the corporate bodies, which appear to me to be monstrous.

The moment Parliament meets you will find me at my post.

PS. It seems to be generally believed, and not denied even by Government itself, that Parliament will meet before Christmas. I depend on hearing from you the moment you are aware of it. From letters I received last night from abroad the Empress of Russia is expected to be at Berlin the next month; whether the Emperor accompanies her or not is not said, but I rather suspect, if not, that a meeting between him and the King of Prussia will take place the first day of September on the frontiers, as the latter is to review the *first* army corps at Königsberg which is to take place in the first week of September. His Majesty, I believe, will have left Berlin ere I reach it, but I shall try to meet him at Stargard when he reviews the second corps d'armée which takes place the 6th or 7th of September. You shall hear from me *all* I know. I rather suspect this meeting has to do with the state of Spain. I hear the poor are up in arms against the Poor Law Bill and the magistrates both in Sussex and Oxfordshire declare they can't act upon it; a pretty *state of things*.

Wellington to the Duke of Cumberland, 24 August 1834

Walmer Castle. I have received your Royal Highness's commands of the 23rd. Your Royal Highness may rely upon receiving the earliest intelligence of any intended meeting of Parliament that I may hear of. There is one maxim about Parliament that is I believe invariable, and that is that meet when it will, it will sit as long as it is convenient for members to remain in town, unless Government should have finished its own business so as to be able to prorogue it at an early season of the year.

In time of war it is sometimes necessary to assemble Parliament before Christmas in order to obtain votes of money. A similar necessity may occur founded on the state of Ireland, as it did in 1819 founded on the riots at Manchester, when some extraordinary measures of law were necessary, which were passed before Christmas. But if such necessity should not exist I don't believe that this Government would [deem] it convenient to meet the reformed Parliament at an earlier period of the year than their predecessors [deemed] it convenient to meet the unreformed one.

There are certainly some reasons why they should desire to meet Parliament at an early period, of which the principal one is that the House of Lords would not be so well attended as at a later period. But on the other hand they would have to take care what they should attempt, even in the House of Commons. An adverse division before Christmas would leave them entirely at the King's mercy. He could form a Government, dissolve his Parliament and meet a new one in time to pass the supplies of the year. I entertain no doubt that those who have to decide this question of early meeting know all this as well as I do; and that they will not meet till the usual time. Indeed if I mistake not Lord Brougham told us as much.

Your Royal Highness's history of the prorogation speech is very curious, and I don't doubt true. It accounts for the nature of it; and for the omission of all topicks of interest. This transaction ought to shew the King what he can do if he pleases.

The Earl of Roden to Wellington, 25 August 1834

Tollymore Park. Private and confidential. I received your two letters of the 19th and 20th instant and return you many thanks for your suggestions with respect to our proceedings which I hope to act on, and propose drawing up a declaration in such moderate but firm language that cannot be gainsaid by any well-wisher to the Protestant cause. I am also most anxious about providing a fund to protect the clergy by law in their rights and property next November when a year's tithe will become due to them. I send you the *Warder* newspaper of today with my proposition and intentions as I stated them at our last meeting at the Conservative Society and which I hope you will be kind enough to read.

With respect to the representative peerage and Lord FitzGerald's claim, I trust there is no need of my assuring you that any suggestion or wish of yours would be attended to most anxiously by me, and if you needed a proof even as respects the object in question, I think on the late occasion our nomination and support of Lord Downes because we knew him to be connected with you, would be sufficient; the same reason would lead me in the present instance to comply with your wishes after Lord Bandon is secured, which I believe is pretty well understood to be the case as to the next vacancy. But I am bound to say that though Lord FitzGerald is a very old friend of mine, he is not popular with our party here and certainly has not come forward *lately* in our cause as many others have done who formerly had taken the same line of politicks; therefore the difficulty of obtaining for him the same support we got for Lord Downes is very evident. I agree fully with you, that we should not allow of a split in our party or else the Government candidate would walk in; but if Lord FitzGerald intends offering himself after the next vacancy, it is very necessary he should take some part with us and openly come forward to support our objects. Our friends are most ready to receive every gentleman that comes to them, nothing could be more strongly proved than this; in the reception Lord Downshire met with from our people at the meeting on the 14th and the rapturous applause Lord Glengall received from so large a company of the resident proprietors of Ireland who were assembled at the dinner on the 15th proved that the manly and open avowal of his sentiments and the expression of his changed view of things rendered him most welcome to be enrolled in their ranks.

I state this to you in perfect confidence and with a sincere desire to meet your wishes. I will sound our friends on the subject but I cannot shut my eyes to the objections that will be made.

Wellington to Sir George Murray, 25 August 1834

Walmer Castle. I am very much obliged to you for the perusal of the inclosed letter.

I am inclined to write to Prince Metternich to beg him to recommend your friend Mr. Drummond to the Pope's government. Let me know his names; and exactly what is his object. I will manage that he should get the letter through the Austrian Minister at this Court.

NLS ADV MS 46.8.16, ff 157, 158.

Captain Edward MacArthur to Wellington, 26 August 1834

House of Lords. It occurring to me that, at a period when public attention is turned to the subject of emigration, it might not be unacceptable to your Grace to receive *genuine* accounts of one of the quarters to which that tide is setting, I take the liberty of putting up the accompanying observations respecting the colony of New South Wales, on the greater part of which, and it appears to me the whole, I might venture to assure your Grace, as being myself intimately connected with that colony, every reliance is to be placed.

Draft reply 31 August 1834. Compliments. The Duke returns his thanks for the tracts which he has sent him on emigration.

The Earl of Roden to Wellington, 26 August 1834

Dublin. We had one of the most powerful and effective meetings on Thursday that I ever beheld. There were upwards of 6,000 persons present, consisting of all the rank and property in the country. Our dinner yesterday to Winchilsea was most effective, and I hope the sentiments then expressed will get out to the publick. Our Protestant case is so desperate we are going to establish large meetings in Ulster. It was truly gratifying to receive from such a body of the landlords of Ireland as have attended in Dublin this week that the House of Lords have acted in full conformity to their wishes by rejecting the Tithe Bill, and the feeling of the clergy on the subject is fully as strong: we are in a tremendous state in this country, and every exertion must be made or we are gone. The Protestants of Ireland feel most grateful to

645

you for your late exertions in their favour. and we cannot but rejoice in being connected with you.

Wellington to the Rev. George Rowley, 27 August 1834

Walmer Castle. I told you when I was at Oxford that I expected that we should hear more of attacks upon the universities of this kingdom whatever might be the result of the measure at that time under the consideration of Parliament; and that the form in which these attacks would be made would be in that of committees to enquire. You will have seen in the newspapers lists of notices of motions to be brought under the consideration of the House of Commons in the next session; which include either three or four for committees to enquire into every branch of the administration of the universities; and of the colleges and houses of which each is composed.

Even in the House of Lords Lord Radnor has given notice of a motion which has for its object to fix by law the age at which youths are to be required to affix their signature to the Thirty-nine Articles.

I think therefore that I may safely say that the expectations which I told you that I entertained will not be disappointed. Such enquiries are inconsistent with justice, and with the independent enjoyment of property, unless rendered necessary by some flagrant abuse which it is not pretended exists. But neither the universities nor any of the established institutions of the country now enjoy the advantage of being protected by the Crown; and we must not conceal from ourselves that in the House of Commons of these days such arguments will not be listened or attended to. A majority, acting under the influence of the Ministers of the Crown, will agree to appoint committees of enquiry, in the same spirit in which a majority agreed to the Dissenters admission bill.

It will rest with the universities to determine whether they will or not submit to the inquisitional power of this leviathan House of Commons. I think that the question ought not to be decided till it will be necessary; and I don't now advise submission. But of this I am certain that whether the universities and the colleges of which they are composed determine that they will submit their affairs to the inquisition of committees of the House of Commons or not, it is absolutely necessary that they should look into them, consider them well; and be prepared for a publick exposition of them.

I don't pretend to understand your affairs. But I must say that I should be the last man to advise you to concede any principle; or to alter any regulation considered necessary for maintaining your institutions and establishments on the footing on which they were placed by their founders.

But it is represented that there are many of your statutes that are becoming obsolete; others of which it is said that a practice contrary thereto has grown into use by custom, if it has not been positively enjoined by authority. It is stated that in some of the establishments the statutes and ordinances of the founders are not strictly obeyed. That in others a construction has been given to the statutes inconsistent with the publick benefit and the objects of the institution for purposes of private advantage. I know nothing; but I tell you what is said. I recommend to the heads of houses to look through the statutes of the university and to take measures to repeal every regulation that has become obsolete, has fallen into desuetude, or of which a practice contrary thereto has become in use; and that they should each in his own institution enter in detail into the whole of their regulations, compare each with the practice; and consider the actual relation between regulation and practice; and that remedial measures should be adopted and put in train of execution if there should be found any deviation of practice from the letter and spirit of the regulation.

I shall be at Stratfield Saye from the beginning of November till the meeting of Parliament; and I need not say how happy I shall be to receive there any gentleman of the university; nor how ready to give my advice and assistance to any who may require my counsel in this revision of their affairs, which I urge all to make. One consequence of such revision must be to enable the university and its colleges to determine whether they will or not submit to an inquisition by committees of the House of Commons upon sure grounds; and with a certainty that, determine which way they may, it will be without loss of reputation.

I now come to advert to the subject of the motion in the House of Lords of which notice has been given by Lord Radnor.

The difficulties under which those labour who defend the practice, under the statutes of the University of Oxford, are first that the statutes themselves provide that there is an age at which the signature of the youth to be matriculated ought not to be affixed to the Thirty-nine Articles; thus admitting that there should be a previous understanding of their meaning. But secondly it is contended that the signature of the youth upon matriculation does not convey assent excepting upon authority of the Church of which the signer is a member. If this assertion be true where is the use of the limitation of age provided in the statute? A youth under the age might sign, as well as one required to sign. Then comes the question at what age is the signature of the Articles to be considered as a test of understanding them; and of assent to them?

I happen to know that there are many conscientious men who have graduated at Oxford who do not approve of the practice of signing the Thirty-nine Articles upon matriculation; and that some of the heads of the Church would wish if possible to see some other test adopted.

In the late debate the Bishop of Exeter threw out the suggestion of an alteration, viz. that a declaration should be made by the candidate for matriculation that he had been educated as and was a member of the Church of England.

I confess that I am no friend to changes of any description; and particularly not to sudden changes. Supposing that it is thought expedient to make any change I would suggest this for consideration. First that the candidate for matriculation should certify and declare that he had been educated as and was a member of the Church of England. Secondly that he should be examined as to his knowledge of the Church catechism, the Lord's Prayer, the Creed etc.; and thirdly that he should farther declare his desire to be instructed in the Thirty-nine Articles with a view to affixing his signature to them as the evidence of his assent to their truth.

Then that he should be called to sign the Articles after examination at a more mature age when confirmed; preparatory to taking his degree.

I think that something of this kind would answer all the purposes of signing the Articles as explained; and would not be liable to the objections, to which that mode is liable, of certifying that the candidate is a member of the Church of England; and it would moreover have the effect of demonstrating to the publick that the education at the University of Oxford is really and bona fide a religious education.

I have troubled you at great length but there is one more point of a general nature to which I must draw your attention in case you should make any revision of your affairs; and that is to the facility which young men find in incurring debt at Oxford. I have received many letters upon this subject each detailing some terrible case of ruin, in some instances of a whole family, in every one of the prospects of the youth himself; and although I confess that I can suggest no remedy I could not write to you at all without adverting to this branch of the subject.

I don't believe that the Vice-Chancellor could refuse to put in execution the law in relation to a member of the university who should be of the legal age. But even if he could the debts of the members of the university would become debts of honour; and the youth who should not pay them would be ruined in reputation as effectually as he is in fortune under existing circumstances.

However it is not desirable that the University of Oxford should come to be considered in the country as a place of education only for the aristocracy of rank and wealth; and knowing how much feeling exists in the publick mind and among reasonable people upon this part of the subject I earnestly recommend it to the serious attention of yourself, and the heads of houses, who understand all the detailed difficulties of the subject better than I do.

The Rev. George Rowley to Wellington, 29 August 1834

Oxford. I will take care that your Grace's communication received this morning shall meet with the earliest and most serious consideration. I *myself* conceive that at the time of matriculation subscription to the Declaration of Uniformity, with an expression of readiness to receive religious instruction, instead of subscription to the Thirty-nine Articles, would answer every purpose, and remove all reasonable objections among the friends of the university. But I cannot of course answer for the opinions of others.

I believe the minds of most here are pretty well made up as to the authority of a commission of enquiry in private colleges (in one of which, if not in more, a solemn oath of secrecy is imposed by the founder) and as for the university there is very little information to be given. Its revenues arise almost entirely from the annual contributions of its members, and the statutes, which are framed by the university itself, are open to the inspection of all who wish to see them. When it becomes necessary, however, to take any positive step, every precaution must be used to insure the correctness of our proceedings.

The *necessary* expenditure of the young men is by no means large, not equalling that which occurs in some of our public schools. Every endeavor is in most colleges used to prevent extravagance, and I do not believe that any positive enactments would be sufficient for that purpose. Where it does occur to any extent, it is nine times out of ten owing to the unwillingness of parents to second the measures of the authorities here. This has always been a subject of complaint and I fear, do what we can, will still continue so to be. I cannot, however, discuss it at large in a letter.

Wellington to Lord FitzGerald, 29 August 1834

Walmer Castle. Private and confidential. After I saw you I wrote to one of my Conservative friends in Ireland in respect to your claims to be elected a representative peer upon the vacancy after the next that will occur, the next being understood to be promised to Lord Bandon.

I think the answer that I have received is favourable; so favourable that I recommend to you to take measures quietly to obtain for yourself support; and I beg you to let me know who are the persons whom an application from me would be likely to influence.

I will not conceal from you however that there is a great deal of prejudice existing against you; as I dare say there is against me for the same cause.

However there cannot be a doubt that we never intended to extinguish tithes, or to destroy the Church of England in Ireland. I believe that we could prove that our measure was adopted in a great degree to insure the support of Parliament to those measures thought necessary to establish and maintain peace and security for all descriptions of property and particularly for the Church in Ireland.

That is our object now. Our views and our measures, if we could propose and carry them, would be different now from those which we might have proposed in 1830 and 1831. But our objects are the same as they were. We support the Church of England in Ireland not only as a system of religion, but as one of property and of imperial policy.

I don't know what Lord Downshire did or said. But the Conservatives are quite satisfied with him.

I could not say what Lord Glengall said. They are equally satisfied with him. Nor could I ask you to conceal your opinion upon bygone transactions.

But I do recommend to you on your arrival in Ireland not to make yourself a party to all the nonsense and bombast that passes at these Conservative meetings, but to declare loudly your opinion on the conduct of the Government and on the measures which they are pursuing in Ireland. I think that by this course, which if I am not mistaken will be entirely consistent with your own opinions and feelings, you will conciliate the support of a great majority of the Conservative peers; and will facilitate and secure your return to the House of Lords.

Addressed to: The Lord FitzGerald, Cheltenham.

Wellington to the Earl of Roden, 29 August 1834

Walmer Castle. Private and confidential. I have received your letter of the 25th. I have written to Lord FitzGerald and have desired him to take his measures quietly to secure for himself votes for the vacancy in the Irish representative peerage next after the first, which it is understood will be filled by Lord Bandon.

I am convinced that Lord FitzGerald entertains the same opinion that I do about affairs in Ireland. It is not necessary to enter into bygone affairs and I think it very possible that he would not like to attend at publick meetings at which the discussion might turn upon subjects in which there was a difference of opinion.

But there can be none now, and I think that you will find that the Conservatives in Ireland have not a more willing, as they certainly have not a more able co-operator than Lord FitzGerald.

I have read your speech in the *Warder*. I had before read a report of it in other places. But I confess that it does not come up to the point which I have in view.

My opinion is that if you associate in the manner and in the terms stated in my letter to you of the 19th August, not only you will save the Church but yourselves. You will very soon find that all proprietors will be anxious to become members of your association, not excluding the great Whig absentee lords and even Lord Duncannon himself.

Besides I am anxious to excite for you a feeling in this country. The Irish gentlemen are not in favour in this country, most particularly in this subject of the Church and of tithes. They are suspected of supporting the Church for selfish motives and of coveting the tithes themselves. This suspicion is unjust and a plain manly course would remove it entirely and would obtain for the Irish Church the support of all England.

I don't know what to say to your subscription to defray legal expenses. Is it legal? Will the Irish gentlemen in general subscribe? Is it expected that composition for tithes, or tithes can be collected in consequence of legal process, every other mode having failed, and the Government being in the field against you and in league with the Roman Catholics and other factions to defeat the payment of tithes with a view to the destruction of the Church and the attainment of other political objects. If you had an association such as I described, I think that you ought to look to attain some good by legal process. You would insure the payment of a good deal of the dues of the Church, and you would not be without the aid of subscriptions in Ireland as well as here for your legal expenses as well as to assist in the support of the clergy.

The Earl of Aberdeen to Wellington, 31 August 1834

Haddo House. I thank you for the account which you have given me of the close of the session, as well as of the proceedings which have taken place since. It coincides pretty much with the notions I had received from other quarters; but I really think that our position, both at home and abroad, becomes more extraordinary every day. Notwithstanding all we hear of reaction, the readiness of the country to approve of revolutionary principles appears to be as great as ever. It is clear that the House of Lords forms the only effectual obstacle to the success of these principles; and the part which it is to act becomes proportionately more difficult. I presume that the rejection of the Irish Tithe Bill was a case which did not admit of any option; and of course there must be questions which do not admit of compromise; but the conduct of the House throughout the session has been on the whole most judicious, and must have added to its weight and influence.

I heard that the King had resisted the desire of his Ministers to allude in the Speech to the rejection of the Tithe Bill; and from an authority which may be considered as equivalent to that of the King himself, although I do not know that it is the better on this account. It may be thought extraordinary that Lord Melbourne should have supported such a proposition; but from him I am satisfied that we have nothing to expect, and that he will sacrifice every principle without scruple or hesitation to suit the convenience of the moment. In this respect, he is perhaps the most dangerous person who could fill the office of Minister, as people are disposed to trust his conservative language and his known opinions, to which he will not himself adhere for a single instant should it be convenient to abandon them.

We are to have the Chancellor very shortly in this part of the country. They are going to give him a dinner at Aberdeen, which in such a place will no doubt be numerously attended. Some radical lawyers and merchants, with a muster of the regular Whig retainers in this and the neighbouring counties, will swell the number; but there will be little enough of the property and respectability of the country.

Although no one troubles his head about foreign affairs, it is not possible to forget the Peninsula. I understand that in case of assistance being necessary for the support of the Queen of Spain, the force is to be composed of Portuguese troops; and that this is stipulated in a new convention, or in articles supplementary to the Quadripartite Treaty, signed before Talleyrand left London.

There are some questions arising in the east which may render it more difficult to prevent hostility. The situation of Mehemet Ali I believe is greatly changed for the worse; and the Sultan is consequently become more enterprising. It is likely before the meeting of Parliament that we may see important events both in the east and in the west.

I had not heard of Peel's intention of going abroad for the remainder of the recess, but it is likely enough. He never, I think, was out of England, and it is natural that he should wish to see a little of the world, while he is able to do so. He wrote to me lately to ask me to go and shoot in Staffordshire about the middle of September, so that his absence cannot be very long. I am much better than when I saw you last in London, and hope to improve during my stay here. My movements are very uncertain, but I have no great wish to remain in Scotland during the winter.

PS. You will hear more of the state of publick opinion in Scotland from others who mix more in the world; but in a party sense, the improvement is manifest. In this county the proportion of our friends among the newly registered voters is five to one.

Memorandum by the Bishop of Exeter on Dissenters taking degrees, August 1834

The petition seems to derive its main importance from the circumstance of its being presented by His Majesty's Prime Minister, who has deemed it right to give to it the additional distinction of personally announcing the intention of presenting it several days beforehand. In itself, a petition signed by fifty members of a body consisting of 4,000 could hardly be deemed very important, either as an indication of the sentiments of that body on the great points adduced in the petition, nor on any other account. In truth, so far as the sentiments of the body of the University of Cambridge are concerned, the fact of the petitioners, not more than an eightieth part of the body in number, coming to Parliament by themselves rather than seeking the co-operation of the body of the large, seems to prove a consciousness on their part that the university at large is opposed to their view.

But let us examine what is the state of facts relative to the matters of complaint on the part of Dissenters, as respects the University of Cambridge.

Dissenters are not excluded by any demand of subscription to articles, or other test, from admission to the university, nor from the fullest participation in all the instruction there afforded.

They share in the honors of the university on equal terms with other students.

It is true that they cannot take degrees in the university without subscribing the Thirty-nine Articles. But on what ground shall the legislature interpose to alter this? The university is a chartered corporation with power to make laws for its own government. One of its laws is that, while it admits all persons to be instructed in it, it will not admit any but members of the Church of England to rule and officiate in it. Is there anything of that obvious unfairness and unreasonableness, which alone can justify an interference with chartered rights? Does it tend to counteract the design of its incorporation and founders? Directly the contrary: it cannot be denied that the university as one corporation was originally incorporated and has always been upheld as a body specially connected with the Church of England, whether unreformed or reformed. The various separate corporations, the different colleges and halls which it comprises were all founded and endowed as seminaries of the Established Church. Their founders have made the academic degrees in all cases, and the actual taking Holy orders in many cases, the conditions on which individuals shall be permitted to have or to retain fellowships. The university therefore, by requiring a test of churchmanship as an indispensable qualification for a degree, does, in fact, protect and promote most faithfully the design of its own incorporation and the munificent and pious purposes of the founders and benefactors of its several colleges.

By admitting Dissenters to matriculation and full share of instruction it goes as far as it can go in concession, without departing from fidelity to its own inherent and fundamental duties.

If it be said that, the universities being national institutions, it is right that they should be made to expand their former contracted views with what is called the encreased liberality of the age, it may be asked in what sense are they *national*? Simply and merely because the meretricious and able manner in which they have fulfilled the purposes of their pious founders has attracted the honor of the whole nation to them, and has caused them to acquire the sanction of royal favour and royal charter. They are not national in the sense of being in any degree maintained or upheld at the *national charge.* On the contrary, they are made, as universities, to be sources of special revenue to the country. For although in two or three instances professorships or lectureships are endowed out of the public purse, the few hundreds that are expended in this way are reimbursed by as many thousands produced to the State by taxes on the degrees conferred there.

Hitherto the case has been treated as it affects the University of Cambridge principally or conjointly with that of Oxford: but its separate bearing on *Oxford* is incalculably more important.

At Oxford, subscription to the Thirty-nine Articles is required as a condition at matriculation. What is the object of this requisition? Does it imply that the party is accurately acquainted with, and from knowledge and inquiry assents to, the various propositions contained in these articles? Certainly not. It is a mere and bare subscription, implying that he who makes it is, bona fide, a member of the Church of England. To object to it because of the ignorance of the young person who makes it, would be no more reasonable than to object to a still younger person saying the Apostles' Creed, as if that implied a full knowledge of, and assent to, the propositions contained in it. In either case, the person simply declares his acceptance, on the authority of those whom his age and circumstances have made it his duty to regard with respect and deference.

But it is at Oxford an indispensable, aye, and a primary part of academic instruction to give an adequate knowledge of the Articles, their foundation in Scripture, their history, and the reasons for which they were ordered.

This is not mere theory, much less mere pretence. For upwards of *thirty years,* since a real and effectual reform took place in the studies of the University of Oxford, it has been the practice of the university to require, and it has been the increasing habit of the several colleges to afford the means of attaining, an adequate acquaintance with not only the general evidences of Christian truth, but also with all that is essential to the faith of a *Church of England Christian.*

So true is it, that this is made an indispensable and primary part of academic instruction, that the public examinations for degrees always commence with this particular; and if there be not satisfactory evidence given by the candidate of his having made due proficiency in this essential point, his examination does not proceed: his knowledge of arts and sciences, his classical scholarship be they what they may, are not even enquired into. The candidate is rejected.

The consequence has been most satisfactory. At first, instances not infrequently occurred of young men being rejected as unfit for their degree, because they could not satisfy their examiners on this primary subject of enquiry; and returning at a subsequent time (after an interval necessarily of several months) redeeming their failure, and obtaining by their splendid attainments in classical and scientific knowledge the highest honors which the university could bestow. I could name among my own lay friends more than one such instance: individuals who have borne high office in the State, or been distinguished among the most eminent political oeconomists of the day.

Such instances, I am told, occur very rarely now, because the system of instruction having been long established and having pervaded the whole course of education in the several colleges (in many of which it constitutes the principal matter of the terminal examinations called *collections*) it now commonly happens that the candidates at the public examinations for degrees are found to bear to each other about the same proportion in their qualification of religious knowledge as they bear in their general attainments.

The result of these considerations is that for the Dissenters to demand admittance to the University of Oxford and the attainment of its degrees, without subscribing to the Articles of the Church of England, is, in effect, to demand that the whole system of instruction and education in the university be abandoned for the purpose of accommodating them.

And what are the grievances which Dissenters endure in consequence of not being able to obtain admission into one of our universities, or degrees at either? In the first place, they lose the benefit (as far as

Oxford is concerned) of the best education in the country. Be it so; it is a condition inseparable from their creed.

Secondly, they cannot have a share in the endowments of the various colleges in the university. To be sure, they cannot. The founders intended that they should not partake of their bounty, and the law of the land respects all the reasonable intentions of such founders, and upholds the bodies which are faithful in observing them.

Thirdly, they are subject to divers degradations in their honest and honourable professions. If they are physicians, they cannot become members of the College of Physicians, unless they have graduated in medicine at Oxford or Cambridge, because that body thinks fit thus to provide for the honor of the profession by reserving this privilege as an inducement to those who enter into it to obtain that primary education, which in England has always been esteemed the highest and the best. (The restriction, indeed, is not absolute, for associates, who have not so graduated, may be admitted by special favor, and several are actually admitted, when they become very highly distinguished.) But, be this as it may, be the exclusion founded on a reasonable or an unreasonable ground, it is not the act of the universities, but of the College of Physicians; the remedy of the evil, if it be an evil which few dispassionate persons will consider it, is to be sought not by thrusting Dissenters into the universities, but by requiring the College of Physicians no longer to exclude them from that society.

Again, in the law, Masters of Arts of Oxford or Cambridge are called to the Bar two years earlier than those who have no such degrees. This, too, is not the act of the universities, but of the governors of the Inns of Court, who seem to have exercised a sound discretion, and to have consulted for the honor of the profession by making the regulation. If, however, the legislature think otherwise, let them remove the grievance in the only effectual and proper manner by requiring the Inns of Court to withdraw the privilege conceded to their academic students.

Wellington to the Earl of Roden, 1 September 1834

Stratfield Saye. Since I wrote to you last I have seen O'Connell's letter of the [25th] which was published in the London papers of the 30th August. It certainly appears as if he and I were working precisely on the same ground. He to persuade the Roman Catholicks, demagogues, Radicals and others to take a course which shall obtain countenance and support in England for the destruction of the Church of Ireland immediately and ultimately for ulterior objects; and I to suggest measures which shall obtain the same countenance and support for the Protestants, and shall save their Church.

In the course of the discussion in his letter he lets out a few secrets which are well deserving of your attention. The first is that he is not satisfied with the Irish Government: that is to say the Lord-Lieutenant. In this sentiment I suspect that he is the mouthpiece of the mountain division of the Government; and that the Lord-Lieutenant will very soon be recalled; and that at all events there will never be another.

Indeed when the Secretary of State is an Irish nobleman residing in Ireland, and that Mr. O'Connell undertakes, as he does in this letter, to govern Ireland there cannot be much necessity for a Lord-Lieutenant. Indeed it will be more convenient to the House of Commons that the only organ of authority in that country should be one of its members. Accordingly I consider the office of Lord-Lieutenant put down.

But he has informed the publick plainly of another fact which is very important and which is well worthy of the attention of the Protestants of Ireland; and that for the first time the Roman Catholicks have the Government on their side in the contest for the attainment of their objects; which objects are too plainly stated in that letter to require repetition here.

You will see therefore, and I hope that the Protestants of Ireland will see how important it is that they should work in earnest and upon sound principles to save themselves. I consider that the foundation of your strength is England. You must look to England for support and protection; and so guide your measures as to obtain that advantage. It is obvious that you cannot look to the administration. You must look to the great mass of the nation. It is clear that O'Connell views the matter in the same light. He attacks you not by the name of Protestants of the Church of England, although the destruction of the supremacy of the Church of England is his object; but as Orangemen. He knows, he almost avows the fact in the letter, that in a question in Ireland between Protestants and Roman Catholics the people of England will take the part of the Protestants. He is quite right; all classes and sects will do so.

But there will be a difference of opinion about tithes; or a little more or a little less of Church reform; and nobody will care a pin about the run at Orangemen. Nobody knows what is the meaning of the society of Orangemen or its objects. Everybody understands the necessity of maintaining the Protestant religion, the supremacy of the Church of England, the settlement of property in the country and the union between Great Britain and Ireland; but nobody sees the necessity for maintaining the Orange society.

I know how difficult it is in dealing with parties to convince any party that it is superfluous; that affairs can be better transacted without its agency; and that its continued existence is injurious.

But it is fit that you should see the truth; and I earnestly intreat you to read O'Connell's letter with attention; and you will see that he is of the same opinion with me; and that in order to be permitted to destroy the supremacy of the Church of England in Ireland he makes his run at the Orangemen.

I contend then that your object should be to keep the Orange Society (if it exists) out of sight. Form your association upon the very broadest basis, the protection of the rights and property of all from the attack meditated and proclaimed and directed against the highest interests of society. Declare your determination and bind yourselves to each other to pay their dues to the clergy of the Church of England in Ireland and to afford them every support and assistance in the power of each of you to recover those dues from others; and pledge yourselves to maintain with your lives and fortunes the union with Great Britain as established by law and the King's government in Ireland.

Something of this sort, very short and very pithy and above all generally signed, and not made publick till generally signed, will do more to put the Protestant cause on its true grounds and to obtain protection and support for it in England, and thus to overthrow O'Connell, than anything you can do.

I have observed in your debates that some of your principal men have attacked absentees. There is no man more sensible than I am of the injury done to Ireland by the absence from the country of men possessing large properties within it. But we must take things as they are. We must have the Church of England in Ireland; the settlement of property in Ireland must be maintained. How can we pretend to enjoy these advantages, if we don't maintain the union with Great Britain? If united with Great Britain, men possessing large properties in Ireland must be permitted to reside in England if they think proper. God send that the Protestants of Ireland may regain political influence and power sufficient to enable them to regulate this or any other detail of government. The object now is existence; and to take such a position as to enable you to contend for it with advantage. The Protestants are on the defensive; and should keep clear of details which do not affect that great object of all their existence, or do not tend to prevent the execution of the avowed designs of their adversary.

You may rely upon it that the first step in the road to subscriptions and everything else is an association such as I have described.

Although I have written you a very long letter, I will venture to intrude upon you for a moment longer to point out the mode in which I think that you ought to proceed in order to obtain an assent to and the signature of your proposed association.

The greatest obstruction in your way will be terror. You can very safely in the north form such an association; and sign anything. I doubt whether the Protestants in the south of Ireland can or will. I would recommend to you therefore to begin in the north; and not to make publick your proceedings till you will have got so many signatures as to render your association respectable. You will judge from correspondence with your friends at what time you ought to extend it to Dublin and to the south and west of Ireland. But I should say that I would start on the ground of not publishing the signatures in any county or district in which a desire should be expressed that they should not be published.

I think that you should lose no time in commencing your operations. You have two months to November by which time it is desirable that some progress should be made.

The Earl of Winchilsea to Wellington, 1 September 1834

Eastwell Park. A public dinner is to take place at Canterbury on Thursday, the 25th instant, in commemoration of His Majesty's late declaration to support the constitution in Church and State, which I hope will be most numerously and respectably attended by the gentlemen and yeomen of the eastern part of the county.

I have been requested by the stewards, to which I beg to add my sincere wishes that it may be in your power to comply with our request, to express their hope that your Grace will favor us with your company upon this occasion.

Wellington to Sir Robert Peel, 2 September 1834

Stratfield Saye. I have no intention of going to the north; and although I would go with pleasure to see you, I am very sorry that it is not in my power to do so between the 6th and 14th.

I am under the necessity of returning to Walmer Castle in the beginning of next week, to receive some persons who are coming there at that time.

I have heard reports ever since the prorogation of Parliament of the intention to meet again before Christmas. But I believe that they were to be attributed to surmises founded on the short period of the first prorogation.

Lord Brougham might have thought it desirable that he should be present when the second prorogation should take place; and he most probably fixed a day on which it would be convenient to himself to attend. At all events the first prorogation being for a short time is no indication of an early meeting of Parliament.

There can be no reason for an early meeting of Parliament, excepting the want of money; and in modern times the only meeting that I recollect was in the autumn of 1819, excepting the year 1830 which was the first Parliament of the reign. I perfectly recollect that in the year 1819 we met early, not for the want of money, but on account of the serious riot at Manchester, of the impression which it made in the country; and in order to propose to Parliament the six Acts.

Lord Rosslyn seemed to think that the state of the West Indies would require an immediate advance of money; and that a vote would be necessary. I should think not; and that not only they have the means of raising the money, but have made use of them.

Unless they quarrel with O'Connell about his parliament in Dublin called a Liberal club, I don't think that there is likely to be any event in Ireland to induce the Government to call Parliament before the usual time.

ADD MS 40309, ff 270, 271.

Wellington to the Rev. George Rowley, 2 September 1834

Stratfield Saye. I have this day received your letter of the 29th. I could not have explained myself correctly regarding the probable proceedings in Parliament. I did not write with the paper before me; and I may not have recollected correctly the notice given in the House of Commons. As well as I recollect it was notice of a motion for the appointment of a committee to enquire etc. This is a very different proceeding from an address to the Crown to appoint a commission to enquire.

The proceeding of a commission may easily be resisted. The party has only to decline to answer. The commission can receive no power from the Crown to enforce answers.

A committee of the House of Commons assume powers. They report to the House for contempt a party who should refuse to answer; and the House would imprison for contempt. This course would not have been taken by what is called the unreformed House of Commons. Indeed that House would not have entered upon such proceedings. But this House of Commons will do anything that is arbitrary.

I have not explained myself as I ought about the debts of the young men. I don't believe that anything can be done to check expense. The only remedy that I have ever heard mentioned is the omission of the Vice-Chancellor to give to the creditor the protection and assistance of the civil magistrate to recover from the undergraduates and bachelors of the university. But I stated in my letter the objections which occurred to me to that course of proceeding.

Thomas Baker to Wellington, 3 September 1834

26 Hart Street, Bloomsbury Square. Your Grace may recollect my having taken the liberty to address you on the subject of the prevailing evil influence of the periodical press, stating my strong conviction not only that something should be done, but that if properly done it would be with effect to check the evil. Your Grace did me the honour to reply, stating your opinion that as all periodical publications were commercial speculations (part of my plan was to establish a daily morning paper conducted by superior talent) and conducted solely on commercial principles they were not likely to accomplish any moral or political good: this was, as I gathered from the reply, the opinion your Grace held. While I admit the premises to be correct, I hope to be excused when I say that I cannot allow the conclusion to be just. I have however from that time allowed the subject to rest, except indeed that it has occupied my thoughts; but having read a most excellent article in *Blackwood's Magazine* of this month on the subject, embodying, as it does, the views I then took, both as to the nature of the evil and the necessity of a corrective, as well as the probability of success, I am induced again to bring the subject before your Grace, referring you to the article. If the Lord Chancellor's observation to the peers was correct, 'pass the Poor Law Bill or your estates are in danger', how much more true is the remark: check the evil influence of the press among the middling and lower classes, or they will subvert everything in a general wreck. The *enemies* of order are numerous, active and persevering, its *friends* are powerful, but their power is only powerful as it is influential. This point is however so well argued in *Blackwood*, that I doubt if anything could be said to improve it. If a powerful influence were set in motion and lightly directed, it would in time produce incalculable good. It may be slow in its progress, it may be some time, commencing as it must with the heads of society, ere it would reach the lowest classes; but passing from one grade to another, it would in time accomplish this and, like capillary attraction, continue its slow, silent course, until it shall have reached the extremity.

I shall be allowed to confirm the correctness of the views I then held and presented to your Grace by reference to the *Standard*, a paper much improved in its character and is I am satisfied working great good by the talent, at least principally, that is employed in it, but likewise by its unvarying consistency and its strict adherence to truth; a morning paper is now wanting, established on the same principles and conducted with the same ability and consistency. My views are not confined to this one object, but if an association were formed it would direct its attention to other modes of counteracting the evils of the Radical press.

Wellington to the Earl of Aberdeen, 4 September 1834

Stratfield Saye. I have received your letter of the 31st August.

I understand that the arrangement between England and France in respect to Spain was in four articles. By the second article it was stipulated that England was to employ her fleet to blockade the coasts of Biscay. France was to blockade the entrances of Spain by the Pyrenees. Portugal was to send to Spain the assistance of troops.

It was very soon discovered that blockade by sea was the exercise of the right of a belligerent. England was not a belligerent. The lawyers informed the Cabinet that the execution of the proposed blockade would lead to unpleasant discussions with other powers, and might be resisted even by the King's subjects unless aided by other measures which would require an Act of Parliament! The resource was to employ Portuguese ships. But it was soon discovered that Portugal could not blockade any more than we could without risk of quarrel with all Europe including ourselves and France! Portugal, therefore, was forbidden to blockade, in the greatest possible haste. Louis-Philippe then is left to himself; and it is said that his subjects in Languedoc don't at all like the interruption of the communication with Spain. In respect to the Tithe Bill we could not do otherwise than we did. In the first place the bill itself was abominable. There was not one principle in it to which we ought not to have objected. Secondly, I could not have commanded our majority if I had allowed the second reading to pass unopposed. A committee in the House of Lords is always a matter of difficulty; and in a bill in which every clause must have been altered the management of the committee would have been impracticable.

After all the bill would have been thrown out. The Government themselves would have thrown it out of the House of Lords, aided by our friends. The mischief in Ireland as resulting from the loss of this bill would have been the same. But there would have been the additional mischief that the Conservative majority in the House of Lords would have been lost; at least would not have been under my direction.

I have been endeavouring to persuade Lord Roden to turn his Protestant meetings in Ireland to some purpose besides that of making speeches.

If the Irish Protestants would associate and pledge themselves to each other and to the world to protect the lives, rights and properties of each other and of all; to pay the clergy their dues, and to assist and protect them in recovering the same from their neighbours and dependants; and their lives and fortunes to maintain the Union with Great Britain and to aid and support the King's Government in Ireland, they would go far towards creating a feeling in their favour in this country which would be of use to them.

It is curious enough that O'Connell and I were working at the same point at the same moment. He, notwithstanding that he has the Government at his back, writes that in a question between Protestants and Catholics in Ireland, the people of England will take the side of the Protestants. He says therefore run at Orangemen! I advise upon the same principle as he does. Conciliate the people of England to your cause. Be just towards the clergy. Fight your battle on the ground of the Protestant religion, the settlement of property, and the union with Great Britain. Throw overboard the Orange Society or keep them concealed, as they are only a party among yourselves, about whom nobody knows anything, or cares; and if you don't succeed you will at least have placed yourselves on your real grounds.

PS. September 5th. I have just received accounts from Portsmouth that Donna Francesca died on the morning of the 4th at eleven o'clock. Mr. Byng wrote that Lord Palmerston was ready to send through France to Don Carlos any accounts of her death that the Princess de Beira might wish to send. This is on a par with everything else!

ADD MS 43060, ff 121–125. *Copy in Wellington Papers.*

Wellington to the Earl of Winchilsea, 4 September 1834

Stratfield Saye. Private and confidential. I have received your letter respecting the dinner at Canterbury. I have kept myself quite clear of any publick measure on the subject of the King's speech to the bishops on the 28th of May. I have done so first because Lord Grey stated in his place in the House of Lords that no Minister had advised it. Secondly because on the very day that the King delivered it he accepted the resignations of four of his Ministers tendered to His Majesty because they found that his Government were about to take a course in direct contradiction to the sentiments contained in the said speech to which course they could not be parties. Thirdly because His Majesty at that very time signed a special warrant to authorize the Great Seal to be put to the commission of enquiry into the Irish Church, of which the object avowed in the House of Commons was to take the first step to carry into execution Mr. Ward's resolution, which had caused the retirement of the four Ministers, and is of itself in fact the forerunner of the destruction of the Church. I conclude from all this either that the King did not make the speech; or that if he spoke as was stated that he did, he had forgotten his sentiments; or he had altered his opinions; or, which is the most probable of all, that he had not strength to act according to them.

Whatever might be the cause it appeared to me that it did not become me as Chancellor of the University, or in any other capacity, to let the publick believe that I felt confidence in declarations in which I felt that none could be placed. I think that what passed upon the Irish Tithe Bill must have tended to shew that at least as far as the Church of England in Ireland was concerned the King did not consider himself or the Government bound by the declaration in his speech to the bishops on the 28th May. But I have gone farther to elucidate this matter. I have had not less than 150 petitions and addresses to present to the King upon this speech. I took an opportunity of letting the King know what I felt upon the presentation of these addresses from his subjects. That I was apprehensive from what I saw of the measures of His Majesty's Government and the acts carried on in His Majesty's name that the expectations of his subjects founded upon His Majesty's Speech would not be fulfilled; and that I felt very unwilling to present these addresses. I was informed in answer that the King had made the speech in question in the usual manner of all his predecessors. That no copy of it had been made, and that none ought to have reached the publick; and that it had not been the practice to consider such speeches as the groundwork of addresses to His Majesty.

I have stated all this detail to you not in any hope of inducing you to alter your course in relation to this speech, but to make it clear to you how I stand. If I am to attend this meeting it must be in celebration of and congratulation for the speech; and to encourage hopes and expectations from it. But truly I entertain none; but I have declared that such is my feeling upon this speech as well to the Vice-Chancellor of Oxford as to the King himself. I have not gone farther, as it is no part of my duty to check any feeling which the speech might have produced, although I could not encourage such feelings. From all this you will see that I cannot with propriety attend the meeting at Canterbury. I don't wish to state the real reason, because I will not injure the King in the publick opinion; but I will take that opportunity of performing an engagement in another part of the country; and I will write you that my engagements will not permit me to attend the meeting.

Although I have written you so long a letter I must add that since the year 1830 I don't know of any transaction that has given me so much pain as this speech to the bishops. I understand that many persons are beginning to feel what it really was; and that they are exceedingly displeased.

The Rev. George Rowley to Wellington, 4 September 1834

Oxford. On referring to the notice paper for the next session of Parliament, I find that Colonel Williams is to move for an address to the King, that he will signify his pleasure that the universities shall no longer act under the letters of James 1st, etc.; Mr. G. W. Wood, the Dissenters admission bill; Mr. Tooke for an address for the London University charter; and Mr. Wilks, an address for a commission of inquiry into the Universities of Oxford and Cambridge. So far as I am aware James 2nd was the only one of our Kings who endeavoured to interpose his direct authority in the proceedings of this university. The subscriptions against which Colonel Williams's motion is directed are imposed by statute, which I do not think anything short of a compulsory Act of Parliament will induce the Convocation to repeal; and till it is repealed no Vice-Chancellor can act in opposition to it, without perjuring himself. I trust we may yet escape a commission from the House of Commons. But should such be issued, the course to be pursued here would still remain a matter for most serious consideration.

The only debts which can be recovered in the court here from minors are such as would be recoverable in the ordinary courts of law; and not all of these, but such alone as are incurred for articles not forbidden by the university authorities. Thus Mr. Fletcher West is in confinement for a debt of £110. But in as much as it is owing for gigs and horses, which articles are interdicted to the junior members (however little efficient in practice such prohibition may be) no tradesmen could recover from *them* in the courts here one farthing of such a bill.

Your Grace does not seem to be aware, as I judge from an expression in the note received this morning, that the Vice-Chancellor seldom or ever presides personally in the court, an assessor being especially appointed for that purpose. This however makes no difference in the proceedings.

The Earl of Roden to Wellington, 4 September 1834

Tollymore Park. I am very much obliged to you for your kind letter and all the counsel you give me, which I should be most anxious to follow. I do not however altogether understand the mode you would adopt and it would be much more satisfactory if I could have half an hour's interview with you on the subject. I am obliged to be in London on some urgent private business the week after next for a few days, and if you could arrange an opportunity for my seeing you, I think much benefit might arise to the success of our undertaking. I leave this for Dublin on Monday next to attend a meeting of the Conservative Society on Tuesday, so I shall be obliged to you to direct your answer to me there. This last letter of O'Connell's has opened the eyes of many apathetic gentlemen to the real state of the case as respects the objects of the enemies of Protestantism in Ireland.

Wellington to Thomas Baker, 4 September 1834

Compliments to Mr. Baker. The Duke does not at all doubt of the influence of the press or of the mischief which it has done. He does however entertain great doubts of the efficiency of any remedy yet proposed; and at all events the Duke is personally so little interested in any of the publications of the day as to have long determined that he would have nothing to do with any question relating to the daily press.

Undated. Docketed From Mr. Baker, September 4, respecting the press, and the answer.

Lord FitzGerald to Wellington, 8 September 1834

Malvern. Having left Cheltenham, I did not immediately receive your Grace's letter, which lay in the post office there.

I cannot well express how much obliged I have felt by it; nor need I assure you how sensible I am of the interest you have shewn, with respect to my being chosen a representative peer, or how grateful I am, as well for the advice you have given me, as for the steps you have already taken to promote my election.

In adopting that advice, I have *only* to declare and act upon the principles on which I have acted during my whole life. I see for Ireland, and for England too, no safety but in upholding the Conservative principle. In Ireland we know how connected that principle is with the interests and maintenance of Protestantism. The Protestantism of Ireland, however, is not best maintained by lamenting or condemning the past concession to the Roman Catholics, for the object of that settlement was to give strength to a Protestant government, and not to weaken it.

I am prepared, without reference to seeking support from the ultra lords, to declare in terms as strong as any of them could use my adherence to those Protestant principles on which alone your Grace and Sir Robert Peel vindicated that concession to the Catholics, by which I firmly believe, had it not been for the consequences of the folly and resentment of the ultras in Parliament, the Church establishment, as well as all the establishments of the empire, would have been strengthened and improved.

I am ready to denounce the King's Ministers as the King's worst enemies, and to oppose them whenever and wherever I can. But I am glad that you disapprove as much as myself of my taking part in intemperate meetings and bombastic harangues. They are not required to prove sincerity, least of all that of a man who has probably written more in support of Conservative principles in Ireland than all those honourable lords combined.

But I shall act strictly in the view and in the spirit which your Grace recommends, and I hope whenever I enter the House of Lords, that those who may support me will have no reason to regret their choice.

I quite feel that it would be to no purpose my thinking of the privilege until after the pledges to Lord Bandon are fulfilled. I doubt that, then, unless in deference to your wishes, I should have much chance of Lord Roden, Lord Farnham, Lord Longford, etc.

I am told that the most unforgiving with respect to the Roman Catholic question are Lord Clancarty and his connexions. But many, perhaps most, of those Lords would be influenced, I presume, by the Duke of Cumberland. I am sure that Lord Thomond, Lords Ely and Enniskillen would go with your Grace. Of course the great majority of the *English Irish*, who are peers of both kingdoms, would do the same and would support the candidate for whom you were anxious.

The Duke of Gloucester, who was at Cheltenham, suggested to me that I ought to be a candidate, saying that unluckily he was pledged to Lord Bandon for his first vote, but that he hoped I would offer myself for the *second* vacancy. I told him that I should not think of interfering with Lord Bandon or *any peer* whom the majority of the Conservative party were inclined to support. In that I would never split that party. I mentioned to him that I had your Grace's kind and friendly wishes in my favor, and he concluded by not only offering me his own vote, but added that he would endeavour to impress on others that there was no other avenue for me into Parliament, and that they should contrive to bring me in. He begged of me further to mention this to your Grace, as his own suggestion. It certainly was so, for I should never have dreamed of canvassing His Royal Highness.

I will not tire you with a longer letter, but will avail myself of the permission which your Grace gave me to write to you from Ireland, where I shall be in a few days, as soon as I am informed of the real state of the country.

The universal opinion, I am told, is that Mr. O'Connell is the absolute adviser (dictator, perhaps I should say) of Lord Duncannon.

The Earl of Winchilsea to Wellington, 8 September 1834

Eastwell Park. I beg to return you my best thanks for your obliging letter, and I must candidly confess that I cannot in any way meet the reasons which you have advanced for not giving us the pleasure of your company on the 25th instant. I still cling to a hope that His Majesty was sincere at the time that he made his declaration to the bishops of his attachment to our institutions in Church and State and of his determination to uphold them, and that he gave his consent to the Irish Church Commission without fully understanding the object and tendency of the pernicious measures. I sincerely trust that I shall not find myself mistaken in the opinion which I have formed, that there is still sufficient feeling and sound principle throughout the country to uphold the leading and essential features of the Constitution in Church and State, and that when conviction takes place, which I am convinced is daily gaining ground in the public mind, that it is the intention of the present Government to subvert these institutions, that such a spirit will be aroused throughout the country, which if generally expressed may check the Ministers and the House of Commons in their mad career of revolution and may enable the House of Lords more successfully to oppose the most dangerous parts of the proposed changes and reforms, whatever they may be, and materially restore that balance to the Constitution which the measures of the last two or three years have so nearly destroyed.

I should feel much gratified if I could induce you to give me and Lady Winchilsea the pleasure of receiving you at Eastwell during the buck-catching and doe-shooting season, which commences on the 10th of November and will leave it to any time after that day more agreeable to you. I will endeavour to persuade our friend Lord Camden to join you if you would be kind enough to inform me about what time we might expect to have the pleasure of seeing you.

Wellington to the Rev. George Rowley, 8 September 1834

Walmer Castle. I believe I mentioned that I had not before me the newspaper when I wrote upon the probable interference of Parliament in your affairs. I thought it was to be a motion for a committee of enquiry in the House of Commons. It appears that it is for an address to His Majesty, that he will be graciously pleased to issue his commission to enquire. This is a very different affair as I explained in my last letter. I am pretty certain however that a committee was mentioned. The truth is that we are in this difficulty whatever may be the mode of proceeding. The Crown and its Ministers, instead of protecting the established institutions of the country, take the lead of the party in the House of Commons whose object is to subvert them. The institutions of the country are safe and have a chance of fair play only in the House of Lords. It is for this reason that I have earnestly advised a revision of all your establishments; and an alteration, gradual as may be desired, of whatever it may appear to be desirable to alter. We shall not get to the end of our difficulties in one year; or possibly even in ten. But your establishment must be perpetual; and I am anxious that it should be placed on such ground as that every reasonable man in the country should be satisfied.

Of course I knew that the Vice-Chancellor could not always preside in what is called his court. I think I understand clearly how the case of the debts stands.

The Earl of Roden to Wellington, 11 September 1834

Dublin. I had the pleasure of receiving your letter of the 1st of September on the 7th instant, the morning before I left Tollymore Park, and my constant occupation since my arrival in this city, considering with gentlemen from all parts of the country the situation of our Protestant affairs, has prevented my replying to you immediately. I cannot enter into the subject of your communications without first expressing in the strongest manner my grateful thanks for all your thoughts about us, the anxiety you evince in our behalf and the clear views you take of the dangers that surround us; but I think you expect from the remedy you propose a result which I fear the state of parties amongst us, the extreme apathy of some, and the violent prejudices of others will very seriously tend to obstruct. It is evident that O'Connell's view is to prejudice the people of England against the Irish Church and the Protestant population, and you have justly observed that it was with this end he classes all Protestants under the name of Orangeists and declares there are but two parties in the country: the repealers and the Orangemen. I fully agree with you that our defence must be on a much broader base than any political club or institution could include. I feel that valuable as I think is the Orange Institution, to which I will refer by and by, it is impossible to suppose that under present circumstances it could be admitted as the basis of an association which would be likely to include all the Protestant force of the country; nor indeed do I know what would: we are unhappily so divided amongst ourselves and there is such a blindness to the awful situation in which we stand. Your proposition of a declaration (if I understood it right) would be more likely to receive the sanction of the many were it carefully worded than perhaps any other measure that could be suggested; but, as I said, the greatest caution would be necessary with wording, as I am sorry to say, even in the north, there is a great cry amongst the Protestant farmers, etc. against tithes, so that at all our publick meetings we are obliged to speak on the general ground of Protestantism as opposed to error to keep them fully with us. I think you are mistaken in supposing that the southern Protestants would be afraid to sign any document expressive of Protestant principle; I believe they are more forward even than those of the north in the open avowal of their opinions. But to return to the Orange Institution, I think you are not aware of the numbers they consist of, or the spirit that animates them. I agree with you to keep them out of sight would be prudent and to convince them that *at present* we could do better without them would be desirable, but they are a class of persons so determined, so jealous, and so suspicious, and all this in the best cause, that it is no easy matter to keep them quiet and yet to preserve that spirit and devotedness which is so peculiar to their character. Their numbers are near 200,000. I believe O'Connell has for the last three or four years endeavoured to get them over on the question of repeal; at one period there was a shaking amongst them on the subject in consequence of the desertion of their leaders and the passing of the Procession Bill. At this period some of my noble friends and others saw with me the danger that was overhanging us: that if O'Connell got over this body of men to his opinions on the question of repeal, the affair was settled; we therefore felt that the only way of averting such a calamity was to unite ourselves to the Institution, and our union with that body of men frustrated the design of O'Connell; and the Orange body are the most forward defenders of the Constitution of the country and the unity of the empire.

It is the knowledge of this band being in existence and being ready at any moment to turn out in defence of the law and for the protection of their brother Protestants which, in many instances, keeps O'Connell's party from bursting all restraint in those parts of the country where Protestants are few. I feel convinced in some parts of Ireland if this check of Orangeism was removed, so impotent is the Government the destruction of Protestant life would be fearful; and I believe so great is the fear and influence of the Orange system that its effects extend even to those parts of the country where it does not exist. Thus you will see the difficulty there must be in keeping such a body out of sight and this will account for the course that has been adopted which, being unaware of the circumstances, you might be ready to condemn. I perfectly agree with you respecting the topics of absenteeism and detail which may have been introduced by our speakers. The object was not to assert that a gentleman of property in Ireland had not full liberty to leave when pleased, but in the first place that the absentees should contribute towards the necessities of their tenants and that in the next place they should know that if the Church property was rendered insecure it was not very probable that theirs would be safe. I do not think our friends meant to go further than this.

I have troubled you with a very long letter and yet I have much more to say, but I must defer it till I have the honor of seeing you. I intend being in London on Wednesday or Thursday next, where a letter will find me at the Carlton.

The Earl of Aberdeen to Wellington, 17 September 1834

Haddo House. You may probably have seen some account of the Chancellor's exhibition at Aberdeen, which on the whole was comical enough. In the various speeches which he made his great difficulty was to satisfy his Radical hearers, who were numerous, without alarming his friends who call themselves Conservatives. All that he said became a mass of inconsistency; and each sentence contradicted the other. The most impudent thing was his appeal to you, of whom he spoke civilly, and his confident belief that you would agree in the immense increase of power, glory and prosperity which the country had received, both abroad and at home, since you left office. Nothing astonishes me more than the barefaced assurance with which the most direct falsehoods are asserted and apparently believed by political men. There is really a species of moral obliquity in the country, by which truth is distorted and common justice no longer recognized.

It would appear that the Government are not disinclined to take the lead in the works of destruction with which the country is threatened. The letter of O'Connell to Lord Duncannon is an event, even in these times of abominable licence. He tells Lord Duncannon that he desires to assist him in reforming the House of Lords by peaceably and legally converting that body into an elective senate. And this is addressed to the Secretary of State for the Home Department! No man can prevent another from writing to him in terms the most culpable, and it would be hard to make the person receiving such a letter responsible for its contents. But in this case, it is different; the parties are friends, known to be such, and who profess to agree generally in their political opinions. Unless it should be specifically contradicted by Lord Duncannon we have good reason to believe that the Secretary of State is not adverse to the project of destroying the House of Lords.

If you succeed in turning Protestant meetings in Ireland to some better account, you will perform an invaluable service; but it will be difficult; for I apprehend that the persons to whom you refer are more impracticable than anything we possess in this country. There is no doubt that to conciliate the good feeling and good wishes of the people of England, to inspire them with the notion that a community of interest exists between the two countries and that we are equally bound to resist injustice and oppression, and to protect life and property in both ought to be the great object of those who wish to see a better state of things in Ireland. It is impossible to deny, however, that there is a good deal of indifference in England respecting Irish affairs. The conduct of the Protestant landlords towards the Church has very often been as bad as possible; and the whole establishment is on that footing which makes it difficult for the people of this country to regard it precisely in the same light as their own. It will not be easy to persuade the people of England that the fate of the Church in Ireland must in a great measure decide what is to become of their own; but the Government have shewn their prudence by abstaining from any direct attack upon the Church in England, to which the attachment is certainly much stronger than they imagined. As to the notion of a repeal of the Union and separation, there will be a general feeling of disgrace and ignominy connected with it, which, independently of all political interests or considerations, will prevent the people from entertaining it for a moment.

I hear from various quarters that it is expected some change will take place in the composition of the Ministry. These reports, it is true, are frequently prevalent while Parliament is not sitting, and may have no foundation; but, in this instance, they come from something like good authority; and especially it is said that Lord Palmerston will not continue in his office until the next session. These supplementary articles of the Quadripartite Treaty respecting blockade are really astonishing. One would have thought that after the embarrassment arising from the illegal blockade of the coast of Holland, notwithstanding the tacit acquiescence of the great powers of Europe, the Government would not have contrived to put themselves into a situation of still greater difficulty of the same kind. But it is a melancholy fact that of late the obligations of publick law, as well as the faith of treaties have been disregarded. We trust to force and menace to carry our object, and care little for right and justice. The moral feeling of the country is thoroughly corrupted abroad, as well as at home.

I had a confirmation of the opinion of our Government entertained by Talleyrand, and which shews that he does not refrain from expressing it in Paris as in London. The Duc de Laval writes to me, 'Ce qu'il y a de bizarre, c'est que ce que vous me mandez en mépris et dégoût sur la situation de vos affaires se trouve l'expression des opinions de l'oncle et de la nièce magicienne qui nous sont arrivés ces jours-ci.'

I hear that Don Pedro is so ill that it is scarcely possible he should last long. His death might lead to complete republican government, for a time, in Portugal, and greatly promote it in Spain, where it appears to be making some progress already. It seems impossible, however, that these two countries should not soon return to really monarchical principles. We are likely to have important events there, and elsewhere, during the next few months, for nothing seems anywhere to be settled.

The Earl of Roden to Wellington, 17 September 1834

London. I arrived in town last night and received your kind letter of the 15th; your communication of the 9th has also reached me in due course. I feel it so important that you should be made fully acquainted with the real state of things in Ireland since our meeting, and that you should be fully aware how much we coincide in your views, that I purpose accepting your kind invitation to Walmer and propose leaving town tomorrow morning by the steamboat for Margate, from whence I am told I can get to Walmer by six or seven o'clock at furthest. I am anxious clearly to understand your view of the association referred to and to put it in progress as soon as the sketch of it is decided upon. I have promised to attend my friend Winchilsea's dinner at Canterbury on the 25th, but I am anxious some progress should be made in your suggestion, otherwise I might have deferred going to Walmer till immediately before or after the 25th.

The Marquess of Downshire to Wellington, 18 September 1834

Easthampstead Park. I have to thank you for your letter of the 4th and to express our regrets at your not being at Stratfield Saye at the time of the archery meeting here last Friday. It went off very well.

When I last wrote to you I was not fully aware of the state in which the Irish tithe subject stood and of the necessity of giving the notices to the clergy previous to the 29th of August last, under Mr. Stanley's Act, and which my agents properly did; at the meeting in Dublin the subject was not much spoken of, and being on a journey, it escaped my recollection. The preparation to come under the Act had been however carefully made the winter before and nearly compleated on my part, and that of Lord Hertford I believe, and other proprietors in Down and Antrim; and therefore but little remained to do this year but to give the notices and to arrange with the tenantry to pay to [the landlords] the tithes with the rents instead of to the clergy, as heretofore. If I had any hesitation since the passing of the Act to take upon myself the payment, it arose from the necessity under which I am placed to provide punctually for heavy annual demands upon me and expectation of legal expences and trouble which *might* arise among the numerous tenants, whose tenures of land vary in nature and duration so generally in Ireland, but I had no doubt of the absolute necessity of every person of property joining in that country to check and defeat the inroads which the agitators are making upon all property, lay and ecclesiastical, and I shall therefore cheerfully submit to any risk which may be incurred by placing myself under the Act in question.

I am very glad that Lord Roden is to be at Walmer Castle, and I beg to enclose with this note a letter for him. How true it is, as you have said in your letter, that there is a great deal of oratory but little done in Ireland. It is the nature of the people and the circumstances in which they are placed, which cause the state of things complained of, but the more your advice is taken and your views acted up to firmly the less this objection will be felt. The resistance already made to Mr. O'Connell has done much good. County meetings are wished, and if they are well managed and temperately contained, there will be less objection to them.

Lady Salisbury left us yesterday quite well.

Wellington to the Marquess of Downshire, 20 September 1834

Walmer Castle. Lord Roden left this for London about an hour before your letter arrived this morning. He intends to go to see you before he returns to Ireland.

I think that you will find him disposed to take measures which shall have the effect of bringing the Protestants of Ireland to concur in an intelligible principle on which they can act together with honor to themselves and advantage to their country.

Wellington to the Earl of Aberdeen, 21 September 1834

Walmer Castle. I think that you wrote your letter of the 17th before you had seen the report of the proceedings at the feast at Edinburgh.

It appears to me that Lord Durham has cut from under Lord Brougham's feet the ground on which he stood in all his orations up to that moment; and three members of the Cabinet who spoke after Lord Durham declared their adherence to Lord Durham's views. I entertain no doubt therefore that we shall have plenty of measures in a state of preparation previous to the meeting of Parliament; and that Brougham will throw overboard his Conservative policy and language. But I think that the principal field of battle will be Ireland. I have had

Lord Roden here and have made some progress with him; but not quite so much as I could wish.

I suspect that the Irish Government are about to commit a terrible outrage, which if these Irishmen could manage anything with dexterity might have the effect of opening the King's eyes to his danger.

They have had a Privy Council lately in Dublin consisting of the Secretary of State, the Lord Lieutenant and the Chief Secretary; and they called to their council Sir Hussey Vivian who was at the time engaged in a tour of inspection in the south of Ireland. If anybody will read with attention O'Connell's correspondence with Lord Duncannon, he will see that the great object of all is the destruction of Orangemen. My opinion is then that the object of this council is to disarm the yeomanry of the north of Ireland. They would not call Vivian to discuss the selection of a new judge, the removal of the Attorney-General or the other objects of O'Connell's letter. The subject of discussion must have been a military operation; and there is no other which this council could have in contemplation, excepting that which I have mentioned. Such a measure would render them infamous certainly; and the best of it is that it must, in this case, originate in Irish councils. There has been no assembly of the Cabinet in London, and the question cannot have been there considered.

I think that if the Irish noblemen and gentlemen can manage any question well they will alarm the Court, as well as the country in general upon the consequences to be expected from this measure.

I quite concur in your view of the state of the publick mind upon all questions. To tell you the truth, I am inclined to believe that that which for the last fifty years has been allowed to have so much weight in the publick councils, I mean publick opinion, was in fact the opinion of the party in opposition to the Government, or, in other words, of the Dissenters from the Church of England. It is quite certain that in every remarkable instance in which the publick opinion, as it was called, prevailed in deciding the course taken in the publick councils, the Dissenters were of that opinion. This was the case in all the slavery questions up to the very last; in many of the questions respecting the first revolutionary war, such as negociations for peace, etc.; and in all the recent questions of parliamentary reform.

The Dissenters from the Church are now looking to political objects of their own, which they hope to attain through the weakness or agency of the present Ministers. They shut their eyes to all the impolicy, disasters, disgrace, immorality and infamy of the existing system; which would have occasioned noise enough if we had been in office. But our friends, and the Conservatives in general whatever may be their opinions and feelings upon what they see going on, are not accustomed to notice such matters in the way in which we have known them to be noticed by the publick; and if they did, the administration, feeling that they have the support of a majority in Parliament elected as this House of Commons has been, and knowing that those who formerly influenced or rather composed the publick opinion have other objects to look to, would consider such declaration of opinion of about as much value as they do a resolution or a declaration of opinion by the House of Lords.

I don't see how there can be any farther change of the Government without bringing into office such men as Tennyson, Parnell, Hume, Cobbett, etc. There is nobody in the House of Lords excepting Lord Radnor who could do anything: and he makes a miserable figure when he is to do anything but make captious remarks on preceeding speeches.

I cannot but think that if Lord Spencer was to die we should see a dissolution of the Government or a state of things in the House of Commons which would prove to the common sense of mankind that the system could not continue. Till then they will go on very much as they have hitherto, be the partial changes what they may.

ADD MS 43060, ff 126–128. *Copy in Wellington Papers.*

The Duke of Buccleuch to Wellington, 21 September 1834

Forest Lodge, Blair Atholl. I write a few lines to tell you what I have heard of Lord Grey's dinner in Edinburgh. The Whigs are in great force about it, and to their party this meeting may be of the greatest benefit and it is one of their most politic proceedings; it is by this excitement alone that they can keep together that support which the waywardness of their friends renders so doubtful. The *unwashed* however were not of the same opinion as their washed leaders, and it was with great difficulty that some of the trades were persuaded to take a part in the procession; some of the trades refused altogether, and those that did attend had but very few followers besides those carrying their banners and emblems of their different crafts.

The day was beautiful and everyone turned out to see the fun, but there was no cheering, and not one hat in a hundred moved to welcome the man of the people.

The mob was most orderly, as an Edinburgh mob always is when assembled for peace, and I am told their order and regularity was most gratifying to see; but the dismal parade of the trades and their want of support and followers excited the ridicule of all parties except those benefiting by it. The dinner-room was very well got up and managed, and certainly Mr. Hamilton who superintended the erection of it deserved great credit, but the Whig account of the dinner and speeches surpasses everything. Never was there, according to their report, so glorious a display of oratory, talent and united feeling; the speeches however of some of the members of the Administration did not quite agree. The Chancellor's appearance was not agreeable, I am told, and not at all wished for; and Lord Grey's personal friends were not well pleased at it. Lord Grey's progress has been nearly as well worthy of record as the Lord Mayor's to Oxford. Any one who knows the towns he has passed through and the persons who have addressed him and to whom he has replied cannot but feel sorry that he should have been persuaded to expose himself to so much ridicule, and to take his reception in the small blackguard village of Coldstream and the other places he passed through as a test of the feeling of the country would be quite absurd. We have lost a most zealous and steady supporter in Edinburgh by the death of Blackwood, the publisher of *Blackwood's Magazine*: his loss will be much felt both in Edinburgh and elsewhere; he was a man of considerable influence there, and one who was respected by all parties. The registration courts as far as I have heard have finished with a result highly in our favour; my brother has a majority of above eighty on this year's registration: this will make him quite safe, and so is Selkirkshire, but I am not so sanguine about this county, i.e. Perth. They are trying to get up a dinner to Sir George Murray, which I am sorry for, for it is not likely to succeed to such an extent as to do good, and a failure would be of immense injury to him. Berwickshire is also in a ticklish state. Sir Hugh Campbell is not popular there and Marjoribanks, brother of the late Member, has married Miss Robertson of Ladykirk, an heiress, and has settled in the county and will contest the next election, and, I am told, with great chance of success. Among the devices carried in the procession to Lord Grey's dinner was a neat model of a door-frame, with the door half open, and beneath was inscribed in gilt letters, 'The door is now open and the people have got the key'; there were some others of the same nature. Lord Grey and the Chancellor met at Sir John Dalrymple's, where they were on a visit for a couple of days, and the account I got was that they were like a couple of dogs always at the watch lest one should bite the other, and were barely civil to one another. I met the Chancellor at Dunrobin: he was not particularly civil in his remarks upon his colleagues, calling Lord Palmerston a stupid fool for not sending a proper ambassador to Petersburg, and Lord Melbourne an idle dog for not doing something else. He was rather amusing, very noisy and talkative, and not insensible to the charms of good whisky.

Edward Drummond to Wellington, 27 September 1834

Stratford Place. At the earnest solicitation of Sir John Pechell, one of the Members for Windsor, I have promised to request your Grace to read the accompanying papers, relative to the projected railway from Paddington to that town. I have told him not [to] expect that I should endeavour to extract an opinion which may be construed into a pledge, either to support or oppose the measure in question; but I consented to lay the papers before your Grace with reference to an impression now existing (from what passed in the House of Lords during the progress of the Great Western Railway Bill) that yourself and other influential peers are opposed to any project of the sort, *as tending to affect the property of the Crown in the neighborhood of Windsor.* So long as any doubt remains upon this point, they deem it to be a question worthy of their consideration whether they shall proceed to take any steps whatever in furtherance of their object.

I know not how I can justify myself for troubling your Grace at all upon the subject. The only way I can *account* for it is that Sir John Pechell obtained the promise *after* dinner at his house at the Admiralty, strongly urging me to do so in consequence of his not having the honour of your Grace's acquaintance.

Enclosure: In the last session of Parliament the inhabitants of Windsor opposed the Great Western Railroad Bill, with a view to drive the promoters of that measure to adopt a line, which was pointed out to them, passing near the town of Windsor, on the southern side.

They proved that the line proposed by them was cheaper, better, shorter, more level, and less opposed than that of the Great Western

Company, and better adapted, to the extent of it, for a railway communication with Bristol; that it was entirely unobjected to by the Provost and fellows of Eton College, and that, although it proposed to pass under the Long Walk, by an underground passage very much below the surface, the ingress and egress of which are both without the bounds and beyond the view or hearing of any part of the royal grounds, the inhabitants of Windsor had the full concurrence and sanction of the Crown and of the Office of Woods for that purpose, as appears by the accompanying document from that office.

The Great Western Bill was thrown out on the second reading in the House of Lords, and subsequently every endeavour has been made to induce that company to adopt the southern line, which was expressly designed to promote the privacy of the royal domain, and to preserve the quiet of the College of Eton, and which was cordially approved by the Provost and fellows, in contradistinction to the Great Western or northern line, which would render Eton a thoroughfare for communication between the town of Windsor and the depot of the railroad. All overtures have been rejected, upon the plea that noble lords will not sanction any measure affecting the Crown property in the neighbourhood of Windsor.

The municipal authorities and inhabitants of Windsor (backed by the authorities of Eton) deeply lamenting that the existence of this feeling, or the report of its existence, should be the means of depriving them of the advantages of a measure which has been studiously and anxiously designed to meet the sanction and approval of His Majesty, the Commissioners of Woods, and the College of Eton, have ventured to ask such an intimation of your Grace's feelings and opinion on the point as may determine them in embarking in a distinct measure for procuring for their town the advantages desired, or as may reconcile them to the abandonment of the town of Windsor to the neglect, which the want of a suitable accommodation with the metropolis will consign it, leaving it in its present insular position; whilst other towns of inferior note and attraction will be brought, by the railroad, into closer connexion and communication with London.

Wellington to Edward Drummond, 1 October 1834

Walmer Castle. I voted, but, as well as I recollect did not speak against the Western Railway in the last session of Parliament; principally because there was not time to obtain the consent of the parties injured as they conceived by this incompleat scheme, or to hear their objections to it. I am under no engagement and have formed no resolution to oppose that or any other scheme in the next session of Parliament which may have for its object a publick convenience. The engineer has lately written to me to desire to converse with me upon this subject. I have advised the company first definitely to fix the plan of their road and the course which they propose that it should take; next that they should endeavour to satisfy proprietors and other parties likely to entertain objections to such a plan, as they have His Majesty and the Commissioners of Woods and Forests in relation to Windsor Park and Frogmore. The policy of the law of England is to give to every individual the service and exclusive enjoyment of his property. It may be convenient to take it from him for publick objects. But the advantage to be acquired ought to be quite certain. The individual whose property is to be taken ought to have ample compensation and moreover every measure ought to be adopted to lessen the nuisance and inconvenience of the work for the advantage of which the property is proposed to be taken. Effectual security has been given that this shall be done in Windsor Park; and I must say that I can see no reason why the smallest proprietor should be treated in respect to his property with less ceremony than the Sovereign.

I have in these few lines chalked out what I conceive to be my duty as a member of the House of Lords in such questions. I need say no more.

The Duke of Cumberland to Wellington, 3 October 1834

Berlin. I have been prevented writing to you sooner from having been attacked during the manoeuvres here with the ague, a complaint very general among our troops here, and which prevented my being able to attend the three last days' manoeuvres here. I however attended the three first days here, as also those at Stargardt in Pomerania. I think I never saw the troops in higher and better order, and though I was originally in doubt as to the efficiency of the cavalry of the *landwehr*, I was, after very scrutinously observing them at Stargardt, convinced that they will prove very useful even as they are now constituted, namely forming regiments of their own, but if *I* was consulted I think that by doubling the strength of the present regiments, and throwing one half of their *landwehr* men into them, they would be turned to more advantage, and in talking this over with experienced generals of cavalry here, they agree with me. As to the landwehr infantry they are in fact the cream of the army as they are all men who have served three years constantly [?] with the regiments, and as every battalion has its *landwehr* battalion, thus the King has very judiciously constituted each regiment and its landwehr to form upon service one brigade, consisting of *six* battalions, a thousand rank and file per battalion, making consequently each brigade 6,000 men strong; each of the eight *corps d'armée* can be collected in itself in a week or ten days and from six to seven weeks marched to any given point. I abstract from these eight corps that of the Guards, which forms the ninth and is equally strong in numbers. I do not believe that in all Europe there is any army equally constituted as to efficiency in every way equal to this one, or in which you will find all classes of officers better educated, or more uniform in every point. I think I never saw His Majesty in better health; he inquired a great deal after you, and said that as long as you and the Conservatives remained united as we are, thank God, *now* there are still hopes.

I found on my arrival here a very false but strong impression afloat that both you and Peel had been proposed by His Majesty to form a new Government, and that both of you had declined this; I instantly denied the fact and explained that *no* such proposal had *ever* been made to either, but through Lord Melbourne a new question whether you would coalesce, they forsooth not giving up one point; which was the fact, *since* this was done on purpose to impress the world here that the Conservatives were *not* able to form any Government, and that the Radicals were still the favourites. They are very indignant here, and I think with reason, at the appointment of Sir George Shee as minister here to replace Lord Minto, a man as yet unproven in the diplomacy, and as this is considered one of the first and principal courts in Europe, it is certainly treating them very cavalierly, and what makes it the more striking is that Lord William Russell who has been already in that capacity at Lisbon has just been appointed to Studtgardt, which is considered a minor court; and he being a man of rank and a military character would have been according to my humble opinion and knowledge of the *carte du pays* here much more acceptable in every way to the court here. Our minister here, I believe, had his audience of leave yesterday, when he presented his letters of recall; and to finish his diplomatic career with éclat, what do you think he did? You know I told you that he was considered the puppet of the French minister here; now to improve this, conceive only after *his* having given up his house and sold all his furniture here almost a fortnight ago, instead then of taking either apartments in an hotel here, or hiring lodgings for the time, he goes and establishes himself under the roof of this same Bresson, the French minister, as his guest. *Now* is this not too disgusting and plainly proves the footing these two gentlemen have been. Never certainly was *our* present Government held I believe in greater detestation or contempt than it is at this moment, and though to a British heart it is painful to be forced to own this, alas I see it too plainly to disguise it from myself. What do you say to the speeches and scenes in *North Britain*; how Grey can have made such a fool of himself and lowered his character by thus dancing over the world I own I am surprised; but not in the least at Brougham's buffoonery and as to his speeches they are in perfect accordance to all I knew and expected of him. His ridiculous and base praise of my brother too insulting and degrading. You will be happy to hear that my son, George, is going on very well; he is immensely grown, reaching now up to my eye-brows: in fact during the eight months I have been absent he has grown *four* inches. The Duchess and George both desire their kindest regards to you.

We have young Cranborne here; Gräfe has seen him, and though he cannot and will not as yet give a decided opinion, yet he has now put him under a cure of magnetism, which is to rouse the power of the eye, and this appears already to have had some effect.

Lord Francis Egerton to Wellington, 3 October 1834

Oatlands. I was about writing to you yesterday to announce to you what I thought you would be glad to hear, when Lady C[harlotte] told me she had written. Lady Francis has been doing very well since the event and as she was remarkably strong before it I hope will recover soon. I am going to send you the first volume of an history of the Polish war. I have mislaid the second, but dare say I shall find it if you find the first worth attention. It is by an officer named Soltyk who seems to have been sufficiently mixed up in the transaction to be able to tell a good [deal] of the truth if he chooses. It has left on me the impression that if they could have turned out one really superior man they would have had a much better chance against Russia than I ever thought they had; and it has confirmed to me the truth of an observation of Auguste d'Arenberg's in the last conversation I ever had with him, that Poland never does produce a great man, or an officer fit for anything beyond the command of a regiment.

I see by the French papers that some of their liberals are starting the notion of making a separate kingdom of Guipuzcoa and the frontier provinces of Spain. I almost doubt whether the suggestion be not a wise one in the absence of all other probable solution of the present *bagarre*.

John Wilson Croker to Wellington, 12 October 1834

West Molesey, Surrey. I have a letter from Lord Hertford at Frankfurt: he was going by the Tyrol, into Italy and *to Naples*, for if he does not, he says 'he must lose Charlotte, the cleverest and best of children'. But how he is to live at Naples *with* Lady Strachan—or *without* her—I know not. She and her Pico went off *suddenly* from Paris the day before Lord Hertford set out for Brusselles. It seems that *Lord Yarmouth* had some row with her Ladyship at Paris and *said something* to her, that it was thought Pico, as a husband, ought to take notice of; instead of which they most *prudently* decamped: I used the word not *ironically*, for even if Picolillis had all the spirit in the world (and I have heard that he is a noted duellist and good shot) Lady Strachan *could* not allow him to fight Lord Yarmouth. Nor could Lord Hertford, if he could have stopped it, have permitted Lord Yarmouth to fight Lady Strachan's husband. In short the whole thing is an imbroglio through which I do not see poor Lord Hertford's way.

I have a letter from Peel who is in town, but sets out on Tuesday: he is not decided how far or for how long he is going. I fear that I shall not be able to go up to see him tomorrow, as he has asked me to do.

I am going into Cornwall the end of this week to hold a duchy court at Truro, as deputy Lord Warden, a troublesome and disagreeable job, which I accepted to please Lord Hertford, who was worried at the idea of being obliged to stay in England and go down into Cornwall to hear a stannary appeal. I shall be back about the 26th.

PS. As your Grace is sometimes kind enough to take notice of humble neighbours, I venture to ask a favor of that kind: there is one of the senior clerks in the Admiralty, by name Mr. Henry Bedford, a great friend of mine and an excellent Tory and I would add, but that it is no *distinction*, a great admirer of your Grace. He has gone to spend his holidays at Dover and if your Grace had an opportunity of asking him to dinner, I am sure he would be delighted and honored above all things. If it should not be convenient, there is no harm done, *for he does not even know that I am aware of his being at Dover*. I only heard by accident and knowing how much he would be flattered by so great an honor I venture to mention him to your Grace, though I do not well see how you are likely to fall in with him. He lives at No. 7 Marine Parade. He is one of a family that have been long in the public offices. The Bedfords have been in the Exchequer ever since Walpole's days. I found this man very young in the Admiralty (put in I fancy by Lord Maryborough) and I promoted him as rapidly as I could, for without being a genius he is clever and gentleman-like.

The Duke of Gloucester to Wellington, 12 October 1834

Bagshot Park. I have this day received a copy of the resolutions passed at a meeting of the beneficed clergymen deputed from several dioceses in Ireland, which I observe it was agreed should be transmitted to the chancellors of the two English universities. Of the importance and utility of the clerical society in Ireland there can be no doubt, and I am very desirous of consulting with your Grace upon the subject, and shall be much obliged to you if you will be so good as to communicate to me your sentiments respecting the proper course for us to pursue in consequence of this communication.

Dr. Allen, formerly tutor to Lord Althorp, is certainly to be the new bishop. I am not acquainted with him.

Bickersteth was offered to be Solicitor-General, but has positively refused.

I find that the King of the French is extremely displeased at the intended marriage of the Queen of Portugal with the Duc de Leuchtenberg, which our Ministers have encouraged. I think they are right, as under existing circumstances, Austria as I understand having declined the proposal for a son of the Archduke Charles to be the husband of Donna Maria, it does not appear to me that for our interests a more suitable person would be found than the one selected, as our great

687

object must be to prevent a French prince being seated on the throne of Portugal.

PS. Have the goodness to direct to me to London.

Mr. Moore, a brother of Lord Mountcashell who married a sister of Lord Clinton, is made a canon of Windsor in the room of Dr. Clarke.

The Earl of Aberdeen to Wellington, 12 October 1834

Haddo House. The mountebank exhibitions of the Chancellor in various parts of Scotland, as well as the dinner given to Lord Grey in Edinburgh, have excited a strong feeling among the Conservatives; and have created a general desire to have some meetings of the same kind, which it is not possible to controul. A dinner is to be given to Murray next week by his constituents at Perth; and it has also been determined to give one to my brother in this county, which I have no doubt will be very numerously attended: probably by near a thousand persons, comprising a very great proportion of the rank, property and respectability of the district. I should have been rather disposed to check this meeting, had it been possible, as not arising from any very obvious cause, and having the appearance of being merely a set off against the Whig dinners; but I found that the people were quite determined, and that any interference would have been injurious.

It certainly appears that the general state of political feeling has been gradually improving throughout this country. We had last week at Aberdeen a great meeting of the Highland Agricultural Society. This institution is not only not political, but men of all parties belong to it, and no allusion is ever made to anything which can produce a difference of political opinion. We had between seven and eight hundred persons at dinner; and contrary to all rule and precedent, your health was given, and was certainly received with as much enthusiasm as I ever witnessed upon any occasion. This is not a bad sign, for a great many Whigs were present.

I admire your perseverance in endeavouring to make something rational of the Irish Orangemen. The attempt would be deemed almost hopeless by anyone but yourself, but in the crisis which is approaching in Ireland, everything will depend on the character of the Protestant proceedings. The Government appear to be a little frightened at the progress of O'Connell, and shew some reluctance to an entire submission to his influence. After the manner, however, in which three Cabinet Ministers expressed themselves at Edinburgh, in direct opposition to the policy of the Government itself, and to the declarations of one of their own colleagues, it is impossible to feel any confidence, or even to guess what is likely to be the principle of their conduct. In these cases, the worst and most wicked opinions are the most calculated to prevail with men who are without any high sense of duty or principle, for they are apparently easy, and they have the advantage of overcoming for the moment, the pressure of some present difficulty. At all events, I think it probable that our Ministers may do whatever they like in their foreign affairs; for very few understand anything of these questions, or take any interest respecting them. And this is natural enough. When everything at home is threatened, and in jeopardy, we cannot expect people to think much of France and Spain.

Don Pedro's death will I suppose speedily bring the affairs of Portugal, and perhaps of the Peninsula, to a crisis. If Palmella could maintain himself, and exercise the full authority of his station, his conduct would probably be rational and moderate, and there might still be a chance of something like order and security in his wretched country. But he is a ruined man; and what is worse, a man without firmness of character or principle, who must yield to what Lord Grey calls 'the pressure from without', which I fear he will do without much reluctance. Should he resist, it is impossible that the Portuguese ministry, as at present constituted, can have a long existence; and even if he should march with the Jacobins, it is not likely to be much prolonged. I see our French friends, and those too, who usually speak the language of their Government, are already beginning to cry out against the appointment of Palmella, as likely to be the means of restoring English influence in Portugal!

The war in the Basque provinces seems still to retain the same character, without any appearance of leading to decisive results. But the appointment of Mina is a considerable step made in the progress of revolution. Will he be able to act with more effect, or prove more successful than his predecessors?

The Earl of Rosslyn to Wellington, 13 October 1834

12 Chapel Street, Grosvenor Place. I have heard that it is believed or at least reported in Berlin that the Duke of Cumberland is active and very

689

instrumental in exciting the opposition of the Crown Prince to the Government of the King by encouraging and suggesting the highest notions of government in contradiction of the more moderate views of the King and Ancillon. I know not how far this is true, but I cannot help fearing that his restless and violent disposition is but too likely to lead him into such a scrape.

At all events it is right to put you in possession of the report.

There is a rumor in Dublin that O'Connell has had a communication from Littleton to say that it was impossible to carry the removal of Blackburn from the office of Attorney-General. This I think more likely to be invented than to have happened. If it be true O'Connell will bring it out. I have read his last letter with care and compared it with the two Acts of the 2nd and 3rd, c. 119, and of the 3rd and 4th of the King, c. 100, and I cannot help fearing that there is much in the remarks he makes upon Stanley's Acts. But although he holds out threats and insinuates obscurely some difficulties and dangers to the landlords who take upon themselves the payment of tithes, I cannot discover any serious or solid objection to that course of which he appears to me to be afraid.

The King I hear was delighted with the exhibition on Saturday and kept as many of his party till Monday as he could.

There seems to be a strong suspicion that the fire in the plantations of Windsor Park, or rather perhaps in the Forest, was occasioned by some of the cadets from Sandhurst.

They mean to try the man of the Coldstream by a general court martial, and it is supposed that it is probable that that there will be a conviction, and sentence to be shot. I much doubt the sentence, and still more the execution of it if it be passed.

I have, I believe, subdued the fever, and have been out on horseback.

Wellington to the Duke of Gloucester, 14 October 1834

Walmer Castle. I have not received the copy of the resolutions to which your Royal Highness refers as having passed at a meeting of the beneficed clergymen in Ireland. But I conceive that it would be very desirable that we should give in this country every support, countenance and assistance in our power to the Irish clergy.

In my opinion the question has materially altered since the last session of Parliament. The noblemen and gentlemen of Ireland have come forward very handsomely in support of the Church of England in Ireland. They are very right in doing so, as it is quite clear first that they will have as much to pay very nearly in the shape of tax according to the plan proclaimed by Mr. O'Connell as they would have to pay in tithes honestly due to the clergy, and secondly I think that the Protestants of Ireland must by this time have discovered that if they cannot maintain the Church of England in Ireland, they cannot expect to keep their properties. Thus, then, putting out of the question altogether the higher duty of preserving the Church as a system of religion, it is the interest of the gentlemen of Ireland to preserve it, if they mean to preserve their properties.

The same argument applies to the preservation of the Church of England in Ireland, if it is the King's desire to retain the English dominion over Ireland.

I believe that the marriage of the Duc de Leuchtenberg with the Infanta Donna Maria is contrary to the fundamental law of the Portuguese monarchy. Her Majesty ought to marry a Portuguese nobleman.

Wellington to the Duke of Cumberland, 15 October 1834

Walmer Castle. I am very much obliged to your Royal Highness for your letter and I sincerely congratulate you upon the favourable prospects of Prince George's recovery of his sight.

Nothing can surprise a person who observes what is going on in these days. But I should think that the King's servants ought to endeavour to conciliate foreign powers at least by appointing proper persons to represent His Majesty at their respective courts.

I am happy to read so favourable an account of the Prussian army. I have always entertained the highest opinion of it. It has the advantage of having gentlemen for its officers.

We are going on in this country much as usual. There exists a general uneasiness about something, nobody knows what, and dissatisfaction with everything. I take the truth to be that people require to be governed and discover that there is no security in the enjoyment of anything in the absence of all government, which is pretty nearly the state in which we live in England.

I think that in Ireland affairs are improving. The Protestant noblemen and gentlemen have, I understand, generally come forward and have declared their intentions to pay in future the composition for tithes on their estates. These intentions have excited O'Connell a good deal, and he has written two or three very violent letters which shew sensibly he feels the consequences of this step on the part of the proprietors. In fact it puts an end to the tithe affair altogether. He has consequently threatened them with the non-payment of rent. I won't say what will be the consequence of his attempting to succeed in this object in these times, because I don't think that any man can venture to foretell anything. But in other times conspiring to withhold rents or even the payment of tithes would have brought the affair in Ireland to a fair trial of strength.

Your Royal Highness is quite right: no offer was made to me or to Sir Robert Peel to enter the King's service. We were desired to consider of a proposition to form an administration on an extended basis made to Lord Melbourne, which Lord Melbourne in his answer deemed to be impracticable. Indeed this answer was so decided that I did not think it necessary (nor did Sir Robert Peel) to enter into the consideration of the subject. We gave detailed answers only after having been again called upon to do so by the King.

I confess that my opinion is that it will be very difficult, if it is at all possible, to carry on the affairs of government in this country by means of the legislature as now formed. Those who undertook in the year 1830 to reform the Parliament did not, I believe, intend to do more than exclude their rivals from power for ever. But they proposed more than they intended to carry, and they ended by carrying a great deal more than they had proposed.

The consequence is that they have destroyed the government of their country. It was the men of property, the men of education, industry, talent, popularity, birth or any notoriety who heretofore wielded the power of this monarchy. They have not at present among them a particle of political influence. If you find one who has carried an election you will learn upon enquiry that it has been by some popular trick which ought not to be practised, or pledge which ought not to have been made, and not by the influence of character or property. I said when the Reform Bill was carried that I knew of but one man who would have a secure, independent seat, and that was Sir Robert Peel. The fact has turned out to be strictly true. What must become of a country, in the government of which not only the property etc. have no influence, but in which the possession of property, talents, etc. will be a cause of exclusion?

We are on the high road of all revolutions. We are travelling upon it in our own way by one course of law without commotion or disturbance, because the King and his authority are at the head of the movement and of the revolution. Accordingly at the moment which Messrs. Stanley and Co. or Lord Grey and his family hesitated about going forward with the carriage, they were thrown out without ceremony, as Lord Lansdowne and Lord Brougham and others will be, in their turn, when they will hesitate. The revolutionary carriage still continues its movement even with increased velocity and certainly without inconvenience, notwithstanding the loss of these able guides, and so it will in future. Nobody will stop it, till it runs the usual revolutionary course, and those who have caused the mischief will have discovered that it is as injurious to themselves as they intended it should be to others. I consider therefore that all attempts to form a Government to be fruitless.

Wellington to the Earl of Aberdeen, 16 October 1834

Walmer Castle. I had heard of and had observed your Conservative meetings in Scotland; which I believe do just as much good as this, and no more. They remind the world that there is such a thing as a Conservative party remaining in the country; and that if they don't like the destruction of the institutions of the country, they will find some of the same opinion as themselves. I don't think that any meeting can do much more than that. However, the numbers tend to shew either that there is a change of opinion in the country; or, what is I believe more near the truth, that there were many more opposed to the destruction of the old constitution of the country than was imagined, or than dared to avow their opinion.

It has been so generally reported that I was going to Scotland to attend these meetings, and I have been invited to go to so many houses and to attend at so many meetings at places on the road that I have found myself under the necessity of advertising that I was not going.

You will see that my plan in Ireland is tolerably successful. I have not heard from Ireland lately; and I know of no details, excepting what I see in the newspapers. I don't know whether you read O'Connell's letters. If you should you will see that he is absolutely writhing under the infliction of the success of this plan. My opinion is that we shall take the tithes entirely out of the fire. Accordingly O'Connell tells the gentlemen if you do take upon yourselves to pay the tithes to the clergy and endeavour to recover from your tenants, you shall have no rent! He has thus touched upon a very tender point, which in fact involves the whole question in Ireland. The Government must decide whether they will or not allow any man or any number of men in Ireland to resist the payment of rent to their landlords, whether by active and open rebellion, or by measures called passive resistance. I think that the Protestants are beginning to have sense enough to see that if they lose the Church of England they will very soon lose their estates!

I know well what many of the Ministers will decide upon this point of the rents. Littleton has already told the Irish gentlemen that their rents could not be maintained at their existing rate. But thank God! we have a House of Lords; and if the Irish noblemen and gentlemen will only be true to themselves I'll engage that we will carry them triumphantly through their difficulties.

I have had a good deal of intelligence from Spain. Rodil is considered as beat by Zumalacarregui; and is put out of his command. Mina, who is stated to be labouring under a mortal disorder which must carry him off in a short time, is expected to perform miracles. If he should not, it is stated that that part of the country must be ruined and abandoned. The country in general is stated not to be disposed towards Don Carlos. But it is labouring under other evils: the cholera; very general inundations; bankruptcy; and, I may add, the mad love of the Queen Regent for a fellow of the name of Muñoz, with whom she lives secluded at the Prado; and the folly of the principal men in the country in thinking that they can establish in Spain anything like the British or even the French constitution.

How they are to get out of their difficulties I cannot say.

In respect to Portugal I understand that the French Ministers object to the marriage with the Duc de Leuchtenberg, and the continental powers do the same. This marriage is certainly contrary to the fundamental law of the country. The Emperor of Austria is said on that ground to have declined to give his consent to a marriage between Donna Maria and the Archduke Charles's son. I don't exactly recollect the terms of the protocol. But it is said that the Duc de Leuchtenberg is excluded as being one of the Bonaparte family.

So that here is another nice affair into which our liberality is getting us.

I have heard that the Duke of Cumberland has been meddling in troubled waters in Prussia; that is to say encouraging the Prince Royal to be less liberal than the King, who is not exactly an example of liberalism.

I have heard from the Duke; and there is no trace of such affair in his letter. I know besides that there is no person better acquainted with the Duke's character, or more upon his guard in his relations with him than the said Prince Royal. I should say more so even than the King.

I have not heard any more news. Peel is gone abroad. He has not decided to what place, nor how long he will stay. He went from London to Calais yesterday.

ADD MS 43060, ff 129–131. *Copy in Wellington Papers.*

The Duke of Gloucester to Wellington, 16 October 1834

Hall Barn Park. I had this morning the pleasure of receiving your Grace's letter and I entirely agree with you in all the sentiments you express in regard to the Church of England in Ireland; and I am quite of your opinion that we should in this country give every support and countenance to the Irish clergy.

I shall not take any step respecting the resolutions that have been sent to me, and which had not reached your Grace when you wrote, but which I can have no doubt will be very shortly sent to you, till I hear again from you, as I am desirous that we should act exactly the same upon this occasion. I shall therefore be much obliged to your Grace, when you have read these resolutions, to inform me whether you do not think that the expression of our approbation and of our interest in the success of the society should be accompanied by a donation. In the papers that have been transmitted to me there is not a list of the subscriptions; I am therefore totally at a loss to know what sort of sum would be expected.

There is a report which I have heard from several quarters of considerable dissentions in the Cabinet.

Sir Gore Ousely tells me that he had proposed to your Grace to meet me here and that you were unable to come. It causes me great regret not to have had the satisfaction of passing these days with you.

The Earl of Roden to Wellington, 16 October 1834

Dublin. Private. I know you will be anxious to hear of our proceedings. I am glad to say the declaration is advancing in its progress for signatures and, make no doubt, before the meeting of Parliament it will be a most respectable document. But you will have observed some Protestant meetings which have taken place of a most important nature, and one particularly in the county of Cork at Bandon, where Lord Bandon collected a body of 5,000 Protestants in his park who entered into resolutions and signed petitions to the legislature expressive of their apprehension of the present position of affairs, and I must beg to call your attention to a requisition from the county of Down for a meeting on the 30th instant: you will see it in yesterday's *Evening Mail* which I think you take. The meeting will be an immense one, I apprehend. The town of Hillsborough probably will not hold it, and consequently we shall have to adjoin to the race-course of the Maze which is near there, if the day is fine. Every resident gentleman in the county of Down of any respectability have signed the requisition, except Lord Annesley and Lord Bangor who have refused me. If the weather is favourable I think it will be one of the finest sights and display of Protestant strength that was ever shown in one county in Ireland. Lords Downshire and Londonderry are both coming over to attend it. I make no doubt this meeting will be followed by many others. The fund for the recovery of the rights of the clergy is getting on very prosperously and the landlords are taking upon themselves the payment of the tithes, I trust very extensively. I hear nothing of the disarming of the Protestant yeomanry, and their legal appointments seem to be as little objectionable as we could have expected. Anything was better than Perrin being appointed to office, and it was of great importance that Mr. Blackburne should remain; our people are in much better spirits than they were, and if we can but get the question of tithes untouched upon, or rather not objected to by a Presbyterian force in the north, I have every hope. I will communicate to you from time to time as circumstances may occur which may interest you, and in the meantime I would beg of you look occasionally into the *Evening Mail* newspaper which is the organ of our party and represents as accurately as possible the passing events of these most important times to this country.

Wellington to the Earl of Roden, 18 October 1834

Walmer Castle. I see some very satisfactory accounts from Ireland of Protestant noblemen and gentlemen undertaking to pay the tithe composition on their estates; and I sincerely hope that that spirit is spreading. From the *writhings* of O'Connell as expressed in his letters, and the new mischief which he has suggested, I am inclined to suspect that he finds the inclination to pay the composition more general than he imagined and that a new course of agitation must be commenced.

To be sure, when one sees that he proposes a tax of 9d. in the pound on rent to be paid instead of composition of tithe, a landlord must be worse than mad who would rob the Church for so trifling a bribe.

There is nothing so clear as that the only security for property as held under the Act of Settlement and for the convention between Great Britain and Ireland is the security and the supremacy of the Church of England in Ireland.

I wish that Mr. Boyton's speech was published in a pamphlet. I would get it reviewed here, and it would do a great deal of good. Let us have plenty of information of facts regarding the state of the country, its outrages, etc. before the meeting of Parliament.

I see that the clergy are doing something for themselves in Dublin. The Duke of Gloucester has written to me upon the subject, having received a letter, a paper from them. I have not yet received one. I think that I can do them some good at Oxford.

Wellington to the Earl of Roden, 20 October 1834

Walmer Castle. I was impatient to hear from you and I wrote to you last week. I have since received your letter of the 16th and I am happy to learn that you are so well satisfied.

Since I wrote I have learnt that the language of the Government is one of great apprehension respecting the state of the tithe question, least the landlords of Ireland should involve themselves. They take this from O'Connell. I know that this is the language of Lord Duncannon.

Let us have as much accurate account of outrages as possible.

I got the Dublin *Evening Mail* and will attend to it.

PS. I think that you might make some use of O'Connell's plan to levy a land tax instead of tithe as announced in his letter.

The Rev. Arthur Henry Glasse to Wellington, 23 October 1834

5 York Place, Brompton. The circumstances under which I venture to address your Grace are these:

It has been in agitation for several months to establish a monthly publication on a novel principle, chiefly for the purpose of keeping the public press under proper controul, but also for the noticing and investigating abuses which it probably suits the purposes of the editors of the present day to pass over in silence. The conductor of the work has been editor and proprietor of a very successful work for the last seven years, in the county of Warwick, and his principles are strictly Conservative; he has arrived in London purposely to superintend and carry into effect this project. Unfortunately the sinews of war are wanting, for although Sir Robert Peel and two other gentlemen have together with myself subscribed towards it, the expenses of establishment, type, etc. are so great that £50 are yet required. Unfortunately we do not find the same energy in the majority of those attached to constitutional principles as in those opposed to them. Would that the Conservatives borrowed the zeal of their combatants and hallowed it with truth!

Allow me to state to your Grace that further than as a subscriber and an occasional contributor on theological subjects, I shall not be personally interested in the success of *The Argus.* I have, however, a thorough conviction that should it be conducted 'wisely and well', that the beneficial effects that must accrue from it are as certain as its success.

Should this brief and I fear abrupt announcement cause your Grace to require further particulars, it would give me great satisfaction to be allowed to lay them before you.

The Earl of Roden to Wellington, 24 October 1834

Tollymore Park. Nothing can be more satisfactory than the way everything is going on here now. The proposed great meeting of Down seems to have given life to everything in the north of Ireland and, I hear, is extending its influence over the south and west. If the day is fine it will be the greatest meeting of Protestant strength ever beheld in Ireland and I am sure not less than 50,000 will attend. The gentry are to march in at the head of their respective people. A large field in the neighbourhood of Hillsborough on the roadside has been chosen and hustings are now erecting. I attended a meeting of the committee of management the day before yesterday for the purpose of submitting to them a copy of the resolutions which they begged of me to prepare, and which they adopted. I hope you will approve of them; if you see anything that requires alteration, be so kind as to let me know: as our meeting is not till Thursday there will be ample time. We have contending parties to deal with here which makes it rather difficult to frame resolutions suited for all, but the kind way I am received by all parties and the attention they give to any suggestion of mine is most gratifying to me. They will come out from Hillsborough and meet me, though I have done what I can to prevent it, as my object would be not to give cause for jealousy to any party who may be present.

I observe your wish to have a pamphlet of Boyton's speech; all our proceedings are most carefully published in a little penny magazine, which comes out weekly. I enclose you in four covers the four numbers which have already come out, where Boyton's and O'Sullivan's speeches are given most accurately. If you think they could be disseminated with effect through England and would point out the best manner, I would order some to be sent. I will send you the last number when we get it next week which I believe contains the speech of Boyton to which you refer, but if you will look over what I send you now, perhaps you may find it there already. I shall take advantage of your permission to write to you from time to time and will desire the clerical returns, to which you refer, to be sent to you. I think you may be of essential service to the clergy at Oxford.

Enclosure: Most Private. Resolutions proposed for adoption at the Down meeting, on 30th October, with the movers and seconders.

1st   Marquess of Downshire
       Matthew Forde, Esq.
Resolved:
    That the state of this country for some time past, the wild doctrines which are propagated respecting property, and the mode whereby the laws may be resisted or evaded, the combination which prevails against the loyal and well-disposed and which in many districts of the other provinces enforces obedience to its dictates by all the excesses of savage punishment, are calculated to excite the utmost anxiety

and alarm in the minds of all classes of His Majesty's peaceable subjects.

2nd   Marquess of Londonderry
       Lord Arthur Hill
Resolved:
   That it appears to this meeting that the minds of a large portion of the population of Ireland have been unsettled by the acts of evil-disposed men, and expectations have been raised that the period is at hand in which their efforts are to succeed in severing Ireland from the Government of Great Britain and establishing a domestic legislature, which would create such derangement of the constitution, affecting all classes, as would throw political power exclusively into the hands of a popish faction.

3rd   Earl Clanwilliam
       Sir Robert Bateson
Resolved:
   That the expectations of the Roman Catholic population and the apprehensions of the Protestants are principally excited by the influence which dangerous and seditious leaders palpably exercise over His Majesty's Ministers and the legislature itself, and every concession thus made manifestly tends to advance the ultimate triumph of the enemies of the constitution.

4th   Viscount Castlereagh
       Revd. Mr. Anderson, Presbyterian minister
Resolved:
   That the consequences resulting from the unsettled state of affairs are most calamitous: a great portion of the population in various parts of Ireland is withdrawn from the wholesome pursuit of industrious occupation and plunged into the commission of barbarous crime, while the peaceable subjects of the King are victims to these atrocities, and their continued insecurity promotes rapid emigration even from this comparatively tranquil district.

5th   Revd. Holt Waring, clerk
       Roger Hall, Esq.
Resolved:
   That petitions be sent to King, Lords and Commons.

6th   Colonel John Ward
          Hugh Moore, Esq.

Resolved:

That we have witnessed with the utmost satisfaction the proceedings of the Protestant meeting in Dublin on the 14th of August, we approve of the resolutions entered into by our Protestant brethren of Cavan, we rejoice at the recent meeting at Bandon, we answer their call made on us in their fifth resolution, and pledge ourselves to co-operate with them in repelling the assaults of the common enemy of our religion and our liberties; that we deeply sympathize with our southern brethren in all their sufferings, and that in any trials to which they may be exposed the appeal of the Protestants of the south and west shall be faithfully responded to by their Protestant brethren in Ulster.

7th   Earl of Roden
          Revd. John White, Presbyterian minister

Resolved:

That we pledge ourselves to co-operate with each other during the difficulties by which we are threatened, to aid and assist our fellow countrymen and all loyal subjects in every practicable manner to maintain the rights of property and the union with Great Britain as established by law, to uphold the integrity of the Protestant Church, the free profession of the gospel of Christ, the unrestricted use of God's holy word by persons of every class and age, the stability of the Protestant institutions of the realm, and the King's authority therein.

Lord FitzGerald to Wellington, 26 October 1834

Dublin. I have taken the liberty of sending to your Grace the copy of a pamphlet, which has produced an extraordinary sensation in Ireland.

It is the avowed work of a Roman Catholic priest, holding a parish in their Church, in the county of Cork.

Under the character of presenting to the public views of what he terms 'ecclesiastical finance' and of proving the necessity of a State endowment for the Romish clergy, the Reverend Mr. Croly has divulged the most extraordinary system of exaction, as well as the most remarkable picture of a corrupt priesthood and a demoralized people that we have ever had exhibited.

The Catholics are in a state of great excitement at this publication, which appears at a moment most favorable for the Established Church, and they are the more incensed at the truths that are told, because the exposure is made with great fearlessness and ability.

With respect to our own Church question, it is satisfactory to see proofs of the feeling which has been called forth. The number of the Protestant landlords who are undertaking for the payment of the tithes on their respective estates is encreasing daily. The clergy are in high spirits. I am assured by some of them that they prefer the bill (Mr. Stanley's, and the powers which they derive under it) to *any other*; that they are armed with immense power under it, and do not despair of weathering the storm. Their strongest support, however, is in the Protestant feeling, which is, I hope, effectually roused.

The proceedings in Down in the present week will confirm that spirit.

I do not believe, notwithstanding the letters that appear, that there is any real rupture between the Government and Mr. O'Connell. When the tribute is collected, I doubt not but that he will be again a *ministerialist*.

I had a letter from Lord Bandon, asking for my vote as a peer and stating that Lord Roden had applied to him to vote for me, on the second vacancy in the representation. This is the result of your kind intervention with Lord Roden and the Conservative lords, and I feel very grateful for it. Of course I shall give my support on the first vacancy to Lord Bandon, and shall obtain for him any vote that I can. Lord Roden had not informed me that he had been canvassing his friends for me, which marks his conduct as still more handsome and more gratifying to me.

The Rev. Edward Cardwell to Wellington, 27 October 1834

St. Alban's Hall, Oxford. Though I have no doubt that the Vice-Chancellor will have written to your Grace on the same subject, I still feel it to be my duty to make some report of what passed this morning at the board of heads of houses, in connexion with the important matters, which your Grace has been pleased to lay before us. As one of the heads of halls also, it is the more incumbent on me to offer our thanks to your Grace for the valuable communication you have made to the board.

The first point considered was the propriety of adopting some other test on matriculation in the place of subscription to the Thirty-nine

Articles. It was determined that nothing should be done hastily in so important a matter; but I have great pleasure in thinking, from the sentiments expressed, that your Grace's recommendation has made a strong impression on the board, and that some measure in conformity with it will be brought before Convocation during the present term.

On the question of examining into the present condition of our statutes, it will I expect be proposed at the next meeting of the board that a committee should be appointed for the purpose; but I am not clear that that plan will be preferred to the much less effective method of leaving individuals to find out faults or deficiencies, and discussing the cases separately as they arise. But halls are circumstanced differently from colleges. With regard to the former, your Grace is not only the Chancellor of the whole corporation to which they belong, but also their visitor, acknowledged by them in the light of founder. Any suggestion therefore which your Grace may address to the heads of houses with respect to their internal government, will be received by the principals of halls as having the nature of a command.

Halls have no private statutes; but there is a collection of rules (entitled *Statuta Aularia*) in the appendix to the statute-book of the university, which were intended to supply the place of private statutes, and together with the general statutes of the university form the law by which the halls are governed. These *Statuta Aularia* were, I believe, put into their present form in the chancellorship of Archbishop Laud, and contain, as might be expected, some injunctions which it would be expedient to modify, and others which may well be omitted altogether. I conceive that this must be done, if at all, by means of the Convocation, in the manner in which statutes are passed for the government of the university at large. It is most gratifying to me that an inquiry, which appears to me to be so desirable, should have obtained so high an authority in its favour.

It is my intention to propose that the heads of halls should be appointed a committee to examine into the present condition of the *Statuta Aularia*, with reference to the several points mentioned by your Grace, and to report thereon to the board. Our proceedings will necessarily be slow; but there will be so much to be said in our favour, that they will, I trust, ultimately be successful. If we should be able to make our statute-book a real and practical code of laws (which, I fear, it can scarcely now be considered to be) we shall be indebted for the change mainly to the valuable counsels of your Grace.

John Wilson Croker to Wellington, 28 October 1834

Kensington Palace. May I trouble your Grace to look over the second page of the printed paper which I inclose and to tell me whether what I there say of your Grace is correct and proper. I am always anxious to preserve *historical truth* and particularly in all that relates to you and I find that correcting such misstatements, by a counter statement in the *Quarterly Review* has had in numerous instances an excellent effect. What I have said is I know, in substance correct, but Your Grace may wish to see it otherwise worded.

I am just come up from Cornwall where I have been holding a stannary court as deputy for Lord Hertford.

I heard of him yesterday at Munich in rather better spirits: no mention of the lady, who is, of course, at Naples.

I regret to hear that poor A. Baring's accident continues to look serious; there is a wound which they are not able to heal. I have been invited to come there three several times and each time they have been obliged by a relapse to put me off.

I am going next week to Sudbourne. We have some corporation business to do, else I should not have accepted the invitation till I had known from your Grace whether you intend to go there this season.

May I beg you to return the paper to this address: you may write as you please on the margin.

Wellington to Rev. Edward Cardwell, 29 October 1834

Walmer Castle. I have received your letter of the 27th, and I am delighted to find that the board of the heads of houses have not disapproved of the suggestions which I made to them in my correspondence with the Vice-Chancellor, founded upon my experience in Parliament and in the transactions of the political world. It was my duty to suggest what I have done, it will be theirs to decide upon the course which they will take and its principle as well as in its details, and they will find me ready at all times to assist them with my opinion on any point on which they may consult me.

I shall be in Hampshire in the course of about a fortnight from this time. We may reckon upon four months more of time to consider whether any thing and what ought to be done. But although we have time it will be desirable not to lose any of it.

Wellington to John Wilson Croker, 29 October 1834

Walmer Castle. I have looked over your sheet. You will see my notes in the margin.

The usual form of communication with the British Government by foreigners is through the Secretary of State. Upon points of importance the foreign ministers desire to communicate with the First Minister and I was in the habit of communicating with all of them verbally. I likewise wrote some letters to Ministers of sovereigns abroad in answer to theirs and sent them after laying them before the Cabinet: such as a letter to the French Secretary of State in 1828 upon the Russo-Greek affair and a letter to Don Miguel in 1830, which has been published, and I carried on the correspondence with the Marquis de Palmella about Terceira, as he, having no official character, would not be listened to according to the usual forms of office. But otherwise I never interfered, excepting with my advice and opinion as every other Minister might. I wrote a great number of the papers in the Greek collection and many others. But they do not appear to be mine more than those of others. I recollect to have seen Laval upon the subject of the Algiers affair, to have had a long conference with him of which I wrote a report for the Cabinet. But this was very early in the transaction. I think before the session of 1830. The result of that conference and of the other measures in consequence was to prevent the French from making use of the Pasha of Egypt in their expedition to Algiers. I am very sorry to hear of Mr. Baring's state of health; should they not move him to town? or have the best London advice for him in the country?

I declined to go to Sudbourne and excused myself as I was so much engaged.

The Duke of Gloucester to Wellington, 30 October 1834

Bagshot Park. Not having heard from your Grace since I had the pleasure of writing to you this day fortnight, I conceive that the resolutions passed at a meeting of the beneficed clergy in Ireland have not been communicated to you, which is the more extraordinary as I observe in the newspapers a letter from the Archbishop of Canterbury acknowledging their receipt; and at that meeting it was resolved that they should be forwarded to him and to all English prelates and likewise to the two chancellors of the English universities. Having now received them nearly three weeks, I do not think that I can delay sending an answer. It does not appear by the Archbishop's letter that he has sent a donation.

I was much disappointed at not meeting your Grace yesterday at the chapter of the Bath, where I was in hopes I should have had the satisfaction of seeing you.

The Earl of Roden to Wellington, 31 October 1834

Belvoir Park, Belfast. I came here last night after our great meeting at Hillsborough. Nothing could have been more satisfactory in every point of view; the numbers were very great and the respectability of landed proprietors not to be surpassed in any country in the world. You will find a tolerable account of it in the *Evening Mail*. The zeal and devotedness of our lower orders was most delightful and I doubt much whether it would be possible to get such a meeting in England. We had, according to calculation, about 10,000 men *round the platform*, which held 350 of the gentry. The whole road to Hillsborough and the town were also quite filled with persons who made up two-thirds of the meeting, so I think we may say *really* that there were about 30,000 people assembled at the meeting. The sentiments expressed by the speakers were warmly responded to by the people, and the Revd. Doctor Cook, a Presbyterian minister of great talent and influence, made one of the most efficient, and certainly at this time for the Church one of the most important speeches that could have been delivered. Everything seemed to favour us and I trust the effect both in England and Ireland will be obvious. The deputations from our Conservative Society go to England on the 20th of next month, when they are invited to attend the meeting at Liverpool, and at Bristol on the 26th. The enthusiasm of the Protestant multitude yesterday was very great and several of the merchants of Belfast came out to thank me for the interest which had been excited and the life which had been given to their trade by the movement which has been made in Protestant feeling, which they say has already given much more confidence amongst them. I think it very probable that the success of our meeting will induce others to come forward, and I am going into Belfast today to organize a great provincial meeting of Ulster to be held in the town of Belfast in the course of the month of January, so as to wind up our course before the meeting of Parliament.

I need not say how much obliged to you I always am for your kind suggestions as to the policy of our proceedings. Lord Clanwilliam was with us yesterday and, as one of our committee men, most active and useful. He told me he wrote to you last night, after the meeting, but I thought you would also wish to hear from me on the subject.

Benjamin Wyatt to Wellington, 31 October 1834

London. I trust that your Grace will forgive the liberty I take in trespassing upon you for a few minutes on the subject of such new buildings as may eventually be undertaken, in consequence of the late disastrous fire at Westminster.[1]

As it strikes me to be probable that, with a view to the construction of new Houses of Parliament, some committee of the Privy Council, or of the House of Peers, or of both houses united, may be formed for the purpose of considering the best place to be adopted, and for superintending the execution of the same; and as your Grace would, in such case, very probably be a member of that committee, I am anxious without further loss of time, to state to your Grace my hope that my name might be included among the architects to be called upon for designs on the occasion, assuring your Grace that I should be most sensible of the great obligation conferred on me by any steps which your Grace (either as a member of the supposed committee, or otherwise) should feel yourself justified and at liberty to take, in furtherance of my object in that respect.

In the event of any new building upon a comprehensive scale being undertaken for the purpose above referred to, whatever should be the site and style of architecture of such building, two objects at least I think present themselves as indispensably connected with the work: first, that the plan, in all its provisions and details, should be as perfect as experience and the ingenuity of man can render it, with respect to the facilities of business and the healthy and convenient accommodation of the two great bodies of the legislature; and secondly that the sober, chaste magnificence of the structure should be such as, at once, to render it a monument of the national taste, and an index of the state of the 'fine arts', at this time, in England. In addition, also, to these two

---

[1] The Houses of Parliament were destroyed by fire during the night of 16 October 1834.

indispensable objects, if the site of the buildings lately destroyed by fire should ultimately be decided on as the best for the new edifice, a third desideratum would then present itself, equally indispensable with the other two: namely that Westminster Hall should be so cleared from the excrescences which now surround it, as to stand forth in isolated majesty, amid the new pile (whether that pile should be of Norman character or not) maintaining its own intrinsical sublimity and interest, uncontaminated and undiminished by the contact of unworthy counterfeits, which, whilst intended to harmonize with, should in fact, as heretofore, grievously detract from their venerable prototype.

It will not escape your Grace's discernment that the present circumstances, as regards this locality, are widely different from those attendant on any former works connected with the various alterations and additions, which have, from time to time, taken place, as appertaining to the Houses of Parliament; for on all antecedent occasions the scope has been confined to adding a bit in one place and making a patch in another; which has, in some instances (and, in point of principle, most reasonably) led to the imitation (however imperfectly effected) of the ancient works, in designing the new ones; and has, in other instances (and not a few) afforded lamentable opportunity for the introduction of the most whimsical and incongruous trash that ever emanated from the caprice or sterility of any artist's brain; but, upon the present occasion a wide and tempting field is laid open for the execution of an uniform and consistent and, in every sense of the term, magnificent structure. The advantages obviously desirable in the way of fine feature from the adjacent bank of the Thames, the magnitude and interesting character of Westminster Hall, the propinquity and solemn aspect of the Abbey, the extent of the ground, with its various local circumstances and associations, all combine to facilitate and induce the production of one of the noblest and most imposing buildings in the world, in every particular of multifarious internal aptitude, and genuine and unequivocal external majesty and good taste, well suited to and worthy of the great council of the most enlightened and the greatest nation that ever yet existed.

Such is the building which the late calamity affords an opportunity of constructing; and I have not a doubt that your Grace will concur with me in feeling that to accomplish this great object in a satisfactory manner every preliminary question connected with the site, or the style of architecture, should be discussed with the most cautious and impartial deliberation; and that, in the selection of the design to be executed, no hasty or mistaken preferences or efforts of individual favor should be allowed to operate.

In soliciting your Grace's favorable notice of my pretensions to the distinction specified in the commencement of this letter, your Grace will, perhaps, permit me to remark that I have, at different times, been engaged in many important and arduous works in the line of my profession; and that, in no one instance, within my knowledge, has any architectural design of mine become a subject of animadversion or unfavorable criticism; but, on the contrary, those designs have invariably obtained for me a most gratifying tribute of unqualified, disinterested and spontaneous applause.

With respect to the heavy misfortune which fell upon me two years ago, through the misconduct and breach of faith of a relative, for whom I had become responsible to a very large amount, I should hope that a calamity thus hurled upon me by another—not attributable to any misconduct of my own, and from which no man, I believe, ever emerged with his principles of probity and honor more unsullied—would not be mixed up with my professional qualifications, either as regards talent or integrity, in any way to prejudice my fair pretensions to compete on any occasion with other professional men in the same pursuit.

Since your Grace last did me the honor to converse with me on my professional prospects, I have had the good fortune to be employed upon an extensive and important work for the Duke of Sutherland at his house in the Stable Yard; and although my employment in that instance is not without a very unpleasant drawback, it brings with it some great advantages, and helps considerably to sustain my hope that, by habitual industry, punctuality and perseverance in business, aided by the patronage of some few powerful friends, I shall ultimately rise above the first adverse consequences of my late misfortune.

The work in which I am engaged for the Duke of Sutherland extends to making the whole of the *designs* and *working drawings* for the completion of his house (including the design for the new attic story) whilst the superintendance of their practical execution is committed to Sir Robert Smirke.

The Duke's exact reasons for this arrangement I have never either ascertained or enquired, but from what has been stated to me, from very credible authority, I have cause to believe that those reasons rest very principally on a most erroneous impression that an architect requires a larger accumulated capital than I at present possess, to enable him to execute with facility and promptitude that portion of duty over an extensive work, which in this instance his Grace has allotted to Sir Robert Smirke. Regarding this impression as a mere mistake into which it is perhaps natural enough that his Grace should have fallen; and at the same time having received from him the most flattering approbation of my designs, together with many marks of kind consideration and good will, I cannot but acknowledge that I feel sincerely obliged to the Duke of Sutherland for that portion of his work which he has committed to my charge; and when I reflect on the fact that any good clerk of works could perform the duties assigned to Sir Robert Smirke in this instance; but that no clerk of works in existence could duly discharge those which are allotted to me, I neither feel mortified nor degraded by the arrangement.

I dare say that your Grace is perfectly aware that an architect's business does not require realized and accumulated *capital* to carry it on; it is for the contractors—the builders and master tradesmen—to purchase large stocks of material, and to pay journeymen artificers' wages; but an architect requires no stock in trade, has no journeymen artificers to pay, and needs no funds to conduct his business in all its branches and departments, beyond such as shall be adequate to the current expenses of his dwelling house, his person and his drawing office.

Such being the fact, it is obvious that if the honor and integrity of my principles be not compromised (and they never have been impeached, and are not impeachable) I am as eligible now, whilst I can manage to defray the expenses of my office, as ever I was for any employment in the line of my profession.

I hope that your Grace, considering the difficult position in which I am placed—that my life has been one of unremitting industry, that I have acquitted myself satisfactorily in a variety of laborious and confidential duties, as well out of as in my present profession, and that the evils are perilous which everyone, not in full prosperity, has more or less to combat in the prejudice of some and the positive and malignant hostility of others—will make allowance for the liberty I take in troubling your Grace with this letter; and forgive the trespass, as arising out of a natural (and I hope not blamable) anxiety to strengthen and give effect to my own immediate exertions by patronage so elevated and so powerful as that of your Grace.

The Earl of Aberdeen to Wellington, 2 November 1834

Haddo House. I very much agree with you in your estimate of the utility of Conservative meetings generally. The local effect, however, of some of them is certainly valuable. We have just had an instance of this at Aberdeen, where a dinner was given to my brother by his constituents, similar to that given to Murray at Perth. We had an attendance of more than seven hundred persons, which at this season of the year, and considering the nature of the country, was very respectable. It comprised a very large proportion of the wealth and respectability of the county, with some of the lower class of freeholders, who had been converted from Whiggery. The good I anticipate from it is the security of the county at the next election. I do not know that there was much danger, under any circumstances; but I should hope there would now be no attempt at an opposition. The demonstrations of the mob, properly so called, are certainly become more friendly in this part of the world.

I have not heard what took place at Lord Durham's dinner at Glasgow; but I presume in such a town there never can be any want of Radicals. He is not likely to be able to command his temper; and in that case, we may look for some useful kind of exhibition. I lately met Ellice at the Duke of Bedford's in the Highlands; he did not affect any sympathy with Lord Durham; nor indeed did he appear to think well of the position of the Government; but it is not from what he says that it is possible to know what he thinks.

We are waiting for an explanation of the fire, if explanation we shall ever have. I confess that I anticipate much greater mischief than the mere destruction of the two houses of Parliament. Many changes must now be made from necessity, which would have been resisted, or probably never attempted; and these will lead imperceptibly to the adoption of others more important and more injurious. Something will depend on the place where the Parliament may meet. I suppose the King will be very anxious to get rid of Buckingham House; but if it is ever to be fitted up as a palace, there will be an enormous expense incurred, both in destroying and restoring. In ordinary times an event like this would have injured the stability of a Government.

I see that the papers announce the return of Talleyrand; should this be correct, he will still for some time to come be the only representative of a great power in England. There seems to be a change of men about to take place at Paris; and probably the loss of Gérard will be of some importance to the Government. They must be uneasy and embarrassed by the proceedings in Spain. Matters are going too far, and the complexion of things at Madrid is becoming too republican for the peace and safety of Louis-Philippe. His card is a difficult one to play in the Peninsula. A revolution may be a good and a profitable thing for him; but a Jacobinical anarchy cannot accord with his plan of government.

It is not easy to understand the state of the Spanish war; but according to all appearances it may last for the rest of our lives; and I suppose these people, when once they are used to it, have no objection to this mode of existence.

The Earl of Clanwilliam to Wellington, [2 November 1834]

When a man speaks only once in forty years, he does not like to have platitudes put into his mouth which he never uttered; and as I have at last found a paper that does not play me this trick, I am ridiculous enough to send it to you. There is also a good report of Dr. Cook's very clever speech.

On looking back at our meeting, I think one of its essential features was the organization (and of which I claim the merit) by which we brought a very large proportion of the people to Hillsborough in bodies headed by the larger proprietors, who started at the head of their tenants and met bodies of 'neighbours and friends' at points announced by printed circular placards. Lord Roden thus came in with some say five, others eight thousand, and all of us in proportion. I am quite certain that this will, for a long time to come, be a bond of union available between me and the 2,000 who made my tail. To be sure, this would not be so feasible in England where the farms are four and five times larger than here. Another local result from the meeting will be the making the orthodox Presbyterians more steadily draw together with the Church of England. There was not one outrage, or even row after the meeting.

Undated, but docketed 2 November 1834 by Wellington's secretary. The meeting at Hillsborough took place on Thursday, 30 October.

The Earl of Rosslyn to Wellington, 3 November 1834

12 Chapel Street, Grosvenor Place. Private. I am very glad to hear that you are quite well, and I can perfectly understand the annoyance you receive from the incessant notice of the newspapers and interminable correspondence with which you are assailed; but the fact is that it is a tax which you must submit to pay for the unexampled pre-eminence to which you have raised yourself. Your health is a great public concern, and your opinions are of the highest interest to all. Some may fear you, and perhaps hate you, as the greatest and perhaps the only effectual obstacle to their plans for subverting all the valuable institutions of the country; many, very many, look up to you as the only hope upon which they can rest any rational chance of its salvation; and all friends and adversaries look to you with respect and admiration.

Public dinners are undoubtedly a great curse when you are compelled to suffer them; but on the other hand, when given to the Radicals they furnish much information and some amusement. I think the quarrel between Brougham and Durham is now nearly irreconcilable. I agree with you that Lord Howick and his brother are likely to throw themselves into Durham's party, if it were only from hatred and resentment to Brougham and Althorp; and in that case I think Grey will take no part.

Sir James Graham told me that Melbourne and the Chancellor have had a very hot dispute respecting the presentation to the living of Battersea, vacated by the promotion of Dr. Allen to the see of Bristol, Brougham claiming it as a Crown living under £20 per annum, in the King's book; Melbourne claiming it as a living devolved to the Crown by the appointment of a bishop, and consequently one upon which the King's pleasure is to be taken through him. The living, in ordinary circumstances, is in Lord Spencer's patronage, is worth from £1200 to £1800.

The Board of Works are beginning their operations to fit up the Painted Chamber and the Court of Requests (our old house) for the two houses.

The King however has not abandoned his scheme of fixing the Parliament, with all its appurtenances, permanently in Buckingham House. He sent a messenger to the Speaker to order him to attend him at Windsor on Friday, and he gave him orders to visit and examine the new palace and the adjoining grounds with a view to ascertain how far it might be practicable or convenient to establish both houses there with all their offices and accompaniments, and requiring him to report to *him directly*.

His Majesty wrote on the same night to Sir John Hobhouse to notify this commission so given, and to order him to furnish every assistance and information his department could afford to the Speaker in the execution of it. His Majesty also wrote to Lord Melbourne to acquaint him with the directions given to the Speaker.

Blore has been required to wait upon the Speaker today with all the plans and drawings, and the examination will take place today and Wednesday.

The Speaker, although he could not refuse to obey His Majesty's commands, stated that he could not presume to offer any opinion upon the expediency of removing the two houses from their ancient site, or, if removed, upon the propriety of placing them in or about the new palace, both because these are matters to be decided by His Majesty's prerogative with the advice of his responsible Ministers, and that he from long habits and old associations must be subject to great prejudices upon the point, but that he would obey the King's commands, if invited, to the enquiry and examination of how far the buildings could be adapted for the reception and accommodation of Parliament, if it should be ultimately resolved to place them in or about Buckingham House; for it seems to be supposed that the actual room for the sitting of one or both may be in addition to the palace. I thought it might interest you to know the true history of this curious transaction.

From all I can hear the King has been talking most bitterly against the Chancellor and publickly expressing his delight in the caricature of the rope dancer.

You know how little value I set on all such conversation; but I believe he is at present very full of this plan for the settlement of Parliament. He rests a great deal upon the absurdity and inconvenience of making any temporary building upon the old site, if it be in contemplation to erect the new edifice in nearly the same situation.

The Rev. Edward Cardwell to Wellington, 3 November 1834

St. Alban's Hall, Oxford. In continuation of my letter of Monday last, and presuming that your Grace is desirous of knowing all that occurs in connection with the important questions brought, under your Grace's direction, before the board of heads of houses, I have to state that at the meeting of this morning there was much conversation, and that the only point actually discussed was put into the following form, 'Is it expedient that any change should be made in the mode of admitting members of the university, as far as concerns subscription to the Thirty-nine Articles?' I regret to say that contrary to the expectation created on Monday last, the question was decided in the negative, the numbers being 10 and 7. It is intended however to propose at our next meeting a form of declaration in lieu of the present subscription; and it will probably be also proposed by way of amendment that a declaration should be made explanatory of the subscription, and the subscription itself should be continued. These matters occupied so much time that no other business was transacted.

Wellington to the Archbishop of Armagh, 3 November 1834

Walmer Castle. I have received two letters from the Duke of Gloucester pressing me to give my opinion upon the measures to be adopted by His Royal Highness and myself as Chancellors of the Universities of *Oxford* and *Cambridge* upon the subject of certain resolutions of the clergy in Ireland which are referred to both and of which His Royal Highness has, and I have not, received the communication.

The question upon which I wish to have your Grace's opinion, concluding that I shall receive the paper in question, is what is the course that you would wish or recommend that the Chancellors of the universities should follow and with what object in view.

I have already since the recess had some correspondence with Lord Roden upon Church affairs in Ireland and he did me the honor of coming here to converse with me upon them. I earnestly urged that he should take advantage of the enthusiasm which appeared to prevail at certain of the meetings of the Protestants in Ireland and make an effort to obtain something like an association, having for its avowed object to protect all, including the Church, in their rights and properties, and an engagement that they would each pay their dues to the Church and exert all their influence with their friends and neighbours and dependants to do the same. I have since urged upon Lord Roden's attention the expediency of the Irish landlords taking this course; and it is quite obvious that do what they may they will be taxed nearly to the amount of the tithe demandable by the Church, and it is better to pay the Church than pay others.

I told Lord Roden that which I am convinced is the truth. There will be no feeling here for the Irish Church or for Irish property unless it is made quite clear that the Irish gentry are making every exertion in their power to save the Church of England in Ireland from the ruin with which it is threatened. As soon as it will appear that the Irish gentry are not only not to gain by this system of oppression, but that they are disposed to make and are making every effort to relieve and assist the clergy, I think I could do a great deal not only in the universities but in the country at large to produce a feeling in their favour.

I have seen a good number of advertisements of the names of noblemen and gentlemen who had come forward to pay the tithes of their estates; and Lord Roden has told me that the disposition to do so is generally prevalent. I have likewise perused a letter from O'Connell which contains a stronger proof of the efficiency of such a system, if it could be generally adopted. Your Grace would probably let me know whether you have heard that many had determined that they would pay the tithes on their estates, and in general what is [the] state and what the prospects of the clergy in Ireland at the present moment. The Duke of Gloucester has enquired from me whether it is wished that we the Chancellors, and eventually that the universities, should subscribe towards any fund to be formed by the Association of Clergymen in Dublin. I don't think that it is quite clear from what I have seen in the newspapers and I shall be much obliged to you if you will let me know.

From what I have above stated, your Grace will observe that I am not very sanguine in my expectations of the amount of a subscription till the publick will be satisfied in respect to the conduct of the Irish noblemen and gentlemen.

Wellington to Lord FitzGerald, 3 November 1834

Walmer Castle. I was very much obliged to you for Dr. Croly's pamphlet; and your letter. I had read the pamphlet with much interest. I am not surprised to learn that it makes an extraordinary sensation.

He states the evil and his notion of the remedy. What he does not state is the mode in which the remedy can be applied. There lies the difficulty of the case. It has its relations with our ecclesiastical position not only in Ireland but in England and Scotland.

I have been very anxious about the advantages to be derived from the feeling which has been manifested in Ireland in favour of the Church; and I urged Lord Roden at a very early period to avail himself of the excitement which had been raised to obtain from the Protestant nobility and gentry some declaration and act which would give real aid to the Church; and which I warranted to him would do the Protestants more good in this country and excite a more general interest in their favour and in support of the connection than anything they could do.

I am happy to learn your opinion of the result up to this moment; and I confess that I hope still more, if the Protestant nobility and gentry will act with prudence and discretion.

I earnestly recommended that the Orangemen should be kept in the background; and it is curious enough that O'Connell and I should have found each other on the same grounds in more than one part of this discussion.

He makes all the Protestants of Ireland Orangemen. I say keep yourselves clear of the Orangemen. He says that in an Irish question between Protestants and Roman Catholics all England will go with the Protestants. I say the same. He adds England will not support the Orangemen. I say the same.

I confess that it is not easy to throw overboard such a party as the Orangemen; and we must suffer a little inconvenience from former follies. But keep them out of sight. Don't allow them to bluster and bully. Put forward men of moderate principles and good conduct. Do a great deal; and say but little; and above all support the Government in all that is right and give them every assistance in maintaining order; and do not attempt to undo what has been settled; and the Irish Protestants will soon find themselves in a position very different from that in which they have been lately.

I should agree with you in respect to O'Connell and the Government, if he had not written to Lord Durham. He has thus drawn the sword and thrown away the scabbard.

The quarrel between Brougham and Lord Durham is in earnest. Great efforts were made to prevent disclosures at Glasgow, and Lord Grey was brought to interfere. I should suspect from this interference and from what Lord Durham said that they are more apprehensive of the progress that we are making in this country, in Scotland and in Ireland than I think they have reason to be; and that they do not think that they can venture to quarrel amongst themselves openly. Lord Durham says so clearly.

They have however quarrelled in reality. Will much advantage be acquired from the concealment of the quarrel? Some may be derived from the concealment for a time of the circumstances under which the Reform Bill was brought in and passed. But the existence of the quarrel cannot be concealed and no advantage can be derived from the attempt to conceal it.

This letter is the original, which was subsequently returned. There is also a copy in the Wellington Papers.

The Rev. Charles Boyton to Wellington, 4 November 1834

Glendoaen, Letterkenny. Upon my return home today I found a letter of Lord Roden's, dated the 24th of October, in which he says that your Grace thought it would be advantageous if a speech containing some statements in reference to the outrages going forward for some time in Ireland were published. There are only two of these to which your Grace I think can refer: one was published, and I have written to Dublin to have it forwarded to Walmer in covers, under an ounce in weight. The second to which it is likely the reference is made has not been printed by itself, but shall shortly be sent in like manner.

I take the liberty of writing directly to your Grace, instead of communicating through Lord Roden, as this would add three or four days to the delay already incurred.

Would you be good enough to say in any of your communications to Lord Roden whether Lord Wellesley's dispatches and the police reports presented to the House of Lords last spring, and from which your Grace and Lord Grey both read extracts, have ever been printed in the proceedings, or if they are to be got at. I have not been able to find any peer here who can give me this information.

Your Grace, I understand, refers to the necessity of collecting, against the opening of Parliament, facts about the outrages. Now there is a great difficulty of doing this. If the reports of the inspectors of police were moved for, the case must come out. I take the liberty of repeating an occurrence which recently took place while I was in Dublin, which will shew that the system is still going forward. Mr. Littleton was visiting Mr. Crampton, the Surgeon-General, at his place near Dublin, when the following conversation took place. He said, 'There never was such a country in history as Ireland, or such a system of cold-blooded assassination. You may take a map of Ireland and draw a line dividing the Protestant from the Catholic part of it; you may paint the latter a deep crimson and shade off the boundary line, as the population mingles, till you come into the Protestant portion of it. And that', he said, 'would represent the state of crime and its locality.' 'How many murders', he added, 'do you think are averaged in this country?' Mr. Crampton said he did not know; he supposed two a week. 'No', said the other, 'they average two a day'; adding, 'the public hear nothing of this. The police returns of murders to Government average two a day.' He went on to make Mr. Crampton name a day, and his daughter who was present named another, and he said he would, when he got home, state the numbers which had been reported for each of those days. And his letter in reply stated three murders to have been committed on each of the days in question.

If this be true, and I have reason to believe it quite accurate, the police returns (if the Government would give them) would make an extraordinary document, more particularly if the original reports of the subconstables be furnished as they were to the tithe committees of 1832, for the detail gives a reality and power, which general descriptions fail to do.

Wellington to the Rev. Edward Cardwell, 5 November 1834

Walmer Castle. I am very sorry indeed for a decision to which the board have come, more particularly upon so close a division. It may be relied upon that the matter cannot remain as it is after what has passed. However I will support and maintain whatever may be decided.

I wish that the board could know what is passing in the world; they would see the necessity for considering the opinions of moderate men.

William Burge to Wellington, 6 November 1834

Lincoln's Inn. According to that system of delusion by imposition which the present ministry have been practising ever since the Jamaica legislature passed their slavery abolition Act, I dare say the newspapers will be made to represent everything there as going on most prosperously.

Now I send your Grace, from a mass of letters which I have received by the packet today, one which gives the *least unfavorable* account of the present disorganized state of Jamaica. The writer is an experienced planter and his description is confirmed by every other letter I have received. Indeed he falls far short of others in the anticipation of the evils which await the colony. Would your Grace believe that after divesting the local magistracy of all authority, which they have supplied by stipendiary magistrates; and although there are twenty-one parishes, which though called parishes are large English counties, none less in extent than the county of Bedford, there are only thirty stipendiary magistrates for the whole island? They literally cannot hear one-third of the complaints of apprentice and manager which ought to be promptly decided. On the estate of the President of the Council a party of apprentices set fire to the buildings in the very presence of the special magistrates.

The Government have given £12,500 to send out some Baptist missionaries, who were suspected of having instigated the late rebellion; but not one member of the Church of England has been yet sent.

Knowing the interest your Grace takes in the welfare of the colonies and how zealously and powerfully you laboured to avert those evils which you predicted, I have thought your Grace would like to know what really is the state of Jamaica. The other colonies are in the same situation. It is my firm conviction that, unless some very decisive and effectual means are adopted to counteract the present disposition of the negroes and to promote something like industry, Jamaica and the other colonies will cease to be inhabited by any Europeans.

Lord Sligo's private secretary has come home by this packet and I am sorry to perceive in his Lordship [a w][1]ant of discretion and judgment in some of h[is late][1] proceedings.

PS. Fearing the enclosure might be too much for a frank, I have sent it under a separate cover to your Grace.

Viscount Mahon to Wellington, 7 November 1834

Hôtel des Iles Britanniques, Rue de la Paix, Paris. The dissolution of the ministry which has just taken place in France induces me to think that

---

[1] Paper torn.

your Grace may not be displeased to hear some particulars of that event and tempts me to take the liberty of addressing you.

From a very authentic source of information, which I abstain from naming in a letter, I can assure your Grace that the common idea of the amnesty having caused this dissolution in the Cabinet is unfounded. It is true that Marshal Gérard retired on that ground. But after his retirement there was no longer any schism between the rest on that account; and it was agreed either that there should be no amnesty at all or that it should appear as a legislative act sanctioned by the two chambers and not as a mere royal *ordonnance*.

The cause of the subsequent resignations is to be found in the personal rivalry of M. Thiers and M. Guizot. Both of them were in a very similar position: both mere writers before the revolution of 1830, and both raised by that event, the first from a newspaper office and the second from a professor's chair, into high administrative functions. From this very similarity a great degree of competition and a strong feeling of hatred had arisen between them. On the retirement of Marshal Gérard, each as a trial of strength attempted to name the new President of the Council, M. Thiers proposing Count Molé and M. Guizot his old friend, the Duke de Broglie. Neither party being inclined to recede, all have gone out; and the King, as your Grace already knows, has desired Count Molé to form a new Cabinet.

It is considered very doubtful whether Count Molé can succeed. In all probability he will connect himself with M. Thiers and those other ex-Ministers who may have voted for Count Molé as President; and it is rumoured that he will endeavour at once to conciliate and remove the Duke de Broglie by offering him the embassy to England. The King's own wish is to have Marshal Soult as Minister of War, but it is not yet known whether the Marshal, who is not now in Paris, would be inclined to return to office.

I have particularly endeavoured to ascertain how far the return of Soult might affect the Spanish question; and I understand that he was always strongly, though not publicly, opposed to any intervention on the part of France, and one day said in Council that he would sooner cut off his right hand than send a single soldier into Spain. The King takes at present precisely the same view.

The want of any able men to put forward is represented to be extreme. The revolution of 1830, by converting so many noisy declaimers into governing statesmen, has laid bare their incapacity and shown how much more easy it is to overthrow than to rebuild or to maintain. Nearly all the *liberal* reputations of France have been already shipwrecked on the rock of office. To this must be added that a very large majority of the upper classes and nearly all the old families are averse to the present dynasty and will not serve it, so that Louis-Philippe is compelled in all his combinations to overlook the highest and to descend several steps in the social scale. From both these causes combined there is felt, I understand, the greatest possible want of efficient men.

M. Dupin is sometimes spoken of, but those who know him best say that he is quite unfit for office from his fretfulness, his impatience and his inconsistencies. Like another celebrated man nearer home, he is no less volatile than able and very dangerous if either attacked or confided in. As one instance of his roughness I may mention that the other day at Compiègne, being in a carriage with the Duke of Orléans, that young prince began to praise his father's government: '*Il parle beaucoup trop!*' was the only answer of Dupin. Certainly nothing could be more true but also nothing more indiscreet. And moreover, to a prince who chatters fifteen hours a day, no one who is not a good listener and is not blessed with patience can be a successful minister.

Having mentioned the Duke of Orléans, I may observe to your Grace that I hear his abilities are much superior to what is commonly supposed. This I learn on the authority of M. Arago, who being in violent Republican opposition has no motive for flattery. He was speaking of it to an acquaintance of mine when crossing the other day from Dover to Calais: he said of the Duke of Orléans, '*Soyez sûr qu'il est plein d'intelligence*', and he added that he (Arago), having been professor at some college or lyceum where the young duke was pupil, had found that out of 200 essays given in on some occasion that of His Royal Highness was fifth or sixth in merit. From other quarters I hear that the Duke has taken great pains to conciliate and please the army, and not without success.

It is very remarkable at present how completely the whole newspaper press of Paris is arrayed against the Government. I am sure it is no exaggeration to say that Charles X in the two last and most unpopular years of his reign had not less of this kind of support. At that time too there were few, if any, direct attacks upon the sovereign; now there are daily very rough and insulting ones. The theatres likewise take a wide and pernicious range both as to religion and politics; as to the former, even the most sacred subjects are brought upon the stage.

Two extracts from today's play-bill will convince your Grace of this:[1]

L'ENFER

Satan	St-Ernest
L'archange	Lajariette
Un Marchand	Montigny
Puck	Guilluy
Ariel	Vigel
L'Envie	François
Une juive	mesdames Sophie
Lilith	Maria
La Mort	Honorine
La Paresse	Héloïse
La Luxure	Léonie
L'Orgueil	Adèle
La Colère	Laure
La Gourmandise	Irma

LE JUGEMENT DERNIER
(Epilogue)

Le juif	Montigny
Barrabas	Emile
L'archange	Lajariette
Le démon	St-Ernest
Napoléon	Léon
Marc-Aurèle	Gilbert
Franklin	Alexandre
Le Tems	Laplaine
La Prière	Sophie

I rejoice very much to hear that your Grace appears in such good health at Walmer Castle. We intended to have been at Deal before this time, but have been a good deal delayed by Lady Mahon's indisposition and were kept for eight days at a little town between Geneva and Paris; however she is now, thank Heaven, quite well.

---

[1] Pasted on to the letter.

The Earl of Rosslyn to Wellington, 8 November 1834

Chapel Street, Grosvenor Place. I have very little new to tell you. The Speaker visited the palace with Blore the day before yesterday, and found that there was no room in the building that would accommodate either house of Parliament, but much more than enough for all other purposes connected with both. The King, I hear, still clings to the hope of disposing of the new palace in that manner; but he has not yet received the Speaker's report.

Ellice's resignation is declared and his language is extremely strong against Durham.

The Privy Council have agreed upon their reports upon the inquiry into the causes of the fire; and the examination leaves no doubt that it was accidental and arose from burning the tallies.

I had been invited by a letter from Lord Melbourne to attend the examination, with the Speaker, Lord Camden, Lord Strangford, and others not of the Ministry, and I was again summoned upon my return to town.

When the examination was completed the Speaker, the Judge-Advocate and I were requested to prepare a précis of the evidence and draw up the report, which under the circumstances I did not think it right to decline, more especially as the press and some of our eager partisans were very much disposed to impute the fire to design and to give credit to Mr. Cooper's testimony, who swore he had heard of the fire at Dudley within three hours of its breaking out. His story has been completely disproved, and all the circumstances of any importance to it clearly negatived by other witnesses. I go to Middleton today.

Sir Robert Gardiner to Wellington, 8 November 1834

Melbourne Lodge, Claremont. I venture to send your Grace the enclosed extract of a letter just received, as it announces the fulfilment of nearly all the results foreseen and predicted in former letters, written in the first days of general anxiety on the slave question. It is otherwise no more than a confirmation of the public intelligence, but it comes from unerring authority.

Enclosure: Jamaica, 23 September 1834.

We are far from being settled: the great want of means which I mentioned in my last, as to magistrates to make the new system work, becomes every day more apparent. We have already lost four; and with the work laid down for them, no strength or constitution can stand. It would be impossible in any country; but in this broiling place it's out of the question. It is in fact cruel to make these magistrates perform a duty, with certain death before them. Besides, the income, which to be sure is but a secondary consideration in the matter, is totally inadequate to the situation. Unless some change is made, *and immediately*, by the Government at home, and a system hit on of employment by wages, *this island is gone*. The determination on the part of the negro not to do more than he likes is general; and the new magistrates know nothing, and can know nothing, of what actually constitutes a proper day's work. There is no disposition to resist overtly; but, what is much worse, they are all passive: they turn out at the proper hours, for instance, but *work* they will not.

Wellington to the Rev. Charles Boyton, 9 November 1834

Walmer Castle. I am very much obliged to you for your letter of the 4th. I had already received the little pamphlet and I shall be very anxious to receive the other to which you refer.

It is very desirable that these and some other matters relating to Irish affairs should be well reviewed in the *Quarterly Review* which will come out at the commencement of the session of Parliament, in order to draw the publick attention to the truth. Among these I propose to include the papers laid before the House of Lords in the last session of Parliament. I will send you a copy of these papers as soon as I return to London.

Your anecdote of the interview between Mr. Littleton and Mr. Crampton is very interesting. I should doubt the truth of the statement of the former that two *murders* were committed every day. Two or three outrages called insurrectionary certainly are. The police reports as laid before Parliament by the existing administration are made up in the same, or nearly the same form as at the period when I was in office, and I don't think that the present administration have till lately had any interest in falsifying them. On the contrary, they had always a case to make out to support some measure proposed. The increase of this description of crime appears on the face of these police reports to be enormous compared even with the worst of the times when I was in office. But I will have an endeavour to obtain a correct report, made up to the last moment when Parliament will meet.

I am very anxious to know how the Church in Ireland will get on in the course of this and the next month.

The Rev. Edward Cardwell to Wellington, 10 November 1834

St. Alban's Hall, Oxford. In continuation of the reports made by me to your Grace on the two former meetings of the weekly board, I beg to state that the proceedings of this morning have been more satisfactory than might have been expected from the resolution of Monday last.

In the first instance it was proposed that a declaration should be added to the present method of subscription (on admission into the university) and explanatory of the meaning of it. This motion had only one voice in its favour. It was then proposed that the following declaration should be made in lieu of subscription: 'I A.B. declare that I maintain, so far as I know, the doctrines and discipline of the united Church of England and Ireland, as expressed in her Thirty-nine Articles; that I will conform to her worship; and am ready and willing to be instructed in her articles of faith, according to the statutes of this university.' This motion was carried by the majority of 1, the numbers being 11 and 10. Five members of the board were absent (two from old age, and three from illness), four of whom would probably have been opposed to the motion. It is apprehended that an attempt will be made on Monday next to neutralize what has been done.

I afterwards proposed that a committee should be appointed to examine into the Aularian Statutes, with reference to the points suggested by your Grace, and to report thereupon to the board. There was a decided unwillingness to appoint a committee; but I was reminded that it was still open for myself or any other member of the board to bring forward any specific alterations.

From this and other symptoms I fear it is not probable that any general revision of the statutes of the university will be attempted.

Princess Lieven to Wellington, 10 November 1834

St. Petersbourg. Je trouve bien triste, monsieur le Duc, d'être si loin de vous; mais il est plus triste encore d'en être oublier. Mes meilleurs souvenirs d'Angleterre sont ceux auxquels vous êtes associés; mon amitié pour vous est aujourd'hui comme elle était dans ces bons tems; permettez-moi donc de venir réclamer mes titres à votre bon souvenir. Dites-moi un mot et permettez-moi de ne pas m'oublier.

L'Empereur a eu un vif regret de ne point vous voir arriver. Vous manquiez a cette superbe cérémonie de la colonne, dernier hommage rendu à la mémoire d'Alexandre. Mais il vous a fallu assister aux derniers moments du parlement *dernier* dans toute la force du terme, puisque la destruction matérielle est venue rejoindre à une destruction morale presque consommée. C'est une frappante catastrophe et qui doit avoir agi fortement sur les esprits en Angleterre. Pour moi, de bien loin, j'en ai été vivement émue. Tout est donc réformé, même cette vieille arène si pleine de grands et glorieux souvenirs. Ma pensée est bien plus en Angleterre qu'elle n'est ici. Je m'occupe de vous, monsieur le Duc. Je vois que vous êtes occupés du massacre des innocens. Quand donc chasserez-vous autre chose que des bêtes?

Je pense un peu à la péninsule aussi. Quoique Don Pedro soit une espèce de débarras je doute beaucoup que le Portugal en aille mieux. Palmella manque de deux choses essentielles: du caractère et du bonheur.

Quant à l'Espagne c'est le chaos. Banqueroute, choléra, guerre civile, rien n'y manque. Ferdinand a fait un beau cadeau à l'Espagne par son testament. Louis-Philippe essaye de faire de la royauté d'autrefois. Je souhaite que cela lui réussisse. En se consolidant il assure le maintien de la paix; et elle est bonne à tout le monde.

L'Empereur est amoureux de sa femme. Il est allé la voir pour quelques jours à Berlin. Voilà tout le secret d'un voyage auquel on va en attribuer mille autres. Mon mari n'a pas accompagné son jeune élève. C'est des courses de courrier qui ne vont plus à soixante ans. L'Empereur sera de retour dans dix-huit jours; l'Impératrice et le Grand Duc au commencement de décembre. J'ai le très grand plaisir, monsieur le Duc, de voir ici le Marquis de Douro. L'Empereur l'attendait à Moscou et j'ai bien regretté qu'il n'y soit pas allé pendant ce séjour du maître qui a été bien brillant. A son retour il n'a fait que traverser Petersbourg, de sorte que ce ne sera qu'à son retour de Berlin qu'il verra votre fils.

Nous avons trois pieds de neige, un ciel noir; mais j'ai une maison bien belle et bien chaude: il faut essayer de ne pas regarder par la fenêtre.

Adieu, monsieur le Duc; je ne vous demande qu'une seule faveur, mais elle m'est bien chère: ne m'oubliez pas et aimez-moi un peu.

John Wilson Croker to Wellington, 11 November 1834

The Grange, Alresford. In one of your late letters you mentioned that you had heard an indifferent account of Mr. Baring, which was quite true: he has been very seriously troubled with his leg, but is now mending. Bad setting the original fracture and bad country surgery occasioned a sore which was for a long time very obstinate and gave a good deal of uneasiness, but it has now granulated and is, I believe, all but healed.

I came here yesterday, and he was consulting me about houses by the seaside at Anglesey Ville, near Gosport, where I was this summer, but today's post brought a letter from Sir Robert Wilson, conveying your Grace's kind offer of Walmer Castle which I presume will be thankfully accepted because it has an inestimable advantage in Mr. Baring's condition, which no seaside lodging-house could have: that the accommodation is all on *one floor*; for, poor fellow, he can only move in wheelchairs.

We hear today that Lord Spencer is dead and that Lord John Russell has resigned *in Ellice's train*; this last circumstance I was not prepared for; but I had heard three months ago that Johnny was going; but why he and Ellice should go *together* I know not.

The King talks very slightingly of Brougham and is, I really believe, a little piqued at being made Brougham's Scotch *hobby-horse*.

I return to Molesey on Friday.

PS. Peel, I hear, passed through Milan the 28th.

Alexander Baring to Wellington, 11 November 1834

The Grange, Alresford. Permit me to express my grateful acknowledgment for the very kind interest you have been so good as to take in the sufferings which have kept me confined for the last three months. Sir Robert Wilson writes to Mrs. Baring that you have even added to our obligations by the friendly offer of Walmer Castle for a short residence by the seaside, which I am advised to make to complete my perfect recovery. If I were quite sure that this very acceptable proposal would not on further consideration expose you to inconvenience or interfere with any other disposal you might wish to make of this delightful maritime residence, I should be tempted to the indiscretion of accepting it. The truth is that I am recovered from my accident and am about to dismiss my surgeons, but it will take me some time to perfect my walking, and a house, and still more a castle where I should not have to climb up and down stairs, would be a very great benefit, to say nothing of the superiority over ordinary lodging-houses at this season of the year. If Wilson has made no mistake and if nothing has since occurred to alter your plans, Mrs. Baring and I will therefore thankfully accept this great act of kindness for three or four weeks between this and Christmas, always however on the positive condition that you turn us out at a day's warning if anything occurs to make a resumption of your castle desirable.

PS. The news of Lord Spencer's death reaches us this morning. This is an event of great importance and must add immensely to existing difficulties. The hold of Althorp on the House of Commons is a feature in our position seldom sufficiently appreciated. I do not see who is to take his place.

Viscount Mahon to Wellington, 11 November 1834

Paris. The new Ministry being at last appointed, I take the liberty of addressing to your Grace some further information on that subject.

In my last letter I believe I mentioned to your Grace that great doubts were entertained whether Count Molé could succeed in forming a Cabinet. The difficulties he encountered from personal piques and rivalries proved even more formidable than had been expected and induced him in four and twenty hours to throw up his commission. He was succeeded by M. Humann, and M. Humann as some say, but this does not rest on very sure authority, by M. Guizot. All these attempts at reconstruction failed, the refusals received were very numerous, and I understand moreover that some very unbecoming scenes took place, even in the royal presence, from several of the ex-Ministers abusing one another violently face to face. Under these circumstances Louis-Philippe, losing patience, determined to form his Cabinet himself; that is, instead of entrusting its selection to some individual, he picked out individuals according to his own fancy, from various parties, without any previous concert or combination and perhaps even no personal acquaintance between them. The result has been that curious piece of patchwork which your Grace will see in the papers and which has filled everyone here with the utmost surprise.

It will, I think, strike your Grace that, distinguished as France has been in the revolution by great generals and skilful diplomatists, she has never yet during thirty years had at the head of her war and foreign departments such utterly undistinguished names. Who, out of the sphere of the French Court, ever heard of Messrs. Bernard and Bresson? Everybody goes about and asks who they are. M. Bernard it appears was a good officer under Napoleon who was so mortified at the fall of his master that he went into voluntary exile in America till the revolution of 1830, since which Louis-Philippe has named him his aide-de-camp. M. Bresson is never supposed to have shown any great diplomatic ability; he is living quietly at Berlin, where as your Grace knows there is not much to negotiate, and may very possibly decline the dangerous honour designed him.

One ministerial office (Public Instruction) is still left open. It has been offered to M. Sauzet, an eminent lawyer at Lyons, and his answer is expected. M. Sauzet is chiefly known as having pleaded in defence of the Ministers of Charles X who signed the *ordonnances* and if he accepts he will sit in the same Cabinet with M. Persil who impeached them!

The Duke of Bassano has taken very little active part in politics since the restoration and even under Napoleon was, I believe, chiefly known as the ready and obedient organ of the imperial will. It is on a similar principle that Louis-Philippe is said to have selected not only him but his colleagues. The King is determined to have good listeners: men who will not interrupt his harangues nor contradict his ideas, servants to execute and not counsellors to guide. At least, if this be not the principle of the new ministerial assemblage, it would be difficult to name any other. It has no one common quality or designation; it is a collection of names never before joined together and bearing the same resemblance to common Ministries as a mob does to a regiment. There is only one opinion as to the weakness and instability of the new administration, unless its existence should be prolonged beyond all reasonable calculations by the division of its adversaries.

As to the comparative strength of parties, either in the chambers or in the country, it is very difficult to obtain anything like positive information, and I would not intrude upon your Grace's time with vague conjectures. On this topic the people one speaks to are very apt to answer according to their wishes and to exaggerate the strength of those with whom they agree. I think, however, that I can observe that the King has entirely lost whatever degree of personal popularity he may ever have possessed with any party, but that the great body of the nation are wearied with agitation and determined to have quiet and order; and that therefore at this moment they would steadily resist attempts at change in any direction. I think too that the national animosity against England has very much declined, as far at least as one can judge from outward appearances. Their gross ignorance of everything connected with our country still continues the same. The newspapers daily teem with the most absurd instances of this. I inclose one paragraph which may probably surprise your Grace, if any proof of French ignorance can.[1]

GAZETTE DE FRANCE. November 8, 1834

Il y eut quelque temps en Angleterre une secte connue sous le nom des anti-vivans. Les membres de cette corporation se donnaient la mort pour les motifs les plus frivoles. Deux gentlemen *se tuèrent à peu de jours de distance; l'un avait laissé sur son bureau ces mots:* I am tedious, *et l'autre ceux-ci:* It is too cold.

The Archbishop of Armagh to Wellington, 11 November 1834

Armagh. I beg your Grace to accept my thanks for the kind interest which your letter of the third evinces on behalf of the Irish Church. In answer to your Grace's question as to the course which it is wished that the chancellors of the English universities should follow, in consequence of having received a copy of resolutions passed by a society recently formed in Dublin for assisting the Irish clergy in the recovery of their rights, I take the liberty of suggesting that it is the object of the Clerical Society to lay before the British public and those influential bodies, more especially, which have the closest connexion with the Established Church the real state to which the Irish branch of that Church is reduced by illegal combinations, and to point out the necessity of active co-operation on the part of the English friends of the Church for preserving the clergy from a total loss of income. It is hoped by these and similar remonstrances the members of the English

---

[1] Pasted on to the paper.

Church will be made to feel that theirs is a common cause with that of their brethren in Ireland. And it is considered that a formal declaration published by the universities, expressive of their sympathy in the sufferings of the Irish Church and of their sense of the common danger with which not only ecclesiastical but every other species of property is menaced, should a lawless resistance to the just claims of the clergy be sufficed to prevail much longer unchecked by the exertions of government, would awaken the public mind as to the impolicy of the temporizing measures which have been adopted in Ireland. Such a declaration, it is felt, would afford a most seasonable support and consolation to the Irish Church in this crisis of embarrassment and danger. It would amount to a protest against the supineness with which the attacks on life and property have been regarded by the Government; and it might contain a resolution to stand by the Irish Church, the integrity of which has been solemnly ratified by the Act of Union, and the permanence of which is alike demanded on every principle of policy and religion. It is possible that the example of the universities would be followed by other constitutional bodies in England or perhaps by the clergy generally, and thus call out a demonstration of public feeling which it will be unwise in the Government to resist. The Irish radicals would thus learn that in their attempts to overthrow the Irish Church and to effect a repeal of the Union, measures which they now avowedly connect, they will have to combat not only the feeble efforts of the Irish Church left to its own means of protection but the united strength of what is most powerful and respected in Great Britain. The line which the Clerical Society has marked out for its operations is to encourage the formation of similar associations for mutual support in the several dioceses, to procure and communicate such authentic information as may enable our friends in Parliament to advocate the case of the Church on its true grounds, and to obtain legal opinions on the difficulties that may occur in the recovery of ecclesiastical income and the most prudent method of enforcing its payment. Your Grace is aware that a Conservative Society has been already formed in Dublin by many distinguished laymen. The exertions of this society have been eminently serviceable to the Irish Church by manifesting the rank and quality of its supporters, by encouraging landlords to take upon themselves the liability of tithe, and by affording pecuniary aid to the Clerical Society in the prosecution of its purposes. The recovery of tithe, where resistance is so general and where every device of chicanery is to be encountered, will be necessary attended with a heavy expense, ruinous to individual clergymen. For common support the clergy have, I believe, in most dioceses taxed themselves at the rate of 5 per cent., payable by instalments on their parochial income, a measure which is considered not open to legal objections. It is a tax which your Grace will observe is on an income still in jeopardy and which by the most successful exertions cannot be received for many months to come. Meanwhile, as your Grace will find by the accompanying letter from Lord Duncannon in answer to a memorial which I also transmit, the Government are about to press on the clergy for the first instalment of the monies advanced under the Act of last session for their relief. The embarrassment thus occasioned by the vigorous enforcement of the Government claims may be readily imagined: a 5 or so per cent., it is to be feared, will be inadequate to defray the expense of the collection. But in transmitting to the chancellors of the universities a copy of their resolutions, it was not so much the object of the Clerical Society to obtain an encrease of their funds as to secure a sanction of their measures and a bold profession of adherence to a cause in which all property and all principle, civil and religious, are at stake.

I am happy to inform your Grace that your prudent and just suggestions to Lord Roden and the heads of the Conservative party appear to have had their due weight, as in very many instances the Conservatives have shewn themselves forward to follow up their professions by throwing themselves between the clergy and the refractory tithe-payer. But I still fear that the landlords who have manifested the sincerity of their declarations by their acts will be found few in number when compared with those who stand aloof and take no part whatever in a danger, which if not averted will speedily come home to themselves in the form of resistance to rent and repeal of the legislative union. An account however of the landlords who have taken upon themselves the liability is preparing, and as soon as I receive it, I will forward it to your Grace.

PS. Please to direct to Armagh, and if not inconvenient frank your letters.

First enclosure: Memorial to the Lord-Lieutenant.

The undersigned archbishops and bishops request most respectfully to represent to his Excellency, the Lord-Lieutenant, the great anxiety and uneasiness felt by the clergy of Ireland on the subject of the debt due by them on the 1st of November, for the first instalment of the loan advanced by Parliament, on account of the arrears of tithe and tithe composition for the years 1831 and 1832 and for the tithe and composition of 1833. The prelates beg further to represent that the loan was accepted by the clergy in the full persuasion that, by restoration of order and of obedience to the laws, or by some equitable arrangement for the composition of tithe, they would have been able to recover these arrears and to provide for the payment of the instalments as they became due. But the disposition to resist the collection of tithe composition still so openly manifested and avowed in several parts of Ireland must be well known to Government, as well as the depressed state of the markets with respect to all matters of agricultural produce, which greatly increases the present difficulty of collection. Even in peaceable times the clergy in general did not demand the tithe composition due in November until the months of January, February and March. The determination therefore on the part of Government to enforce from the clergy payment at the time required by the 3 and 4 William IV c. 100 must involve the clergy in extreme difficulty and embarrassment. The clergy feel grateful to Government for the relief afforded to them, which proved most seasonable under the distressing circumstances to which resistance and combination had reduced them, and they feel satisfied that you! will not increase those difficulties and embarrassments which they lent their aid to remove.

October 30, 1834.

John G. Armagh	Robert Clogher
Richard Dublin	J. Elphin
Richard Cashel	J. Dromore
Power Tuam	Richard Derry
Nathaniel Meath	Richard Down and Connor
Charles Kildare	Thomas Leighlin and Ferns
George Kilmore	S. Cork and Ross

Second enclosure: Marquess Wellesley to the Archbishop of Armagh, 4 November 1834

Dublin Castle. Your Grace may be assured that I have received the representation of the archbishops and bishops, transmitted by your Grace, with every sentiment of respect which so high an authority demands from me. His Majesty's Government has not been insensible to the difficulties and embarrassments in which the clergy of Ireland must be involved at this period of time, unless some equitable arrangements had been previously made by law for the final settlement of the question of tithes. Accordingly after having provided for the immediate relief of the clergy by a temporary loan of one million sterling, a bill was introduced into Parliament under the direction of Government for the permanent relief of that body, by which in the first place such of the clergy as had availed themselves of the temporary loan of one million sterling were absolved altogether from their debt to the Crown, accruing on the 1st of November 1834. The payment of the first instalment was charged on the landowners, but was postponed by that bill until the 1st of November 1835. The unappropriated surplus of the sum of one million (which was calculated to amount to £300,000[1]) was rendered applicable to the payment of arrears of tithe on composition still due to the clergy for the years 1831-2-3; and such of the clergy as might take relief from this source were to be in the same manner absolved from repayment to the Crown, and the debt was to be charged on the owners of the first estate of inheritance on the land. The Crown was then charged with the collection both of rent charges and instalments, and ample security was given to the clergy throughout Ireland for receiving £77.10.0 per cent. on the amount of the composition due to each. Your Grace will observe that under this plan an arrangement was contemplated for the final settlement of the loan of a million advanced to the clergy, without any further pressure for repayment. Thus His Majesty's Government has manifested the most sincere desire not only to relieve the clergy of Ireland from all immediate distress but to provide effectually for the interests of that body by an equitable and permanent arrangement. The failure of this arrangement for the present has produced all the difficulties which were foreseen, and which have been most deeply lamented by His Majesty's Government, more especially because those embarrassments are now beyond the reach of any immediate remedy. The Act of 3 and 4 William IV c. 100 is imperative with respect to the repayment of the instalment due on the 1st of November 1834; nor is it in the power of the officers of the Crown (without the authority of a new law) to relieve the parties affected by the law now in force. The time and mode

[1] MS: £3,000,000.

of requiring this repayment have been the subject of communication between this Government and the Government of England; and I will direct the Chief Secretary in a few days to communicate to your Grace the instructions which have been received from the Treasury on these points. Your Grace cannot doubt that I will submit the representation of the archbishops and bishops to His Majesty's Government without delay. I am persuaded that the same anxious solicitude for the relief of the clergy of Ireland, which I have expressed, will prevail in the King's councils in England; but I am grieved to add my apprehension that no effectual remedy can at the present moment be provided for this evil. I earnestly trust that on the meeting of Parliament all parties will unite in a calm, dispassionate and steady endeavour to effect the final settlement of a question, every branch of which is now so clearly traced that no reasonable obstacle can arise to obstruct a fair and impartial discussion, and a just and equitable decision of all its details. Until such a decision shall be established by law, no peace nor order nor prosperity can be expected in Ireland; and above all, no effectual protection can be given to the permanent security, dignity and happiness of the clergy. It is no less a high obligation of duty toward my sovereign and my country than a sincere and deeply rooted sense of affection and grateful attachment, which renders me desirous of promoting the true interests and welfare of the clergy. This principle has been, and ever will be the fixed rule of my conduct, by which all the measures of my Government must be constantly guided; and it is my earnest request to your Grace that you will be pleased to communicate this declaration to the archbishops and bishops who have signed the representation presented to me by your Grace.

Copy.

Third enclosure: Edward John Littleton to the Archbishop of Armagh, 8 November 1834.

Dublin Castle. When your Grace placed in my hands the representation of the archbishops and bishops of Ireland to the Lord-Lieutenant of their desire that the Government would suspend any call for payment of the instalments due on the loan recently made to the clergy, I was directed by the Lord-Lieutenant to transmit a copy of it without delay to the Secretary of State for the Home Department. His Excellency has since received from Lord Duncannon a communication in reply, of which I have now the honor to enclose to your Grace a copy. *Copy.*

Enclosure to the above: Lord Duncannon to Marquess Wellesley, 3 November 1834.

Whitehall. I have had the honor to receive a letter from the Chief Secretary for Ireland, by your Excellency's directions, conveying to me the resolutions of the prelates of Ireland. And I can only observe that, however anxious His Majesty's Government may be for the best interests of the Church, and however deeply they may feel for the distress and embarrassment of a portion of the clergy, they cannot reproach themselves of the expectations under which the prelates state the loan to have been accepted have not been realized. His Majesty's Government having in the last session unsuccessfully proposed to Parliament a bill, which, in their opinion, tended to the restoration of order and obedience to the laws, which would have made an equitable arrangement for the composition of tithes and have relieved the clergy from the repayment of the loan, I can only refer your Excellency to the provisions of the Act of Parliament (3 and 4 William IV c. 100, section 19) which rendered the demand of repayment on the part of the Secretary imperative. *Copy.*

Fourth enclosure: Newspaper publication of the communication made from the meeting of the archbishops and bishops to the Clerical Society, in Dublin, 30 October 1834.

Wellington to the Duke of Gloucester, 14 November 1834

London. I write your Royal Highness one line to tell you that Mr. Dwyer, the secretary of the Ecclesiastical Association, has sent me the printed paper, a copy of which your Royal Highness has received, and a letter giving a very satisfactory account of the affairs of the Church in Ireland.

But I have not heard from the Lord Primate, however, nor does Mr. Dwyer tell me in what manner it is wished that the friends of the Church of England in Ireland resident in this country should promote the views of the association. I conclude, however, that money will be what they will want although they do not say so. At all events money will do them no harm, and I propose to subscribe to any fund that they may have. I don't know that I can do anything else.

The Earl of Mansfield to Wellington, 14 November 1834

Scone. I must trouble you with one line merely to thank you for your kind recollection of Mr. Sayer Holbrook, who I hope will conduct himself in a way to justify the recommendation. I wish I could send you any news, but you will have seen the account of the Aberdeen and Perth meetings which went off very well. In this country our friends have gained confidence and many are beginning to avow sentiments which they always entertained, but from apprehension of violence were forced to conceal. I should think that Sir George Murray's majority at the next election would be increased. The disposition of the towns is bad, but even in the town of Perth, of which the provost and magistrates are Whigs or Radicals, there is an altered feeling, and next year it is probable that the wish will be strongly expressed for the introduction of some Tories into the council.

Sir Henry Wheatley to Wellington, 14 November 1834

¼ past 9 o'clock. St. James's Palace. I have received the enclosed letter by express from Brighton with directions from the King to deliver it into your Grace's hands should you be at Apsley House; if not, to forward it without delay by a messenger; and finding on enquiry that your Grace left London this morning for Stratfield Saye, I lose no time in obeying His Majesty's commands by sending the enclosed by a messenger, who has orders to receive your Grace's further commands.

First enclosure: Sir Herbert Taylor to Wellington, 14 November 1834.

2 p.m. Brighton. I have been honored with the King's commands to send your Grace the inclosed letter, and I beg you to add for your convenience that His Majesty's breakfast is in general over about 10, and that he goes to luncheon at two, and drives out between that hour and three, but never before luncheon. He returns between 4 and 5 and dines at seven.

Second enclosure: The King to Wellington, 14 November 1834.

Brighton. The King requests that the Duke of Wellington will attend him here at his earliest convenience as His Majesty is desirous of consulting his Grace upon the arrangements which the approaching dissolution of the present Government must call for.

His Majesty considers it unnecessary to enter further into the subject until he shall have the pleasure of seeing the Duke of Wellington.

APPENDIX

The King's speech to the Irish bishops, 28 May 1834

On the 28th of May, the day which is observed as the anniversary of His Majesty's birth, the Irish bishops, headed by the Archbishop of Armagh, presented to the King an address against hasty innovations in the Church, to which were said to be appended upwards of 1,400 clerical names, including seventeen out of the twenty prelates of Ireland. After expressing their conscientious belief in the purity and Christian authority of the doctrine, the liturgy, and government of the united Church of England and Ireland, they deprecated the introduction of undefined changes and experiments in a Church so pure in doctrine and apostolical information, whose religious services were endeared by long usage to the devotional feelings of its members. . . .

To this address His Majesty did not return the common formal answer; but, after a short conversation with the prelates, he spoke to them thus,

'I now remember you have a right to require of me to be resolute in defence of the Church. I have been, by the circumstances of my life and by conviction, led to support toleration to the utmost extent of which it is justly capable; but toleration must not be suffered to go into licentiousness—it has its bounds, which it is my duty, and which I am resolved, to maintain. I am from the deepest conviction attached to the pure Protestant faith, which this Church, of which I am the temporal head, is the human means of diffusing and preserving in this land. I cannot forget what was the course of events that placed my family on the throne which I now fill. These events were consummated in a revolution which was rendered necessary, and was effected, not, as has sometimes been most erroneously stated, merely for the sake of the temporal liberties of the people, but for the preservation of their religion. It was for the defence of the religion of the country that the settlement of the Crown was made which has placed me in the situation which I now fill; and that religion, and the Church of England and Ireland, the prelates of which are now before me, it is my fixed purpose, determination, and resolution to maintain. The present bishops, I am quite satisfied (and I am rejoiced to hear, from them and from all, the same of the clergy in general under their governance) have never been excelled at any period of the history of our Church by any of their predecessors, in learning, piety, or zeal in the discharge of their high duties. If there are any of the inferior arrangements in the discipline of the Church, which, however, I greatly doubt, that require amendment, I have no distrust of the readiness and ability of the prelates now before me to correct such things; and to you, I trust, they will be left to correct, with your authority unimpaired and unshackled. I trust it will not be supposed that I am speaking to you a speech which I have got by heart; no, I am declaring to you my real and genuine sentiments. I have almost completed my sixty-ninth year, and though blessed by God with a very rare measure of health, not having known what sickness is for some years, yet I do not blind myself to the plain and evident truth, that increase of years must tell largely upon me when sickness shall come. I cannot, therefore, expect that I shall be very long in this world. It is under this impression that I tell you that while I know that the law of the land considers it impossible that I should do wrong,—that, while I know there is no earthly power which can call me to account—this only makes me the more deeply sensible of the responsibility under which I stand to that Almighty Being before whom we must all one day appear. When that day shall come, you will know whether I am sincere in the declaration which I now make, of firm attachment to the Church, and resolution to maintain it. I have spoken more strongly than usual, because of unhappy circumstances that have forced themselves upon the observation of all. The threats of those, who are enemies of the Church, make it the more necessary for those who feel their duty to that Church to speak out. The words which you hear from me are, indeed, spoken by my mouth, but they flow from my heart.

Annual Register, 1834, pp. 43–4

Lord Grey's speech in the House of Lords, 6 June 1834

Duke of Newcastle. It is reported that an Administration either is, or is about to be, formed on principles entirely adverse to the Established Church of this country. If we require evidence of the fact, it is to be found in the secession of certain late members of the Cabinet, who, in a manner highly honourable to themselves, have refused to participate in those measures of spoliation and injury to the Church, which their colleagues have, in a way so much to be condemned, brought forward;

and their conduct in doing which, I venture to say, will draw down upon them the malediction, not only of those who are witnesses of their acts, but of those who will come after them. I say, my Lords, that the present Administration is founded on principles hostile to the Church of England. All your Lordships have heard of the speech which was made by his most gracious Majesty to the bishops on a late occasion— a speech quite worthy of the glorious and venerated sire of our present Monarch. Now, my Lords, here I say arises the discrepancy, because on the one side we have an Administration formed on the decisive principle of opposition, and injury, and persecution to the Church of England; and on the other, we have His Majesty, determined to uphold the religious institutions of the country, which he has sworn, by the most solemn asseveration to preserve .Then, my Lords, I call upon the noble earl at the head of His Majesty's Government to explain to your Lordships and the country the grounds on which his Administration is formed. I ask the noble earl and his colleagues whether they mean to force the conscience of the King—to violate the conscience of their Sovereign? . . . I ask His Majesty's Ministers whether it is their intention to attempt to control His Majesty, and to induce him to forswear his most solemn engagements?

Lord Grey. I certainly, my Lords, am not inclined to dispute the privilege which any noble lord in this house possesses of putting a question to His Majesty's Ministers, nor shall I ever be unwilling to answer such questions. I must however say upon the present occasion, both that the question itself is a very strange one, and that the ground upon which it is founded is still stranger, and in direct opposition to the forms of your Lordship's house. The noble duke, first of all, assumes that there is what he calls a discrepancy between certain declarations made by His Majesty, and the constitution of the present Administration. With respect to the speech supposed to have been made, I can say nothing at all. Not having advised His Majesty upon the subject, being in no way responsible for it, not knowing by whom it was reported, or on what authority addressed, I can say nothing but this:—if that speech declared His Majesty's determination to uphold the Church, I am certain it expressed truly the feeling and determination of His Majesty on that important subject. My Lords, allow me further to say, that with respect to the inference which the noble lord appears to draw,—from what premises I know not,—that there is in the constitution of the present Administration something inconsistent with that declaration of the

Sovereign to support the Church, I must take leave to give to that assertion the most positive contradiction. The noble duke refers to the secession of some persons who were lately members of His Majesty's Administration. My Lords, nobody regrets that secession more than I do—nobody has, both upon personal and upon public grounds, more reason to regret it than I have—but, I am sure, after leaving His Majesty's councils upon grounds on which they in conscience, and in honour, and in duty, felt themselves compelled to act, that they will give me credit for entertaining an equally sincere desire with them-selves—though upon certain points of opinion we may differ—I am quite sure they will give me credit for an equally sincere desire with themselves, to uphold the security of the Protestant Church.

My Lords, more than this I will not say upon the present occasion, as probably we shall soon have—possibly on this very night—an opportunity of going more at length into the circumstances connected with the question: but I must protest, distinctly and decidedly, against any interpretation which the noble duke or any other peer may put upon the changes that have unfortunately recently taken place in His Majesty's councils. I protest against the noble duke or any other peer putting an interpretation upon those changes, which may lead to the conclusion that there is, on the part of those who remain in His Majesty's confidence, any other than a sincere desire to maintain by such means as they think necessary for that purpose, the efficiency, the dignity, and the usefulness of the Established Church. My Lords, so much for the general allusion of the noble duke. I must say, however, that the manner in which his question was put, was not a little extra-ordinary; for, my Lords, what was the question? The noble duke calls upon me,—unworthily placed at the head of His Majesty's councils, to answer this singular question—a question so singular, that I believe it never before entered the mind of man to put it to any person, in this or any other house of Parliament. The noble duke asks us whether the Administration is founded upon the principle of forcing His Majesty's conscience. My Lords, is it possible that the noble duke can have considered such a question for a moment? Is it possible that the noble duke can have anticipated any but one answer to it? The noble duke may think the measures of His Majesty's Administration incon-sistent with the duty which they owe to His Majesty, the country, and the Church; he may condemn them as loudly and vehemently as he pleases, but can he believe that any man here could deliberately entertain such a question but one, namely—that he never had attempted, and never could attempt to put any force on His Majesty's conscience? My Lords, if the attempt could be made, I can answer for it that if any person—a member of the present Administration or otherwise—were at any time to propose to His Majesty anything that he thought inconsistent with those duties which he owes to his people as their protector and their father, he would reject the proposal with indignation; and such persons could not continue for an instant longer in His Majesty's councils.

My Lords, I have thought it necessary to say thus much in answer to the question of the noble duke, which I hold to be improper, because I consider it was founded on grounds inconsistent with the orders of the house; and having answered it, I shall be ready to meet any charge—as it has been described by the noble lord opposite—which that noble duke, or any other peer, can fairly bring against me. If, as the noble duke says, the present Ministers are unworthy of the confidence of this house, the proper course for that noble duke to pursue—the course which he is bound, in duty and in honour, in my opinion, to take—is to move an address to His Majesty, praying him to remove those Ministers from their places—a motion, my Lords, which I shall be prepared to meet, and upon the result of which I shall be ready to act in such manner as my duty shall point out.

J. H. Barrow, *Mirror of Parliament*, 1834, iii. 2075

INDEX

Gloucester, William Frederick, 2nd—
contd.
150, 257, 279, 361, 402, 403, 418,
496, 519–20, 575, 669
letters from, 687, 695, 705
letters to, 690, 737
Wellington's relations with, 280, 287,
586–7
and Ultra Conservatives, 353
as Chancellor of Cambridge
University, 484, 509, 715–16
Goderich, Frederick John Robinson, 1st
Viscount (1833 1st Earl of Ripon),
43, 427, 559, 639
memorandum by, 59–61
and slavery emancipation, 45–6, 53–7,
65–6, 68, 145
Goldsmid, Isaac Lyon (1841 1st Bt.)
letters from, 82, 551
letter to, 552
Goodall, Rev. Joseph, Provost of Eton
College
letter from, 450
Gordon, Hon. Alexander Hamilton, 301
Gordon, George, 5th Duke of
letter from, 403
Gordon, James Edward, Captain R.N.
(M.P. 1831–2), 223
Gordon, Sir James Willoughby, 1st Bt.,
General, 417
letter from, 294
Gordon, Hon. William, M.P., 688, 711
Gordon-Cumming, Sir William Gordon,
M.P.
letter from, 144
letter to, 154
Gormanston, Jenico Preston, 12th
Viscount, 36, 152
Gort, Charles Vereker, 2nd Viscount, 19,
36, 40, 93, 150
Gosford, Archibald Acheson, 2nd Earl of,
10, 36, 40, 151, 281
Goulburn, Henry, M.P., 16, 19, 39, 286,
526, 531, 539
letters from, 404, 410
letters to, 406, 412
Gräfe, Albrecht von, oculist, 293, 391,
685
Graham, Sir James, 2nd Bt., M.P., 390,
427, 552, 713
Graham, John [?], Major, 93rd Foot [?],
563
Granard, George Forbes, 6th Earl of, 35,
41, 151

Grant, Sir Alexander Cray (M.P. 1840)
('Chin' Grant), 45, 281, 361
letters from, 72, 80, 226
letter to, 75
Grant, Charles, M.P., 13, 288, 408, 427,
456–7
Grant, 'Chin', *see* Grant, Sir Alexander
Cray
Grant, Robert, M.P. (1834 K.C.H.),
Judge Advocate-General, 493
Granville, Granville Leveson-Gower,
1st Earl, British Ambassador to
Paris, uncle of Lord Francis
Egerton, 492, 506
Graves, William Thomas, 3rd Lord, 51
Gray, Francis, 14th Lord, 31
Great Dunham, Norfolk
petition from, 459
Greene, Rev. William
letter from, 581
Grenville, William Wyndham, 1st Lord
his illness and death, 362–3, 366, 376,
378, 420
Gressenhall, Norfolk
petition from, 459
Greville, Lady Charlotte (née Cavendish-
Bentinck), mother-in-law of Lord
Francis Egerton, 685
Grey, Charles, 2nd Earl, Prime Minister,
33, 39, 43, 53, 58, 69, 74, 143, 197,
199, 287, 431, 484, 539, 553, 566,
569, 575, 718
letters from, 274, 598
letter to, 274
and William IV, 44–5, 375, 418
and Irish Church reform, 64, 65, 72,
75, 263
rumours of his resignation, 112, 263,
377
and the Mutiny bill, 164, 168, 171,
175–6, 178, 189, 205
and foreign policy, 202–3, 344, 417,
422, 423, 424–5, 426, 427, 434, 540
divisions in his Cabinet, 390, 423,
424–5, 426, 427, 428, 693, 713,
717
and the King's speech to the Irish
bishops, 596, 608, 665, 742–5
his visit to Scotland, 679, 685, 688
Grey, Hon. Charles, son of preceding,
713
Grey, Edward, Bishop of Hereford
letter from, 635
letter to, 636

Mayers, John, clerk of General Assembly, Barbados, 613

Mayo, John Bourke, 4th Earl of, 33, 40, 150

Meath, Bishop of, *see* Alexander

Meath, John Chambre Brabazon, 10th Earl of, 35, 40, 151

Mehemet Ali, Pasha of Egypt, 100, 321, 381–3, 653

Melbourne, William Lamb, 2nd Viscount, 46, 50, 71, 113, 286, 375, 427, 460, 470, 625, 639, 724
 letters from, 10, 94, 134, 141, 462, 470, 493, 602
 letters to, 133, 141, 446, 461, 464, 483, 485, 490, 491, 599, 604
 comments on the King's project for a coalition, 602–4, 692
 Aberdeen on, 652
 Brougham on, 681, 713

Melville, Anne (née Saunders), Viscountess, wife of following, 499

Melville, Robert Saunders Dundas, 2nd Viscount, 38
 letters from, 31, 498
 letter to, 506

Mendizabal, Juan Alvarez, Spanish statesman, 336, 339

Merewether, Henry Alworth, serjeant-at-law
 letters from, 604, 636
 letter to, 605

Messiah, The
 Wellington attends performance of in Westminster Abbey, 585

Methodists
 their number in Manchester, 549–50

Metternich-Winneburg, Clement Wenceslas L., Prince, Austrian Minister for Foreign Affairs, 336, 495, 645
 Lord Clanwilliam on, 297–8

Mexborough, John Savile, 3rd Earl of, 19, 35, 40, 94, 113, 150

Midleton, George Brodrick, 4th Viscount, 36, 40, 150

Midsomer Norton, Somerset
 petition from, 596–7

Miguel, Dom, contender for Portuguese crown, 78, 81, 300, 319, 329, 335–41, 347, 380, 515, 639

Miles, William, M.P. for East Somerset, 534

Milltown, Joseph Leeson, 4th Earl of, 35, 40, 152

Milton, Hampshire
 petition from, 565

Mina, Francisco Espozy, Spanish general and politician, 353, 354, 689, 694

Minto, Gilbert Elliot-Murray-Knynynmound, 2nd Earl of, minister to Berlin, 298, 302–3, 343–344, 371–2, 541–2, 684

Minuzzi, Colonel, Spanish politician, 329

Mitford, Norfolk
 petition from, 459

Moberly, Rev. George (1869 Bishop of Salisbury), 557

Molé, Louis-Matthieu, Count, French statesman, 721, 729

Molesworth, Richard Pigott, 7th Viscount, 36, 40, 50, 63, 91, 150

Monk, James Henry, Bishop of Gloucester, 195

Monson, Frederick John, 5th Lord
 letter from 275
 letter to, 284

Montalivet, Marthe-Camille Bachasson, Count de, French politician, 494

Monteith, Henry (M.P. 1820–31), 291

Montrond, Casimir, Count, French diplomat, 37

Moore, Hon. and Rev. Edward George, Canon of Windsor, 688

Moore, Hugh, of Rowallane, co. Down, 701

Moreno, General, Governor of Malaga, 586

Morgan, Henry, clerk in navy pay office, 573

Morgan, Thomas
 letter from, 579
 letter to, 583

Morillo, Lieutenant-General Don Pablo, Count of Carthaginia, 329

Morning Advertiser, 69

Morning Chronicle, 69, 88, 216, 427, 554

Morning Herald, 69, 95, 98, 289–90, 340

Morning Post, 15, 16, 25, 290, 296, 361, 364, 563, 587
 Editor committed by House of Lords, 585

Morpeth, George William Frederick Howard, Viscount, M.P. (1848 7th Earl of Carlisle), 45

Morrison, James, M.P., merchant, 566, 594

Morton, George Sholto Douglas, 17th Earl of, 433

Stronge, Helen, Lady (widow of the Rev.
Sir James Stronge, 1st Bt., and wife
of William Holmes, M.P.), 394, 398
Stuart de Rothesay, Charles Stuart, 1st
Lord, 427
Sturminster Newton, Dorset
petition from, 532
Sudbourne Hall, Suffolk, seat of Lord
Hertford, 704, 705
Sugden, Sir Edward Burtenshaw, M.P.
(1852 1st Lord St. Leonards), 196,
289, 377, 555
Sullivan, Rev. L.
letter to, 135
Sumner, John Bird, Bishop of Chester,
195
Sutherland, George Granville Leveson-
Gower, 2nd Duke of, 639, 709–10
Sutton, Rev. Thomas, vicar of Sheffield
letter from, 583
Swan, Rev. Francis
letter to, 599
Swanton Morley, Norfolk, 459
Symonds, Rev. James, curate of
Ormesby, Norfolk, 531

Talbot, Charles Chetwynd, 3rd Earl
letter from, 394
and Chancellorship of Oxford
University, 361–2, 367, 368–9, 370,
376, 378, 379, 421
Talbot, Hon. John, son of preceding,
368–9, 395
Talleyrand-Périgord, Charles Maurice
de, French Ambassador in London,
37, 43, 52, 344, 397, 492, 494–5, 640,
675, 711
Taticheff, Dmitri Paulovitch, Count,
Russian Ambassador to Vienna,
297–8
Taunton, Rev. George, Rector of
Stratford Tony, Wilts., 294
Taunton, Sir William Elias, Recorder of
Oxford, a mistake for Rev. G.
Taunton (q.v.), 294
Taylor, Sir Herbert, private secretary to
William IV, 403
letters from, 163, 203, 597, 598, 608,
611, 612, 624, 635
letters to, 156, 169, 208, 596, 611
Teignmouth, John Shore, 1st Lord, 36,
40, 151
Temperance movement
in army, 386–8, 392–4

Temple, Octavius, Major (father of
Archbishop Frederick Temple and
grandfather of Archbishop William
Temple)
letter from, 47
letter to, 57
Templetown, John Henry Upton, 1st
Viscount, 36, 41, 151
Tendring, Essex
petition from, 543
Ten Hours Factory Bill
Richard Oastler on, 222
Tennyson, Charles, M.P., 679
Tenterden, John Henry Abbott, 2nd
Lord, 639
Tatham, Rev. Edward, late Rector of
Lincoln College, Oxford, 522
Teynham, Henry Francis Roper Curzon,
14th Lord, 83
Thiers, Louis-Adolphe, French
statesman and historian, 434, 495,
500, 721
Thomas, Rev. Vaughan, chaplain
Corpus Christi College, Oxford,
625
letter from, 521
Thomond, William O'Bryen, 2nd
Marquess of, 35, 40, 150, 669
Thompson, Robert, clerk in Admiralty,
573
Thomson, Charles Edward Poulett,
M.P. (1840 1st Lord Sydenham),
14, 288, 436, 439, 555, 576, 638
Thornhill, Thomas, of Fixby Hall,
Yorks., 566
Threlfall, Miss E. B., of Bath, 238
Thurlow, Rev. Edward, curate of
Lound, Suffolk, 531
Times, The, 37, 69, 95, 117, 201, 263, 290,
375, 382, 409, 426–7, 524, 526
Todd, Henry John, Archdeacon of
Cleveland
letters from, 588, 610
letter to, 608
Tooke, William, M.P., 667
Tottenham, Lord Robert Ponsonby,
Bishop of Clogher, 734
Tower of London, 195, 244, 575
Transportation, 324
Tremlett, Rev. Daniel, of Rodney
Stoke, Somerset
letter from, 534
Trench, Hon. Power, Archbishop of
Tuam, 734

Printed in England for Her Majesty's Stationery Office by Butler & Tanner Ltd., Frome and London
Dd503643 K12 9/75